36⁰⁰

Logistical
Management

Logistical Management

A Systems Integration of
Physical Distribution Management
and Materials Management

Second Edition

Donald J. Bowersox

Graduate School of Business Administration
Michigan State University

Macmillan Publishing Co., Inc.
New York

Collier Macmillan Publishers
London

Earlier edition copyright © 1974 by Macmillan Publishing Co., Inc.
A portion of this material has been reprinted from *Physical Distribution
Management*, First Edition, by Edward W. Smykay, Donald J. Bowersox, and
Frank H. Mossman, © 1961 by Macmillan Publishing Co., Inc.; Second
Edition, by Donald J. Bowersox, Edward W. Smykay, and Bernard J. La Londe,
copyright © 1968 by Macmillan Publishing Co., Inc.

Macmillan Publishing Co., Inc.
866 Third Avenue, New York, New York 10022

Collier Macmillan Canada, Ltd.

Library of Congress Cataloging in Publication Data

Bowersox, Donald J
  Logistical management.

  Bibliography: p.
  Includes index.
  1. Physical distribution of goods—Management.
2. Materials management. I. Title.
HF5415.7.B66   1978   658.8′7   77–4670
ISBN 0-02-313110-1 (Hardbound)
ISBN 0-02-978530-8 (International Edition)

Printing: 4 5 6 7 8   Year: 4

ISBN 0-02-313110-1

Preface

For over two decades, I have had the good fortune to participate actively in the formative years of business logistics. During this time, I have come to have a deep respect for the complexity of logistical performance and for its importance to the maintenance and growth of the free-enterprise system. To have the opportunity to attempt to describe the current content and future direction of this dynamic aspect of professional management is both a deeply felt privilege and a responsibility.

The history of the preparation of *Logistical Management* goes back to 1958. As many readers are aware, the first edition (published in 1974) was actually my third effort to describe the direction and dimension of an emerging field. The first effort, published under a different title and presented in 1961, was a collaboration with two other authors and was the initial attempt to integrate corporate physical distribution activities in a single book. In 1968 the work, again a collaboration, was substantially rewritten as a new book because of the vast changes that had occurred in the field during the intervening seven years. The first edition of my *Logistical Management* itself contained a great deal of the material I contributed to the two earlier works. However, by 1974, the horizons of subject content had once again expanded so as to make a new and broader approach to subject matter development desirable. The viewpoint of total logistics has been further developed and refined in this second and heavily revised edition of *Logistical Management*.

Logistical Management is presented as a systems integration of physical distribution management, materials management, and internal inventory transfer. With the exception of manufacturing processing, business logistics is viewed as involving overall management of all aspects of physical movement to, from, and between facility locations that constitute the operating structure of the enterprise. I hope that the text, as an introduction to logistics, has achieved two fundamental objectives. First, the selected materials present a comprehensive description of existing logistical practice within the private and public sectors of society. Second, a conceptual approach is provided that illustrates how the discipline is likely to mature during the initial years of the student's career.

It would be impossible to list all the individuals who have made significant contributions to the contents of this book. Special thanks are due to Professors Donald A. Taylor of Michigan State University, Thomas A. Staudt of Chevrolet Motor Division of General Motors Corporation, and Arthur E. Warner of the University of South Carolina, all of whom served as graduate chairmen for the author. In addition, for their specific aid with the manuscript, particular appreciation is due Professors Frank Mossman, John Hazard, Douglas Lambert, Robert Monczka, and George Wagenheim of Michigan State University, Bernard J. La Londe of The Ohio State University, Brian O'Neil of the University of Miami, Jim Johnson of the University of Tulsa, and Omar Keith Helferich of Cleveland Consulting Associates. I am also pleased to acknowledge the guidance over the years of three close friends who counsel freely: Walter L. Jeffrey, Vice Chairman of the E. F. MacDonald Company; Robert J. Franco, President of Spector Industries, Inc.; and Mark Egan, former Executive Director of The National Council of Physical Distribution Management; and the influence of two former mentors who are deceased: Edward A. Brand and George A. Ramlose.

I have been an active member of The National Council of Physical Distribution Management since its inception, and it would be impossible to elaborate the contributions of the many NCPDM members who have been of assistance in the preparation of this manuscript. In addition, over the past eleven years, those managers who have attended the annual Michigan State University Physical Distribution Executive Development Seminar have been exposed to the basic concepts developed in the text and have given freely of their time and experience.

The roll of those who teach various aspects of logistics around the world has expanded so as to make acknowledgment of key individuals impossible. To this group in general, and in particular to Professors E. Grosvenor Plowman of the University of Maine, Robert Pashek of Pennsylvania State University, Ernest Williams of Columbia University, and Lester Waters of Indiana University, I express sincere appreciation for their dedication to the objective we all serve. In addition, I am grateful for the support of my colleagues at Michigan State University whose advice and assistance made it possible to complete this manuscript.

It is difficult to pinpoint the continuous contribution that a teacher receives from his students over the years. In many ways, the final day of judgment of a professional career comes in the seminar room. I have been fortunate to have the counsel of a great many outstanding young scholars who currently are making their marks upon the academic and business worlds. In particular, I wish to acknowledge the assistance of all the doctoral students who participated in simulation research dealing with LREPS and SPSF over the past decade. Two graduate assistants, John T. Mentzer and Jeffrey Sims, have provided substantial assistance in the preparation of this revision.

I wish to single out the contribution of Felicia Kramer, who once again has served as coordinator of manuscript preparation. Felicia, who typed, edited, and prepared the manuscript art carried a burden over and above her normal assignment that is deeply appreciated. David Close made a substantial contribution to the manuscript through preparation of mathematical and statistical examples. His contribution is particularly notable in Chapters 11 and 12.

Finally, every author has an understanding family, or the preparation of a manuscript would be impossible during the demanding years of life. In my particular case, this book is dedicated to Carol for reasons she full well understands.

With so much able assistance, it is difficult to offer any excuse for the shortcomings that might follow. However, the faults are solely my responsibility.

D. J. B.

The Logistician

Logisticians are a sad and embittered race of men who are very much in demand in war, and who sink resentfully into obscurity in peace. They deal only in facts, but must work for men who merchant in theories. They emerge during war because war is very much a fact. They disappear in peace because peace is mostly theory. The people who merchant in theories, and who employ logisticians in war and ignore them in peace, are generals.

Generals are a happily blessed race who radiate confidence and power. They feed only on ambrosia and drink only nectar. In peace, they stride confidently and can invade a world simply by sweeping their hands grandly over a map, pointing their fingers decisively up terrain corridors, and blocking defiles and obstacles with the sides of their hands. In war, they must stride more slowly because each general has a logistician riding on his back and he knows that, at any moment, the logistician may lean forward and whisper: "No, you can't do that." Generals fear logisticians in war and, in peace, generals try to forget logisticians.

Romping along beside generals are strategists and tacticians. Logisticians despise strategists and tacticians. Strategists and tacticians do not know about logisticians until they grow up to be generals—which they usually do.

Sometimes a logistician becomes a general. If he does, he must associate with generals whom he hates; he has a retinue of strategists and tacticians whom he despises; and, on his back, is a logistician whom he fears. This is why logisticians who become generals always have ulcers and cannot eat their ambrosia.

—Author unknown
Made available by Major William K. Bawden, RCAF.

Contents

PART Four *Logistical System Administration and Organization*

Integrated Logistical Management

Logistical Management

The subject of this book, logistical management, is unique because it is one of the oldest and also one of the newest enterprise activities.[1] Logistical activities—facility location, transportation, inventory, communication, and handling and storage—have been performed since the beginning of commercial specialization. It is difficult to visualize any marketing or manufacturing that would not require logistical support.

The newness of logistics stems from a totally different and integrated approach to management that began to emerge during the 1950s. *Modern logistics* is defined as

the process of strategically managing the movement and storage of materials, parts, and finished inventory from suppliers, between enterprise facilities, and to customers.[2]

---

[1] The term *logistics* is not qualified specifically as business or military. The basic concepts of logistical management are applicable throughout private and public enterprise activities. Over the years, common titles used to describe all or parts of the material discussed in this text have been *business logistics, physical distribution, materials management, physical supply, logistics of distribution, marketing logistics, rhochrematics,* and *total distribution.*

[2] In 1976 the National Council of Physical Distribution Management modified its 1962 definition of *physical distribution management* as follows: "Physical distribution management is the term describing the integration of two or more activities for the purpose of planning, implementing and controlling the efficient flow of raw materials, inprocess inventory and finished goods from point of origin to point of consumption. These activities may include, but are not limited to, customer service, demand forecasting, distribution communications, inventory control, material handling, order processing, parts and service support, plant and warehouse site selection, procurement, packaging, return goods handling, salvage and scrap disposal, traffic and transportation, and warehousing and storage." Although this definition does not incorporate the specific managerial titles used in this text, it does reflect the need for total movement management from point of materials procurement to location of finished product distribution.

The objective of logistics is to deliver finished inventory and material assortments, in correct quantities, when required, in usable condition, to the location where needed, and at the lowest total cost. It is through the logistical process that materials flow into the vast manufacturing complex of an industrial nation and products are distributed through channels of distribution for consumption.

Logistical performance provides time and place utility. Such utility represents an important aspect of business as well as governmental operations. All forms of organized behavior require logistical support. Value, in the form of timely availability, is added to either materials or products as a result of the logistical process. Such value is costly to achieve. Although difficult to measure precisely, the annual logistical expenditure of the United States exceeds 20 per cent of the total gross national product. In other words, for every trillion dollars of GNP, the national logistical bill exceeds $200 billion annually.[3]

This book is concerned with logistical management. In the broadest sense, the scope of logistical management involves everything that moves to, from, and between the operating facilities of an enterprise. To achieve an orderly flow of products to the marketplace, managerial attention must be directed to the design of a logistical system and then to its operation. Therefore, *logistical management responsibility* is defined as

The managerial responsibility to design and administer a system to control
the flow and strategic storage of materials, parts, and finished inventory to the
maximum benefit of the enterprise.

The goal of logistical performance is to achieve a predetermined level of manufacturing-marketing support at the lowest possible total cost expenditure. The logistical manager has the fundamental responsibility for planning and administering an operating system capable of realizing this goal. Within this broad responsibility of system planning and administration, a multitude of detail and complex tasks exist. The hallmark of logistics is integration of the varied dimensions and demands for strategic movement and storage.

This initial chapter introduces and defines the basic concepts involved in logistical management. Attention is first directed to a brief review of forces contributing to the development of contemporary logistics. Then an overall perspective of integrated logistics is presented. The final section offers a specific statement of the logistical mission. The chapter summary provides a synthesis of subjects developed in subsequent chapters.

Toward Integrated Logistics

Prior to 1950, the typical enterprise treated the process of logistical management on a fragmentary basis. Although a great many authors acknowledged

---

[3] Author's estimate based on figures provided by U.S. government publications and industry reports.

the fundamental importance of logistics to marketing and manufacturing, no formalized or integrated managerial concept prevailed.[4]

From the beginning of the Industrial Revolution, our national capacity to mass-produce and mass-market far outstripped our capacity to mass-distribute. The advent of the marketing concept intensified the chaotic nature of logistical operations. The priority which modern marketing placed upon (1) extensive line-item proliferation, (2) selling identical products through a wide variety of marketing channels and different types of retailers, and (3) the widespread offering of product-contained services, combined to create a *need* for a new and less expensive approach to the physical support of marketing. The following quote from a 1954 speech of the late Paul D. Converse provides a general appraisal of the situation prevailing during the early 1950s.

. . . in the study of marketing and the operation of marketing departments and businesses a great deal more attention is paid to buying and selling than to physical handling. In fact, the physical handling of goods seems to be pretty much overlooked by sales executives, advertising men, and market researchers. . . . problems of physical distribution are too often brushed aside as matters of little importance. I have for years been reading business and economics magazines. Such publications over the years have devoted relatively little space to physical distribution.[5]

The neglect and subsequent late development of logistics can be logically attributed to at least two major forces. First, prior to the time that computers were commonplace and before quantitative techniques were widely available, there was no reason to believe that the overall integration of logistical activities would improve performance. The 1950s were destined to witness a major change in logistical management practices. Neither computers nor quantitative techniques were to be denied the fertile area of logistical applications. There is little doubt that computers and quantitative techniques have been as effectively utilized in logistics as in any other management area.

---

[4] Numerous early references to logistics can be located in the literature. Arch W. Shaw, *An Approach to Business Problems* (Cambridge, Mass.: Harvard University Press, 1916), pp. 101–10, discussed the strategic aspects of physical distribution. Other early references are found in Fred E. Clark, *Principles of Marketing* (New York: Macmillan Publishing Co., Inc., 1922); Theodore N. Beckman, *Wholesaling* (New York: The Ronald Press Company, 1926); Ralph Borsodi, *The Distribution Age* (New York: Appleton-Century-Crofts, 1929); and Richard Webster, "Careless Physical Distribution: A Monkey-Wrench in Sales Management Machinery," *Sales Management*, Vol. 19 (July 6, 1929), p. 21. For a comprehensive review of early literature, see Bernard J. La Londe and Leslie M. Dawson, "Early Development of Physical Distribution Thought," in *Readings in Physical Distribution Management* (New York: Macmillan Publishing Co., Inc., 1969), pp. 9–18. The historical review presented in this introduction is updated from an article by the author originally published in 1969; see Donald J. Bowersox, "Physical Distribution Development, Current Status, and Potential," *Journal of Marketing*, Vol. 33 (January 1969), pp. 63–70.

[5] Paul D. Converse, "The Other Half of Marketing," *Twenty-sixth Boston Conference on Distribution*, Boston, 1954, p. 22.

A second major force contributing to modification of traditional practices was the existence of a prolonged, volatile economic climate. The extended profit squeeze of the early 1950s, characterized by recessions, created a managerial environment conducive to the development of improved cost control. Integrated logistics offered a fertile area for realizing cost reduction.

Thus technology, as well as need, changed abruptly during the 1950s. The development of integrated logistics is reviewed in three time periods during which revised attitudes and practices emerged regarding movement and storage management.

1956 to 1965—A Decade of Crystallization

The period from 1956 to 1965 was the decade during which the integrated logistical concept crystallized after years of relative obscurity. Four major developments solidified this crystallization: (1) development of total cost analysis, (2) development of the systems approach, (3) increased concern for customer service, and (4) revised attention to distribution channel arrangements. A brief discussion of each follows.

DEVELOPMENT OF TOTAL COST ANALYSIS.   In 1956 a specialized study of air freight economics provided a significantly new integrative concept.[6] The study, in an effort to explain the economic justification for high-cost air transport, introduced the concept of total cost analysis. Total cost was presented as a measure of *all* expenditures required to accomplish a logistical mission. The authors illustrated that the high freight rates characteristic of air transport could in selected situations be more than offset by reductions in inventory holding and warehouse operation costs.

The concept of total cost, although basic, had not previously been applied to logistical economics.[7] Probably because of the economic climate of the times, the result was increased attention to the total cost evaluation of logistical problems. Subsequent refinements provided a comprehensive identification of cost components and further developed the measurement techniques of functional cost analysis.[8]

---

[6] Howard T. Lewis, James W. Culliton, and Jack D. Steel, *The Role of Air Freight in Physical Distribution* (Boston: Division of Research, Graduate School of Business Administration, Harvard Univesity, 1956).

[7] The total cost concept, developed in greater detail in Chapter 8, is a specialized form of break-even analysis. For some early applications, see J. Brooks Heckert and Robert B. Miner, *Distribution Costs* (New York: The Ronald Press Company, 1940), Chap. 15; and Donald R. Longman and Michael Schiff, *Practical Distribution Cost Analysis* (Homewood, Ill.: Richard D. Irwin, Inc., 1955), pp. 35–37.

[8] In particular, see Marvin Flaks, "Total Cost Approach to Physical Distribution," *Business Management*, Vol. 24 (August 1963), pp. 55–61, and Raymond LeKashman and John F. Stolle, "The Total Cost Approach to Distribution," *Business Horizons*, Vol. 8 (Winter 1965), pp. 33–46. For a more recent application, see Douglas M. Lambert and Bernard J. La Londe, "Inventory Carrying Costs," *Management Accounting*, August 1976, pp. 31–35.

DEVELOPMENT OF THE SYSTEMS APPROACH. It is difficult to trace the exact origins of the systems approach.[9] However, the concept of total integrated effort toward the achievement of predetermined goals was ready-made for logistical analysis. Whereas total cost analysis offered a method for evaluating alternative combinations of logistical activities, the systems concept provided an analysis framework.

The first general articles on logistics relied heavily upon the systems approach.[10] In particular, the systems approach highlighted the deficiency of treating logistical activity centers as isolated performance areas.

When evaluated from a systems viewpoint, integrated logistics creates a new requirement for compromise between and among traditional managerial policies. For example, manufacturing desires long production runs and low procurement costs. In contrast, logistics raises questions concerning the total cost commitment of these practices. The traditional financial position favors low inventories, a practice that could force the arrangement of logistical activities into a less than satisfactory total cost structure. With respect to marketing, traditional preference is for finished goods inventory staging and broad product assortments in forward markets. Such anticipatory logistics may be in direct conflict with the most economical total system evaluation. The significant point made by the above illustrations is that logistical considerations must be included in total system planning. The basic belief that integrated system performance produces superior end results in comparison to noncoordinated activity became a primary focal point of logistical planning.

INCREASED CONCERN FOR CUSTOMER SERVICE. By the mid-1960s, the horizons of integrated logistics began to expand. During this period, management emphasis shifted from cost to customer service performance.[11] The result was a more realistic evaluation of logistical service with respect to manufacturing

---

[9] For an early discussion of the systems approach to problem solving, see Geoffrey Gordon, *System Simulation* (Englewood Cliffs, N.J.: Prentice-Hall, Inc., 1969), Chaps. 1 and 2; Jay W. Forrester, *Principles of Systems* (Cambridge, Mass.: Wright-Allen Press, 1969); Stanford L. Optner, *Systems Analysis* (Englewood Cliffs, N.J.: Prentice-Hall, Inc., 1960); Stanely F. Stasch, *Systems Analysis for Marketing Planning and Control* (Glenview, Ill.: Scott, Foresman and Company, 1972); Van Court Hare, Jr., *Systems Analysis: A Diagnostic Approach* (New York: Harcourt Brace Jovanovich, 1967); and/or Robert H. Kupperman and Harvey A. Smith, *Mathematical Foundations of Systems Analysis* (Reading, Mass.: Addison-Wesley Publishing Company, Inc., 1969).

[10] For example, see Harvey N. Shycon and Richard B. Maffei, "Simulation—Tool for Better Distribution," *Harvard Business Review*, Vol. 38 (November–December 1960), pp. 65–75; Donald D. Parker, "Improved Efficiency and Reduced Cost in Marketing," *Journal of Marketing*, Vol. 26 (April 1962), pp. 15–21; J. L. Heskett, "Ferment in Marketing's Oldest Area," *Journal of Marketing*, Vol. 26 (October 1962), pp. 40–45; and John F. Magee, "The Logistics of Distribution," *Harvard Business Review*, Vol. 40 (July–August 1962), pp. 89–101.

[11] For examples, see Peter Drucker, "The Economy's Dark Continent," *Fortune*, Vol. 72 (April 1962), pp. 103–104; William Lazer, "Distribution and the Marketing Mix," *Transportation and Distribution Management*, Vol. 2 (December 1962), pp. 12–17; and Wendell M. Stewart, "Key to Improved Volume and Profits," *Journal of Marketing*, Vol. 29 (January 1965), pp. 65–70.

and marketing. To support marketing plans or manufacturing operations several different logistical systems can be utilized. Each can be expected to provide a different level of operational support and will involve significantly different resource commitments. To develop an effective and efficient logistical system the relationship of cost and service must be simultaneously evaluated. The management task is to develop a logistical operation capable of attaining required service performance at the lowest possible total cost.

REVISED ATTENTION TO DISTRIBUTION CHANNEL ARRANGEMENTS. An additional aspect of logistical significance from 1956 to 1965 relates to overall channel arrangements. Most logistical systems were initially studied from the vantage point of a single or vertically integrated enterprise. During the crystallization decade, considerable attention focused on the recognition that logistical activities and responsibilities seldom stop at the point of ownership transfer.[12]

An overall perspective of integrated logistics illustrates that significant costs may occur as a result of the practices of individual enterprises engaged in a channel arrangement. The interface of two or more individual logistical systems may result in excessive cost generation and customer service impairment for the overall channel. Even if individual logistical systems are fully compatible, the total cost for the channel may escalate rapidly as a result of duplicated efforts. A great deal of the impetus toward understanding channel relationships resulted from the classic work of Wroe Alderson.[13] The functional approach he provided served to revive, expand, and update the contributions of early marketing scholars concerning the relationships of risk and degree of advanced commitment in logistical operations.[14]

A new approach to channel-wide logistical evaluation resulted from an examination of information lags and product commitments inherent in channel organizations. In 1958 Forrester introduced the dynamic analysis of channel relationships.[15] In terms of physical flow, Forrester illustrated the channel-wide impact of information upon inventory fluctuation and accumulation. Until this contribution the impact of time had been generally neglected in logistics in favor of facility location. The integration of time and location offered a more balanced approach to logistics which took integration of spatial and temporal forces into consideration.

In summary, the study of integrated logistics is relatively new. The development of sophisticated tools of analysis and high-speed computers provided

---

[12] The issue of legal ownership is critical to transaction analysis. Logistical responsibility may extend long after the time of actual ownership transfer. For an expanded treatment, see Chapter 2, pages 36–39.

[13] Wroe Alderson, *Marketing Behavior and Executive Action* (Homewood, Ill.: Richard D. Irwin, Inc., 1957).

[14] In addition to references in footnote 4, see Percival White, *Scientific Marketing Management* (New York: Harper and Row, Publishers, 1927).

[15] Jay W. Forrester, "Industrial Dynamics," *Harvard Business Review*, Vol. 36 (July–August 1958), pp. 37–66; or Jay W. Forrester, *Industrial Dynamics* (Cambridge, Mass.: The MIT Press, 1961).

the capability to improve logistical operations. In addition, the economic climate of the period encouraged cost reduction. The result was a decade during which the concept of integrated logistics crystallized.

Although many factors contributed to logistical development, four had particular significance. First was the development of total cost analysis. Second was the application of systems technology. The systems approach provides a way to study complex relations, and total cost provides the measurement device. A third factor of development was greater realization that logistical performance could, in fact, stimulate revenue generation as a result of customer service performance. Finally, development was also assisted by increased awareness of the importance of timing, risk, and commitment of logistical resources in the overall distribution channel.

1965–1970—A Period of Testing for Relevancy

By the mid-1960s logistical managers had available a rather segmented, but theoretically sound, approach to guide planning. The flurry of attention that Converse perceived as a critical need in 1954 had become a reality.

The period from 1965 to 1970 was the time during which the basic concepts of logistics were to be tested. The result was that benefits predicted became reality and the logistical concepts passed the test of time. Emphasis focused on operating results as countless firms began to implement integrated logistics. Within a single enterprise, initial emphasis was typically placed on one or the other of the two main operating aspects of the logistical system.

From the marketing orientation, physical distribution management emerged as the integrated approach to finished inventory movement. Among those concerned with physical distribution, emphasis centered on the logistical support of customer orders.[16]

In contrast, materials management developed as the applicational area for procurement and manufacturing.[17] Emphasis in materials management centered around the orderly flow of raw material and component part supply to manufacturing operations.

1970–1978—A Period of Changing Priorities

The years from 1970 to 1978 represented a period of prolonged uncertainty in almost every dimension of enterprise activity. For the first time since World War II, the availability of energy became a matter of critical concern. Energy

---

[16] The aspects of logistics dealing with physical distribution management operations are discussed in Chapter 3, pages 56–65.

[17] For examples, see Robert E. McGarrah, *Production and Logistics Management* (New York: John Wiley & Sons, Inc., 1963), and James L. Heskett, Robert M. Ivie, and Nicholas A. Glaskowsky, *Business Logistics* (New York: The Ronald Press Company, 1973). Dean S. Ammer, *Materials Management*, rev. ed. (Homewood, Ill.: Richard D. Irwin, 1970).

shortages, coupled with rising prices for fuel and petroleum-based materials, culminated in widespread shortages of many basic materials and manufactured products. Logistics faced a need to improve energy productivity since the activities involved in transportation and storage are among the largest and most visible energy consumers.[18]

The crises of the decade extended beyond energy to a major concern with ecology. Once again, logistics activities ranked high among the major potential sources of environmental pollution.

Finally, the economy failed to withstand the many strains that were characteristic of the decade, ranging from Watergate to the demise of the eastern railroads. By the early 1970s the U.S. economy fell into a deep recession during which unemployment reached heights surpassed only during the Great Depression. The recession of the early 1970s created a situation which has been labeled "stagflation."[19] In terms of growth, the economy became stagnant. However, at the same time inflation continued at rates unprecedented within the United States.

The impact of the eight-year period upon the development and implementation of logistical concepts was significant. Almost overnight, enterprise priorities and related programs to cope with the ever-changing situation shifted from *servicing demand* to *maintaining supply*. Top management attention was forced to procurement by the sheer consequences of failure. The result was the rapid advancement of the materials management professional. Whereas the physical distribution profession grew from the potential of the marketing concept, the materials management profession matured from the impact of supply discontinuity. In response to an immediate need, traditional methods of material procurement changed overnight. In replacement, a new systems orientation based upon time-phased movement and long-term commitment emerged. Emphasis began to focus on pre-action control rather than reaction. In other words, rather than planning operations to react to marketing needs, management began to formulate plans around the maintenance of continuous manufacturing and processing given a high probability of material shortages.

From a technological perspective, the early 1970s was one of the most prolific periods of research and development in computer models for logistical system design and control.[20] Logistical models of all types with substantial capabilities became a reality.

The events of the period also confirmed a growing realization that significant logistical problems often have an organizational and institutional base

[18] Donald J. Bowersox, "Guide to Marketing and Distribution in an Energy Deficient Economy," *Frozen Food Age*, March 1975, p. 40.

[19] *Stagflation* is defined as simultaneous stagnation in growth of gross national product and inflation.

[20] For a review of system models, see Robert G. House and George C. Jackson, *Trends in Computer Applications in Transportation and Distribution Management* (Columbus, Ohio: Ohio State University, 1976). A review of specific techniques applicable to transportation and logistics can be found in Frank H. Mossman, Paul Bankit, and Omar Keith Helferich, *Logistics Systems Analysis* (Washington, D.C.: University Press of America, 1977).

rather than a technical base. Attention began to be directed to an evaluation of third party logistical arrangements as new ways were examined to cope with the growing complexity of logistical support.[21]

Finally, perhaps the most significant impact of the period was the institutionalization of various aspects of logistics within the organizational structures of countless private and public enterprises. The concepts had been proven to be viable contributors to the attainment of enterprise objectives. The integrated logistics concept provided a means to cope positively with uncertainty.

Beyond 1978—Toward Integrated Logistics

The decades ahead offer the prospect of even greater payoffs from the full implementation of logistical management. In retrospect, some of the critical necessities that stimulated the materials concern were exaggerated but many were not. The challenge for the future is to integrate the inherent complexities of physical distribution and materials management operations. As currently constituted, each represents a partial solution to an important operating requirement. The only relevant perspective is one that places primary emphasis on attainment of enterprise goals. The primary challenge for the future is to develop a *single* logic to guide the orderly, efficient storage and flow of inventory from material sourcing, through the manufacturing complex, throughout the distribution channel, and to the customer. Integrated logistical management provides such a logic and is becoming more common for at least five reasons.

First, there is a great deal of interdependence between both operational areas which can be exploited to the advantage of the enterprise. The perspective of a *total* movement/storage system provides a higher order of trade-offs and greater synergistic potential. The potential to integrate includes far more activities than if physical distribution or materials management are viewed alone. For example, backhaul situations exist where transportation equipment used for customer delivery can also be used to pick up purchases. Even if direct backhaul potential does not exist, separation of physical distribution and materials management often results in facility and personnel duplication within the enterprise. Prior to integrated logistical management it was not unusual for the corporate transportation department to service the requirements of both physical distribution and materials procurement. However, rarely did such integration occur in other operational areas of logistics. Faced with ever-increasing labor cost, logistical managers must develop methods to substitute capital for labor intensive processes. Logistical operations are among the most labor intensive performed in an enterprise. Complete integration

[21] James L. Heskett, "Sweeping Changes in Distribution," *Harvard Business Review*, March–April 1973, pp. 123–32; or see Donald J. Bowersox, "Showdown in the Magic Pipeline: Call for New Priorities," Presidential Issue, *Handling and Shipping*, Fall 1973, pp. 12–14.

of physical distribution and materials management increases the likelihood for realizing substitution of capital for labor.

A second reason for supporting integrated logistics is that the narrower concepts of physical distribution and materials management create the potential occurrence of a negative or dysfunctional interface. To a significant degree, the two concepts place operational priorities on diametrically opposite goals. The advent of either as a dominant philosophy of logistical management creates the potential for classical suboptimization.

A third reason to integrate the activities of physical distribution and materials management is that the control requirements for each type of operation are similar. Such controls are referred to in this text as *logistical coordination*. The objective of logistical coordination is to reconcile the different operational demands placed upon distribution and materials management.

A fourth reason for the integration of logistical operations is an increasing awareness that many trade-offs exist between manufacturing economies and marketing requirements that can be reconciled by a well designed logistical system. The dominant pattern of manufacturing is to produce products in various sizes, colors, and quantities in *anticipation* of future sale. The *postponement* of final assembling or model characteristics to some later point in the order processing cycle can greatly reduce risk and increase overall enterprise flexibility. Innovative new systems are emerging to make use of logistical facilities to reduce the anticipatory nature of traditional logistical systems. Such systems are discussed in Chapters 9 and 15.[22]

A fifth, and perhaps most significant, reason for integrated logistics is that the requirements of today's and tomorrow's logistical mission no longer can be overpowered by deployment of pure hardware technology. The challenge for the coming decades is to develop *new ways* of satisfying logistical requirements, not simply attempting to perform *old ways more efficiently*. The broad perspective of integrated logistical management is a prerequisite to attainment of this breakthrough.

As a result of the five reasons discussed above, the field of logistics has and will continue to be managed on an integrated basis. This text is written on the assumption that full integration of all logistically related operating systems into one highly coordinated effort will materialize. The next section provides a brief review of such an integrated logistical process.

Integrated Logistics

The concept of integrated logistics consists of two interrelated efforts: (1) logistical operations, and (2) logistical coordination. Each effort is reviewed.

---

[22] See pages 281 and 458. Also, for applied examples, see Walter F. Friedman, "Physical Distribution: The Concept of Shared Services," *Harvard Business Review*, March–April 1975, pp. 25–36.

Logistical Operations

The operational aspect of logistics is concerned with management of the movement and storage of enterprise materials and finished products. As such, logistical operations are viewed as commencing with the initial transportation of a material or component part from source of procurement and terminating with the final delivery of a manufactured or processed product to a customer or consumer.[23] For a large manufacturer, logistical operations may consist of thousands of movements, which ultimately culminate in the delivery of products to an industrial user, retailer, wholesaler, dealer, or other marketing intermediary. For a large retailer, logistical operations may commence with the purchase of products for resale and terminate either with consumer pickup or with delivery to the consumer's home. For a hospital, logistics starts with procurement and ends with full support of surgical and recovery operations. The significant point is that regardless of the size and type of enterprise, logistics requires a great deal of management attention. For discussion, logistical operations are divided into three categories: (1) physical distribution management, (2) materials management, and (3) internal inventory transfer.

The process of *physical distribution management* is concerned with movement of product to customers. In a physical distribution sense, the customer is viewed as the final stop in the marketing channel.[24] The availability of product is a vital part of the marketing efforts for each channel member. Even a manufacturer's agent, who does not typically own inventory, must depend on product availability to perform expected marketing responsibilities.[25] Unless a proper assortment of products is delivered when needed and in an economical manner, a great deal of overall marketing effort may be in jeopardy. It is through the physical distribution process that the time and space of customer service become an integral part of marketing. Thus physical distribution links an enterprise with its customers. To support the wide variety of marketing systems that exist in a highly commercialized nation, many different physical distribution systems are utilized by individual enterprises. In total, such systems link together manufacturers, wholesalers, and retailers into marketing channels which provide product availability as an integral aspect of the overall marketing process.

Materials management, sometimes referred to as physical supply, is concerned with the procurement and movement of materials, parts, and/or finished inventory from geographical points of purchase to manufacturing or assembly plants, warehouses, or retail stores.[26] Depending upon the situation, the process of acquisition is commonly identified by different titles. For the manufacturer, the process of material acquisition is typically called *purchasing*.

[23] Logistical operations is structured to include physical distribution management, materials management, and internal inventory transfer.

[24] Chapter 3 develops this concept in greater detail; see pages 65–70.

[25] For a detailed development, see Appendix IV.

[26] To this author's knowledge, the term *physical supply* was first used by Heskett, *op. cit.*

In government circles, acquisition is traditionally referred to as *procurement*. At the retail and wholesale levels of overall marketing, the title *buyer* represents the most widely used term. Acknowledging that operational differences do exist concerning each specific purchasing situation, in this text the term *procurement* is used to refer to all types of purchasing. The term *material* is used to identify and differentiate inventory moving inbound to an enterprise, regardless of its degree of readiness for immediate resale. The term *product* is used to identify finished inventory. Thus *material* relates to inventory with respect to inbound flow, and *product* is used to identify inventory for outbound customer shipment. The fundamental difference is that a product results from whatever value is added to material as a consequence of the enterprise's manufacturing, sorting, or assembly.

Similar to physical distribution, materials management is concerned with availability of the desired material assortment where and when needed. Whereas physical distribution is concerned with outbound customer shipments, materials management is concerned with the inbound support of manufacturing, sorting, or assembly. Under select situations, such as a grocery manufacturer shipping to an integrated retail chain, one firm's physical distribution is another firm's materials management. Although similar or even identical transportation movements are involved, the degree of managerial control and associated risk related to the shipment varies substantially between the manufacturer and the integrated chain.

The process of *internal inventory transfer* concerns control over semifinished components as they flow between stages of manufacturing, and the initial movement of finished product to warehouses or retail outlets. Inventory transfer has one significant distinction when contrasted to physical distribution or materials management. Whereas both physical distribution and materials management deal with the uncertainty of market forces, inventory transfer operations are limited to movement within and ostensibly under the complete control of the enterprise. The uncertainties introduced by random customer ordering, erratic vendor performance, or critical material shortages are removed from the management of inventory transfer. Thus from the viewpoint of operational planning, the separation of transfer from inbound or outbound movement provides an opportunity for more optimal allocation of transfer capability. Because of the captive nature of inventory transfer, potential cost saving benefits run the great danger of being obscured by organization and functional responsibility.

From the perspective of the total enterprise, these three areas of logistical operations overlap substantially. However, viewing each as a distinct dimension of movement provides the opportunity to capitalize upon the particular circumstances surrounding each effort while maintaining a coordinated effort. One prime concern of integrated logistical management is the coordination of these three types of movement. The three movements combine to provide operational management of materials, semifinished components, and products moving between locations, supply sources, and customers of the total enterprise. In this sense logistics is concerned with the strategic management of total movement and storage.

Logistical Coordination

Logistical coordination is concerned with the identification of movement requirements and the establishment of plans to integrate overall logistical operations. Coordination is required to establish and maintain operational continuity. Within the three areas of logistical operations, substantially different movement circumstances exist with respect to size of order, availability of inventory, and urgency of movement. The primary function of logistical coordination is to reconcile these differentials.

Logistical coordination involves planning and control of operational matters. Coordination is divided into four areas of managerial concern: (1) product-market forecasting, (2) order processing, (3) operational planning, and (4) procurement, or materials requirement planning.

The establishment of objectives to guide logistical operations requires that estimates be compiled concerning future sales expectations and inventory requirements. The formulation of a statistical estimate of future sales is the primary concern of *product-market forecasting*. The planning horizon of a product-market forecast is relatively short, with a maximum time duration of one year (three months is most typical). Forecasting what will be purchased by specific customers or in specific markets is the initial step in operational planning. Almost all procurement, manufacturing, and distribution undertaken by an enterprise is in *anticipation* of future sale. For example, materials are procured in *anticipation* of undertaking specific manufacturing and assembly, in *anticipation* of an order, which itself is in *anticipation* of future consumer demand. Product-market forecasting constitutes a firm's initial effort to reconcile, program, and, if possible, postpone the anticipatory process inherent in a free market system.

In contrast to forecasting, *order processing* constitutes a "here and now" measure of marketing activity. In a sense, order processing represents the realization of sales that were anticipated by the forecast. The arrival of a customer order initiates the physical distribution process which, when completed, provides the logistical effort necessary to support marketing.

Order processing, including up-to-date information regarding the nature of demand, is an essential aspect of logistical coordination. First, it creates a command status that renders the logistical system dynamic. Second, the order provides a factual source of information to assist in adapting current and future forecasts. Seldom, if ever, is a product-market forecast directly on target. The more typical case is a degree of over- or under-estimate of anticipated sales. The integration of order processing information into logistical coordination provides an ongoing source of reconciliation between what was anticipated and what is in fact occurring.

To coordinate logistical activity, the forecast and current experience derived from order processing should ideally be synthesized. This synthesis is referred to as *operational planning*. The operational plan integrates what the enterprise is capable of doing with what management decides to attempt in the future. The plan specifies how the enterprise will deploy available resources over a specified period. The time period covered by an operational plan varies depending upon the enterprise. For example, buying and merchandising for retailers are normally of short duration, approximately 30 to 90 days, and closely associated with seasonal and holiday periods. In contrast, production plans for manufacturing firms often detail alternative processing and assembly capabilities and schedule specific utilization of capacity for as long as a one-year period provided that no major discrepancy is experienced between forecasted and experienced sales activity. The main point is that the operational plan provides managerial direction to the overall enterprise and details specific logistical activities.

The fourth aspect of logistical coordination is identified as either *product procurement* or *materials requirement planning* depending upon the specific procurement situation. If a finished product is being purchased for eventual resale, the typical situation in retailing or wholesaling, the term *product procurement* is utilized. The coordination of manufacturing and material procurement is, in contrast, typically a multiple stage process which entails more complex time phasing than either retail or wholesale buying. Thus the term *materials requirement planning* is used to discuss coordination of this aspect of logistics.[27]

In product requirement situations, the merchant buyer is concerned with deciding what, how much, and when to purchase inventory which ultimately will be resold to consumers or other marketing intermediaries. For example, a department store menswear buyer would be expected to make purchases of suits, slacks, sport coats, and other garments that fit the season and style trends for each upcoming period covered by the operating plan. Such items are often acquired in a one-time purchase to cover the overall merchandising period.

In addition, several stock units such as socks, undergarments, and shirts are purchased initially to establish a basic inventory and are reordered as stocks deplete. Thus product procurement deals with obtaining products to satisfy an *independent demand* situation. The menswear buyer must purchase in anticipation of future sales and according to an overall merchandise plan sometimes referred to in trade terminology as an "open-to-buy." Only a limited degree of certainty exists regarding the retailers' ultimate capability to sell the merchandise purchased at the planned profit. To help cope with the uncertainty of independent demand, business institutions purchasing for resale typically utilize reorder point inventory control systems.[28]

Procurement and short-term scheduling in manufacturing typically require

[27] Materials requirement planning is discussed in greater detail in Chapter 4, pages 105–106.
[28] See Chapter 4, pages 99–104.

a great deal more coordination than procurement for resale. Thus material requirements planning (MRP) has been developed to assist management in the time phasing of acquisition and conversion in a manufacturing or assembly situation. Given the master plan, MRP provides an organized methodology for coordinating the utilization of manufacturing capability (*production scheduling*), and timing the availability of material and component parts (*material procurement*). In a manufacturing or assembly situation, the specific material plan and the short-term production schedule result from MRP. Unlike the resale situation which was categorized by *independent demand*, the MRP procedure is based upon the assumption of *dependent demand*.

The operating plan is assumed to represent an authoritarian position concerning the range of activities planned for the immediate future. Thus, in an MRP application concerned with scheduling material procurement and production, limited uncertainty is experienced regarding demand or the time frame during which such demand will materialize. If the operating plan is modified, which is typically the case, appropriate recalculation of material requirements and time phasing is necessary.

The situation of dependent demand and the associated techniques of MRP are not always applicable to material procurement situations. In periods of prolonged material shortage, rapidly rising prices, or anticipated work stoppages, to name a few uncertainties that confront procurement, appropriate contingency strategies are necessary. For example, one such strategy might be to build up a speculative inventory. Although the buildup of a speculative inventory is a vital concern of materials management, such contingency buildup involves a commitment that typically exceeds the boundary of logistical management authority. From the viewpoint of the enterprise, it is necessary to perform all logistical coordination functions to assure fully integrated performance. The following summary illustrates the integration of logistical operations and coordination.

Integrated Logistics—An Overview

To clarify the operational and coordination concerns of logistical management, the overall concept is summarized by Figure 1-1. The boundaries of enterprise logistical activity are represented by solid lines which identify market interface points. The concerns of operations and coordination are separated by the vertical line of alternating dots and dashes. At the top of Figure 1-1 revenue generating markets are classified as consumer and customer locations. A *consumer* is contrasted from a *customer* based upon the purchase reason. Customers purchase either for purposes of resale or material input. Thus, customers typically are retailers, wholesalers, and manufacturing firms. In contrast, the primary consumer markets are households and institutional product users.

The left side of Figure 1-1 reflects the operational aspects of logistics. Logistical operations begin as early as the initial transportation routing of

FIGURE 1-1
Logistics of the Enterprise

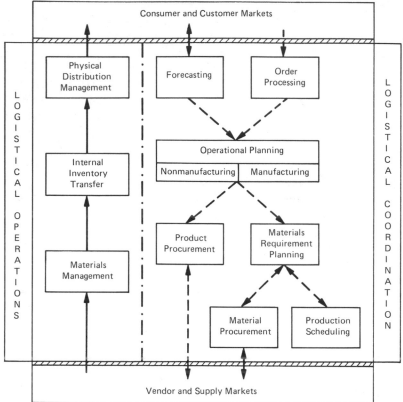

inbound material and may continue to the time of final product delivery. The flow of material and product from source to destination is illustrated by the solid vertical lines moving toward the market. These boundaries of logistical operations represent interface points between different organizations. As such, the boundaries illustrated by the double lines in Figure 1-1 are matters of *interorganization concern.*[29]

The right side of Figure 1-1 illustrates the process of logistical coordination. Coordination constitutes information flow which is illustrated by the vertical broken lines. Unlike physical movement which flows *to* the destination market, coordination flows exist from both selling and buyer markets. In the case of product-market forecasting and order processing, the information flow is of

---

[29] *Interorganizational* refers to relationships between two different and legally independent enterprises. See Chapter 14, pages 451–452.

vital concern in operational plan formulation. Similarly, feedback from vendor to supply markets is vital to maintaining flexibility. The exact use of operational plan information as an input to acquisition planning or materials requirement planning is a function of the independent or dependent nature of demand. Similar to physical flow, information flow transcends the boundary of intra-firm logistical management. Therefore, interorganizational management at information interface points is a major concern of logistical management.

The basic concept illustrated in Figure 1-1 is not limited to business nor is it unique to a specific type of enterprise. The dual areas of operations and coordination are found in all types of institutions which function in a specialized society. All political-economic societies have logistical requirements regardless of their reliance upon either free or controlled market allocation systems. Logistics is universal to the process of growth and survival.

The Logistical Mission

The logistical mission of an enterprise is to develop a system that meets service policies at the lowest possible dollar expenditure. The logistical system is primarily concerned with support of manufacturing and marketing operations. At the policy level, the critical question is to determine the desired level of performance and determine the associated cost of logistical operations. Thus, the planning of logistical support involves two policy considerations: (1) service performance, and (2) total cost expenditure. The challenge is to establish a balance between performance and cost that results in attainment of the desired return on investment or other specified goals of the enterprise. This balance is the logistical policy which in turn provides the managerial mandate for guiding system design.

Logistical Performance

With respect to total performance, almost any level of logistical service can be obtained if an enterprise is willing to pay the price. For example, a full-line inventory could be situated in close geographical proximity to all major customers. A fleet of trucks could be held in a constant state of delivery readiness. To facilitate communications, a special communication line could be installed between the customer's facility and the supplier's distribution warehouse. Under this hypothetical situation, a customer's order could be delivered within a matter of minutes. The availability of inventory could be set even higher by consigning merchandise to each customer. Although this hypothetical service situation might constitute a sales manager's dream, such extreme performance is neither practical nor necessary to support most marketing and manufacturing systems.

Logistical performance is, in the final analysis, a question of priority and cost. If a specific material is not available when required by the manufacturing system, it may necessitate a plant shutdown, with resultant cost and possible loss of sale. The penalty of such a failure is great. Therefore, the priority placed upon performance in such situations is typically high. In contrast, a two-day delay in delivery of a product to a grocery chain store warehouse may cause little more than a supermarket delivery scheduling problem. Therefore, within limited ranges, the priority placed upon performance in the second situation will not be as severe, because the penalty for failure is not as drastic.

Logistical performance is measured with respect to availability, capability, and quality. *Availability* involves the system's capacity to consistently satisfy material or product requirements. As such, availability deals with inventory level. As a general rule, the lower the frequency of planned stockouts, the greater the investment in average inventory.

Capability of logistical performance refers to the elapsed time from receipt of an order to inventory delivery. Performance capability consists of the speed of delivery and its consistency over time.[30] Naturally, all firms desire to provide customers fast delivery programs. However, a rapid delivery is of little value unless it is consistently achieved. It may substantially hinder a firm to promise second-day delivery if in actual performance the standard is achieved only a small percentage of the time. As will be illustrated, an enterprise on the receiving end of a logistical system values consistency over speed of service.

Performance *quality* relates to how well the overall logistical task is completed with respect to damage, correct line items, and resolution of unexpected problems. There is no point in speedy and consistent delivery of a damaged product or the wrong order. Thus quality relates to the maintenance of low error rates and the resolution of problems over time.

Performance standards should be established on a selective basis. Some products are more critical than others because of their importance to the purchaser and their profitability. The stated level of delivery performance should be realistic. In general, firms tend to be overly optimistic when stating performance standards. Inferior or substandard performance in adherence to an unrealistic service policy might well cause greater operating and customer problems than the statement of less ambitious goals.

Logistical Cost

For a considerable period of time, it has been in vogue to talk about profit centers within the modern enterprise. The logistical system should be viewed as a cost center. As with all other expenses, every effort must be made to hold expenditures to a minimum. Logistical costs have a direct relationship to the

---

[30] The terms "performance cycle" and "replenishment cycle" are used interchangeably. See Chapter 3, pages 53–56.

service performance policy. The attributes of high availability, fast and consistent capability, and high quality each has associated costs. The higher each of these aspects of total performance, the greater the cost of logistical operations.

A significant planning problem stems from the fact that logistical cost and increased performance have a nonproportional relationship. A firm that supports a service standard of overnight product delivery at 95 per cent consistency may confront nearly double the logistical cost of one that develops a program of second-morning delivery at 90 per cent consistency. The same firm committed to a delivery policy of overnight service at greater than 95 per cent consistency could easily dissipate profits by attempting to provide performance which is possibly not needed, expected, or even wanted by customers.

Logistical System Balance

The typical enterprise will find that the best overall relationship between logistical performance and cost is one that balances reasonable performance levels and realistic cost expenditures. Very seldom will either the lowest total cost or the highest service performance system constitute the best logistical goal.

Significant advances have been made in the development of tools to aid management in the measurement of cost-performance trade-offs. A sound policy can be formulated only if it is possible to estimate expenditures for alternative levels of system performance. Likewise, alternative levels of system performance are meaningless unless viewed in terms of marketing and manufacturing requirements. Arriving at a statement of the logistical mission is the task of policy formulation and planning.

Summary

The concept of integrated logistics is relatively new to enterprise management. The growth of logistics has resulted from an acute need to improve movement and storage efficiency. This growth has been stimulated by a vast array of technological developments. The decades ahead offer the prospect of even greater payoffs from full exploitation of integrated logistics.

Overall logistical management is concerned with operations and coordination. Operations deals with strategic movement and storage. To complete the total operations mission, attention must be directed to the integration of physical distribution, materials management, and internal inventory transfer. These three areas combine to provide operational management of materials, semifinished components, and products moving between locations, supply sources, and customers of the enterprise.

The mission of the logistical system is measured in terms of total cost and performance. Performance measurement concerns the availability of inventory, capability in terms of delivery time and consistency, and quality of effort. Logistical costs have a direct relationship to performance policy. The higher each is, the greater will be the total cost of logistics. The key to effective logistical performance is to develop a balanced effort between the service performance provided and the cost expended.

In total, this first chapter has introduced and traced the development of the basic concepts and ingredients of integrated logistical management. The text is divided into four parts. The objective of Part One is to introduce the scope and subject detail of integrated logistics. Following this overview chapter, the remaining chapters of Part One describe a systems orientation to logistical operations and control. Chapter 2 provides a detailed treatment of the channel setting of logistical performance and elaborates the systems concept as the integrative logic. In Chapter 3 the nature of logistical operations is detailed. The final chapter of Part One, Chapter 4, develops logistical coordination.

The subject matter of Part Two concerns the typical components or parts of a logistical system. Chapter 5 is concerned with transportation. In Chapter 6 the elements of inventory are treated. In Chapter 7 material handling and storage are covered.

Part Three is concerned with logistical policy formulation and planning. The foundations of logistical costing are developed in Chapter 8. Chapter 9 presents basic considerations in formulating a customer service strategy. Chapter 10 treats planning procedure. In Chapter 11 attention is directed to techniques available to assist management in the design of a logistical system. Chapter 12 reviews and illustrates techniques available to assist in short-term operational planning and management.

In Part Four, the emphasis shifts to administration and organization. Chapter 13 is devoted to administrative control. Chapter 14 treats organization. Chapter 15 presents one view of potential future dimensions of the logistical profession.

Thus the subject matter development begins with a comprehensive discussion of logistical management (Part One), followed by a detailed treatment of the fundamental components that combine to form the logistical system of the enterprise (Part Two). At the conclusion of the first two parts, the stage will have been set for in-depth treatment of the two fundamental responsibilities of a logistical manager: logistical planning (Part Three) and management (Part Four).

The decision to focus this text at the individual enterprise level made it necessary to select subjects of concern to overall logistical management and omit others from explicit coverage. Three such omissions are noteworthy.

First, all logistical managers have a specific stake in the maintenance of a viable national transportation system. The determination of national policy and the encouragement of sound public investment in the transportation infrastructure require the active involvement of logistical professionals in all levels of government. Issues of macrotransportation are not specifically discussed at any point in the text material. Chapter 5 presents a background discussion of the transport infrastructure and regulatory framework within which logistical systems must be designed. This material also introduces the reader to major issues of national concern.

Second, many logistical managers have an active responsibility for multinational materials management and physical distribution. All indications suggest greater involvement in the international logistical arena can be expected during the years ahead. At the present time it is difficult to make generalized statements concerning multinational logistical patterns. Selected materials are presented in Chapter 7 in the sections dealing with containerization. However, with the exception of transportation and containerization, most import-export arrangements are highly specialized. Therefore, at the possible sacrifice of total subject coverage, attention concentrates on domestic logistical operations.

Third, the text does not extensively discuss the important subject of logistical ecology. Various aspects of logistical systems, particularly transportation and packaging, are potential causes of environmental pollution. On the positive side, the logistical delivery system is one of the nation's most available resources to be applied toward solving ecological problems. For example, solid waste disposal and package material recycling depend upon effective "backward" logistical movement for successful transfer of society's waste to processing points. The prime reason for not including logistical ecology, once again, is an inability to generalize regarding developments and responsibilities.

Final notes concerning subject matter development are the format used to integrate locational analysis and theory and the extensive footnote cross-referencing. The network of facilities used in a logistical system provide and limit the potential for operating effectiveness and efficiency. To a large degree, facility location influences all components of the logistical system. To stress these interrelationships at the most relevant point, locational considerations are discussed at several points throughout the text. In Chapter 2 the network concept of fixed facilities is introduced in a discussion of the logistical system concept. Its treatment is also an integral part of Chapter 5's coverage of transportation. The integration of spatial and temporal considerations in the formulation of logistical policy is developed in depth in Chapters 8 and 9. Techniques to assist managers in selecting specific locations are covered in Chapter 11. The basic issues involved in manufacturing plant location and associated checklists are treated in appendixes. Although this format spreads the treatment of location throughout the text, it has the advantage of developing the salient aspects of location as an integral part of each impacted subject matter.

Finally, throughout the text, extreme care has been taken to cross-reference the location of subject matter through footnotes. The integrated nature of logistical management results in a particular subject being relevant at several different points.

Questions

1. Discuss reasons why no formal or integrated concept of logistics prevailed prior to 1950.
2. What is the basic logic of the total cost concept?
3. How can customer service performance influence total enterprise profitability? Does the same concept relate to public enterprise?
4. What is the meaning of the following statement: "The only relevant operating perspective is one that places primary emphasis on corporate goals"?
5. Describe the differences among logistics, physical distribution, materials management, logistical coordination, and transportation.
6. What is meant by the statement that the logistical management responsibility involves both system design and administration?
7. What reasons can you give for the lack of attention to internal inventory transfer in the traditional organizational structure of the business enterprise?
8. Illustrate the difference between *product* and *material* as used in Chapter 1.
9. Why is full realization of the impact of *anticipation* important to logistical planning?
10. Does the statement that the firm should seek to realize logistical performance at the lowest total cost mean that an over-all effort should be made to design and administer a logistical system of lowest total cost?

Logistical Systems

Introductory comments stressed that the primary objective of logistical management is to develop integrated operations. Management of individual logistical activities is often under the direction and control of various departments within an enterprise. Such diffusion of responsibility increases the possibilities for duplication and waste, and sometimes hinders mission accomplishment. Similarly, information flow between organizational units may be fragmented enough to jeopardize logistical coordination. The fundamental belief that integrated system performance will produce an end result greater than is possible from noncoordinated performance is the focal point of the integrated logistics concept. Systems technology provides a disciplined method for achieving integration.

The objective of this chapter is to describe the environment within which logistical performance must be planned and executed. The initial section provides an overview of the enterprise in a competitive environment. It is important to develop a proper perspective of how logistical management relates to other operating units of an enterprise as well as its posture with respect to the external competitive environment. From this broad perspective, attention is directed in the second section to relationships that result from involvement in a distribution channel. The third section develops the basic postulates of the systems concept. The systems concept provides the integrative logic for planning logistical performance within a competitive industry structure and a cooperative channel setting. The fourth section briefly reviews the operational components of a logistical system. The chapter concludes with a description of selected patterns of logistical operations commonly found in modern enterprises.

Before proceeding, some cautionary comments are in order regarding organization. Managers are acutely interested in organizational arrangements because they directly reflect responsibility and, therefore, title, compensation, and power. Implicit in the statements of Chapter 1 regarding duplication and waste was the assumption that if all management responsibility for logistics was grouped into a single organizational unit, integrated control would automatically improve. This assumption is misleading, in that it emphasizes structure rather than results. It can be readily observed that formal organization alone is not sufficient to guarantee results. Some of the most effective logistical operations function without formal organizational grouping under a single management unit. However, other enterprises with formal logistical groups also achieve superior results. Thus, any generalization regarding proper organization is unreliable.

Individual organization structures vary depending upon the specific mission, available personnel, and resource capabilities. Some basic patterns of organizational structure are available and will be presented later as managerial guides. However, discussion and development of organization is deferred until Chapter 14. *At this stage the objective is to foster a philosophy of operation that stimulates all levels of management within an enterprise to think and act in terms of integrated logistical capabilities and economies.*

Integrated Logistics, the Enterprise, and a Competitive Environment

The proper perspective from which to initiate review of logistical performance is to gain an understanding of internal and external forces that influence design of an enterprise's logistical system. Figure 2-1 illustrates the environmental setting for logistical planning. The logistical system is illustrated as one link or part of an enterprise operating system.

In addition to logistics, Figure 2-1 illustrates the other primary systems of a typical enterprise. In essence, the logistical system is but one of four basic operating areas. Logistics, marketing, production, and finance are all important parts of the enterprise operating system. Just as logistical operations and coordination must be integrated, so must the four areas of the enterprise operating system function as a totality.

External to the enterprise are environmental business forces that limit flexibility of corporate design. Together these forces form an ecological environment for the enterprise. They include (1) industry structure, (2) geomarket differentials, (3) government and legal regulation, (4) network of service industries, (5) competitive tactics, (6) logistical channel alliances, (7) economic conditions, and (8) transaction channel alliances.[1]

---

[1] Because of comprehensive treatment of environmental forces in other texts, the various forces illustrated in Figure 2-1 are not developed in great detail. For an expanded treatment, see Thomas A. Staudt, Donald A. Taylor, and Donald J. Bowersox, *A Managerial Introduction to Marketing*, 3rd ed. (Englewood Cliffs, N.J.: Prentice-Hall, Inc., 1976), pp. 56–65.

FIGURE 2-1
The Enterprise—A Competitive Environmental Setting

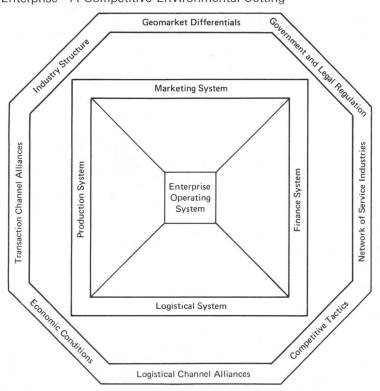

In competition, the enterprise is viewed as a goal-seeking organization functioning within and adjusting to environmental constraints. Over a given planning period, environmental constraints remain relatively constant. The enterprise and its competitors modify corporate programs in an effort to obtain greater shares of the market for the particular product assortment offered. The enterprise that gains favor in the eyes and behavior of buyers enjoys a differential advantage over competitors. This advantage may be rapidly eliminated by competitors, or it may be retained over a substantial period of time. To the degree that a differential advantage prevails, the recipient firm gains lasting distinctiveness and long-run goal achievement.

The complexities of total activity are important only to the extent that an enterprise is able to focus all effort on transactions. To enjoy a sustained series of desirable transactions requires the efficient integration of all resources. If an enterprise is to survive, all systems—marketing, production, finance, and logistics—must function as a totality. Viewed in isolation, each system or any of its activity centers has no justification. Only to the extent that any given part contributes to the total effort does that given part—or the total effort—gain economic justification.

Viewing enterprise activity as a total system of goal-directed action has become customary. Equally accepted is an overall enterprise marketing orientation as an underlying philosophy of management. This market orientation does not presume to place marketing on a pedestal but to underscore the importance of markets in enterprise planning. Transactions are accomplished in the marketplace. Transactions are essential to survival. Therefore, all action must be geared to the transaction.

Within the enterprise the logistical system is essential to completion of the transaction. Those enterprises enjoying logistical efficiency gain an advantage in cost and service that is difficult to duplicate. Enterprises that achieve an integrated network of facilities, transportation capacity, inventory deployment, communication, and handling and storage in harmony with the financial, marketing, and production efforts of the corporation stand the best chance of gaining a long-range differential over competition.

Such a balance of components within the logistical system and to the remainder of the enterprise is subject to constant adjustment. In the long run, quicksands of economic and institutional change may render an existing system inadequate. This inadequacy may result in increased costs or loss of competitive advantage to rival enterprises.

Logistics in a Channel Context

One of the basic realizations about specialization of trade is the fact that no single enterprise can be self-sufficient. Regardless of the size of an enterprise and the vastness of its operation, it must rely upon other firms to provide selected services and material requirements. Thus, prior to discussing design of an enterprise's logistical system, attention is directed to selected aspects of the channel environment.

Among the least understood areas of business are the institutional and activity groupings referred to as *distribution* or *marketing channels*. Distribution structure is of fundamental importance, because the channel is the arena within which marketing and logistics culminate customer transactions. The American Marketing Association defined the distribution channel as the structure of intracompany organization units and extracompany agents and dealers, wholesale and retail, through which a commodity, product, or service is marketed.[2] Others have defined the distribution channel as a grouping of intermediaries who take title to a product during the marketing process, from first owner to last owner.[3]

Figure 2-2 provides a graphic illustration of the typical alternatives found in

---

[2] Ralph S. Alexander, *Marketing Definitions: A Glossary of Marketing Terms* (Chicago: American Marketing Association, 1960), p. 10.

[3] Theodore N. Beckman and William R. Davidson, *Marketing*, 7th ed. (New York: The Ronald Press Company, 1962), p. 44.

FIGURE 2-2
Typical Channels of Distribution

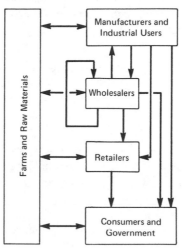

institutional arrangements at all levels of the marketing process. Of particular interest in Figure 2-2 are the many institutions products or materials may pass through and the alternative paths they can follow between original owner and final buyer. For example, retail stores may purchase from all levels of supply, from farm to wholesaler.

One advantage of a channel flow graph is that it places the multiplicity of institutions used in modern marketing into a logical sequence. However, the simplicity of the flow diagram understates the complexities involved in selecting a channel structure for an individual enterprise. Appendix IV provides a more comprehensive review of the various ways channels of distribution are treated in marketing literature. To fully understand the importance of channel considerations in operational system design it is important to view the logistical process in a multienterprise structure.

The Channelwide Logistical Process

As previously noted, the logistical channel consists of a number of independent enterprises which combine to deliver product and material assortments to the right location at the proper time. A number of functions must be performed jointly by all channel members in the logistical process. From the total channel viewpoint, these functions should be performed with a minimum of duplication. The following discussion expands the basic components of the single enterprise logistical system to include multiple enterprises functioning in a channel context.

Logistical flow in a channel is analogous to the mechanics of a ratchet wrench. Physical movement is best designed for economies of one-way movement toward final customer location. Although products often have to be returned from retailer to manufacturer, such reverse movement is an expensive exception rather than the rule.[4]

ADJUSTMENT.   The *adjustment function* has received considerable attention in marketing literature.[5] Adjustment is concerned with the creation of an assortment of goods. At some geographical point or points in the logistical process, goods must be concentrated, selected, and dispersed to the next level in the logistical channel.

Concentration refers to the collection of large lots of a single good or large groupings of several goods earmarked for final sale in an assortment. A manufacturer's distribution warehouse is a prime example of a logistical concentration point. Large shipments of products produced at each factory are transferred to the distribution warehouse. The distribution warehouse, in turn, holds such concentrations until an order is received for a particular assortment.

The process of grouping individual products into an assortment is referred to as *selection*. The selection process results in a custom grouping of products to satisfy one customer's specifications. Manufacturers commonly offer customers mixed carloads or truckloads of products based upon the functional capability to select in an economical manner. Such custom-selected shipments allow customers to carry the minimum necessary inventory of all items in the product line and to retain the benefits of the lower freight rates per unit that result from volume shipments.

Dispersement consists of placing selected assortments in the right place at the proper time. Dispersement represents the final level of performance and is directly related to customer service in the logistical process.

The particular enterprise performing the overall adjustment function may be company-operated or a specialized middleman. Wholesalers find economic justification in performing the adjustment function and thereby reducing risk on the part of other channel members. Over the past several years merchant wholesalers have increased at the very time when vertical integration by large retailers and manufacturers was to have eliminated their basis for economic

---

[4] For examples, see C. G. Golucke and P. H. McGaukey, *Comprehensive Studies of Solid Waste Management*, Public Health Service Publication 2039 (Washington, D.C.: Government Printing Office, 1970); William G. Zikmund and William J. Stanton, "Recycling Solid Wastes: A Channels-of-Distribution Problem," *Journal of Marketing*, July 1971, pp. 34–39; and Omar Keith Helferich, Vernon Hoffner, and Douglas E. Gee, "Dynamic Simulation Model for Planning Solid Waste Management," *International Pollution Control Journal*, 1972 Pilot Issue, pp. 40–49.

[5] This concept has long standing in marketing literature. Two early treaments are found in Percival White, *Scientific Marketing Management* (New York: Harper & Row, Publishers, 1927), and Fred E. Clark, *Readings in Marketing* (New York: Macmillan Publishing Co., Inc., 1924).

justification.[6] It would appear that the economies of vertical integration may not offset the corresponding loss of innovative specialization and risk spreading. The strategically placed merchant wholesaler is able to perform the adjustment function for a number of different retailers and manufacturers, thereby reducing the risk as well as the number of transactions required in the total logistical channel.[7]

TRANSFER.   The *transfer function* consists of the mechanics of concentration and dispersement. A single good or an assortment of goods must be physically transported to support transactions. In the collection phase of the adjustment function, the typical transfer consists of large, limited commodity shipments. In the dispersement phase, the typical transfer will be smaller shipments of an assortment of products. As a general rule, transfers related to dispersement will be more costly than transfers related to concentration.

STORAGE.   The *storage function* occurs in the logistical channel because a great deal of concentration, sorting, and dispersement is performed in anticipation of future transactions. Under conditions of uncertainty in demand and supply, the logistical process must develop certain hedges to be able to satisfy future transaction requirements.

The risks inherent in storage may be the greatest of all logistical functions, because damage and obsolescence can occur when inventories stand idle. A continuous logistical flow from processing through adjustment and on to final consumption would involve less risk for all channel members. However, in a buyer's market, continuous movement is seldom achieved. At some point in the logistical channel, storage of at least a temporary nature will be required.

Because of related risks, the storage function is normally spread out among enterprises that make up the channel. Each enterprise is willing to assume the minimum amount of storage necessary to support its transaction activities. Because the total concentration of any one product tends to be reduced as the product moves through consecutive adjustments, it is not surprising to find that manufacturers are frequently forced to assume the largest share of product storage. In a given channel containing a manufacturer, a wholesaler, and a retailer, negotiating who will perform storage and have risk exposure is one of the areas of greatest potential conflict.

HANDLING.   The *handling function* is one of the most costly aspects of channel performance. Once a concentrated lot or an assortment of goods reaches a stopping point, shuffling begins. Cartons are moved in, placed, moved about,

[6] Reavis Cox, *Distribution in a High-Level Economy* (Englewood Cliffs, N.J.: Prentice-Hall, Inc., 1965), p. 56.

[7] In marketing literature this relationship is referred to as *the principle of minimum total transactions*. For an expanded treatment, see Staudt, Taylor, and Bowersox, op. cit., pp. 279–80, and Margaret Hall, *Distributive Trading* (London: Hutchinson's University Library, 1961). Also see Figure EIV-6, page 507.

moved about more, and finally moved out. The objective is to reduce handling in the logistical channel to an absolute minimum. Each handling operation has a separate and unique cost. Consequently, the fewer the total handlings in the channel, the lower the total cost. Channel structures requiring the movement of product or material through several different facilities represent one of the most excessive areas of logistical duplication.

COMMUNICATION. *Communication* is a two-way function in the logistical channel. In one direction, messages relay the need for logistical action. In the other direction, communication monitors progress toward desired end results. Channel communication is continuous as products are transferred, adjusted, and stored in anticipation of future transaction requirements. Communications also exist between the transaction channel and the logistical channel with respect to assortment, quantity, location, and time of exchange.

At the outset it was noted that the total logistical channel was similar to a ratchet wrench in design concept, with primary emphasis on forward movement to terminal user locations. A forward movement that requires subsequent reversal can be very costly to the total channel of exchange. From initial stimulant to feedback, the direct costs of communication are overshadowed by the resultant cost of a faulty message.

Because a great deal of logistical action is initiated in anticipation of future transaction requirements, communications containing an overly optimistic appraisal of potential may stimulate a fever of ultimately useless work. Recent analysis of communication between channel members suggests that such anticipation has a tendency to amplify as it proceeds between consecutive intermediaries in a logistical network.[8] Each such error in appraisal of transaction requirements creates a disturbance for the total logistical channel. Faced with such a disturbance, the total channel may enter into an oscillating corrective pattern, resulting in a series of over- and under-adjustments to real market requirements.

By the very nature of its mission, a logistical channel must be sensitive to transaction requirements. The system stands ready to initiate the logistical process upon receipt of a stimulating message. Extreme care must be taken to structure communication with a high degree of reliability.

Interorganizational Considerations

Because a sequence of functions must be performed in the logistical process, it is not surprising that a number of individual enterprises combine to create a channel. Only through coordination can transaction requirements be fully satisfied. Each organization exists for a reason and performs services in

---

[8] See Thomas W. Speh and George D. Wagenheim, "Retailer Logistical Problems: Impacts on Supplier Marketing Strategy," in Robert G. House and James F. Robeson, eds., *Interfaces: Logistics, Marketing, and Production,* Proceedings of the Sixth Annual Transportation and Logistics Educators Conference (Columbus, Ohio: Ohio State University, 1976), pp. 83–110.

anticipation of a return on investment and effort. Unnecessary duplication of functions in the channel impairs the total efficiency of the combined effort. Over the long run each channel member enjoys rewards or suffers losses based upon the success of the overall logistical channel.

Enterprises that make up the logistical channel are specialists in performing one or more exchange functions. Specialization by function increases efficiency and spreads risk. However, risk in an exchange network is never equally spread among participants. The greater the degree of specialization the intermediary has in the performance of logistical functions, the less risk that specialist will assume in overall performance.

A motor carrier performing a single transfer function in a channel incurs relatively little risk with respect to the ultimate transaction. Carriers will attempt to hedge risk involvement in any single logistical channel by performing similar functions for a variety of channels. A retailer or a merchant wholesaler incurs risk in the sale of a single manufacturer's products. Each attempts to hedge this risk by offering a total assortment much broader than any single manufacturer's product mix.

In contrast, a processor or manufacturer of a single product line may risk his enterprise's survival on the capabilities of a single distribution channel. This disproportionate risk among channel members is of central importance in logistical planning. Some channel members have a deeper vested interest in the ultimate accomplishment of successful exchange than others. Therefore, members with a greater vested interest are forced to play a more active role and assume greater responsibility for channel performance.

Without guidance, a great many logistical costs may be rapidly accumulated by functional duplication. In addition, costs may be unfavorably influenced by enterprises with very little at stake in the channel. Such costs must be controlled if the channel is to realize maximum efficiency. Control in a logistical channel is difficult to realize, because the only alternatives to ownership are persuasion or coercion.

Ownership control consists of vertical integration, by a single enterprise, of two or more consecutive links in the logistical channel. The ultimate in vertical integration in a logistical channel is the manufacturer shipping via private transportation to vertically integrated warehouses and retail outlets. Such complete vertical integration is rare. The exact extent to which vertical integration has materialized during the past two decades is difficult to appraise. As noted earlier, merchant wholesalers have tended to increase in number rather than decrease. Ample evidence exists that the selling intermediaries have undergone more dramatic vertical integration than the logistical specialists.[9]

Even when a firm is vertically extended with respect to integrated wholesaling, the services of a specialized transfer intermediary rarely can be eliminated. Sears Roebuck and Montgomery Ward use extensive common carrier

[9] Cox, op. cit., p. 55.

transportation in addition to their own vast fleet of private and contract transportation. It is doubtful that a firm could ever be fully integrated in a complex society.

Tactics of persuasion and coercion are the most practical methods other than ownership for directing and controlling logistical activities. This need for common action under leadership guidance has been referred to as "super-organization management."[10] The prerogative of spearheading coordinated activity often goes to the channel member with the greatest economic power, and that economic power most often rests with the channel member directing activities at the point of transaction creation. Domination by virtue of economic leverage comprises what are termed *vertically controlled* (in contrast to *vertically owned*) *operations*. In many situations, an enterprise coordinates the activities of specialized intermediaries through market strength. The name *channel captain* has been suggested for the enterprise able to stimulate interfirm coordination.[11]

Although all enterprises in a logistical channel desire to cooperate, individual profit orientation and legal barriers tend to create conflict. In addition, a degree of conflict exists over who in the channel is willing to assume responsibility for performance of the more risky logistical activities. The enterprise with the greatest economic power often is the one least directly concerned with the welfare of the specific channel. Under such conditions, economic power is often used to shift risk rather than stimulate coordination.

Conflict resolution in distribution channels receives substantial attention in the literature.[12] Detailed treatment is beyond the scope of this text; the essen-

[10] J. L. Heskett, "Costing and Coordinating External and Internal Logistics Activities," unpublished paper presented to the joint seminar, The Railway Systems and Management Association and The Transportation Research Forum, Chicago (October 6, 1964).

[11] E. Jerome McCarthy, *Basic Marketing: A Managerial Approach*, 5th ed. (Homewood, Ill.: Richard D. Irwin, Inc., 1974), pp. 389–90.

[12] For a selection of examples, see J. C. Palamountain, Jr., *The Politics of Distribution* (Cambridge, Mass.: Harvard University Press, 1955); Valentine Ridgeway, "Administration of Manufacturer–Dealer Systems," *Administrative Science Quarterly*, March 1957, pp. 464–83; Bruce Mallen, "Conflict and Cooperation in Marketing Channels," in L. George Smith, ed., *Reflections on Progress in Marketing*, Proceedings American Marketing Association (Chicago: American Marketing Association, 1964), pp. 65–85; Bert C. McCammon, Jr., "Alternative Explanations of Institutional Change and Channel Evolution," in Stephen A. Greyser, ed., *Toward Scientific Marketing Proceedings* (Chicago: American Marketing Association, 1963), pp. 477–90; Bert C. McCammon, Jr., "Perspectives for Distribution Programming"; Donald J. Bowersox and E. Jerome McCarthy, "Strategic Development of Planned Vertical Marketing Systems"; and James L. Heskett, Louis W. Stern, and Frederick J. Beier, "Bases and Uses of Power in Interorganization Relations"; all published in Louis P. Bucklin, ed., *Vertical Marketing Systems* (Glenview, Ill.: Scott, Foresman and Company, 1970); Bert Rosenbloom, "Conflict and Channel Efficiency: Some Conceptual Models for the Decision Maker," *Journal of Marketing*, July, 1973, pp. 26–30; and Louis P. Bucklin, "A Theory of Channel Control," *Journal of Marketing*, January 1973, pp. 39–47. For selected examples from recent literature, see Robert F. Lusch, "Sources of Power: Their Impact on Intrachannel Conflict," *Journal of Marketing Research*, Vol. 13 (November 1976), pp. 382–88; Shelby D. Hunt and John R. Nevin, "Power in a Channel of Distribution: Sources and Consequences," *Journal of Marketing Research*, Vol. 11 (May 1974), pp. 186–93; and Louis W. Stern and Adel El-Ansary, *Marketing Channels* (Englewood Cliffs, N.J.: Prentice-Hall, Inc., 1977).

tial point is that the ultimate survival of a channel may depend upon constructive leadership. Future improvements in marketing efficiency will increasingly require concern with channel group objectives rather than preoccupation with individual channel member programs. This total channel perspective is particularly important to the logistical aspects of distribution channels. This interdependence is developed in greater detail in the next section.

Nature of Logistical Channels

Completion of the logistical process requires the utilization of a broad range of enterprise facilities and intermediary specialists. A *facility* is defined as an organizational unit engaged in the performance of all or some part of the logistical process. Thus a distribution warehouse or a company-managed truck are logistical facilities. However, either one also may be an *intermediary specialist*. The warehouse may be public, and the truck may be owned and operated by a common carrier. The intermediary specialist is an independent business operated for profit. In the design of a logistical system, the services of an intermediary specialist can be substituted for those provided by the enterprise. The objective is to select the proper combination of facilities and specialists to meet objectives at the lowest total cost.

Two factors are of critical importance in planning logistical channels. First, planning must encompass the total channel rather than a single enterprise. Second, care must be exercised to select intermediary specialists for reasons of logistical competence rather than marketing capability only. Each of these considerations will be discussed.

RANGE OF CHANNEL PLANNING.   The traditional approach to channel planning seldom extended beyond the legal boundaries of the enterprise, because normal control and profit measurement end when a product is transferred to a new owner. Depending upon conditions and terms of sale, exchange of legal ownership is usually accomplished immediately before or after the final physical transfer of the product. However, in special cases, such as consignment selling, a product's physical exchange may be completed long before the legal ownership exchange.

The logistical process does not end once ownership transfer occurs. It does not end when the product is turned over to the next level in the distribution channel or even when it is delivered to a buyer, unless all conditions of the transaction are satisfied. Ultimate responsibility for physical distribution or materials management does not end until the product in question is finally accepted by the person, family, or enterprise that will utilize it. Practitioners agree that a product is not fully distributed until no additional physical transfer is possible. Some of the most difficult logistical problems are those arising from handling and moving returned products. Such products may be returned for damage, improper performance, or even late delivery. Therefore, to properly direct logistical activities, planning horizons must transcend the total distribution channel.

Many significant costs of logistics occur between enterprises engaged in a distribution channel. As noted earlier, the control of such costs may rest with an intermediary specialist who has very little risk or vested interest in the overall success of the marketing or logistical process. For example, an infrequently used common carrier who takes 20 days to transfer a shipment scheduled for three-day delivery and delivers in split quantities of the original shipment may substantially increase total distribution costs.

In addition, many costs—such as inventory holding expense—may accumulate from duplicated effort at various levels within a channel. Duplication increases the cost of total marketing, and adjustments in channel arrangement may be justified on the basis of a single firm's cost-control program. Such modifications, however, may increase the costs of all other enterprises in the channel and seriously hinder the ability of the total channel to survive. Consequently, logistical planning should be channel-wide in perspective.

As previously indicated, the main reason for an enterprise's limitation to within legal boundaries is the desire for control and profit. When an enterprise limits consideration to controllable limits within a channel, in effect it operates under artificial conditions of vertical integration.[13] Such control effort normally stops when ownership transfer occurs. This deficiency of legal limits, if extended to all enterprises, could have a detrimental impact on overall channel performance.

INTERMEDIARY SELECTION.   A second factor of prime importance in channel planning involves caution in selecting specialized intermediaries for reasons of logistical competence. Traditionally, when an enterprise decided to locate a branch or district sales office, it was almost axiomatic that a field inventory be located at the facility. If an enterprise selected a market plan to utilize a specific wholesaler, it was assumed that the same wholesaler would inventory a full line product assortment.

This single-structure system ignores the possibility that a very effective marketing intermediary may not be either an effective or an efficient logistical intermediary. Successful marketing of an enterprise's product may require a wide range of channels to effectively reach various market segments. Using the same structure for logistical flows may force small uneconomical shipments upon the physical distribution system. Substantial economies of scale and related advantages might otherwise be realized in physical flow. The most suitable structure for marketing channels may not, and often is not, satisfactory for logistical operations.

The Concept of Channel Separation

The term *structure* is widely used to describe a number of interrelationships which are part of, but subordinate to, the whole. Thus the arrangement and

---

[13] The term *vertically controlled* is adopted to describe a situation in which the next level of a channel is operationally controlled through purchase relationships to the extent that two independently owned enterprises function as a single entity.

interrelationship of a logistical system's components is properly viewed as the system's structure. In logistical channels, structure relates to the framework for processing basic flows which pass through the channel. Careful analysis and classification of such flows provides the basis for specialization of effort.

Several authors have developed the idea of flow separation within the overall structure of the distribution channel.[14] The present approach singles out two flows. To achieve a satisfactory marketing process, a flow of transaction-creating efforts and a flow of logistical efforts must exist and be coordinated. There is no reason why these two flows must transpire sequentially through the same network of intermediaries. These two flows, logistical and transaction-creating, are considered primary. All other flows in the total distribution channel are viewed as secondary.

The logic for separation of logistical fulfillment and transaction creation is based on the notion that no positive legal or economic laws require simultaneous treatment or performance.[15] Factors that tend to increase or decrease the total cost of physical flow have no real relationship to ownership boundaries, only an artificial one. Conversely, advertising, credit, personal selling, and other transaction-creating efforts of marketing have a significant influence upon the economics of physical flow. The responsiveness of each primary flow to specialization is unique to the circumstances surrounding that flow. In any given marketing situation, primary flows may best be accomplished by intermediary specialists. The most effective network for achieving profitable transactions may not be the most efficient arrangement of exchange intermediaries. Based upon specialization in primary flow, the total distribution channel is classified as containing transaction and logistical channels.

The transaction channel consists of a group of intermediaries engaged in the process of trading. The goal of the transaction channel is to negotiate, to contract, and to administer trading on a continuing basis. The full force of creative marketing action exists within the transaction channel. Participants in transaction-channel activities are marketing specialists, such as manufacturing agents, salesmen, jobbers, wholesalers, and retailers.

The logistical channel contains a network of intermediaries engaged in the functions of adjustment, transfer, storage, handling, and communication. Participants in this channel are logistical specialists. They are concerned with solving problems of time and space.

---

[14] A number of authors have developed the flow concept; contributions of noteworthy mention in this author's opinion were presented by Roland Vaile, E. T. Grether, and Reavis Cox, *Marketing in the American Economy* (New York: Ronald Press, 1952); Ralph F. Breyer, "Some Observations on Structural Formation and Growth of Marketing Channels," in Reavis Cox, Wroe Alderson and Stanley J. Shapiro, eds., *Theory in Marketing* (Homewood, Ill.: Richard D. Irwin, Inc., 1964), pp. 163–75; George Fisk, *Marketing Systems* (New York: Harper & Row, Publishers, 1967), pp. 214–79; and Louis P. Bucklin, "Postponement, Speculation, and the Structure of Distribution Channels," *Journal of Marketing Research*, February 1965, pp. 26–31.

[15] The notion of transaction versus exchange is based on John R. Commons, *The Economics of Collective Action* (New York: Macmillan Publishing Co., Inc., 1950).

FIGURE 2-3
Distribution Channel—Logistical and Transaction Separation

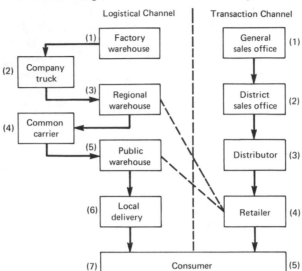

EXAMPLES OF SEPARATION.   Figure 2-3 illustrates the concept of separation for the distribution of color television sets. In this situation the transaction channel consists of five links: (1) general sales office, (2) district sales office, (3) distributor, (4) retailer, and (5) consumer. The logistical-channel design consists of seven links: (1) factory warehouse, (2) company truck, (3) regional warehouse, (4) motor common carrier, (5) public warehouse, (6) local delivery, and (7) consumer. Only at the point of transaction completion, the consumer, do the two primary channels merge.

Figure 2-3 illustrates additional significant points. In the logistical channel, three specialized intermediaries are involved in distribution of the product. These three specialists are: at level 4, a common-carrier motor firm; level 5, a public warehouse; and level 6, a specialized local delivery firm. Three levels of physical distribution operations take place in the logistical channel using organizational facilities of the producing enterprise. The television sets are warehoused at the factory, transported in company trucks, and stored in a regional warehouse before any specialized intermediary ever participates in the logistical channel.

The distributor, level 3 in the transaction channel, plays a unique role. The distributor, while never physically handling the television sets, has legal title from the time the sets leave the company warehouse (level 4, logistical channel) until they are delivered to the consumer. Of course, the distributor could elect to warehouse in a private facility but in this example has selected to use a public warehouse specialist.

The retailer illustrated is only one of many who sell the line of television sets. The retailer displays limited sets and offers next-day delivery to consumers who enter into a transaction. Delivery is then made from the distributor's stock in the public warehouse, using the services of a specialized local delivery intermediary. When sets are required for display in the retailer's store, they may be obtained by the distributor from the factory's regional warehouse (level 3, logistical channel) or from stock in storage at the public warehouse (level 5, logistical channel). These two possibilities are illustrated as connections between the two channels utilizing common-carrier transportation.

Retailers commonly limit stocks to display models. Sales are negotiated with a commitment to deliver a specified model and color at a particular time and place. Although the transaction is initiated at a retail store, physical exchange may be completed by direct customer shipment from a warehouse strategically located many miles from the point of transaction.

An additional example of separation is the factory branch office that carries no inventory. The office exists for the sole purpose of transaction creation. The physical exchange between seller and buyer may move in a variety of combinations of transport and storage, depending upon value, size, bulk, weight, and perishability of the shipment. Generally, no economic justification exists for locating warehouses and inventories with each branch office. The network of branch offices is best selected to facilitate maximum transaction impact. The selection of logistical intermediaries is designed to achieve the desired physical performance and economies.

A final example of separation comes from the rapidly growing mail-order industry. An order placed at a local catalog desk may be drop-shipped from a distant factory directly to the buyer's home. Although the flow pattern described is only one of many observable arrangements in mail order, all such systems are designed to create separation and thereby the opportunity for specialization.

Interdependence of Transaction and Logistical Activities

The concept of separation of transaction flows and logistical flows should not be interpreted to mean that either can stand alone. Both must be completed as the basis for a satisfactory sale. Both are essential to the marketing process. The major argument in favor of separation of transaction and logistics is that it increases the structural opportunities for specialization.

Separation does not necessarily require different enterprises to enjoy the benefits of specialization. The same intermediary may be very capable of performing both transaction and logistical activities. The degree of individual enterprise separation depends upon the necessity for specialization, economies of scale, available resources, and managerial capabilities.

Transactions are never complete until the logistical process is fully administered. Depending upon the category of goods—convenience, shopping, or speciality—the logistical process may start in anticipation of, be simultaneous with, or follow after negotiation is initiated.[16] The final logistical act occurs in accord with specifications established during the negotiation phase of the transaction. Such specifications relate to time, location, or terms of transfer. Given specifications, minimization of logistical expense is essential to achieve a mutually satisfactory transaction.

Benefits of efficient logistics are not limited to cost reduction. By achieving time and place utility, logistics can enhance transaction capabilities.[17] The ability to promise and provide dependable delivery of a proper assortment serves as a stimulant to purchase agreement and routinization.

Conclusion—Logistics Channels

The logistical process typically requires the coordinated effort of a number of different and often independent enterprises. The channel role of such specialists ranges from providing a specific service to assuming full entreprenurial risk. Regardless of how the channel is organized the functions of adjustment, transfer, storage, handling, and communication are necessary to complete the logistical process. While individual enterprises can be eliminated in channel design, the functions of logistics cannot. When more than two enterprises jointly perform logistical functions, the potential of duplication is introduced into the channel.

The typical channel has a number of enterprises participating. In such situations, the question of interorganizational coordination is an important point of channel design. The resolution of conflict and the negotiation of joint risk is an essential aspect of formulating a logistical strategy.

A useful design concept when arranging logistical channels is to separate structures for transaction and logistical flow. The objective of separation is to increase specialization. It is important to realize three features of the concept of separation: (1) both transaction and logistical flows are highly interrelated, (2) the transaction flow establishes the nature of requirements placed upon the logistical flow, and (3) the same legal institution may perform both flows under a separated structure.

Given the perspective of competitive environment and the nature of channel arrangements, attention is now directed to the formulation of the logistical affairs of a specific enterprise. The integrative logic is the systems concept.

---

[16] This classification is widely used in marketing to describe conditions surrounding the availability of consumer goods in the marketplace. Different exchange channel considerations relate to each, which, in turn, may dictate different timing in actual physical distribution performance with respect to transaction.

[17] For a discussion of time and space utility, see James L. Heskett, "Spatial and Temporal Aspects of Physical Distribution," in Peter D. Bennett, ed., "Marketing and Economic Development," *Proceedings of American Marketing Association*, 1965, pp. 679–87; and James L. Heskett, "A Missing Link in Physical Distribution System Design," *Journal of Marketing*, October 1966, pp. 37–41.

The Systems Concept

The exact origins of the systems approach to problem solving are difficult to trace since the concept of a system is closely related to all forms of organized activity.[18] The first significant applications of systems analysis, however, developed during World War II. Faced with the challenges of global war, scientists developed an organized methodology to guide the research and development of complex physical and organizational problems. This approach is now commonly referred to as *systems analysis*. Technical aspects of logistical design are treated in Part Three. However, a basic understanding of the systems concept is desirable for a full appreciation of integrated logistics.

The systems concept stresses total integrated effort toward the accomplishment of a predetermined objective. Such objectives for a logistical system can be varied. For example, the objective might be the lowest cost operation or the most consistent method of customer service. Given the stated objective, a system capable of obtaining the desired results can be designed.

Under the systems approach, attention is directed to the interaction of all parts of the system. These parts are referred to as *components* of the system. Each *component* has a specific function to perform for attainment of the objective of the total system. To illustrate, consider a precision high-fidelity stereotape player. Many components are combined into an integrated system for the single purpose of reproducing sound. The speakers, the transistors, the amplifier, and other components only exist to the end that their combined performance results in the desired quality of sound.

From this basic review some principles can be stated concerning systems in general. First, the performance of the total system is of singular importance. Components exist and are justified only to the extent that they enhance total system performance. Second, components need not possess optimum design on an individual basis, because emphasis is based upon their integrated relationship in the system. Third, a functional relationship exists between components which may stimulate or hinder combined performance. This relationship is called a *trade-off*. Finally, it is explicit that components linked together as a system can, on a combined basis, produce end results greater than that possible through individual performance. In fact, the desired result may be unattainable without such synergistic performance.

These principles are basic and logically consistent. Without question, a logistical system with balanced integration of all component parts should be able to attain greater results than one lacking coordinated performance. However, although logical and indisputable in concept, an effective application of the systems approach is operationally difficult.

Until recently, the activities of logistics often were performed within enterprises on an individual basis. For example, transportation and inventory

---

[18] See page 7 for a brief historical review of the systems concept.

were managed by separate organizational units with little effort toward integration. To the degree that such isolated performance exists, a serious barrier to the realization of fully integrated benefits may also exist. In the final analysis, it matters little how much is spent for an individual component—transportation, for example—as long as the overall logistical objectives are achieved at the lowest total cost expenditure.

One useful way to view the potential of logistics as an enterprise-wide support system is to disregard organizational arrangements. Placing primary emphasis upon the cross-functional arrangement of system components permits maximum creativity in system design without involvement in traditional organizational hangups.

Logistical System Components

Five components combine to form the logistical system: (1) facility location structure, (2) transportation, (3) inventory, (4) communication, and (5) handling and storage. While these components are similar to the logistical process functions discussed earlier in this chapter, attention will be directed now to the performance of specific logistical tasks by the individual enterprise.[19] Keep in mind, however, two important factors when viewing components from the vantage point of the single enterprise.

First, while an enterprise desires a high degree of congruity with others in a distribution channel, such alliances are limited to agreements on common interorganizational policies and programs. Risk for performance of logistical functions will be accepted only to the extent that it corresponds with the organization's goal attainment or counterbalance of power. Decisions as to who will perform which functions in a distribution channel are therefore matters for negotiation. Once these negotiations are stabilized, they in effect become logistical operating parameters. Each individual enterprise involved in a marketing or purchasing situation, given negotiation of transaction conditions, must legally make its own arrangements in implementing its share of the channel's overall logistical responsibility. The outcome of such negotiations forms the base for planning the logistical system. It also follows that an individual enterprise may be engaged in the various functions of logistics to varying degrees and therefore will be more or less involved in each of the five system components.[20]

Second, service firms such as transportation carriers or public warehouses often play an important role in the logistical system of an enterprise. In essence, such intermediary specialists represent substitute arrangements for the performance of specific logistical functions by the enterprise itself. While

[19] In this sense the individual enterprise is viewed as one participant within the channel of distribution.

[20] The degree of involvement in each logistical activity area depends to a large degree upon the enterprise's vertical integration.

for-hire specialists only assume limited risk for performance, when included in a logistical system they are assumed willing to accept a degree of managerial direction and control from their customers.

Thus consideration of logistical system components often extends beyond the normal organizational structure of the single enterprise to include distribution channel alliances and potential utilization of for-hire specialists. Attention is directed initially to the basic components common to all logistical systems.

Facility Structure

Classical economic analysis had been deficient in that it neglected the importance of facility location to operating performance. When economists studied supply-and-demand relationships within a variety of market structures, location advantages and transportation cost differentials were often assumed to be either nonexistent or equal among competitive firms.[21] Business, in contrast, cannot neglect the impact of location structure upon its ability to realize an adequate return on investment. The network of facilities selected by an enterprise's management is fundamental to ultimate logistical results. The number, size, and geographical arrangement of facilities operated or used bear a direct relationship to the enterprise's customer service capabilities and corresponding logistical cost outlay.

That a great deal of disparity exists between geographical market areas is an accepted fact. The top 10 trading markets in the United States account for over 42 per cent of potential product sales or services.[22] It follows that any enterprise marketing on a national basis must give serious attention to the location of fixed facilities near these prime consumer markets. A similar geographic disparity exists in raw-material and component-parts markets or source locations.

A realistic appraisal of competition makes it clear that all business transactions must be developed within and between a given framework of location points. The facility network of an enterprise represents a series of locations to which and through which material and products move. For planning purposes, such facilities include production plants, warehouses, and retail stores. If the specialized services of transportation firms or public warehouses are employed, the facilities of these specialists are considered a significant part of the network.

The importance of selecting the best possible network of facilities cannot be overemphasized. Although relocation of all facilities at one time would be inconceivable for an enterprise, considerable latitude remains in location selection and facility design over a period of time. The selection of a superior

---

[21] The classical assumption of economics is often referred to as the "Anglo-Saxon bias." See Appendix II for a detailed development.

[22] Derived from U.S. Department of Commerce census statistics. The capability to provide overnight delivery service from the top 10 trading markets is over 90 per cent to potential product sales or services in the United States.

set of locations can result in a substantial competitive profit advantage. The degree of logistical efficiency attainable is directly related to and limited by the facility network.

Transportation

Given a facility network, transportation provides the connecting link. Transportation and traffic management have received considerable attention over the years. Almost every enterprise of any size has a traffic manager responsible for administration of its transportation program.

Generally, an enterprise has three alternatives in establishing transportation capability. First, a private fleet of equipment may be purchased or leased. Second, specific contracts may be arranged with transport specialists to provide contract movement service. Third, an enterprise may engage the services of any legally authorized transport company that offers point-to-point transfer at specified charges. These three forms of transport are known as *private*, *contract*, and *common carriage*. From the logistical system viewpoint, three factors are of primary importance in establishment of the transport service capability: (1) cost, (2) speed, and (3) consistency.

The *cost* of transport accrues from the actual payment for movement between two points, plus the expenses related to owning in-transit inventory. Logistical systems should be designed to minimize the transport cost in relation to the total system cost. However, as will be illustrated later, this does not mean that the most inexpensive method of transportation is always desirable.

Speed of transportation service is the time required to complete a movement between two locations. Speed and cost are related in two ways. First, transport specialists capable of providing faster service will charge higher rates. Second, the faster the service, the shorter the time interval during which materials and products are captured in transit.

Consistency of transportation service refers to the measured time performance of a number of movements between two locations. In essence, how dependable is a given method of transportation with respect to time? In many ways, consistency of service is the most important characteristic of transportation. If a given movement takes two days one time and six the next, serious bottlenecks can develop in the flow of goods which impair inventory control. If transport capability lacks consistency, safeguards in terms of inventory safety stocks must be provided in the system to protect against service breakdowns. Transport consistency influences both the seller's and buyer's overall inventory commitment and related risk.

In the design of a logistical system, a delicate balance must be established between transportation cost and quality of service. In some circumstances low-cost slow transfers will be preferred. Other conditions may require faster methods. Finding the proper transportation balance is one of the primary objectives of logistical system analysis.

Three aspects of transportation should be kept in mind as they relate to the logistical system. First, facility selection establishes a structure or network that limits the range of transport alternatives and determines the nature of the transfer effort to be accomplished. Second, the cost of physical transfer involves more than a carrier's freight bill for movement between two locations. Third, the entire effort to integrate transport capability into a logistical system may be defeated if the service is sporadic and inconsistent.

Inventory

The requirement for transport between facilities is based on the inventory policy followed by an enterprise. Theoretically, an enterprise could stock each and every item carried in inventory in the same quantity at every facility. Few enterprises, however, would follow such a luxurious inventory program, since the total cost would be prohibitive. The objective of inventory integration into the logistical system is to maintain the lowest quantity of items consistent with customer service goals. Excessive inventories can compensate for errors in the design of the basic system and may even help overcome poor administration of logistical activities. However, inventory used as a crutch will result eventually in increased total cost.

Logistical programs should be initiated with the objective of committing as few assets to inventory as possible. The answer to a sound inventory program is found in selective deployment centering on four factors: (1) customer qualities, (2) product qualities, (3) transport integration, and (4) competitor performance. Each of these factors is discussed briefly.

Every enterprise selling to a variety of customers is confronted with a range of relative profitability. Some customers are very profitable and others are not. Such profitability stems, for example, from range of product-line purchases, volume of purchases, price, marketing services required, and the support activities necessary to maintain an ongoing relationship. Highly profitable customers constitute the core market of an enterprise. Inventory policies should be designed to protect core customers by providing rapid and consistent logistical service.

Most enterprises experience a substantial variance in the volume and profitability of individual products within a product line. Often, the typical enterprise with a wide assortment finds that 20 per cent of the products marketed account for 80 per cent of the profit. Given this variance, a realistic appraisal should be made of the reason low-profit items are carried in the assortment. On the surface, it would seem obvious that an enterprise would want to provide a high degree of consistent delivery service on highly profitable products. Less profitable items, however, may be necessary to provide full-line service to profitable customers. Therefore, all factors must be considered when selectively developing inventory policy. Many enterprises find it desirable to hold product inventories on slow-moving or low-profit items at a centralized distribution warehouse, utilizing rapid transportation methods when these items are ordered by a customer.

Selection of a product assortment to be stocked at a specific facility will have a direct impact on transportation cost. Most transportation rates are based on shipment size. Thus it may be sound policy to stock more items at a specific facility to generate larger-volume shipments. The corresponding savings in unit transportation cost may more than offset the increase in unit inventory holding cost.

Finally, inventory stocking programs are not created in a competitive vacuum. An enterprise will be more desirable to do business with if it has the ability to provide rapid delivery of a complete assortment of products. Therefore, inventory may be placed in a specific warehouse to improve logistical impact even when such commitments increase cost. Such inventory policies may result from an effort to gain a differential advantage over a competitor or to neutralize one that a competitor currently enjoys. The strategy of competitively stimulated inventory stocking increases in direct relationship to the ability of customers to substitute various competitors' products.

Material inventory exists in the logistical system for different reasons than finished product inventory. The four aspects discussed above regarding finished products do not necessarily relate to material inventories. With MRP time phasing, the critical objective is to maintain production schedule continuity with a minimum commitment to inventory holding.[23]

An understanding that an integral relationship exists among facilities, transportation, and inventory is fundamental. With inventory, it is desirable to be as selective as possible in policy development.

Communication

Communication is an often-neglected activity in the logistical system. In the past such neglect was due in part to the lack of data-processing and data-transmission equipment capable of handling the necessary flow of information. A more important reason, however, has been the lack of understanding regarding the impact rapid and accurate communication can have upon logistical performance.

Deficiencies in the quality of information can result in countless problems. Such deficiencies fall into two broad categories. First, information received may be incorrect with respect to appraisal of trends and events. Because a great deal of logistical flow takes place in anticipation of future transactions, an inaccurate appraisal can result in inventory deficiency or inventory over-commitment. Second, information may be inaccurate with respect to a specific customer's needs. An enterprise that processes an incorrect order confronts all the costs of logistics without the resultant sale. Indeed, the costs are often compounded by the absorbed cost of returned inventory and, if the sales opportunity still exists, another attempt to provide the proper assortment.

[23] MRP is discussed in greater detail in Chapter 4, pages 105–106.

The speed of information flow is also directly related to the integration of facilities, transportation, and inventory. It makes little sense for a firm to accumulate orders at a local sales office for a week, mail them to a regional office, send them to the data-processing department, assign them to a distribution warehouse, and then ship them via air for fast delivery. Perhaps a direct phone call would have been justified from the customer's office, if such rapid order transmittal would have resulted in faster delivery at a lower total cost. Once again, it is a question of balance among all components of the logistical system.

Two managerial tasks are directly associated with logistical communication. The first is customer order processing. An order is a critical information flow which represents the prime input to the logistical system. The second task is order control: administration of an order until it is correctly received by a customer in undamaged condition. On-time shipment of a customer order is not sufficient logistical performance. The order must also be acceptable in quality and in the quantity promised.

The more efficient the design of a firm's logistical system, the more sensitive it is to disturbances in information flow. Fincly balanced systems have no extra inventory holdings. In such situations, safety stocks are maintained at the minimum level based on transportation capability. Incorrect information can cause a serious disturbance in system performance, and delays in communication flow can amplify the error, causing a series of oscillations in the system for over- and undercorrection. Communication renders a logistical system dynamic. The quality and timeliness of information are the prime determinants of system stability.

Handling and Storage

Four of the components of a basic logistical system—facility location, transportation capacity, inventory allocation, and communication network—are subject to a variety of alternative design arrangements, each of which has a degree of potential effectiveness and a limit in attainable efficiency. In essence, these four activity centers provide a system structure for integrated product flow. The final area of design—handling and storage—also represents an integral part of the logistical system but does not fit the neat structural scheme of the other components. Handling and storage permeates the system and directly relates to all aspects of operation. It involves the flow of inventory through and between facilities with such flow initiated only in response to a product or material need.

In a broad sense, handling and storage involves movement, packaging, and containerization. Handling accounts for a great deal of the cost of logistics in terms of operations and capital expenditure. It stands to reason that the fewer times a product has to be handled in the total process, the less restricted and more potentially efficient will be the total physical flow.

To facilitate handling efficiency, a grouping of cans, bottles, boxes, or whatever are combined into larger cartons. This *master carton* performs two functions. First, it serves to protect the product throughout the logistical process. Second, the master carton serves as a primary load, allowing handling of one larger package rather than a multitude of individual units.

For efficient handling, master cartons are grouped into large lots. These large lots may be then banded with steel strapping, combined with tape, shrink-wrapped, stocked into a wire cage, or stacked on a wooden pallet. These grouping devices provide a load of sufficient size to justify specialized material-handling equipment.

Technically, the term "container" includes any device used for grouping, ranging from a can used to protect pineapple to a 40-foot sea–truck box loaded on a ship in Hawaii for ultimate delivery in Lansing, Michigan. However, *container* is used here to describe loadings containing more than one master carton.

When effectively integrated into an enterprise's logistical operation, handling and storage can substantially reduce problems related to speed and ease of movement thoughout the system. In fact, several enterprises have been able to design unit loads to move large assortments of products from the production line directly to a customer's shelf. Although such programs carry a proportional expense, if properly developed they may more than pay for themselves through reduced handling, lower transportation costs, improved customer relations, and overall efficiency.

Conclusion—Logistical Components

The main strength of logistics evolves from the development of techniques and concepts for treating components on an integrated basis. Systems technology provides the framework for evaluating alternative logistical designs on a total cost basis. A systems orientation stands in direct contrast to the traditional approach of treating the activities of logistical management on a separate or diffused basis.

In a strategic context, the central focus of logistics is the commitment to inventory. Products and materials are properly viewed as a combination of form, time, place, and possession utilities. Inventory has little value until form is placed at the right time at a location which will provide the opportunity to enjoy possession. If a firm does not consistently meet the requirements of time and place closure, it has nothing to sell. Unless such time and place closure is efficiently achieved, profits and return on investment may be jeopardized. Until the utilities of time and place are achieved, little, if any, value has been added by the logistical process.

Typical Logistical Systems

The many facets of logistics make the design of an operating system a complex assignment. In designing a system with an acceptable balance of performance and cost, management must always keep in mind that any system will require constant adjustment. Thus flexibility becomes an important part of system design. When one considers the variety of logistical systems around the world that service widely diverse markets, it is astonishing that any design similiarity exists from one situation to the next. However, all systems have two characteristics in common. First, they are designed to encourage maximum inventory flow. Second, the systems must be designed within the existing technological state of development of the logistical system components. Technological limits for the performance of major logistical activities result in common patterns among systems. Three basic patterns stand out as the most widely utilized for logistical operations: (1) echelon systems, (2) direct systems, and (3) flexible systems.

Echelon Systems

The term *echelon* implies that the flow of products or materials proceeds through a series of consecutive locations as it moves from origin to final destination. Such steps involve accumulation of inventory in warehouses. Thus the essential characteristic of an echelon system is that inventory is stocked at one or more points prior to arrival at its final destination.

Two common echelon patterns are the establishment of break-bulk and consolidation warehouses in physical distribution systems. The break-bulk warehouse receives large-volume shipments from a variety of suppliers for assortment into combinations required for individual customers or retailers. The food distribution centers operated by major grocery chains, such as Kroger, A & P, Safeway, and Jewel, are prime examples of break-bulk points. The consolidation distribution warehouse is normally operated by an enterprise that produces a product line at different production plants. Consolidation of all products at a central point makes it possible to ship large volumes of the complete product. Major food-processing firms, such as Quaker, Pillsbury, Del Monte, and General Foods, are prime examples of enterprises using consolidation points.

Echelon systems employ warehouses in order to combine a wide variety of products into a single large-volume shipment. Additionally, inventories are held in field location for rapid delivery of customer orders. The echeloned situation favors warehousing in order to enjoy benefits of high volume while providing complete product assortment. Rapid delivery can be realized without a warehouse network. However, when volume is sufficient, a network of strategically located field inventories often provides the best balance of service performance and cost economies.

Direct Systems

Contrasting with the echelon pattern are systems operating *direct* to final destination from one or a limited number of central inventory accumulations.

Direct-distribution enterprises find that their particular marketing efforts can be best supported by a central inventory from which customer orders are filled. Direct-product-distribution systems often utilize high-speed transport and electronic order processing to overcome geographical separation from customers. Examples of direct shipments are carload to customer movement and consumer mail-order deliveries. Direct-shipment systems are commonly used to satisfy material acquisitions, owing to the large size of the average shipment from vendor to procurement source.

Flexible Systems

The most common logistical systems are those combining the principles of the echelon and direct systems into a *flexible* operating pattern. As noted earlier, inventory selectivity is encouraged in the design of a logistical system. Some products or materials may be held in warehouses; others may be distributed directly. In many cases, the nature, composition, or order size may determine the location from which a customer will be serviced.

For example, one enterprise supplies after-market replacement automobile parts to support its new-car distribution. Its system is designed to warehouse inventories at various distances from prime markets. The slower the part turnover, the more centralized the inventory. The slowest moving parts are held at a central location, which directly supplies the entire world.

A second enterprise, which supplies industrial replacement parts, follows a completely opposite distribution policy. In order to rapidly meet unexpected demands, this enterprise inventories sufficient quantities of all slow movers at each distribution warehouse. In contrast to the first firm, fast- and medium-turnover products are supplied on a regular basis directly to customers from plants and central supply centers.

The difference in policies is explained when one examines the market that each enterprise serves and the degree of product differentiation each enjoys. The automobile enterprise faces extensive competition on replacement parts for new models. However, as the original product ages, the competition decreases, making this enterprise the sole supplier. The industrial parts enterprise, on the other hand, sells a product with very little style deterioration and a high degree of competitive substitutability. In this enterprise's market, a supplier is measured by purchasing agents in terms of how fast unexpected production breakdowns can be remedied.

Each enterprise faces a different marketing problem, and each utilizes a different flexible logistics policy with respect to warehousing finished product inventories.[24] Each enterprise must study its own logistical requirements to determine the pattern that will best satisfy its service requirements at the lowest total cost.

---

[24] The potential of flexible operations is discussed further in Chapter 8, pages 279–281.

Summary

The systems approach is essential to a comprehensive analysis of the logistical requirements of an enterprise. To facilitate logistical performance, facility structure, transportation, inventory, communication, and handling and storage must be highly coordinated. Such coordination has three levels of concern: (1) within the overall logistical system; (2) within the enterprise in terms of a balanced effort with marketing, manufacturing, and finance; and (3) within the competitive environment faced by the enterprise.

The process of integration requires coordination with other organizations within the overall distribution channel. The distribution or marketing channel is of fundamental importance to physical distribution because the channel is the area within which marketing and logistics culminate in customer transactions. The notion of loosely aligned middlemen linked together in pursuit of joint opportunity is not consistent with the logic of efficient logistical systems. One way to increase marketing efficiency is to improve physical movement within the distribution channel. Advantages in operation may result when physical flow is separated from other flows in the total distribution process. The development of a specialized network of exchange intermediaries allows maximum control and economies of specialization in physical flow.

Many enterprise costs of replenishment are hidden between departments of an enterprise, are not necessarily under the control of any given department, and are extremely difficult to identify. In addition, little consideration has been given to problems of coordinating and controlling logistics beyond the legal limits of control of an individual enterprise. Most physical distribution flow proceeds from production to consumption through specialized enterprises linked as a logistical channel. Each of these independent units or links may perform an excellent individual job of physical distribution, even though, as a totality, the overall channel suffers from expensive duplication. Therefore, the proper planning of an enterprise's logistical effort must transcend the total channel.

As a total grouping of enterprises, a logistical channel must perform a specific sequence of functions in order to support transaction-creating efforts. The total channel is in effect, then, an integrated network with well-defined objectives. The most effective total channel is one capable of meeting objectives and controlling the flow of materials and finished goods in accordance with time and space demands. The nature of logistical operations within a specific enterprise is the subject of Chapter 3.

Questions

1. As shown in Figure 2-1, why do corporate managers have various degrees of control over the environmental forces that form the ecology of the enterprise in comparison to the managerial factors?

2. What is the concept of separation and how does it lead to potential increases in overall operating efficiency?
3. Why are exchange activities dependent upon the transaction channel for formulation of operational specifications?
4. Discuss risk with respect to the performance of the channel functions of exchange. Why is risk disproportionate among channel members?
5. Contrast vertically owned and vertically controlled distribution systems. What is the concept of channel leadership, and how does it influence the design of a logistical system?
6. Would you agree that all organized behavior is to some degree systems-oriented? Describe the concept of trade-off and illustrate why it is an integral aspect of the systems concept.
7. Illustrate from your experience an example of failure to solve a problem on a total systems basis.
8. Why is location selection fundamental to the design of a logistical system?
9. Explain the difference between speed and consistency of service in transportation.
10. Why would a firm normally expect to find that 20 per cent of its products account for 80 per cent of its sales? Why do you think such relationships are significant to logistical planning?

Logistical Operations

The essence of logistical management is a balanced integration of all components that form the logistical system. As indicated in Chapter 1, balanced integration is ideally realized by arranging the logistical operation to achieve the desired service performance at the lowest possible total cost. One way to develop a deeper understanding of the nature of integrated logistical operations is to visualize all activity as taking place within a complex structure of performance cycles. This chapter presents, develops, and illustrates the performance-cycle concept as it applies to physical distribution, materials management, and inventory transfer operating systems.

The initial section of Chapter 3 examines the integral nature of a performance-cycle orientation to logistical operations. The proposition presented is that, regardless of its size and complexity, a logistical system can be explained and understood in terms of its inherent structure of performance cycles. While the physical distribution system may have a significantly different mission than the materials management operation, both systems must be organized to function as a series of performance cycles. Following development of the performance-cycle concept, the remaining sections of the chapter discuss and illustrate specific features of physical distribution management, materials management, and internal inventory transfer operations.

Logistical Performance Cycles

Visualizing logistical operations as a grouping of performance cycles provides a basic orientation which can be used for design analysis and operational administration.[1] At the most basic level, each set of vendors, enterprise facilities,

---

[1] The term *performance cycle* is used interchangeably with *lead time* and *replenishment cycle*. Types of logistical performance cycles are illustrated in Figure 3-1.

and/or customer locations engaging in any form of logistical activity must be interconnected by communication and transportation. The specific facility locations within a performance cycle are identified as *nodes*. The communication and transportation aspects of the performance cycle are identified as *links*.

In addition to nodes and links, a logistical performance cycle must be supported by a *level* of inventory which is an integral part of the operating system. Such inventory committed to the system consists of average investment to cover reorder time plus safety stock.[2]

Finally, a performance cycle must be faced with an *input/output* requirement in order to function in a dynamic manner. The *input* to a performance cycle is the volume of product or material orders the system handles. If the average level of demand for performance is great, a substantial volume of throughput will be experienced. The net result will be a broad range of design alternatives. Similarly, a high-volume throughput system will in all probability require a variety of performance cycles to satisfy overall requirements. If input is not large, the complexity of the network will be reduced. The design options will also be reduced, since little opportunity will exist to aggregate volume movements between any two nodal points.

System *output* relates to the capability of a structure of performance cycles to satisfy operational requirements. To the extent that individual operational requirements are satisfied, the performance cycle structure is *effective* in accomplishing its stated mission. *Efficiency* is the expenditure of resources necessary to render the overall logistical system effective.

Depending upon the purpose of the particular performance cycle, all activities may or may not be under the complete control of the enterprise. For example, internal inventory transfer cycles typically will be under complete control. However, performance cycles related to physical distribution and materials management normally include performance controlled by separate corporations.

It is also important to realize that the frequency of logistical activity will vary greatly among performance cycles. Some may exist to support a one-time purchase or sales activity. In this case the cycle is designed, implemented, and then abolished. In contrast, other performance cycles function almost continuously. An additional complicating element is that any single location in a logistical system may be involved in several hundred different performance cycles. For example, the warehouse facility of a hardware wholesaler might receive merchandise from many manufacturers on a more-or-less regular basis.

When one considers an enterprise of national or multinational scope, marketing a broad product line to many customers, engaged in basic manufacturing and assembly, and procuring raw materials and components from a variety of sources, the notion of a performance cycle linking every pair of locations may be difficult to comprehend. It is almost impossible to guess how

[2] This relationship is developed in Chapter 6, pages 154–155.

FIGURE 3-1
Logistical Performance Cycles

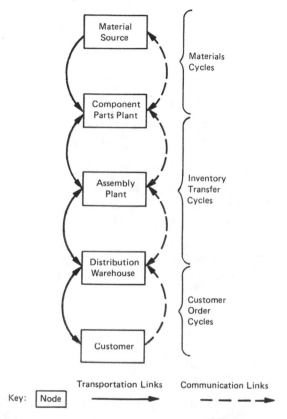

many individual performance cycles exist in the logistical systems of General Motors or Sears Roebuck.

Regardless of the number of performance cycles an enterprise uses to satisfy its logistical requirements, the important point is that each cycle needs to be designed and operated individually. A performance cycle orientation is an important first step toward understanding an enterprise's logistical requirements. In essence, the performance cycle structure provides a framework for implementation of the systems approach discussed in Chapter 2.

Figure 3-1 illustrates the performance-cycle concept in terms of basic application in each of the logistical operating systems. Figure 3-2 illustrates the more complex network of performance cycles one would expect to find in a multiecheloned and flexible linkage structure.

Three points are significant in the performance-cycle approach to understanding logistical arrangements. First, the performance cycle has been identified as the fundamental concept around which integration of logistical

FIGURE 3-2
Structure of a Multiecheloned Flexible Logistical Network

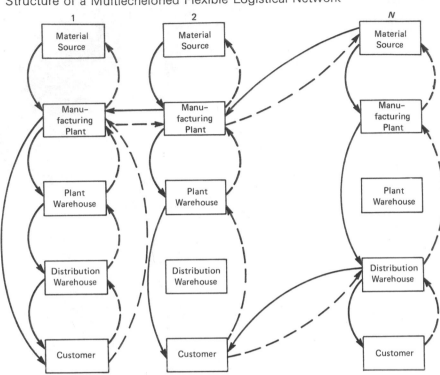

functions is achieved. Second, the concept of performance-cycle structure is basically the same whether one is concerned with physical distribution, materials management, or inventory transfer. Third, regardless of how vast and complex the total logistical system structure, the essential working aspects of its anatomy can be identified and illustrated in terms of individual performance-cycle structures.

Attention is now directed to the specific nature of operations associated with physical distribution, materials management, and inventory transfer.

Physical Distribution Management Operations

Physical distribution management is the aspect of overall logistics concerned with the processing and delivery of customer orders. Physical distribution is essential to marketing because timely and economical product delivery is necessary for profitable transactions. The process of marketing can be broadly divided into transaction-creating and physical fulfillment activities. Physical distribution is primarily concerned with the physical fulfillment activities.

The development of physical distribution systems to support modern marketing is a dynamic aspect of management, because an enterprise constantly changes parts of its marketing mix in an effort to gain and hold a competitive advantage in the marketplace.[3] This section of the chapter is devoted to a general review of modern marketing as it interrelates with and encompasses physical distribution. The objective is an in-depth understanding of the integral nature of physical distribution operations to an enterprise's marketing effort.

A Marketing Perspective

In today's business climate the predominant philosophy of enterprise planning is a marketing orientation.[4] Such an orientation is designed to underscore the need for successful penetration of markets and the importance of profitable transactions to enterprise survival. This posture, referred to as the *marketing concept*, emerged during the shift from a seller's market to a buyer's market following World War II.[5]

The marketing concept is a market-based planning philosophy dedicated to identifying customer needs and mobilizing enterprise resources to serve selected needs.[6] The marketing concept starts with the goal of satisfying consumer needs at a profit, and all systems of the firm must be integrated toward this fundamental goal. If an enterprise is to survive, all systems— marketing, production, finance, and logistics—must function as a totality aimed at generation of a stream of profitable transactions.[7] The marketing concept provides the integrative force in corporate planning.

Three basic pillars support the marketing concept: (1) customer needs are more basic than products, (2) products must be viewed in an end-use context, and (3) volume is secondary to profit. Each of these will be discussed briefly.

The notion that customer needs are more basic than products places a priority upon studying market opportunities to determine which products are needed and will be purchased. Products that can be manufactured economically may or may not be sold profitably, depending upon customer needs. All products will die over time as new and better methods of satisfying consumer needs are discovered through research and development. Thus the marketing concept starts with an in-depth study of markets in order to discover potential product opportunities. Once a market opportunity is isolated, a product may or may not materialize, depending upon the feasibility of successful production, adequate financial resources, physical distribution capability,

---

[3] For a full development of this competitive rivalry, see Thomas A. Staudt, Donald A. Taylor, and Donald J. Bowersox, *A Managerial Introduction to Marketing*, 3rd ed. (Englewood Cliffs, N.J.: Prentice-Hall, Inc., 1976), pp. 3–17.

[4] J. B. McKitterick, "Profitable Growth—The Challenge to Marketing Management," speech before the 45th National Conference of the American Marketing Association, June 20, 1962.

[5] The term *buyer's market* refers to a situation where the buyer has considerable freedom of choice between product alternatives.

[6] Staudt, Taylor, and Bowersox, op. cit., Chap. 2.

[7] Ibid.

and marketing skill. The opportunity for profitable transactions initiates in the marketplace—customer needs are more basic than products.

For successful marketing, products must be viewed in an end-use context. This second pillar of the marketing concept stresses that products be placed in a context where customers can readily make the transition from concept to use. Once again the integration of total available resources is required. Four economic utilities add value to a product in a use context: form, possession, time, and place utility. The form utility of a product is generated in the manufacturing process. Marketing creates possession utility in the product by informing the potential customer of the availability of the product and facilitating the transaction phase of the overall process. Physical distribution creates time and place utility. Thus marketing can specify the color, shape, and style of the product and create a convenient and economical transaction between buyer and seller. Manufacturing can build a high-quality product at the lowest possible unit cost. It remains for physical distribution to ensure that the right product is at the right place at the right time. Profitable transactions will materialize only if all four utilities are integrated in an end-use context.

The final pillar of the marketing concept highlights the importance of stressing profitability rather than volume in selecting priorities.[8] The important measure of success is not the number of units sold during the planning period but the degree of profitability resulting from accumulated transactions. Therefore, variations in all forms of utility offered—form, possession, time, and place—can be economically justified if a particular segment of the market is willing to pay for the adjustment in offering. Markets consist of many different segments, each of which has a particular product preference. The refinement of market segmentation and product differentiation acknowledges that all aspects of an offering are subject to modification when justified on the basis of profitability.[9] The integrated marketing concept provides the foundation for planning overall operations for all facets of the enterprise.

Many attempts have been made to describe the activities of managerial marketing. For purposes of illustration, the functional approach developed by Staudt, Taylor, and Bowersox is adopted. These authors describe integrated managerial marketing in terms of nine functions to be accomplished if profitable transactions are to materialize. They are: (1) market delineation, (2) purchase behavior motivation, (3) product-service adjustment, (4) channel

---

[8] McKitterick, op. cit.

[9] The classic article on this point is Wendell R. Smith, "Product Differentiation and Market Segmentation as Alternative Marketing Strategies," *Journal of Marketing*, July 1956, pp. 3–8. Also see Theodore Levitt, "Marketing Myopia," *Harvard Business Review*, July–August 1960, pp. 45–56. More recent treatments are found in R. C. Blattbey and S. K. Sen, "Market Segmentation Using Models of Multidimensional Purchasing Behavior," *Journal of Marketing*, Vol. 38 (October 1974), pp. 17–28; J. T. Plummer, "The Concept and Application of Life Cycle Segmentation," *Journal of Marketing*, Vol. 38 (January 1974), pp. 33–37; and Harvey N. Shycon and Christopher R. Sprague, "Put a Price Tag on Your Customer Serving Levels," *Harvard Business Review*, July–August 1975, pp. 71–77.

selection, (5) physical distribution, (6) communications, (7) pricing, (8) organization, and (9) administration. Table 3-1 provides a brief definition of the managerial point of emphasis in each function.

TABLE 3-1
Managerial Functions of Marketing Defined

1. The *market delineation function*—the determination and measurement of potential purchasers and their identifying characteristics.
2. The *purchase behavior motivation function*—the assessment of those direct and indirect factors that underline, impinge upon, and influence purchase behavior.
3. The *product-service adjustment function*—those activities required to match the product-service offering with the market in which it is to be purchased and consumed.
4. The *channel selection function*—the selection and organization of institutions through which the product-service offering is made available to the marketplace.
5. The *physical distribution function*—the actual movement of goods from points of production to points of consumption.
6. The *communications function*—the design and transmitting of information and messages between the buyer and seller to the end that the most favorable climate for the seller is created in the marketplace.
7. The *pricing function*—the determination and administration of prices that meet the objectives of the enterprise.
8. The *organization function*—the structuring and incentive of human resources.
9. The *administration function*—the formulation of operating procedures and standards to control pretransaction and transaction performance and the measurement of post-transaction feedback to generate satisfactory marketing performance on a continuing basis.

Source: Adapted from Thomas A. Staudt, Donald A. Taylor, Donald J. Bowersox, *A Managerial Introduction to Marketing*, 3rd ed. (Englewood Cliffs, N.J.: Prentice-Hall, Inc., 1976), p. 53.

This brief review of managerial marketing from a functional viewpoint stresses the role of marketing as one part of the enterprise engaged in implementing the marketing concept. Two points are of particular importance. First, a clear distinction should be kept in mind between a market-oriented philosophy of planning as contrasted to those functions associated with the performance of the marketing job. Second, it is important to realize the integral nature of physical distribution operations to marketing performance. Although logistics has been introduced as a major system of the enterprise incorporating physical distribution, clearly considerable overlap exists between the logistical job and the marketing job. This integral relationship can be clarified by a discussion of the typical enterprise's marketing strategy.

Logistics in Strategic Marketing

The marketing strategy of an enterprise is a plan which guides the deployment of resources toward the attainment of specific objectives. Given the objectives, the marketing strategy specifies the activities the enterprise will undertake. This combination of activities is called the *marketing mix*.[10] To formulate a marketing mix, distribution, communication, and pricing must be integrated. The critical managerial task in formulating a strategic marketing plan is to determine how much effort to apply to each aspect of the marketing mix. The fundamental concern of logistics in the marketing mix is physical distribution. The management task in physical distribution is to coordinate a relationship between company facilities and middlemen which will result in completion of the time and place aspects of marketing. The result will be that both goods and their titles are moved to the market.

Obviously, considerable overlap exists among the marketing concept, the marketing mix, and the functions of managerial marketing. The marketing concept is the umbrella for the enterprise's goal-oriented planning perspective. The marketing mix and the functions of managerial marketing relate specifically to activities necessary for successful marketing. Both stress the integral nature of physical distribution within the firm's marketing effort.

Physical Distribution Performance

From the foregoing discussion it is clear that physical distribution is far more than a passive support for marketing. In addition to economical delivery, the level and response to customer service represent one of the elements of potential competitive superiority within the integrated marketing mix.

The marketing mix must be dynamic with respect to changes in the marketplace and competition. Thus the level and response aspects of customer service will differ depending upon the specific situation confronted. In this final section physical distribution performance is examined in terms of dynamics, flexibility, and complexity.

TACTICAL ADJUSTMENT ACROSS PRODUCT LIFE CYCLE. Perhaps the best illustration of the need for dynamic physical distribution performance is the product life cycle. The product-life-cycle concept has been developed by marketing planners to illustrate the varying competitive conditions which can be expected to exist during the market life of a product.[11]

Figure 3-3 illustrates a four-stage product life cycle: (1) introductory, (2) growth, (3) saturation–maturity, and (4) obsolescence–decline. Detailed discussion of all marketing ramifications associated with each stage of the life cycle is beyond the scope of this book. Our illustrations, however, empha-

---

[10] For initial development of this concept, see William Lazer and Eugene J. Kelley, eds., *Managerial Marketing: Perspectives and Viewpoints*, 2nd ed. (Homewood, Ill.: Richard D. Irwin, Inc., 1962), p. 413.

[11] For an interesting discussion of overall marketing strategy during the product life cycle, see Theodore Levitt, "Exploit the Product Life Cycle," *Harvard Business Review*, November–December 1965, pp. 81–94, or John E. Smallwood, "The Product Life Cycle: A Key to Strategic Marketing Planning," *Business Topics*, Winter 1973, p. 30.

FIGURE 3-3
Product Life Cycle Concept

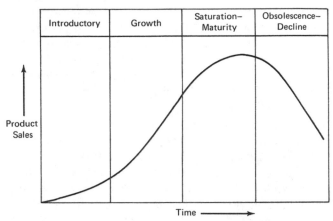

size that the marketing mix of a firm will be different in each stage and that expectations concerning physical distribution performance will also vary.

During the introductory stage of a new product, a high level and response of physical distribution performance is desirable. Since initial distribution of the product is to be developed, a high premium will be placed on having an available stock for customers to draw upon and providing rapid and consistent service on replacement orders. For example, a retail chain may add a new product but invest in only a slim stock. If the product gains customer acceptance, rapid and positive reorder will be required. Marketing communication cost is also high during the introductory stage as potential customers are informed of product availability and persuaded to purchase. Product unavailability during this critical time could dilute the total impact of the marketing effort. Thus during the introductory stage physical distribution plays a prominent role in the integrated marketing offering. Since the market position is not secure, shipment sizes will tend to be small and the frequency of orders erratic. Consequently, the physical distribution costs associated with providing the necessary level of service will be high.

During the growth stage of the product life cycle, the product has gained market acceptance and sales become more predictable. Physical distribution emphasis during the growth stage shifts from a high level of customer service to a more balanced service/cost design. Thus standards of both level and response will be reduced provided that a substantial per unit reduction in physical distribution cost can be realized. Characteristic of the growth stage is expanded market coverage and a high level of profitability in transactions. Terms and conditions of sale will be adjusted to reflect economies associated with physical flow and efforts made to encourage maximum efficiency. During the growth stage, particularly near the end of the stage and prior to intensive competition, the enterprise will experience maximum latitude in controlling physical distribution performance to reflect low total cost.

The saturation–maturity stage is characterized by intense competition. The product faces extensive competition from a variety of substitutes, with price competition a characteristic tactic. Physical distribution performance during the saturation stage can be expected to become highly selective. Competitors will adjust their service performance to provide high levels of availability and response to major customers. Higher expenditures will be allocated to physical distribution performance to assure service to those customers who represent the core of the enterprise's market.

The product's volume declines during the obsolescence–decline stage of the product life cycle. During this period, management is faced with a decision on whether to close out the product or to continue distribution on a restricted basis. During this stage, the physical distribution system must support existing business while avoiding excessive risk in the event that the product is discontinued. Minimum risk thus becomes more important than achieving the lowest cost per unit of physical distribution performance.

The product life cycle illustrates the variety of physical distribution strategies that may be implemented at different times. No "must do" rules exist. Physical distribution performance, like all other elements of the marketing mix, must be altered to meet the market and competitive situation. The level and response of performance will change over time, and the enterprise's willingness and ability to absorb physical distribution cost will also vary across the life cycle.

PERFORMANCE FLEXIBILITY AND COMPLEXITY. As the foregoing discussion of product life cycle indicates, the degree of customer service and associated total cost of physical distribution must be adjusted to the marketing situation. In addition to change across time, the physical distribution system must maintain flexibility and adjust to complexity at any specific point in time. Supporting a single product throughout one life cycle is rather clear. The more prevalent situation, however, involves physical distribution support of multiple products being serviced to different markets through multiple channels. In such a complex situation a physical distribution system must be flexible and capable of coping with change. Some examples are provided in the remainder of this section.

New Product Support. Physical distribution support of new product introduction was briefly discussed under the introductory stage of the product life cycle. It was pointed out that the system would be expected to provide a high level of availability and rapid response during the introductory period. In addition, some aspects of coordinating physical distribution support with introductory communications were noted.

The extent of new product activity anticipated for the future is worth discussion. In the past, growth was easily generated from existing products or acquisition of other enterprises. The pattern for growth in the future, however, appears to be oriented to new product development. This change in emphasis is important to physical distribution for at least three reasons.

First, greater emphasis on new product development means that the physical distribution system will need to accommodate a wider variation in product line. Special handling, transportation, and packaging requirements will increase also as the product line expands, forcing greater flexibility upon the system. Should the expanded product line require special equipment, such as refrigerated trucks or rail tankcars, the task of physical distribution planning and coordination will become more complex.

A second consideration is the requirement to service many different markets through multiple channels. With an expanding market offering, products probably will become more specialized and sold to smaller and highly service oriented market segments. To reach these markets, a firm may need to use several different exchange and transaction channels. The result will be small product volume flowing through any specific channel and less opportunity to aggregate volume for cost reductions.

A final implication of increased new product introductions stems from the knowledge that marketing is far from an exact science when it comes to the development of new products. As noted earlier in this chapter, the development of new products requires an interpretation of customer needs. In addition, the potential product must be projected into a use context for an effective communication program to inform and persuade potential buyers. In more than half the cases of new product development, the product offered does not experience sufficient longevity in the marketplace to repay its development cost. From a physical-distribution-operations viewpoint, it is difficult to project which products will win or lose. Extreme care must be taken not to influence product failure by being unable to support the product during critical points of introduction. On the other hand, inventory stockpiling and advanced physical distribution of products to support sales that never materialize can be extremely expensive. Physical distribution operations must be handled with care with respect to new product planning. Distribution planning for new products can be expected to increase during the years ahead.

Customer Service Myopia. Just how much customer service should be provided to support the overall integrated marketing mix is a complex question. The system capacity to provide both high levels of availability and rapid and consistent response to customer orders is costly. Chapters 8 and 9, which deal with the formulation of logistical policy, will illustrate that the cost of improving the level of customer service performance increases at a far faster rate than the corresponding service increases. Therefore, enterprises offering extremely high degrees of customer service will confront high total costs of physical distribution.

Failure on the part of managers to appreciate the relationship of incremental customer service and associated cost can result in commitments to high degrees of performance. The ideal result is the selection of a service level and response that will support sales without setting standards so high as to endanger performance. This proper degree of service can be determined only by experimentation and a willingness to formulate a policy regarding customer service to be offered.

With modern physical distribution technology, almost any degree of service can be provided if an enterprise is willing to pay the cost. In fact, most firms attempt to provide service in excess of that necessary for successful marketing. One of the major tasks in physical distribution planning is to replace the tendency to overservice with a sound approach to the determination of necessary customer service. The desire to place a warehouse in every customer's backyard or to place consignment inventories in anticipation of sales must be replaced with a systematic approach to the design of a physical distribution system. Such design should be based upon cost–revenue benefit analysis.[12] Overcoming customer service myopia is one of the most difficult tasks of physical distribution planning.

Scrambled merchandising. In today's economy, retailers sell wholesale, wholesalers sell retail, hardware stores sell soft goods, department stores sell food, food stores sell appliances, they all sell toys, and discount stores sell everything. This new structure of retailing is often referred to as *scrambled merchandising* or *channel jumping*.

Scrambled merchandising is not restricted to retailing. Finished goods often move to the same retailer from wholesalers, distributors, jobbers, assemblers, and direct from producers. In some cases, goods bypass retailers altogether and move directly to consumers. These changing patterns of shipment have forced substantial alterations in the physical distribution systems of individual enterprises.

To accommodate multiple-channel physical distribution, many manufacturers and retailers have been forced into operating distribution warehouses. To a significant degree, manufacturer warehouses have replaced many of the specialized wholesalers, such as drug and hardware, who were once the dominant distribution channel members. Such specialized intermediaries were unable to service adequately the distribution patterns of multiple channels.

Thus today's complex business arena demands that an enterprise provide physical distribution service within many different channels. The simple task of delivering almost all manufacturing output to a few wholesalers has been replaced by a variety of physical fulfillment systems delivering to numerous customer warehouses and, in many cases, direct to retail stores. Under multichannel distribution, less volume is delivered to any one location, which often results in higher per unit costs. On the other hand, customer demands for high degrees of service are more direct, since no middleman exists between manufacturer and retailers in many channels. The practice of channel jumping has simultaneously increased the complexity of physical distribution and reinforced the need for flexibility in operations.

[12] See Chapter 9, pages 268–269 for an expanded discussion.

Materials Management Operations

The aspect of overall logistics concerned with the procurement of raw materials, parts, and merchandise for resale is materials management. Materials management is essential to manufacturing because timely and economical delivery is necessary to maintain efficient and continuous production. Raw materials and parts constitute the highest single cost expenditure of enterprises engaged in basic manufacturing. From the viewpoint of wholesale or retail establishments, the steady availability of merchandise is essential to profitable performance. Therefore, extreme care is necessary to assure that procurement meets quality specifications and is performed at the lowest possible total cost.

The perspective of materials management presented in this chapter includes all aspects of logistical support ranging from manufacturing to retail replenishment. Among various levels of procurement the manufacturing support situation is the most complex application of integrated materials management. In addition to raw materials and parts, a typical enterprise must procure a variety of other items, such as supplies and equipment. In nonmanufacturing situations, a variety of retail and mechandising enterprises exist that do not engage in any form of manufacturing but do, in fact, have a great stake in economical procurement. The basic concepts of materials management apply directly to all procurement situations.

Objectives of Materials Management

The focal point of materials management is to provide continuity and stability in procurement. The fundamental objective is to provide the correct assortment of materials, parts, or merchandise for resale to the desired location, when needed, and in an economical manner. The efficient support of manufacturing engages all logistical components. Thus the materials management subsystem, similar to physical distribution and inventory transfer, involves transportation, inventory warehousing, communications, and handling and storage.

Materials management activities initiate from the operating plan. The operating plan provides a statement of requirements to support manufacturing or marketing operations and contains specifications concerning when and for what facility the items are to be procured. The task of materials management is to satisfy economically the requirements outlined during operational planning.[13]

The actual formulation of the operations plan is not recommended as a materials management responsibility. The plan is ideally formulated as part of logistical coordination. The sequence of events that culminate in the plan is discussed in the next chapter. At this point it is sufficient to note that the

[13] See Chapter 1 for the relationship between materials management and operations planning, pages 13–17. In manufacturing the term *master schedule* or *master plan* often is used to identify that portion of the operations plan related to production activities.

operations plan is formulated on the basis of sales forecasts, order-processing information, and the master production schedule.[14]

Given the operations plan, materials management is concerned with achieving six interrelated objectives. [15] Each objective will now be discussed.

BEST PRICE PROCUREMENT. Foremost, materials management is concerned with procuring the required raw materials, parts, and products for resale at the best possible price. The best possible price may not always be the lowest price available in the market place. Naturally, price must be viewed in terms of consistent quality and continuity of supply.

A great deal of the effort of materials managers involves price negotiation and cost reduction. Most prices are negotiated, and to determine a fair price it may be necessary to study supplier operations to develop a detailed understanding of supplier costs. Such an understanding of cost is also integral to decisions regarding whether a firm should continue to purchase externally or consider internal manufacture of the part.[16]

With raw materials, the best price may well change as a function of supply and demand.[17] The timing of purchases must be based on an appraisal of most likely future prices as well as the cost associated with maintaining stockpiles. A substantial element of risk is involved in procurement, which can make hedging economically justifiable at times.

SUPPLY CONTINUITY. The maintenance of a continuous supply is an essential aspect of materials management. To avoid erratic availability it may be necessary to establish standing commitments with vendors to assure continuous supply. Such commitments are made in advance of formulation of a specific operations plan. Thus materials management is involved in projecting

[14] The sales forecast, combined with customer orders, formulates the basic manufacturing assignment. The production schedule determines when, where, how much, and at what point in time they will be produced. See page 106.

[15] The exact functions will vary depending upon author's coverage; for example, see Lamar Lee, Jr., and Donald W. Dobler, *Purchasing and Materials Management*, rev. ed. (New York: McGraw-Hill Book Company, 1971); Wilbur B. England, *The Purchasing System* (Homewood, Ill.: Richard D. Irwin, Inc., 1967); E. S. Buffa, *Production Inventory Systems: Planning and Control* (Homewood, Ill.: Richard D. Irwin, Inc., 1968), Dean S. Ammer, *Materials Management*, rev. ed. (Homewood, Ill.: Richard D. Irwin, Inc., 1970); Wilbur B. England, *Modern Procurement Management: Principles and Cases*, 5th ed. (Homewood, Ill.: Richard D. Irwin, Inc., 1970); and Stuart F. Heinritz and Paul V. Farrell, *Purchasing*, 5th ed. (Englewood Cliffs, N.J.: Prentice-Hall, Inc., 1971).

[16] For a comprehensive discussion of the factors involving the make-versus-buy decision, see England, op. cit., pp. 71–81; J. W. Culliton, *Make or Buy*, Division of Research Study 27 (Boston: Harvard Business School, 1956); and Alfred G. Oxenfeldt, *Make or Buy: Factors Affecting Decisions* (New York: McGraw-Hill Book Company, 1956). For further discussion and illustration, see Chapter 12, pages 370–372.

[17] Raw-material speculation so as to realize an "appreciation" value on material stockpiles is less frequently practiced today than it was in the past. Nevertheless, the supply–demand relationship in the market has a major impact on evaluation of "best price." See Lee and Dobler, op. cit., pp. 106–11.

availability and taking appropriate steps to protect the interests of the enterprise.

The serious nature of maintaining continuity is easily understood when one considers the present high cost of manufacturing disruption. If the shortage of materials or parts causes a work stoppage, in most cases the burden of manufacturing cost continues because of labor contract commitments and capital investment in plant facilities. In addition, an unplanned work stoppage will have a direct impact upon marketing performance and consequently on cash flow. At the very least, the orderly processes of physical distribution will be disrupted as emergency measures are taken to maintain continuity in customer order processing.

QUALITY MAINTENANCE.   Although materials, parts, and products planned for resale are normally procured to standard specifications, considerable variations in quality may exist between supply sources. A fundamental responsibility of materials management is to select the sources that most consistently meet quality specifications. In addition, a quality-control program must be maintained to safeguard against quality deterioration once a source commitment has been made. A sudden quality variation in a major material or part can cause a prolonged work stoppage.

The emphasis on quality control has increased substantially in recent years as a direct result of broader interest in consumer protection. Manufacturers are increasingly faced with assuring customers as well as channel participants that their products meet performance and safety standards. Maintaining this commitment starts with quality control of materials and parts. This is clearly evident in the history of automotive recalls. To date, most recalls are the result of subassembly failure.

LOW LOGISTICAL ACQUISITION COST.   Another objective of materials management is to design and operate a highly efficient system for acquiring items procured. To accomplish this objective, materials managers must integrate transportation, inventory, ordering communication, and storage and handling into a balanced support system. In this respect the logistical cost required to gain possession must be carefully evaluated in source or vendor selection. Although a particular vendor may offer the lowest purchase price for a quality part, the logistical cost may prohibit the firm from doing business with that vendor.[18]

In the next section the material cycle is discussed, so further elaboration on acquisition cost is not necessary at this point. However, keep in mind that the expansion of managerial concern to the performance of the total logistical

---

[18] For an excellent example, see James L. Heskett, Robert M. Ivie, and Nicholas A. Glaskowsky, Jr., *Business Logistics* (New York: The Ronald Press Company, 1973), pp. 171–93.

support system is the primary difference between materials management and traditional purchasing.

RESEARCH AND DEVELOPMENT ASSISTANCE. A prime responsibility of materials management is to be on the lookout for new ideas in product design engineering. This aspect of materials management requires a continuous search for new and better ways of meeting specifications and the assimilation of new technology into the enterprise. Because materials management representatives have regular contact with sources, trade shows, and specialized purchasing publications, they are generally in a better position than others in the management group to acquire information on new developments.

For example, a change in technology could allow a specific part to be produced with a cheaper material or by a less expensive process, with the result of lower total cost and/or higher reliability. Thus materials management can recommend changes in specifications that appear to be justified economically for review by the manufacturing research and development department.

MAINTAINING SUPPLIER RELATIONS. A final objective of materials management deals with the development and maintenance of a positive relationship with suppliers. Suppliers may also be important customers for many large enterprises. Therefore, an element of reciprocity often will be involved in materials management decisions. Provided that the five objectives already discussed can be satisfied, there may be sound business reasons for encouraging reciprocal arrangements.[19]

Another benefit of goodwill with vendors concerns the inevitable emergencies that develop regardless of how well the operations plan is established. The ability to compensate for sudden failure of a supply source or to increase production rapidly may depend upon the willingness of suppliers to modify their operations substantially. At times it may be necessary to cancel outstanding commitments or return materials or parts when actual sales lag behind forecasts or when a product is discontinued. The ability to get full vendor cooperation in such situations is in part a question of economic leverage. However, if a positive relationship exists between the materials management group and the supplier, such situations can be handled with a minimum of friction.

The Material Cycle

The concept of the material cycle is useful in planning and designing the materials management system.[20] Several distinct activities are required to maintain an orderly flow of materials and parts into manufacturing operations. These are (1) sourcing, (2) order placement and expediting, (3) transportation,

[19] See Lee and Dobler, op. cit., pp. 91–97.

[20] For an expanded discussion, see J. H. Westing, I. V. Fine, and C. J. Zenz, *Purchasing Management: Materials in Motion*, 3rd ed. (New York: John Wiley & Sons, Inc., 1969).

and (4) receiving and inspection. These specific activities are required to complete the procurement process. Once materials, parts, or resale products procured are in the possession of the enterprise, storage, inventory control, and materials handling are required to complete their flow into the manufacturing or retail complex.

In many ways, the material cycle is similar to the customer-order-processing cycle involved in physical distribution. However, three important differences exist.

First, delivery time, size of shipment, method of transport, and value of the products involved changes substantially in the material cycle. Generally, materials management requirements result in very large shipments, which may be transported by barge, deep-water vessels, multiple-car trains, and truckloads. While exceptions do exist, transport emphasis in the material cycle is placed on realizing movement at the lowest cost. The lower value of materials and parts in contrast to finished products means that a greater potential trade-off exists between cost of maintaining inventory in-transit and low-cost modes of transport. Since the cost of maintaining materials and most parts in the supply pipeline is relatively lower per day than the cost of maintaining finished products, there is no benefit in paying premium rates for faster transport. Therefore, lead times in the material cycle will be longer than those in customer-order-processing cycles.

A second major difference is the lack of middlemen in the material cycle as contrasted to the finished-product marketing channel. In Chapter 2 the marketing channel was viewed from a number of vantage points.[21] A channel structure consisting of many middlemen is normal for marketing and physical distribution. In physical distribution planning, any particular enterprise is only one participant in an overall channel which must achieve several specified functions through the combined efforts of all members. In contrast, the manufacturing material cycle is far more direct than the typical marketing channel. Materials and parts are purchased directly from the source and the procuring firm has little interest in the steps necessary to realize purchase source availability. The utilization of more direct channels is an important factor in design of the materials management system.

Finally, since the customer-order-processing cycle handles orders at the convenience of customers, random ordering must be accommodated in the design of the physical distribution system. In contrast, the materials management system *places* orders. The degree of control is therefore far greater in the material cycle as a result of a substantial reduction in uncertainty.

The three major differences in the material cycle as contrasted to the customer order cycle are receptive to more orderly programming of logistical activities. The major uncertainty in the material cycle exists in the appraisal concerning the probability of future significant price changes or disruptions in supply.

[21] See pages 28–41 and Appendix IV.

Internal Inventory Transfer Operations

Internal inventory transfer is concerned with the movement required to integrate the physical distribution and materials management operations within an enterprise. Materials management's primary objective is maintaining an orderly and economical flow of raw materials and externally purchased merchandise into the enterprise. Physical distribution management operations are concerned with customer order processing and delivery. Substantially different movement requirements exist between physical distribution and materials management.

Specialization of physical distribution management and materials management within a single enterprise creates a gray area in control between the flow of material to manufacturing plans and the flow of finished production to customers. Inventory transfer reconciles this gray area. The movement of product, materials, and semifinished parts and components between enterprise facilities is the responsibility of inventory transfer operations.

The most significant inventory transfer requirement deals with coordinated logistical performance within the enterprise. From the viewpoint of marketing, products must be consistently available from manufacturing sources to provide high levels of customer service. The level of product availability in turn depends upon decisions made with respect to production scheduling and the capability to transfer component parts between facilities. Another aspect of internal inventory transfer is the initial allocation of products from manufacturing plants to field warehouses. If allocation is inaccurate, adequate inventory may exist within the firm, but it may be located a substantial distance from where it is required.

The identification of internal inventory transfer as a distinct operating area is a relatively new concept in logistical management. The justification is that physical distribution and materials management, as well as transfer operations, should be designed within a particular set of objectives and constraints. Therefore, to realize maximum benefits, the allocation of logistical effort and control within each performance area should vary within a single enterprise, although it is desirable to standardize as much as is practical.

Logistical organizations which place prime emphasis on physical distribution and materials management may run a considerable risk of neglecting selected aspects of internal movement. Or, if not completely neglected, inventory transfer may be handled in part by physical distribution and materials management, with the result that an opportunity for specialization is overlooked in the logistical system design.

The area of transfer has one major difference in comparison with either physical distribution or materials management operations. Internal inventory transfer is captive to the enterprise, whereas the other two areas must deal with the uncertainty of external procurement sources and customers. Greater overall control is thus possible in the transfer area. *Maximum exploitation of this control is the prime justification for separate treatment of inventory transfer as a distinct operating area.*

The internal transfer system initiates operational control over components, semifinished products, and finished products when they are released from initial manufacturing. Its purpose is to control the movement and storage of components and semifinished goods between stages of manufacturing and finished inventory to and between warehouses utilized by the enterprise. As such, inventory transfer serves as a safety valve between all manufacturing plants and field inventories.

In sequence, in a manufacturing organization, materials management provides raw materials and externally purchased semifinished components when and where needed. Once the manufacturing operation is initiated, subsequent interplant movement of materials or semifinished products is classified as internal inventory transfer. Transfer operations are restricted to dock-to-dock movement and any intermediate storage required. When production is completed, inventory transfer arranges for initial allocation of inventory to the warehouses which service customer orders. Unless inventory is subsequently shuffled between warehouses, the transfer task is completed when inventory is turned over to physical distribution operations.

In a multiplant manufacturing firm, the inventory transfer system often constitutes a vast network. To the extent that a number of different manufacturing plants participate in various stages of production and fabrication leading to final production, numerous handlings and transfers will be required prior to final product availability. With finished inventory allocation, products may flow directly from manufacturing plants to field warehouses or they may be funneled through a series of intermediate warehouses for purposes of accumulating product assortments. Thus the complexity of inventory transfer may far exceed that of either the physical distribution or materials management operations.

As noted earlier, the inventory transfer system has one major difference in contrast to either physical distribution or materials management. Transfer operations are limited to movements within and under the control of the enterprise structure. Therefore, in conducting transfer activities, the uncertainties introduced by random-order entry and erratic vendor performance are removed from operational planning, permitting more optimal allocation.

Summary

This chapter has reviewed the three areas of logistical operations: physical distribution management, materials management, and internal inventory transfer. Each aspect is critical to the accomplishment of integrated operations. To stress the similarities of each type of logistical operations, the initial part of the chapter was devoted to a discussion of performance-cycle structure. Various aspects of the performance cycle were discussed in terms of nodes, links, level, and input/output, as well as effectiveness and efficiency in operation. The critical point of the discussion was that the performance-cycle structure provides a framework for implementation of the systems approach to integrated logistics. To stress the particular nature of each type of logistical operation, each operational area was then further developed.

Physical distribution operations are an integral aspect of the overall marketing strategy of the enterprise. Physical distribution management is concerned with strategic movement of products *out* of an enterprise to is customers. To fully appreciate the importance of customer order delivery, the marketing concept, the marketing-mix, and the managerial functions of marketing were presented. Specific aspects of physical distribution performance over time were discussed to stress the dynamic qualities of logistical support of marketing programs.

Next, attention focused on materials management performance. The operational task of materials management is the procurement and timely movement of raw materials, component parts, and finished inventory *into* an enterprise. Although substantial differences exist between raw-material and finished-product procurement, each process is guided by the same basic considerations. The six fundamental objectives of procurement were then reviewed in terms of the material cycle.

Finally, attention was directed to internal inventory transfer operations. Inventory transfer is concerned with movement *between* enterprise facilities. To a degree, inventory transfer balances the requirements of physical distribution and materials management. A point of significant interest in system design is that inventory transfer is captive to the enterprise and does not need to deal with the uncertainty of external procurement and customers.

Although each area of logistical operations is unique, there are similarities. Perhaps the greatest common denominator is reliance upon the same logistical system components to complete movement and storage requirements. Viewing the total logistical system on an integrated basis requires a great deal of coordination. The nature of logistical coordination is the subject of Chapter 4.

Questions

1. Describe the logistical network concept. Why would a logistical network have many different performance cycles?
2. What are the relationships among nodal points, linkages, and inventory in a system network perspective?
3. Describe the similarities and differences of the order-processing cycle in comparison to the materials management and internal inventory transfer cycles.
4. How does physical distribution become an integral part of a firm's marketing mix? Is this consistent with the concept of overall logistics developed in Chapter 1?
5. What is meant by best price procurement?

6. Discuss the role of logistical cost in the acquisition of raw material and component parts.
7. How does physical distribution fit into the marketing-mix concept?
8. Why would a firm under certain circumstances elect to purchase a component part even though it could manufacture it more economically?
9. Discuss the different priorities placed on physical distribution performance during the product life cycle.
10. What is the impact of scrambled merchandising and channel jumping on the design of a physical distribution system?

Logistical Coordination

Logistical coordination is concerned with the establishment of requirements and specifications which integrate overall logistical operations. Materials management has the primary objective of maintaining an orderly flow of externally purchased items into the enterprise. Physical distribution operations are concerned with outbound delivery of products to customers. Internal inventory transfer serves to balance operations by managing the movement of semifinished goods between stages of manufacturing and finished inventory to and between warehouses utilized by the enterprise. *The function of logistical coordination is to assure that all movement and storage is completed as effectively and as efficiently as practical.*

When an enterprise performs substantial operations in both physical distribution and materials management, there is little doubt that a high degree of coordination is necessary. Since the managerial activities that can be directed to realize effective coordination are often in existence within an enterprise, improved logistical coordination does not require the creation or formation of new activities. Rather, existing activities must be performed with their impact upon logistical cost and performance foremost in mind. A clear perspective of the importance of coordination is the primary purpose of this chapter.

The chapter initially deals with forecasting. Next, order processing is developed. The combination of forecasting and order processing provides source information concerning the level, nature, and pattern of customer demand. This information represents a vital input to the formulation of the operational plan discussed in the third section. The treatment of logistical coordination is concluded in the final section, which presents a discussion of product procurement and material requirement planning. Each represents a methodology for guiding procurement which is unique to the nature and planned use of the item being purchased.

Forecasting

The fundamental input to planning and coordinating logistical operations is a forecast of customer demand. Such demand is independent of the enterprise in that potential customers are free to choose what they want and when they want it. Forecasting represents the manner in which an enterprise seeks to limit the impact of future uncertainty on operations. The demand forecast provides the linkage between the enterprise and its market environment. The desired result of forecasting is a common set of expectations among all managers concerning expected level of future business activity and anticipated sales performance of individual products. To be useful in logistical coordination, the overall demand forecast must be detailed to the individual product level. This level of forecasting is referred to as *product-market sales forecasting*.[1]

Two procedures are available to arrive at product level demand. First, an overall forecast of demand can be completed and geographically distributed to market areas. Once aggregate demand is segmented on a geographic basis, it can be broken down to product detail using historical records, salesmen's estimates, and other available information about specific markets. The end result is a formal statement of individual product sales expectations by market areas. When all product-market estimates are aggregated, they reconcile to the initial overall demand forecast.

A second approach is to apply forecasting techniques directly to the market area in an effort to generate product level demand. From this procedure, the overall forecast of the enterprise is realized by aggregation of individual product-market estimates.

Logistical coordination requires as accurate an estimate of individual product-market demand as possible. Although forecasting is far from an exact science, more and more enterprises are relying on mathematical and statistical forecasting techniques. Forecast procedures will vary depending on planned use, period covered, and level of detail.

The purpose of the forecast techniques discussed in this section is to generate expectations concerning future demand to be placed upon the combined physical distribution, inventory transfer, and materials management operations.

---

[1] For a detailed discussion of this level of forecasting, see Donald J. Bowersox et al., "Short Range Product Sales Forecasting," Proceedings, 14th Annual Conference of the National Council of Physical Distribution Management, Chicago, 1976.

Therefore, only mathematical and statistical techniques capable of individual product demand estimates are discussed. The term *forecast* is used exclusively to refer to these formal procedures for estimating future demand. All other methods of arriving at estimates concerning future demand are referred to as *predictions*.

The time horizon projected in logistical operational forecasts is normally one year or less. Depending upon the plan's intended use, forecasts may be required on a daily, weekly, monthly, quarterly, semiannual, or annual basis. A recent survey of 161 companies revealed that the most popular forecast period is one month.[2] While the forecast time period will vary between enterprises, the important requirement is that the basic planning horizon be selected to accommodate logistical operations.

Finally, with respect to level of detail, the purpose of the forecast is to develop an estimate of product requirements in individual markets. In the formulation of procurement plans and production schedules, the combined forecast for several markets provides an overall statement of operational requirements.

In presenting two commonly used categories of mathematical–statistical forecast techniques, the simplifying assumption is made that a single product is being forecasted in a single market. In actual practice, several thousand forecasts may be required to get a fix on overall demand. The two techniques discussed are (1) regression, and (2) time-series analysis.

Regression

Forecasting by regression consists of estimating the sales of an individual product based upon information regarding one or more other factors. If the product forecast is based upon a single factor, it is referred to as simple regression analysis. The use of more than one forecast factor is referred to as *multiple regression.*

The use of regression simply means that the forecast of future sales is based upon a correlation of one event to another. No cause–effect relationship need exist between the product's sale and the independent event if a high degree of correlation is consistently present. However, the most reliable use of regression forecasting of sales is based on a cause–effect relationship.

Since multiple regression is covered in depth in all business statistics textbooks, the present treatment is limited to the logic of regression forecasting. The reader not familiar with regression is advised to review the technique in a basic source.

The initial step in a regression-based forecast is to accumulate past sales history for the product to be forecasted. Given a reasonable sales history, the average monthly sales and standard deviation of sales around the average

[2] "Sales Forecasting Practices: An Appraisal," *Experiences in Marketing Management* 25 (New York: National Industrial Conference Board, 1970), p. 23.

FIGURE 4-1
Example of Monthly Unit Sales

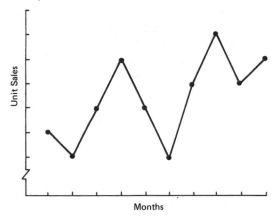

should be calculated to determine the general distribution of historical sales. A typical pattern of monthly sales is illustrated in Figure 4-1.

The mean or average monthly sale is determined by the formula

$$\bar{x} = \frac{\sum\limits_{i=1}^{n} S_i}{n}$$

where

$\bar{x}$ = average sales

s = monthly sales

i = sales of individual months for $1 \cdots n$

n = total number of months of data available

The standard-deviation formula is

$$\sigma = \sqrt{\frac{\sum fd^2}{n}}$$

where

σ = standard deviation

f = frequency of event

d = deviation of events from mean [which is equal to $(S_i - \bar{S})^2$]

n = total number of months of data available

Once the average monthly sales and standard deviation are determined, it is possible to evaluate the degree of dispersion or likelihood that future months' sales will be nearly equal to previous months' sales. If the standard deviation is small, it may be possible to make a forecast based upon average sales. If the deviation is large, some other method of forecasting must be used.

Regression forecasting assumes that monthly sales can be correlated to another factor, which will result in a forecast with a smaller standard deviation than the prediction obtained using basic probability analysis.

The second step is to collect data concerning the independent factor which will provide a better forecast. Assume for purposes of illustration that the objective is to forecast aviation propeller replacement sales. There is reason to believe that a positive correlation exists between total hours flown by private aviation in previous months and future months' propeller replacement sales. To test this assumption, historical data are collected on private aviation hours flown and an attempt is made to establish a correlation relationship. The independent data must be lagged to accommodate the time interval between cause and effect. Assume that the appropriate time lag is three months.

The third step, once the data on private aviation are collected, is to plot the results in the form of a scatter diagram. Although it is not necessary to develop a scatter diagram, such a display makes it easier to observe a positive correlation. Figure 4-2 provides an example where monthly total hours flown by

FIGURE 4-2
Scatter Diagram for Regression Forecasting

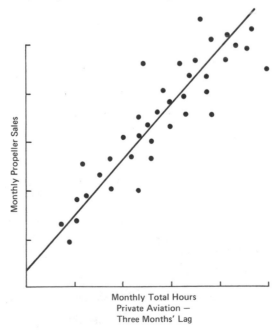

Monthly Propeller Sales

Monthly Total Hours
Private Aviation —
Three Months' Lag

private aviation lagged three months is the independent variable, and monthly propeller sales is the dependent variable.

The fourth step is to fit the solid line displayed on Figure 2-4 to the data plotted in the scatter diagram. The assumption is made that a linear relationship exists; therefore, the regression line is established by the formula

$$S = a + bx$$

where

S = predicted value of propeller sales associated with total monthly hours flown

x = monthly hours flown

a, b = coefficients of the regression equation

Fitting the regression line resolves to finding the values for a and b that will minimize the sum of the squared deviations. Once the relationship of monthly sales and flying hours is determined, the regression line can be fitted and a three-month forecast of the expected sales is obtained.

A final step in regression forecasting is to determine if a reduction in standard deviation has resulted from the use of regression analysis as opposed to the use of a moving average. This will help appraise the net gain realized from the attempt to correlate sales to an independent event.

The strength of the relationship between the dependent variable (sales) and the independent variable (flying hours) can be estimated by measuring the coefficient of correlation. The coefficient of correlation between two variables is determined by the formula

$$r = \frac{n \sum_i x_i y_i - \sum_i x_i \sum_i y_i}{\sqrt{\left[n \sum_i x_i^2 - \left(\sum_i x_i\right)^2\right]\left[n \sum_i y_i^2 - \left(\sum_i y_i\right)^2\right]}}$$

where

r = coefficient of correlation

x_i = independent variable

y_i = dependent variable (formerly noted as s; changed to y to conform to standard notation)

Correlation is measured by the regressive-line fit between the independent variable and the dependent variable. The closer the value of the coefficient of correlation to $+1$, the higher the correlation.

Several assumptions underlie the use of regressive analysis for forecasting.[3]

[3] For an expanded discussion, see M. Hamburg, *Statistical Analysis for Decision Making* (New York: Harcourt Brace Jovanovich, 1970), p. 540.

The most significant are:

1. The basic relationships of x and y are linear.
2. The regression error is randomly distributed.
3. The values of y are independent and express no autocorrelation.

Regression analysis provides an adequate method for forecasting product sales in many situations. However, it is subject to seasonal effects that could dilute the direct value of the forecast. The most serious limitation is that it may not be possible to isolate a cause–effect relationship that has an acceptable coefficient of correlation. Using multiple regression for a broad number of product forecasts in numerous markets could be a cumbersome task.

Time-Series Analysis

Time-series analysis includes a variety of forecasting techniques which analyze the pattern and movement of historical data to establish recurring characteristics. Based upon specific characteristics, techniques of varying sophistication can be used to forecast future values of the data. Four techniques of time-series analysis are discussed in order of increasing complexity. They are (1) moving averages, (2) exponential smoothing, (3) extended smoothing, and (4) adaptive smoothing.[4]

MOVING AVERAGES.   *Moving-average forecasting* is a two-step procedure. First, the average value of a series of data covering specific time periods, such as average weekly sales, is calculated. Second, the average value is used in conjunction with the trend of the data to forecast future sales. Each time a new period of actual data becomes available, it replaces the oldest time period's data. Thus the number of time periods is held constant.

The concept of moving average is expressed as

$$\bar{X}_M = \frac{\sum_{n=1}^{n} st_i}{n}$$

where

$\bar{X}_M$ = moving average

st = sales per time period; time periods are identified by the appropriate subscript

n = total number of time periods

[4] This section draws heavily on Steven C. Wheelwright and Spyros Makridakis, *Forecasting Methods for Management* (New York: Jon Wiley & Sons, Inc., 1973) and Robert G. Brown, *Smoothing, Forecasting, and Prediction of Discrete Time Series* (Englewood Cliffs, N.J.: Prentice-Hall, Inc., 1963).

Although a moving average is easy to determine, it has several obvious limitations. The most significant are that it relies upon an average of change to forecast, it is unresponsive or sluggish to change, and finally, a great many historical data must be maintained and updated to calculate forecasts. In the previous section dealing with regression analysis the notion of average sales and the measure of standard deviation around the average were discussed. If the standard deviation is large, average or mean value cannot be relied upon to render useful forecasts.

To partially overcome these deficiencies, weighted moving averages have been introduced as refinements. Exponential smoothing represents a form of weighted moving average.

EXPONENTIAL SMOOTHING. *Exponential smoothing* bases the estimate of future sales on the accuracy of the previous sales estimate. The new forecast is a function of the old forecast incremented by some fraction of the differential between the old forecast and actual sales realized. The increment of adjustment is called the *alpha factor* (α). The basic format of the model is

$$F(t) = F(t - 1) + \alpha[D(t - 1) - F(t - 1)]$$

where

F = forecasted sales for a time period

t = forecast time period of constant duration

D = most recent demand

α = alpha factor

To illustrate, assume that the forecasted sales for the most recent time period were 100 units and actual sales experienced were 110 units. Further assume that the alpha factor being employed is 0.7. Then, substituting,

$$
\begin{aligned}
F(t) &= F(t - 1) + \alpha[D(t - 1) - F(t - 1)] \\
&= 100 + 0.7(110 - 100) \\
&= 107
\end{aligned}
$$

Thus the new forecast is for a product sales volume of 107 units.

The prime advantage of exponential smoothing is that it permits a rapid calculation of a new forecast without substantial historical records and updating. Thus exponential smoothing is highly adaptable to computerized forecasting. In exponential smoothing the forecast responds quickly to changes in demand. If demand remains stable, the process is still as accurate as the basic averaging method.

The essential need in exponential smoothing is to determine the value assigned to the alpha factor. If a factor of 1 is employed, the net effect is to assume the most recent demand as the forecast of expected demand. A very low value, such as .01, would have the net effect of reducing the forecast to almost a simple moving average. Large alpha factors make the forecast very sensitive to change and therefore highly reactive. Low-alpha factors tend to react slowly to change and therefore provide sluggish or delayed reaction. Thus exponential smoothing does not eliminate the need for judgmental decisions. In selecting the value of the alpha factor, the user is faced with a trade-off between eliminating random fluctuations or having the forecast fully respond to demand changes.

EXTENDED SMOOTHING.   The basic exponential smoothing technique can be extended to include the impact of sales trend and seasonality in deriving the sales forecast.[5] When either trend or seasonality is included in the forecast, it is termed *double exponential smoothing*. If both are included, the technique is called *triple exponential smoothing*.[6] Both represent examples of extended smoothing.

Trend represents the long-range pattern of sales, which may reflect either a prolonged increase or a decrease in expected sales over time. Further, the trend may be at a constant or accelerating rate of change.

Seasonality, in contrast to trend, represents an increase or decrease in sales which is expected and of a short-term nature. Factors causing seasonality are such things as weather, holidays, or traditional periods of selected activities.

The fundamental objective of extended exponential smoothing is to take into account the impact of trend and seasonality when specific values for these variables can be identified. The method of calculation is the same exponential procedure used in arriving at the basic forecast.

ADAPTIVE SMOOTHING.   *Adaptive smoothing* encompasses a regular review of the validity of the alpha factor. The value of the smoothing constant is frequently reviewed after the fact to determine the exact alpha value that would have resulted in a perfect forecast. Once determined, the alpha factor currently in use is replaced by the one that would have produced an accurate forecast. Alternatively, any other value can be manually inserted as the smoothing constant. Thus managerial judgment is partially replaced by a systematic and consistent method of updating in determining an alpha factor.

More sophisticated forms of adaptive smoothing include an automatic tracking signal to monitor error in the smoothing constant. When the signal is

---

[5] P. R. Winters, "Forecasting Sales by Exponentially Weighted Moving Averages," *Management Science*, Vol. 6 (April 1960), pp. 324–42.
[6] Brown, op. cit.

tripped, the constant is automatically adjusted to reduce the error. As the forecast error is eliminated, the tracking signal automatically returns the smoothing constant to its original value.

Order Processing

The study of information systems within an enterprise is a relatively new phenomenon. The communications message is the trigger mechanism for the entire logistical system. The quality and speed of information flow facilitates integration of the basic logistical system components. Conversely, a poor communication network, which allows order bottlenecks or information errors to go undetected, can create havoc within the logistical system. Such errors amplify and distort stockout problems, production schedules, and inventory accumulation patterns.

Further, it is axiomatic that the more sophisticated the logistical system design, the more vulnerable it is to any internal or external communication malfunction. Take, for example, a zero-based inventory system, in which an order is placed following an item sale for replacement delivery. In such a system there is no safety stock at the retail level. The shoe retailer, for example, stocks one pair of a particular style of men's shoes in size 11D. When this pair of shoes is sold, a replacement order is placed. The retailer is out of stock of this particular size and style until the replenishment order is received from the warehouse. In such a system the lag between sale (impulse) and order replenishment (response) must be dependable, or a prolonged out-of-stock situation could develop at the retail level. In this type of inventory system, the only way to ensure rapid response is through an efficient communications network. Enterprises using the zero-response type of inventory frequently rely on high-speed store-to-distribution center communication. The effect of a communication delay, either through mechanical failure or transmission error, can be serious. Delay increases the probability of an out-of-stock condition at the retail store and possible amplification of these problems throughout the supplier channel.

With the advent of the high-speed computer, new opportunities for effective use of communication in logistical operations have emerged. Communications deals with the speed and accuracy of messages. Time in the logistical system is both limited and inelastic.[7] If time is not fully utilized, it cannot be retained for the future. The more rapidly a specific task can be performed in the logistical system, the more time is made available for performance of other activities.

Two aspects of time influence the performance of all logistical components.

---

[7] Richard R. Mead, "The Time Dimension and the Order Cycle," in C. McConaughy and C. J. Clawson, eds., *Business Logistics Policies and Decisions* (Los Angeles: University of California, 1968), p. 118.

The first is the time expected to elapse while performing a specified activity, such as order transmittal. The second concerns message delay, experienced as a result of a variety of causes.

With today's level of information technology, a message can be transmitted with almost no elapsed time. Time saved in information transmission can be made available for the performance of other logistical activities. Since time is expensive, the cost associated with rapid receipt of a customer order may be more than offset by savings realized in other logistical areas.

For example, assume that the total time elapsed in servicing a customer consists of three days for order transmittal, two days for warehouse processing, and one day for transport. Air freight is used to keep the total delivery time down to six days. An investment in data communications transmitting equipment integrated into warehouse operations could easily reduce transmittal and processing time to one day, which would allow five days for delivery. Given five days for possible outbound shipment, a number of options less expensive than air freight might be available to perform product delivery within a total elapsed time of six days. The resultant transportation rate savings in such a situation could be more than adequate to offset the added cost of data communications.

The second impact of time upon communication concerns delay. Delay simply means that the message does not arrive when expected. Such delays can have a substantial impact upon logistical system performance. In particular, customer service can suffer as a result of stockouts, and production scheduling can be disrupted because of material or parts shortages.

The classical analysis of the impact of communication time and delay upon industrial performance was made by Forrester.[8] Figure 4-3, selected from his work, illustrates the impact of time lags in amplifying inventory and production requirements within an overall distribution channel. The chart displays the interrelationship among sales, inventory stocks at various levels in the distribution channel, and production output. Some assumptions on time lags and functional relationships in the system are made, and the simulated impacts upon important variables in the system are presented. In Figure 4-3 the assumption is made that a sales increase of 10 per cent occurs in January. This, in turn, peaks out in March as a 16 per cent increase in distributors' orders from retailers. Manufacturing operations peak out at plus 40 in May.

The entire chart illustrates the impact of time delays in amplifying inventory and production requirements of an enterprise. Note that the same process, in reverse, would probably occur if sales dropped 10 per cent in early January.

Figure 4-3 illustrates the vital role of timely communications between production, logistics, and marketing. If the marketing department develops a program that will result in a 10 per cent increase in sales, it is important to ensure physical distribution support of the program. Any anticipated shift in

[8] Jay W. Forrester, *Industrial Dynamics* (Cambridge, Mass.: The MIT Press, 1961), and "Industrial Dynamics," *Harvard Business Review*, July–August 1958, p. 43.

FIGURE 4-3
Response of a Simulated Production-Distribution System to a Sudden
10 Per Cent Increase in Sales at the Retail Level

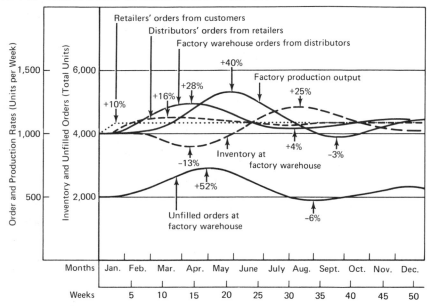

sales not carefully coordinated with manufacturing and logistics could result
in lost sales due to stockouts or higher costs due to overtime and expedited
shipments. Careful monitoring of the logistical system can reduce these
amplifications through rapid relay of customer orders into adjusted production
schedules.

The Communication Function in Logistical Management

Generally, the communication network has the same role as the other components of the logistical system. All exist in integrated performance to balance
customer service and total logistical cost. However, the method by which a
communication network achieves these objectives varies somewhat from the
other logistical components. The communication network has four links. The
first link consists of inbound communication in the form of a customer order,
purchase order for raw materials or parts, or product transfer request. The
second link in the system coordinates information with other enterprise units
that are influenced by the order. The third link is the command function,
which initiates activity. The fourth link is the control phase, where management establishes and monitors feedback to ensure desired logistical system
performance. Each aspect of the total communication network is discussed in
greater detail.

ORDER TRANSMITTAL.   A variety of methods exist to accomplish the task of
order transmittal. Some common methods utilized are personal delivery, mail,
teletype, and various forms of telephone transmittal. Telephone order transmittal ranges from personal calls to automated data transmission. Each method
of order communication can be classified according to speed, cost, dependability, and accuracy of message delivery. Table 4-1 presents a comparative
ranking of methods.

TABLE 4-1
Relative Characteristics of Alternative Order Transmittal Methods

Type	Speed	Cost	Dependability	Accuracy
Personal delivery	Moderate	High	High	Moderate
Mail	Slow	Low	Low	High
Teletype	Fast	Moderate	Moderate	High
Telephone				
Personal	Fast	High	High	Moderate
Data	Fast	High	High	High

As a general rule, the more rapid a form of order transmittal, the more
costly it is per message unit. High-speed order communication may be desirable
when rapid replenishment of inventory is necessary or when fast order transmittal can result in more economical performance in other areas of the overall
logistical system. When evaluating the speed of order transmittal, keep in
mind that no logistical activity can begin until the order arrives at the processing point.

Any increase in order-processing speed should result in reduced inventories
throughout the system. A decrease in the performance cycle time reduces
reaction time to a customer order and consequently permits lower safety
stocks. If a supplier can reduce order processing time from 10 to 5 days, there
will also be a reduction in transit inventory. In this respect, there is a direct
cost trade-off between increased communication cost and inventory level.
However, as safety stocks are reduced and the system is brought into delicate
balance, it becomes more vulnerable to any communication or information
malfunction.

Alternative methods of order transmittal can be evaluated for dependability
by the consistency of message delivery. In a sense, dependability is a mechanical measure of performance. As a general rule, the longer the time of message
delivery, the greater the inconsistency of average performance.

Inaccuracy in order transmittal results from human involvement. Written
methods of order transmission using a standard format will be more accurate
than verbal methods. The degree of accuracy will increase when data is
coded and verified for mechanical transmission.

A number of methods can be used to detect errors in order transmission and improve accuracy of data. Mechanical detection devices are available to perform consistency checks in the transmission of data. A computer can be programmed to select for managerial review any orders exceeding certain established ranges in quantity or cost. Computers can also be programmed to check cost extension, product codes, and other order details. In general, the more often a piece of information is handled, the greater the chance of error in communication. This is particularly true for manual transmission of information.

In summary, logistical operations are initiated with the transmittal of an order. Available methods of order communication can be evaluated with respect to speed, cost, dependability, and accuracy. Regardless of the method selected to transmit orders, it is desirable to limit the options and derive benefits of simplicity and routinization. There are three principles of order transmittal. First, the time span for order transmittal should be as consistent as possible, considering the risks of system malfunction and consequent stockout problems. Second, order transmission should be as direct as possible, with a minimum of change in order form and intermediate relay. Third, whenever possible, customer orders should be transmitted by mechanical rather than manual means, to minimize human error.

INTERNAL COORDINATION. The second function of the logistical communication system is to ensure a timely and accurate flow of information to management areas outside logistics. Useful information derived from customer orders is often needed by other units of the organization. For example, sales reports and market evaluation data can be generated in a more timely and accurate manner when orders first arrive than at any other time in communication flow. Finance and accounting are concerned, for purposes of cash-flow management, with anticipated accounts receivable, credits granted, and purchases.

In a sophisticated logistical communication system, a great deal of the coordination surrounding order processing is accomplished automatically. For example, production scheduling may be linked directly to order processing and warehouse inventory control in order to level out production and realize an orderly overall manufacturing process.[9]

In summary, logistical communication has an impact on many functions within the organization. A network must be designed that will ensure adequate two-way communication between logistics and other functional areas of the enterprise.

LOGISTICAL COMMAND. After an order has been processed, the communication system must prepare logistical work directives. Inventory must be assigned, customer credit cleared, assignment to a warehouse completed, and shipping

_____

[9] For an expansion, see Chapter 2, pages 42–48.

instructions and documentation formulated. Similar logistical tasks must be specified in filling materials management orders and inventory transfer requests. This activity is called the *command function.*

The command function is extremely important in logistical operations because it activates system components. Unless the command function is accurate and timely, a great deal of inefficiency can result in logistical operations. The command function can be performed automatically through an integrated data-processing system in which inventories are automatically updated and shipping instructions prepared and released, or it can be done manually through verbal or written instructions. Modern logistical systems rely heavily upon automated communication command functions.

Command activities generally are limited to the logistical system. When common carriers and public warehouses are included as system components, logistical commands will extend outside the enterprise to ensure proper performance.

In summary, communication command initiates logistical performance. The efficiency of the logistical performance system depends upon the timeliness and accuracy of command.

MONITOR AND CONTROL.   If the logistical communication system is used as a monitoring device, management must establish specific systems which ensure feedback. Feedback is the return of information for management review of all logistical activities requiring monitoring. These activities always relate to some aspect of customer service or to the cost of system performance. It is one thing to promise a customer service level of two-day delivery for 95 per cent of the orders and another to make certain that this target level has been achieved. A multiplant or multiproduct supplier generally will not review each individual delivery to each customer but rather design a review on an exception basis. Standards might be established to allow plus or minus one-day delivery deviation from programmed customer service levels. The only items reviewed are those exceeding the upper or lower limits of this range.

A similar review procedure can be designed to evaluate vendors, transportation suppliers, back orders, and damaged merchandise on a continuous basis. Exception reports from logistical monitoring also can be transmitted to other functional areas of the firm. For example, a listing of warehouse shipments expressed as turnover rates over time might be of interest to purchasing or marketing in evaluating suppliers or customers.

Another advantage of monitoring is the identification of developing trends. Shifts in color preferences and sizes, regional demand, and competitive actions can be identified by closely observing movement within the physical distribution system. Properly reviewing and evaluating this information and relaying it to decision points within the firm can result in a more accurate reaction to unanticipated or uncontrollable factors in the marketplace. It is a flexible management tool with which informed adjustments can be made to the total marketing program of the enterprise. The net effect of monitoring and control is a reduction of amplification and distortion in the logistical system. Additional aspects of performance measurement are discussed in Chapters 9 and 13.[10]

INTEGRATED PERFORMANCE.   The four links of the logistical communication system are essential to overall performance. The fundamental purpose of an automated order-processing system is to integrate the four linkages into a coordinated logistical information system. Figure 4-4 illustrates the basic concept of the logistical information system.

FIGURE 4-4
Logistical Information System

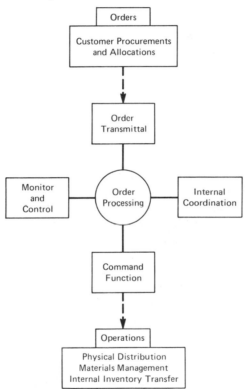

Automated Order Processing

In today's highly competitive environment, few organizations of any size rely on manual methods of order processing. Three potential benefits encourage the trend toward automated processing. First, the total order processing time can be substantially reduced, thereby lowering total logistical cost and increasing

[10] See pages 265 and 431.

customer service. Second, the accuracy of processing and overall administration is much higher in automated systems. Third, the high cost of clerical help has resulted in greater productivity gains from the use of automated systems. This trend toward automated order processing has resulted in considerable research and development in terminal equipment, data-transmission capability, and computerized processing programs.

No two automated order-processing systems are identical. Because of the vast differences in operational requirements, the automated order-processing system which constitutes the communication component of the logistical system should be highly customized. In this section a generalized concept of automated order processing is presented rather than an actual system.[11]

Figure 4-5 illustrates a generalized concept of the automated order-processing system. A total of 17 specific parts of the system are joined together and identified. The four connector links are identified by alpha designators. The processing system is initiated by an order (INPUT) and is completed when either a shipment or a purchase order is logistically processed (OUTPUT). Each aspect of the system is briefly discussed.

TERMINALS (1).   Terminals are the hardware utilized to originate the order in the system. The assumption is made that some form of data transmission is employed. If not—for example, if orders are transmitted by government mail— the system starts at point 3.

The rate of development in data-transmission terminals has been phenomenal since the mid-1960s. Just a few years ago the only device capable of transmitting orders was the teletype. Today a wide variety of devices are available within a reasonable price range. Most terminals in use transmit over standard voice-grade telephone lines by first encoding messages on punch cards, paper tape, or magnetic tape. The orders are encoded from hard copy and verified for accuracy. In a technical sense, the terminal merely transmits the message once it is encoded in data-processing format. The encoding and transmitting hardware is called the *terminal*.

In some systems order transmittal is completed directly from computer to computer without encoding or external terminal devices. Internal computer communication capacity is commonly available in third-generation hardware. Such capacity allows simultaneous handling of a number of transmission lines. When the computer is directly linked with a number of terminals, terminals can be dialed automatically and polled in sequence without manual intervention.

Most data-transmission systems require manual intervention at the terminal location. Either the operator transmits an order directly to the receiving location, or a number of orders are prepared for transmission at a specified time. Either way, the system would not be classified as real time unless the entire order processing was completed during the on-line time. Real-time processing will be discussed later.

---

[11] The generalized system illustrated is based on a situation characterized by a broad product line and a large quantity of orders.

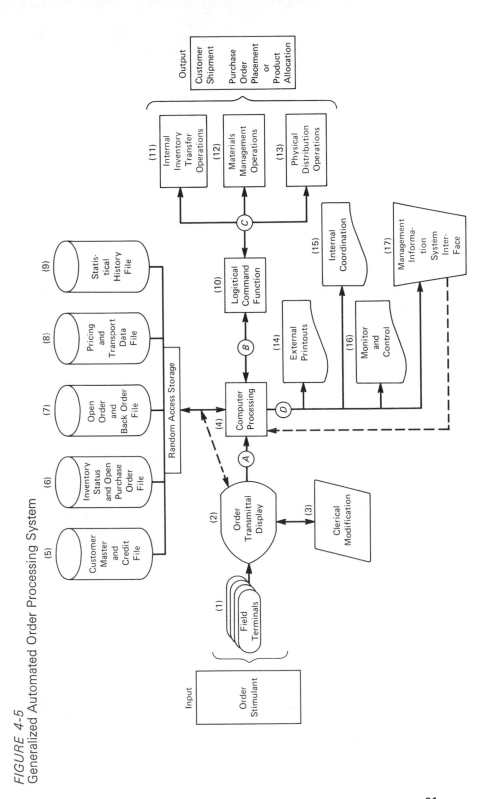

FIGURE 4-5
Generalized Automated Order Processing System

91

A recent development gaining widespread attention is the P-O-S (point-of-sale) terminal. Primarily in retail establishments, the traditional cash register is replaced by a device that encodes unit data while the customer transaction is in process. These terminals allow a firm to automatically encode small-ticket transactions and accumulate the data for effective inventory replenishment. Several types of P-O-S terminals are currently marketed, and numerous retailers have tests under way. Some experts predict that more than half of the retailing industry will be using P-O-S terminals and related information-processing systems by the mid-1980s.[12]

Specifics on the various terminals for order transmittal are not as important as the basic concept. Under all forms of terminal application, telecommunication is being employed to move order requirements rapidly into the processing system. In this sense, the use of a telephone for verbal order placement is classified as a terminal. Many automated order-processing systems make a toll-free area 800 telephone number available to customers so that orders can be called directly to the processing location.

ORDER TRANSMITTAL DISPLAY AND CLERICAL MODIFICATION (2 AND 3). Orders generally do not flow directly from input terminals into the automated order-processing system. For a number of reasons, it may be desirable to intercept the order for editing or adding information prior to processing. An increasingly popular method of intercept is a unit that provides a picture display of the order in place of hard-copy reproductions.

A number of display units are available and are usually referred to as CRT (cathode-ray tube). The CRT displays the total order and allows the option of entering or extracting data. In Figure 4-5 a dashed two-way arrow connects the order display unit (3) with the various random-access files of the computer processor. This linkage illustrates that it is possible to display selected information from computer files on the CRT for immediate identification of customer, credit, inventory, back- or open-order status, or stastical data. Thus, if a customer is on line, information concerning all aspects of order processing can be provided immediately.

For example, assume that a customer calls in an order to a CRT operator by telephone. Once the order is encoded, it is possible to read out inventory availability and to inform the customer when delivery can be expected. In fact, many systems reserve inventory for specific customers at this point of order processing.

---

[12] "Chains Unlock Flood Gates for POS Systems," *Chain Store Age*, February 1972, pp. E23–E32. The anticipated growth has not materialized as dramatically as anticipated. For an interesting discussion of the progress of product coding in the retail food industry, see Alan L. Haberman, "A Proposal to Institutionalize the Food Industry's Ongoing Effort for Productivity," Proceedings, National Association of Food Chains 1976 Distribution Clinic (Washington, D.C., 1976), pp. 102–13; and Gilbert D. Harrell, Michael D. Hutt, and John W. Allen, *Universal Product Code* (East Lansing, Mich.: Division of Research, Michigan State University, 1976).

The alert reader will note that the CRT is, indeed, a terminal unit located at a different geographical point from the field terminals. In fact, some field terminals utilize CRT equipment. Therefore, the combined function of parts 1 through 3 of the order-processing system is to capture the order and render it ready for processing. The first link of the logistical communication network is then complete at connector point *A* of the system.

COMPUTER PROCESSING AND RANDOM-ACCESS STORAGE (4–9). The computer and its associated hardware is the heart of the automated order-processing system (4). Most computer systems used in order processing have random-access capabilities, permitting random extraction of data from storage files, disks, or drums, which can be merged to formulate a completed order. Although a number of files may be incorporated in an order-processing system, five interrelated types of data are common to most systems.

The customer master and credit file (5) contains complete information on the customer being serviced. Of particular importance are credit-limit data, which can be checked automatically and updated during order processing. The exact data contained in this file will vary considerably. If multiple customer locations are serviced by the logistical system, all should be identified in the file. In some applications, customer detail goes only so far as to require the entry of a code number to complete all necessary order detail. The extent of data contained in this file will depend upon the frequency and size of the customer's purchases.

The inventory status and open-purchase-order file (6) is perhaps the most critical file in order processing. This file contains the inventory on hand at all warehouse facilities within the logistical operating system. The inventory control system is implemented by use of data contained in this file.

The open-order and back-order file (7) provides the status of orders in process within the logistical system. An order is retained in this file while it is moving through the warehouse and transportation components of the logistical system. If the firm back-orders merchandise it cannot provide at the time of original order, a record is maintained in this file.

The pricing and transportation data file (8) provides the information necessary to create the customer billing invoice. Depending upon the size, quantity, selection of products, or destination, the order may be shipped prepaid or collect. A great deal of sophistication exists in the extension of pricing and transportation data at the time of order processing. Several firms route the shipment, apply appropriate rates, and extend the total freight bill at this point in the logistical process. Some go so far as to pay carriers without the rendering of a freight bill. If discounts are offered by the firm, normally they are applied from data contained in this file.

The final file (9) concerns the retention of statistical history. The purpose of this file is self-explanatory. The standard practice is to retain short-term history in the integrated order-processing system for later generation of operational reports and forecasts. The amount and type of data generated by the logistical communication system is a vital aspect of the overall corporate information data base.

In total, the computer processor merges all data in terms of response to an order and completes the necessary processing to initiate logistical performance. The command function assigns operating tasks.

LOGISTICAL COMMAND FUNCTION (10). The policies and operating rules of the logistical system are applied by the command linkage. In essence, the command function identifies the tasks that various logistical operating systems must perform in order to carry out enterprise policy. The communication system does not formulate policy; it consistently implements the policy formulated by management. The logistical command function represents nothing more than the established operating policy expressed in usable decision rules.

For example, the command function provides the criteria for review of inventory status so as to initiate materials management and product allocation operations. In physical distribution operations, appropriate instructions direct customer orders to specific warehouses and arrange for necessary transportation to ensure delivery as specified.

LOGISTICAL OPERATING SYSTEMS (11–13). Physical reaction to order processing occurs when any of the three operating systems is given a performance assignment. Without extensive elaboration, the reader should note that communications facilitate operational performance within the transportation, inventory warehousing, and material-handling components of each logistical operating system. Communication between the command function and the operating systems is two-way for purposes of file update and system monitor and control.

EXTERNAL PRINTOUTS (14). A variety of documents which flow outside the enterprise may be required to complete the logistical communication process. The most common are shipment notifications, invoices, and purchase orders. One benefit of automated systems is that invoices can be prepared and mailed simultaneously with order processing, thereby substantially reducing cash-flow lags.

INTERNAL COORDINATION (15). A third linkage of the logistical communication system is internal coordination. As noted earlier, a number of areas of the enterprise require information of a logistical nature for the performance of their operational assignments. This information can be provided by daily, weekly, or monthly reports generated from the statistical history file.

MONITOR AND CONTROL (16). The final link of the automated order-processing system is concerned with the performance of the overall logistical system. This linkage is monitor and control.

In automated order-processing systems, data are processed at speeds which allow discovery and interpretation of trends while they are forming. This information can be tapped at will by all levels of administrative control. All experience has been incorporated into the data statistical bank and the potential exists to examine any control or design problem from all dimensions. This link can be likened to a control nerve center.

This control nerve center is similar to an air-traffic-control system. Central management has direct up-to-date status information concerning all units of the logistical system. From a central vantage point, interrogation may be initiated on the status and performance of individual units of the system at any geographical point. Performance can be evaluated with respect to the operating plan, allowing fast and efficient management response to any externally or internally generated change.

The daily sequence of logistical data provides a continuous two-way flow of information between all activity locations and the point of central data bank maintenance. All transactions and records are stored in central data files prepared from the original documents. Status reports can be developed as desired, and selected trend or special diagnostic reports can be generated as frequently as necessary. The essence of an information system is that all transaction documents are originated in a format that permits direct posting into data files. This posting results in a total information reservoir which contains relevant data in breadth as well as depth concerning logistical system status and performance. Management reporting is developed in greater detail in Chapter 13.[13]

TIME CONNECTORS (*A–D*).   Within Figure 4-5, four connectors illustrate the speed with which data flow into and out of the automated order-processing system. Data flow can be instantaneous or subjected to a degree of predetermined delay. In the logistical sector of an enterprise, operations are carried on at widely separated locations. This geographical separation creates a need to collect and disseminate information rapidly.

Three groups of information flow can be identified, based upon speed: (1) batching, (2) short-interval sequencing, and (3) real time. Batching involves grouping data until sufficient volume is generated at a given location to justify entry into the tele-data-processing system. Short-interval sequencing involves collection of information for a specific time period—one day, for example—with entry into the system at the end of the specified period, regardless of volume. Real-time processing consists of direct contact among all locations, with immediate entry of information as generated. A daily sequence of data entry is adequate for most logistical systems. At the present time the cost of maintaining a broad real-time information network is generally prohibitive.

MANAGEMENT INFORMATION SYSTEM INTERFACE (17).   A final comment concerns the interface of logistical communication and the overall management information system. The logistical information system is part of a larger

---

[13] See pages 434–440.

communication network, and provisions must be made to transmit and receive data from the enterprise's information system.

Two factors, increasing information technology and management's recognition of information potential, have given impetus to a philosophy of management information systems. A management information system may be defined as "an integrated intelligence system designed to permit management by exception, based on timely information, randomly available, and guided by rigorously determined relationships and decision rules."[14]

When discussing a logistics information requirement, then, it should be remembered that it is part of an overall information system. One author has identified three major elements of a typical management information system: (1) logistics or physical distribution information system, (2) financial information system, and (3) personnel information system.[15] Each of these major elements can be further broken down into subsystems. In the logistics information system, subsystems might include procurement, raw-material inventory control, production scheduling and control, finished-goods inventory control, and order processing.[16]

Operational Planning

Demand forecasts, updated by timely information from order processing, provide the major inputs to the formulation of the enterprise's operational plan. The operational plan is directly linked with product procurement and materials requirement planning. The nature of this linkage in commercial organizations varies between manufacturing businesses and enterprises purchasing merchandise for resale, such as wholesalers or retailers.

Prior to discussing manufacturing and resale operational planning in more detail, one important point requires elaboration. The operational plan represents a time-phased statement of the enterprise's planned activities. As such, the plan integrates growth objectives, forecasts, and all forms of information into a concise statement. Once stated, the operational plan represents the transition from independent to dependent demand.[17]

Demand for a given item is *independent* when it is not dependent upon the demand for another item. For example, demand for a refrigerator is not dependent upon the demand for household furniture. Demand is dependent when

---

[14] This definition, although presented in 1961, is a valid explanation of the objective of an information system. Roger Christian, "The Total System Concept," from a speech delivered before the 14th Annual International Systems Meeting, October 1961, p. 8.

[15] John Dearden, "How to Organize Information Systems," *Harvard Business Review*, March–April 1965, pp. 65–73.

[16] John Dearden, *Computers in Business Management* (Chicago: Dow Jones–Irwin, Inc., 1966), p. 122.

[17] For an expanded discussion, see Joseph Orlicky, *Material Requirement Planning* (New York: McGraw-Hill Book Company, 1975), pp. 22–29. For product procurement, the situation is independent. For materials and parts procurement, the situation is dependent.

the quantity of a specific component is directly based on the demand for an end product or subassembly, as in the relationship of axles to automotive assembly. The essential characteristic of dependent demand is that it can be calculated given the operational plan.

Dependent demand illustrates the vertical sequence in the procurement or manufacture of specific items. Requirements are expressed in direct quantity such as cases of corn or tons of coal necessary to meet end-product requirements. In manufacturing situations, vertical dependence may extend through several organizational levels. Horizontal dependent demand is a special situation where an attachment, promotion item, or operator's manual is included with each item shipped. In this situation the item demanded is not required to complete the manufacturing process but may be necessary to complete the marketing process.

The important point to remember is that the estimated demand for the item to be purchased for resale or to be manufactured is initially determined by a combination of forecasting, order processing, and operational planning. However, once the plan is formulated, component-parts requirements or insertions to the product can be directly calculated and do not need to be forecasted separately.[18] If substantial changes develop in forecasting or order processing, it may be necessary to modify or regenerate the operational plan. However, the dependent demand status of procurement does not change. Specifics related to the resale and manufacturing environments are now developed further.

The Retail Wholesale Environment

Buying merchandise for resale does not involve the same level of time phasing found in manufacturing systems. However, procurement for resale is complicated by the wide span of products purchased. Size, color, and label assortments in a grocery store can exceed 12,000 items, and over 50,000 items is not unusual for a department store. The idiosyncracies of products, seasons, and markets require careful product procurement (PP).

The nature of PP varies by industry practice and category of goods. While the integrated logic of PP is not as refined as MRP, several concepts are important to implementing the operational plan for resale purchases: (1) economic order quantity, (2) safety stock, (3) reorder control, and (4) fashion/promotion procurement. Each will be discussed.

ECONOMIC ORDER QUANTITY. The *economic-order-quantity* (EOQ) concept balances the cost of maintaining inventory against the cost of ordering. The

---

[18] For varied MRP applications, see George W. Plossl and Oliver W. Wright, *Materials Requirement Planning by Computer* (Washington, D.C.: American Production and Inventory Control Society, Inc., 1971); Robert M. Monczka, Philip L. Carter, and Richard F. Gonzales, "Materials Requirements Planning: Implementation Scenario for a Successful User," unpublished paper, Michigan State University, 1976; and Jeffrey G. Miller and Linda G. Sprague, "Behind the Growth in Materials Requirement Planning," *Harvard Business Review*, September–October 1975, pp. 83–91.

key to understanding the relationship is to remember that average inventory is equal to one-half order quantity. Therefore, the larger the order quantity, the larger the average inventory and consequently the greater the maintenance cost per year. Likewise, the larger the order quantity, the fewer orders required per planning period and consequently the lower the total ordering cost. The EOQ formulation finds the exact order quantity at which the annual combined total cost of ordering and maintenance is at the lowest point for a given sales volume. Figure 4-6 illustrates the basic relationship. The point at which ordering cost and maintenance cost intersect represents the lowest total cost. The exact quantity that should be ordered to enjoy economical relationships can be determined by dividing the number of orders into the annual volume.

The reader should carefully observe Figure 4-6 with respect to the shape of the total cost curve in the range of minimal value. Over a considerable range the total cost curve is relatively flat, which indicates that it would require a substantial change in either ordering or maintenance cost to result in a minor change in EOQ.

If in a particular situation inventory costs cannot be isolated with exact precision, the usefulness of EOQ is not diluted. Likewise, the recalculation of

FIGURE 4–6
Economic Order Quantity

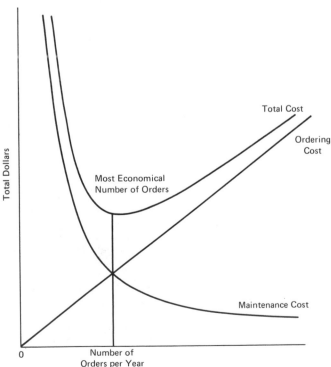

EOQ need be performed only when a notable change occurs in cost or anticipated sales volume. The specific uses and limitations of EOQ are discussed
in greater detail in Chapter 6.[19]

SAFETY STOCK. *Safety stock* refers to a specific quantity of inventory placed
into the system to protect against unexpected delivery delays or greater than
anticipated sales. Unlike the time-phased MRP programs in the manufacturing
environment, PP programs are based on the probabilistic attainment of a
customer service level somewhat less than 100 per cent.

The strategic nature of safety stock is developed in substantial detail in
Chapter 9.[20] The important point stressed at this time, however, is that
inventories which support resale systems normally incorporate a safety stock
strategy as an integral part of the PP program. The amount of safety stock in
a given logistical system will depend upon service-level objectives, order time,
order-time variance, and number of facilities stocked with a given inventory
unit.

REORDER CONTROL. The combination of EOQ and safety stock policy sets
the standard for the mechanical process of reordering. Reorder merchandise
consists of items purchased on a regular basis as part of a basic product
assortment. Examples of reorder items are those stocked by grocery stores,
appliance dealers, and hardware stores. As the name implies, reorder items
are purchased on the basis of their future expected rate of sale.

A variety of inventory reorder systems exist; however, most are based on
either the perpetual or periodic methods. The following section reviews each
method and presents some concepts regarding modification of the basic
methods.[21]

Perpetual Review. An inventory control approach based on perpetual
review is basically a reorder-point system. To utilize this type of control
system, an accurate accountability is necessary of all units of a particular
stockkeeping line. If the line is broad, computer assistance is necessary to
implement the perpetual concept effectively. The perpetual approach is
described as follows:

$$\text{ROP} = S_s + \bar{S}dR$$

where

$$\text{ROP} = \text{reorder point}$$

$$S_s = \text{safety stock}$$

---

[19] See pages 159–167.
[20] See pages 272–279.
[21] The following section draws upon M. K. Starr and D. W. Miller, *Inventory Control:
Theory and Practice* (Englewood Cliffs, N.J.: Prentice-Hall, Inc., 1962).

$\bar{S}d$ = average expected daily sales

R = duration of expected inventory replenishment cycle

Thus, with an expected replenishment cycle of 10 days, expected average sales of 5 units per day, and a safety stock of 32 units to cover uncertainty, the ROP would be as follows:

$$\text{ROP} = S_s + \bar{S}dR,$$
$$= 32 + 5(10)$$
$$= 82 \text{ units}$$

and average inventory would be

$$\bar{I} = S_s + \frac{Q}{2}$$

where

$$\bar{I} = \text{average inventory}$$
$$S_s = \text{safety stock}$$
$$Q = \text{order quantity}$$

Implementing an economic order quantity of 50 units, average inventory would be as follows:

$$\bar{I} = S_s + \frac{Q}{2}$$

$$= 32 + \frac{50}{2}$$

$$= 57 \text{ units}$$

Most illustrations throughout this text are based on a perpetual review system with a fixed reorder point. The reorder formulation is based on two assumptions: (1) purchase orders for the item under control will be placed whenever the reorder point is reached, and (2) the method of control provides a continuous monitoring of inventory status. If these two assumptions are not satisfied, the method of perpetual review must be modified.

Periodic Review. An inventory control system based upon periodic review assumes that the status of items will be reviewed at a specified time. For example, the status of a particular item may be reviewed only every 20 days. Therefore, modifications in the basic reorder point must be implemented to take into consideration the fixed time interval of review.

The periodic concept is described as follows:

$$ROP = S_s + \bar{S}d\left(R + \frac{P}{2}\right)$$

where

$$ROP = \text{reorder point}$$
$$S_s = \text{safety stock}$$
$$\bar{S}d = \text{average expected daily sales}$$
$$R = \text{duration of expected inventory replenishment cycle}$$
$$P = \text{review period, days}$$

Since inventory status counts are completed only periodically, any particular item could fall below the desired reorder point during or within the review period. Therefore, the assumption is made that the inventory will fall below ideal reorder status prior to the periodic count approximately one half of the time. Assuming a review period of 20 days and using conditions similar to those of the perpetual example, the ROP then would be as follows:

$$ROP = S_s + \bar{S}d\left(R + \frac{P}{2}\right)$$

$$= 32 + 5\left(10 + \frac{20}{2}\right)$$

$$= 132 \text{ units}$$

Implementing an economic order quantity of 50 units, average inventory could remain 57 units. However, because the review period is of greater duration than the replenishment cycle, the order quantity would have to be increased to accommodate the 10 days' difference. Average inventory thus would become 82 units. Because of the time interval introduced by periodic review, periodic control systems generally require larger average inventories than perpetual systems.

Modified Control Systems.   As expected, variations and combinations of the basic periodic and perpetual control systems have been developed. Most common are the replenishment-level system and the optional replenishment system. Each is briefly noted to illustrate the range of modified systems available for control purposes.

The *replenishment-level system* is a fixed-order-interval system that provides for periodic review but in short intervals. With complete status on inventory similar to the perpetual concept, an upper limit or replenishment level for reordering is established. The review period is added to the lead time and the replenishment level is defined as

$$L = S_s + \bar{S}d(R + P)$$

where

L = replenishment level

S_s = safety stock

$\bar{S}d$ = average daily sales

R = duration of expected inventory replenishment cycle

P = review period, days

The general reordering rules become

$$O = \begin{cases} L - I & \text{if } R < P \\ L - I - q_o & \text{if } R > P \end{cases}$$

where

O = order quantity

L = replenishment level

I = inventory status at review time

q_o = quantity on order

R = duration of expected inventory replenishment cycle

P = review period, days

Assuming a review period of 5 days, average expected sales of 5 units, safety stock of 32 units, and a replenishment cycle of 10 days:

$$\begin{aligned} L &= S_s + \bar{S}d(R + P) \\ &= 32 + 5(10 + 5) \\ &= 107 \text{ units} \end{aligned}$$

Since the replenishment cycle is greater than the review period, it would be necessary to take into consideration outstanding orders. Assume that one order is outstanding for 25 units and the inventory status at time of review is 25 units. Then

$$\begin{aligned} O &= L - I - q_o \\ &= 107 - 25 - 25 \\ &= 57 \text{ units} \end{aligned}$$

If the review period had been greater than 10 days, assume 20. Then

$$L = S_s + \bar{S}d(R + P)$$
$$= 32 + 5(10 + 20)$$
$$= 182 \text{ units}$$

and

$$O = L - 1$$
$$= 107 - 25$$
$$= 82 \text{ units}$$

Under the replenishment-system concept, the size of order is determined without reference to the economic order quantity. Emphasis is placed upon maintaining inventory levels below a maximum, which is the replenishment or order-up-to level. The maximum is protected as an upper level since inventory will never exceed the replenishment level and can only reach the replenishment level if no unit sales are experienced between the order communication and update. Under these conditions the average inventory becomes

$$I = S_s + \tfrac{1}{2}\bar{S}dP$$

The *optional replenishment system* is sometimes referred to as Ss or the *min-max system*. Similar to the replenishment system, the optional system substitutes a variable order quantity for the economic order quantity. However, a modification is introduced to limit the lower size of the variable order quantity. As a result, inventory is controlled on a perpetual basis between an upper and lower range. The upper range exists to limit maximum accumulation of inventory, and the lower limit serves to protect against small orders. The basic ordering rule becomes

$$O = L - 1 - q_o \quad \text{whenever} \quad I + q_o \text{ is } < \text{ROP}$$

Do not order if $I + q_o$ is $> \text{ROP}$.

FASHION/PROMOTION PROCUREMENTS. The special situations surrounding fashion and promotion buying stand in contrast to reorder control purchasing, which is dominated by relatively stable product lines. Specific fashion and promotion items are purchased on a one-time basis with the anticipation that they will be sold within a specified time period. Such items are highly seasonal or fad-oriented.

To the extent that the acquisition plan consists of fashion/promotion items, the traditional program used to monitor and control is the open-to-buy. The open-to-buy is a dollar amount or budget which each buyer is permitted to commit to purchase of a line of resale items. The total of the open-to-buy budgets represents the enterprise's acquisition plan for this category of merchandise.

The Manufacturing Environment

Production scheduling and overall materials and supplies procurement are the end results of the operations plan in a manufacturing environment. Such a plan must take into consideration manufacturing capabilities and the process utilized at each production plan.

The first is the job shop, in which the manufacturing function is spread across a number of work stations. Each work station performs a specific task in the production operation, such as stamping or machining, and each passes the product or component to the next work station. Under job shop processing, the flow of work does not proceed uniformly through successive stages, because of the variable time required to complete each process. Therefore, specific work stations may perform similar processes on a number of different products or components, while others may be limited to processing a single item.

The second type of manufacturing process has a production line orientation. Under this arrangement all functions required to manufacture a product are performed in sequence. Although the assembly line is primarily a product-line manufacturing process, this type of production is characteristic of all processes in which several manufacturing stages are continuous.

From the viewpoint of operations planning, the job shop provides the greatest flexibility, since it is not linked to a specific product. Therefore, with a reasonable lead time a variety of products can be produced by a job shop. The degree of flexibility will vary between different job shops. Some have the capability of adapting on a per job basis. Others must complete sufficient processing once a station is activated to spread the tooling costs and to realize the economy of scale for which the machinery was designed.

The product-line manufacturing process has limited flexibility, since it is oriented to producing a specific product at a continuous, high-volume rate. Many continuous-process manufacturing facilities produce on a 24-hour, seven-day-per-week basis and have no flexibility with respect to the product produced. Large paper-processing plants are prime examples of this manufacturing category.

Whereas the job shop can be regulated on the basis of anticipated product order, the product-line process is committed to a volume orientation. Many variations exist where the features of these two processes are combined to achieve a balance between flexibility and economy. One way of combining the two processes is to use the maximum number of similar components in a variety of end products. Another technique is to postpone painting, accessory addition, and other superficial aspects of production to the final stage of the manufacturing process.

No matter what type of manufacturing process a firm has, it is considered relatively fixed in the short run. A statement of manufacturing capabilities provides the flexibility that can be adapted in the process of operational planning. In particular, the operational plan should include but is not limited to:

1. Identification of which products can be produced at specific plants.
2. A statement of the lead time required for changeover.
3. A statement of economic lot size of production.
4. A statement of the relative cost and desirability of producing a specific product at alternative manufacturing plants (when it is capable of being produced at more than one).

The complexity of the operational plan will vary greatly, depending upon the nature of the enterprise. Generally, the more complex the manufacturing process, the more rigid the plan will be. In situations where different job shops are linked with product-line assembly plants in a multiecheloned network production sequence, lead-time requirements may make it impossible to switch product assignments in less than several months.

MATERIALS REQUIREMENT PLANNING. The material-requirement-planning (MRP) system consists of a set of logically related procedures, decision rules, and records designed to translate the operations plan into a production schedule and a time-phased statement of materials requirements.[22] The MRP procedure evaluates inventory on hand and on order in terms of gross requirements and then identifies additional procurement requirements according to lot-sizing rules for each item.[23] The MRP approach accepts as given the characteristics of the manufacturing process and product bill-of-materials structure. Its purpose is to seek maximum efficiency in production by ensuring that appropriate work priorities are maintained.

An MRP system of coordination requires that all inventory items be capable of identification and that their lead times for procurement and manufacturing be known and relatively dependable. To accomplish this control, the system requires computerized processing similar to the automated order-processing system.

The unique feature of MRP is that it incorporates a dimension of time into traditional systems of inventory stock status. With time-phased capability, the MRP system provides two significant outputs vital to overall logistical coordination: (1) statement of materials requirements, and (2) production schedule.

Statement of Materials Requirements. The material requirements statement summarizes procurements, cancellations, or expedite actions required to support planned manufacturing. The actual procurement activity is a materials management responsibility included in logistical operations.

---

[22] Orlicky, op. cit., p. 21.
[23] Ibid., pp. 120–37.

The time-phased listing of materials which leads to procurement and transfer requirements results from MRP analysis. Given the operations plan, a *bill of materials* explodes in detail the specification of required products and materials. Explosion consists of identification and purchase lot sizing of the aggregate quantity of materials and parts required to manufacture or assemble the scheduled production. Since one of the ingredients in the formulation of the bill of materials is the procurement lead time, the result of the explosion analysis is the material plan ranked by recommended sequence of purchasing.

Lot-sizing requirements when procuring materials and components do not always fit the basic assumptions underlying the EOQ formulation. The EOQ assumption is that usage is continuous and occurs at a more-or-less uniform rate. In contrast, procurement support of manufacturing typically occurs at uneven time intervals and in discrete quantities which vary in size. The typical EOQ approach does not offer a convenient way to balance economical lot sizes with procurement requirements. Several *discrete-lot-sizing* techniques have been developed as solutions to this problem.[24] Specific techniques are discussed in Chapter 6 in conjunction with a more detailed treatment of inventory.[25] The important point to note at this time is that the manufacturing environment most often requires a specialized approach to quantity lot sizing.

Production Schedule. A second output of the MRP system is the conversion of sequenced requirements into the production schedule. Whereas the operational plan was based on anticipated customer demand as forecasted, the production schedule is based on more timely appraisal of customer activity (order processing) and is constrained by the availability of materials and component parts as determined from materials management operations. Thus the finalized schedule incorporates all available information to formalize and direct manufacturing operations.

The purpose of the production schedule or final assembly schedule is to determine the products to be produced, how much of each to produce, and in what time interval or sequence to assure availability at the lowest possible unit production cost.

Both logistical coordination and manufacturing organizations have a major interest in operations planning. The appropriate demarcation of responsibility lies with what and how much will be produced, not how or where it will be manufactured. Logistical coordination is concerned with *what* and *how much* will be produced within a given time period and the time sequence of its planned availability. Manufacturing is concerned with *where* and *which way* the product will be manufactured or assembled.

Summary

The combination of managerial activities required to integrate physical distribution management, materials management, and internal inventory

---

[24] Ibid.
[25] See pages 164–166.

transfer operations is referred to as logistical coordination. The function of logistical coordination is to assure that all of the movement and storage required in logistical operations is completed as effectively and efficiently as practical.

Two primary methods of forecasting—regression and time-series analysis—were reviewed as alternative ways to forecast future logistical operating requirements. The type of forecast required is short-run and at a detailed level. This forecasting is referred to as product-market sales forecasting.

To supplement the forecast, constant updates of factual data are available from the order-processing system. The communication message represents the trigger mechanism for the entire logistical system. To facilitate understanding of the importance of communication, the overall process was functionally described as possessing four links: (1) order transmittal, (2) internal coordination, (3) logistical command, and (4) monitor and control. Building upon integration of the four communication linkages, an example of an automated order-processing system was presented.

Demand forecasts, updated by timely information from order processing, provide the major inputs to the formulation of the enterprise's operations plan. The operations plan synthesizes all available information into a time-phased statement of activities planned by the enterprise. The way the plan is used to complete the logistical coordination process varies in manufacturing and retail and wholesale operations.

The retail–wholesale environment represents a unique set of procurement requirements in that the typical purchase item is a finished product and the range of stockkeeping units is expansive. The logic used to guide retail–wholesale procurement deals with independent demand and was identified as product procurement. In implementation of the PP logic four concepts are noteworthy: (1) economic order quantity, (2) safety stock, (3) reorder control, and (4) fashion/promotion procurement.

In the manufacturing environment, primary emphasis is placed upon scheduling production and planning material requirements to satisfy dependent demand. To assist in this complex task, software programs have been developed. The MRP system, working with the most current data available, provides two major outputs: (1) the statement of materials requirements, and (2) the short-term production schedule. The requirements statement becomes the blueprint for materials management operations. The production/assembly schedule is the blueprint for manufacturing operations.

In total, the chapter has integrated the communication and planning functions necessary to coordinate logistical operations. In Part Two the components of the typical logistical system are examined in detail.

Questions

1. What is the justification for placing product-market unit forecasting in the logistical coordination group?

2. What is the fundamental difference between the use of regression analysis and exponential smoothing in forecasting?

3. Discuss the range of sensitivity of alpha factors in an exponentially smoothed forecast. How does adaptive smoothing assist in the selection of alpha factors?

4. What is meant by zero-response communication and when would you consider it to be effectively used in a logistical system?

5. Discuss the relative capabilities of various techniques available for order transmittal.

6. What is the logistical command function and how does it relate to the order-processing system?

7. Discuss the potential of P-O-S terminals in relation to order cycle and inventory control.

8. Discuss and illustrate the differences between independent and dependent demand.

9. What role does economic order quantity play in material requirements planning?

10. What is the purpose of the bill of materials in material requirements planning?

PART Two

Components of
Logistical Systems

Elements of Transportation

Transportation provides logistical system geographical closure by linking facilities and markets. In most firms more dollars are spent on transportation than on any other single element of logistical operations. Total expenditures on intercity freight in the United States in 1976 were over $80 billion and are projected to exceed $200 billion by 1990.[1] Naturally, the ratio of transportation cost to total logistical cost varies among industries. Industries that produce high-value products such as cameras, jewelry, and electronics have low transport cost as a percentage of sales. In contrast, coal, iron ore, basic chemicals, and fertilizers have high relative transport cost.

The requirement for transportation services varies greatly from industry to industry. For some basic commodities, transportation requirements are in terms of total trains. In automobile logistics, the most common method of transport is the trilevel railcar. Several hundred trilevel railcars are required to transport a single week's production from an assembly plant. In iron ore

[1] This estimate does not include local trucking. Based upon *Transportation Facts and Trends*, 12th ed. (Washington, D.C.: Transportation Association of America, July 1976) and *1972 National Transportation Report*, Department of Transportation, and *Summary of National Transportation Statistics*, Department of Transportation, November 1972. All freight movement in 1975 was estimated to be $136 billion.

111

transport, ships and barges moving on the Great Lakes and inland waterways may satisfy requirements most economically. To the meat packer, transportation means refrigerated railcars or truck trailers. For the crude oil producer, transportation centers around pipelines. For the retailer, United Parcel Service may constitute the primary method of customer delivery. In contrast, a producer of electronic components may use air freight for product delivery.

Many transportation options are available for product or raw-material movement in a logistical system. In addition to for-hire transportation, an enterprise may decide to operate private transportation or enter into a contract with a transport specialist. This chapter provides an overview of available transportation services. The chapter development places emphasis on the range and cost of available transportation services.

The first section of this chapter provides an overview of the transport infrastructure in terms of modal characteristics. Various transport modes are classified based on operating characteristics and legal alternatives. The second section reviews the common-carrier rate structure and describes special or accessorial services important to logistical operations. The final section covers special aspects of traffic management and administration.

Transportation Infrastructure

In this section infrastructure is viewed in terms of the legal variety and relative characteristics of individual transportation modes and multimodal systems.

Modal Variety and Relative Characteristics

The term *mode* is used to identify basic methods of transportation. The five basic transportation modes are rail, highway, water, pipeline, and air. The relative importance of each mode can be measured in terms of mileage, traffic volume, traffic revenue, and the nature of traffic composition. Each mode is reviewed with respect to these relative measures.[2]

RAIL. Historically, railroads have handled the largest number of ton-miles within the continental United States. As a result of the early establishment of a comprehensive rail network connecting almost all cities and towns, railroads dominated intercity freight tonnage through World War II. This early superiority resulted from the capability to transport large shipments economically, frequent service, and a somewhat monopolistic position. However,

---

[2] For more detail, see D. Phillip Locklin, *Economics of Transportation*, 6th ed. (Homewood, Ill.: Richard D. Irwin, Inc., 1972). Also John Hazard, *Transportation Management, Economics, and Policy* (Cambridge, Mass.: Cornell Maritime Press, Inc., 1977) and *White Paper on Transportation* (Washington, D.C.: Transportation Association of America, 1976). Statistics throughout this section are from the sources listed in footnote 1.

with the advent of serious competition since World War II, the railroad's share of ton–miles and revenues has been declining.

In 1975 railroads transported 36.5 per cent of total intercity ton–miles. The 1975 rail share was nearly equal to the 1970 share, and projections to 1985 indicate that rails will continue to transport between 35 and 37 per cent of total intercity ton–miles for the foreseeable future. This stabilization of market share represents a major accomplishment compared to the 1947 to 1970 period, during which railroads reported a steady decline in market share. In terms of total share of intercity ton–miles, railroads transported 54.0 per cent in 1947, 39.2 per cent in 1958, 38.8 per cent in 1965, and 35.9 per cent in 1970. The decline in share of revenue was even more significant, dropping from almost 40 per cent in 1950 to less than 20 per cent in 1970. In 1975 the railroad share of for-hire revenue was estimated at approximately 18 per cent.[3]

The miles of railroads in service once ranked number one among all modes. In 1975 the total miles of railroad was under 200,000 miles, fourth among modes and exceeding only inland water. Although this change in relative mileage between modes is not surprising, it is important to realize that since World War II the absolute miles of railroads have continued to decline. For example, 220,000 miles were reported in operation in 1960, contrasted with 209,000 in 1970. This decline in railroad mileage has continued into the 1970s as a result of a concentrated effort on the part of the railroads to abandon low-volume trackage.

The capability of railroads to transport very large tonnages efficiently over long distances is the main reason they continue to command significant intercity tonnage and revenue. Railroad operations experience high fixed costs with extensive equipment, rights-of-way, switching yards, and terminals. This fixed capacity, coupled with the nature of rail power, results in a relatively small variable operating cost. The replacement of steam by diesel power reduced the railroad's variable cost per ton–mile, and electrification offers a potential for even greater reductions. A minimal amount of power, combined with limited labor, allows a large volume of traffic to be transported considerable distances at low variable cost per ton–mile.

In recent times the character of traffic transported by rails has shifted from a wide range of commodities to an emphasis on extracting industries, heavy manufacturing, and agricultural commodities. However, even in these categories a significant share of tonnage has been lost to competitive carriers. The greatest sources of railroad tonnage are the raw-material-extracting industries located a considerable distance from improved waterways. Switching and car-tracing problems have created serious operational dilemmas for railroads; the average speed between terminals is approximately 20 miles per hour.[4]

Despite operational problems, the inherent fixed-variable cost structure of

---

[3] *Transportation Facts and Trends*, op. cit.

[4] For a comprehensive discussion of railroad operating characteristics and problems, see George E. Harmon, *Transportation: The Nation's Lifelines* (Washington, D.C.: Industrial College of the Armed Forces, 1966).

railroads still offers economic superiority for numerous long-haul movements. This distance advantage is one reason why western railroads have been able to maintain revenues and tonnage better than their eastern counterparts. Since the 1950s, railroads have tended toward a policy of market segmentation by eliminating small-shipment (LCL) traffic and several accessorial services. To provide improved services to major rail users, progressive railroads have concentrated on the development of specialized equipment, such as the enclosed trilevel automobile car, cushioned appliance cars, unit trains, and new pricing techniques.

These examples are by no means a comprehensive review of recent railroad innovations, but they are characteristic of the attempts being made to retain and improve railroad's share of the market. However, the plight of the railroads continues and is causing grave national concern. In 1971 rail passenger service was nationalized for all effective purposes with the creation of the National Railroad Passenger Corporation (AMTRAK), a government-backed corporation. The loss of intercity passenger revenue was not a serious concern to the railroads, which had less than 3 per cent of the total market. However, in the opinion of many transportation experts, the creation of Amtrack represented the first step toward overall nationalization. Following the financial demise of the Penn Central in 1970 a series of bankruptcies occurred among railroads operating largely in the eastern and midwestern United States. On April 1, 1976, seven bankrupt railroads became part of the Consolidated Rail Corporation (CONRAIL). CONRAIL was culminated by the Railroad Revitalization and Reform Act which allocated $2.1 billion for reform. It is clear that significant change will occur in traditional concepts of railroading. The issues of survival or nationalization and the resultant form of a viable rail network are of prime concern to logistical planning.

HIGHWAY.   Highway transportation has expanded rapidly since the end of World War II. To a significant degree the rapid growth of the motor carrier industry has resulted from greater flexibility of door-to-door operation and greater speed of operation in comparison to railroads.

In 1975 expenditures on intercity freight moved by for-hire truck exceeded $25 billion, which was greater than the combined total for rail, air, water, and pipeline. In terms of relative increase, motor carriers transported 5.2 per cent of total ton–miles in 1947, 12.5 per cent in 1958, 14.6 per cent in 1965, 15.9 per cent in 1970, and 19.7 per cent in 1975. Forecasted market share of intercity ton mileage is projected to remain around 20 per cent.

Motor carriers have flexibility in that they can operate on all types of highways. The 1975 improved highway mileage available to motor carriers exceeded 3 million miles, which was greater than the combined total of all other modes of transport.

In comparison to railroads, motor carriers have relatively small investment in terminal facilities and owned right-of-way. Although the cost of license fees and tolls experienced in operation is considerable, these expenses are related to the number of over-the-road vehicles in operation. The variable cost per mile of motor carrier is high because of the requirement that a separate power unit be operated for each trailer.[5] Also, the amount of labor is high because of restrictions by the drivers and substantial dock labor at shippers' locations and at carrier terminals. The net result is a structure of low fixed cost coupled with high variable cost. In comparison to railroads, motor carriers are more economically adapted to handling smaller shipments moving shorter distances.

The character of motor carrier traffic leans heavily toward the manufacturing and distributive trades. In particular, the motor carriers have made significant inroads into rail traffic associated with medium and light manufacturing. Because of the flexibility of store–door delivery, motor carriers have captured almost all freight moving in the distributive industries from wholesalers or warehouses to retail stores. In fact, the greatest source of competition to motor common carriers in this aspect of freight is the private or contract-operated truck.

The prospects for maintaining relative market share in highway transport remain bright. By 1975, with the exception of small package goods, almost all less-than-10,000-pound shipments (LTL) moving in intercity freight were captive to the motor carrier industry. This phase of traffic alone was capable of generating over 60 per cent of the revenue and more than 45 per cent of the tonnage of motor common carriers.

The motor carrier industry, however, is not without substantial problems. The primary difficulties relate to the increasing cost of labor as reflected in equipment replacement, driver wages, maintenance, and, in particular, platform and dock wages. The labor settlement of 1970, after a prolonged strike, had a substantial impact on labor rates, with a subsequent increase in motor carrier rates. The 1973 labor settlement, which could not immediately be offset by a rate increase owing to Phase III inflation controls, created a major problem for many carriers. The trend was further amplified by the 1976 contract settlement. Although accelerating labor rates influence all modes of transport, the labor-intensive nature of motor carrier operations causes the impact to be felt severely. To counteract this trend, carriers have placed a great deal of attention on improved line-haul scheduling that bypasses ter-minals, overhead billing systems, mechanized terminals; double-bottom line-haul operations that pull two trailers by a single power unit; and utilization of coordinated transport systems, such as trailer on flat car (TOFC) to perform a portion of line-haul movement.

Perhaps the greatest threat to the common motor carrier industry is over-the-road transportation by shipper-owned trucks or by specialized carriers that perform transport services for shippers under contract. In 1975 over 50 per cent of all intercity truck tonnage was hauled in private fleet

---

[5] Some variations exist wherein more than one trailer may be pulled in a double-bottom or truck–train arrangement, which exceeds 40 feet of combined trailer length.

operations.[6] The low-fixed-cost structure of motor carrier operations encourages easy entry. Common-carrier entry can be blocked by other common carriers because each must gain explicit operating authority from the Interstate Commerce Commission in the form of a Certificate of Public Convenience and Necessity.[7] However, private transportation need only comply with the federal, state, and local safety and licensing laws. Increasing indications are that the ICC will relax entry requirements for common carriers as a result of pressures for regulatory reform.

It is apparent that highway transportation will continue to function as the backbone of logistical operations for the foreseeable future. The area of greatest importance to logistical planning concerns increasing rates and special charges associated with shipments under 10,000 pounds.

WATER. Water is the oldest form of transport. The original sailing vessels were replaced by steamboats in the early 1800s and by diesel power in the 1920s. A distinction is generally made between deep-water and navigable inland water transport. Domestic commerce centers on the Great Lakes, canals, and navigable rivers.

In 1975 water transport accounted for 22.6 per cent of total intercity tonnage. Its relative share of intercity tonnage was 31.3 per cent in 1947 and 31.7 per cent in 1958. Tonnage declined to 27.9 per cent in 1965 but increased by 1970 to 28.4 per cent. This short-term increase did not stabilize. Market share dropped by 5.8 per cent by 1975. Forecasted market share by 1985 is 18.4 per cent of total intercity tonnage. The water transport share of revenue has been less than 2 per cent of intercity freight revenue since 1955.

The exact miles of improved waterways in operation depend in part on whether coastwise and intercoastal shipping are included. Approximately 26,000 miles of improved inland waterways were operated in 1975. Fewer miles of improved inland waterways exist than of any other transportation mode.

The main advantage of water transport is the capacity to move extremely large shipments. Deep-water vessels are restricted in operation, but diesel-towed barges have a fair degree of flexibility. In comparison to rail and highway, water transport ranks in the middle with respect to fixed cost. The fixed cost of operation is greater than that of motor carriers but less than that of railroads. The main disadvantage of water is the limited degree of flexibility and the low speeds of transport. Unless the source and destination of the movement are adjacent to a waterway, supplemental haul by rail or truck is required. The capability of water to transport large tonnage at low variable

[6] Donald J. Bowersox and Bernard J. La Londe, *Competitive Transportation Study, Phase I, Patterns of Motor Carrier Growth, 1960–1980* (Washington, D.C.: Regular Common Carrier Conference, September 1974), and Robert M. Butler, "RCCC Board Terms Private Trucking Fastest Growing Competitive Threat," *Traffic World* (April 26, 1976), p. 21.

[7] Issued by the federal government and most state government units.

cost places this mode of transport in demand when low freight rates are desired and speed of transit is a secondary consideration.

Freight transported by inland water leans heavily to mining and basic bulk commodities, such as chemicals, cement, and selected agricultural products. In addition to the restrictions of navigable waterways, terminal facilities for bulk and dry cargo storage and load–unload devices limit the flexibility of water transport. Labor retrictions on loading and unloading at dock level create operational problems and tend to reduce the potential range of available traffic. Finally, a highly competitive situation has developed between railroads and inland water carriers in areas where parallel routings exist.

Inland and Great Lakes water transport will continue to be a viable alternative for future logistical system design. The full potential of the St. Lawrence Seaway has not yet been realized with respect to domestic freight.[8] The slow passage of inland river transport can provide a form of warehousing in transit if fully integrated into overall system design. Improvements in ice-breaking equipment appear on the verge of eliminating the seasonal limitations of water transport.

PIPELINE. The initial pipelines were in operation in domestic commerce in 1865. Although growth was not dramatic, by 1947, 9.5 per cent of intercity tonnage moved by pipeline. A major increase in utilization occurred between 1947 and 1958, when the percentage of total intercity freight ton–miles jumped to 16.5 per cent. In 1956 pipeline transport constituted 18.7 per cent of total intercity tonnage, 19.6 per cent in 1970, and 21.0 in 1975. The forecasted market share for 1985 is 26 per cent. Thus, the pipeline currently represents the fastest-growing transportation mode. A great deal of this growth is directly attributable to the energy crises which resulted in direct government subsidies for a substantial increase in capacity such as the Trans-Alaska pipeline.

The most frequent commodity transported by pipelines is petroleum. In 1960, 190,944 miles of pipeline were operational in the United States. By 1970 that figure had jumped to 218,671 miles. The operational figure was estimated as 223,583 miles in 1974.[9] Pipelines have the distinction of having the highest fixed cost and the lowest variable cost among all the transport modes. The high fixed cost results from the right-of-way for the pipeline, construction, and requirements for control stations and pumping capacity. Since pipelines are not labor-intensive once constructed, the variable cost of operation is extremely low.

The basic nature of a pipeline is unique in comparison to all other modes of transport. It operates on a 24-hour basis, seven days per week, and is limited only by the need to change over commodities or conduct emergency and

---

[8] For more detail concerning research on this subject, see John Hazard, "The Second Decade of the Seaway," *Transportation Journal*, Summer 1970, pp. 33–40.

[9] *Transportation Facts and Figures*, op. cit., p. 31.

preventive maintenance. The obvious disadvantage is that a pipeline is extremely limited with respect to commodities. Experiments on moving solid products in the form of slurry or in hydraulic suspension continue to be conducted, but petroleum products remain the main commodity of pipelines for the immediate future.

AIR.   The newest, most glamorous, and by far the least utilized mode of transport is air freight. The glamor of air freight lies in the speed with which a shipment can be transported. A coast-to-coast shipment via air between two major cities takes only hours, rather than days as with other modes of transport. Likewise, the trade-off of air freight for other elements in the logistical system, such as field warehousing, has attracted considerable attention to the potential of air freight.

Air transport still remains more of a potential than a reality. Although the mileage is almost unlimited, in 1975 air freight accounted for only 0.2 per cent of all intercity ton–miles and about 1 per cent of revenue. Air transport capability is limited by lift capacity and availability of aircraft. To date, most intercity air freight has been transported on scheduled passenger flights, with the subsequent reduction of both capacity and flexibility in freight operations. The high cost of jet aircraft, coupled with the erratic nature of freight, has limited the assignment of existing aircraft to all-freight operations. Likewise, research and development on special-purpose cargo aircraft, such as STOL-capable aircraft and cargo helicopters, had lagged because of the slow maturation of high-volume air freight.

The fixed cost of air transport is not high in comparison to rail, water, and pipeline. Airways and airports are generally developed and maintained with public funds. Likewise, terminals are normally maintained by local communities. The fixed costs of air freight are associated with aircraft purchase and the requirement for specialized handling systems and cargo containers. Air transport ranks second only to highway with respect to low fixed cost. On the other hand, variable cost is extremely high for air operations, as a result of fuel, maintenance, and the labor intensity of both inflight and ground crews.

No particular commodity dominates the traffic carried by air freight operations. Perhaps the best distinction is that most freight handled is on an emergency, rather than a routine, basis. Most firms will utilize scheduled or nonscheduled air cargo movements when the situation justifies high-cost movement. Products with the greatest potential for regular air movement are those with high value or extreme perishability. When the marketing period for a product is extremely limited, such as with Christmas or high-fashion items, air transport may be the most economical method for logistical operations.

The prospects for increased utilization of air cargo in logistical operations remain promising. Although movement by air requires prior and subsequent land movement, the speed of service possible between two distant points can reduce overall logistical costs by sufficient margins to offset the added cost of air transport.

Modal Comparative Analysis

Figure 5-1 provides a distribution of intercity freight movement by each mode from 1947 through 1970 and forecasted to 1985. Table 5-1 ranks the modes on the basis of revenue per ton–miles. Air leads the five modes, with a revenue figure of 21.88 cents per ton–mile. The differential between rail and truck is over 6 cents per ton–mile, whereas the differential between water and rail is only slightly greater than 1 per cent per ton–mile.

In terms of composition of traffic between modes, the value and bulk of the product and length of haul are the prime determinants of modal choice.

FIGURE 5-1

Distribution of Intercity Freight Movement by Modes, 1947–70, Forecasted to 1985

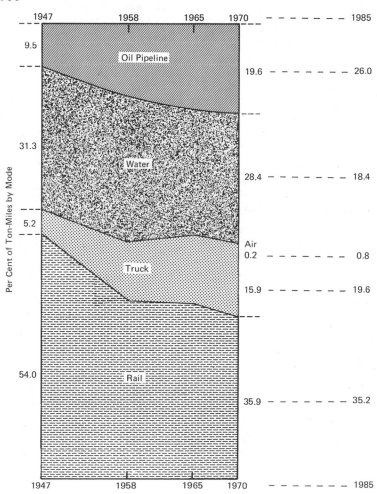

TABLE 5-1
Comparative Average
Revenue—Five Basic
Transportation Modes
(cents per ton–mile)

Air	21.88
Truck	7.70
Rail	1.43
Water	0.30
Pipeline	0.27

Considering air and pipeline in a special category, the composition of freight tendered among truck, rail, and water would be expected to prefer truck as the value increases and water as the bulk increases.

Figure 5-2 provides the U.S. Department of Transportation projection of annual growth rate by mode during the 1970s and 1980s.

Modal Classification

The basic modes of transportation have been reviewed in terms of historical development and share of intercity ton–miles and freight revenue. The essential operating characteristics of each mode were noted, including the relationship of associated fixed and variable cost structures. Table 5-2 summarizes the operating characteristics of each mode with respect to speed, availability, dependability, capability, and frequency of service.

Speed, of course, refers to the elapsed time for intercity movement, and air cargo is the fastest of all modes. Availability of service refers to the ability of a mode to service a given pair of locations. Highway carriers are the most capable in terms of availability. Dependability of operations refers to potential variance from expected or published delivery schedules. Pipelines, because of their continuous service, rank highest in dependability. Capability is the

TABLE 5-2
Relative Operating Characteristics—Five Basic
Transportation Modes

Operating Characteristic	Transportation Mode				
	Rail	Highway	Water	Pipeline	Air
Speed	3	2	4	5	1
Availability	2	1	4	5	3
Dependability	3	2	4	1	5
Capability	2	3	1	5	4
Frequency	4	2	5	1	3

FIGURE 5-2
Projected Annual Growth Rates by Mode, 1970–80 and 1980–90

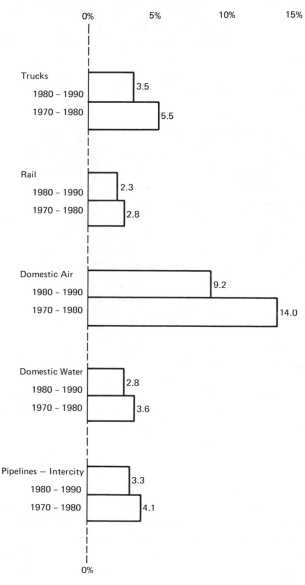

ability of a mode to handle any transport requirement, and water transport is the most capable. The final classification is frequency, which relates to the quantity of scheduled movements. Pipelines, again because of their continuous service between two points, lead all modes in frequency.

As Table 5-2 shows, the rapid growth of highway transport can be explained, at least in part, by its high ranking across characteristics. Operating on a highway system that comprises over 3 million miles, motor carriers rank first or second in all categories except capability. Although substantial improvements in motor capability resulted from relaxed weight limitations on interstate highways and approval of the practice of pulling tandem trailers, the prospect that motor transport will surpass rail or water capability in the immediate future is not realistic.

Legal Forms of Transportation

In addition to classifying transportation alternatives on the basis of mode, another common grouping is based on the legality of carrier operating rights. Each carrier must comply with some form of legal authorization to transport goods and commodities. The four basic types of legal carrier are common, contract, private, and exempt. Each type of carrier may exist within any basic mode of transportation. For regulatory reasons, a single for-hire transportation firm will generally operate utilizing a single mode. However, more than one type of legal transport within a mode can often be found.

The category of legal transportation represented most often consists of the common carriers. A common carrier is a company that offers to transport property for revenue at any time and any place within its operating authority without discrimination. A common carrier is authorized to conduct for-hire transportation after receiving a Certificate of Public Convenience and Necessity from the appropriate regulatory agency. Common carriers are required to publish for the public all rates charged for transport services. These rates must be identical for similar movements of freight. The operating authority received by a motor common carrier may include transport of all commodities or may limit transport to specialized commodities such as steel, household goods, or computers. In addition, the operating authority specifies the geographical area the carrier may service and indicates if such service is to be on a scheduled or nonscheduled basis.

Contract carriers perform transport services on a selected basis. Although contract carriers must receive authorization in the form of a permit, such permits provide limited and for the most part less specific operating authority than do those for common carriers. The basis for contract cartage is an agreement between a carrier and a shipper calling for the carrier to provide a specified transportation service at an agreed-to cost for the shipper. The business agreement of contract becomes the basis for the contract carrier to receive his permit. The permit authorizes the contract carrier to transport specified commodities over specified routes. The contract carrier may transport for more than one shipper and is not required to charge the same rate for all shippers. Each agreement to transport requires regulatory approval.

Exempt carriers do not confront direct regulation with respect to operating rights or pricing policies. Exempt carriers, however, must comply with licensing and safety laws of the states in which they operate. If the exempt carrier is engaged in interstate movement, rates must be published. Exempt carriers for motor and water originated in the agricultural sector, when unprocessed farm products were authorized for hauling to processing centers. Today, exempt carriers operate in a broader range of commercial activity. Exemptions are also granted on the basis of area and to select associations. An example of area exemption is in local cartage within the commercial zones surrounding municipalities. In a controversial and contested ruling in early 1977 the ICC dramatically expanded commercial zones. In the case of municipalities with populations of 1 million or more, the commercial zone was expanded from 5 to 20 miles from municipal limits.

An association exemption refers to shipper alliances for the purpose of aggregating numerous small shipments at a buying center for transport to the shipper locations in one consolidated shipment. The two modes mainly engaged in exempt cartage are highway and water.

Private carriage consists of a firm providing its own transportation service. The firm must own or control through lease the transport equipment and be the bona fide owner of the goods or commodities transported. In addition, the act of transporting goods must be incidental to the primary purpose of the business. Although private transport does not come under the regulatory laws of the federal or state governments, it is subject to license, safety, and weight restrictions. Private trucking has increased significantly during the past decade, and all forecasts indicate continued rapid expansion. The flexibility and economy of a private truck operation customized to the needs of a particular shipper is difficult to match by a common-carrier operation.

Although the distinction between the legal forms of transport is slight, the related restrictions can have considerable impact upon logistical system design. From the perspective of logistical planning the main considerations between legal types are the degree of restriction, the extent of financial commitment, and the flexibility of operation.

The degree of restriction refers to the law that surrounds the operation of each form of cartage. For instance, the private carriage of one subsidiary of a conglomerate cannot legally transport goods of another subsidiary in backhaul. However, substantial pressure is being exercised for changes in legal restrictions to increase the flexibility of private truck utilization.[10]

---

[10] For examples of proposed change in regulatory posture, see "Transportation Freedom from Regulation," *Business Week*, May 12, 1975, pp. 74–80. The particular re-regulation provision noted is the backhaul exemption, which permits selected commodities to be transported by nonregulated carriers. Current proposals call for substantial liberalization of "what" constitutes a legal backhaul. In particular, pressure is mounting to permit subsidiaries to be treated like divisions for purposes of backhaul.

The extent of commitment refers to the degree of financial involvement or obligation which the shipper has to the carrier. The least amount of commitment is experienced with common carriers, since an agreement reached for each shipment specifies the obligations of all parties. Contract operations have a greater degree of commitment in the sense that the typical contract between the carrier and the shipper is of six months' to one year's duration. It is important to point out that the degree of involvement normally associated with both common and contract carriers is variable-cost in nature and is directly associated with the tonnage transported. In private transport, the extent of commitment is longer and involves both fixed cost of equipment and variable cost of operation. The duration of obligation can be reduced by equipment leasing. However, this form of financing only influences the cash flow related to equipment purchase and does not relieve the extent or magnitude of obligation. The commitment associated with exempt cartage is difficult to generalize, since it can range from very little to extensive.

The greatest latitude in terms of flexibility is naturally associated with private transport. However, it should be noted that failure to schedule private transport in an economical and routine manner can be a pitfall leading to costly operations. Exempt and contract cartage rank second to private carriage for operational flexibility. Since the contract operator is captive to the shipper, a great deal of direction can be exercised in operational scheduling. The number of common carriers, in excess of 15,000 motor carriers alone, means that the availability of service is great. However, the shipper does not legally enjoy a large degree of flexibility concerning the common carriers' operation. While the common carrier must service all shippers on an equal basis and at a common price, the prudence of good management dictates that the common carrier will design service around the requirements of large and frequent shippers located within the operating territory.

The vitality of a sound national transportation system rests with common carriers, the backbone of the transport network. Most enterprises utilizing private, exempt, and contract carriers also tender frequent shipments to common carriers. In fact, the largest users of private trucking are usually the largest users of common-carrier transport. The general belief among professional traffic managers is that every effort should be made to utilize the common-carrier network capacity. Using contract carriers assigns responsibility to a management that has the sole task of operating transport capacity.

Multimodal Transportation Systems

To this point the transportation infrastructure has been viewed with respect to basic modes and legal classification. The student of logistics soon learns that every generalization has an exception. Two major areas of exception are the auxiliary users of for-hire transport and coordinated arrangements. An examination of each is necessary for an overall understanding of the transportation infrastructure. These two additional classifications of transportation supply are grouped under multimodal systems because they frequently utilize more than one mode of transport.

AUXILIARY USERS. *Auxiliary users* are transportation companies that, in effect, work in transportation in a manner somewhat analogous to wholesalers.[11] They purchase a major share of their intercity or line-haul transport from the legal forms of transport. In some situations they operate their own over-the-road equipment by special authorization of regulatory agencies. It is common practice for auxiliary users to operate as exempt carriers within the commercial zone of municipalities for purposes of pickup and delivery.

The economic justification of auxiliary users is that they offer shippers lower rates for movement between two geographical points than would be possible by direct shipper utilization of common carriers. A more detailed explanation of the peculiarities in the common-carrier rate structure that provide the opportunity for auxiliary transport will be discussed later in this chapter. It is emphasized here that the enabling conditions for auxiliary transport are the existence of minimum charges, surcharges, and less-than-volume rates.[12] A quantity of small shipments from various shippers is aggregated by the auxiliary user, who then purchases intercity transportation on a volume-rate basis. The auxiliary users then offer the shipper a rate that is lower than the common-carrier rate for the shipment size. The profit margin of the auxiliary user is the per pound difference between the rate charged the shipper and the transport service purchased from the carrier. In some cases auxiliary users charge even higher rates than shippers could obtain directly from primary carriers. The justification for higher charges is faster delivery and more complete service. The three main auxiliary users are freight forwarders, shipper associations, and parcel post.

Freight forwarders are a quasi-legal form of transport in the sense that they are subjected to federal regulation and are treated as common carriers. They accept the full responsibility for performance on all shipments tendered to them by shippers. Freight forwarders are common in surface and air cargo. In both cases they consolidate small shipments and then tender a bulk shipment to common carriers for transport. At the destination the freight forwarder splits the bulk shipment back into the original shipments. Local delivery may or may not be included in the forwarder's service. The main advantage of the forwarder is a lower rate per hundredweight and, in most cases, speedier transport of small shipments than would be experienced by direct tender to a common carrier.

Shipper associations are similar in operation to the freight forwarder. However, as the name implies, shipper associations are voluntary nonprofit entities with membership centered around a specific industry in which small-shipment purchases are common. Department stores, for example, often participate in shipper associations, since a large number of different products

[11] See Chapter 2, pages 35–36, and Appendix IV.
[12] See pages 135–136.

may be purchased at one location, such as the garment district in New York City. The basic idea is that a group of shippers establish an administrative office at a point of frequent merchandise purchase. The staff at the office arranges for all members' purchases to be delivered to a central location. When sufficient volume is accumulated, the staff arranges for consolidated shipment to the association's membership base city. As indicated earlier, some associations operate their own intercity transportation, with the legal status of an exempt carrier. Each member is billed on a proportionate basis to traffic moved plus a prorated share of the association's operating cost.

The U.S. Postal Service operates surface and air parcel service. The charges for parcel post are based on weight and distance. Generally, parcels must be delivered to the post office at a point of shipment origination. However, in the case of large users and when it is to the convenience of the government, post office service may be provided on the premises of the shipper. Intercity transport is accomplished using air, highway, rail, and even water, and the legal forms utilized in parcel post include common and contract cartage. Delivery is provided at the destination by the Postal Service. The importance of parcel service cannot be overemphasized. One of the fastest-growing forms of marketing in the United States is nonstore retailing, in which orders are placed by telephone or mail from catalogs for subsequent home delivery. The bulk of nonstore retailing for home delivery which transcends a local municipal area is transported via parcel post and United Parcel Service.

The auxiliary forms of transportation utilize the services of one or more of the legal forms of transport to various degrees, and all major modes except pipelines. However, they do not represent coordinated transportation.

COORDINATED TRANSPORTATION. *Coordinated transportation* refers to two common carriers representing different modes providing joint point-to-point service on a regularly scheduled basis. Many efforts have been made over the years to combine the inherent advantages of different transport modes into single-shipment movement. Initial attempts at modal coordination trace back to the early 1920s. Such services became more common during the 1950s.

Technically, coordinated transportation could be arranged among all basic modes. Descriptive jargon is popular—piggyback, fishyback, trainship, and airtruck have become standard transportation terms. The important distinction of coordinated arrangements is that the line-haul portion of the shipment is split between two different modes.

The best known and most widely used coordinated system is the trailer-on-flatcar (TOFC), commonly known as *piggyback*. As the name implies, a motor carrier trailer is placed on a railroad flatcar for some portion of the intercity line haul.

A variety of piggyback service plans are available. However, not all railroads offer each. The basic plans are summarized in Table 5-3.[13]

---

[13] This table is adapted from Charles A. Taiff, *Management of Traffic and Physical Distribution*, 5th ed. (Homewood, Ill.: Richard D. Irwin, Inc., 1972), Chap. 18.

TABLE 5-3
Summary TOFC Plans

Plan I. Railroad movement of trailers or containers of common motor carriers, with the shipment moving on one bill of lading and billing being done by the trucker. Traffic moves under rates in regular motor carrier tariffs.

Plan II. Railroad performs its own door-to-door service, moving its own trailers or containers on flat cars under tariffs usually similar to those of truckers.

Plan II$\frac{1}{2}$. A combination of plans II and III whereby the railroad furnishes the trailer but the shipper performs the terminal service.

Plan III. Ramp-to-ramp rates based on a flat charge, regardless of the contents of trailers or containers, usually owned or leased by freight forwarders or shippers. No pickup or delivery is performed by the railroad.

Plan III$\frac{1}{2}$. The same as plan III except one instead of two trailers per car at 60 per cent of the rate.

Plan IV. Shipper or forwarder furnishes a trailer or container-loaded flatcar, either owned or leased. The railroad makes a flat charge for loaded or empty-car movement, furnishing only power and rails.

Plan V. Traffic moves generally under joint railroad–truck or other combination of coordinated service rates. Either mode may solicit traffic for through movement.

Containers also move via TOFC service. Containerization will be discussed in greater detail in Chapter 7. The basic concept is that goods are enclosed in a protective container to facilitate handling during transit from origin to destination.[14] The containers are placed on flatcars similar to trailers, except that containers are generally smaller than trailers and do not have undercarriages. A special label has been applied to container-on-flatcar service— COFC.

As noted earlier, TOFC is just one type of coordinated transport currently in operation. One of the oldest is fishyback, when over-the-road trailers or containers are loaded on ships or barges for long-distance transport. Such services are provided in coastal waters between Atlantic and Gulf ports, Great Lakes to coastal points, and along inland navigable waterways.

Because of the economic potential of linking two modes in a coordinated effort, the concept appeals to shippers and carriers alike. In fact, several authorities have suggested that the only way to maintain a strong common-carrier network is to encourage and foster increased multimodal combinations. Efforts toward increased multimodal coordination are of prime interest to logistical planners, because such developments increase the options available for efficient spatial closure. The next decade should witness expanded development of coordinated arrangements. The greatest deterrent to growth in the past has been a tendency among modal representatives and regulatory agencies to protect the status quo rather than to participate in the innovative process.

---

[14] See pages 205–209.

The trend of shippers away from for-hire transport should challenge this protective attitude among common carriers concerning coordinated transport.

Package Services

One type of transportation service that represents an important part of the transport infrastructure does not fall neatly into any of the preceding classification schemes. Several localized carriers offer package delivery services within the commercial zones of metropolitan areas under the category of exempt carriers. Some carriers offer package delivery services on an intrastate and interstate basis. The best known of these carriers are United Parcel Service (UPS) and Bus Parcel Service.

The original service offered by UPS was contract delivery of local shipments for department stores. In this sense the service was limited to delivery of merchandise to consumers. During the last decade, UPS has made substantial inroads into overall package movements, both in materials management and physical distribution. Since inception UPS has been constantly expanding the scope of its overall operating authority. The basic concept is that individual packages conforming to specified size and weight restrictions may be shipped intercity via UPS. Shipments may include up to 10 individual packages. By specializing in a specific size of package, UPS has been able to provide overnight service between most cities within 150 miles. Unlike parcel post, UPS provides both pickup and delivery service.

A second major package service is offered by various bus companies that provide intercity passenger transport. These firms have found an increasing demand for station-to-station parcel transport on scheduled bus service. Bus parcel does not include pickup or delivery service.

The growth of parcel service has attracted considerable interest in transport circles, since inroads are being made into the serious small-shipment problem confronting the distributive industries.[15] Of particular interest here is not UPS or bus parcel service per se, but the advent of specialized carriers who develop an operating system customized to a specialized market segment. One example is Federal Air Express that provides a network of jet aircraft for rapid movement of critical materials. Similar developments have taken place within the limited certificate common carriers for shipments larger than package goods. There is every indication that specialization of carriers will continue.

Summary—Transport Infrastructure

The transportation infrastructure available to the logistics planner in the United States is superior to that of any other nation. Although problems

[15] For an interesting analysis of the small-shipment situation, see James C. Johnson, "An Analysis of the Small Shipments Problem with Particular Attention to Its Ramifications on a Firm's Logistical System," *ICC Practitioner's Journal*, July–August 1972, pp. 646–66.

do exist within and between the modes, the shipper has many choices with respect to how a particular shipment will be transported between two locations. Within the five basic modes, several legal forms exist. In addition, auxiliary users, coordinated arrangements, and specialized carriers exist to round out the alternatives. The task in design of a logistical system is to select from among available alternatives the combined transport mix that best fits logistical needs.

Ultimately, the selection of transportation mix must be fully integrated into the overall logistical effort in order to design a balanced system. However, in evaluating the potential transportation mix, the value or service rendered by a specific combination of carriers must be measured in terms of corresponding cost. The next section discusses the common-carrier rate structure.

Common-Carrier Rate Structure

A comprehensive treatment of all aspects of common-carrier rates is beyond the scope and intent of this brief overview. The primary purpose of the following is to introduce the basic logic and prevailing structure of common-carrier rates.

The initial section provides a brief history and review of interstate regulatory authority associated with common-carrier rates. Next, the most common types of rates are discussed. The final section reviews special services that carriers provide which are important to logistical planning.

Regulatory Rate Making

All legal forms of transport are subject to some degree of regulation. Common and contract carriers are subject to direct authorization of operating rights, acceptable rates, and safety regulation if they operate in interstate commerce. If carriers' activities are limited to a single state, regulatory control is maintained by state agencies. Of particular interest in this section is the influence of regulation with respect to rate making. Federal economic regulation affects 100 per cent of rail and air ton–miles, 80 per cent of pipeline, 43.1 per cent of trucking, and 6.7 per cent of domestic water carriers.[16]

BRIEF HISTORY OF INTERSTATE REGULATION. The purpose of interstate regulation is to scrutinize the activities of common and contract carriers in the public interest. Since railroads dominated the early overland transportation network, they initially enjoyed the privileged position of a near-monopoly. Individual states maintained the legal right to regulate discriminatory practices within their borders, but no federal regulation existed until the "Act to Regulate

---

[16] Derived from the *1972 National Transportation Report*, op. cit., pp. 2–44. To obtain a clear view of the regulatory responsibilities within the executive and legislative branches of the federal government, see *Transportation Facts and Trends*, op. cit., pp. 33–36.

Commerce" was passed on February 4, 1887.[17] This initial act was the forerunner of the regulatory structure of today. It created the Interstate Commerce Commission (ICC), which remains the chief transportation regulatory agency of the federal government.[18]

The gradual delineation of the federal government's regulatory power over carrier rate making resulted from a series of enactments and judicial decisions from 1900 through 1920.[19] At the turn of the century, serious competitive conditions resulted from independent rate making among carriers. Although the ICC had the authority to review groups of rates with respect to their just and reasonable nature after the rates were placed into effect by individual carriers, no regulation existed over proposed rate making. Attempts at joint rate making by railroads had been declared illegal, and in 1903 the railroads supported the passage of the Elkins Act. This act reduced under-the-table rebates and special concessions, and increased the penalty for departing from published rates. It did not, however, eliminate the cause of discriminatory practices—independent and nonregulated rate making.

The passage of the Hepburn Act in 1906 began to establish federal regulatory powers over rate making. The just-and-reasonable-review authorization of the 1887 act was expanded to include examination of maximum rate levels. However, the regulatory posture remained *expost* until passage of the Mann–Elkins Act in 1910. This act permitted the ICC to rule on the reasonableness of proposed rates and to suspend them when the proposed rates appeared discriminatory.

The posture of modern rate regulation was completed with the passage of the Transportation Act of 1920. The review power of the ICC was expanded to prescribe minimum as well as maximum reasonableness of rates, and the commission was instructed to assume a more aggressive nature concerning proposed rates. The original Act To Regulate Commerce was modified to instruct the commission to initiate, modify, and adjust rates as necessary in the public interest. The 1920 act also changed the name of the 1887 act to the Interstate Commerce Act.

Several additional acts related to transportation have been enacted. With few exceptions their primary objective was to clarify issues related to the basic acts of 1887 and 1920. In 1935 the Emergency Transportation Act further instructed the ICC to set standards with respect to reasonable rate levels. Motor carrier competition was now a prime factor. In 1935 the Motor Carrier Act placed the regulation of common-carrier highway transportation under

[17] For an early history of legislative attempts prior to 1887, see L. H. Hanley, *A Congressional History of Railways in the United States, 1850–1887*, Bulletin 342 (Madison, Wis.: University of Wisconsin, 1910).

[18] In recent years the ICC has been subjected to considerable review and evaluation by both Congress and critics of government regulation. Some have called for abolishment of the commission. However, the contents of the 1976 Surface Transportation Act, which Congress reviewed extensively, continue to support the concept and scope of the ICC as the principal regulatory agency of the federal government.

[19] The discussion that follows is based upon that presented by Locklin, op. cit., pp. 208–38.

the jurisdiction of the ICC. This act, which became Part II of the Interstate Commerce Act, defined the basic nature of the legal forms of common, contract, and exempt motor carriers.

In 1938 the Civil Aeronautics Act established the Civil Aeronautics Authority (CAA) as the ICC's counterpart for regulating air transport. The powers and charges of the CAA were somewhat different from those of the ICC, in that the act specified that the CAA would promote and actively develop the growth and safety of the airline industry. In 1940 the functions of the original CAA were reorganized into the Civil Aeronautics Board (CAB) and the Civil Aeronautics Administration, now known as the Federal Aeronautics Administration (FAA). In addition, the National Advisory Committee on Aeronautics was formed in the mid-1930s and in 1951 became known as the National Aeronautics and Space Administration (NASA). Through the 1960s NASA concentrated attention on aerospace. However, NASA is specifically charged with the responsibility for increasing aviation safety, utility, and basic knowledge through the use of science and technology. Thus the CAB regulates rate making, the FAA administers the airway system, and NASA is concerned with scientific development of aerospace, commercial, and civil (private) aviation.

The regulation of pipelines has not been as clear cut as that of railroads, motor carriers, and air. In 1906 the Hepburn Act declared that selected pipelines, primarily oil, were in fact common carriers. The need for regulation developed from the early market dominance that Standard Oil Company gained by developing crude oil pipelines to compete with rail transport. In 1912 the ICC took action, which was upheld by the Supreme Court, to convert private pipelines into common carriers. While there are substantial differences between pipeline and other forms of regulation, for all effective purposes, the ICC fully regulates pipeline traffic today. Interestingly, the greatest difference in pipeline regulation is that these common carriers are allowed to transport goods owned by the carrier.

Regulation of water transport prior to 1940 was extremely fragmented. Some regulation existed under both the ICC and the U.S. Maritime Commission. In addition, a series of specific acts had placed regulation of parts of the domestic water transport network under particular agencies. The Transportation Act of 1940 placed under the ICC jurisdiction over domestic water transportation and gave the Federal Maritime Commission authority over water transport in foreign commerce and between Alaska and Hawaii and other U.S. ports.

It is important to understand that the ICC *does not* set or establish rates for carriers under its regulatory jurisdiction. Rather, the ICC reviews and either approves or disapproves rates. Carriers under federal regulation are exempt from the antitrust provisions of the Sherman, Clayton, and Robinson–Patman Acts with respect to collaboration in rate making. Such exemption is provided by the Reed–Bulwinkle Act of 1948, which permits carriers to participate in rate-making bureaus. Cooperative rate making is common

TABLE 5-4
Scope of Federal Economic Regulation of Interstate Transport by Mode

Mode	Author-izing Statute	Agency	Functions Regulated		
			Rates	Carrier Agreements	Entry
Railroads	IC Act, Part I	ICC	Max-min-precise	Permitted	PCN[a]
Motor trucks	IC Act, Part II	ICC	Max-min-precise	Permitted	PCN,[a] permit
Buses	IC Act, Part III	ICC	Max-min-precise	Permitted	PCN[a]
Domestic water carriers	IC Act, Part III	ICC	Max-min-precise	Permitted	PCN,[a] permit
Surface freight forwarders	IC Act, Part IV	ICC	Max-min-precise	Permitted	Permit
Petroleum pipelines	IC Act, Part I	ICC	Max-min-precise	Permitted	Not controlled
Air carriers Domestic	FA Act	CAB	Max-min-precise	Not permitted	PCN[a]
International	FA Act	CAB	Not directly controlled	IATA agreement	PCN,[a] presidential approval
Air freight forwarders	FA Act	CAB	Discrimination only	Not permitted	Operating authority
Noncontiguous maritime	Merchant Marine Act, 1933	FMC	Max-min-precise	Permitted (limited)	Not controlled
International maritime	Merchant Marine Act, 1916	FMC	Not directly controlled	Permitted	Not controlled
Maritime freight forwarders	Merchant Marine Act, 1916	FMC	Not directly controlled	Permitted	Licensed

Source : Table III-1, *1972 National Transportation Report*, U.S. Department of Transportation, pp. 2–44.

[a] PCN, Certificate of Public Convenience and Necessity.

	Functions Regulated				
Service	*Exit*	*Merger*	*Finance*	*Reporting*	*Exemptions*
Car service only	PCN,[a] train discontinued	Controlled	Controlled	Specified	None
Not controlled	PCN[a]	Controlled	Controlled	Specified	Agricultural commodities, local transport
Not controlled	PCN[a]	Controlled	Controlled	Specified	None
Not controlled	PCN[a]	Controlled	Controlled	Specified	Bulk commodities
Not controlled	Not controlled	Controlled	Controlled	Specified	Shipper associations, minor carrier groups
Not controlled	Not controlled	Not controlled	Controlled	Specified	None
Little control	PCN[a]	Controlled	Controlled	Specified	Air taxi, agricultural commodities
Bilateral agreements	PCN[a]	Controlled	Controlled	Specified	None
Not controlled	Not controlled	Controlled	Controlled	Specified	None
Not controlled	Not controlled	Not controlled	Not controlled	Specified	Nonliner services
Not controlled	Not controlled	Not controlled	Not controlled	Specified	Nonliner services
Little controlled	Not controlled	Not controlled	Not controlled	None	None

among all modes, in line with their specific bureau's standardized procedure. Motor carriers, for example, utilize eight rate-making bureaus to coordinate the establishment and publication of new or modified rates. The action of the bureaus is subject to ICC sanction.

Over the years a maze of federal agencies has been created to assist in various phases of overall transport regulation. In 1968 the Department of Transportation (DOT) was formed by Congress in an effort to draw the majority of transport-related agencies together under a single administrative head at cabinet level.

Although the primary concern in this treatment is rate regulation, it is important to realize that national transportation policy has a direct impact on the vitality of the common-carrier infrastructure and prevailing rates charged for services. Existing national transportation policy is stated in the Amended Interstate Commerce Act, the Merchant Marine Acts, the FAA Act, The Department of Transportation Act, the administrative actions of the ICC, court decisions, and economic messages of various presidents.

Table 5-4 summarizes the scope of federal economic regulation of interstate transport by mode. A review of the table shows that overall regulation goes far beyond rate regulation.

A concentrated attempt is currently being made to review and modify existing national transportation policy in light of the demands and requirements of contemporary society. In 1972, 1974, and 1976 the Department of Transportation introduced legislation to modify the scope of regulation of common carriers. Particular re-regulation legislation has centered on the railroad and trucking sectors of the common-carrier industry. Upon assuming office as chairman of the Interstate Commerce Commission in 1977, A. Daniel O'Neal appointed a special task force to recommend ways in which the ICC could internally improve the regulation of motor carriers. The report, commissioned on June 2, 1977, was completed in 34 days and offered 39 reform proposals. This particular report is significant because it represents the first major effort on the part of the ICC to take the major lead in motor carrier regulatory reform away from DOT. There is little doubt that the regulatory posture of this industry will undergo change in the future, but the exact nature and magnitude of the change are difficult to predict.[20]

[20] For varied opinions regarding the eventual outcome of potential regulatory revamping, see *Analysis and Criticism of the Department of Transportation Motor Carrier Reform Act* (Washington, D.C.: American Trucking Association, 1976); Rupert L. Murphy, "Private or For-Hire?" *Distribution Worldwide*, September 1975, pp. 39–41; Stephen Tinghitella, "The Day the ICC Died," *Traffic Management*, December 1975, p. 14; Jim Dixon, "The Spectre of Distribution," *Distribution Worldwide*, September 1975, pp. 29–30; and Harry J. Newman, "The Key to Reform is Gradualism," W. Doyle Beatenbough, "There Is Room for Improvement"; Lee Cisneros, "Regulation Is Simply the Balance Wheel"; J. B. Speed, "There Has To Be a Cross-Subsidization of Freight Rates"; B. A. Franzblau, "There Must Be a More Rational Approach"; Tom Cornelius, "Deregulation Would Cause a Chaotic Situation"; W. Stanhaus, "Our System Can Be Improved"; and E. Grosvenor Plowman, "The Need Is for Rational Regulatory Improvement," all in "Deregulation, Reregulation, or Status Quo?" *Distribution Worldwide*, September 1975, pp. 31–38.

Common-Carrier Line-Haul Rates

Common carriers utilize three types of line-haul rates: (1) class, (2) exception, and (3) commodity. Each type of rate will be reviewed.

CLASSIFICATION AND CLASS RATES. The term *class rate* evolves from the fact that all products transported by common carriers are classified for purposes of transportation pricing. The classification scheme simplifies the number of transportation rates charged by common carriers; it does not fix the monetary rate charged for movement of a particular commodity. In standard transportation terminology a specific product classification is referred to as its *rating*. The charge in dollars and cents per hundredweight to move a specific product classification between two locations is referred to as the *rate*. The specifics of freight classification and rate tariffs are discussed in greater detail in the last section of this chapter.

Once the classification rating for a product is identified, the applicable rate per hundredweight between any two points can be determined from the tariff. All products legally transported in interstate commerce can be shipped via class rates. The actual price charged for a specific shipment is normally subjected to a minimum charge and may also be subject to a surcharge or an arbitrary assessment.

The *minimum charge* represents the lowest total charge a shipper can pay for a specific shipment regardless of weight. To illustrate, assume that the applicable class rate is $2/cwt (hundredweight) and the shipper wants to ship 100 pounds to a specific location. If no minimum charge existed, the total cost of transport would be $2. However, with an assumed minimum charge of $5 per shipment, the cost for completing the shipment would be the minimum. Thus, under the assumed conditions, the minimum charge renders all shipments from 1 to 250 pounds equal in transportation cost.

An *arbitrary* is a special assessment added to a shipment charge. In some cases, such arbitraries exist to provide carriers special compensation for servicing selected destinations or areas. Arbitraries are particularly common in the South, where added charges have traditionally been placed upon all shipments in a particular weight category. In other cases, the applicable rates to specific destinations are published in terms of a hundredweight charge to a major city plus an arbitrary charge for delivery beyond.

An additional charge, often added for small shipments, is a *surcharge* to help cover the cost of carrier handling. The surcharge may be a flat charge or a sliding scale based on the size of the shipment. Class rates, minimum charges, arbitrary charges, and surcharges form a pricing structure which, in various combinations, is applicable between all locations within the continental United States. The general classification provides a base rating for all products. Thus the classification and class rate structure combine to form a generalized pricing structure for rail and motor common carriers. Because of the general nature of class rates, they represent the highest transport prices.

EXCEPTION RATES. *Exception rates*, or exceptions to the classification, are special rates published to provide shippers lower rates than the prevailing class rate. The original purpose of the exception rate was to provide a special rate for a specific area, origin–destination, or commodity when either competitive or high-volume movements justified a downward rate adjustment. Rather than publish a new tariff, an exception to the classification was established.

Just as the name implies, when an exception rate is published, the classification that normally applies to the product is changed. Such changes may be the assignment of a new class or may be a percentage of the original class. Technically, exceptions may be higher or lower, but most exception rates are reductions from class rates. Unless otherwise noted, all services associated with the movement remain the same as the class rate when a commodity moves under an exception rate.

COMMODITY RATES. When a large quantity of a product moves on a regular basis between two locations, the common procedure is to publish a *commodity rate*. Commodity rates are special or specific rates published without regard to classification. These rates are normally published on a point-to-point basis and apply only on the products specified in the tariff.

At one time most rail freight moved via exception rates. Today commodity rates dominate. Commodity rates are less prevalent in motor carrier tariffs. Whenever a commodity rate exists, it supersedes the corresponding class or exception rate.

CONCLUSION—LINE-HAUL RATES. The three main line-haul rates form the nucleus of the motor and rail common-carrier rate structures. Each of the other modes has specific characteristics applicable to their tariffs. In water, specific tariff provisions are made for cargo location within the ship or on the deck. In addition, provisions are made to charter total vessels. Similar specialized provisions are found in air cargo and pipeline tariffs. Auxiliary users and package services publish tariffs specialized to their service.

Thus, although this section describes the most frequently used common-carrier line-haul rates in a logistical system, it does not provide a comprehensive treatment.

Special Rates and Services

A number of special rates and services provided by common carriers are of particular importance to logistical operations. This final section describes some important examples.

FREIGHT-ALL-KINDS RATES. Rates for *freight-all-kinds* (*FAK*) are important to physical distribution operations. Under FAK rates, a mixture of different commodities is delivered to a single or a limited number of destinations. Rather than charge each classification of freight within the shipment its appropriate rate, an average rate is applied for the total shipment. In essence, FAK rates are line-haul rates since they replace class, exception, or commodity rates. Their purpose is to simplify the paperwork associated with the movement of a mixture of commodities. As such, they are of particular importance in distribution from warehouses to retail stores.

LOCAL, JOINT, PROPORTIONAL, AND COMBINATION RATES. Numerous *special rates* exist that may offer transportation savings on particular freight movements. When a commodity moves under the tariff of a single carrier, it is referred to as a *local rate*. If more than one carrier is involved in movement of the freight, a *joint rate* may be applicable wherein the freight moves on a through bill of lading even though multiple carriers are involved in the actual transport. Because many motor and rail carriers operate in restricted territory, it may be necessary to utilize the services of more than one to complete a shipment. Utilization of a joint rate can offer substantial savings over the use of two or more local rates to complete a shipment.

Proportional rates are in fact special price incentives to utilize a published tariff that applies only to part of the desired route. If a joint rate does not exist and proportional provisions do, the cost of moving a shipment under the proportional arrangement will be lower than combining local rates. Proportional provisions of a tariff are most often applicable to origin or destination points beyond the normal geographical area of a local tariff. They provide a discount on the local tariff, thereby resulting in a lower overall freight charge.

Combination rates are similar to proportional rates in that two or more rates may be added when no published local or joint rates exist between two locations. The rates may be any combination of class, exception, and commodity rates. The utilization of combination rates often involves several technicalities, such as intermediate rules and aggregation of intermediates, which are beyond the intent of this treatment. The use of combination rates substantially reduces the cost of an individual shipment. In most cases that involve regular movements, the need to utilize combination rates is eliminated by the publication of a through rate.

TRANSIT PRIVILEGES. *Transit privileges* are, with some exceptions, limited to railroad operations. A transit privilege permits a shipment to be stopped at an intermediate point for processing. When transit privileges exist, the shipment is charged a through rate from origin to destination plus a transit privilege charge. From the viewpoint of the shipper, the use of this specialized service is restricted to specific geographical areas once the product enters in transit service. Therefore, a degree of postponement is lost when the product is placed in transit because the area of final destination can be altered only at significant added expense, or, at the least, loss of the through rate and assessment of the transit charge. Finally, the utilization of transit privileges increases the paperwork of shippers both in terms of meeting policing requirements of railroads and ultimate settlement of freight bills. The added cost of administration must be carefully weighed in evaluating the true benefits gained from utilizing a transit privilege.

DIVERSION AND RECONSIGNMENT.   For a variety of reasons, a shipper, or for that matter the *consignee* (receiver of shipment), may desire to change routing, destination, or even consignee of a shipment once it is in transport. This flexibility can be extremely important. It is a normal practice among certain types of marketing middlemen to purchase commodities with the full intention of selling while in transit with subsequent diversion or reconsignment.

Diversion consists of changing the destination of a shipment while it is enroute and prior to arrival at the originally planned destination. *Reconsignment* is a change in final consignee prior to delivery. Both services are provided by railroads and motor carriers for a specified charge.

DEMURRAGE AND DETENTION.   Demurrage and detention are charges assessed by carriers when freight cars or truck trailers are held beyond a specified loading or unloading time. The term *demurrage* is used by the railroads for delay in excess of 48 hours in returning a car to service. Motor carriers use the term *detention* to cover similar delays. In the case of motor carriers, the permitted free time is specified in the appropriate tariff and will normally be limited to a few hours. The assessment of a penalty charge is mandatory on the part of carriers and is subject to ICC policing and fine if not properly administered.

From the viewpoint of logistical operations, the degree of demurrage and detention experienced must be carefully administered. Situations exist wherein it is desirable to pay the assessment in order to gain more operational time in processing a particular shipment. In effect, the boxcar or trailer can be used as temporary warehouse space by payment of demurrage or detention charges.

ANCILLARY OR ACCESSORIAL CHARGES.   Motor and rail carriers offer a wide variety of services that can be of extreme importance in planning a logistical operation. Diversion, reconsignment, transit, demurrage, and detention are examples of special services singled out earlier. The list of additional special services is almost unlimited. Of particular importance to logistics are environmental, special equipment, and special delivery services.

Environmental services refer to special control of freight while in transit. Icing, refrigeration, ventilation, and heating to prevent freezing are examples of controlled-environment transport. *Special equipment charges* refer to per trip assessment for the use of specific equipment which the carrier has purchased for the economy and convenience of the shipper. The *special delivery* services provided by carriers are particularly important to logistical operations. One category of special service is most common among motor carriers, who provide door-to-door delivery. At destination, motor carriers will provide split delivery where a load is delivered to more than one destination. Under specified tariff conditions, pickup and delivery will be extended to points beyond those normally considered part of the point-to-point line-haul service.

Although this brief coverage of special services is not all-inclusive, it does provide examples of the services carriers will provide. Thus the role of carriers in logistical operations can be far greater than simply a means of transportation.

Transportation Administration

With the advent of the logistical concept, responsibilities for exacting traffic management have increased substantially. In the past it was not unusual for the traffic manager to be strictly responsible for transportation purchasing. However, in the new context, traffic management duties frequently involve packaging, materials handling, inventory management, warehousing, and other areas of logistics.

Regardless of the exact scope of authority, under the logistical concept the traffic manager will become more involved with other corporate activities, such as marketing, production, and finance. The recent awareness of total logistical systems has created confusion regarding the proper role of traffic management. Transportation management is only one part of overall logistical management, but it is one of the most important aspects of total control.[21]

This section reviews the role of traffic management in a logistical organization. Because many books are devoted to this subject, the content here does not constitute a detailed professional development of the field of traffic management. The objective is to familiarize the nonprofessional reader.

Traffic Administration

The administration responsibility of traffic management consists of day-to-day control of freight movement. In cases where all movements are by for-hire carriers, this responsibility consists of purchasing and movement control. If an enterprise operates private equipment, the traffic department is responsible for administration and scheduling of equipment. In both cases traffic management must provide a transport service that meets logistical requirements. These system requirements relate to speed of service, size of order to be shipped, and assignment of the specific plant or warehouse to make the shipment. The operating standards for transport are given and must be met to achieve logistical goals. However, the research responsibility of traffic management, discussed in the next section, outlines the way a traffic department can take an active role in setting logistical standards.

---

[21] For a selected review of duties and approaches to modern traffic administration, see Robert V. Delaney, "The Effective Use of the Private Fleet," James K. McConnell, "Developing a Transportation Strategy," Phillip Catalano, "A Study of the Traffic Department Organization at Steelcase, Inc.," and Jack L. Collins, "Cost Reduction Opportunities Through Improved Consolidation," all in Proceedings, 14th Annual Conference of the National Council of Physical Distribution Management, Chicago, 1976.

The administration of transportation consists of (1) freight classification, (2) obtaining lowest rate for a given movement consistent with service requirements, (3) equipment scheduling, (4) documenting, (5) tracing and expediting, (6) auditing, and (7) claims.

FREIGHT CLASSIFICATION. All products normally transported are grouped together into uniform classifications. The *classification* takes into consideration the characteristics of a product or commodity that will influence cost of handling or transport. Similar products are grouped into a class, thereby reducing the wide range of possible ratings to a manageable size. The particular class that a given product or commodity receives is its *rating*. A product rating is not the price that must be paid to have the product transported. The rating is the product's classification placement. The actual price to be paid is called the *freight rate*. As will be explained, the rate is printed in pricing sheets called *tariffs*. Thus a product's rating is used to determine the freight rate.

Motor carriers and rail carriers each have independent classification systems. The motor carrier system is the "National Motor Freight Classification," and rail classifications are published in the "Uniform Freight Classification." The motor classification has 23 classes of freight; the rail system has 31. In local or regional areas, individual groups of carriers may publish additional classification listings.

Classification of individual products is based on a relative percentage index of 100. Class 100 is considered the normal class, with other classes running as high as 500 and as low as 35 in the national motor freight system. Each product is assigned an item number for listing purposes and then a class rating. As a general rule, the higher a class rating, the higher the transportation cost of a product. Thus a product classified as 400 would be approximately four times more expensive to transport than a product rated as class 100. Products are also assigned classifications based upon the quantity shipped. Less-than-carload (LCL) or less-than-truckload (LTL) shipments of identical products will have higher ratings than carload (CL) or truckload (TL) shipments.

To illustrate, assume item 70660 from the National Motor Freight Classification, described as "carpet or rug cushions, cushioning or lining, sponge rubber, in wrapped rolls." Item 70660 would fall into the general product grouping 70500, "floor coverings or related articles." For LTL shipments, item 70660 has a $77\frac{1}{2}$ rating, whereas in TL shipments it is assigned class 45, provided that a minimum of 30.2 hundredweight is shipped. Many products will also be assigned different ratings based upon packaging. Sponge rubber cushions may have a different rating when shipped loose, in bails, or in boxes than when shipped in wrapped rolls. Thus a number of different classifications may apply to the same product, depending upon where it is being shipped, the size of the shipment, the transport mode being used, and the packaging of the product.

One of the major responsibilities of the traffic department is to obtain the best possible rating for all products shipped by the enterprise. Although there are differences in rail and motor classifications, each is guided by classification rules. These rules are similar. However, the rail rules are more comprehensive and detailed than those for motor freight classification. It is essential that members of a traffic department have a comprehensive understanding of classification rules. The general rules handle all normal situations and specific rules are available as exceptions to the general rule.

It is possible to have a product reclassified by written application to the appropriate classification board. These boards review proposals for change or additions with respect to minimum weights, commodity descriptions, packaging requirements, and general rules and regulations. All changes other than corrections in classification require public hearings prior to publication. All interested parties are provided an opportunity to be heard prior to acceptance or rejection of the proposal. After the proposal is accepted or rejected, methods of appeal are provided.

An alert traffic department must take an active role in classification. Many dollars can be saved by finding the correct classification for a product or by recommending a change in packaging or quantity shipped that will reduce the rating of an enterprise's product.

FREIGHT RATES.   Earlier in the chapter, a description of basic transportation rates and rate regulation was presented. For any given shipment it is the responsibility of the traffic department to obtain the lowest possible rate consistent with service requirements. Determination of transport cost by method of movement—rail, air, motor, pipeline, parcel post, United Parcel, freight forwarders, and so on—is found by reference to tariffs. In this connection it is important that the traffic department have adequate access to current tariffs. The most important information resource available to the traffic department is its tariff library. Many tariffs exist and relevant ones must be kept up to date for all changes and modifications.

As indicated several times throughout this text, the lowest possible cost for transportation may not be the lowest total cost of logistics. The traffic department must seek the lowest rate consistent with service standards. For example, if two-day delivery is required, the traffic department seeks to select the method of transport that will meet this standard at the lowest possible cost.

EQUIPMENT SCHEDULING.   One major responsibility of the traffic department is scheduling, either for common carriers or private transportation. A serious operational bottleneck can result from carrier equipment waiting to be loaded or unloaded at a shipper's dock.

Railroads and motor carriers each have special charges for equipment delay beyond normal times allowed in the tariffs. As a general rule, demurrage and detention should be held to a minimum, because they represent a penalty charge that increases total cost. However, in special cases, it may be desirable to pay delay penalties in order to reduce other expenses. For example, demurrage charges may represent a favorable trade-off if overtime can be reduced. Each situation must be evaluated on the merits of the alternatives. The objective is to eliminate special service charges unless they reduce other costs.

DOCUMENTATION.   Several documents are involved in transportation management. Two of the most important are the bill of lading and the freight bill.

BILL OF LADING.   The *bill of lading* is the basic document in the purchase of transport services. It serves as a receipt for goods shipped through the description of commodities and quantities detailed on the document. For this reason, accurate description and count are essential. In case of loss, damage, or delay, the bill of lading provides evidence for damage claims.

The bill of lading specifies the terms and conditions of carrier liability and includes all possible causes of loss or damage except those defined as acts of God. It is important that these terms and conditions be clearly understood, so that appropriate actions may be taken in the event of inferior performance.

There are variations in bills of lading. In addition to the *uniform* bill of lading, others commonly used are order notify, export, livestock, and government. It is important to select the correct bill of lading for a specific shipment.

An *order-notified* or *negotiable* bill of lading is a credit instrument. It provides that delivery not be made unless the original bill of lading is surrendered to the carrier. The usual procedure is for the seller to send the order-notified bill of lading to a third party, usually a bank or credit institution. Upon payment of the invoice value of the goods, the credit institution releases the bill of lading to the buyer. The buyer then presents it to the common carrier, who in turn releases the goods.

An *export* bill of lading permits the domestic use of export rates, which are sometimes lower than domestic rates. Thus, when a shipment is being moved domestically for export, savings in transport might be enjoyed. An export bill of lading also permits greater time at the port for transfer of freight from a railcar to a ship. In many cases the export bill also eliminates the need for special broker services at the port facility.

Government bills of lading may be used when the product is owned by the U.S. government. A government bill of lading allows the use of *Section 22 rates*, which are normally lower than regular rates.

The named individual or buyer on a bill of lading is the only bona fide recipient of goods. A carrier is responsible for proper delivery according to instructions contained in the document. In effect, title is transferred with accomplishment of delivery.

FREIGHT BILL.   The *freight bill* represents a carrier's method of charging for transportation services performed. The freight bill is derived from information contained on the bill of lading. It may be either prepaid or collect. A *prepaid* bill means that transport cost must be paid for prior to the transportation performance, whereas a *collect* shipment shifts payment responsibility to the buyer.

Freight bill payment periods vary. Motor carriers must bill shippers within seven days of delivery and the shipper must pay the carrier within an additional seven days after receipt of the bill. In the case of rail, 96 hours are allowed for carloads and 120 hours for LCL shipments. Unless credit arrangements have been made with carriers, collect shipments are payable upon delivery.

A great deal of transportation administration is involved in preparation of bills of lading and freight bills. Several shippers and carriers are working together to reduce this administrative burden. Some firms elect to pay at the time of creating the bill of lading, thereby combining the two documents into one. Such arrangements are based upon financial analysis of the relative benefits of advanced payment to reduce paperwork costs. Many attempts are also under way to produce all documents in the required number of copies simultaneously. This has become more practical with the advent of computer facilities to aid in document preparation.

TRACING AND EXPEDITING. Another important responsibility of transportation management is tracing and expediting. Shipments committed to the vast transportation network of the United States are bound to go astray or be delayed en route from time to time. Most large carriers maintain a tracing department and a computerized service to aid shippers in locating a shipment. The tracing action must be initiated by the shipper's traffic department, but once initiated, it is the carrier's responsibility to provide the desired information.

Under conditions of exacting product movement control, the shipper may desire to expedite a given shipment to overcome some unexpected change of events. Under these conditions the shipper is often provided a "pro" number, which corresponds to the carrier's waybill and vehicle number. Identification of the shipment's pro number allows rapid location at the point of destination terminal and transfer terminals.

AUDITING. Auditing of freight bills is another important function of the traffic department. Owing to the complexities involved in finding the correct rate, the probability of an error in rate determination is higher in purchasing transportation than in most other purchasing decisions. Given the fact that transportation costs in the United States exceed $100 billion, a 1 per cent error in rate calculation will result in a potential billion dollar loss to either carriers or shippers.

The freight audit is of two types: preaudit and postaudit. A *preaudit* determines the proper rate and charges prior to payment of a freight bill. A *postaudit* makes the same determination after payment.

Auditing may be either external or internal. If external, specialized freight auditing companies are used whose personnel are usually assigned to specific commodity groupings. This is generally more efficient than the use of internal personnel. Payment for an external audit is usually based on a percentage of the revenues reclaimed through overcharges. It is crucial that a highly ethical firm be employed for this purpose, because valuable marketing and customer information is contained in the freight bill, and corporate activities may be adversely affected if it is not held confidential.

A combination of internal and external auditing is frequently employed. The division of this activity is based upon the freight bill. Thus, for a bill of $600, a 10 per cent error results in a $60 recovery, but for a $50 bill a 10 per cent error results in only a $5 recovery. Bills with the larger recovery potential are typically handled internally.

External versus internal auditing may also be affected by the size of the firm and the degree of rate computerization. Large traffic departments are in a position to have specialized clerks for auditing purposes. Firms on computerized systems of freight payment can build in appropriate applicable rates on a large majority of points and weights. In that case automatic checks on proper payment can be made by computer programs designed for that purpose.

CLAIM ADMINISTRATION. When transportation services or fees do not meet the predetermined standards, shippers can make claims for restoration. Naturally, carriers and shippers desire to prevent as many claims as possible. Most claims can be settled between the carrier and shipper without resort to a higher authority. However, when necessary, the framework for third-party settlement is detailed.

In general, claims break down into two categories: (1) loss and damage, and (2) overcharge–undercharge. Loss and damage claims represent a shipper's demand for carrier payment of partial or total financial loss resulting from improper fulfillment of the transport agreement. Charge claims result from a variation in charges from those published in tariffs.

A specialized body of rules applies to the proper procedure for claim filing and the responsibility of the parties involved. A discussion of this detail is beyond the present intent. Two factors regarding claim administration, however, are of primary importance. First, detailed attention should be given claim administration, because such recoveries will be realized only by aggressive shipper programs. Second, the emergence of a large volume of claims indicates that the carriers selected are not performing their specified service obligation with the desired consistency. Regardless of the dollars recovered by claim administration, the breakdown in customer service performance from loss and damage claims damages the shipper firm's reputation with customers.

Traffic Research

Beyond traffic administration, the traffic department carries a research responsibility with respect to the transport area and to the overall logistical system. Most traffic managers are capable of performing the administrative responsibilities of transportation. However, the true distinction of professionalism between traffic managers is their capability in traffic research.

Traffic research is divided into two areas of responsibility. The first represents activities to improve the cost of transportation services and/or the quality of service received. The second constitutes activities aimed at improving the logistical effort of the firm.

TRANSPORT SERVICES RESEARCH. Traffic managers should always be on the lookout for information to improve carrier service or obtain lower freight rates for a certain quality of service. This means that an aggressive program of performance measurement and rate negotiation should be a continuing function of transportation research.

Carrier performance measurement is perhaps one of the least developed areas of traffic research. Information is normally accumulated in the number of claims with individual carriers as tracing occurrences. However, shippers should also attempt to measure how well carriers meet stated service obligations. Such obligations involve (1) equipment availability, (2) tracing efficiency, (3) expediting capability, and (4) transit consistency.

Among these four measures of performance, the one most difficult to obtain reliable information about is transit consistency. In Chapter 6 the subject of inventory control is developed and it is pointed out that one vital aspect of control systems is the lead time required to obtain replenishment. Regardless of how fast a supplier is able to ship, if the transport carrier provides inconsistent delivery, problems in inventory control will result. Likewise, sales can be lost and production lines shut down if carriers fail to meet their service obligation. Generally speaking, the smaller a given shipment, the greater the service variance between consecutive shipments. Thus, while a truckload or carload shipment may regularly meet published schedules, the same efficiency may break down in LTL or LCL shipments. Some carriers are superior to others, and the task is to determine which carrier is most consistent.

One shipper purchasing from a number of suppliers for delivery to several warehouses obtains this information as follows. When suppliers ship, they are required to record the date and other critical information on a postcard. When the order arrives at the warehouse, it is noted on the daily data transmitter to the central purchasing headquarters. Both dates are retained in a computer file by individual carrier along with a statement of expected performance. The variation between actual and expected performance is determined by a simple computer routine and the average performance is calculated and updated on a regular basis. At specified intervals, the performance record of each carrier is printed in report form and forwarded for traffic management review.

This consistency report, coupled with statistics on equipment availability, tracing, and expediting performances, provides valuable information for evaluation of carriers. Unless this information is collected on a routine basis, it is difficult to be specific or take corrective action about erratic carrier performance.

Another vital area of transport research is negotiation, both formal and informal. In formal negotiations, shippers must participate actively in proceedings before regulatory boards. Such proceedings may be aimed at achieving improvements in rates, ratings, or service provisions of a specific tariff, or they may be aimed at preventing undue price increases or service detailments proposed by carriers. Informal negotiations consist of direct relationships between shippers and carriers. Despite the fact that transportation is a highly regulated industry, a great deal of latitude does exist between carriers and shippers. The effectiveness of both formal and informal negotiation will depend upon the shipper's ability to support proposals with accurate and complete information. Such information can only be collected by a well-administered research and analysis program. One very important area of transport research, therefore, is the constant review of carrier performance and continuous examination of beneficial changes in existing classifications and tariffs.

LOGISTICAL SYSTEM RESEARCH.   For any given operating period, traffic management is expected to provide the required transportation within the stated transportation budget. However, it is also traffic management's responsibility to look for ways in which transportation can be used effectively to reduce total logistical costs. For example, a slight change in packaging may open the door for negotiation of a lower classification rating for a product. Although packaging costs may increase, this added expense may be offset by a substantial reduction in transportation cost. Unless such proposals evolve from the traffic department, they will go undetected in the average firm.

As indicated earlier, transportation is the highest single cost area in most logistical systems. Because of this cost and the dependence of the logistical system on an effective transport capability, the traffic department must play an active role in future planning.

Summary

The critical nature of transportation to logistical operations can be developed from a number of perspectives. Transportation provides spatial closure for the logistical system by linking geographically separated facilities and markets. Transportation is a total cost-reducing factor in the sense that expenditures for transport services allow greater specialization and economies in the process of manufacturing and marketing.

The transport infrastructure consists of five basic modes of transport. Rail, highway, water, pipeline, and air transport can be compared on the basis of speed, availability, dependability, capability, and frequency of service, as well as fixed and variable costs. Within these modes, legal forms of transport identify specific carriers as common, contract, private, and exempt. In addition, multimodal transport exists in the form of auxiliary users and coordinated systems. Finally, the transport infrastructure includes a number of firms which provide package services. The task in the design of a logistical system is to select from among all alternatives the combined transport mix that best fits the need of a particular enterprise.

The common-carrier rate structure provides a basis for evaluating the benefits in overall logistical operations in terms of corresponding cost. Common-carrier rates are controlled by interstate regulatory authority. Specific common-carrier line-haul rates can be grouped as class, exemption, and commodity rates, and a wide variety of special rates and services exist which are of particular importance to logistical operations.

Transportation management is sufficiently specialized to constitute an area of detailed professional administration essential to logistical operations. The final section of this chapter provided a short review of the duties and responsibilities of traffic management within the overall logistical management organization. A distinction was made between the duties of an administrative nature and those related to research and development. Perhaps the greatest demands on professional traffic management rest with research and development. It is in the area of transport services and basic system research that the skills of the traffic management group are vital. Many benefits of integrated logistical effort are first recognized and accomplished by aggressive and innovative traffic management. Chapter 6 focuses attention on the basic nature of inventory.

Questions

1. Describe the various modes of transportation and the concept of intermodal movement.
2. Describe the differences among common carriers, private carriers, and contract carriers in terms of fixed and variable costs of operation.
3. Why is a strong carrier system considered essential to national growth and defense?
4. What has been the major shift in orientation in transportation regulation from the passage of the initial act in 1887 to the proposed Surface Transportation Act of 1976?
5. Why is the Reed–Bulwinkle Act considered important to transportation pricing, and what current forces have subjected the provisions of that act to critical review?
6. Discuss the difference between class commodity and exception rates. What is the role of classification in determination of rates?
7. Why are transit privileges integral to the formulation of distribution systems?
8. Discuss the importance of demurrage and detention to the carriers and shippers.
9. Why would a freight-all-kinds rate be of extreme importance to an enterprise engaged in delivery of a broad product line from its warehouse to its retail stores?
10. What would be the major implications for the transportation industry and shippers if transportation were deregulated?

Elements of Inventory

Inventory is one of the riskiest decision areas in logistical management. Commitment to a particular inventory assortment and subsequent market allocation in anticipation of future sales represent the vortex of logistical operations. Without the proper assortment of inventories, serious marketing problems can develop in revenue generation and customer relations. Likewise, inventory planning is critical to manufacturing operations. Raw-material shortages can shut down the production line or modify the production schedule, which, in turn, introduces added expense and the potential of finished product shortage. Just as shortages can disrupt planned marketing and manufacturing operations, overstocked inventories also create problems. Overstocks increase cost and reduce profitability through added warehousing, capital tieup, deterioration, excessive insurance, added taxes, and even obsolescence.

Inventory management seeks to achieve a balance between shortage and excess of stock within a planning period characterized by risk and uncertainty. The principles of inventory management are developed in this chapter. The first section presents an overview of function and risk related to inventory decisions. The second section deals with inventory policy and control in a replenishment-cycle context.[1] Inventory cost is examined and economic order

[1] See Chapter 3, pages 53–56.

quantity is elaborated. The replenishment cycle is then examined as the inventory planning perspective. The following section considers sales uncertainty. Statistical probability is introduced as a technique for establishing safety stocks under a variety of situations. In the next section, uncertainties in sales and performance cycle duration are treated as independent but compounded variables in the formulation of safety stock policy. The final section treats special issues related to selectivity in inventory management as related to customer service.

Nature and Functions of Inventory

Formulation of an inventory policy requires an understanding of the role of inventory in a manufacturing–marketing enterprise.[2] In this section the functions of inventory are examined first. Next, the degree of risk with respect to width, depth, and duration of inventory decisions is reviewed.

Functions of Inventory

The basic function of inventory is simply stated: to increase profitability through manufacturing and marketing support. The ideal concept of inventory would consist of manufacturing a product to a customer's specifications. Such a system would not require stockpiles of raw materials or finished goods in anticipation of future sales. While a zero-inventory manufacturing–distribution system is not practical, it is important to remember that each dollar invested in inventory should be committed to achieve a specific objective.

Inventory is a major area of asset deployment which should be required to provide a minimum return on capital investment. A measurement problem exists, however, since the typical corporate profit-and-loss statement does not adequately display the true cost or benefits gained by inventory investments.[3] Lack of measurement sophistication makes it difficult to specify the desired inventory level. Thus conflict exists concerning the appropriate level of inventory commitment and allocation. Financial management has a tendency to want inventories as low as practical to improve cash flow. Marketing desires adequate finished-goods inventories to protect against stockouts or back orders. The manufacturing department is inclined to large stockpiles of raw materials and components to assure against production disruptions.

[2] For a variety of background discussions, see John F. Magee, *Production Planning and Inventory Control* (New York: McGraw-Hill Book Company, 1958); M. K. Starr and D. W. Miller, *Inventory Control: Theory and Practice* (Englewood Cliffs, N.J.: Prentice-Hall, Inc., 1962), E. S. Buffa, *Production-Inventory Systems: Planning and Control* (Homewood, Ill.: Richard D. Irwin, Inc., 1968); and G. Hadley and T. M. Whitin, *Analysis of Inventory Systems* (Englewood Cliffs, N.J.: Prentice-Hall, Inc., 1963).

[3] Douglas M. Lambert, *The Development of an Inventory Costing Methodology* (Chicago: National Council of Physical Distribution Management, 1976), p. 3, and *Inventory-Carry Cost, Memorandum 611* (Chicago: Drake Sheahan/Stewart Dougall, Inc., 1974).

Generally, most enterprises carry an average inventory which exceeds their basic requirement. This generalization can be understood better through a careful examination of the four prime functions underlying inventory management.

GEOGRAPHICAL SPECIALIZATION.   One function of inventory is to allow *geographical specialization* of individual operating units. Owing to factors of production such as power, raw materials, water, and labor, the economical location for manufacturing is often a considerable distance from areas of demand.[4] For example, tires, batteries, transmissions, springs, and so forth are significant components in automobile assembly. With geographical separation, each automobile component can be produced on an economical basis and then, through internal inventory transfer, fully integrated in assembly.

The function of geographical separation is also related to assortment collection in finished goods physical distribution. Manufactured goods from various locations are collected at a single warehouse in order to offer customers a single mixed product shipment. This is a prime example of geographical separation and integrated distribution made possible by inventory.

Geographical separation permits economic specialization between the manufacturing and distribution units of an enterprise. To the degree that geographical specialization exists, inventory in the form of raw materials, semifinished goods or components, and finished goods is introduced to the logistical system. Each location requires a basic stock. In addition, in-transit inventories are necessary to link manufacturing and distribution. Although difficult to measure, the economies gained by geographical specialization are expected to more than offset the added cost of inventory and transportation.

DECOUPLING.   A second function of inventory is to provide maximum efficiency of operations within a single facility. This function is referred to as *decoupling*.[5] Stockpiling work in process within the manufacturing complex permits maximum economies of production without work stoppage. Likewise, production to warehouse inventory allows economy of scale in manufacturing. Warehouse inventory produced in advance of need permits distribution to customers in large-quantity shipments at minimum freight rates per unit.

The decoupling function of inventory permits each product to be manufactured and distributed in economical lot sizes. In terms of marketing, decoupling permits products manufactured over time to be sold as an assortment. Thus decoupling tends to buffer the operations of the enterprise. Decoupling differs from geographical specialization. Decoupling enables increased efficiency of operation at a single location, while geographical specialization includes multiple locations.

[4] See Appendix II.
[5] Buffa, op. cit.

BALANCING SUPPLY AND DEMAND.   A third function of inventory is *balancing*, which concerns elapsed time between consumption and manufacturing. Balancing inventory exists to reconcile supply availability with demand. The most notable examples of balancing are seasonal production and year-round consumption. Orange juice is one such product. Another example of year-round production and seasonal consumption is antifreeze. Inventories in a balancing capacity link the economies of manufacturing with variations of consumption.

The managerial reconciliation of time lags in manufacturing and demand involves a difficult planning problem. When seasonal demand is concentrated in a very short selling season, manufacturers, wholesalers, and retailers are forced to take an inventory position far in advance of the peak selling period. For example, in lawn furniture manufacturing, production must be in high gear by early fall for units that will not be sold until the following spring or summer. In early January and February manufacturers' inventories peak and start to decline as orders for furniture begin to flow through the marketing channel on their way to wholesalers and retailers. Retail sales begin in early spring and hit a peak between Memorial Day and Labor Day. However, after July 4 the retail market shifts from a seller's market to a buyer's market. Price competition dominates as retailers attempt to reduce inventory and eliminate seasonal carryover. Thus, from a retailer's viewpoint, an inventory position for the entire selling system must be planned six months prior to the peak selling season. Any attempt to supplement inventories after Memorial Day is risky.

Although lawn furniture is an extreme example of seasonal selling, almost all products have some seasonal variation. Inventory stockpiling allows mass consumption or mass manufacturing of products regardless of seasonality. The balancing function of inventory requires investment in seasonal stocks which are expected to be fully liquidated within the season.[6] The critical planning problem is how much to stockpile to enjoy maximum sales without running the risk of carryover into the next selling season.

SAFETY STOCK.   The *safety stock* or *buffer stock* function concerns short-range variation in either demand or replenishment. A great deal of inventory planning is devoted to determining the size of safety stocks. In fact, most overstocks are the result of improper planning of safety stocks.

The safety stock requirement results from uncertainty concerning future sales and inventory replenishment. If uncertainty exists concerning how much of a given product will be sold it is necessary to protect inventory position. In a sense, safety stock planning is similar to purchasing insurance.

Safety stock protects against two types of uncertainty. The first type of uncertainty (type I) is concerned with sales in excess of forecast during the replenishment period. The second type of uncertainty (type II) concerns

[6] This type of buying is often referred to as *promotional buying*.

delays in replenishment. An example of type I uncertainty is the sale of more units per time period than estimated. Type II uncertainty results from a delay in order receipt, order processing, or transportation during replenishment.

Statistical and mathematical techniques for aiding managers in planning safety stock are developed later in the chapter. At this point it is important to realize that the probability and magnitude of each type of uncertainty can be estimated. The safety stock function of inventory is to provide a specified degree of protection against both types of uncertainty.

SUMMARY—INVENTORY FUNCTIONS. The four functions of inventory are geographical specialization, decoupling, balancing supply and demand, and safety stock. These functions define the inventory investment necessary for a specific system to perform to management objectives. Given a specific manufacturing–marketing complex, inventories planned and committed to operations can be reduced only to a minimum level consistent with performing the four inventory functions. All inventories exceeding the minimum level represent excessive commitments.

At the minimum level, inventory invested to achieve geographical specialization and decoupling can be modified only by changes in the facility location and operational processes of the enterprise. The minimum level of inventory required to balance supply and demand relates to the difficult task of estimating seasonal requirements. With experience over a number of seasonal periods, the inventory required to achieve marginal sales during high periods of demand can be projected fairly well. A seasonal inventory plan can be formulated based upon this experience.

The inventories committed to safety stocks represent the greatest potential for improved performance. Commitments to safety stocks are operational in nature. They can be adjusted rapidly in the event of error or a change in policy. A variety of techniques is available to assist management in planning safety stock commitments. Therefore, this chapter focuses on a thorough analysis of safety stock relationships and policy formulation.

Inventory Risk

The holding of inventory to achieve any of the above noted functions is risky. It is important to understand that the nature and extent of risk varies depending upon an enterprise's position in the distribution channel.

RETAIL INVENTORY RISK. For a retailer the management of inventory is fundamentally a buying and selling process. The retailer purchases a wide variety of products and assumes a substantial risk in the marketing process. The retailer's inventory risk can be viewed as wide but not deep. Because of the high cost of store location, the retailer places prime emphasis on turnover or velocity of sales.

Although retailers will assume a risk position on a variety of products, their position on any one product is not deep. Risk is spread across more than 10,000 stockkeeping units in a typical supermarket. A discount house with general merchandise and food often exceeds 25,000 stockkeeping units. A full-line department store may have as many as 50,000 stockkeeping units. Faced with this width in inventory, retailers can be expected to attempt to reduce their risk by pressing manufacturers and wholesalers to assume greater and greater inventory responsibility. Pushing inventory "back up" the marketing channel has resulted in retailer demands for fast delivery of mixed-product shipments from wholesalers and manufacturers. Specialty retailers, in contrast to mass merchandisers, normally experience less width of inventory risk because the lines they handle are narrower. However, specialty retailers must assume greater risk with respect to depth and duration of inventory holding.

WHOLESALE INVENTORY RISK.   The risk exposure of wholesalers is narrower but deeper and of longer duration than that of retailers. The merchant wholesaler purchases in large quantities from manufacturers and sells in small quantities to retailers. The economic justification of the merchant wholesaler is the capability to provide a merchandise assortment produced by different manufacturers. Often, when such products are seasonal, the wholesaler is forced to take an inventory position far in advance of the selling season, thereby increasing depth and duration of risk.

One of the greatest hazards of wholesaling is product-line expansion to the point where the width of inventory risk approaches that of the retailer while depth and duration of risk remains characteristic of wholesaling. For example, traditional full-line hardware and food wholesalers have faced a difficult situation during the past decade. Expansion of product lines has increased the width of inventory risk. In addition, their retail clientele have forced a substantial increase in depth and duration by shifting inventory risk in the marketing channel. The pressure of product-line proliferation, more than any other single factor, has forced a decline in general wholesalers with replacement by specialized operations.

MANUFACTURER INVENTORY RISK.   For the manufacturer, inventory risk has a long time dimension. The manufacturer's inventory commitment starts with raw material and component parts, includes work-in-process, and ends with the finished goods. In addition, finished goods often must be transferred to warehouses in close proximity to wholesalers and retailers prior to sale. Although a manufacturer may have a narrower line of products than retailers or wholesalers, the manufacturer's inventory commitment is relatively deep and of long duration.

If an individual enterprise plans to operate at more than one level of the distribution channel, it must be prepared to assume additional inventory risk. For example, the food chain that operates a regional warehouse assumes risk related to the wholesaler operation over and above the normal retail operations.

To the extent that an enterprise becomes vertically integrated, inventory must be managed at all levels of distribution. The management of echeloned inventories characteristic of vertically integrated firms is complex because of a need for multi-level policy formulation and control. Regardless of whether the inventory problem confronted is at the manufacturing, wholesaling, or retailing level, or whether it is single level or echeloned, the same basic techniques and principles of inventory management apply.

Elements of Inventory Policy

Inventory policy consists of guidelines concerning what to purchase or manufacture, when to take action, and in what quantity. The development of sound policy is the most difficult area of overall inventory management. The focal point of policy formulation is the establishment of average inventory commitment.

Average inventory consists of the finished products, raw materials, components, and work-in-process held over time in logistical facilities. From a policy viewpoint the appropriate level of inventory must be determined for each facility. Average inventories consist of base and safety stock.

Base stock is the portion of average inventory that results from the replenishment process. In Chapter 4 the concept of economic order quantity (EOQ) was introduced to determine the amount of an item to order. The average inventory held as a result of the order process is referred to as base stock. Another commonly used term to identify this aspect of inventory is *lot size stock.*[7] *Given the reorder formulation, average base stock equals one-half order quantity.*[8]

The second part of average inventory is the stock held to protect against uncertainty at each location. This portion of inventory, as noted earlier, is called *safety stock.* The basic premise of safety stock is that a portion of average inventory should be devoted to cover short-range variation in demand and replenishment. *Given safety stock, average inventory equals one-half order quantity plus safety stock.*

A subject of special interest is the ownership of in-transit inventory. This portion of total inventory is referred to as *transit* or *pipeline inventory.* Transit inventory is necessary to accomplish replenishment. A specific enterprise may or may not have legal ownership of transit inventory depending upon terms of purchase. If purchase is f.o.b. destination, inventory in transit is not owned. The opposite is true when merchandise is purchased f.o.b. origin. Under conditions of f.o.b. origin, transit inventory should be treated as part of average inventory. The determination of *how much* inventory to hold and the delineation of *when* and in *what* quantities to order are the primary concerns of inventory policy.

---

[7] In this text these terms are used interchangeably.
[8] For the initial discussion of EOQ, see Chapter 4, pages 97–99.

Inventory control is a mechanical procedure for implementing an inventory policy. The accountability aspect of control measures how many units are on hand at a specific location and keeps track of additions and deletions to the basic quantity. Accountability and tracking can be performed by manual or computerized techniques.[9] The primary differentials are speed, accuracy, and cost.

One major problem in applied inventory management is failure to separate the formulation of policy from control. The formulation of inventory policy is an executive responsibility. The determination of policy guidelines integrates inventory with all other aspects of logistics. In turn, all other functional areas of the enterprise are influenced by the implementation of inventory policy through logistical performance. Inventory control performance is a logistical coordination responsibility. While effective inventory control is essential for smooth operations, problems in control normally do not create the same disruption or failure to achieve goals as problems of improper policy. The remainder of this chapter focuses on various aspects of inventory policy formulation.

Relationship of Performance Cycle and Average Inventory

In initial policy formulation, it is necessary to determine how much inventory to order at a specified time. For purposes of illustration, assume the following conditions. First, the performance cycle duration has a high degree of time consistency. Second, the daily rate of sales during the replenishment is constant. For example, the performance cycle is always 20 days and the rate of sale is always 10 units per day. Third, as a matter of managerial preference, no more than one order per product is outstanding at any time. Although such assumptions concerning certainty remove the complexity involved in the formulation of inventory policy, they serve to illustrate basic principles.

Figure 6-1 illustrates these relationships. This type of chart is referred to as a *sawtooth diagram*, because of the series of right triangles. Since complete certainty exists with respect to replenishment and usage, orders are scheduled to arrive just as the last unit is sold. Thus no inventory beyond average base stock is held in the system. Since the rate of sale in our example is 10 units per day and it takes 20 days to complete inventory replenishment, a sound reorder policy would be to order 200 units every 20 days. Given these conditions, terminology related to policy formulation can be identified.

First, the reorder point is specified as 200 units on hand. Order size would have no reason to exceed 200 units. Every time an order is received, an additional order for 200 units is placed.

Second, average base inventory is 100 units, since stock on hand exceeds 100 units one half of the time (10 days) and is less than 100 units one half of the

[9] See Chapter 4, pages 93–94.

FIGURE 6-1
Inventory Relationship Constant Sales and Performance Cycle

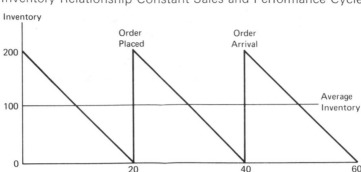

time. In fact, average base inventory is equal to one half of the 200 order quantity.

Third, assuming a work year of 240 days, 12 purchases will be required during the year. Therefore, over a period of one year, 200 units will be purchased 12 times (2,400 total units). Sales are expected to equal 10 units 240 times (2,400 total units). An average base inventory of 100 units is planned. Thus the inventory turn will be 12 times.

In time, the sheer boredom of such routine operations would lead management to ask some questions concerning the arrangement. What would happen if orders were placed more frequently than once every 20 days ? Why not order 100 units every 10 days ? Why order as frequently as every 20 days ? Why not reorder 600 units once every 60 days ? Assuming that the inventory performance cycle remains a constant 20 days, what would be the net result of each of these alternative ordering policies on reorder point, average base inventory, and inventory turnover ?

The policy of ordering a smaller volume of 100 units every 10 days means that two orders will always be outstanding. Thus the reorder point would remain 200 committed units on order to service average daily sales of 10 units over the 20-day inventory cycle. However, average base inventory on hand would drop to 50 units, and inventory turnover would increase to 24 times per year. The policy of ordering 600 units every 60 days would result in an average base inventory of 300 units and a turnover of approximately eight times per year. These alternative ordering policies are illustrated in Figure 6-2. Despite this analysis, a dilemma would still exist concerning the most desirable ordering policy.

An exact policy concerning order quantity can be calculated by balancing the cost of ordering and the cost of maintaining average base inventory. EOQ provides a specific answer to the balancing of these two critical groups of cost. By determining the EOQ and dividing it into forecasted annual demand, the

FIGURE 6-2
Illustration of Variable Order Quantity and Average Inventory

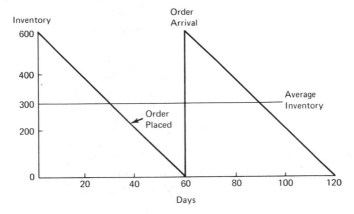

Example: Order 600

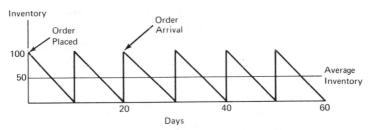

Example: Order 100

frequency and size of order that will minimize the total cost of inventory is identified. Prior to reviewing EOQ, it is necessary to identify costs typically associated with ordering and maintaining inventory.

Identification of Inventory Costs

Because inventory is related to all aspects of logistical operations, it is difficult to isolate the cost of inventory ordering and maintenance. In fact, accounting practice is to group inventory costs. The net result is that the functional cost of inventory is difficult to isolate for purposes of policy formulation.

MAINTENANCE COSTS. The accounts traditionally included in the cost of maintaining inventory are taxes, storage, capital, insurance, and obsolescence.[10] The costs associated with taxes and insurance are relatively easy to determine.

[10] Lambert, op. cit., p. 57, provides a detailed review of accounts.

Insurance cost is a direct payment based upon estimated risk or exposure over time. Tax cost is a direct levy normally based on inventory holding on a specific day of the year or average holding over a period of time, depending upon local laws.

Storage cost must be allocated to specific products, since it is not related directly to inventory value. Depending upon the type of warehouse facility used, public or private, total storage charges may be direct or it may be necessary to impute costs. With privately owned facilities, the total annual depreciated expense of the warehouse must be reduced to a standard measure such as cost per day per square or cubic foot. The cost of total annual occupancy for a given product can then be assigned by multiplication of daily occupied space times the standard cost factor accumulated for the year. This figure can then be divided by the total number of units of merchandise processed through the facility to determine the average storage cost per merchandise unit. In assignment of such costs, care must be taken to make appropriate allowances for idle space.

Obsolescence cost is calculated on the basis of past experience. The type of obsolescence of concern in inventory planning is the deterioration of product while in storage which is not covered by insurance. Obsolescence also can be expanded to include marketing loss when a product becomes obsolete in terms of model design. Again, care must be exercised to avoid costs not directly related to the inventory procurement decision. The assignment of obsolescence cost should be approached with caution and should be limited to direct loss related to storage. Charges related to obsolescence should be expressed on a per unit basis similar to storage cost.

The most controversial aspect of maintenance cost is the appropriate charge to place on invested capital. Experience with a variety of enterprises indicates figures ranging from the prevailing prime interest rate to 25 per cent.[11] The logic for using the prime interest rate or a specified rate pegged to prime is that cash to replace capital invested in inventory can be purchased in the money markets at that rate. Managerially specified interest rates are based on a target return on investment expected from all dollars available to the enterprise. A dollar invested in inventory loses its earning power, restricts capital availability, and prohibits optional investment.

General confusion results from the fact that many top managements have not formulated a clear-cut capital cost policy to be applied uniformly in decision making. For logistical planning, the cost of capital must be thought out clearly, since the final rate of assessment will have a profound impact on system design. Low cost of investment will tend to encourage multilocations and liberal inventory allocations. High costs will have the opposite effect, almost to the point of restricting expansion.[12]

[11] For a list of 13 different approaches to arriving at this figure, see Lambert, op. cit., pp. 24–25.

[12] In Chapter 8, pages 246–252, the impact of inventory cost on facility location is examined in detail.

The cost of maintaining inventory involves management judgment, estimation, assignment, and a degree of direct measurement. The final figure should be expressed on an annual basis as a percentage value to be applied to average inventory. Determination of maintenance cost across a broad group of products or raw materials requires substantial analysis. While cost of capital can be applied to average inventory holdings, expenses associated with taxes, insurance, storage, and obsolescence will vary, depending on the specific attributes of each product. Once agreement has been reached on the appropriate assessment for maintenance, the figure should be held constant during logistical system analysis.[13]

ORDERING COSTS.   The cost of placing an order consists of estimating the full expense of inventory control, order preparation, order communication, update activities, and managerial supervision. Similar to maintenance cost, ordering costs are built up for each element of expense until a total cost of order placement is obtained. The combined figure should include assignment of a share of fixed cost related to order preparation plus the direct variable cost associated with ordering. For example, if the total fixed cost associated with ordering activities is $550,000 per year and the historical pattern has been the placement of 220,000 orders per year, the fixed-cost factor per order would be $2.50. The variable cost of placing an order—direct communication cost and supplies—would represent a calculated cost which, when combined with fixed cost, would result in a total cost per order.

A great deal of difference exists among organizations concerning what it costs to place an order. The important element is to include all costs in assignment of fixed and variable expenses. Once the total cost of placing an order is estimated, the typical assumption is to hold it constant regardless of how many orders are placed during a planning period. This assumption of linearity is not typically accurate. However, as long as order quantity remains fairly constant from one planning period to the next, only a limited error is introduced.

Calculating Economic Order Quantity

The most efficient method for calculating economic order quantity is mathematical.[14] Earlier in this section a policy dilemma was faced regarding whether to order 100, 200, or 600 units. The answer can be found by determining the applicable EOQ for the situation. The necessary information is contained in Table 6-1.

To benefit from the most economical purchase arrangement, orders should be placed in the quantity of 300 units rather than 100, 200, or 600. Thus, over

---

[13] This is developed in greater detail as an aspect of management procedure in logistical strategic planning. See Chapter 10, pages 298–300.

[14] See Chapter 4, pages 97–99, for a graphic presentation of EOQ.

TABLE 6-1
Factor-Input EOQ Sample Formulation

Annual sales volume	2,400 units
Unit value at cost	$5
Maintenance cost	20% per year
Ordering cost per order	$20

the year eight orders would be placed and average base inventory would be 150 units.

To calculate the above, the standard formulation for EOQ is

$$EOQ = \sqrt{\frac{2C_o S}{C_m U}}$$

where

$$C_o = \text{cost per order}$$

$$C_m = \text{cost of maintenance per year}$$

$$S = \text{annual sales volume, units}$$

$$U = \text{cost per unit}$$

Substituting from Table 6-1,

$$EOQ = \sqrt{\frac{2 \times 20 \times 2400}{0.20 \times 5.00}}$$

$$= \sqrt{96,000}$$

$$= 310 \qquad \text{(rounded to 300)}$$

Total ordering cost would amount to $160 and maintenance cost $150. Thus, after rounding to allow ordering in multiples of 100 units, annual reordering and maintenance costs have been equated.

Referring back to Figure 6-1, the impact of ordering in quantities of 300 rather than 200 can be observed. The EOQ of 300 means that additional inventory in the form of base stock has been introduced into the system. Average inventory has been increased from 100 to 150 units on hand.

Based upon examination of the relationship of the inventory-performance cycle, inventory cost, and economic order formulations, several basic relationships useful for inventory planning have been introduced. First, the EOQ is found at the point where annualized order cost and maintenance cost are equal. Second, average base inventory will equal one-half order quantity. Third, to retain no more than one order outstanding at a time, the duration of the replenishment cycle should be equal to or less than the EOQ divided by average daily sales. Fourth, the value of the inventory unit, all other things being equal, will have a direct relationship on the duration of the performance cycle in that the higher the value, the more frequently orders will be placed.

Some EOQ Complications

The straightforward simplicity of the EOQ formulation does confront some difficulty in application. The most persistent problems are those related to various adjustments necessary to take advantage of special purchase situations. Three typical adjustments are (1) volume transportation rates, (2) quantity discounts, and (3) other adjustments. Each category will be discussed briefly.

VOLUME TRANSPORTATION RATES. In the EOQ formulation discussed, no consideration was given to the impact of transportation cost upon order quantity. When products are purchased f.o.b. destination and the seller pays transportation cost for delivery to the inventory location, such neglect may be justified. However, when the item is procured f.o.b. origin, the impact of transportation rates upon total cost must be considered when determining order quantity.

As a general rule, the greater the weight of an order, the lower the cost per pound of transportation cost from any origin to destination.[15] A freight-rate discount for larger-size shipments is common to both truck and rail and is found in class, exception, and commodity rates. Thus, all other things being equal, an enterprise naturally will want to purchase in quantities that offer maximum economies in transportation expenditure. Such quantities may be larger than the purchase quantity that would otherwise constitute the EOQ.

Increasing order size has a twofold impact upon inventory cost. Assume for purposes of illustration that the most desirable transportation rate is obtained when a quantity of 480 is ordered as compared to the EOQ-recommended order of 300 calculated earlier.[16] The first impact of the larger order is to increase the average base inventory from 150 to 240 units. Thus ordering in larger quantities increases inventory maintenance cost.

The second impact is a decrease in the number of orders required to satisfy annual requirements. Given the modification, the frequency of orders required to realize the maximum economies of transportation in the example will be five.

To complete the analysis it is necessary to formulate the total cost with and without transportation savings. While this calculation can be directly made by modification of the EOQ formulation, direct comparison provides a ready answer.[17] The only additional data required are the applicable freight rate

---

[15] For an expanded discussion, see Chapter 5, pages 135–136.

[16] For purposes of determining transportation rates, the quantity of units must be converted to weight.

[17] For an expanded discussion, see John L. Coyle and Edward J. Bardi, *The Management of Business Logistics* (St. Paul, Minn.: West Publishing Co., 1976), pp. 67–92.

TABLE 6-2
Modified Input EOQ to Accommodate
Transportation Volume Rates

Annual sales volume	2,400 units
Unit value at cost	$5
Maintenance cost	20% per year
Ordering cost/order	$20
Small-shipment rate/unit	$1
Large-shipment rate/unit	$0.75

for ordering in quantities of 300 and 480. Table 6-2 provides the data necessary to complete the analysis.

Table 6-3 provides the analysis of total cost. Taking into consideration the potential transportation savings by purchasing in larger lot sizes, total annual cost by purchasing 480 units five times per year rather than the EOQ solution of 300 units eight times per year results in a $570 saving.

TABLE 6-3
EOQ Modified to Accommodate Volume Transportation
Rates

	Alternative I: EOQ = 300	Alternative 2: Modified Order = 480
Maintenance cost	$ 150	$ 240
Ordering cost	160	100
Transportation cost	2,400	1,800
Total cost	$2,710	$2,140

The impact of volume transportation rates upon total cost of procurement cannot be neglected. In the example above, the rate per unit equivalent dropped from $1 to $0.75, or by 25 per cent. In actual practice, freight–weight breaks may not drop that abruptly. However, it is common to have multiple weight breaks applicable between any given origin and destination. Under such situations, the cost-per-hundredweight range, from minimum shipment LTL to carload minimum weight, may far exceed 25 per cent. Thus any EOQ must be tested for transportation cost sensitivity across a range of weight breaks if the merchandise is purchased f.o.b. origin.

A second point illustrated in the data of Table 6-3 is the fact that rather substantial changes in the size of order and the orders placed per year resulted in only modest change in total cost of maintenance and ordering. The EOQ quantity of 300 had a total annual cost of $310, whereas the revised order quantity had a comparative cost of $340. EOQ formulations are only sensitive to substantial changes in order cycle or frequency. Likewise, substantial changes in cost factors are necessary to result in a major impact on the economic order quantity.

Finally, three factors regarding inventory cost under conditions of f.o.b. origin purchase are noteworthy. First, f.o.b. origin means that the buyer assumes full risk on inventory exposure at time of shipment. Depending upon time of required payment, this could mean that transit inventory is part of the firm's average inventory and therefore subjected to an appropriate charge.[18] It follows that any change in weight break leading to a shipment method with a different in-transit time should be assessed the added cost or savings as appropriate in the total cost analysis.

A second factor regarding transit time and related inventory is that when purchasing f.o.b. destination, no direct liability is associated with transit inventory. However, as will be pointed out shortly, the length and consistency of transit time as well as the quantity of inventory in transit are major factors when planning inventory under conditions of uncertainty.[19]

The final factor deals with the addition of transportation cost to the value of inventory for purposes of correct maintenance costing. Table 6-3 is not totally correct in that the transportation cost per unit is not added to the value of the inventory for costing purposes.[20] Thus the savings possible from buying in larger quantities are understated.

QUANTITY DISCOUNTS. An analogous situation to transportation volume rates is when the item purchased is subject to quantity discounts. Table 6-4 illustrates a sample schedule of discounts. Quantity discounts can be handled directly with the basic EOQ formulation by calculating total cost at any given volume-related purchase price to determine associated EOQs. If the discount at any associated quantity is sufficient to offset added cost of maintenance less reduced cost of ordering, then the quantity discount offers a viable alternative.[21] It should be noted that quantity discounts and transportation volume rates each affect larger quantity purchases. This does not mean

TABLE 6-4
Example of Quantity Discounts

Cost	Quantity Purchased
$5.00	1–99
4.50	100–200
4.00	201–300
3.50	301–400
3.00	401–500

[18] In such situations, the cost of money invested in inventory should be appropriately charged provided that it is paid for f.o.b. origin.

[19] See pages 175–178.

[20] Lambert, op. cit.

[21] The exact calculation is a form of break-even analysis. See Chapter 11, pages 336–338.

that the lowest total cost purchase will always be larger than would otherwise be the case under basic EOQ.

OTHER EOQ ADJUSTMENTS. A variety of special situations may occur which will require adjustments to the basic EOQ. Examples are (1) production lot size, (2) multiple-item purchase, (3) limited capital, and (4) private trucking. In all adjustment situations the focal point of attention is total cost of the basic EOQ in comparison to the modified purchase condition.

Discrete Lot Sizing

Not all inventory control situations require procurement to support uniform usage rates that are common in EOQ reorder situations. In manufacturing situations the demand for a specific component tends to occur at irregular intervals and for varied quantities. The irregular nature of usage requirements results from demand being dependent upon the production schedule. At the time of manufacturing, the necessary assembly parts must be available. Between requirement times, no need exists to maintain inventory of the component in stock if it can be obtained when needed.[22] Inventory servicing of *dependent demand* requires a modified approach to the determination of order quantities, which is referred to as *discrete lot sizing*. The identification of the technique as "discrete" means that the procurement objective is to obtain a quantity of a component that equals the net requirements at a specific time. Because component requirements fluctuate, purchase quantities using discrete lot sizing will vary between orders. A variety of lot sizing techniques are available. In this section we will briefly present (1) lot-for-lot, (2) period order quantity, and (3) time-series lot sizing.

LOT-FOR-LOT. The most basic form of discrete ordering is to plan purchases to cover net requirements over a specified period. No consideration is given to the cost of ordering under the *lot-to-lot* methodology. In one sense, lot-to-lot sizing is pure dependent-demand-oriented, since no economies of discrete ordering are considered. Once manufacturing requirements are identified, no additional lot sizing is performed. The basic technique is often used when the item being purchased is inexpensive and the requirements are relatively small and irregular.

PERIOD ORDER QUANTITY. The *period-order-quantity* (POQ) technique builds upon the logic of EOQ. The POQ technique performs three steps to accomplish component procurement. First, the standard EOQ is calculated. Second, the EOQ quantity is divided into the forecasted annual usage to determine the frequency of ordering. Third, the number of orders is divided into the

---

[22] George W. Plossl and Oliver W. Wight, *Materials Requirement Planning by Computer* (Washington, D.C.: American Production and Inventory Control Society, 1971), p. 6–8.

relevant time period (52 for weeks or 12 for months) to express the order quantity in time periods covered.

To illustrate, carry forward the data from Table 6-1 which resulted in an EOQ of 310. To adjust to a 12-period year, the POQ technique would be as follows:

$$\text{EOQ} \quad\quad = \quad 310$$

$$\text{Forecast} \quad = 2{,}400$$

$$\text{Orders per year} = \frac{2{,}400}{310} = 7.74$$

$$\text{Order interval} \quad = \frac{12}{7.74} = 1.5$$

Under the POQ application, orders will be planned approximately every six weeks. The typical order will be 310 units unless planned usage has not materialized or order duration requires procurement for advanced periods.

The main advantage of the POQ approach is that it takes into consideration the cost of maintenance and thereby reduces carryover inventories to a minimum. The disadvantage is similar to basic EOQ, in that derived demand needs to be continuous to realize the full potential.

TIME-SERIES LOT SIZING. The fundamental objective of time-series lot sizing is to combine requirements over several periods to arrive at a procurement logic. The time-series approach is dynamic because the order quantity is adjusted to meet best estimate requirements. This dynamic approach is contrasted to basic EOQ, which is static in the sense that the order quantity, once computed, continues unchanged in the planned purchasing activity.[23]

The key to dynamic lot sizing is that requirements are expressed in varying quantities across time rather than in usage rates per day or week, as is typical of the basic EOQ. Given substantial usage fluctuation, fixed order quantities must give way to a lot sizing system that can calculate an economical order given changing and intermittent usage.[24] Three such techniques are widely discussed in the literature and are briefly reviewed: (1) least unit cost, (2) least total cost, and (3) part-period balancing.

The *least unit cost* seeks to identify a combination of requirements over a number of periods that will result in the lowest cost per piece. Starting with the net requirements of the initial period, each future period is evaluated on a per unit basis to arrive at the combined quantity for a given number of periods wherein the unit cost is minimized. Thus, order quantities and frequency will vary substantially as a function of the least-unit-cost determination.

---

[23] Thomas Gorham, "Dynamic Order Quantities," *APICS Production and Inventory Management Journal*, First Quarter, 1968.

[24] Plossl and Wight, op. cit., p. 7.

The least-unit-cost approach does provide a way to overcome the static features of EOQ and POQ. The main shortcoming is that unit cost may experience wide variation between time periods that would not be evaluated using the least-unit-cost methodology.

The *least-total-cost* approach seeks the quantity that will minimize total cost for successive periods. In this sense, least total cost, which is the balancing of ordering and carrying, is similar to EOQ in objective. The fundamental difference is that order interval is permitted to vary to seek least total cost. The least-total-cost calculation is based upon a ratio of ordering to maintenance cost (CO/CMU), called the *economic part-period*. The economic part-period defines the quantity of a specific component which, if carried in inventory for one period would result in a maintenance cost equal to the cost of ordering. The least-total-cost technique selects order sizes and intervals that most nearly approximate the economic part-period calculation. Thus, order sizes will remain fairly uniform; however, substantial differences will occur in elapsed time between order placement. The least-total-cost technique overcomes the failure of the least unit cost to consider trade-offs across the overall planning period.

Part-period balancing is a modified form of the least-total-cost technique that incorporates a special adjustment routine called *look ahead/look back*.[25] The main benefit of this feature is that it extends the planning horizon across more than one ordering point to accommodate usage peaks and valleys when calculating order quantities. Adjustments are made in order time or quantity when a forward or backward review of more than one order requirement indicates that modifications to the economic part-period may be beneficial. The typical procedure is to first test the *look-ahead* feature to determine if more time will result in approximation of the economic part-period quantity. *Look back* is typically utilized if look ahead leaves the lot size unchanged. In this sense, look back means that a future order, which under the economic part-period rule would normally be scheduled for delivery during the fourth period, would be advanced if earlier delivery would reduce total cost. The net result of incorporation of the look ahead/look back feature is that it renders the application of the economic part-period concept to a simultaneous review of multiple periods.

CONCLUSION—DISCRETE LOT SIZING. The varied approaches to discrete lot sizing all seek to overcome assumptions of uniform usage characteristic of basic EOQ calculations. Whereas EOQ results in a uniform order quantity that may be ordered in a fixed or variable time interval, discrete-lot-sizing techniques seek greater flexibility to accommodate irregular usage. The techniques reviewed have had varying degrees of success in meeting the basic objective of discrete lot sizing.[26]

[25] J. J. DeMalteis, "An Economic Lot Sizing Technique: The Part-Period Algorithms," *IBM Systems Journal*, Vol. 7 (1968), pp. 30–38.
[26] Joseph Orlicky, *Materials Requirement Planning* (New York: McGraw-Hill Book Company, 1975), pp. 120–37.

Planning the Performance Cycle

The task of managing inventory consists of policy formulation and unit control during a performance-cycle period. Logistical performance cycles link all inventory stocking locations in an enterprise with locations supplying raw material or finished products. The overall cycle from an inventory viewpoint consists of order communications, order processing, transportation, and inventory update. The performance times for the four elements combine to create total elapsed time required for replenishment.

As a first approximation of the performance cycle, the expected time duration required to complete each element can be added together. For example, if expected order-communication time is two days, order processing three days, transportation five days, and inventory update one day, then the anticipated duration of the performance cycle would be 11 days. Thus, if expected average daily sales is 10 units per day, it would be necessary to reorder when stock on hand and stock on order reached a combined total of 110 units.

Two basic methods of replenishment exist: periodic and perpetual. Under a *periodic* ordering system, orders are placed at fixed time intervals. For example, an order is placed on a specific day each month based upon inventory on hand and inventory currently on order. Under a *perpetual* system, orders are placed when the quantity of inventory reaches a level (reorder point) just sufficient to handle planned sales requirements during replenishment. Under a perpetual system as many orders as necessary can be placed during a specific time interval.[27]

No specific relationship exists between the length of the performance cycle and the finalized order quantity. If the economical order quantity is less than expected sales during replenishment, then more than one order typically will be outstanding at a time. If the order quantity is greater than expected sales during replenishment, then at selected times no orders for that specific item will be outstanding.

An operating goal is to keep the performance cycle as short and consistent as possible when implementing an inventory policy. The reason for this emphasis on rapid and consistent service will become clear as we consider the ramifications of sales and replenishment uncertainty.

Evaluating Sales Uncertainty

Although it is useful to review basic inventory relationships under conditions of certainty, formulation of inventory policy must take into consideration the realistic situation of uncertainty. One of the main functions of inventory is to provide safety stock protection against uncertainty.

---

[27] It would be useful to relate periodic and perpetual replenishment to the various types of buying discussed in Chapter 4, pages 99–104.

As noted earlier in this chapter, two types of uncertainty have a direct impact on inventory policy. Type I concerns the fluctuation in rate of sales during the inventory performance cycle. Type II deals with variations in the length of the inventory performance cycle. In this section sales uncertainty is treated with respect to setting safety stocks when the duration of the inventory performance cycle is assumed constant. In the next section both types of uncertainty are handled on a simultaneous basis.

Nature of Sales Uncertainty: Type I

The purpose of unit sales forecasting is to project sales during the inventory performance cycle. Even with good forecasting, sales during the replenishment typically will exceed or fall short of anticipated sales. To provide protection against a stockout when sales exceed forecast, safety stock is added to base inventory. Under conditions of sales uncertainty, average inventory is defined as one-half order quantity plus safety stock. Figure 6-3 illustrates

FIGURE 6-3
Inventory Relationship Sales Uncertainty and Constant Performance Cycle

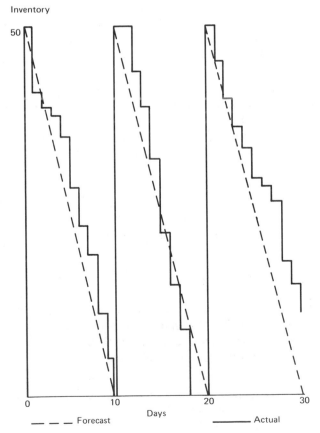

an inventory-performance cycle under conditions of sales uncertainty. The dashed line reflects the forecast. The solid line illustrates inventory on hand from one cycle to the next. The task of planning safety stock consists of three steps. First, the likelihood of stockout must be gauged. Second, sales potential during periods of stockout must be estimated. Finally, a policy decision is required concerning the degree of stockout protection to introduce into the system.

Assume for purposes of illustration that the inventory performance cycle is 10 days. Historical experience indicates that daily sales range from zero to 10 with average daily sales of 5 units. The economic order is assumed to be 50, the reorder point is 50, the planned average inventory is 25, and sales during the performance cycle are expected to be 50 units.

TABLE 6-5
Typical Sales Experience During Three Replenishment Cycles

	Forecast Cycle 1		Stockout Cycle 2		Overstock Cycle 3	
Day	Sales	Accumulated	Sales	Accumulated	Sales	Accumulated
1	9	9	0	0	5	5
2	2	11	6	6	5	10
3	1	12	5	11	4	14
4	3	15	7	18	3	17
5	7	22	10	28	4	21
6	5	27	7	35	1	22
7	4	31	6	41	2	24
8	8	39	9	50	8	32
9	6	45	Stock-out	50	3	35
10	5	50	Stock-out	50	4	39

Table 6-5 provides a recap of actual sales history over three consecutive inventory performance cycles. During the first cycle, while daily sales experienced considerable variation, the average of 5 units per day was maintained. Total sales during cycle 1 were 50 units, as expected. During cycle 2 sales totaled 50 units in the first 8 days, resulting in an out-of-stock. Thus no sales were possible on days 9 and 10. During cycle 3 sales reached a total of 39 units. The third performance cycle ended with 11 units remaining in stock. Over the 30-day period total sales were 139 units, for an average daily sales of 4.6 units.

Based on the history recorded in Table 6-5, management can observe that stockouts occurred on 2 of 30 total days. Since sales never exceed 10 units per day, no possibility of stockout exists on the first 5 days of the performance cycle. Stockouts could occur on days 6 through 10, on the remote possibility that unit sales on the first 5 days of the cycle averaged 10 units per day and no inventory is carried over from the previous period. Since over the three performance cycles 10 units were sold only once, it is apparent that the real risk of stockout occurs only during the last few days of the performance cycle and then only when sales have exceeded the average by a substantial margin.[28]

Some approximation is also possible concerning the amount of sales that could have been enjoyed had stock been available on days 9 and 10 of cycle 2. A maximum of 20 units could have been sold if inventory had been available. On the other hand, it is remotely possible that even if stock had been available, no sales would have occurred on days 9 and 10. Based on average sales of 4 to 5 units per day, a reasonable appraisal of lost sales is from 8 to 10 units.

It should be apparent that the degree of risk related to stockouts created by variations in sales is limited to a short time and includes a small percentage of total sales. However, management will want to take some protective action to realize available sales and to avoid the risk of possible deterioration in customer relations. Although the sales analysis presented in Table 6-5 helps toward an understanding of the problem, the appropriate course of corrective action is still not clear. Statistical probability can be used to assist management in the development of a safety stock policy.

Application of Statistical Probability

The sales history over the 30-day period has been arranged in Table 6-6 in terms of a frequency distribution. The main purpose of a frequency distri-

TABLE 6-6
Frequency of Sales

Sales/Day	Frequency (days)
Stockout	2
Zero	1
One unit	2
Two units	2
Three units	3
Four units	4
Five units	5
Six units	3
Seven units	3
Eight units	2
Nine units	2
Ten units	1

[28] In this example, daily statistics are used. An alternative, which is technically more correct from a statistical viewpoint, is to utilize performance related to reorder cycles. The major limitation of order cycles is the length of time required to collect the necessary data.

bution is to make an appraisal of variation around the average daily sales. Given an expected average of 5 units per day, sales exceeded average on 11 days and were less than average on 12 days. An alternative way of illustrating a frequency distribution is by a bar chart, as in Figure 6-4.

FIGURE 6-4
Historical Analysis of Sales History

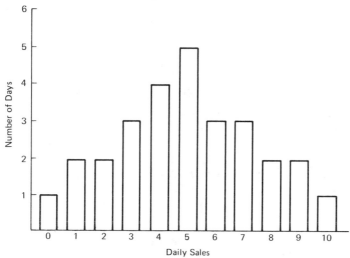

Given the historical frequency of sales, an exact calculation is possible of how much safety stock would be necessary to provide a specified degree of protection. Probability theory is based on the random chance of a given occurrence out of a large number of occurrences. In the situation illustrated, the frequency of occurrences is 28 days. Although in actual practice more than 28 events would be desirable, a limited sample will illustrate the application of probability theory to setting safety stocks.

The probability of occurrences can be expected to assume a pattern around a measure of central tendency, which is the average value of all occurrences. While a number of frequency distributions are utilized in inventory control, the most basic is the *normal distribution*.[29]

A normal distribution is characterized by a symmetrical bell-shaped curve, illustrated in Figure 6-5. The essential characteristic of a normal distribution is that three measures of central tendency are identical. The mean (average) value, the median (middle) observation, and the mode (most frequently observed) value all have the same numerical value. To the extent that these

[29] For a useful discussion of the application of statistical concepts to logistical problems, see Harry J. Bruce, *How to Apply Statistics to Physical Distribution* (Philadelphia: Chilton Book Company, 1967).

FIGURE 6-5
Normal Distribution

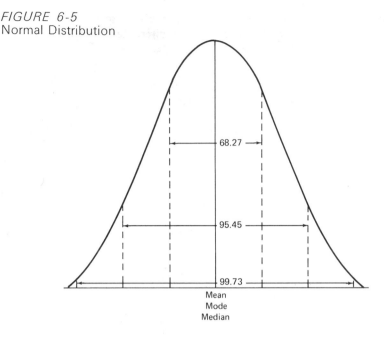

three measures are the same or nearly identical, a frequency distribution is classified as normal.

The basis for prediction using a normal distribution is the standard deviation of observations around the measures of central tendency. The *standard deviation* is a measure of dispersion of events within specified areas under the normal curve. With ± 1 standard deviation, 68.27 per cent of all events occur. Within ± 2 standard deviations, 95.45 per cent of all events occur. At ± 3 standard deviations, 99.73 per cent of all events are included. In terms of inventory policy, the standard deviation provides a means of estimating the safety stock required to provide a specified degree of protection above the average sales.

The first step in setting safety stocks is to calculate standard deviation. The formula for standard deviation is

$$\sigma = \sqrt{\frac{\sum fd^2}{n}}$$

where

σ = standard deviation

f = frequency of event

d = deviation of event from mean

n = total observations available

The necessary data to determine standard deviation are contained in Table 6-7. Substituting from Table 6-7,

$$\sigma = \sqrt{\frac{181}{28}}$$
$$= \sqrt{6.46}$$
$$= 2.54 \text{ (rounded to 3)}$$

TABLE 6-7
Calculation of Standard Deviation of Daily Sales

Units	Frequency (f)	Deviation from Mean (d)	Deviation Squared (d^2)	fd^2
0	1	-5	25	25
1	2	-4	16	32
2	2	-3	9	18
3	3	-2	4	12
4	4	-1	1	4
5	5	0	0	0
6	3	$+1$	1	3
7	3	$+2$	4	12
8	2	$+3$	9	18
9	2	$+4$	16	32
10	1	$+5$	25	25
$n = 28$	$\bar{x} = 5$			$\sum fd^2 = 181$

Owing to the inability to add stock except in complete units, the standard deviation of the data in Table 6-7 is rounded to 3 units. In setting safety stocks, 2 standard deviations of protection, or 6 units, would protect against 95.45 per cent of all events included in the frequency distribution.

However, in setting safety stocks, the only situations of concern are the probabilities concerning events that exceed the mean value. No problem exists concerning adequate inventory to satisfy sales equal to or below the average. Thus, on 50 per cent of the days, no safety stock is required. Safety stock protection at the 95 per cent level will, in fact, protect against 97.72 per cent of all possible events.

In order to use statistical probability in setting safety stocks, it is important to test the compatibility of the historical data with the expected theoretical frequency distribution. Although the frequency distribution illustrated in Figure 6-4 or Table 6-6 is very similar to a normal distribution, this may not always be the case. In other situations where the actual data are exponential, binomial, Poisson, or nearly normal, a test of goodness of fit should be completed.[30] One such test is the chi-square (χ^2) test of fit, the formula for which is

$$\chi^2 = \sum_{i=1}^{k} \frac{(o_i - e_i)^2}{e_i}$$

where

$$\chi^2 = \text{measure of fitness}$$
$$o_i = \text{observed frequencies}$$
$$e_i = \text{expected frequencies}$$

If the value of χ^2 is zero, the fit between the historical data and the theoretical expectation would be perfect. The larger the value of χ^2, the increasingly poorer the fit.

Statistical tables are available to assist in the acceptance or rejection of theoretical distribution as a valid statistical representation.[31] While the inventory planner does not need to understand the full process, the planner should be assured of a valid *fit* prior to utilizing statistical probability in establishing safety stock.

The preceding example illustrates how statistical probability can assist with the quantification of type I uncertainty. However, sales are not the only source of uncertainty. Therefore, attention is now directed to a combined treatment of sales (type I) and replenishment (type II) uncertainties.

Treatment of Combined Sales and Performance-Cycle Uncertainty

The inventory performance cycle has been identified as the combination of order communication, processing, transportation, and update. These elements create an information and physical product flow between two locations. The integrated performance cycle forms the central context for planning inventory policy. Up to this point, all discussions related to safety stock have assumed a constant time value for the duration of the performance cycle. For example, in the illustrations concerning the establishment of safety stocks to cover sales uncertainty, the duration of the cycle was assumed as a 10-day constant. The more typical situation confronting the inventory planner is illustrated in Figure 6-6, where both sales (type I) and inventory-performance-cycle (type II) uncertainties exist. In this section the nature of uncertainty concern-

---

[30] For example, see Robert Schlaifer, *Probability and Statistics for Business Decisions* (New York: McGraw-Hill Book Company, 1959), or any standard statistical text used in business research courses.
[31] Ibid.

FIGURE 6-6
Combined Sales and Performance Cycle Uncertainty

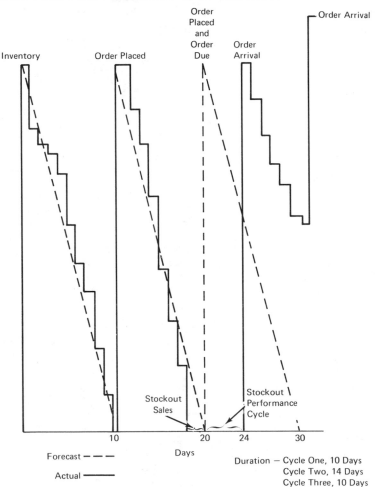

Forecast — — —

Actual ——————

Days

Duration — Cycle One, 10 Days
Cycle Two, 14 Days
Cycle Three, 10 Days

ing the performance cycle is reviewed, and methods are introduced for estimating combined probabilities of both types of uncertainty.

Nature of Performance-Cycle Uncertainty: Type II

Uncertainty in performance-cycle duration simply means that inventory
policy cannot be based on consistent delivery. The planner should expect
that the time duration of the replenishment will have a high frequency around
the average and be skewed in excess of the planned duration.

From a planning viewpoint, it would be possible to establish safety stock policy around the minimum possible days, the average expected days, or the maximum possible days of the inventory performance cycle.

Using the minimum or maximum limits, the resultant safety stock would be substantially different. Remember that safety stocks exist to protect against sales uncertainty during replenishment. Consequently, policies centered around minimum performance value would provide inadequate protection, and those formulated around maximum value would result in excessive safety stocks.

If the impact of type II uncertainty is not evaluated statistically, the most common practice is to formulate safety stock policy on the planned or average experienced replenishment days. However, if substantial variation in performance-cycle duration is experienced, formal evaluation is necessary. In manufacturing planning situations dealing with derived demand, the major form of uncertainty is the performance cycle.

TABLE 6-8
Calculation of Standard Deviation of Replenishment-Cycle Duration

Performance Cycle (days)	Frequency (f)	Deviation from Mean (d)	Deviation Squared (d)²	fd²
6	2	−4	16	32
7	4	−3	9	36
8	6	−2	4	24
9	8	−1	1	8
10	10	0	0	0
11	8	+1	1	8
12	6	+2	4	24
13	4	+3	9	36
14	2	+4	16	32
				$\Sigma fd^2 = 200$

$$N = 50 \qquad \bar{x} = 10$$

$$\sigma = \sqrt{\frac{\Sigma fd^2}{N}} = \sqrt{\frac{200}{50}} = \sqrt{4} = 2 \text{ days}$$

Table 6-8 presents a frequency distribution of performance cycles. Although 10 days is the most frequent experience, replenishment ranges from 6 to 14 days. If one wishes to consider the full range of cycle possibilities, the standard deviation is 2 days, if we assume that fitness exists between the data in Table 6-8 and a normal distribution. In other words, we would expect that total cycle time would fall within 8 to 12 days 68.27 per cent of the time.

From a practical viewpoint, when cycle days drop below 10, no immediate problem exists with safety stock. If the actual performance cycle was consistently below the planned over a period of time, then adjustment of expected duration would be in order. The situation that is of most immediate concern is when the time duration of the performance cycle exceeds the expected value of 10 days.

From the viewpoint of the probability of exceeding 10 days, the frequency of such occurrences from the data in Table 6-8 can be restated in terms of performance cycles greater than 10 days and equal to or less than 10 days. In the example data, the standard deviation would not change because the distribution is normal. However, if the actual experience had been skewed in excess of the expected cycle duration, the theoretical distribution most appropriate may have been a Poisson distribution.[32] In Poisson frequency distributions the standard deviation is equal to the square root of the mean. As a general rule, the smaller the mean, the greater the degree of skewness in the Poisson distribution.

Treating sales uncertainty (type I) and performance-cycle uncertainty (type II) consists of combining two independent variables. The duration of the cycle is, at least in the short run, independent of the daily demand. However, in setting safety stocks, the joint impact of the probability of individual variation in each must be related.

TABLE 6-9
Frequency Distribution—Types I and II Uncertainty

Sales Distribution		Replenishment-Cycle Distribution	
Daily Sales	Frequency	Days	Frequency
0	1	6	2
1	2	7	4
2	2	8	6
3	3	9	8
4	4	10	10
5	5	11	8
6	3	12	6
7	3	13	4
8	2	14	2
9	2		
10	1		
	$n = 28$	$n = 50$	
	$\bar{x} = 5$	$\bar{x} = 10$	
	$\sigma_s = 2.54$	$\sigma_r = 2$	

Table 6-9 presents a summary of sales and performance-cycle performance. The key to understanding the potential relationships of the data in Table 6-9 is, if the cycle is six days in duration, total demand during the six days

[32] Ibid.

could range from 0 to 60 units of sales. On each day of the cycle the sales probability is independent of the previous day, and so forth for the six-day duration. Assuming the full range of potential situations, total sales during replenishment could range from 0 to 140 units. With this basic relationship between the two types of uncertainty in mind, safety stock requirements can be determined by either numerical or simulated procedures.

Numerical Compounding: Types I and II Uncertainty

The exact compounding of two independent variables involves multinomial expansion. While this type of procedure requires extensive calculations when the data approximate the scope of that illustrated in Table 6-9, the solution provides a direct measure of encountering various levels of usage during the replenishment cycle. The method of compounding two variables involves an expansion of the general type[33]

$$p(fm) = [p(S_1) + p(S_2) + \cdots + p(S_n)]fm$$

where

$$f = \text{replenishment cycle}$$

$$s = \text{sales-replenishment-cycle duration}$$

$$m = \text{number of replenishment cycles}$$

$$n = \text{number of sales levels per day}$$

$$p = \text{probability of an event}$$

Expanding an equation of this type would determine the exact probabilities for all possible sales during all performance-cycle durations. The resultant probabilities can then be used to set safety stocks by setting the desired level of protection corresponding to a probability of stockout.

A more direct method is to relate the standard deviations of the two frequency distributions in order to approximate the combined standard deviation of the two sets of data:

$$\sigma c = \sqrt{\bar{P}\sigma s^2 + \bar{S}^2 \sigma P^2}$$

[33] This expansion is presented in Robert B. Fetter and Winston C. Dalleck, *Decision Models for Inventory Management* (Homewood, Ill.: Richard D. Irwin, Inc., 1961), pp. 50–52. To fully understand this expansion, it is necessary to refer also to pages 105–6. A similar approach to expansion is found in James L. Heskett, Nicholas A. Glaskowsky, Jr., and Robert M. Ivie, *Business Logistics*, 2nd ed. (New York: The Ronald Press Company, 1973), pp. 312–13. To illustrate this type of expansion in the example of this chapter would require calculation of a range from 0 to 140 units.

where

σ_c = standard deviation of combined probabilities

$\bar{P}$ = average performance cycle

σ_p = standard deviation of the performance cycle

$\bar{S}$ = average daily sales

σ_s = standard deviation of daily sales

Substituting from Table 6-9,

$$
\begin{aligned}
\sigma_c &= \sqrt{10.24(2.54)^2 + (5.28)^2(2)^2} \\
&= \sqrt{66.06 + 111.51} \\
&= \sqrt{177.57} \\
&= 13.32 \qquad \text{(rounded to 13)}
\end{aligned}
$$

Thus, given a frequency distribution of daily sales of from 0 to 10 units per day and a range in performance-cycle duration of 6 to 14 days, 13 units of safety stock would be required to satisfy 68.27 per cent of all probable relationships. To protect at the 97.72 per cent level it would be necessary to plan a safety stock of 26 units.

In terms of average inventory, no safety stock would require 25 units, whereas protection for both types I and II uncertainty would require 51 units. An average inventory of 51 units would be sufficient to provide a combined 97.72 per cent protection against the independent possibility of daily sales or performance-cycle variation. Table 6-10 summarizes the alternatives

TABLE 6-10
Summary of Alternative Assumptions Concerning Uncertainty and
Impact on Average Inventory

	Order Quantity	Safety Stock	Average Inventory
Assume constant $\bar{x}$ sales and constant $\bar{x}$ performance cycle	50	0	25
Assumes sales protection $+2\sigma$ and constant $\bar{x}$ performance cycle	50	6	31
Assume constant $\bar{x}$ sales and $+2\sigma$ performance-cycle protection	50	20	45
Assume joint $+2\sigma$ for sales and performance cycle	50	26	51

confronting the planner in terms of assumptions and corresponding impact on average inventory.

Simulating: Types I and II Uncertainty

As an alternative to numerically compounding types I and II uncertainty, the joint relationship of sales and performance cycle variation can be approximated by using *Monte Carlo simulation.*[34] The Monte Carlo technique consists of selecting values for representative performance cycles and corresponding sales levels on a random basis. Although Monte Carlo requires a large number of observations to establish safety stock policy, the procedure can be extremely useful when frequency distributions related to either sales or performance-cycle history are not known or do not have a good fit to either normal or Poisson distribution.

To illustrate the Monte Carlo procedure, Table 6-11 recaps historical statistics similar to those of Table 6-9, with the addition of probabilities and random numbers. The probability related to each indicates the frequency with which that value would be expected to occur over a large sampling. For example, with respect to daily sales, sales of 5 units would be expected to occur 17 out of 100 times. The accumulated probability is also displayed and indicates the number of times the value of the occurrence would be equal to or less than a particular value. For example, 60 out of 100 times the daily sales value would be expected to be equal to or less than 5 units. In addition, random numbers proportional to the frequency of each event have been displayed in Table 6-11.

The Monte Carlo process consists of selecting a random number for an inventory performance cycle. A random number can be selected from a table of numbers or generated by a computer. To illustrate, assume that the random number 386 is selected for the inventory performance-cycle duration. The corresponding value is 9 days. Next, random numbers for 9 individual days of sales are selected. Table 6-12 illustrates two rounds of Monte Carlo simulation where the random value of the performance cycle was selected as 9 and 11 days, respectively. In order to simulate a complete approximation of the joint relationships of types I and II uncertainty, a sample of several hundred performance cycles and related sales would be required for reliability.

If the purpose of the simulation is formulating a safety stock policy, then only selections where average sales during the performance cycle are greater than average expected need be considered. For example, if expected average sales are 5 units per day and the expected performance cycle is 9 days, all simulations with total sales of less than 45 units can be dropped from the analysis. All situations in which simulated average sales exceeded the value of expected average sales during replenishment would be tabulated for purposes of formulating a safety stock policy.

[34] Fetter and Dalleck, op. cit., pp. 52–54.

TABLE 6-11
Summary of Demand and Performance-Cycle Probabilities for Monte Carlo Simulation

Daily Unit Demand	Frequency Probability	Probability ≤ Demand	Random Number	Performance-Cycle Duration	Frequency Probability	Probability ≤ Duration	Random Number
0	0.04	0.04	001–040	6	0.04	0.04	001–040
1	0.07	0.11	041–110	7	0.08	0.12	041–120
2	0.07	0.18	111–180	8	0.10	0.22	121–220
3	0.11	0.29	181–290	9	0.17	0.39	221–390
4	0.14	0.43	291–430	10	0.20	0.59	391–590
5	0.17	0.60	431–600	11	0.17	0.76	591–760
6	0.11	0.71	601–710	12	0.12	0.88	761–880
7	0.11	0.82	711–820	13	0.08	0.96	881–960
8	0.07	0.89	821–890	14	0.04	1.00	961–1,000
9	0.07	0.96	891–960				
10	0.04	1.00	961–1,000				
	$N = 28$	$\bar{S} = 5$			$N = 50$	$\bar{S} = 10$	

TABLE 6-12
Example Results of Monte Carlo Simulation: Two
Observations

Performance-Cycle Duration: R386 = 9 days		Performance-Cycle Duration: R721 = 11 days	
Random Number	*Unit Sales*	*Random Number*	*Unit Sales*
097	1	796	7
542	5	520	5
422	4	805	7
019	0	452	5
807	7	685	6
065	1	594	5
060	1	481	5
269	3	124	2
573	5	350	4
		916	9
		085	1
$\sum s = 27$		$\sum s = 56$	
$\bar{S}p = 3$		$\bar{S}p = 5.09$	

The Situation of Dependent Demand

Prior to reviewing the strategy of the customer service availability level, clarification is needed regarding safety stocks in dependent situations.[35] The essential aspect of dependent demand is that inventory requirements can be calculated. Dependent demand, therefore, does not require forecasting, since uncertainty is eliminated. It follows that no specific safety stock is necessary to support a time-phased procurement program such as MRP.[36] The basic notion of time phasing is that parts and subassemblies need not be carried in inventory as long as they are available when needed.

The case for no safety stocks under conditions of dependent demand rests on two assumptions: (1) that procurement replenishment will be constant (no type II uncertainty), and (2) that vendors and suppliers will maintain adequate inventories to always satisfy 100 per cent of purchase requirements (functional shift of type I uncertainty). The second assumption may be operationally attainable by virtue of volume-oriented purchase contracts which assure vendors and suppliers of eventual purchase.[37] In such cases the safety stock requirement still exists even though the liability has been shifted.

[35] Orlicky, op. cit., pp. 22–25.

[36] This lack of need for safety stock is conceptually correct. However, in practice, safety stocks are used in MRP systems. See Orlicky, op. cit., pp. 7–9, and Plossl and Wight, op. cit., pp. 9–10.

[37] The practice became more common as a result of the material-shortage periods of the early 1970s.

The assumption of lead-time certainty is more difficult to accept. Even in situations where private transportation is used, an element of uncertainty is always present. The practical result is that safety stocks do exist in most dependent demand situations.

Three basic approaches have been used to introduce safety stocks into a system coping with dependent demand.[38] First, a common practice is to put *safety time* into the requirements plan. Thus a component is ordered one week earlier than needed to assure timely arrival. A second approach is to increase the requisition by a quantity specified by some estimate of expected forecast error. For example, it is assumed that forecast error will not exceed 5 per cent. This procedure is referred to as overforecasting top-level demand. The net result is to increase procurement of all components in a ratio to their expected usage plus cushion for forecast error. Components common to different end products or subassemblies under the overforecasting technique will naturally experience greater quantity buildups than single-purpose components and parts. To accommodate for the unlikely event that all common assemblies will simultaneously require safety stock protection, a widely used procedure is to set a total safety stock for the item at a level less than the sum of 5 per cent protection for each potential use.[39] The third method is to utilize the previously discussed statistical techniques for setting safety stocks directly to the component rather than the item of top-level demand.

The essential point is to recognize that safety stocks *are* normally required under conditions of derived demand. Techniques are available to assist in planning manufacturing safety stocks.

Establishing Customer Service Availability Level

Regardless of the method used to determine the probability of stockout during performance cycle, customer service availability boils down to the establishment of a safety stock level.[40] If the exact probability distribution of stockout is known, then safety stocks can be set to cover or satisfy a specified number of sales. Such safety stock policy is established by evaluation of the statistical distribution of stockouts resulting from combined uncertainties.[41]

It is important to realize that the size of safety stocks increases as higher and higher levels of stockout protection are desired. In Figure 6-7 the relationship between stockout protection and average inventory is illustrated. At lower levels of desired protection a substantial degree of protection is enjoyed with relatively low investment in safety stocks. As the desired level of protection

[38] Plossl and Wight, op. cit., pp. 31–33.
[39] Ibid.
[40] See Chapter 1, pages 19–21, and Chapter 9, pages 269–279, for an expanded discussion.
[41] This was discussed on pages 178–182 of this chapter.

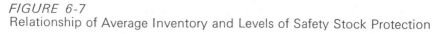

FIGURE 6-7
Relationship of Average Inventory and Levels of Safety Stock Protection

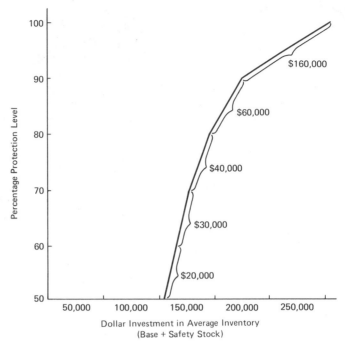

increases, the size of investment necessary to gain each increment of added protection increases.

Table 6-13 illustrates the degree of incremental protection realized and typical inventory requirements for setting safety stocks at various levels within the range 1 to 3 standard deviations. To achieve protection at each of the selected levels of from 1 to 2 standard deviations, approximately a 4 per cent increase in inventory was required. In other words, it requires about a 12 per cent increase in inventory to obtain 1 standard deviation of protection. However, at the first-standard-deviation level, 34.13 per cent of protection is gained above the mean value for a 12 per cent increase in inventory. Moving from 1 to 2 standard deviations, the percentage of protection gained is 13.59. From the 2- to 3-deviations level, the gain is down to 2.14. A rule to keep firmly in mind is that the incremental protection diminishes as safety stocks increase. Assuming all other things are equal, the ideal or optimal level of safety stock would protect each item in the line to the point where the marginal cost of protection equals the marginal revenue gained by the last unit sold.

If the specific inventory situation includes a policy of back-ordering customer orders, the associated costs should be considered when establishing safety

TABLE 6-13
Safety Stock Protection at Various Levels of Standard Deviation

Safety Stock Set at Standard Deviation	Degree of Protection	Incremental		Increase over Average Inventory[a]
		Protection	Inventory	
1.0	84.13	34.13	12	12
1.3	90.32	6.19	4	16
1.6	94.52	4.20	4	20
2.0	97.72	3.20	5	25
2.3	98.93	1.21	3	28
2.6	99.53	0.60	4	32
3.0	99.86	0.33	4	36

[a] Inventory requirements based upon example of sales uncertainty used in this section. Although degrees of protection related to standard deviation are applicable to all normal distributions, related inventory requirements are special to each situation.

stock policy. For example, a back-order will require duplicate order processing, added administrative cost, wasted marketing effort, and loss of profit contribution on available cash flow when unable to fill an order. These cost factors can be eliminated by maintaining high inventory availability. Once again, the solution is found at the point of equating appropriate marginal costs and revenue. For practical planning, a high degree of selectivity must be exercised in establishing safety stock policy across a broad product line. Not all items have the same degree of importance. The task in establishing sound safety stock policy is to classify the inventory line on the basis of enterprise objectives.

The fine-line classification of a product line can be based on a variety of measures. The most commonly used are sales, profit, unit value, usage rate, and critical nature of the item. By classifying the overall product line, different safety stock policies can be established for each product grouping. Those groups of extreme importance can be assigned high safety stock protection. In contrast, those with limited importance can be given little or no safety stock protection.

Classification by sales volume is one of the oldest methods employed to establish selective safety stock policy for an inventory line. In most marketing situations a small percentage of products account for a large percentage of sales. This generalization is often called the 20/80 rule: 20 per cent of the products account for 80 per cent of the sales. The most common sales classification is to rank-array and then group products into categories labeled, for example, ABC. Table 6-14 presents a rank array of 20 products with three classification groupings. With fine-line classification, safety stock policies can be set for each group to assure that the fast-moving products are afforded the lion's share of protection.

TABLE 6-14
Fine-Line Classification on Basis of Sales

Product Identification	Annual Sales (in thousands)	Per cent Total Sales	Accumulated		Classification Category
			Sales (%)	Products (%)	
1	$45,000	30.0	30.0	5	A
2	35,000	23.3	53.3	10	A
3	25,000	16.7	70.0	15	A
4	15,000	10.0	80.0	20	A
5	8,000	5.3	85.3	25	B
6	5,000	3.3	88.6	30	B
7	4,000	2.7	91.3	35	B
8	3,000	2.0	93.3	40	B
9	2,000	1.3	94.6	45	B
10	1,000	0.7	95.3	50	B
11	1,000	0.7	96.0	55	C
12	1,000	0.7	96.7	60	C
13	1,000	0.7	97.4	65	C
14	750	0.5	97.9	70	C
15	750	0.5	98.4	75	C
16	750	0.5	98.9	80	C
17	500	0.3	99.2	85	C
18	500	0.3	99.5	90	C
19	500	0.3	99.8	95	C
20	250	0.2	100.0	100	C
	$150,000				

In special situations the classification system used to develop safety stock policy may be based upon multiple factors. For example, sales, profitability, and critical nature could be weighted together in a combined index. The level of safety stock protection is then assigned according to the weighted rank array.

For classification on the basis of unit usage, it is important to realize that a differential will exist in a product line between total dollar sales and unit movement. Often items with a high frequency of unit sales during an inventory performance cycle account for only a small percentage of total dollar sales. Grouping of such items into broad categories can relieve the task of setting safety stocks.

With respect to unit value, it is important to keep in mind that high-value items are more expensive to protect than items with lower value. The reader should recall that the higher the unit value and the greater the sales rate, the more frequently orders would be placed under the rules of economic order quantity. The ideal inventory performance cycle would be short for items having high value and high usage. Therefore, the need to provide safety stocks for sales uncertainty during replenishment is reduced.

The key to selective establishment of safety stocks is to realize from the outset that different products have various degrees of importance. Variations in the desired inventory performance cycle and in the degree of stockout protection during the cycle should be programmed in the best interest of meeting planned objectives.

Summary

In summary, the basic functions of inventory have been identified as geographical separation, decoupling, balancing supply and demand, and safety stock protection against uncertainty. The risk related to inventory holding by level of the channel of distribution was discussed. In addition, a basic distinction was developed between inventory policy and control. Base and safety stock determinations are the prime concerns in formulating inventory policy.

The concept of economic order quantity, first introduced in Chapter 4, was further developed as the prime determinant of how much to order. Essential to the measurement of order quantities is the identification of costs related to ordering and maintenance. Several special adjustments to the basic EOQ were noted, with special emphasis on volume transportation rates and quantity discounts. In addition, a discussion was devoted to discrete-lot-sizing techniques commonly used in manufacturing procurement situations.

A critical aspect in formulating inventory policy is the determination of the appropriate performance cycle. The performance cycle is the basic planning perspective used for formulating inventory policy. As a general rule, performance-cycle duration should be kept as short and as consistent as possible.

Next, type I uncertainty, which concerns sales during replenishment, was introduced. Statistical probability was illustrated as a technique to cope with such uncertainty. The following section introduced type II uncertainty, which concerns variation in the performance cycle. Methods for handling both types of uncertainty on a numerical and simulated basis were discussed. The section concluded with a brief discussion of safety stock requirements for dependent demand.

The final section of the chapter discussed basic managerial considerations when selecting a specified level of inventory availability as one aspect of overall customer service performance. The key to effective inventory control is selectivity. In total, the chapter was designed to provide a working knowledge of inventory. Emphasis was placed on the policy aspects of inventory. Even greater attention will be paid in Chapters 8 and 9 to the strategic implications of inventory. Chapter 7 focuses attention on storage and material handling.

Questions

1. Where does the cost of carrying inventory show on the traditional profit-and-loss statement of the enterprise?
2. Is it safe to say that safety stocks are the prime cause of overstocks?
3. Discuss the disproportionate risk in the holding of inventory by retailers, wholesalers, and manufacturers. Why has there been a trend to push inventory back up the channel of distribution?
4. Describe the difference between discrete and EOQ lot sizing.
5. Why is the performance cycle a critical concept in formulating inventory programs?
6. Describe the difference between type I and type II uncertainty.
7. Under conditions of uncertainty, describe the relationship between economic order quantity and order-cycle duration.
8. How much protection would a firm be providing in percentage terms if safety stocks were set equal to 2 standard deviations?
9. Discuss the importance of selectivity in the formulation of inventory policy.
10. How does Monte Carlo simulation assist in the formulation of inventory policy?

Elements of Storage and Material Handling

Storage and material handling does not fit into the neat classification scheme of transportation and inventory because it involves all aspects of the logistical components. For example, material handling involves inventory as it flows through warehouses and as it is being transported. Such material handling is initiated in response to an order within the physical distribution, materials management, or inventory transfer system. The main concern of this chapter is the development of a unified approach for the treatment of handling and storage throughout the logistical system.

A major problem in logistical operations during the past several decades has been the level of attainable labor productivity. The basic nature of raw materials, parts, and finished goods flowing through and between a vast network of facilities makes logistics labor-intensive.

In the simplest sense, productivity is a ratio of physical output to physical input. To increase productivity, it is necessary either to obtain greater output with the same effort or to maintain existing output with a reduction in effort.

Labor productivity growth is influenced by the boom and recession pattern of business which has been characteristic of American industry since the early 1950s. When business is extremely good and the economy approaches full employment, output per man-hour falls as marginal workers are employed. The logistical sector of the enterprise gets more than its fair share of such new employees because few, if any, skills are required to perform many logistical tasks. When business activity plummets, labor contract provisions and the necessity to continue to handle material and inventory prevent a rapid reduction in payrolls. Separate productivity figures for logistical workers are not available. However, we can assume with confidence that logistical labor productivity has lagged most other areas of privately employed labor. Four factors contribute to this assumption.

First, the sheer number of labor hours involved in logistical operations increases this sector's vulnerability to any drop in output rate per labor hour. Second, the logistics area has not benefited from the extensive substitution of capital for labor which is characteristic of manufacturing. Third, until recently logistical operations have not been managed on an integrated systems basis nor have they received a great deal of top management concern. Finally, two major technological areas of logistics capable of reducing labor input—warehouse automation and domestic containerization—have not reached full potential.

Within the logistical system, material handling is the prime consumer of labor. The application of labor to handling transcends all other areas of the system and accumulates into one of the highest total costs. Because of the relative levels of technological development in other areas of logistical operations, a prime opportunity for improved productivity lies with the technology of handling.

Likewise, in a logistical warehouse primary emphasis is placed on material and product flow in contrast to storage. The warehouse represents the primary arena of handling operations. Therefore, warehouse design is an integral aspect of overall handling efficiency and is also of vital concern in obtaining increased productivity.

In this chapter the traditional functions of packaging, containerization, handling, and storage are treated as a single area of managerial concern. The objective of attaining maximum productivity throughout the logistical system provides the primary logic for grouping these functions. The first section treats packaging. Emphasis is placed on protective packaging aspects rather than marketing or motivation considerations. Attention is then directed to material handling. In the third section, containerization is the focus of attention. Containerization is defined to include all aspects and benefits obtainable from unitization. The final sections of the chapter elaborate on warehouse functions, planning, and establishment of operations. The overall objectives of the chapter are the development of a unified approach to the treatment of handling throughout the logistical system and establishment of the warehousing concept.

The Package in Movement and Storage

Individual products or parts are normally grouped into cartons, bags, or barrels for handling efficiency. These containers will all be referred to as *master cartons*. In the material movement system, the master carton performs two functions. First, the package serves as the basic unit for handling and, second, it protects the product or part from physical damage as it moves through the logistical operating system. Each function will be discussed.

The Benefits of Standardized Packaging

The master carton is the unit which is physically processed through a logistical system. The weight, cube, and fragility of the master cartons in a product line determine the configuration of transportation and warehousing to be utilized. Thus, if the package is not designed as efficiently as is practical for logistical processing, overall system performance will fall short of what otherwise might be accomplished.

Unfortunately, the final package is often based on production and marketing considerations at the expense of logistical requirements. For example, shipping certain products fully assembled, such as motorcycles, will result in a substantial reduction in density. A low-density package means higher transportation rates and greater cubic utilization of warehouse storage space. The proper perspective lies with the definition of "distribution or logistical packaging."[1] In essence, this requires an evaluation of how the package influences all components of the logistical system.

The traditional quantities in which products are sold at wholesale or retail should not be the prime determinant for the manner in which they are grouped into master cartons. There is no law of marketing or pricing that requires master carton packaging in even multiples of six units. The prime objective

---

[1] Walter F. Friedman, "The Role of Packaging in Physical Distribution," *Transportation and Distribution Management*, February 1968, p. 38.

is to arrive at an assortment of master cartons as standardized as possible. Standardization of master carton size facilitates material movement.

The importance of standardization can be illustrated by an example adapted from a shoe retailer. The initial physical distribution system employed by the retailer to ship shoes from the warehouse to retail shoe stores consisted of reusing cartons received from manufacturers for shipping. Individual pairs of shoes were grouped into whatever repack cartons were available. The result was a variety of carton sizes going to each retail store.

The method of order picking used to assemble a store's requirement was to produce a warehouse-sequenced picking list by shoe style and quantity. The shoes were selected in the warehouse, packed into cartons, and the cartons were manually loaded on a four-wheel truck for transfer to the shipping dock. The cartons were then loaded into over-the-road trailers for transport to the retail shoe store. While the order picking list provided a summary of all shoes in the total shipment, it was impossible for the retail stores to determine the contents of any given carton.

Viewing material handling as an integrated system resulted in a major change in the practice of reusing manufacturer cartons, the method of order picking, and material-handling procedures. The revised system was structured around two basic concepts. First, standardized shipping cartons were adopted, which allowed continuous conveyor movement from picking area direct to over-the-road trailers. Second, the integrated system used the computer to cube-out shoe pairs to assure that each standardized master carton was packed to maximum practical usage.

Under the new system, the cubed-out picking list was printed for each carton. After the individual pairs of shoes were placed into the carton, the pick list was attached to the carton, providing a summary of contents for retail store personnel.

The advantages of a standardized carton extended even to the retail store's back room. Because the contents of each master carton were easily determined, it was not necessary to search through many cartons for a particular style or size of shoe. Standardization allowed master cartons to be more efficiently tiered, which reduced back-room congestion. Finally, complete identification of master carton contents facilitated completion of retail inventory and merchandise reordering.

As expected, the new integrated system required the regular purchase of master cartons, since each could be reused only about three times. However, this added cost was more than recovered by reduced labor in order picking, continuous movement of cartons into over-the-road trailers, and more efficient utilization of cubic space in the transportation vehicles. Since each master carton was cubed out to near capacity, dead space was reduced substantially. The standardized carton size was selected for maximum conformity with a 40-foot-high-cube over-the-road trailer, thereby eliminating dead space in stacking. The end result of standardized master carton usage was a substantial reduction in total cost combined with a far more effective material-handling system at both the warehouse and retail shoe store.

This example illustrates both the systems approach to logistical planning and the principle of total cost. However, the most important point to be derived from the example is that master carton standardization facilitated total system integration.

Naturally, few organizations can reduce their master carton requirements to a single size. When master cartons of more than one size are required, extreme care should be taken to arrive at an assortment of units which are compatible. Figure 7-1 illustrates one such concept utilizing four module sizes.[2] Although the master carton sizes are not completely standardized, they are fully compatible.

Of course, logistical considerations cannot fully dominate packaging design. The ideal package for logistical processing would be a perfect cube (equal

FIGURE 7-1
Example and Benefits of the Modular System of Packing

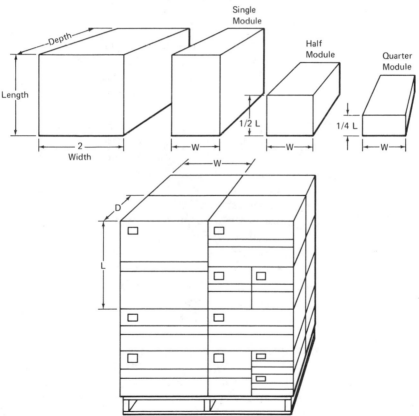

Source: Walter F. Friedman, "The Role of Packaging in Physical Distribution," *Transportation and Distribution Management*, February 1968.

---

[2] Ibid.

length, depth, and width) for maximum density and minimum handling. Seldom will such a package exist. The important point is that logistics should be weighed along with marketing and product design in planning master cartons.

Protective Packaging

A major function of the master carton is to protect the product from damage while it is moving through the logistical system. To a degree, the master cartons also serve as a deterrent to pilferage. Achieving the desired degree of protection involves tailoring the package to the product and selecting the material for package construction. The crucial question is the degree of product protection desired.

For most products, the cost of absolute protection is prohibitive. The determining factors are the value and fragility of the product. The higher the value and the more fragile a product, the greater the economic justification for nearly absolute protection.

The susceptibility to damage of a given package is directly related to the environment within which it is logistically processed. The environment can be divided into two categories: physical environment and element environment.[3] These aspects will be reviewed briefly. A brief discussion then follows on package material selection and damage prevention testing.

PHYSICAL ENVIRONMENT. The first aspect of package environmental analysis concerns the physical nature of the logistical system employed to move a product to its destination. The physical environment both influences and is influenced by the damage potential.

Package damage results from the transportation, storage, and handling systems employed to complete the logistical process. If privately owned and operated transportation is used, the product will move to its destination in a relatively controlled environment. On the other hand, if common carriers are utilized, the product enters a noncontrolled environment. In the latter situation, the product may be handled by one or more terminals and loaded on a variety of vehicles. The less control a firm has over its logistical environment, the greater the precautions required in packaging to prevent damage. The logistical environment thus influences the packaging design decision.

During the logistical process, the product can experience a number of shocks, which could result in loss of usefulness or package identity. The four most common causes of physical damage are vibration, impact, puncture, and compression. Within the logistical system, combinations of these four forms of shock can be experienced whenever a package is in transit or being handled.

---

[3] This distinction is used to separate sources of potential damage to the package while in transit.

In addition, stacking failure can result in considerable damage while the product is in storage. The physical damage that can result from shock ranges from surface scuffing and marring to complete product crushing, buckling, and crackling.

Shock damage can be limited to a significant degree by securing the package while it is in transit. Typical methods of securing are strapping, tiedowns, and various dunnage materials which prevent product shift or absorb vibration and impact shock. The best method of prevention is to load the over-the-road trailer or railcar in a tight pattern to eliminate shifting. Securing and proper loading reduce the damage prevention burden placed on the product package.

As noted earlier, the package requirement also influences logistical system design. The standard shipping practice in electronic data-processing equipment provides an excellent example. Because the basic product is of high value and extreme fragility, a substantial investment in packaging would be required to perform physical distribution using normal common-carrier services. Consequently, electronic data-processing equipment is normally distributed by specialized household movers. The equipment and handling procedures employed by household moving specialists are highly oriented to damage prevention. Therefore, while the cost of transportation is higher, product packaging capable of providing absolute product protection is not required. The product packaging requirement can substantially influence logistical system design.

ELEMENT ENVIRONMENT.   The element environment of a package in the logistical system refers to potential damage from temperature, humidity, and foreign matter. For the most part these environmental factors are beyond the control of logistical management. However, the protective package must be designed to cope with possible adverse conditions during transit.

To illustrate, it is not unusual for a package to be exposed to snow and below-freezing temperatures during loading, to be exposed to rain at an intermediate transfer point, and to arrive at a hot and humid destination. The crucial problem in evaluating the element environment is to determine in advance how the contents of the package will react with respect to instability and deterioration.

Temperature extremes naturally will affect package contents. At very high heat levels, some products will melt, spoil, blister, peel, fuse together, and discolor. Exposed to cold, the contents may experience cracking, brittleness, or complete spoilage. The package can offer only minimal protection from extreme temperatures. For example, frozen foods in prolonged transit cannot be maintained merely by package construction. The package design should, however, accommodate natural environmental elements for a reasonable period of time during the logistical process.

Another impact upon product stability involves water and vapor. The humidity problem is in many ways far more severe than the impact of temperature extremes upon package contents, for two reasons. First, a typical product has extremely limited tolerances for water exposure without causing dissolution, separation, corrosion, or pitting. Second, since for the most part water exposure occurs during transfer between transport carriers or distribution organizations, the package may constitute the product's sole source of protection. Even if the product is protected, the package could very well lose its exterior identification if exposed to excessive moisture.

The foreign-matter elements consist of any damage or loss of content stability caused by miscellaneous factors. For example, package contents can become contaminated or absorb tastes and odors if exposed for prolonged periods to chemical, noxious, or toxic elements. For certain kinds of products extreme care must be taken to protect against insects and rodents. Sometimes the package must protect against deterioration caused by prolonged exposure to air or light.

Many products, such as film, chocolate, confectionery, livestock, and produce, are so perishable that design of logistical systems must be geared to provide controlled environmental movement. Surprisingly, products clearly identified as perishable often do not create as severe an element problem as their more durable counterparts. It is the unexpected short-term excessive temperatures, high humidity, or foreign matter which cause most product damage.

MATERIAL SELECTION AND PACKAGE TESTING. Development of new packaging materials has been one of the most prolific areas of logistical research and development. A vast range of materials is employed in packaging. The most common are corrugated, solid fiberboard, wood, and styrofoam. The question confronted in selecting the optimum package is to determine the degree of protection required to cope with the anticipated physical and element environments. The optimal package design and material would combine to achieve absolute protection without incurring the expense of overprotection.

A common situation is to have a package which is excessive in design or material but does not provide the necessary protection. Arriving at a satisfactory packaging solution involves defining allowable damage in terms of expected overall environment and then isolating a combination of design and material capable of meeting the specifications. The important points are: (1) in most cases the cost of absolute protection will be prohibitive, and (2) package construction is properly a blend of design and material.

The determination of final package design requires a great deal of testing to assure that specifications are satisfied at minimal cost. Such tests can be conducted in a laboratory or on an experimental shipment basis. During the past decade the process of package design and material selection has become far more scientific. To a large degree, care in design has been encouraged due to increased federal regulation on hazardous materials.

Today, computerized environmental simulations can be used to replicate the conditions that a package will experience in the logistical system. Laboratory test equipment is available to evaluate the impact of shock upon the interaction of product fragility and packaging materials and design. New instrumented recording equipment is available which measures severity and nature of shock while a package is in transit. Use of instrumented shipments on a scientifically selected sample of logistical movements can greatly reduce the bias inherent in trial-and-error test shipments.[4]

Material Handling

One extremely encouraging aspect of modern logistics is the concentration of capital investment toward keeping the freight moving. To realize logistical time and space closure, material handling cannot be avoided. It should, however, be minimized. The technical aspects of material handling are extensive and beyond the scope of this text. The following discussion places emphasis upon handling methods and efficiency measurement. A final discussion treats recent developments in automated handling.

Basic Handling Considerations

Material handling in the logistical system is concentrated in and around the warehouse facility. In particular, four warehouse-handling activities must be performed: (1) receiving, (2) transfer, (3) selection, and (4) shipping. These four types of handling are common to the materials management, transfer, and physical distribution operations within a logistical system. The same handling activities are common to in-plant material handling. However, material handling within production and assembly plants is part of basic manufacturing and not an element of logistics movement.

A basic difference exists in the handling of bulk materials and master cartons. Bulk handling is a particular situation where protective packaging normally is unnecessary, but specialized handling equipment is required to unload solids, fluids, or gaseous materials. The following discussion focuses on master carton handling within the logistical system.

Modern handling systems can be classified as mechanized or automated. A combination of labor and handling equipment is utilized in mechanized systems to facilitate receiving, processing, and/or shipping. Generally, labor constitutes a high percentage of the overall input in mechanized systems. Automated systems, in contrast, attempt to minimize the labor element as much as practical by substituting capital investment in equipment. An automated handling system may be applied to any of the basic handling requirements, depending upon the situation. Mechanized handling systems are most common today, but automated systems are increasing and rapid

---

[4] For a discussion, see *5-Step Packaging Development* (Monterey, Calif.: MTS, Inc., 1971).

expansion is predicted for the 1980s. As noted earlier, one factor contributing to low logistical productivity is that automated handling has yet to achieve its full potential.

Mechanized Handling

Mechanized handling systems employ a wide range of handling equipment. The types of equipment most commonly used in logistical operations are powered fork-lift trucks, towlines, tractor-trailer devices, and conveyors.

Powered fork-lift trucks can move loads of master cartons both horizontally and vertically. The pallet, which is discussed in greater detail in the containerization section of this chapter, is a platform (Figure 7-3) upon which master cartons are stacked. A fork-lift truck normally transports a maximum of two pallet loads at a time. Fork-lift trucks are not limited to handling pallets; skids, slip sheets, or boxes may be transported, depending upon the nature of the product.

Many types of fork-lift trucks are available. High-stacking trucks capable of up to 20 feet of vertical movement, palletless side-clamp versions, and narrow aisle models can be found in logistical warehouses. The fork-lift truck is not economical for long-distance horizontal movement because of the high ratio of labor per unit of transfer. Therefore, fork-lifts are most often employed in shipping and receiving, and to place merchandise in high cube storage. The two power sources for fork-lift trucks are propane gas and electricity. Electric-powered fork-lift trucks are becoming most popular, for ecological reasons.

Towlines consist of either in-floor or overhead-mounted drag devices. They are employed with four-wheel trailers on a continuous-power basis.[5] The main advantage of a towline is continuous movement. However, such handling devices do not have the flexibility of either fork-lift trucks or tractor-trailer devices. The most common application of towlines is for order selection within the warehouse. Order selectors or assemblers place merchandise on the trailer, which is then towed to the shipping dock. A number of automated decoupling devices have been perfected which route trailers from the main line to selected shipping docks.

A continuing controversy over the years involves the installation of in-floor or overhead towlines. In-floor installation is costly to modify and difficult to maintain from a housekeeping viewpoint. Overhead installation is more flexible, but unless the warehouse floor is absolutely level, the line may jerk the front wheels of the trailers off the ground and risk product damage.

The tractor-trailer consists of a manned power unit which tows a number of individual four-wheel trailers. The average size of the platform trailers is 4 by 8 feet. The tractor-trailer, like the towline, is used in order selection.

---

[5] Four-wheel trailers are similar to hand trucks or carts that are powered by attachment to the towline.

This device has a great deal of flexibility. It is not as economical as the towline, however, because it requires greater labor participation and is often idle. Experiments have been conducted with radio-controlled tractors and some special applications where the tractor follows a guide strip attached to the warehouse floor. Although remote control has the potential to reduce labor, the majority of tractor-trailer operations are of the conventional type.

Conveyors are used widely in shipping and receiving operations and form the basic handling power for a number of order-selection systems. Conveyors can be classified on the basis of power or gravity and roller or belt movement. The conveyor is flexible, which allows the basic installation to be modified with minimum difficulty. Gravity-style roller conveyors are often set up for a specific shipping or receiving task and in some cases are transported on over-the-road trailers to ease destination unloading. When power-drive and belt configurations are employed, a great deal of conveyor flexibility is sacrificed.

The four types of material-handling equipment discussed here are only samples of the range available for use in mechanized handling systems. Most systems employ a combination of handling devices. For example, fork-lift trucks may be employed for vertical movement while tractor trailers are used for horizontal movement.

Over the years a variety of guidelines have been suggested to assist management in the design of mechanized material-handling systems.[6] The following six guidelines are representative.

1. Equipment for handling and storage should be as standardized as possible.
2. When in motion, the system should be designed to provide maximum continuous product flow.
3. Maximum investment should be in movement, rather than stationary, equipment.
4. Movement equipment should be utilized to the maximum extent possible.
5. In equipment selection, effort should be made to minimize the ratio of dead weight to payload.
6. To the extent practical, gravity flow should be incorporated in system design.

As noted earlier, there is a distinct trend toward automated systems.

Automated Handling

For a number of years automated handling has been long on potential and short on accomplishment. Initial efforts toward automated handling concentrated upon order-selection systems at the master carton level. Recently, emphasis has switched to the development of unit-load high-rise storage and

---

[6] *An Introduction to Material Handling* (Pittsburgh, Pa.: Materials Handling Institute, Inc., 1966), Chap. 4.

information directed handling. Each will be discussed in turn after a brief review of automated handling concepts.

POTENTIAL OF AUTOMATION.   The appeal of automation is that it substitutes capital investment in equipment for labor in mechanized handling systems. In addition to using less direct labor, an automated system will operate faster and more accurately than a mechanized system. Its shortcomings are the high degree of capital investment and the complex nature of development and application.

To date, most automated systems have had to be custom designed and constructed for each application.[7] The six guidelines previously noted for selection of mechanized handling systems are not applicable to automated systems. For example, storage equipment in an automated system is an integral part of the handling capability and represents about 50 per cent of the total investment.[8] The ratio of dead weight to payload has little relevance in an automated handling application.

Although computers play an important part in all handling systems, they are essential to automated systems. The computer provides programming of the automated selection equipment and is used to interface the warehouse to the remainder of the logistical system. Thus the control system will be vastly different if automated handling is utilized. One factor that prohibited rapid development of automated systems earlier was the high cost of minicomputers. Breakthroughs in electronic data processing have eliminated this barrier.

AUTOMATED PACKAGE SYSTEMS.   Initially, automation was applied to master carton selection or order assembly in the warehouse. Because of high labor intensity in order selection, the basic objective was to integrate mechanized and automated handling into a total system.

The initial concept was as follows. An automated selection device was preloaded. The device itself consisted of a series of merchandise racks stacked vertically. Merchandise was loaded from the rear and permitted to flow forward in the "live" rack on gravity conveyors until stopped by a rack door. Between or down the middle of the racks, power conveyors created a merchandise flow line, with several flow lines positioned above each other, one at each level of rack doors.

Upon receipt of an order, punch cards were created for each product to be selected and sorted in rack sequence. The cards were then processed through a reader, which tripped the rack doors in sequence, allowing the desired merchandise to flow forward onto the powered conveyors. The conveyors in turn transported merchandise to an order-packing area for shipment preparation.

---

[7] This particular feature, in all probability, will be an ever-present aspect of customized handling. However, during the past five years, remarkable standardization of systems and hardware has occurred.

[8] *High-Rise Storage* (Boston: Modern Materials Handling, 1971), Chapter 2.

When compared to modern applications, these initial attempts at automated package handling were highly inefficient. A great deal of labor was required at the merchandise input and output phases, and the automated equipment was expensive.[9] Applications were limited to merchandise of extremely high value or to situations where working conditions justified such investment. For example, these initial systems were adopted widely for order selection of frozen foods, where work temperatures are below freezing.

Substantial advancements have been made recently in automated selection of case goods. The automated systems concept employed by the Johnson & Johnson Domestic Operating Company will be described briefly to reflect the current state of development.

At several Johnson & Johnson distribution warehouse facilities, the handling of fast-moving products in master cartons is fully automated from merchandise receipt to placement in over-the-road trailers for shipment. The system uses an integrated network of power and gravity conveyors linking power-motivated live storage. The entire system is controlled by a computer coupled with the inventory and order-processing control systems for the warehouse facility.

Upon arrival, merchandise is automatically routed to the live storage position and inventory records are updated. Upon order receipt, the merchandise desired is pre-cubed to vehicle size and scheduled for selection. At the appropriate time, all merchandise is selected in loading sequence and automatically transported by conveyor to the loading dock. In most situations, the first manual handling of the merchandise within the warehouse is when it is stacked into the transport vehicle.

The solution of the input/output interface problem and the development of sophisticated control systems resulted in a highly effective and efficient package-handling system. The Johnson & Johnson application is representative of the package-handling systems becoming more common today.[10]

AUTOMATED UNIT-LOAD SYSTEMS.   The concept of automated unit-load handling using high-rise storage has received considerable attention recently.[11] The high-rise concept of handling is fully automated from receiving to shipping. Four main components constitute the basic system: (1) storage racks, (2) storage and retrieval equipment, (3) input/output systems, and (4) control systems.

The name *high-rise* derives from the physical appearance of the storage rack. The rack is a structured steel vertical storage area 50 to 75 feet high, with some as high as 120 feet. When one considers that the stacking height of

[9] Ibid.

[10] The package-handling field is currently receiving a great deal of attention. Many experts consider this form of automation to represent the primary research and development focus in automated handling during the next decade.

[11] *High-Rise Storage,* op. cit.

palletized cartons in a mechanized handling system is normally 20 feet, the high-rise potential comes through loud and clear.

The typical high-rise facility consists of rows of storage racks. The rows are separated by aisles running from 120 to over 800 feet. It is within these aisles that the storage and retrieval equipment functions. As described by *Modern Materials Handling,*

the storage and retrieval machine—this marvel of automated control—is basically a cross between the fork truck and the bridge-type stacker crane. It looks like a stacker crane but moves on wheels much like a truck. Locked within an aisle, it travels back and forth hoisting and lowering loads, moving them into and out of storage openings on either side of the aisle.[12]

A variety of storage and retrieval equipment is available. Most require guidance at the top and bottom to provide the vertical stability necessary for high-speed horizontal movement and vertical hoisting. Horizontal speeds range from 300 to 400 feet per minute (fpm) with hoisting speeds of up to 100 fpm or more.[13]

The initial function of the storage and retrieval equipment is to reach the storage position rapidly. A second function is to deposit or retract a load of merchandise. For the most part, load deposit and retraction are achieved by shuttle tables, which can enter and exit from the rack at speeds up to 100 fpm. Since the shuttle table moves only a few feet, it must be able to accelerate and stop rapidly.

In some installations, the storage and retrieval machine can be moved between aisles by transfer cars. Numerous transfer arrangements and layouts have been developed, and transfer units may be dedicated or nondedicated. The *dedicated* transfer car is always stationed at the end of the aisle in which the storage and retrieval equipment is working. The *nondedicated* transfer car works a number of aisles and retrieval machines on a scheduled basis to achieve maximum equipment utilization. The decision as to whether or not to include aisle-to-aisle transfer in a high-rise storage system rests with the economics of throughput rate and number of aisles included in the overall system.

The input/output system in high-rise storage is concerned with moving loads to and from the rack area. Two types of movement are involved. First, loads must be transported from receiving docks or production lines to the storage area. Second, within the immediate peripheral area of the racks, loads must be positioned for entry or exit. The greatest potential handling problem is in the peripheral area. The common practice is to have pickup and discharge stations assigned to each aisle capable of staging an adequate supply of loads to fully deploy the storage and retrieval equipment. For maximum input/

---

[12] Ibid., p. HR-6.
[13] Ibid., p. HR-8.

output performance, it is normal to have different stations for transfer of inbound and outbound loads assigned to the same aisle. The pickup and discharge stations are linked to the handling systems that transfer merchandise to and from the high-rise storage area.

The control system in high-rise storage is similar to that described earlier when discussing automated master carton handling. In the case of high-rise storage systems, a great deal of sophistication in programming and control measurement is required to achieve maximum equipment utilization and rapid command cycles. Recent advancements in the speed and cost of small computers that can be fully dedicated to the high-rise system have, for the most part, eliminated major control system problems.

FIGURE 7-2
High-Rise Warehouse Facility

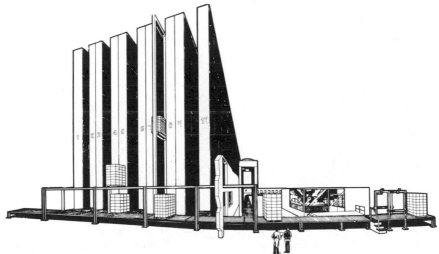

Reproduced by permission of Kenway Engineering.

Figure 7-2 illustrates the concept of a high-rise storage system. Merchandise flowing from the bakery is automatically stacked on 48- by 40-inch pallets and shrink-wrapped to create a unit load.[14] The unit load is then transported to the high-rise storage area by power conveyor. When the load arrives, it is assigned to a storage bin and transferred by power conveyor to the appropriate pickup station. At this point the storage and retrieval equipment takes over and delivers the unit load to its temporary storage location.

In addition to scheduling arrivals and location assignments, the control

[14] For a more detailed description of the system described in Figure 7-2, see James K. Allred, "New Developments in Computer Controlled Warehousing," presented at Materials Management Systems Seminar on Computers and Materials Handling, LaSalle Hotel, Chicago, October 24, 1972.

system handles inventory control and stock rotation. When orders are received, the command control system directs the retrieval of specified unit loads. From the outbound delivery stations, the unit load flows by power and gravity conveyor to the appropriate shipping dock. While retrieval and outbound delivery are being accomplished, all the paper work necessary to initiate product shipment is completed.

This example is just one of an increasing number of high-rise storage systems currently in operation in a variety of industries. They are all designed to increase material-handling productivity by providing maximum storage density per square foot of floor space and to minimize the direct labor required in handling. The highly controlled nature of the system combines reliable pilferage-free and damage-free handling with extremely accurate control.

Information-Directed Handling

The concept of information-directed handling is relatively new and has not been tested extensively. However, the concept is appealing because it combines the control of automated handling with the operational flexibility of mechanized systems.

The information-directed system uses mechanized handling equipment. The typical source of power is the fork-lift truck. In layout and design, the warehouse facility is essentially the same as any mechanized facility. The difference is that all fork-truck movements are directed and monitored by the command of a minicomputer.

In operation, all required handling movements are fed into the minicomputer for analysis and equipment assignment. A computer program is utilized to analyze handling requirements and to assign equipment in such a way that total movement and deadhead movement is minimized. Work assignments are provided to individual fork trucks by printouts picked up at selected terminal locations throughout the warehouse. Tests are also under way to place data terminals on the fork trucks so that work assignments can be transmitted directly to the equipment operator.

Information-directed handling has noteworthy potential in that selected benefits of automation can be achieved without substantial capital investment. The potential for gains in productivity results from substantial reduction in deadhead movements. The main drawback in the concept is the flexibility of work assignment. As a specific fork truck proceeds during a work period it may be involved in loading or unloading several vehicles, selecting many orders, and completing several handling assignments. This wide variety of work assignments increases the complexity of work direction and could decrease the quality of performance.

Evaluating Handling Alternatives

The managerial question faced is whether a handling system should be designed on a mechanized, automated, or combined basis. Generally, the initial cost of an automated system will be higher than that of a mechanized system. An automated system will require less building space, but the equipment investment will be greater. The return on investment from automation is in the reduced cost of operation. An automated handling system, if properly designed and controlled, should outperform a mechanized system in terms of less labor, reduced damage, increased accuracy, and quality of performance in product protection and rotation. In the final analysis, the design to be used should be evaluated on the basis of return on investment, as should any investment decision.[15]

Containerization

An additional aspect of the overall storage and materials-handling is containerization. The term *container* describes the grouping of master cartons for handling or transport. The concept of containerization includes all forms of unitization, from taping two master cartons together to the use of specialized TOFC or other coordinated transport arrangements. All forms of containerization have one basic objective, to increase the material-handling efficiency of the logistical operating system. The present discussion is limited to methods of unitization that extend up to but do not include total vehicle size. The first part of the section discusses unit loads which do not use rigid enclosure. Next, the rigid-enclosure approach to unitization is discussed. Finally, the relative advantages and disadvantages of both are reviewed.

Nonrigid Containerization

As the name implies, the nonrigid containerized load is not protected by complete enclosure. The most common variety is stacking master cartons on pallets for purposes of material handling. A hardwood pallet is illustrated in Figure 7-3. Pallet types and sizes will be discussed first. Next, methods of stacking master cartons on pallets are briefly noted. Finally, alternative ways to secure the unit load on the pallet for transport outside the immediate handling environment are discussed.

PALLET TYPES AND SIZES. Most industry associations have selected a standardized pallet size to be employed as extensively as possible by major firms within the industry. For example, the Grocery Manufacturers of America have adopted the 40- by 48-inch pallet with four-way entry as the recommended configuration for food distribution. Throughout industry, the sizes most frequently used are the 40 by 48, 32 by 40, and 32 by 36 (all dimensions in inches). It is common practice to identify first the dimension of the pallet from which most frequent entry by handling equipment is anticipated. If a

---

[15] *An Introduction to Material Handling*, op. cit., Chap. 5.

FIGURE 7-3
Example of Hardwood Pallet

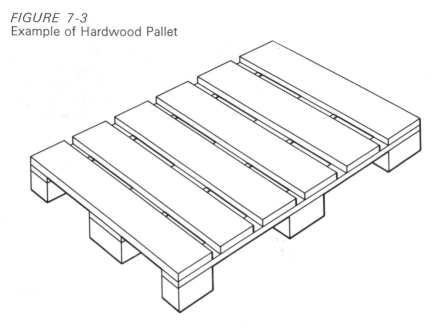

pallet provides four-way entry, it can be moved by handling equipment from any side.

Generally, the larger a pallet, the more economical will be the resultant material handling. For instance, the 40- by 48-inch pallet provides 768 more square inches per stacking tier than the 32- by 36-inch size. Assuming that master cartons can be stacked as high as 10 tiers, the total added unitization space of the 40- by 48-inch pallet is 7,680 square inches, which is 60 per cent larger than the 32- by 36-inch size. The final determination of pallet size should be based upon size of load, compatibility with the handling and transport equipment used throughout the logistical system, and standardized industry practice. With modern handling equipment, few restrictions are encountered in weight limitations.

A wide range of material is used in pallet construction. The most prevalent material is hardwood, but pallets are also constructed from steel, corrugated, plastic, aluminum, and various synthetic materials. The material employed depends a great deal upon the planned use of the pallet. In many situations, the pallet is considered expendable after its initial use. Inexpensive construction is essential for such pallets. A corrugated disposable pallet can be purchased for about $1, whereas a reinforced four-way-entry hardwood pallet will be $10 to 12, depending upon the quality of the material. Pallets constructed from other materials will also vary in price, depending upon material and cost of fabrication.

FIGURE 7-4
Basic Pallet Master Carton Stacking Patterns

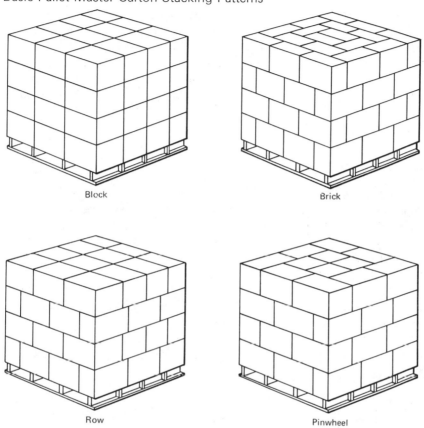

Block

Brick

Row

Pinwheel

Adapted from palletization guides of the National Wooden Pallet Manufacturers Association.

MASTER CARTON STACKING.   Four stacking methods are employed in tiering master cartons on pallets. The block method is used with cartons of equal width and length. With differential widths and lengths, the brick, row, or pinwheel pattern is employed. Figure 7-4 illustrates the four basic patterns. Except for the block method, cartons placed on the pallet are arranged in an interlocking pattern with adjoining tiers placed at 90-degree angles to each other. Load stability is increased by interlocking. The block pattern does not have this benefit.

PALLET LOAD SECURING.   In a number of situations, the stability of the pallet pattern is not sufficient to secure the unit load while it is being handled or while in transit. Standard methods of additional stability include rope tie, corner posts, steel strapping, taping, and glue bonding. Shrink-wrap securing has increased in popularity recently.

Shrink wrapping consists of placing a prestretched plastic sheet or bag over the pallet and master cartons. The material is then heat-shrunk to lock the cartons to the pallet. With shrink-wrap securing, the palletized unit load assumes many of the characteristics of a rigid container, with the exception that the same degree of physical protection is not provided during handling or transit. Other benefits of shrink wrapping are reduced exposure of master cartons to logistical environment, low cost, adaptability to various shipment sizes, and insignificant added weight. The major problem of shrink wrap is waste material disposal.

Rigid Containers

A rigid container is a box within which master cartons or loose products are placed during warehousing and transportation. The premise is that placing merchandise within a container will both protect it and make it easier to handle. The prospects for extensive domestic containerization have been the subject of a great deal of attention since the early 1950s. The potential for increased productivity by containerization is obvious. One expert estimated in the early 1960s that one half of the total cost of transporting domestic goods was spent in shuffling between vehicles, transporting across docks and platforms, in packaging, for loss and damage claims for pilferage, and for insurance.[16] Table 7-1 summarizes the potential benefits of increased containerization.

TABLE 7-1
Potential Benefits of Rigid Containerization

Improves overall material movement efficiency
Reduces damage in handling and transit
Reduces pilferage
Reduces protective packaging requirements
Provides greater protection of product from element environment
Provides a shipment unit that can be reused a substantial number of times, thereby
   reducing waste and the need to dispose of the container

Despite the potential benefits, domestic rigid containerized shipments are not common.[17] A comprehensive study on why domestic containerization has not materialized identified the following four factors as the primary obstacles:

---

[16] Maritime Cargo Transportation Conference, *Inland and Maritime Transportation of Unitized Cargo* (Washington, D.C.: National Academy of Science, 1963), pp. 33–36.

[17] The discussion that follows draws upon Vernon C. Seguin, *An Investigation of the Factors Inhibiting Growth of Containerization in Domestic Surface Freight Shipments* (unpublished Ph.D. dissertation, Michigan State University, 1971).

(1) carrier attitudes and practices, (2) lack of standards, (3) lack of leadership, and (4) lack of coordination.[18]

In contrast, the rapid expansion of container movements in international commerce proves that the concept can work and does hold forth the potential for increased productivity. A challenge for the future is to make domestic containerization a reality.

Integrated Shipping Programs

Although treated separately in this chapter for clarity, packaging, material handling, and containerization represent integral parts of the material movement component of the overall logistical operating system. All three areas greatly influence each other. For example, unitized automated handling cannot be efficiently designed without a high degree of master carton standardization, which in turn provides the opportunity to containerize individual products. This section illustrates some aspects of the interaction of packaging, material handling, and containerization in the context of a total system of movement.

Integrated Customer Shipping Programs

A number of efforts have been successful in developing integrated shipping programs between manufacturing firms and their customers. The impetus for such programs is to combine material-handling capability, transportation, warehousing, inventory policy, and communications into the customer's logistical system. The objective is minimum handling during the exchange of merchandise between two firms. To the degree that exchange interface friction can be reduced, cost savings are possible for both the manufacturer and the customer. This type of integrated exchange is most common in physical distribution.

The General Foods Corporation "Palletized Shipping Program" is an example.[19] Unit loads of General Foods products are shipped to customers on 40- by 48-inch hardwood pallets. In addition to shipping in standardized palletized quantities, the program uses railcars and trucks designed specifically to facilitate unit-load handling. Pallets are exchanged on a loan basis between GFC and customers.

Palletized shipment has many benefits for the customer. First, unloading time and congestion at the customer's warehouse are minimized. Second, products in palletized quantities facilitate material-handling activities at the customer's warehouse. Inbound shipment checking is simplified, and the inventory can be positioned rapidly for order selection. Palletized system

---

[18] Ibid.

[19] L. G. Smiley, *General Foods Palletization Shipping Program* (New York: American Society of Mechanical Engineers, 1964), p. 4.

unloading requires only one fifth as much time as is needed for manual unloading. Finally, damage in transit can be almost eliminated by use of pallet loads and specialized transportation equipment. All these factors mean reduced cost to the customer.

For General Foods, the palletized shipment program permits products to be placed automatically on pallets at the end of the manufacturing line and maintained as a unit load during physical distribution. No manual handling is required during the process. The pallet quantity provides a convenient focus for standardizing order quantities. In turn, carload and truckload prices can be coordinated in terms of gross weight and palletized units. The shipper gains from lower costs and the ability to improve customer service.

Although integrated shipping programs are not limited to food physical distribution, the Grocery Manufacturers of America have been very active in encouraging unitized shipment programs. In many industries, palletized shipments are common in the internal inventory transfer phase of logistics, when shipments are between company facilities. However, for such systems to function efficiently, a high degree of standardization and cooperation is required.

Special Considerations in Material Handling

As expected, the primary focus of material movement is merchandise flowing in an orderly and efficient manner from manufacture to point of sale. However, material-handling systems must also be capable of handling reverse flow within the logistical network.

For a variety of reasons, merchandise may be recalled by a manufacturer or returned to the manufacturer. Normally such return flows are not of sufficient quantity or regularity to justify containerized movement. Therefore, the only convenient method for processing reverse flows is manual handling. To the degree practical, material-handling design should consider the cost and service impact of reverse logistics. Such flows often involve pallets, cartons, and packaging materials in addition to damaged, dated, or excessive merchandise. In addition, ecological pressure to eliminate disposable containers will increase the quantity of returnable bottles moving in the logistical system. Handling and overall logistical systems in such industries will need to handle two-way movement efficiently.

The Concept of Strategic Storage

Traditionally, storage has been an important aspect of economic activity. In the early stages of American development, the economy was comprised of individual households acting as self-sufficient economic units. Consumers performed the storage function and accepted the attendant risks. Meats were stored in smokehouses, and perishable products were protected in underground food cellars.

As transportation facilities developed, specialized economic activity evolved. Product storage was shifted from the household to retailers, wholesalers, and manufacturers. Early literature indicates that the warehouse was initially introduced as a storage unit designed to help satisfy basic marketing processes.[20] Storage was considered necessary to match products with consumers. The warehouse was the location for product storage until demand became sufficient to support distribution. The time utility principle was used to justify this type of storage.[21] The tendency to consider storage a necessary evil resulted in criticism of operating efficiency with little appreciation of the broader logistical spectrum in which warehousing played a vital role. The warehouse served as a static unit in the material and product pipeline. The warehouse function of assorting was noted but given little emphasis. Internal management controls and maximum product turnover received little attention.

Literature of this early era correctly described the situation. Firms seeking to operate effectively between points of procurement, manufacturing, and final consumption gave little attention to internal warehouse operations. The establishment of warehouses was essential for survival, but little emphasis was placed on qualitative storage and handling. Engineering efforts were centered on the major problem of this early era, manufacturing.

The internal operation of early warehouses illustrates the neglect of efficient concepts. These warehouses received merchandise by railcar or truck. The merchandise was moved manually to the storage area and then hand-piled in stacks on the floor. When different products were stored in the same warehouse, merchandise was continually lost. Stock rotation was handled poorly, and products often deteriorated. When orders were received from retailers, merchandise was hand-picked for placement on carts. The carts were then pushed to the shipping area, where the merchandise was reassembled and hand-packed on outbound trucks for delivery.

Because of low labor rates, manpower was used freely, with little consideration given to efficiency in space utilization, work methods, or material handling. Despite their shortcomings, however, early warehouses were necessary to bridge the storage gap between marketing and production.

After World War II, managerial attention shifted toward increasing operating efficiency. Management was forced to justify the traditional warehouse. Forecasting and production scheduling had improved, reducing the need for extensive inventories. Production processes had been perfected, eliminating long time delays during manufacturing. Seasonal production still demanded storage facilities, but the overall need for storage was reduced. The changing character of the retail order, however, supported the need for warehouse facilities. The retail store, faced with the necessity of stocking a variety of products, could not gain the advantages of consolidated shipments. Cost of

[20] Hugh B. Killough, *The Economics of Marketing* (New York: Harper & Row, Publishers, 1933), p. 101.

[21] Theodore N. Beckman and William R. Davidson, *Marketing*, 8th ed. (New York: The Ronald Press Company, 1967).

transportation in less-than-quantity shipments made direct ordering prohibitive. The need for warehouses capable of providing rapid and economical inventory assortment became increasingly important. At the wholesale level, the warehouse became a customizing unit for filling retail orders. Alert firms developed integrated warehouse systems capable of providing increased retail service at reduced operating costs.

Improvements in warehousing at the wholesale level soon were adopted by materials managers. For manufacturers producing multiple products at many locations, warehousing offered a method of reducing raw material and part storage and handling costs, while maximizing production operations. A basic stock of all parts could be maintained at the warehouse, reducing the need to stockpile at each plant. Using volume shipments, products could be transported, when needed, to the warehouse and then to various plants at lower total expense.

A full line of products grouped at the same warehouse also opened the door for mixed carloads to customers. The mixed carload gained marketing importance because it enhanced the reputation of manufacturers who could provide this extra service. For the customer, mixed carloads had two distinct advantages. First, inventories could be reduced because the advantages of consolidation transportation were combined with full product assortments. Second, slow-turnover products could be ordered economically as part of the consolidated shipment. As competition increased, the manufacturer who could provide a mixed carload on 24-hour demand gained a competitive advantage.

Warehousing Functions

The warehouse contains materials, parts, and finished goods on the move. Because the operation is essentially a break-bulk and regrouping procedure, the objective is efficient movement of large quantities into the warehouse and customized orders out of the warehouse. A desirable practice is to have products arrive in and depart from the warehouse within a single working day.

The functions performed in the warehouse may be grouped into movement and storage categories. Movement is emphasized, with storage of secondary concern. Within these two broad categories, movement is divided into four subfunctions and storage into two subfunctions.

Movement Function

In the movement function, quantity shipments are reduced to customized assortments. The four handling activities are (1) receiving, (2) transfer, (3) order selection, and (4) shipping. Each will be discussed.

RECEIVING.   Merchandise and materials normally arrive at the warehouse in carload and truckload quantities. The first movement is unloading. In most warehouses, unloading is primarily manual except for raw materials. Limited automated and mechanized methods have been developed which are capable of adapting to varying product characteristics. Generally, one or two men unload the shipment and if the product is small enough to hand-stack, pallets are used to construct a unit load to maximize movement efficiency. In many cases, conveyors are employed to free vehicles rapidly. Larger merchandise may be unloaded directly from the car or truck for movement into the warehouse. As discussed previously, containerized shipment can reduce unloading time in many situations.

TRANSFER.   There are at least two and sometimes three transfer movements within a typical warehouse. The merchandise is first moved into the warehouse and placed in a designated spot. The inbound movement is handled by fork-lift trucks when pallets are used and fork-lift truck or other mechanical traction for larger unit loads.

A second internal move may be required prior to order assembly, depending upon the operating procedures of the warehouse. If merchandise is stored on pallets, some units may be moved from the receiving dock to a remote storage area. When these products are subsequently selected, they will once more be moved to a specialized selection area. When the merchandise is large or handled in full pallet loads, the second movement may be omitted. In the final transfer, the specialized assortment is moved from the warehouse to the loading dock.

SELECTION.   Selection is the primary function of the warehouse. At this point, movements are aimed at regrouping materials, parts, and products into assorted orders. For a large number of small products, one section of the warehouse may be established as a selection area. Automatic data processing may be used to facilitate billing accuracy. Order pickers then place all items billed on selection carts for transfer to the shipping area.

SHIPPING.   Shipping consists of checking and loading orders for outbound movement. As in receiving, shipments are handled manually in most systems. Shipping full pallet loads has become increasingly popular, as considerable time can be saved in vehicle loading. Some enterprises have experienced considerable transportation savings by shipping unit loads. However, damage in transit may be increased. When delivery trucks are not company-owned, the additional problem of returning empty pallets may offset some of the savings. A checking operation is required when the merchandise changes ownership as a result of shipment. Checking generally consists of item counts, but in some instances a piece-by-piece check for proper brand, size, and so on is necessary to assure proper receipt of all items.

Storage Function

In addition to processing custom or special orders, the warehouse performs two forms of storage: temporary and permanent.

TEMPORARY STORAGE.   As previously noted, primary emphasis is placed upon product flow in the warehouse. Regardless of inventory turnover, all goods received must be stored for some time period. Storage for basic inventory replenishment is referred to as *temporary storage*. Temporary storage duration will vary in different logistical systems, because elapsed time is based upon inventory replenishment. Temporary storage must provide a sufficient quantity of goods to satisfy demand and assure adequate safety reserves.

PERMANENT STORAGE.   *Permanent storage*, a somewhat misleading term, refers only to storage required in excess of inventory for normal replenishment. In some special situations, storage may be needed for several months. The logistical manager should understand the reasons for permanent storage. Warehouse managers should be encouraged to minimize permanent storage and concentrate upon maximum product flow. A modern warehouse stores goods in excess of normal replenishment requirements for five reasons. Each of these is considered to be a special case rather than normal operating procedure.

Seasonal Production.   Regardless of advances in production scheduling, some products are seasonal because of growing periods. If a firm engages in this type of processing, extensive storage may be required during specific periods. Special storage warehouses or public warehouses may satisfy this requirement. Even if the firm does not engage in production but only in retail distribution, it may be necessary to purchase large quantities of seasonal products to assure a year-round supply. Canned tomato products are an example.

Erratic Demand.   When a product with an extreme demand fluctuation is handled, it may be necessary to carry additional supplies to satisfy heavy demand requirements. An example is air conditioners. Because air conditioners are expensive items, retailers prefer to carry small inventories. When a period of high temperatures begins, the manufacturer has a very limited time to distribute additional units.

Conditioning.   Conditioning is required for some products at the warehouse. These products may be retained for a limited period of time in excess of temporary storage. The ripening of bananas is a case in point. Modern food distribution centers include ripening rooms to hold products until they reach peak quality.

Speculation.   The warehouse seldom stores goods for speculative purposes. The degree to which this activity takes place will depend upon the materials purchased. For example, it is not unusual to store grain for speculative reasons.

Realization of Special Discount.   The distribution warehouse often requires space for storage of products offered at special discount. The material manager may be able to realize a substantial reduction during a specific period of the year. Under such conditions the warehouse holds inventories additional to those required for normal replenishment. Manufacturers of fertilizer, toys, and lawn furniture often attempt to shift the warehousing burden to customers by offering off-season discounts.

Storage Alternatives

In considering warehouse alternatives, three arrangements are available: (1) private, (2) public, and (3) combinations of the two. A private warehouse facility is one operated and managed by the enterprise which owns the merchandise handled and stored at the facility. A public warehouse, in contrast, is operated as a service business and offers a range of services on a fee basis.

Public Warehouses

Public warehouses are used extensively in logistical systems. Almost any combination of services can be arranged with the operator of a public warehouse. A classification of public warehouses has been developed based upon the range of specialized operations performed.[22] *Public warehouses* are classified as (1) general merchandise, (2) refrigerated, (3) special commodity, (4) bonded, (5) household goods and furniture, and (6) field warehouse. Of course, many public warehouses offer combinations of these.

In physical distribution, emphasis is placed on the use of public facilities to assist in the development of product assortments. In materials management, emphasis is placed on storage. This treatment is concerned with the distribution capabilities of public warehouses. The distribution public warehouse performs six specialized services: (1) stock spotting, (2) distribution assortment, (3) break-bulk, (4) in-transit mixing, (5) consolidation, and (6) processing. Each of these specialized services will be reviewed.

STOCK SPOTTING. The stock-spotting capabilities of public warehouses are most often used in physical distribution systems. In addition, manufacturers with limited or highly seasonal product lines are partial to this service. Rather than placing inventories year-round in warehouse facilities or shipping direct from manufacturing plants, delivery time can be substantially reduced by advanced movement to strategic cities. Thus a consolidated carload of the firm's product line is *spot-stocked* in a public warehouse, from which customer orders are filled. Utilizing public warehouse facilities for stock-spotting allows inventories to be placed in a variety of markets adjacent to key customers just prior to a maximum period of seasonal sales.

DISTRIBUTION ASSORTMENT. A public warehouse used for complete line *assorting* may be employed by either a manufacturer, wholesaler, or retailer. In this case the public warehouse performs the complete range of warehousing functions and carries stock year-round. Products are stocked in anticipation

---

[22] This form of classification was first developed in John H. Frederick, *Using Public Warehouses* (Philadelphia: Chilton Book Company, 1957). For more detailed discussions, see Charles A. Taft, *Management of Physical Distribution and Transportation*, 5th ed. (Homewood, Ill.: Richard D. Irwin, Inc., 1972), pp. 174–76, and Kenneth B. Ackerman, *Warehousing* (Washington, D.C.: Traffic Service Corporation, 1977).

of customer orders, with customized assortments selected upon order receipt.

The differential between stock spotting and complete line assortment is the degree of warehouse utilization. A firm following a stock-spotting policy will normally have a narrower product line and will place stocks in a wider range of markets on a seasonal basis in comparison to one which uses public warehouses for distribution assortment.

BREAK-BULK. *Break-bulk* public warehouse service is a form of assistance in a logistical system which does not involve storage. A manufacturer can combine orders of different customers within the market area into one consolidated shipment and ship to a public warehouseman. The public warehouse then separates the individual orders and arranges for local delivery. Using a public warehouse in a break-bulk capacity results in volume freight rates and reduces the difficulty of controlling a number of small shipments to a given market.

IN-TRANSIT MIXING. *In-transit mixing* is similar to break-bulk. When product plants are geographically separated, overall transportation charges and warehouse requirements can be reduced with this service. In-transit mixing may involve shipments to one or more customers. Carloads or truckloads are shipped from production plants to the public warehouse, which provides the mixing service. Each large shipment enjoys the lowest possible transportation rate, and the involved products are designated to be mixed for specific customers at the public warehouse.

Upon arrival at the public warehouse, railcars or trucks are unloaded and the proper combination of each product is selected. Shipment is then made to individual customers. The process of in-transit mixing is illustrated in Figure 7-5.

The economies of in-transit mixing have been increased by the development of special transportation tariffs.[23] These special tariffs are modifications of basic storage in-transit privileges. Products are shipped from production plants, mixed and combined with products currently stored at the public warehouse, and then transported to customers under a special through rate. Although freight rates are applied on a commodity basis rather than on a mixed or freight-all-kinds rating, this special provision reduces total freight charges. Specialized public warehouse services of break-bulk and in-transit mixing have the net effect of reducing product storage.

CONSOLIDATION. A relatively new type of service offered by public warehousing is the *multimanufacturer consolidated shipment*. Under this arrangement, the public warehouse consolidates merchandise orders from a number of manufacturers destined for a specific customer as a single transportation shipment. The obvious benefits are the realization of the lowest possible transportation rate and reduced congestion at a customer's receiving dock.

---

[23] See Chapter 5, pages 137–138.

FIGURE 7-5
Public Warehouse In-Transit Mixing

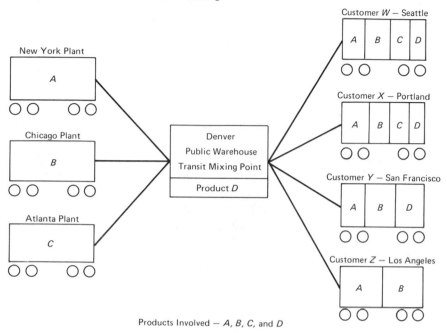

Products Involved — A, B, C, and D

In order to effectively consolidate, each participating manufacturer must be using the public warehouse for either stock spotting or distribution assortment in their physical distribution system. The primary benefit of consolidation is that it combines the logistical flow of several shippers to a specific market area. Through the use of a warehouse consolidation program each individual shipper enjoys lower total distribution cost than could be realized on an individual basis.

PROCESSING.   Recently, a great deal of attention has been directed to the prospect of using public warehouses for selected *light manufacturing* and *processing* activities. Using this procedure, form change can be *postponed* in anticipation of demand formulation. For example, vegetables can be cooked, frozen, packed in large containers, and shipped to field warehouses. Actual packaging into consumer and institutional packs can be postponed until actual rates of inventory usage are experienced.

This example of postponement has two advantages. First, packaging in advance can be reduced to the point of lowest possible risk. Second, overall inventories can be reduced by using the same product to support a number of stockkeeping units.

The concept of postponement has broad implications for system design, which are discussed in Chapters 9 and 15. The important point here is that economic benefits can be realized by services available from public warehouses.

In conclusion, note that a great many of the services available from public warehouses work to eliminate the need for storage. This adaptation of traditional services to contemporary needs is an excellent example of the role of intermediary specialists in modern logistical management.

Private Warehouses

A *private warehouse* may be owned or leased. The decision as to which best fits an individual firm's requirements is essentially financial. Often it is not possible to find a warehouse facility for lease which fits the requirements of a firm. If a considerable amount of material handling is planned for a warehouse, a readily available building may not be conducive to efficient handling. As a general rule, an efficient warehouse should be designed around a material-handling system in order to encourage maximum ease of product flow.

Real estate developers are increasingly willing to build distribution warehouses to a firm's specifications on a leased basis. Such custom construction is available in many markets on a lease arrangement as short as five years.

Combination Systems

As would be expected, many enterprises utilize a combination of public and private distribution warehouses. A private facility is used to cover basic year-round requirements, and public facilities are used to handle peak requirements. Figure 7-6 illustrates the combined concept.

A public warehouse charges on the basis of packages or hundredweight stored or handled. Such charges normally exceed the cost of warehousing equivalent volumes in a private facility. Public warehouse rates must be adjusted to the seasonal demands of a variety of customers. Full utilization of public

FIGURE 7-6
Combined Private and Public Warehouse Facilities

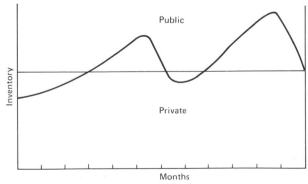

warehouse space through the cycle of annual activities of all customers is remote. For this reason the rate structure of a public warehouse used only for peak overflows will reflect lower efficiencies than a private warehouse designed to handle stable demand.

As a planning rule, if a private warehouse is used it should be designed for full-capacity utilization between 75 and 85 per cent of the time. Thus from 15 to 25 per cent of the time, space will be available to accommodate peak requirements. An enterprise may find that private distribution warehouses can be used best in specific markets, with public warehouses preferable in other market situations. In logistical system design the objective is to determine whatever combination of the two types of warehouses most economically meet customer service objectives.

Comparative Benefits of Public Versus Private Warehouses

In recent years, the traditional role of public warehouses as supplemental storage facilities has changed dramatically.[24] The nature of modern business places a great deal of emphasis on product turnover and the ability to satisfy orders rapidly. To achieve these two benefits, flexibility must be maintained within the logistical structure. Public warehouse management has been very progressive in designing warehouse systems which can be placed at the immediate disposal of logistics managers with little fixed or long-term commitment.

Many public warehouses have formed associations which allow a firm to purchase total order processing and local delivery systems in a number of cities across the United States. In addition to basic warehousing, the associations provide specialized services, such as inventory control and billing.

Some larger public warehouse firms also are expanding their operations to encompass a network of warehouses located in key markets. This trend has the ultimate potential to offer manufacturers a service which is effectively a logistical utility. Under the utility concept, all functions required to service a firm's customers are provided by the public logistics specialist. That is, transportation, order processing, inventory control, warehousing, and selected administrative matters are provided as an integrated service. Although still in the formulation stages, indications are that these multifacility public warehouse networks under one management coordination will increase substantially in number and geographic coverage during the coming decade.

Such innovative trends in public warehousing services are important in the appraisal of whether or not to use public or private warehouse facilities. Traditionally, the decision to use public warehouses was based on relative storage economics and flexibility. In the future, the choice will be based on

---

[24] For an expanded discussion, see Bernard J. La Londe et al., "The Public Warehouse Decision: An Interim Report" (Columbus, Ohio: Division of Research Reprint Series, College of Administrative Science, The Ohio State University, 1973).

the public warehouse organization's ability to perform necessary logistical tasks more effectively and efficiently than private systems.

From an analytical viewpoint, the private versus public warehouse decision is analogous to the procurement decision on making or buying component parts.[25] Private warehouse facilities require substantial investment, and such commitments should provide the same rate of return as other investments of corporate capital. If such prospects do not exist from a total cost perspective, the use of public warehouse specialists should be carefully examined.

A final consideration regarding the use of public warehouse associations and single-ownership networks is the natural reluctance of firms to turn over responsibility for an area as vital as logistics. The risks—potential loss of control, problems in customer goodwill, and the inability to rapidly replace or supplement a system that fails to perform—are the prime reasons given by logistical managers for not adopting single-management public warehouse networks. Although many organizations employ public warehouses exclusively, each facility is under individual management, with logistical network control resting with the manufacturing, wholesaling, or retail enterprise. Whether or not future conditions will change the prevailing attitude and reluctance of public warehouse customers remains to be seen.

Private Warehouse Establishment

Establishing a warehouse involves a series of decisions, which, in total, mold the structure within which the logistical functions will be performed. The following discussion is management-oriented. Managers who have not previously experienced warehouse establishment often repeat the mistakes of others. This brief review provides a working background for managers and indicates the type of information required to establish a warehouse. Decisions made in one area will influence decisions in other areas. Such interrelationships must be recognized to develop an integrated warehouse system.

Planning the Distribution Warehouse

The first decisions confronted are those related to planning the warehouse. The modern concept that a warehouse is an enclosure for a material-handling operation requires detailed analysis before the size, type, and shape of the enclosure can be determined. Too often the building is designed and under construction before the material-handling system is selected. A master plan of related areas such as material handling, layout, space requirement, and design should be developed, and a specific site for the warehouse selected.

---

[25] See Chapter 12, pages 370–372, for discussion and example of make-versus-buy methodology. Taft treats the subject in the context of the warehouse decision. See Taft, op. cit., Chap. 8.

Construction decisions are the most rigid in implementation. They establish the character of the warehouse, which, in turn, determines the degree of attainable handling efficiency.

SITE SELECTION. Location analysis techniques are available to assist in selecting a general area for warehouse location.[26] Once locational analysis is completed, a specific building site must be selected. Three areas in a community may be considered for location: the commercial zone, outlying areas served by motor truck only, and the central or downtown area.

The primary factors in site selection are the availability of services and cost. The cost of procurement is the most important governing factor. A warehouse need not be located in a major industrial area. In city after city, one can observe warehouses among industrial plants, in industrial parks, and in areas zoned for light or heavy industry. This is not necessary, because most warehouses can operate legally under the restrictions placed upon commercial property.

Beyond procurement costs, such setup and operating expenses as rail sidings, utility hookups, taxes, insurance rates, and highway access require evaluation. These expenses vary between sites. For example, a food-distribution firm recently rejected what otherwise appeared to be a totally satisfactory site because of insurance rates. The site was located near the end of the water main. During most of the day, adequate water supplies were available to handle operational and emergency requirements. The only possible water problem occurred during two short periods each day. From 6:30 A.M. to 8:30 A.M. and from 5:00 P.M. to 7:00 P.M., the demand for water along the line was so great that a sufficient supply was not available to handle emergencies. Because of this deficiency, abnormally high insurance rates were required, and the site was rejected.

Several other requirements must be satisfied before the site is purchased. The site must offer adequate room for expansion. Necessary utilities must be available. The site's soil must be capable of supporting the structure and must be sufficiently high to afford proper drainage. Additional requirements may be situationally necessary, depending upon the structure to be constructed. In summary, the final selection of the site must be preceded by extensive analysis.

PRODUCT-MIX CONSIDERATIONS. A second and independent area of quantitative analysis is a precise study of the products to be distributed through the proposed warehouse. The design and operation of a proposed warehouse is related directly to the character of the product mix. Each product should be analyzed in terms of annual sales, stability of demand, weight, bulk, and packaging. It is also desirable to determine the total size, bulk, and weight of the average order processed through the warehouse. These data provide necessary information for determining requirements in warehouse space,

[26] See Chapter 11, pages 339–347.

design and layout, material-handling equipment, operating procedures, and controls.

EXPANSION.   Future expansion is often neglected when an enterprise is considering an immediate extension of its warehouse facilities. Inclusion of a warehouse component into the logistical structure should be based partially upon estimated requirements for future operations. Well-managed organizations often establish 5- to 10-year expansion plans. Such expansion considerations may require purchase or option of a site three to five times the size of the initial structure.

Special construction is often considered to ease expansion without seriously affecting normal operations. Some walls may be constructed of semipermanent materials to allow easy removal. Floor areas, designed to support heavy movements, are extended to these walls in a manner that facilitates expansion.

SELECTION OF MATERIAL-HANDLING SYSTEM.   A material-handling system is one of the initial considerations. Movement is the main function within a warehouse. Consequently, the warehouse is viewed as a structure designed to facilitate maximum product flow. Earlier in the chapter, material-handling alternatives ranging from mechanized to automated were discussed in detail. It is important to stress that the material-handling system must be selected early in the warehouse design stage.

WAREHOUSE LAYOUT.   Layout consists of developing a floor plan that will facilitate product flow, and the layout of a warehouse depends on the proposed system of material handling. The layout and the material-handling system must be planned together.

It is difficult to generalize because of the variety of layouts available to fit specific needs. If pallets are utilized, the first step is to determine the size of the pallets. A pallet of nonstandard size may be desirable for specialized products but, whenever possible, standardized pallets should be used because of their lower cost. The most common sizes are 40 by 48 inches and 32 by 40 inches.[27] In general, the larger the pallet load, the lower the cost of movement per pound or package over a given distance. One fork-lift-truck operator can move a large load in the same time and with the same effort required to move a smaller load. The packages to be placed on the pallet and the related patterns will determine, to a certain extent, the size of pallet best suited to the operation. Regardless of the size finally selected, management should adopt one size for the total operation.

The second step in planning a layout involves the positioning of pallets. There are two methods: (1) ninety degree, or square, and (2) angle. Ninety-

---

[27] In reference to pallets, it is customary to name the dimension that is placed lengthwise of the forks in the lift truck first. Many pallets are designed with four-way entry; consequently, the two dimensions of the pallet may be used interchangeably.

FIGURE 7-7
Alternative Methods of Pallet Placement

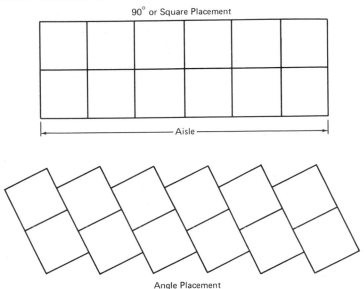

degree, or square, placement means that the pallet is positioned perpendicular to the aisle. Angular placement means that the pallet is placed at an angle. The angles employed range from 10 degrees to 45 degrees, with $26\frac{1}{2}$ degrees most common. Figure 7-7 shows the two methods of positioning. The square method was used in early warehouses because of layout ease. The angle method, however, offers the potential for greater operating efficiency. Aisle width can be reduced because the fork-lift truck can position a pallet in the angle placement system without making a full 90-degree turn. Operating efficiency is increased because of the ease of placement resulting from the shorter turn. Under certain conditions, reduced aisles offset space losses due to angling. The method of pallet placement in a particular layout will depend upon the specific problems experienced.[28] Often the two methods can be combined to arrive at the most efficient overall layout.

Once all details have been isolated, the equipment selected must be integrated into a final layout. The path of product flow will depend upon the material-handling system. To indicate the relationship between material handling and layout, two systems and their respective layouts are reviewed. The following illustrations represent only two of many possible layouts.

[28] For a detailed discussion see Donald J. Bowersox, "Resolving the Pallet Layout Controversy," *Transportation and Distribution Management*, June 1962, pp. 43–46; and Ronald H. Ballou, *The Consideration of Angular Pallet Layout to Optimize Warehouse Space Utilization* (unpublished Master's thesis, The Ohio State University, Columbus, Ohio, 1963).

FIGURE 7-8
Layout A

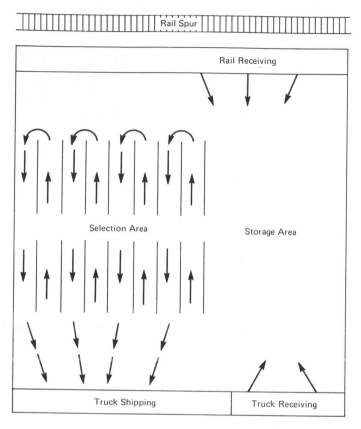

Layout A. Layout A, Figure 7-8, represents a material-handling system with related layout utilizing fork-lift trucks for inbound and transfer movements and tractor-trailers for order selection. The products are assumed adaptable to a palletized operation. This layout is greatly simplified, because offices, special areas, and details are omitted.

The floor plan in layout A is approximately square. The advocates of this particular system feel that a square structure provides the best plan for operating efficiency. As indicated earlier, in some material-handling systems, products are clustered in a specific area of the warehouse for order selection. Such is the case in layout A. This area is labeled the selection area, and its primary purpose is to minimize the distance order pickers must cover when selecting an order.

The selection area is supported by a storage area. When products are received by rail or truck, they are palletized and placed in the storage area. The selection area is then replenished from storage as required. When a compact selection area is utilized, products are placed in this area according to weight, bulk, and velocity characteristics, in an attempt to minimize outbound-movement problems. Special orders are then accumulated by the order selector moving a tractor and trailer through the selection area. The arrows in layout A indicate the flow of product movements.

FIGURE 7-9
Layout B

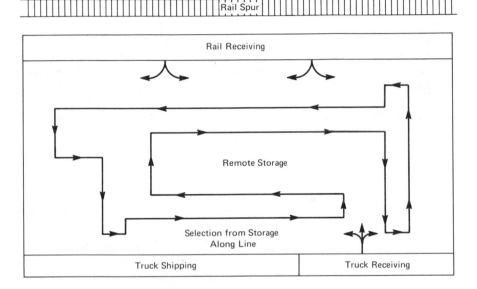

Layout B.   Layout B, Figure 7-9, represents a material-handling system with related layout utilizing fork-lift trucks for inbound and transfer movements and a continuous-movement towline for order selection. Again, products are assumed adaptable to pallets, and the illustration is greatly simplified. The floor plan is rectangular. In a system with a continuous-movement towline, the special selection area is omitted; selection is made directly from storage.[29] Products are moved from rail and truck receiving areas into storage areas adjacent to the towline. The orders are then selected directly from storage and loaded onto four-wheel trucks, which are propelled by the towline. Merchandise is placed in the storage area to minimize inbound movement. Because the towline moves all products with equal efficiency, the weight, bulk, and velocity considerations are not important for outbound movement. The arrows in layout B indicate major product movements. The line in the center of the layout illustrates the path of the towline.

[29] With the minor exception that some products have bulk storage in the center of the warehouse. Such bulk or remote storage occurs when extra-heavy stocks of a given product are procured or for other reasons leading to more permanent storage. See page 213.

As indicated, both layouts A and B are greatly simplified; their purpose is to indicate the relationship of material-handling systems and warehouse layouts.

PRECISE DETERMINATION OF WAREHOUSE SPACE. Several methods are used to determine the exact amount of required warehouse space. Each starts with a sales forecast or some projection of the total tonnage expected during a given period. This tonnage is then used to develop base and safety stocks. Some require consideration of firm and peak utilization rates; others do not. Neglecting utilization rates can result in overbuilding, with corresponding cost increases. It is important to note, however, that one of the major complaints of warehouse supervisors is the underestimate of warehouse size requirements by management. A good practice is to allow 10 per cent additional space to account for increased volume, new products, and so on. Size determination techniques are discussed in Chapter 12.[30]

WAREHOUSE DESIGN. Warehouse design is a special area of planning usually contracted to an architect. Design and construction characteristics must not hinder product flow. Consequently, management must communicate to the architect the need for unrestricted movement. In order to design a warehouse properly, the architect will require specifications for the size of the structure, layout, and predetermined path of material-handling equipment. The material-handling specialist must work closely with the design specialist to develop an integrated system.

Careful attention should be paid to placement of overhead obstructions such as lights, steampipes, sprinkler systems, and heating ducts. These items must be kept above the tiering height if 20 feet of clearance is planned for the material-handling operation. The placement of supporting columns is also an important design consideration. Generally, some latitude exists in positioning, depending upon which ways the columns run in relation to the supporting walls of the structure. Column placement is important to ensure a minimum of restricted storage bays. The floor areas, which must be specially treated for sufficient hardness, depend upon the predetermined path of the material-handling equipment.

These items illustrate just a few reasons why the warehouse must be designed to facilitate product flow. The modern warehouse is founded on the efficient use of every cubic foot of space and available material-handling equipment, and the structure should be designed to stimulate this efficiency.

THE INTEGRATED PLAN. Once management has selected a site and planned the size, layout, material-handling equipment, and design, construction may begin. A small-scale physical model of the proposed structure, using a model and templates, provides a clear three-dimensional image of the proposed structure. A scale of $\frac{1}{4}$ inch equal to 1 foot is a standard size. Such a model will

[30] See Chapter 12, pages 380–386.

help pinpoint minor shortcomings of the proposed structure so that modifications can be made prior to construction.

Initiating Warehouse Operations

To initiate operation, management must stock merchandise, hire personnel, develop work procedures, establish a method of billing and inventory control, and initiate a system of local delivery.

STOCKING THE WAREHOUSE. The ideal procedure to follow when stocking a warehouse is to obtain the complete inventory prior to initiating operations. The individual products to be distributed through the warehouse and the quantities of each in the basic inventory were determined when the warehouse was planned. The problem in stocking is to schedule the arrival of this merchandise to achieve an orderly inbound flow. The time required to initially stock a warehouse depends upon the number and quantity of products to be handled. For a warehouse containing 4,000 or more products, it may take over 30 days to complete initial stocking.

In the storage area, products are assigned in full pallet loads to a predetermined area. Specific products that fall into a designated area can be placed at any point within the area. In the selection area, a coding system using numerical classification and a slot position is used to identify products and positions.

The numerical classification is assigned upon product arrival and is retained as long as the product is held in inventory. The assignment of slots refers to the floor position where merchandise is placed. A slot is merely a predetermined pallet position. Two methods of slot assignment are used: variable and fixed. The variable-slot system allows the product position to be changed each time a new shipment arrives in order to utilize warehouse space efficiently. With the fixed-slot placement system, a permanent position is assigned to each product placed in the selection area. The product retains this position as long as volume of movement maintains the same level. If volume increases or decreases, the product is reassigned. Fixed placement has an advantage over variable-slot placement because it provides a method of immediately locating a product. Regardless of which slot system is employed, each inbound product should be assigned an initial location.

PERSONNEL TRAINING. Hiring and training personnel qualified to operate a warehouse presents a serious problem. Regardless of how efficient the proposed system is in theory, in practice it will be only as good as the operating personnel. Proper training of personnel is necessary to ensure results from the system.

Training is not a difficult task if executed properly. The full work force should begin work prior to the arrival of merchandise. People hired for specific assignments should be fully indoctrinated in their jobs and the role they play in the total system. Examination of the scale model and tours of the actual structure will familiarize the personnel with the system.

After indoctrination, each *group* of employees should be given specific training. Personnel hired to operate a warehouse may be grouped in the following categories: administrators, supervisors, selectors, equipment operators, laborers, and miscellaneous workers (maintenance, salvage, etc.).

When initial stocking begins, the work force receives actual experience in merchandise handling. Normally, the manufacturer supplying the basic material-handling equipment sends an instructor to help train equipment operators. Once the basic inventory is in stock, it is a good practice to spend some time running sample orders through the warehouse. Simulated orders can be selected and loaded into delivery trucks and the merchandise may then be treated as a new arrival and transferred back into stock.

DEVELOPING WORK PROCEDURES.   The development of work procedures goes hand in hand with the training of warehouse personnel. Design of a material-handling system generally includes work procedures. It is management's responsibility to see that all personnel understand and use these procedures.

In the mechanized warehouse, approximately 65 per cent of the floor personnel are employed in some phase of order selection. Modifications of two basic methods of order picking are employed in distribution warehouses: (1) individual selection, and (2) area selection. Under the individual system, one selector completes a total order. This system is not used widely. Its primary application is when a large number of small orders are selected for shipment on the same truck. Under the more commonly used area selection system, each selector is assigned a certain portion of the warehouse and many selectors handle the same order. Because each has a thorough knowledge of the selection area, no time is lost in locating items.

Specific procedures must also be established for receiving and shipping. Merchandise received must be checked to ensure its inclusion into the inventory accounting system. If pallets are used, the merchandise must be stacked in patterns to ensure maximum load stability. Personnel working in shipping must have a knowledge of loading procedures. In specific types of operations, particularly when merchandise changes ownership, items must be checked during loading.

Work procedures are not restricted to floor personnel. A definite procedure must be established for proper handling of inventory control records. Most firms employ some type of automatic data-processing equipment. The purchasing or reordering of merchandise for the warehouse can cause a serious operational problem if proper procedures are lacking. Normally, there is little cooperation between buyers and the warehouse personnel if the facility is operating below capacity. The buyer tends to purchase in the quantity that will afford the best price, and little attention is given to the problem of space utilization. Under such conditions, it will not be long until the warehouse is overstocked and demurrage charges accumulate. The problem can be avoided if the proper procedures are employed.

Buyers should be required to check with the warehouse manager before any abnormally large orders or new products are purchased. Some feel so strongly about this point that buyers are required to obtain a space allotment for all merchandise ordered. An equally serious problem is the quantity of cases ordered at a given time. The buyer should be required to order in pallet-multiple quantities. For example, if a product is placed upon pallets in a pattern containing 50 cases, the buyer should order in multiples of 50. If an order is placed for 110 cases, upon arrival the cases will fill two pallets plus ten on a third pallet. The extra 10 cases will require the same space as 50 and will require the same amount of movement effort. These illustrations indicate a few of the operational bottlenecks that can result from poor work procedures.

SECURITY SYSTEMS.　In a broad sense, security in a warehouse involves protection against merchandise pilferage and deterioration. Each form of security is worth management attention.

Pilferage Protection.　Protection against theft of merchandise has become a major factor in warehouse operations.[31] Such protection is required with respect to employees and as a result of the increased vulnerability of firms to riots and civil disturbances.

All normal precautions employed throughout the enterprise should be strictly enforced at each warehouse. Security begins at the fence. As standard procedure, only authorized personnel should be permitted into the facility and surrounding grounds, and entry to the warehouse yard should be controlled through a single gate. Without exception, no private automobile—regardless of management rank or customer status—should be allowed to penetrate the warehouse yard.

To illustrate the importance of the guidelines stated, the following actual experience may be helpful. The particular firm enforced the rule that no private vehicles should be permitted in the warehouse yard. Exceptions were made for two handicapped office employees. One night after work, one of these employees accidentally discovered a bundle taped under one fender of his car. Subsequent checking revealed that the car was literally a delivery truck. The matter was promptly reported to security, who informed the employee not to alter any packages taped to the car and to continue parking inside the yard. Over the next several days, the situation was fully uncovered, with the ultimate arrest and conviction of seven warehouse employees who confessed to stealing over $100,000 of company merchandise. The firm would have been better off if it would have originally purchased the small transport vehicle that was procured after the incident to provide rides from the regular parking lots to the office for the handicapped employees.

Shortages are always a major consideration in warehouse operations. Many

---

[31] Although no direct estimate of warehouse pilferage in the United States is available, the U.S. Department of Transportation estimated that annual losses due to cargo theft and pilferage ranged from $1.0 to $1.5 billion in 1972. See *1972 National Transportation Report* (Washington, D.C.: U.S. Department of Transportation, 1972), p. 15. In 1977, a conservative estimate of $2.0 billion annual loss was provided by a D.O.T. official.

are honest mistakes in order selection and shipment, but the purpose of security is to restrict theft from all angles. The majority of thefts occur during normal working hours.

Computerized inventory-control and order-processing systems help in the protection of merchandise being carried out the doors. No merchandise should be released from the warehouse unless accompanied by a computer-release document. If samples are authorized for the use of salespersons, this merchandise should be separate from other inventory. Not all pilferage is on a one-by-one basis. Numerous cases have been discovered where organized efforts between warehouse personnel and truckers resulted in deliberate overpicking, or high-for-low-value product substitution in order to move unauthorized merchandise out of the warehouse "in system." Employee rotation, total counts, and occasional complete line-item checks can reduce vulnerability to such collaboration.

A final comment is in order concerning the increased incidence of hijacking over-the-road trailer loads from yards or while in transit. Hijacking has become a major concern during the past decade. Over-the-road hijack prevention is primarily a law-enforcement matter, but in-yard total unit theft can be eliminated by tight security provisions.

Product Deterioration. Within the warehouse, a number of factors can reduce a product or material to a nonusable or nonmarketable state. The most obvious form of product deterioration is damage from careless transfer or storage. Another major form of deterioration is noncompatibility of products stored in the same facility.

Of concern at this point is the deterioration that results from improper warehouse work procedures. For example, when pallets of merchandise are stacked in high cubes, a marked change in humidity or temperature can cause packages supporting the stack to fall. The warehouse represents an environment that must be carefully controlled or measured to provide proper product protection.

A constant concern is the carelessness of warehouse employees. In this respect, the fork-lift truck may well be the worst enemy. Regardless of how often fork-lift truck operators are warned against carrying overloads, some still attempt such shortcuts when not properly supervised. In one situation, a stack of four pallets was dropped off the fork truck at the receiving dock of a food warehouse. Standard procedure was to move merchandise two pallets per load. The value of the damaged merchandise exceeded the average daily profit of two supermarkets. Product deterioration from careless handling within the warehouse is a form of loss that cannot be insured against. Such losses constitute 100 per cent cost with no compensating revenue.

BILLING AND INVENTORY CONTROL. Most firms handling a large number of products with varied turnover characteristics find it economical to employ computers for billing and inventory control. Inputs are prepared for each case of merchandise received at the warehouse. When an order is received, products are listed in order of warehouse placement. For example, if an area method of selection is employed, the order will be grouped by areas and listed in either numerical or slot order for the selector. It is possible to print an inventory of merchandise on hand at any given time. The computer inventory must be checked at times against a physical inventory in order to ensure accuracy in receiving and shipping records.

INITIATING AND PROGRAMMING LOCAL DELIVERY. Most shipments from distribution warehouses are made to customers by truck. When private trucking is utilized, a problem is encountered in scheduling movements to ensure maximum utilization at minimum cost. Routing techniques discussed in Chapter 12 have been developed to assist management in solving this problem.[32] In programming local deliveries, the objective is to minimize the cost of distribution, which may be expressed as a function of vehicle mileage, for example.

SAFETY AND MAINTENANCE. Accident prevention is a paramount concern within the warehouse. A well-balanced safety program should include constant examination of work procedures and equipment to locate and correct unsafe conditions before they result in accidents. Accidents occur when workers become careless or are exposed to mechanical and/or physical hazards. The floors of a warehouse may cause accidents if not properly cleaned. During normal operation, rubber and glass deposits collect along aisles and, from time to time, broken cases will cause product seepage onto the floor. Proper cleaning procedures can reduce the risk of accidents from these hazards. Work environment safety has become a major concern of government under such programs as OSHA and cannot be neglected by management.

A preventive maintenance program is necessary for material-handling equipment. Unlike production machines, movement equipment is not stationary, and it is easy to neglect proper maintenance. A preventive maintenance program requiring a periodic check of all handling equipment should be installed.

MEASURING WAREHOUSE EFFICIENCY. Maintaining warehouse efficiency requires measurement techniques and standards for evaluation. Several measures of warehouse efficiency are available. The two most popular are physical and dollar evaluations.

Physical Systems of Efficiency Measurement. Physical systems of measurement consist of unit and weight evaluations. For example, a unit measure may be cases moved per work-hour or pallets per work-hour. Generally, a tabulation is made of units handled in each functional area of the warehouse. The physical unit system of measurement is also a convenient method for evaluating individual employees.

[32] See Chapter 12, pages 398–410.

Weight systems employ a popular measure referred to as tons per work-hour (usually written TPWH). TPWH may be computed for the total warehouse or for individual functional areas. Normally the TPWH figure for the total warehouse is obtained by adding together the tons of merchandise received (TR) and shipped (TS) and then dividing the sum by the number of total direct handling hours. The formula is

$$\text{TPWH} = \frac{\text{TR} + \text{TS}}{\text{hours}}$$

In some special cases where the shipment is by truck, it is not necessary to include loading time. Normally, the merchandise is delivered to the dock, and the motor carrier assumes the responsibility for loading. When this is the case, the TPWH should be figured excluding loading hours.

Dollar System of Efficiency Measurement. The most widely used dollar measure is one expressing warehouse expense as a percentage of the cost of merchandise delivered to the warehouse during a given period. Weighting the relative dollar figures to a percentage figure partially omits the problem of changing dollar values between time periods. The problem of different rates of change in prices and wages still exists. The dollar system is also inadequate for measuring efficiency between two warehouse systems because of regional cost differences.

MEASUREMENT STANDARDS. The selection of standards presents a delicate management problem. The standard is the primary reason for measuring various activities. The various measures result in figures that may be compared to standards, thereby determining whether specific functions or employees deviate substantially from the expected level of activity.

A performance standard can be set only after one has a thorough knowledge of all particulars relating to the job. Extreme care should be taken in making warehouse comparisons on the basis of physical measures and related standards. Management should realize that there is no such thing as an absolute standard for measuring warehouse efficiency. Figures vary substantially between warehouses, depending upon methods of calculation and the various details of operation. Each warehouse should be considered as a special operation, and specific standards should be established on the basis of the potential of that operation. Physical standards do offer a convenient means of making internal employee comparisons. For example, order selectors may be evaluated to point out which workers are exceptionally fast or slow. The results of such an evaluation may be compared with accuracy figures to determine which selectors require additional training and supervision.

Regardless of which system of standards is employed, if applied to evaluate various workers, it should represent a reasonable goal rather than an optimum effort. Setting standards is a difficult problem which deserves management attention. Only if measuring techniques are consistently applied and performance standards realistically developed will management have a true picture of warehouse efficiency.

Summary

The primary concern of this chapter was to develop an integrated approach for the treatment of handling and storage. Materials handling facilitates flow throughout the logistical system. The activities of material handling are prime consumers of labor. Because labor productivity has been dropping, considerable attention is focused on the improvement of material handling efficiency.

The master carton is the nucleus of the material-handling function. Extreme care must be taken to prevent product design and marketing from dominating package design. Logistical system factors must also be considered. From a logistical perspective, the greater the degree of package standardization achieved, the more inherently efficient the material-handling function. To this end, a modular system of packaging is a noteworthy goal. The protective aspects of packaging consist of selecting a design and material capable of coping with physical and element environmental influences. Although absolute protection will in most cases not be necessary, the package should be scientifically designed to satisfy clear-cut protective specifications.

A great deal of attention is being directed to keeping freight on the move. A wide choice of handling equipment and systems is available to process individual master cartons and unit loads. All have one objective—to eliminate unnecessary handling. The choice among mechanized or automated handling systems depends upon the nature of the task confronted and the relative capital investment cost benefits.

While recent advancements in automated handling are encouraging, similar prospects are not materializing for containerization. The main advancements in domestic containerization are centered upon nonrigid containers and coordinated transport arrangements.

The warehousing concept has caused a dramatic change in the range of available logistical systems. By utilizing the principles of warehousing, better service often can be rendered at lower cost. When product storage is required, it can be accomplished at strategic locations in the product-flow pipeline. A wide variety of public warehouse capacity and services are available for hire in logistical operations.

With the completion of Chapter 7, each of the basic components of the logistical system have been covered in detail. The essence of integrated logistics is that decisions related to communication, transportation, inventory, and storage and handling be treated on a combined basis. Unfortunately, not all markets can support a warehouse operation. Therefore, the number of facilities, their location, and the product mix carried at each is a primary concern of logistical system design. Part III deals with the formulation of logistical policy and plans.

Questions

1. Discuss the role of master cartons in a material-movement system.
2. What benefits can be gained by a modular system of packaging?
3. In basic handling, describe the role of a unit load.
4. Why have automated handling systems failed to reach their potential?
5. What is the major justification for high-rise storage?
6. Discuss the differences between rigid and nonrigid containers. What is the role of shrink-wrapping in the development of unit loads?
7. What is meant by the statement that the warehouse should merely consist of a set of walls enclosing an efficient handling system?
8. Describe fixed- and variable-cost considerations of private versus public warehousing. Is this similar to the difference between private and common transportation carriers?
9. Discuss the importance of specialized services provided by public warehousemen in the formulation and design of a distribution system.
10. Under what conditions would one combine private and public warehousing in a single distribution system?

CHAPTER 8

Foundations of Logistical Policy— Total Cost Analysis

The essence of logistical management is to achieve balanced integration of all components in the logistical system. As indicated in Chapter 1, balanced operations must be achieved at three levels within the enterprise. First, within each of the operational areas of the overall logistical system the components of facility location, communication, transportation, inventory, and storage and material handling must be integrated. Next, to achieve maximum overall efficiency, physical distribution management, internal inventory transfer, and materials management must be coordinated into a corporate logistical effort. Finally, the total logistical effort must be coordinated and integrated with the marketing, manufacturing, and financial efforts of the enterprise.

The objective of Chapter 8 is to develop the framework for formulating logistical policy. As such, the contents of the chapter begin to synthesize the material of the first seven chapters and serve as the prerequisite to the discussion of service strategy. This chapter deals with the integration of the first two levels of a logistical system based upon total cost analysis. The spatial aspects of transportation are combined with the temporal aspects of inventory in a system integrated by total cost. Integration at the third or corporate level requires that desired performance criteria be planned within the constraints of available resources. Integration at this third level is reserved for Chapter 9.

The initial section of the chapter reviews the fundamental forces involved in system integration. In the following two sections spatial and temporal relationships are developed separately. In the second section the relationship of transportation and facility location is developed. The third section develops the relationship of inventory and facility location. In the fourth section the

237

total cost implications of transportation and inventory are integrated with respect to facility location. From a temporal and spatial viewpoint, integration is accomplished by quantification of total cost relationships. The final section deals with procedures and problems in implementing total cost analysis.

Logistical System Integration

As noted earlier, relationships within a logistical system can be classified as spatial or temporal.[1] The spatial structure relates to the combination of facilities and linkages. The temporal structure of the logistical network relates to inventory levels and flow rates. It is important to realize that a logistical system could be designed on the basis of either spatial or temporal economics. In fact, locational decisions traditionally have been solved without consideration of inventory level and flow rate.[2] The objective in such cases was the selection of a network of facilities that realized minimum transportation cost. Likewise, most attempts to plan inventory decisions assume as given the basic facility structure.[3]

From the viewpoint of logistical system design, the interrelationship of spatial and temporal factors should be evaluated on a simultaneous basis. One of the major contributions of logistical analysis to modern business practice has been the practical attainment of such simultaneous treatment.

Transportation Economies and Facility Location

Prior to the availability of low-cost overland transportation, most of the world's commerce was transported by water. During this early era, commercial activity centered around port cities, and overland transport of goods was costly and slow. For example, if a young lady in one of the far western states wanted to be married in an eastern store-purchased dress, the lead time for ordering could exceed 9 months. Although the need for fast and efficient transportation existed, it was not until the application of steam power to water and the invention of the steam locomotive in 1829 that the transportation technological revolution began in the United States. Today, the transportation system of the United States is a highly developed network of rail, water, air, highway, and pipeline services. Each transport alternative provides a different type of service which can be utilized within a logistical system.

[1] See following sections of this chapter. This material is based on Donald J. Bowersox, "The Integration of Spatial and Temporal Factors in Physical Distribution System Design," *Der Markt*, 1972/1, pp. 4–8.

[2] For example, see Edward J. Taaffe and Howard L. Gauthier, *Geography of Transportation* (Englewood Cliffs, N.J.: Prentice-Hall, Inc., 1973).

[3] For example, see Robert B. Fetter and Winston C. Dalleck, *Decision Models for Inventory Management* (Homewood, Ill: Richard D. Irwin, Inc., 1961).

The importance of transportation services to economic development has been recognized since at least the middle of the nineteenth century, when the German economist von Thünen developed "The Isolated State."[4] To von Thünen, the primary determinant of economic development was the price of land and the cost of transport to market. The price of land resulted from the relative cost of transport and the ability of a product to command a price capable of absorbing transport cost. His basic thesis was that the value of specific produce at the growing location decreases with distance from the primary selling market.

Following von Thünen, Weber generalized location theory from an agrarian to an industrial society.[5] Weber's theoretical system consisted of numerous consuming locations spread over an area and linked together by linear weight–distance transportation costs. With respect to materials, Weber developed the two major categories of localized and ubiquities. Ubiquities were those raw materials found in all locations which could not in themselves serve to command location. Localized raw materials consisted of mineral deposits found only in selected locations. Based upon an analysis of the relative weight of localized raw materials and finished products, Weber developed a "material index." The material index was a measure of the proportion of the weight of localized raw materials to the weight of the finished product. Each type of industry, based on the material index, could be assigned a "locational weight." Utilizing these two measures Weber generalized that specific industries would locate at the point of consumption if the manufacturing process was weight-gaining, near the point of raw-material deposits if the manufacturing process was weight-losing, and at an intermediate point or location of convenience if the manufacturing process was neither weight-gaining nor -losing.

Several location theorists followed von Thünen and Weber. The most notable contributions toward a general theory of location have been presented by Lösch, Hoover, Greenhut, Isard, and Webber.[6] All these authors have highlighted the importance of geographical specialization in industrial location, including a thorough development of the fundamental importance of transportation.

In the most basic sense, transport capacity makes goods and commodities available that must be mined or produced elsewhere. Without economical transportation a community would have to be self-sufficient. The consequence

---

[4] Joachim von Thünen, *The Isolated State* (Rostock, 1842–1863; reprinted Jena, 1921).

[5] Alfred Weber, *Theory of the Location of Industries*, Carl J. Friedrich (trans.) (Chicago: University of Chicago Press, 1928).

[6] August Lösch, *Die Räumliche Ordnung der Wirtschaft* (Jena: Gustav Fischer Verlag, 1940); Edgar M. Hoover, *The Location of Economic Activity* (New York: McGraw-Hill Book Company, 1938); Melvin L. Greenhut, *Plant Location in Theory and Practice* (Chapel Hill, N.C.: University of North Carolina Press, 1956); and W. Isard et al., *Methods of Regional Analysis: An Introduction to Regional Science* (New York: John Wiley & Sons, Inc., 1960); W. Isard, *Location and Space Economy* (Cambridge, Mass.: The MIT Press, 1968); and M. J. Webber, *Impact of Uncertainty on Location* (Cambridge, Mass.: The MIT Press, 1972).

would be limited variety of products, high prices, and inefficient utilization of resources.

From the vantage point of logistical planning, transportation links geographically dispersed manufacturing, warehousing, and market locations into an integrated system. As such, transportation provides spatial closure and permits specialization. Transportation should be viewed as cost-reducing in the sense that expenditures permit greater economies in the processes of manufacturing and marketing.

Warehouse Location Patterns

The prime locational decision in a logistical system design centers on warehousing. The warehouse exists if it can render service or cost advantages in a given market. Determination of the number and geographic locations of warehouses is determined by production locations and markets to be penetrated.

Warehouses represent one part of a firm's overall effort to gain time and place utility. From a total system viewpoint, retail or customer locations represent the final point of product distribution. Thus the warehouse location is justified only if it increases sales and marketing impact or reduces total cost.

Manufacturing locations are the originating point of the value-creation process. A refined body of knowledge concerning the location of manufacturing facilities has emerged over the years. Today, management can draw upon analytical sophistication tempered by sound theory to guide the selection of plant locations offering maximum economic and competitive benefits.[7]

Logically, three types of locational patterns evolve when warehouses are utilized. Using a classification developed by Hoover, these may be identified as market-positioned, production-positioned, or intermediately positioned.[8]

MARKET-POSITIONED WAREHOUSES. A market-positioned warehouse's functions are replenishment of inventory for retail stores and merchandise delivery to consumers. The warehouse, located near ultimate product consumption, affords maximum transport consolidation economies from distant shipping points with relatively short product movements in local delivery. The geographic market area served from a market-positioned warehouse depends on the required speed of inventory replenishment to customers, size of average order, and cost per ton of local delivery.

Market-positioned warehouses may be owned by the retailer, the manufacturer, or independently. The mission of the warehouse varies depending upon the ownership arrangement. Retailer-owned warehouses are designed to serve as break-bulk points for products purchased from various sources. Because the product line processed through retailer-owned warehouses is extremely

---

[7] Melvin L. Greenhut and H. Ohta, *Theory of Spatial Pricing and Market Areas* (Durham, N.C.: Duke University Press, 1975).
[8] Hoover, op. cit., p. 35.

wide, the magnitude of demand for a given product need not be much of the warehouse's total volume.

The average retail store, large or small, does not have sufficient demand to order inventory in consolidated quantities directly from manufacturers. Retail product lines, manufactured or processed at widely scattered manufacturing locations, are usually extensive. In order to obtain rapid inventory replenishment of this broad product line, the retailer normally requires the services of a warehouse.

The purpose of the warehouse is to consolidate purchases from distant procurement points and replenish inventory to retail outlets. A warehouse strategically located to provide a cost-and-service benefit to retail stores is best located near the outlets it serves. This allows maximum advantages of consolidated shipment with relatively short local delivery. Therefore, retail store location modifies warehouse location.

Good examples of market-positioned warehouses are found in the food industry. The modern food warehouse usually is located near the point of highest sales concentration. At this location, local deliveries are held to a minimum average length of haul. Delivery times determine the proximity of the warehouse to the most distant retail outlet. The Kroger Company, for example, operates two distribution warehouses to serve the Michigan market. If two-day or overnight service were acceptable, one warehouse could satisfy demand requirements. In the food industry, maximum local delivery of approximately 150 miles is desirable.

This description of market-positioned warehouses represents one location pattern. The basic premise, their location close to the market served, rests upon the need to replenish customer inventory rapidly and at the lowest cost.

PRODUCTION-POSITIONED WAREHOUSES. A production-positioned warehouse is located close to production plants in order to act as a collection point for products manufactured at different plants. The fundamental reason for production-positioned warehouses is the manufacturer's desire for maximum service to customers. Quantities of products from each plant are shipped to the collection center, from which customer orders are filled.

When customer orders are received, merchandise is shipped in the mixture necessary to satisfy customer requirements. Strategic location of warehouses with respect to manufacturing plants allows mixed carloads to move to customer locations at consolidated transport rates. A customized carload order may be shipped to a customer faster than smaller quantities, thus allowing rapid replenishment and lower basic inventories. This mixed-carload service stimulates purchase of products that would normally move under less-than-volume rates. Therefore, the advantage of a production-positioned warehouse is the ability to furnish superior service for a total product assortment. If a manufacturer can offer all products in custom assortments at consolidated transportation rates, a competitive differential advantage may be gained in customer service.

Several major food-processing firms currently operate production-positioned warehouses. Leading examples are Pillsbury, Johnson & Johnson, General Foods, and Nabisco. At Nabisco, a shipping branch warehouse is located adjacent to each bakery. Quantities of all major products are maintained at each warehouse, thereby allowing full-service shipments from each.

INTERMEDIATELY POSITIONED WAREHOUSES. Warehouses located between customers and manufacturing plants are classified as intermediately positioned. These warehouses, similar to production-positioned warehouses, find economic justification in increased customer service.

Industrial location theory points out that plants producing a particular product often must locate near required raw material.[9] For production economy reasons, firms may be faced with geographically decentralized production plants.

When products from two or more plants are sold to a single customer, a collection warehouse may be established at an intermediate location. By grouping all products in the line, a firm can deliver mixed shipments with the advantages noted earlier.

Warehouse Justification

From the preceding discussion it is clear that warehouses enter a logistical system only when a differential advantage results from their inclusion between manufacturing site and final product destination. Differential advantage gained by adding warehouses results from a distribution cost or service benefit to a given market.

ECONOMIC JUSTIFICATION. A basic economic principle underlying the use of warehouses to serve a market area is consolidated shipment. A manufacturer may initially sell f.o.b. over the market area. However, if the shipment tends to be smaller than that necessary to enjoy volume rates, economic justification may exist for establishing a warehouse.

For example, assume that the average shipment size is 500 pounds and the rate between the manufacturing plant and a market for shipments of the product is $3.28 per hundredweight. Each shipment made direct from the manufacturing location to the market would have a transportation cost of $16.40. Assume that the volume rate for shipments of 20,000 pounds between the manufacturing plant and the market is 76 cents/hundredweight and that the cost of local delivery within the market area is 50 cents/hundredweight. Under these conditions, products shipped to the market via quantity rates and distributed locally would cost $1.26 per hundredweight or $6.30 per 500-pound shipment. Thus, if the warehouse facility and associated inventory level costs could be established for less than $10.10 per 500-pound shipment or $2.02

---

[9] Greenhut, op. cit., p. 117.

FIGURE 8-1
Economic Justification of a Single Warehouse Facility Cost per CWT

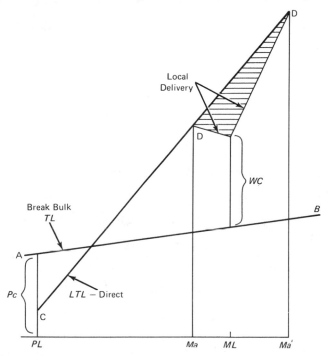

per hundredweight, the overall cost of distributing to the market would be reduced. Under these conditions a warehouse might reduce total cost.

Figure 8-1 illustrates the basic principle of warehouse economic justification. *PL* is identified as the manufacturing location and *ML* is the warehouse location within the market area. The vertical line at point *PL* labeled *Pc* reflects the processing cost associated with the preparation of a 500-pound LTL shipment and a 20,000-pound truckload shipment. The slope of line *AB* reflects the truckload freight rate from *PL* to and beyond *ML*, which are assumed to be linear with distance.[10] The vertical line labeled *WC* at point *ML* represents the cost of warehousing and associated inventory maintenance. The lines labeled *D* reflect the varied cost of local delivery from the warehouse located at *ML* to customers located within the area *Ma* to *Ma'*. The slope of line *CD* reflects the less-than-truckload rate from *PL* to customers located between the plant and the boundary *Ma'*. The shaded area represents the locations to which shipment of 500-pound lots would be more economical

---

[10] As explained in Chapter 5, pages 135–136, this assumption of linearity does not reflect typical common-carrier freight rates. Also see the same qualification related to the applicability of linear programming to logistical problems, Chapter 11, pages 347–354.

via the warehouse than direct from the plant to the customer. It would make no difference from the viewpoint of total cost if customers located at points Ma and Ma' were serviced from the manufacturing plant or the warehouse, assuming equal delivery capability.

As a general rule, warehouses would be added to the logistical system in situations, where

$$\sum \frac{Pc_v + Fr_v}{N_{\bar{x}}} + Wc_{\bar{x}} + Ld_{\bar{x}} \leq \sum Pc_{\bar{x}} + Fr_{\bar{x}}$$

where

Pc_v = processing cost volume shipment

Fr_v = freight cost volume shipment

$Wc_{\bar{x}}$ = warehousing cost average shipment

$Ld_{\bar{x}}$ = local delivery average shipment

$N_{\bar{x}}$ = number of average shipments per volume shipment

$Pc_{\bar{x}}$ = processing cost of average shipment

$Fr_{\bar{x}}$ = direct freight cost average shipment

The only limitation to this generalization is that sufficient volume of shipments be available to justify the cost of the warehouse facility. The impact of the annual volume would be reflected in the warehousing cost of the average shipment. As long as the total cost of warehousing including local delivery is equal to or less than the total cost of direct shipment to customers, the facility is economically justified.

In situations where the flow rate consists of orders too small to enjoy volume freight rates, the general relationship of transportation cost to location is illustrated on the left side of Figure 8-2. The total transportation cost will reduce as warehouse locations are added to the logistical network. The reduction in transport cost results from consolidated volume shipments to warehouses coupled with short-haul small shipments from warehouse locations to customers. At the low point on the transportation cost curve the number of facilities required to enjoy the lowest total cost of transportation is identified.

If facilities are added beyond the optimum number of warehouses, total cost will increase. The main reason for the cost increase is that the quantity of consolidated volume shipments to each warehouse decreases, which results in a higher rate per hundredweight. In other words, the frequency of small shipments inbound to warehouses increases. Finally, as more and more warehouses are added to the network, the benefit of consolidated shipments is diminished and total transportation cost increases at an increasing rate.

FIGURE 8-2
Transportation Cost As a Function of the Number of Warehouse Locations

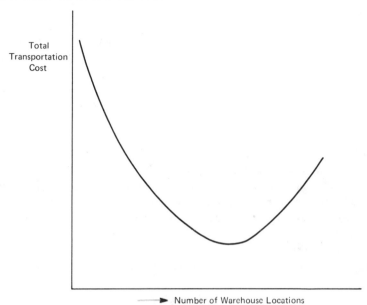

SERVICE JUSTIFICATION.   Warehouses often are vital to the expansion of firms that sell products nationally. Competitive firms sell over a larger total market area in order to realize maximum profitable sales volumes. These competitive conditions probably will compel large producers to concentrate manufacturing plants where low production costs or large amounts of industry demand exist. This is necessary because no individual submarket demands a firm's total production.

The dynamics of spatial competition enter the industry when products begin to gain acceptance in distant markets. The firm finds it desirable to decentralize to support marketing efforts. In highly competitive industries a firm may select to place a warehouse in a particular market area even if operation of the facility adds cost in the short run. The availability of a local inventory permits these firms to replenish consumer inventories more rapidly than major competitors. For customers this means faster order handling and an overall reduction of basic inventories. Thus the firm with warehouses has one more method of gaining a differential advantage. Once a producer obtains sufficient volumes to support a warehouse in a market segment, a permanent location advantage is gained. In addition to transportation economies, firms operating warehouses also gain a customer service advantage in these market segments.

Inventory Economies and Facility Location

Inventory level and flow rate are concerned with achieving temporal closure throughout the logistical system. The framework for planning inventory is the performance cycle. Although the cycle includes transportation, which provides spatial closure, from the viewpoint of inventory the transit capability is measured in terms of time rather than cost.

The average level of inventory required to provide temporal closure consists of base and safety stock. Base stock results from the specified order quantity. The order quantity is based upon a balance of maintenance and ordering cost adjusted to take into consideration volume transportation rates and purchase discounts. As a general rule, the shorter the duration of the performance cycle, the lower the average inventory.

Safety stock provides protection against sales uncertainty (type I) and uncertainty in performance-cycle duration (type II). Both aspects of uncertainty are time related. Type I uncertainty is concerned with usage in excess of forecasted daily sales during replenishment. Type II is concerned with the total replenishment days.

For the total logistical system, average inventory commitment would be

$$\bar{X}Is = \sum_{i=1}^{n} \frac{Qi}{2} + SS_i$$

where

$\bar{X}Is$ = average inventory total network

n = number of performance cycles in the network

Qi = order quantity for a given performance cycle identified by the appropriate subscript

SS_i = safety stock for a given performance cycle identified by the appropriate subscript

Adding locations to a logistical structure increases the number of performance cycles. The question is: What impact will the addition of locations have on average inventory? The impact on transit inventory and safety stock is different.

Locational Impact on Transit Inventory

The impact of transit inventory is significant when purchased f.o.b. origin. In such cases the inventory in-transit represents committed capital. As performance cycles are added to the logistical network, the most common result

FIGURE 8-3
Logistical Network—Two Markets, One Warehouse

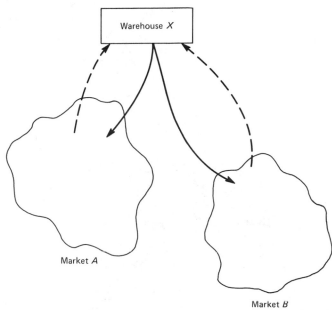

is a reduction in average inventory. Assume that a single product is being sold in markets *A* and *B* and is currently being supplied from warehouse *X*, as illustrated in Figure 8-3. Assume also that the forecasted average sales per day is six for market *A* and seven for market *B*. The performance-cycle duration is 6 days to market *A* and 10 days to market *B*.

With all other things held constant, what will happen to transit inventories if a second warehouse is added, such as illustrated in Figure 8-4? Table 8-1 provides a summary of results. The main change is that the performance cycle to market *B* has been reduced from 10 to 4 days. Thus, the second warehouse

TABLE 8-1
Transit Inventory Under Different Logistical Networks

Forecasted Average Daily Sales	Market Area	Warehouse X Only	Two-Warehouse Facilities		
			Warehouse X	Warehouse Y	Combined
6	*A*	36	36	—	36
7	*B*	70	—	28	28
	$\Sigma A + B$	106			64
	$\bar{X}Ia$	18			18
	$\bar{X}Ib$	35			14
	$\Sigma \bar{X}I$	53			32

FIGURE 8-4
Logistical Network—Two Markets, Two Warehouses

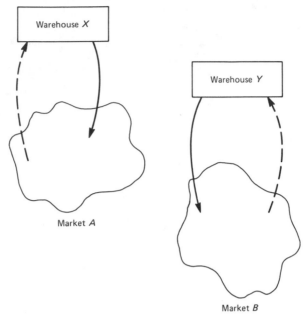

reduced average transit inventory for the network from 53 to 32 units. It should be noted that the second warehouse did not create additional performance cycles on the outbound or physical distribution portion of the logistical flow. However, on the inbound flow each new warehouse requires a replenishment source. Assuming a full product line at each warehouse, the number of performance cycles will increase each time a new warehouse is added. However,

TABLE 8-2
Logistical Structure : One Warehouse, Four Plants

Manufacturing Plant	Warehouse X			
	Performance-Cycle Duration	Forecasted Average Sales	Transit Inventory	$\bar{X}I$
A	10	35	350	175
B	15	200	3,000	1,500
C	12	60	720	360
D	20	80	1,600	800
	57	375	5,670	2,835

TABLE 8-3
Logistical Structure : Two Warehouses, Four Plants

Manufacturing Plant	Performance Cycle Duration	Forecasted Average Sales	Transit Inventory	$\bar{X}I$
		Warehouse X		
A	10	20	200	100
B	15	100	1,500	750
C	12	35	420	210
D	20	30	600	300
	57	185	2,720	1,360
		Warehouse Y		
A	5	15	75	38
B	8	100	800	400
C	6	25	150	75
D	15	50	750	375
	34	190	1,775	888
	$\sum xy = 91$	$\sum xy = 375$	$\sum xy = 4,495$	$\sum \bar{x}xy = 2,248$

the average in-transit inventory for the total system will normally drop each time a new warehouse is added as a result of a total lower number of re-plenishment days.

Assume that warehouse X is supplied by four manufacturing plants whose individual performance cycles and forecasted average usage are as illustrated in Table 8-2. For purposes of comparison, assume a unit value of $5 for all products handled at the warehouses. Utilizing only warehouse X, the average transit inventory would be 2,835 units at $5 each, or $14,175. Table 8-3 illustrates the addition of warehouse Y. Average transit inventory under the two-warehouse logistical structure dropped to 2,248 units or, at $5 each, $11,240. Thus, even though four new performance cycles were added to the logistical system, the average transit inventory was reduced because of the reduction in total replenishment days.

In summary, the addition of facilities generally will have the net effect of reducing the time duration of cycles and thus transit inventory levels. This result, while typical, is not always the case. Each network of locations must be carefully analyzed to determine the exact impact upon average transit inventory. The key to understanding the typical locational impact on transit inventory is that total cycle days are reduced independent of the number of replenishment cycles in the network.

Locational Impact on Safety Stock

From the viewpoint of safety stock the expected result is an increase in average inventory as locations are added to the logistical system. In Chapter 6 the uncertainty related to sales during performance cycle (type I) and performance cycle duration (type II) was evaluated for two frequency distributions. In that example the standard deviation (α) for type I uncertainty was determined to be 2.3, and for type II uncertainty, 2. Compounding the two independent variables resulted in a combined α of 13 units. Thus it was determined that 26 units of safety stock would be required to provide 97.72 per cent of stock availability during the performance cycle, taking types I and II uncertainty into consideration.

The addition of locations to the logistical system impacts safety stock requirements in two ways. First, since the duration of the performance cycle is reduced, the variability in sales during replenishment and the variability in the cycle are both reduced. Therefore, reducing the duration of the performance cycle relieves, to some degree, the need for safety stocks.

The second impact of adding locations has a more serious influence on average inventory. The addition of each new performance cycle creates the need for an additional safety stock. In addition, the statistical data base for determining the required safety stock is reduced in size, with no corresponding reduction in uncertainty. For example, when the needs of several markets can be aggregated as a single requirement, variability of demand can be averaged across markets. In essence, the use of probability allows the unused stock of one market to be used to meet the requirements of other markets.

To illustrate, Table 8-4 provides a summary of monthly sales in three markets on a combined and separate basis. Average sales for the three markets combined is 22 units per month, with the greatest variation above the average in month 6, when sales reached 29 units, 7 over average. Assuming, for ease of illustration, that it is desirable to provide 100 per cent protection against stockout and that total sales of 29 units had an equal probability of occurring in any month, a safety stock of 7 units would be required.

For individual markets, the average monthly sales for markets A, B, and C are 7, 4, and 10 units (rounded). The maximum demand in excess of forecast is for market A, 5 units in month 12; for market B, 3 units in month 8; and for market C, 4 units in month 6. The total of each of these three extreme months equals 12 units. If safety stocks were being planned for each market on a separate basis, 12 units of safety stock would be required in the system as contrasted to 7 units on a combined basis. Thus a total increase in safety stock of 5 units would be required to provide equal protection.

Although this is a simplified example, it illustrates the impact of additional locations on the average level of system safety stock. The important point to understand is that the increase in safety stock results from an inability to aggregate sales across the larger market area. As a consequence, separate

TABLE 8-4
Summary of Sales in One Combined and Three Separate
Markets

Month	Combined Sales All Markets	Unit Sales per Market		
		A	*B*	*C*
1	18	9	0	9
2	22	6	3	13
3	24	7	5	12
4	20	8	4	8
5	17	2	4	11
6	29	10	5	14
7	21	7	6	8
8	26	7	7	12
9	18	5	6	7
10	24	9	5	10
11	23	8	4	11
12	23	12	2	9
Total sales	265	90	51	124
Average monthly sales	22.0	7.5	4.2	10.3
Value greater than average	7	5	3	4

safety stocks must be established for each market which take into consideration
the total impact of local variation in demand.

Generalized Locational Impact on Inventory

The impact upon average inventory of expanding locations in a logistical
system is generalized in Figure 8-5. A reduction in average transit inventory is
assumed as illustrated by the line labeled $\bar{X}t$. The assumption is that a general
linear relationship exists between average transit inventory and the number
of locations in the network.[11]

The curve labeled $\bar{X}ss$ (average safety stock) increases as locations are added.
The actual increase is at a decreasing rate, since the net increase per location
is the added safety stock less the reduction in uncertainty as a result of shorter
replenishment-cycle. This relationship reduces as more and more locations
are added.[12] The total curve represents the summation of the two inventory

[11] Experience with system simulation indicates that the typical result of adding locations is an increase in the number of performance cycles coupled with a decrease in total
days of inventory in-transit. However, exceptions to this relationship have been observed.

[12] This reduction in safety stock results from an increase in homogeneity of demand as
the geographical size of the market area serviced by a facility is reduced.

FIGURE 8-5
Average Inventory As a Function of Number of Warehouse Locations

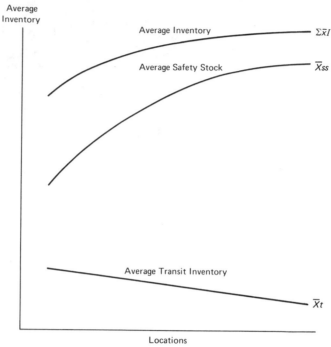

functions. The significant point is that the safety stock function dominates. This results because the average inventory for each performance cycle is the safety stock plus one half of the order quantity and transit inventory. Thus the total inventory increases as the number of locations increases given the same demand and specified service goals.

Total Cost Integration

Over the past several years the total cost concept has received considerable attention in the literature related to logistics.[13] The original application of the concept in logistics was presented by Lewis and Culliton in an illustration of how air freight, the most expensive method of transportation, can result in

---

[13] For complete development of the total cost concept, see Raymond LeKashman and John F. Stolle, "The Total Cost Approach to Distribution," *Business Horizons*, Vol. 44 (Winter 1965), pp. 33–46; or Marvin Flaks, "Total Cost Approach to Physical Distribution," *Business Management*, Vol. 24 (August 1963), pp. 55–61.

FIGURE 8-6
Total-Cost Logistical Network

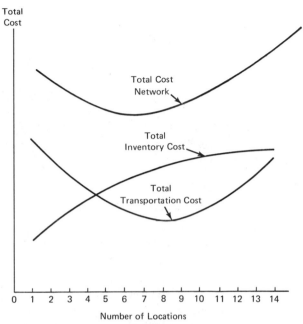

Number of Locations

the lowest total cost of physical distribution.[14] Total cost analysis provides the integrative methodology of logistical system design. Thus the first two levels of integration noted at the start of the chapter are achieved by total cost analysis.

The basic concept of total cost for the overall logistical system is illustrated in Figure 8-6. The low point on the total transportation cost curve is at eight facilities. Total cost related to average inventory commitment increases with each location. The lowest total cost for the overall logistical structure is at six locations.

The identification of the least-total-cost combination illustrates the potential of trade-offs among cost-generating activities. The minimal total cost point for the system is not at the point of least cost for either transportation or inventory. This is the hallmark of integrated logistical analysis.

In actual practice, a great many problems must be overcome for effective total cost analysis. Foremost among implementational problems is that many costs important for logistical systems analysis are not measured or reported in standard accounting systems. A second concern is the fact that a two-dimensional analysis, such as illustrated in Figure 8-6, does not encompass the total

[14] Howard T. Lewis and James W. Culliton, *The Role of Air Freight in Physical Distribution* (Boston: Harvard University, 1956).

complexity of total cost integration. Each of the implementational problems will be discussed.

Implementing Total Cost Analysis

Two important points have been made thus far concerning logistical cost. First, emphasis should always be placed upon total cost. Second, the traditional accounting methods of classifying and reporting cost do not adequately serve the needs of logistical controllership. In this section traditional accounting methods are reviewed briefly to illustrate deficiencies for logistical planning purposes. The section also identifies costs relevant to logistical planning and recommends a classification format.

Traditional Accounting and Logistical Cost Requirements

The two main financial reports in a business enterprise are the balance sheet and the profit-and-loss statement (P&L). The balance sheet reflects the financial position of a firm at a specific point in time. Its purpose is to summarize assets and liabilities of the firm and to reflect the net worth of ownership. The P&L statement reflects the revenues and costs associated with operations over a period of time. As the name "profit and loss" denotes, its purpose is to determine the degree to which operations have been financially successful. Logistical operations influence and are an integral part of both statements. However, for logistical planning, the primary concern is the method by which costs are identified, classified, and reported.

Traditionally, the accountant has been concerned with the preparation of P&L statements which follow accepted accounting practices. It is a financial requirement that major organizations with public investors be audited regularly to assure that accounting practices are standardized and sound. What has resulted over the years is a reporting method designed to meet the requirements of investors and the internal revenue service of federal, state, and local governments. Unfortunately, the conventional methods of profit-and-loss accounting do not satisfy logistical planning requirements.

The first problem results from the fact that accounting practice is to aggregate costs on a standard account basis rather than on a functional basis. For example, the practice of grouping expenses into accounts as salaries, rent, utilities, depreciation, and so on, does not identify functional responsibility. To overcome this deficiency, it is common for the overall P&L statement to be subdivided by managerial or organizational areas of an enterprise in an effort to achieve a measure of each unit's contribution. This process of division helps but does not completely solve the problems of logistical costing.

Internal P&L statements generally group costs along budgetary lines. Thus, costs are provided at an organizational detailed level. The fact that few, if any, logistical operations are unified within a single organizational unit illustrates the deficiency.

The classification of costs on a natural basis also presents a problem. In order to plan logistical operations, it is necessary to get a grasp on costs associated with performing specific tasks. This means that the logistical functions must be identified and costs assigned to each. The data are available in most accounting systems to classify costs by logistical function. Schiff clearly reflects the deficiency in the following paragraph:

> What is of primary concern . . . is the suitability of (logistics) cost reporting for internal use, and failure to identify these costs and classify them as operating expenses can only suggest that management and accountants do not think these costs are important enough to warrant the attention and concern of the receiver of the report or that they can be influenced by the manager to whom the report is addressed. It is difficult to find a logical basis for this position. The costs are identified and assembled in accounts and in all cases they are of significant dollar value to warrant identification. It would take a minimum of effort and re-education to alter the classification wherein freight and other distribution costs would be identified as operating expenses and thus more closely relate responsibility with reported results.[15]

A great deal more logistical functional costing is taking place today than ever before. However, much more managerial attention and research are needed before standardized logistical cost accounting will become a universal practice.

A third deficiency of traditional accounting concerns methods of reporting transportation expenditures. A standard practice in retailing is to deduct freight from gross sales to arrive at a net sales figure. This is the same way discounts and returns are handled and has evolved over the years as a firmly entrenched accounting practice. In part, the practice seems to be based on the belief that freight is a necessary evil about which management can do very little. Once again, Schiff makes the point:

> It would appear that the practice of deducting freight costs from sales imputes such characteristics (namely, a taxlike quality) to freight costs and suggests the inability of the company to influence the cost. But freight costs *can* be influenced by the shipper in many ways. . . . the fact that rates are basically governed by a public agency or a contract does not restrict a company from influencing the total cost by the decision it makes in how it utilizes the service paid for by a pre-determined rate, or by the alternative it chooses. There is, therefore, no justification for deducting freight costs from sales to arrive at net sales. Apart from its lack of rationality, reporting net sales as a basis for analysis precludes responsibility reporting for this large cost and with it any possibility for control. Despite efforts and successes by Traffic Managers in minimizing freight costs, those responsible for creating demand for freight

---

[15] Michael Schiff, *Accounting and Control in Physical Distribution Management* (Chicago: National Council of Physical Distribution Management, 1972), pp. 1–10.

service are free from any responsibility for its incurrence since they are measured by net sales and costs related to net sales.[16]

The problem extends beyond *where* freight is reported. In many purchasing situations, freight is not reported at all. Rather, products are purchased on a delivered basis and transportation costs are buried in the procurement cost of merchandise or material. These practices must be rectified to gain functional control over logistical operations.

A final deficiency in traditional accounting practice is the failure to identify the cost of inventory maintenance. This deficiency has two aspects. First, costs associated with the maintenance of inventory, such as insurance and taxes, are not directly related to inventory decisions, which reduces the importance of this expense. Second, the cost impact of capital invested in inventory is not measured and separated from other forms of interest expense incurred by the enterprise. In fact, if the firm uses internal financing rather than borrowing in the money market, no capital cost at all may be reflected in profit-and-loss reporting.

In summary, several modifications in traditional accounting are required to realize an effective cost base for logistical planning. In particular, the two largest individual cost centers, transportation and inventory, usually are reported in a manner that results in obscure identification. Although the situation is improving, the establishment of an accepted practice for isolating logistical functional costs is a long way from a reality.

Logistical Costing Concepts

Which costs should be identified for purposes of logistical planning, and how should they be identified? One basic problem in logistical costing is to arrive at agreement concerning the specific accounts to be included in a functional classification. A second aspect is to identify the time frame for accumulating costs. Finally, a decision must be reached concerning the manner in which cost data will be structured for managerial use.

Each of the above areas is judgmental. It should be clear from numerous examples throughout the book that the judgment exercised in cost identification and grouping can substantially influence both logistical system design and operation. Therefore, the judgmental factor should be reviewed thoroughly at all levels of management in order to develop a realistic set of specifications.

COST IDENTIFICATION. Generally, all costs associated with the performance of materials management, physical distribution, and inventory transfer should be included in a functional cost-classification system. The total costs associated with transportation, warehousing, inventory maintenance, communication, and storage and material handling should be isolated and grouped functionally.

---

[16] Ibid., pp. 2–3.

Total logistical cost involves three types of specific expenditures: direct, indirect, and overhead.

Direct or *operational costs* are those expenses experienced on an out-of-pocket basis during the performance of logistical activities. Such costs are not difficult to identify. The direct cost of transportation, warehousing, material handling, and some aspects of communication and inventory can be accumulated from traditional cost accounts. Likewise, little difficulty is experienced in isolating the direct administration cost of logistical operations.

Indirect costs are more difficult to identify. These costs are experienced on a more-or-less fixed basis as a result of allocation of resources to logistical operations. For example, the cost of capital invested in real estate, transportation equipment, and inventory—just a few of the areas within the capital structure of logistics—must be reconciled to arrive at a true total cost. The degree to which imputed costs are included in total logistical cost is an area of managerial judgment.

All capital allocated to the logistical system represents a scarce commodity. Therefore, all expenses paid to support investment in the overall logistical operation should be assigned to arrive at a total cost. To the degree that capital investment is internally financed out of the asset base of the enterprise, a charge or hurdle rate for utilization should be imputed and assessed to the total cost of logistics. When such charges are levied, they may range from the prime interest rate to a figure which takes into consideration alternative uses of capital. The judgment applied in arriving at this standard will greatly influence logistical system design. In turn, system design greatly influences operating costs that will be experienced in logistical processing. Thus procedures and standards used in arriving at imputed logistical costs are critical.

The final classification of cost is the allocation of fair-share *overhead*. In total, the enterprise incurs a great deal of expense on behalf of all functional organizational units. A question of judgment is involved in how and to what extent this overhead should be allocated to specific cost centers. One method is to soak up all corporate overhead by direct assignment on a uniform basis to all functional areas. To the other extreme, some firms withhold all allocations to avoid distorting the ability to measure direct and indirect logistical expenditures. Given these extremes, it is impossible to generalize regarding standard practice. From the viewpoint of control, it would appear sound not to allocate any costs that cannot be directly influenced by logistical system design.

The discussion clearly illustrates that considerable gray areas exist in determining the total cost of logistical operations. Which costs are included in total cost is subject to management judgment. As a general practice, a cost should not be assigned unless it is under the managerial control of the logistical organization. Because of the judgmental factor involved, firms in the same industry will report vastly different total costs.[17] It is important to realize

---

[17] For an example, see Douglas M. Lambert, *The Development of an Inventory Costing Methodology* (Chicago: National Council of Physical Distribution Management, 1975).

that such cost differentials may have no direct relationship to the actual efficiency of logistical operations.

COSTING TIME FRAME.   A basic problem in costing which must be reconciled relates to the period of time over which costs are accumulated for measurement. Generally accepted accounting principles call for accrual methods, where an attempt is made to relate revenues and expenditures to the actual performance of services. Significant timing problems are associated with just when to charge for logistical operations. From materials management through physical distribution, almost all logistical operating cost is in anticipation of a future transaction.

To overcome the time problem, accountants attempt to break costs into those which can be assigned to a specific product and those which are associated with the passage of time. Using this classification, an attempt is made to match appropriate product and time period costs to specific revenue generation.

From a logistical perspective, a great many of the costs associated with materials management and inventory transfer operations are absorbed into direct product cost. Thus, because they can be assigned on a specific product basis, inventories can be valued on the basis of fully absorbed cost. Such practices can greatly influence logistical design. In situations where a considerable period of time elapses between production and sales, such as in highly seasonal businesses, significant costs of logistical operations will be disassociated with revenue generation. Unless this potential mismatch is clearly understood and planned for, logistical operations can be significantly mismeasured.

COST FORMATTING.   Logistical costs can be presented in a number of ways for managerial purposes. Three common ways are (1) functional groupings, (2) allocated groupings, and (3) activity-level groupings. Each method is discussed.

To format costs by *functional grouping* means that for a specified operating period all expenditures for direct and indirect logistical services performed are listed by master and subaccount classifications. Thus a total cost statement is derived that can be compared from one operating period to the next. No standard format of functional cost grouping is available to fit the needs of all enterprises. As with organizational structure, logistical functional cost statements should be designed to facilitate control within each unique environment. What is important is to include as many cost account categories as practical and to develop a coding system that will facilitate classification of costs into account categories.

Allocated cost formatting consists of assigning logistical expenditures to a significant measure of physical performance. For example, total logistical cost per ton, per hundredweight, per product, per order, per line item, or some other physical measure provides a basis for comparative analysis between consecutive operating periods.

Activity-level groupings are the most useful for analysis of different logistical system designs. This method of formatting consists of grouping functional costs on the basis of fixed, semifixed, and variable nature as a function of volume throughput. The purpose of classifying on the basis of fixed and variable costs is to approximate the magnitude of change in operating expenditure which will accompany different volumes of logistical performance.

All cost elements that do not vary with volume are classified as fixed. In other words, in the short run, these costs would remain if volume is reduced to zero. Costs influenced by volume are classified as semifixed or variable.

Total Cost Groupings

For purposes of total cost analysis it is recommended that emphasis be placed upon the two main cost groupings that directly influence logistical system design: inventory and transportation. Each of the primary costs is defined in a format sufficiently broad to include the functional relationship to other components of the logistical system. For example, communication cost is included in order processing. Storage and handling cost is included in the maintenance account of overall inventory cost.

In terms of inventory, total cost includes all costs related to maintenance and ordering. Maintenance cost includes taxes, storage in terms of fixed facility cost, capital, insurance, and obsolescence. The cost of ordering includes the full expense of inventory control, order preparation, order communications, update activities, and managerial supervision. The total cost of transportation includes published rates and accessorial charges plus expenses related to the hazards incurred in utilizing the various modes and legal forms of transport and the associated administrative costs.

A summary of total costs of logistical activities is presented in Table 8-5. A number of groupings of logistical accounts have been developed to assist in total cost accounting and analysis.[18]

Thus, from the perspective of total cost accounting, provision must be made to assign all costs related to logistical system design. The technique of grouping costs in association with the major accounts of inventory and transportation highlights the basic cost-to-cost trade-offs and maintains a clear perspective of the critical factors in logistical planning.

Total Cost Limitations

The two-dimensional display in Figure 8-6 represents a single level of sales volume across a single planning period. The assumption is made that all logistical activity consists of an average shipment of a single size. In actual operations neither of these conditions will hold true. First, the nature of logistical network design is not a short-term planning problem. Because of the basic nature of fixed facility decisions, the planning horizon should encompass

[18] Ibid.

TABLE 8-5
Total Cost Grouping by Inventory and Transport Components

Inventory-Related Costs	*Transportation-Related Costs*
Maintenance	Direct
Tax	Rates
Storage	Accessorial charges
Capital	Indirect
Insurance	Liability not protected by carrier
Obsolescence	Managerial
Ordering	
Communication	
Processing, including material	
handling and packaging	
Update activities, including	
receiving and data processing	
Inventory control	
Managerial	

several years of operation with a range of likely annual sales volumes. Second, actual shipment size or order size can be expected to vary substantially around the average shipment size. In fact, the assumption that average shipment size must be less than volume load to economically justify warehouse locations displayed in Figure 8-2 must be relaxed to include direct truckload and carload volume shipments. A realistic approach to planning must consider the range of shipments handled by a variety of logistical methods, based on size and urgency. In practical operations all modes of transportation can be employed and delivery service can be upgraded by selection of a transit method independent of the locational structure. The level of service provided by a given logistical system will depend upon facility location and method of transportation.

The locational selection aspect of planning is far more complex than deciding how many facilities to utilize along a limited scale, as illustrated in Figure 8-6. For example, if a firm is engaged in nationwide logistics, a wide latitude of potential warehouse locations exists. There are 50 states within which one or more distribution warehouses can be located. Assume that the total practical number of warehouses cannot exceed 50 and possible locations are limited to one in each state. Given this range of options, there are 1.1259×10^{15} combinations of warehouses that could be selected in seeking the total least-cost network.

In order to take into consideration the wide range of variables in designing a logistical system, complex models have been developed. Several such models will be discussed in Chapter 11. At this point, the nature of the integrated logistical system design is important from the viewpoint of policy formulation.

The integrated total cost curve must take into consideration all relevant variables that influence system design.

The initial refinement is to introduce a variation in shipment size and transportation alternatives to the two-dimensional analysis contained in Figure 8-6. The refinement requires that a range of two-dimensional relationships be linked, similar to the pages in a textbook. The three variables under consideration are shipment size, transportation mode, and number of predetermined locations. The constants or givens are level of inventory protection, performance-cycle duration, and the specific warehouse locations.

In constructing a more comprehensive analysis, shipment sizes can be grouped in terms of frequency and the transportation mode economically justified to handle each shipment size within the constraint of performance-cycle. For each shipment size a total cost curve is determined. The result is a series of two-dimensional charts, one for each combination of shipment size and associated transportation mode. Next, the individual charts are linked by joining the points of least total cost by a three-dimensional planning curve. In a technical sense, the planning curve is an envelope curve that joins the low total cost points of individual shipment size–transport mode relationships. Figure 8-7 illustrates the basic concept.

The planning curve joins points of total least cost for each shipment size. It does not join locational points. For example, the desirable number of locations for one size of shipment may be more or less than for another. Therefore, further refinement to the problem is necessary. However, two points are important. First, because the level of service and the performance cycle are constants or parameters, the planning curve integrates the logistical structure

FIGURE 8-7
Three-dimensional Total Cost Curve

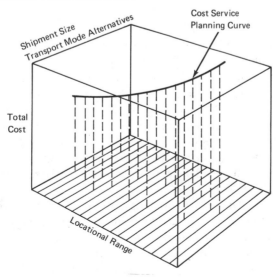

with other operational units of the enterprise. As a result, the planning curve joins points of least cost related to a specified service performance and not necessarily points of total least cost. Second, the entire analysis is conducted with respect to a projected volume of activity.

A further refinement is to identify the specific locations that offer the least cost alternative for each shipment size and transport combination. Assume that the locational range consisted of from 1 to 14 alternatives. Within this range the planning curve will identify a smaller range of desirable locations. In Figure 8-7 the points of least cost for six different combinations indicate that the range of four to eight locations will accommodate the least cost for all shipment size–transport arrangements tested.

Although a compromise is in order for selection of the final number of system locations, the duration of the performance cycle should not be varied. Therefore, the final selection will tend toward the higher number of locations. The final fit of the planning curve ideally will consist of measuring marginal cost changes for each shipment size–transportation mode combination at four, five, six, seven, and eight locations. Providing that within this range the service constraint is attainable, the lowest total cost result after marginal adjustment would be selected.

A final refinement to the planning problem concerns the locational array selected. In the case of Figure 8-7, the best-fit number of locations may not be cost superior to a different sequence of locations. For any given set of locations a least-cost design can be identified. The best practical alternative must be identified from among the different locational sets. While this further refinement requires only comparison of the total cost related to each locational set, the number of potential locational sets is almost unlimited.

Summary

The objective of this chapter was to develop a basic framework for formulating logistical policy. Two fundamental aspects of logistical operations were identified and discussed in detail. Transportation deals with the spatial aspects of logistics and provides the primary justification for including warehouses in a system design. Inventory deals with the temporal aspects of logistics. Average inventory is expected to increase as the number of warehouses in a system increases. Total cost integration provides a methodology for simultaneous integration of these two basic logistical activities. Thus, total cost analysis provides the methodology for integration within and between specific operating areas of logistics.

The formulation of a total cost analysis is not without its practical problems. Foremost is the fact that a great many important costs are not specifically measured or reported in standard accounting systems. A second category of problems related to total cost analysis is the need to consider a wide variety of design alternatives. To develop complete analysis of a planning situation, alternative shipment sizes, modes of shipment, and range of facility locations must be systematically taken into consideration.

These problems can be overcome if care is taken in the formulation of the study assignment. Several guidelines and cautions were reviewed in this chapter. The cost format recommended for total cost analysis is to group all functional costs associated with the categories of inventory and transportation. The significant contribution of total cost integration is that it provides a simultaneous analysis of time- and space-related costs in logistical system design.

Thus far, integrative analysis has proceeded under the assumption that service level is given. In other words, the safety stock cost as illustrated in Figure 8-6 was based upon an assumed level of product availability at each facility within the system. The elements of customer service related to capacity and quality were not explicitly considered in arriving at the total cost integration. The customer service aspects of logistical strategy are treated in Chapter 9.

Questions

1. Describe in your own words the meaning of spatial–temporal integration in logistical system integration.
2. What justification of logic can be presented to support the placement of a warehouse in a logistical system?
3. Why do transportation costs decrease as the number of warehouses in a system increase?
4. Why do inventory costs increase as the number of warehouses in a system increase?
5. In your own words, what is the locational impact of inventory? How does it differ for transit inventories and safety stocks?
6. What is the significant characteristic of the total cost system illustrated in Figure 8-6?
7. In Table 8-5, why are costs associated with all aspects of the logistical system grouped under inventory and transportation?
8. Discuss typical problems confronted in the use of traditional financial statements for purposes of total cost analysis.
9. What is the difference between direct and indirect costs in logistical costing?
10. What additional variable is introduced to total cost analysis in Figure 8-7? Are other modifications desirable? If so, why? If not, why not?

Customer Service Policy

As stated repeatedly, the logistical system exists to provide a service through physical distribution, materials management, and internal inventory transfer operations. Attention is now directed to formulation of policy concerning service. The inclusion of service in the analysis provides the third level of integration. This third and final form of integration is at the enterprise level. Integration at the overall level requires that logistical performance criteria be coordinated within the constraints of all operational units and toward enterprise planning goals.

The total cost approach to logistical policy indentifies the most economical arrangement of warehouses as a function of inventory and transportation cost trade-offs. Beyond pure cost, the primary objective of planning is to determine and provide the overall performance required by marketing and manufacturing. The integration of logistical performance into overall enterprise operations is achieved by expanding the analysis to cost–revenue measurement.

This chapter crystallizes the main theme of this book—that a logistical operating system should be designed to provide a specified level of performance at the lowest associated total cost. In commercial enterprises, the only figure of any significance is the bottom-line profit result. The goal of logistical system design is to increase profit contribution. The initial section briefly reviews the nature of logistical performance. Next, measures of performance are identified. The third section introduces cost–revenue analysis. The next section provides a conceptual approach for formulating a customer service policy. The final section reviews a number of selected operational considerations which should be considered prior to finalization of a logistical policy.

Logistical Performance

In Chapter I the nature of logistical performance was identified to include availability, capability, and quality.[1] The point was made that almost any level of logistical service was possible if the enterprise was willing to pay the associated cost. With respect to the logistical mission of the enterprise, *the mandate for guiding system design is the establishment of a balance between performance and cost that will achieve the desired return on investment or other goals of the enterprise.*

In logistical performance, *availability* is a system's ability to provide a product or material on a predictable basis. Availability in a system results from safety stock policy. *Capability* is the ability to provide a stated speed and consistency of delivery. A system's capability results from the design and dependability of components that make up the performance cycle structure. *Quality* of performance relates to how effectively the logistical task is performed. The maintenance of quality performance is a responsibility of logistical operations measurement.

To be effective a logistical system must have some level of each attribute of logistical performance. It is also necessary to develop performance measures for each aspect of the overall logistical service mix.

Performance Measurement

The measurement and control of service can be approached from a number of vantage points. The approach suggested here is based upon three specific sets of performance measurement data. The first is built around the total order cycle and provides a measure of capability. The second centers on availability. The final measure deals with quality. To avoid redundancy, the discussion is illustrated around the physical distribution performance cycle. Similar examples could be provided for the internal inventory transfer and materials management performance cycles of the total logistical system.

Capability Measurement

The total performance cycle consists of the time measured in days from order placement to shipment receipt. In physical distribution, the cycle should be measured from time of order transmittal to the customer delivery.

---

[1] See pages 19–20.

FIGURE 9-1
Illustration Total Order Cycle Physical-Distribution Single-Echelon Example

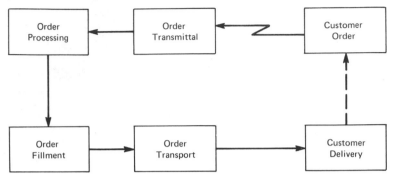

As noted earlier, the physical distribution order cycle confronts a number of uncertainties which complicate performance.[2] The task of capability measurement is to evaluate the impact of these uncertainties upon operational effectiveness.

At the single-echelon level, the typical total order cycle consists of four time elements. They are (1) order transmittal, (2) order processing, (3) order filling, and (4) order transportation. The basic cycle is illustrated in Figure 9-1. A fifth element of time is the degree of delay experienced in the performance of any one or all of the order-cycle elements. Figure 9-2 provides an illustration of the variable time patterns which can be expected in each element as well as the total order cycle. Note that while each form of time distribution in Figure 9-2 is illustrated as a normal statistical distribution, other statistical patterns can be experienced in actual practice.

Using the total order cycle as a capability measurement framework, statistical analysis is possible concerning each element and the total performance time. In Figure 9-2 an individual order can take as few as 4 days and as many as 36 days to reach the customer. The task of capability service measurement is to determine the combined impact and cause of all delays over an operating period. Table 9-1 provides a review of the different measures that can be developed from the total order-cycle framework.

The measures illustrated in Table 9-1 are in no way exhaustive of the capability measures which can be generated. However, they do provide an indication of the usefulness of the order cycle as a capability measurement framework.

Availability Measurement

The most visible measure of customer service is inventory availability. Variation in availability, perhaps more than any other element of performance, is the cause of failure to meet performance standards.

[2] See Chapter 6, pages 175–178.

FIGURE 9-2
Total Order Cycle and Time Distribution of Four Elements

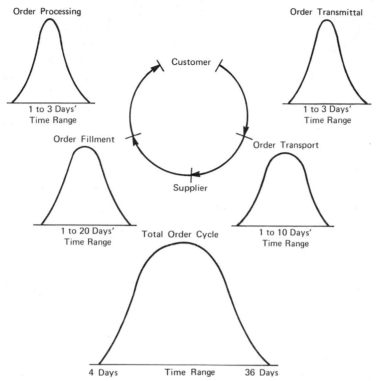

TABLE 9-1
Measurement of Customer Service Capability

1. Average delivery time	A measure of total elapsed time from transmittal to delivery of a number of different customer orders
2. Standard deviation of delivery time	A measure of delivery consistency for a number of different customer orders in terms of average expected time
3. Distribution orders within time intervals	A measure of total orders delivered by time intervals over an operating period
4. Per cent of orders within time intervals	Percentage of total orders delivered by time intervals over an operating period
5. Dollar distributions	Similar to measures 3 and 4, with dollar sales being used rather than orders

A typical measure of inventory availability is the percentage of items out of stock to total items carried in stock. The fallacy in this measure is that it does not take into consideration the velocity movement of various items in the product line. For example, 10 slow-moving items may be out of stock but not create serious problems. On the other hand, one fast-moving item out of stock could cause havoc and result in a flood of customer complaints.

Therefore, the most desirable measures of inventory availability provide an analysis over a time period of performance. For example, orders with one item out of stock, average cases out of stock per order, average percentage availability of all items requested, back-order frequency, and back order recovery rate are indicators that provide a comprehensive and factual measure of inventory availability.

Quality Measurement

Delivery of incorrect or damaged merchandise in a timely manner does nothing to help an enterprise reach its operating goals. The measure of operational quality, similar to the other performance measures, requires analysis over a time period. For example, frequency of incorrect items on an order, shipments to improper locations, percentage of damage incidence by shipments or line items, and damage claims per quantity of shipments are representative of quality measurement indicators.

Cost–Revenue Analysis

The goal of integrated logistical system design is to provide the overall level of performance that will contribute to maximum attainment of enterprise goals. For most commercial enterprises the goal is to maximize profits. The theoretical solution to this design problem is simply stated: continue to increase expenditures for improved logistical performance to the point where marginal cost equals marginal revenue.[3] Although easily stated, marginal equality is difficult if not impossible to accomplish in practice. Some of the major problems are (1) measurement of incremental cost; (2) isolation of logistical performance from the remainder of enterprise performance; (3) inability to make incremental or minor changes in logistical system components, which in fact prohibit a truly marginal solution; (4) inability to modify commitments related to the logistical system quickly, such as leases; and (5) inability to measure revenue elasticity as a function of logistical performance.

Various attempts have been made to approach the marginality solution by identifying the revenue loss when available sales are not realized. The cost of stockout represents logistical expenditure without benefit of revenue

[3] At this point short-run profits would be maximized.

contribution.[4] This approach provides assistance in arriving at a justified level of inventory availability; however, it does not answer the question of what might have been sold with superior logistical performance. Even though measurement and flexibility preclude exact solutions to the marginality problem, the objective of logistical system design is to approximate the ideal solution. The approach recommended is to undertake sensitivity analysis initiating with the least total cost design for the logistical system.[5] A general approach to evaluating the marginal productivity of incremental service level is discussed in the next section.

Formulating a Service Policy

While substantial difficulties exist in the measurement of marginal revenue, the comparative evaluation of service performance and related marginal cost offers a way to approximate an ideal logistical system design. The general approach consists of (1) determination of a least-total-cost system design, (2) measurement of service availability and capability associated with the least-total-cost system design, and (3) conduct of sensitivity analysis of incremental service and related cost in terms of required revenue contribution. Such an analysis is the prime reason why comprehensive system design techniques have been developed. The discussion of such design techniques is the subject of Chapter 11. This part is devoted to a discussion of the logic which underlies the formulation of a service performance policy.

The Least-Total-Cost Design

Just as a physical map of a geographical area shows the elevations, depressions, and contours of land surface, an economic cost map illustrates the differences in the cost of logistics between different areas. Generally, peak costs for labor and government services occur in large metropolitan areas. However, because of geographical demand clusters, total logistics cost resulting from reduced expenditures on transportation and inventory often is at a minimum at these metropolitan points.

At first approximation, a policy of least total cost will seek to select a combination of facilities which will result in lowest fixed and variable costs. Such a system will be designed purely on cost-to-cost trade-offs, with the resultant

---

[4] For a comprehensive study of customer service measurement and practice, see Bernard J. La Londe and Paul H. Zinszer, *Customer Service: Meaning and Measurement* (Chicago: National Council of Physical Distribution Management, 1976).

[5] The idea is further developed in Chapter 10, pages 318–321. Also see William D. Perreault, Jr., and Frederick A. Russ, "Physical Distribution Service in Industrial Purchasing Decisions," *Journal of Marketing*, Vol. 40 (April 1976), pp. 3–10; and Ronald P. Willett and P. Ronald Stephenson, "Determinants of Buyer Response to Physical Distribution Service," *Journal of Marketing Research*, Vol. 6 (August 1969), pp. 279–83.

customer service capabilities a function of cost minimization. In terms of basic relationships, the point of total least cost was illustrated in Figure 8-6. The customer service which results from the least-total-cost system design is referred to as the *threshold* service level.

To establish a threshold service level it is necessary to start the analysis with initial policies regarding minimum *availability* and *capability* expected from the logistical system. A typical first approximation is to permit the service capability to be a function of existing order transmission time, standard order processing time at facilities, and transit time selected on the basis of lowest-cost transportation. For example, products will be routed at the lowest cost for the appropriate shipment size. Given the assumptions above, cycle speed and consistency will serve as the measure of performance capability.

The typical first approximation regarding availability is to assume an acceptable minimum stockout level.[6] For example, if the safety stock availability level is set at the 97.75 per cent protection for the combined probability of type I and type II uncertainty, it would be anticipated that approximately 98 out of 100 items ordered would be available.

Under initial conditions, each customer is assigned a shipment location on the basis of least total cost. In a multiproduct situation, selection of service territories for each facility will depend on the products stocked at each location and the degree of product mixing required on customer orders. Because costs have significant geographical differentials, the service area of any given facility will vary in size and configuration. Figure 9-3 provides an illustration of the assignment of warehouse shipping areas based upon a line of equalized total delivered cost. The irregularity of service territories results from directional transportation cost differentials outbound from the three warehouses.

In Figure 9-3 the warehouses are identified by the letters X, Y, and Z. The cost illustrated at each facility location represents the logistical cost for an average order with the exception of transportation. The differential of average order cost between facilities reflects geographical and individual system differentials.

Around each facility three total cost lines are displayed, at intervals of $1.50, $2.50, and $3.50. The value on the line represents the total cost of logistics, including transportation to points located along the line. The area within a given line can be serviced at something less than the parameter cost displayed at the line. In actual practice, equal total cost lines would be plotted at less than $1 intervals illustrated in Figure 9-3.

The area serviced by each facility is based on lowest total cost. This territory boundary line represents the point of equal total cost between two facilities. Along this line of equal costs, an enterprise would be indifferent on a cost basis as to which warehouse services the specific customer. From the customer's viewpoint, a substantial difference could result in terms of delivery time.

---

[6] A common assumption is to follow industry customer service practice to initiate the analysis.

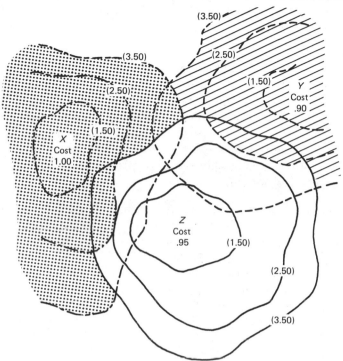

Two conditions are assumed in Figure 9-3. First, the illustration is based on an average order, and thus distribution costs are equated on the average. To the degree that order size varies from the average, alternative territory boundaries based on shipment size will be required. Second, an element of time is included because transportation cost is calculated on the basis of common-carrier rates. Inventory in transit is calculated on standard time. Thus one cannot conclude that delivery times will be constant within territories or that equal total logistics cost will be experienced within service areas.

The fact that a least-cost system is designed for maximum economy does not mean that performance service necessarily is low. The elapsed time from the customer's order placement to product delivery in a least-cost system will be longer on the average than for other types of systems. However, customers located in the heart of the market close to warehouses will enjoy rapid delivery. Because the least-cost array will tend to favor areas of highest demand concentration, a substantial number of customers will enjoy such service.

Given an estimate of expected order cycle time, management will be in a position to make customer commitments concerning expected delivery. Such a statement might be expressed as follows: Order performance for area A will be 10 days from receipt of orders at the warehouse facility. It is our policy to be able to fill 90 per cent of all orders within the 10-day period. The operational performance of a logistical system is measured by the degree to which established service standards are met in practice.

Service Sensitivity Analysis

The threshold service resulting from the least total cost system design provides the base from which sensitivity analysis can be initiated. The basic service capabilities of a system can be increased or decreased by any or all of the following methods: (1) variation in number of facilities included in the system, (2) change in one or more elements of the performance cycle to modify speed or consistency of operations, and/or (3) change in safety stock policy. Each form of modifying threshold service and the expected impact on total cost is briefly discussed.

LOCATIONAL MODIFICATIONS. The facility structure of the logistical system establishes the service which can be realized without changing the speed of the performance cycle or the availability of inventory. To understand the relationship between number of facilities and service time, assume that the measure of logistical service is related to percentage of demand serviced within a specified time interval. The general impact of adding locations to the system is presented in Table 9-2. Several points of interest are illustrated.

First, incremental service is a diminishing function. For example, the first

TABLE 9-2
Service Capabilities Within Time Intervals as a
Function of Number of Locations

Network Locations	Percentage Demand by Performance-Cycle Duration (hours)			
	24	48	72	96
1	15	31	53	70
2	23	44	61	76
3	32	49	64	81
4	37	55	70	85
5	42	60	75	87
6	48	65	79	89
7	54	70	83	90
8	60	76	84	90
9	65	80	85	91
10	70	82	86	92
11	74	84	87	92
12	78	84	88	93
13	82	85	88	93
14	84	86	89	64

five locations provided 24-hour performance to 42 per cent of all customers. This degree of performance is the threshold service related to total least cost. In order to nearly double the percentage of 24-hour service, from 42 to 84 per cent, nine additional locations are required.

Second, high degrees of service are reached much faster for longer performance intervals than the shorter intervals. For example, only four locations can provide 85 per cent performance within the 96-hour performance cycle. Increasing the total locations from 5 to 14 improved the 96-hour performance incrementally only 9 per cent.

Finally, the total cost associated with each location added to the logistical network increases dramatically. Thus, while the incremental service resulting from additional locations is a diminishing function, the incremental cost associated with each new location is an increasing function.

PERFORMANCE-CYCLE MODIFICATIONS. Speed and consistency of service can be varied to a specific market or customer by a modification in one or more elements in the performance cycle. These elements were previously discussed and are illustrated in Figure 9-1. To improve service, telephone ordering and premium transportation can be used on a priority basis. Therefore, geographical proximity and number of facilities do not equate directly with rapid or consistent delivery. The decision to increase service capability by faster performance-cycle operation will involve extensive variable cost. In contrast, service improvement by virtue of added facility structures involves a higher degree of fixed cost and results in less overall system flexibility.

No generalizations can be offered regarding the cost/service improvement ratio attainable from performance-cycle modification. The typical relationship of premium to lowest-cost transportation results in a significant incentive in favor of large shipments.[7] Thus, if order volume is substantial, the economics of logistics can be expected to favor use of a warehouse or consolidation point to service a market area.

The impact of using premium transportation on the least total cost system would be twofold: (1) the transportation cost curve would be shifted up to reflect higher per shipment expenditure; and (2) the inventory cost curve would be shifted down to reflect any reductions in average inventory resulting from lower transit stocks. In almost all cases, the net impact of these cost modifications will be an increase in cost which could be offset only by a variation in facility structure. Such adjustment from the least-total-cost system could be justified only on the basis of higher service levels.

AVAILABILITY MODIFICATIONS. One direct way to vary service level is to increase or decrease the amount of safety stock held at one or more warehouse facilities. The cost ramifications of providing high levels of inventory availability were discussed in detail in Chapter 6.[8] At that point a substantial case

---

[7] See Chapter 5, pages 135–136.
[8] See pages 179–180.

was presented to support the logic of following a policy of planning selective safety stocks to support those items most critical to attainment of operating goals.

The impact of increasing the safety stock across a total system would be a shift upward in the inventory cost curve. The availability relationships can be generalized in the following statements: lower safety stock levels provide a substantial degree of availability; as the desired availability is increased, the safety stocks required to achieve each equal increment of availability increase at an increasing rate.

Finalizing a Performance Policy

Establishment of service standards constitutes a critical managerial policy. This policy is integral to logistical system design because service objectives must be within anticipated cost. Management often falls into the trap of being overly optimistic in their service policies. The result may be an excessively high commitment to customers, followed by erratic performance. This dichotomy results from lack of a realistic appreciation of the total cost required to support high service commitments. The final step in isolating a policy is to relate the cost of incremental service to revenue requirements.

To illustrate, assume that the current system is geared to service at least 90 per cent of all customers at a 95 per cent inventory availability within 60 hours of order receipt. Further, assume that the current logistical system is meeting these objectives at lowest total cost by utilizing five warehouses. Marketing, however, is not happy. Marketing management's opinion is that service capability should be increased to the point where 90 per cent of all customers at 97 per cent inventory availability would receive 24-hour delivery. Top management is faced with a critical policy consideration. Sensitivity tests are in order.

Figure 9-4 illustrates results which might be isolated by such sensitivity testing. Marketing is requesting a 2 per cent improvement in inventory availability coupled with a 36-hour improvement in delivery capability. To achieve these goals, 13 additional warehouses would have to be added to the system. Design analysis, through sensitivity testing, determines that 20 facilities would be the lowest-cost method for achieving the new service standards. The total cost of this expanded service capability is measured on the vertical axis of Figure 9-4 as the distance between points A and B. The total cost of meeting the new managerial service standard will be $200,000 per year greater than current expenditures. If the firm had a before-tax profit margin equal to 10 per cent of sales, it would be necessary to generate additional sales of $2 million to justify the added service on a break-even basis.[9]

---

[9] This relationship is based on the assumption that no change, favorable or unfavorable, would take place in existing fixed cost or variable cost per unit sold as a result of an increase in volume.

FIGURE 9-4
Comparative Total Cost for Seven- and Twenty-Distribution-Point
Systems

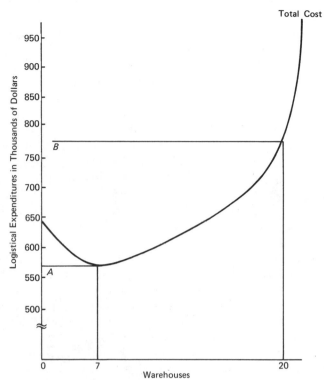

Acceptance or rejection of the marketing proposal for increased service must rest with top management. Policy changes, once adopted, influence logistical design. Regardless of origin—internal or external to the logistics sector—the formulation of new or modified policies will require system modification.

Beyond least total cost, three basic strategies are available to guide system design: (1) maximum service, (2) profit maximization, and (3) maximum competitive advantage. Each basic strategy requires a different system design.

MAXIMUM SERVICE. A maximum service strategy is rarely found. A system designed to provide maximum service usually would not attempt to deliver products faster than on a 24-hour basis.

Emphasis in maximum service shifts from cost to delivery time. Thus a territory division is developed similar to the least-cost service areas illustrated in Figure 9-3. However, the cost lines are transformed into time or service lines. The limits of each facility service area are determined by the capability to provide overnight delivery. As with cost-oriented service areas, time-oriented areas will be irregular because of transport-route configurations.

Total cost variation between least-cost and maximum-service models will be substantial. To service the total U.S. market on an overnight basis would require 30 to 40 distribution facilities or the use of very high-speed, high-cost transportation.

PROFIT MAXIMIZATION. Most business firms aspire to maximize profit in the design of logistical systems. Theoretically, the service area of each facility is determined by establishing a minimum allowable profit margin for customers located at varying distances from the facility. Because the warehouse facility normally will be located in high-volume markets, the greater the distance a customer is located from the service area center, the greater are the costs of logistics. This occurs, not only because of distance, but also because of lower customer density at the periphery of the service area. At the point where the costs of serving peripheral customers result in minimum allowable margins, further extensions of the service territory become unprofitable on a total-cost-delivered basis.[10]

If the customer were offered better delivery service, more of the product assortment might be purchased. Therefore, additional service is introduced, to the point where marginal revenues equal marginal costs. At this point of equilibrium, no additional service is justified economically. Additional service may or may not result from increasing the number of warehouses. The service may be provided best by a supplemental system of direct or dual distribution. The theoretical profit-maximization position is easier to state than to measure in practice. However, equated marginal revenue and marginal cost represents a situation management should strive to approximate.

In the development of a highly profitable system, management is seeking a balance between service and cost. Referring back to Figure 8-6 (page 253), the balance normally will be found along the total cost curve to the right of the least-cost point but considerably short of the point where total costs rise rapidly. For the situation illustrated in Figure 8-6, the profit-maximization system, as a first approximation, could be expected to fall between a network of 6 and 10 warehouses.

Table 9-2 presented a quantification of the service capabilities of the 14 best networks of distribution points in comparison with a hypothetical customer configuration. The actual service gains accruing will vary with each situation. The amount of dollar variation between each of the systems under consideration shows the additional total costs of reaching higher service levels. These dollar estimates provide an assessment of the value of added service against added cost. Given a schedule of these cost–service relationships,

---

[10] From a geographical perspective, this point represents equality of marginal cost and revenue. For an expansion of the territory concept, see Kung-Mo Kuo, "How Far Can a Regional Distributor Reach?" in Robert G. House and James F. Robeson, eds., *Interfaces: Logistics, Marketing, and Production,* Proceedings of the Sixth Annual Transportation and Logistics Educators Conference (Columbus, Ohio: Ohio State University, 1976), pp. 111–27.

management is armed with considerable information to help in the establishment of a performance policy.

MAXIMUM COMPETITIVE ADVANTAGE. Under special situations, the most desirable policy to guide logistical system design may be the accomplishment of maximum competitive advantage. Although there are many cases where systems may be modified to gain competitive advantage, two are developed here to illustrate the range of policy considerations.

Core-Market Considerations. The first case concerns modifications in system structure aimed at protecting major customers from competitive inroads. With a firm capable of providing 42 per cent of the customers with 24-hour delivery at 95 per cent inventory availability, management should be concerned with the welfare of major customers under this service policy.

To illustrate, assume that this firm is typical among those engaged in mass marketing and that 20 per cent of their customers purchase 80 per cent of their product output. Further, assume that 20 per cent of the customers represent 75 delivery or terminal points to be serviced. Is this 20 per cent of core customers included in the 42 per cent of total customers receiving 24-hour delivery? Under conditions of equal customer geographical dispersion, the probability is about 0.5 that the array of 42 per cent of total customers would include all the significant 20 per cent. In other words, one would expect that on the average approximately 40 to 45 of the core customers would get 24-hour service. However, because we know that the system is biased toward location of distribution facilities at points of highest demand, it would be safe to assume that a higher number of core customers would receive prime service.

Once core customers are identified, it is an easy process to isolate the service each receives. Core customers are identified as critical delivery points, and the frequency of service interval is obtained through an interrogation process. Table 9-3 presents the results of a hypothetical interrogative process.

TABLE 9-3
Core-Customer Interrogative Results

Total Core Customers	Number of Core Customers Serviced by Hour Intervals			
	24	36	48	60
75	53	16	4	2

The actual number of core customers receiving 24-hour delivery service is 53. Thus, although 42 per cent of all customers receive 24-hour service, 76 per cent of the core customers receive prime consideration. In addition, the interrogative process points out that the remaining core customers receive varying degrees of service, with two of these critical customers obtaining 60-hour delivery.

Provided that management is inclined to do so, this situation can be rectified by a restatement of objectives. The cost of a system providing 24-hour service to 90 per cent of all customers can be isolated, and management can equate the dollar-and-cents requirements of a core-customer policy.

Several additional systems modifications may be evaluated similar to the core-customer illustration shown. Management may wish to examine service provided to the most profitable customer. Evaluations can be made regarding customers or noncustomers with the greatest potential. In addition, an enterprise may wish to evaluate the incremental cost of providing prime service to the core customers of major competitors. Although all such modifications may increase total cost and decrease short-range profits, the long-range gain may be a substantial improvement in competitive position.

Economically Justified High-Cost Facility. An additional application of design modification to capitalize on competitive situations is the economically justified high-cost facility. This situation is pertinent especially to a small business enterprise. Because of the rigidities inherent in large firms, pricing policies are likely to be inflexible. Present antitrust legislation reinforces these rigidities. The result is that large firms selling in broad geographical markets tend to disregard unique cost and demand conditions in localized markets or find it legally impossible to adjust marketing and logistical systems to accommodate these localized situations. This inflexibility creates opportunities for smaller and localized situations. Such opportunities may encourage smaller firms to make significant modifications in least-cost distribution policies.

Location of a small-scale plant or warehouse facility in a minor market some distance from major competitors results in a localized service more or less insulated from competition. The logic of this special situation was developed under the general discussion of factors influencing distribution facility location. At this time it is sufficient to point out that major firms typically follow one or two courses concerning these localized situations with respect to logistical design.

First, a large enterprise can elect to avoid these localized situations. This policy of concentrating on primary markets can be an opportunity for the higher-cost, smaller firm. Second, major producers may introduce smaller-scale facilities or institute direct logistical systems in an effort to service local demand situations. Following the first policy will result in a system approaching a least-cost configuration. The second policy will require substantial system modification, with higher costs and lower short-range profits. It is interesting to note that firms which adjusted to the localized West Coast situation in the late 1930s find their market position desirable today.

Conclusion—Service Policy Formulation

In summary, integration of the logistical system into overall corporate planning consists of specifying desired performance. This performance is viewed from product availability, performance time, and the probability that the desired delivery service will consistently materialize. The total cost curve defines the point of least cost associated with each level of potential service. From a design viewpoint, the point of total least cost with its associated threshold service capability offers optimum cost trade-offs. From the viewpoint of overall enterprise objectives, incremental service in excess of the threshold level may be justified from the perspective of marketing or manufacturing operations. Thus, service–cost trade-offs may be structured which will result in the logistical network being designed to operate at other than the point of least total cost.

Operational Considerations in Policy Formation

Thus far the discussion dealing with customer service has for the most part related performance capacity to the structural design of the logistical system. In other words, the service performance was directly related to availability, capability, and quality. Each of these service attributes was related to ways to improve performance by modification of the locational structure, performance cycle, or basic safety stock policy. Thus far no notable mention has been made concerning several operating procedures that can be utilized to increase customer service performance. In this section four such operating procedures are introduced and discussed: (1) flexible operations, (2) postponement, (3) reverse logistics, and (4) shipment consolidation.

Flexible Operations

The capability for flexible logistical operations was initially introduced in Chapter 2,[11] and the basic concept behind a flexible operating procedure was illustrated in Figure 3-2.[12] Flexible operations incorporate into basic system design the capability to service customers from alternate shipping points. Flexible operations can be based on two situations: (1) contingency, and (2) standard procedures.

CONTINGENCY FLEXIBLE OPERATIONS. Contingency flexible operation is a form of backup to the desired pattern of logistical performance. A typical situation is when a primary shipping point is unable to provide normal service. For example, a warehouse facility may be stocked out of a specific item with no inventory replenishment planned for arrival in the immediate future. To prohibit a prolonged backorder or to avoid order cancellation a policy may exist to fill all or at least the short items on the order from a secondary shipping point. Such utilization of flexible operations to supplement planned service capability represents a form of marginal analysis. A

[11] See pages 48–50.
[12] See page 56.

secondary source location will typically require higher logistical cost. Thus, the customer will be serviced but at an increased cost, which must be justified by product contribution margin[13] or critical nature of the product to core customer performance.[14]

STANDARD FLEXIBLE OPERATIONS. A form of flexible operational capacity which is gaining in popularity is to incorporate into the logistical system design a standard procedure for shipping the same customer location from more than one logistical facility. This practice of variable origin can result from at least three situations.

First, the customer may be located at or near a point of indifference between two logistical warehouses. Figure 9-3 illustrated the isolation of service territories based on total logistical cost. Those customers who are located at points of nearly equal cost from more than one facility offer an opportunity to fully utilize logistical capacity by alternating shipment origin according to inventory availability, work load, and/or equipment utilization. This form of flexible balancing offers a way to fully utilize capacity and balance work loading of a logistical system based on demand variability.

A second situation wherein an enterprise may deliberately incorporate flexible logistical operations is when specific size customer shipments have different logistical costs from different facilities. For example, the lowest total cost method to provide delivery of a small shipment may be through a warehouse. In contrast, shipments having total weight greater than 10,000 pounds may have the lowest total logistical cost when shipped direct from manufacturing plants. Provided that each alternative method of shipment can meet customer performance standards related to speed and consistency of delivery, total logistical cost will be reduced by planned flexible operation.[15] The recent redesign of the General Foods SDDS logistical structure which ships carload quantities direct from manufacturing plants and LTL quantities from warehouses is a prime example of this form of preplanned flexible operations.[16]

A third form of flexible operations results when an enterprise selects to follow different stocking policies by individual market area or by the echelon structure of the logistical system. The nature of inventory requires that significant judgment be used when deciding which items to place in a particular warehouse. A common practice is to stock selected items in a specific market area with the total line being supported from a secondary facility. For example, a retail store in a small community may stock a limited version of the overall line. When customers desire nonstocked items, the store will accept the order. However, customer shipment will be made from a larger store or a warehouse

---

[13] See Friedhelm Bliemel, "A New Approach for Inventory Decisions in Product Oriented Marketing Strategies," in House and Robeson, op. cit., pp. 130–49.

[14] See this chapter, page 277.

[15] Provided that customer service standards can be satisfied, direct shipment in carload or truckload quantities typically offers the lowest-total-cost method of shipment.

[16] *General Foods Logistic System* (Boston: Intercollegiate Case Clearing House, 1974).

facility. The term "mother store" is often used to describe inventory policies that vary by market area with designated responsibility for backup support.

The variation of stocking policy by echelon level is a common strategy used to limit the degree of anticipatory inventory exposure. Systems that plan multiecheloned stocking strategies normally cannot justify complete line stocking in distribution warehouses. The reasons for echelon stocking range from low profit contribution to high per unit cost of inventory maintenance. One way to operationalize a fine-line classification strategy of inventory management is to differentiate stocking policy by system echelons.[17]

CONCLUSION—FLEXIBLE OPERATIONS. The concept of flexibility in operations can result from contingency planning or standard operating procedures. In each situation the capacity to accurately interrogate inventory status and to quickly switch orders between facilities is a prerequisite to flexible operations. While the use of flexible operations for contingency planning has a long track record, the incorporation of flexible arrangements as a basic part of system design is a new and rapidly growing dimension of logistical management. To a significant degree, a programmed capability of flexible operations can offset the safety stock required to provide customer service from multiple locations.

Postponement

The concept of postponement has long standing; however, practical applications have not materialized until recently in logistical operations.[18] Postponement offers a way to reduce the anticipatory nature of traditional logistical operations. Almost all movement and storage in a logistical system takes place in anticipation of a future transaction. To the degree that the final manufacturing or logistics of a product can be postponed until a customer commitment is obtained, the risk associated with inventory planning is automatically reduced or eliminated. Two types of postponement considerations should be carefully reviewed when formulating logistical operating procedures: (1) form postponement, and (2) temporal postponement.

FORM POSTPONEMENT. The basic concept behind *form postponement* is to retain the product in a neutral status as long as possible in the manufacturing process. Several outstanding examples of form postponement are currently in practice. Mixing colors upon customer request has reduced dramatically the number of stockkeeping units required at retail paint stores. A similar

---

[17] See Chapter 6, page 186.

[18] For example, see Wroe Alderson, "Marketing Efficiency and the Principle of Postponement," *Cost and Profit Outlook*, 3 (September 1950); Wroe Alderson, *Marketing Behavior and Executive Action* (Homewood, Ill.: Richard D. Irwin, 1950), p. 424; Louis P. Bucklin, "Postponement, Speculation, and the Structure of Distribution Channels," *Journal of Marketing Research*, Vol. 2 (February 1965), pp. 26–31; and Thomas A. Staudt, Donald A. Taylor, and Donald J. Bowersox, *A Managerial Introduction to Marketing*, 3rd ed. (Englewood Cliffs, N.J.: Prentice-Hall, Inc., 1976), pp. 281–82.

postponement situation is Sunoco's system to mix gasoline octane grades at the retail pump. In other industries it has become common practice to process and pack product in large bins to postpone product put-up and even label identification until demand stabilizes. Another example of form postponement is the rapidly increasing practice of installing accessories at the automobile and appliance dealer level, thereby customizing products to customer request.

The examples above all have one thing in common. They introduce the capability to reduce the number of stockkeeping units required to support a broad-line marketing effort. Until the product is customized, it has the potential to serve many different end customer requirements.

The impact of form postponement on logistical operations is twofold. First, the quantity of different products moved in anticipation of sale is reduced, and therefore the error of misallocation is reduced. The second, and perhaps more important, impact of form postponement is the increasing trend to use logistical facilities to perform light manufacturing and final assembly operations. To the extent that a degree of specialized talent or economies of scale exist in the preparation of the final product configuration, the process of customization may be best performed one echelon away from the final destination market. The traditional mission of the logistical warehouse is changing rapidly in some industries to accommodate form postponement. A prime example is found in the assembly and final accessory configuration of imported motorcycles.

TEMPORAL POSTPONEMENT.   In many ways temporal postponement is the exact opposite of form postponement. The basic notion of *temporal postponement* is to maintain a full product assortment at a few centralized locations with no forward movement until a customer order is received. Once the logistical process is initiated, it is to a precommitted customer destination. Under the concept of temporal postponement the anticipatory nature of traditional logistics is completely eliminated.

An example of temporal postponement is Sears Store Direct logistical system. Utilizing rapid-order communications, the actual distribution and, in some cases, the basic manufacturing of an appliance is not initiated until a customer order is received. An appliance purchased on Monday in Lansing, Michigan, will be ready for in-home installation on Thursday. However, beginning on Monday the actual order coordination will flow from the Lansing store to the regional store in Detroit, to Sears Tower in Chicago, to Whirlpool Headquarters in St. Joseph, Michigan, to Whirlpool Manufacturing in Findlay, Ohio. The logistical operation will consist of a consolidated overnight truck movement on Tuesday to Detroit with transfer to Lansing during the day Wednesday. The distinct possibility exists that the appliance being sold was not manufactured until Monday night or early Tuesday.

The potential of temporal postponement has resulted from the capability to process and transmit orders with a high degree of accuracy and speed.[19]

[19] See Chapter 4, pages 83–96.

Temporal postponement substitutes rapid processing time for the need to move products to forward stocking points in anticipation of future sale. Unlike form postponement, systems utilizing temporal postponement can retain full manufacturing control and economies characteristic of centralized operations while still meeting customer service requirements.

CONCLUSION—POSTPONEMENT. The two types of postponement offer ways to refrain from final product-market commitment until a customer order is received. Thus they both serve to reduce the anticipatory nature of overall logistics. The two types of postponement arrive at reduced anticipation from opposite directions. Form postponement moves *nondifferentiated* product toward the market with a plan to modify the product to customer requirements at some time during the logistical processes. Temporal postponement involves an effort to avoid any movement of a *differentiated* product until customer purchase commitment is received. The factors favoring one or the other form of postponement hinge on volume, value, competitive practices, economies of scale, and required customer service in terms of speed and consistency of delivery.

Reverse Logistics

A specialized form of logistical operations which is rapidly increasing is movement of products back toward the manufacturer in the channel of distribution. Product recalls have become a common occurrence during the past two decades, owing to increasingly rigid standards of quality control, expiration dating, and clear-cut responsibility for hazardous product consequences. A further need for reverse or return logistical performance is the increasing number of laws prohibiting disposable beverage and food containers.

Unlike the operational impact of flexibility and postponement, reverse movement does not serve to introduce improved logistical productivity. However, reverse movement is justified on a social basis and must be accommodated in logistical system design.

The point of significance in reverse logistical operations may be the need for maximum control when a potential health liability exists. In this sense, a recall program is similar to a strategy of maximum customer service which must be executed regardless of cost. In contrast, reverse logistics of reusable or recyclable containers requires movement utilizing the lowest-total-cost approach. The important point is that no contemporary logistical strategy can be formulated without careful consideration of present and potential reverse logistical requirements.

Shipment Consolidation

A significant opportunity existing in all logistical operations is the potential for reducing transportation expenditure as a result of shipment consolidation.

Quantity discounts are provided for in the published rate structures of common carriers. Generally speaking, the larger the shipment, the lower the freight rate per hundredweight. From an operational viewpoint, three opportunities exist to realize freight consolidation: (1) market area grouping, (2) scheduled delivery, and (3) pool consolidation. The extent to which each can be realized in day-to-day operations must be considered in formulating logistical policy.

MARKET AREA GROUPING. The most fundamental type of consolidation is when small shipments in a specific market area can be consolidated for transportation. This type of consolidation does not interrupt the natural flow of the freight by trying to influence when shipments are tendered to common carriers. Rather, the quantity being shipped to or purchased in a specific market is sufficient to justify a consolidation program.

From a purchasing viewpoint, many firms are participants in cooperatives that arrange joint consolidations. However, the difficulty of market area groupings is to develop sufficient daily volume to realize the benefits of consolidation. To offset the volume deficiency three arrangements are commonly used. First, firms may consolidate shipments to an intermediate point for purposes of line-haul rate savings. At the intermediate point the shipments are separated and forwarded to beyond points on an individual basis. Second, firms may select to delay shipments to realize sufficient volume for consolidation on specific days to the destination market. Third, a given enterprise may join with other firms to form a pooling of small shipments. The last two arrangements are discussed below.

SCHEDULED DISTRIBUTION. Scheduled distribution consists of limiting shipments to specific markets to selected days each week. The scheduled distribution plan is normally communicated to customers in a way that sells the virtue of planned delivery. Thus, the performance cycle is stabilized by a commitment on the part of the shipping firm that orders received prior to the established deadline will be guaranteed of delivery on the day of scheduled distribution.

POOLED DISTRIBUTION. Participation in a pooled distribution plan typically means that a third-party organization is arranging for consolidated shipment.[20] The term *third party* refers to a freight forwarder or a public warehouser who consolidates shipments from many different organizations. While the available pool-type arrangements were discussed in Chapters 5 and 7, they are noted again because of their direct impact upon customer service strategy.[21]

---

[20] For an illustration of the Total Distribution Plan for America third-party consolidation arrangement, see John B. Redmond, "Distribution," *Proceedings, Midwestern Frozen Food Spring Marketing Conference*, May 15, 1976. For overall discussion, see Walter F. Friedman, "Physical Distribution: The Concept of Shared Services," *Harvard Business Review*, March–April 1975, pp. 25–36.

[21] See pages 125 and 215.

Conclusion—Operating Considerations in Policy Formulation

Four types of logistical operating arrangements have been reviewed. Flexible operation provides a method by which contingency or planned operations make use of alternative shipment points to service a specific customer. Postponement offers a logic to reduce the risk of maintaining extensive inventory. Reverse logistical flow represents a "here today" requirement that cannot be neglected in formulating a logistical strategy. Finally, methods of shipment consolidation were reviewed as alternative ways to reduce the cost of small shipments.

The above-noted operational impacts upon the formulation of logistical policy do not represent an exclusive listing. Likewise, their impact upon logistical operations may be complementary or contradictory, depending upon the circumstances. The significant point is a realization that all logistical strategies formulated upon structural arrangements must be tempered by the opportunities and problems in day-to-day operational execution.

Summary

The formulation of a logistical strategy requires that total cost analysis be evaluated in terms of overall customer service performance. Logistical service is measured in terms of *availability*, *capability*, and *quality* of performance. The realization of each service attribute is directly related to logistical system design. To realize the final integration of logistical operations within overall enterprise planning, service ideally should be provided to the point where marginal cost is equaled by marginal revenue. Such marginal balance cannot be achieved in practice. However, the relationship serves as a normative planning goal.

The formulation of a service policy starts from the identification and analysis of the least-total-cost system design. Given an inventory availability level, the service capability associated with the least-cost design is referred to as the *threshold level of service*. To evaluate potential modifications in the least-cost design, several forms of sensitivity analysis were discussed. Three fundamental modifications were identified as ways to vary service levels: (1) variation in the number of facilities, (2) change in one or more elements of the performance cycle, and/or (3) change in safety stock policy. The impact of each type of change was explored in detail.

Next, attention was directed to alternative approaches to finalizing a performance policy. Beyond least total cost, three basic strategies were identified as guides to system design: (1) maximum service, (2) profit maximization, and (3) maximum competitive advantage. Regardless of the strategy selected, the specified level of performance service ideally should be realized at the associated lowest total cost.

From an operating viewpoint, a variety of procedures and concepts influence final performance which are not directly related to the system structural design. Four such operating procedures were discussed: (1) flexible operations, (2) postponement, (3) reverse logistics, and (4) shipment consolidation. The significant point of emphasis was to stress that logistical strategies formulated upon structural arrangements must be tempered by the opportunities and problems of day-to-day operations.

Conceptually, the stage is set for a detailed discussion of logistical planning. Chapter 10 provides a recommended procedure to guide various types of logistical planning.

Questions

1. What measurements typically are used to evaluate logistical performance?
2. Discuss the usefulness of the performance-cycle concept when measuring and evaluating customer service performance.
3. What is the purpose of cost–revenue analysis?
4. What is meant by the level of threshold service of a least-cost system?
5. Why does customer service not increase proportionately to increases in total cost when a logistical system is being designed?
6. In Table 9-2 why does customer service speed of performance increase faster for customers located greater distances from a warehouse facility? What is the implication of this relationship for system design?
7. Discuss the differences between improving customer service through faster and more consistent transportation, higher inventory levels, and/or expanded numbers of warehouses.
8. What is the difference between minimum total cost and short-range profit maximization policies in system design?
9. Under what conditions would a firm design a maximum customer service system?
10. In what ways can customer service performance be improved by incorporating flexible distribution operations into a logistical system design?

Planning Procedure

The implementation of a revised logistical plan normally involves modification of operating procedures and/or substantial change in the existing system network. Depending upon the nature of the planning situation, a great deal of data collection and analysis may be necessary to finalize a plan. The primary purpose of Chapter 10 is to recommend a managerial guide to be followed when conducting logistical planning.

The initial section of the chapter presents a classification of planning situations typically confronted in logistics. Next, the managerial procedure to guide planning is presented and discussed.

Logistical Planning

The logistical manager typically is confronted with three types of planning situations: (1) strategic, (2) operational, and (3) tactical. The basic criteria

TABLE 10-1
Typology of Logistical Planning[a]

Classification	Subtypes	Example	Definition
Strategic planning	Long-range	Logistical system for 1980	A process for dealing with allocation of logistical resources over an extended time frame which is consistent and supportive of overall enterprise policy and objectives
	Project status	Establishment of a corporate regional warehouse system	
Operational planning	Up to one year	Add new item to inventory control system	A process for developing logistical policy and plans to handle routine or regularly anticipated management action in an ongoing organization
	Periodic	Yearly distribution budget	
		Production scheduling	
		Procurement requirements	
Tactical planning	Special support requirements	Material breakdown during new product introduction	A process for short-range adjustment of logistical resources to irregular or unanticipated enterprise, competitive, or environmental conditions
	Contingency support requirements	Maintaining distribution service levels during severe snowstorm	
		Expediting procurement	

[a] Adapted from: Bernard J. La Londe, "Technique and Procedure for Developing the Strategic Plan," *Proceedings NCPDM Fall Meeting,* Chicago, 1970, p. 54.

for delineating between each are the nature of asset commitment, the time duration of the plan, and the likelihood of implementation. Table 10-1 defines and illustrates the various levels of planning. As with any classification scheme, it does not cover all contingencies or planning situations confronted by logistical managers.

Strategic Planning

Strategic planning requires a significant commitment of capital and managerial resources. The strategic plan sets the structure within which operational and tactical plans are cast. Thus, the strategic plan represents a set of guideposts for other types of planning. It is anticipated that implementation of a strategic plan will alter significantly the method of conducting operations. The objective of system redesign strategy is to bring the logistical network to a desired performance level while maintaining the lowest possible associated total cost. The strategic planning procedure and techniques utilized should incorporate the capability to experiment and evaluate among alternative logistical operations prior to commitment to a final system design.

The horizon for strategic planning may extend from the immediate future to 5 or 10 years hence. Once a strategic plan is developed, the implementation period may extend over several years. Substantial modifications to the original plan are usually necessary, because the nature of strategic planning involves a high element of probability that all events anticipated will not materialize. Relatively speaking, as the planning horizon is extended, the degree of certainty concerning conclusions diminishes. Because of the inherent uncertainties of long-range projections, strategic planning is most appropriately viewed as a never-ending process.

Operational Planning

The role of operational planning was noted initially in Chapter 1 and was further developed in Chapter 4. As an indication of its importance to logistical integration, the operational plan is classified in the planning typology at this point; however, managerial development is deferred to Chapter 13, which deals with logistical administration.

The operational plan is the tool used to coordinate the logistical efforts of an organization. It typically covers up to a one-year period. The overall operating plan will have at least three sets of objectives: (1) system modification, (2) performance, and (3) budgetary.

During any operating period, a substantial number of adjustments in system design may be required. These modifications are specified as part of the prevailing strategic plan. For example, a new warehouse may be scheduled for initial construction planning, or an existing facility may be ready to be phased out. Other examples may be the establishment of a private fleet, the installation of a new order-processing system or a changeover in a materials-handling system. Whatever the nature of the requirement, it can be expected that in a dynamic organization, system change will be an integral part of each operating plan.

The performance objectives of the operational plan deal with short-run deployment of capital and managerial resources toward attainment of enterprise goals. The duration of the performance schedule is tied to the basic activities of the enterprise. For example, in manufacturing enterprises the performance schedule typically is based upon the most economical production runs. For retailing firms, seasonal buying patterns and holidays may be the prime determinants of the performance pattern. As a general rule, the more stable or repetitive the operational situation, the greater the time period covered by the performance plan. However, the performance schedule seldom would exceed the time duration of the operating plan. The main data used to formulate the performance plan are the sales forecast as updated by order-processing statistics coupled with product and materials availability feedback from suppliers. In essence, performance objectives coordinate planned activities over short time periods within the operational plan.

The financial aspects of operational planning consist of logistical budgeting. The budgeting process may be completed using several alternative procedures which will be covered in Chapter 13. The primary purpose of the total budget package is to control expenditures while combining all relevant cost centers into a single unified plan.

Because the operational plan covers a short time period, a high probability exists that the events planned will materialize. Those aspects of the total plan dealing with strategic modification are most likely to materialize. The performance scheduling aspects of operational planning have a more-or-less built-in adaptive mechanism because they deal with short intervals within the overall operational planning period. The fact that performance plans are of short duration makes their probability of execution very high. The financial budgeting aspects of operational planning are the least likely to materialize over the specified time period. The very nature of the financial control process would require complete accuracy in overall planning for the budget to exactly balance expenditures on a line-item basis.

The operational plan is the most important tool of integrated logistics. It is the device that brings about the management of total system performance. In terms of resource deployment, the logistical operational plan results in significant expenditures of capital and human resources.

Tactical Planning

Tactical planning consists of a procedure for adapting to irregular or unanticipated events within the operational planning period. A critical question in tactical planning is the determination of the extent to which management pre-acts or reacts to unexpected events. A *pre-act* tactical procedure develops advance contingency plans which detail adjustments to events that were possible but not probable at the time the operational plan was formulated. A *react* tactical procedure is one that develops the mechanism for modifying the operational plan based upon the actual occurrence of the unanticipated event. An ideal tactical planning procedure would incorporate pre-act and react capabilities to be used given the severity of the event. A method for incorporating tactical procedures into the overall process of logistical planning is presented in Chapter 13.

The time period of tactical planning is short because the focus is event-oriented. The implementation period may cover an extended time depending upon the nature of the event. For example, when H. J. Heinz introduced the vacuum-sealed screwtop jar for baby food, all major competitors faced an immediate need to make tactical adjustments to their existing operational plans. Depending upon the nature of the event, the capital and resource

FIGURE 10-1
Logistical Planning Time Perspectives

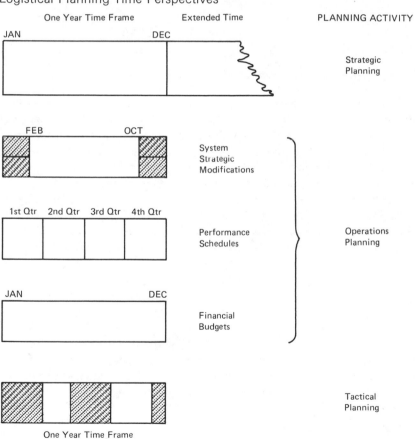

Shaded areas represent inactive time periods.

requirements of a tactical plan may range from minor adjustments to a major change in basic strategy. The degree of significance is the focal point of the procedure elaborated in Chapter 13.

Conclusion—Logistical Planning

To summarize the interrelated aspects of logistical planning, the time horizon of each aspect of logistical planning is illustrated in Figure 10-1. The horizon for strategic planning may extend across many years. The typical operational plan covers no more than a year's activity. The system strategic modifications could require any or all of the time included in the operational plan. In Figure 10-1 the activity is assumed to start in February and end in October. Idle times are indicated by shaded areas. The nature of performance plans depends upon the flexibility of the enterprise involved. Those illustrated in Figure 10-1 encompass quarterly operations. The financial budgets typically will cover the full operating plan; however, they usually include an adjustment procedure to accommodate business trends. Tactical planning periods occur at irregular intervals and last for varying degrees of time.

Managerial Guide to Logistical Planning

Just as there exists no ideal logistical system suitable to the needs of all enterprises, procedures followed in the conduct of logistical planning vary extensively. As one would expect, the procedural format for formulating a logistical strategic plan would be considerably different than that followed when studying the potential modification of a logistical warehouse. However, several definable steps should be considered in most planning situations. The purpose of this section is to present a managerial guide for the planning process. To illustrate the approach, a strategic planning situation is utilized.

Figure 10-2 illustrates a flow diagram of a generalized managerial guide. Each of the major steps recommended is noted with reference to the prime areas of managerial concern. The left-hand side of the flow diagram illustrates the process of (1) heuristic analysis procedures, and (2) continuous adjustment to change. From a managerial viewpoint, a final plan never really exists. The system should be under constant review to take advantage of change. Thus the total process of logistical system planning is a never-ending responsibility subject to change with passing time. Each of the major areas illustrated in Figure 10-2 is discussed in the remainder of this section. Because of the comprehensive nature of strategic planning, the discussion that illustrates the managerial guide is based upon logistical system design.

Feasibility Assessment

Strategic planning begins with a comprehensive analysis of the logistical situation. The immediate managerial concern is to determine what, if any,

FIGURE 10-2
Managerial Guide to Logistical Planning

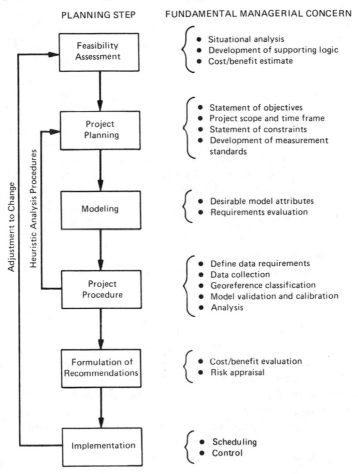

PLANNING STEP   FUNDAMENTAL MANAGERIAL CONCERN

Feasibility Assessment
- Situational analysis
- Development of supporting logic
- Cost/benefit estimate

Project Planning
- Statement of objectives
- Project scope and time frame
- Statement of constraints
- Development of measurement standards

Modeling
- Desirable model attributes
- Requirements evaluation

Project Procedure
- Define data requirements
- Data collection
- Georeference classification
- Model validation and calibration
- Analysis

Formulation of Recommendations
- Cost/benefit evaluation
- Risk appraisal

Implementation
- Scheduling
- Control

Adjustment to Change
Heuristic Analysis Procedures

modifications are needed in the existing logistical operating system and facility structure. The process of evaluating the need and desirability of change is referred to as *feasibility assessment*. The recommended steps in completing the feasibility assessment are (1) situational analysis, (2) development of supporting logic, and (3) cost–benefit estimate. Each is discussed below.

SITUATIONAL ANALYSIS.   Situational analysis involves the collection of facts concerning the logistical requirements confronted by an enterprise and the overall scope of present operation. The typical appraisal involves an internal review, a competitive appraisal, and a technology assessment to determine if a substantial area for cost or service improvement exists.

Internal Review. The purpose of the internal review is to develop a clear understanding of the existing logistical network. In particular, the review is directed at a comprehensive evaluation of the existing system's capabilities and deficiencies. Each aspect of the overall logistical system should be carefully examined with respect to how well its stated objectives are being realized. For example, is the physical distribution support system consistently meeting the level and response of customer service performance desired by the marketing department? Likewise, is the materials management system meeting its goals with respect to supporting manufacturing requirements? Are the primary activities of logistical coordination being conducted in an orderly and integrated fashion? Finally, does an integrated concept of internal inventory transfer which takes maximum advantage of the captive nature of work in-process inventory exist in practice? These and many similar questions form the basis of the self-appraisal involved in the internal analysis. Through this comprehensive review the opportunities that might justify potential system redesign are initially identified.

The specific content of the review is concerned with, but not limited to, such matters as these:

1. Developing a specific understanding of the existing geographical arrangement, capacity, and assignment of all facilities.
2. A careful review of the order-processing systems and procedures employed in the customer service, materials management, and internal inventory transfer performance cycles.
3. Delineation of the internal communication network used to generate management information.
4. Examination of the current policies and control systems utilized to manage inventory.
5. A thorough review of the practices of traffic management, including an evaluation of the full range of common-carrier services available and an audit of private fleet capabilities and condition.
6. Development of a clear understanding of existing material-handling techniques and practices employed in various facilities, including an evaluation of the effectiveness of any existing automated or extensively mechanized handling.
7. Review of existing forecast techniques employed with an appraisal of their effectiveness.
8. Examination of the methods employed to develop production schedules.
9. Delineation of the techniques employed to formulate procurement plans, including evaluation of the overall accuracy of specifications concerning material and part requirements and timing.
10. Evaluation of receiving and inspection procedures.

11. A detailed review of finished products from the perspective of packaging, special handling, relative volume, relative profitability, and existing facility stocking policies.
12. An accounting of existing expenditures for logistical performance by function, including an evaluation of the existing investment and turnover in assets committed to physical distribution, materials management, and internal inventory.

It would indeed be rare if all the above data were available for instant review. Unquestionably, considerable research would be required to assemble data related to each area. The purpose of the review is not data collection. Rather, the review represents a diagnostic look at what is currently taking place in logistical operations as well as a probe to determine the availability of data. Most significantly, the internal review is aimed at the identification of areas where a substantial opportunity for improvement exists.

Competitive Appraisal. The focal point of the competitive appraisal is the external environment within which the logistical system must function. In particular, the competitive analysis is concerned with an appraisal of how well the existing logistical system is functioning in terms of customer requirements, vendor consistency, and competitor practices.

Although an internal review will indicate if the physical distribution operating system is satisfying the marketing organization's requirements, the competitive analysis is aimed at evaluating the fundamental need for existing customer service standards. For example, does the danger of developing a service myopia, as discussed in Chapter 3, in fact exist?[1]

The content of a competitive analysis is concerned with, but not limited to, such matters as:

1. Examination of the logistical systems being used by major competitors in both the materials and finished-goods markets.
2. Evaluation of existing marketing channel arrangements as well as major structural trends, including the presence or absence of separation in the transaction and logistical channels.
3. Quantification of existing and potential customers and supply sources with respect to volume purchased, special logistical requirements, and structure of facilities that must be linked into the logistical system.
4. Measurement of delivery service consistently offered by major competitors.

As with the internal review, it would be rare to find all the data desired about the competitive and market environment readily available. Once again, the purpose of the competitive review is to appraise what is generally needed and to develop a comprehensive insight into the effectiveness of the existing logistical system.

[1] See pages 63–64.

Technology Assessment. As noted earlier, the period during which the concept of integrated logistics matured was dominated by a continuous stream of technological developments.[2] In particular, technologies related to computers and high-speed data transmission have been significant contributors to practical management of integrated logistics. The purpose of the assessment is to evaluate the findings of the internal review and competitive analysis in an effort to measure the extent to which available technology is being utilized.

To illustrate, if no major review has been completed recently regarding the technology of order processing, then substantial trade-off benefits may be available to the enterprise. Such an assessment should be completed with respect to each component of the logistical system as well as the status of overall integration.

DEVELOPMENT OF SUPPORTING LOGIC. The second recommended step in the feasibility assessment is to integrate the findings of the internal review, competitive analysis, and technology assessment into a logic to support strategic plan modification. In many ways the development of a supporting logic constitutes the most difficult part of the strategic planning process. The purpose of the situational appraisal is to provide management with the best possible understanding of the strengths and weaknesses of the existing logistical system. From the comprehensive review three specific end products are desired.

First, a determination must be made if sufficient areas for improved logistical performance exist to justify detailed research and analysis. In a sense, completion of the situational analysis provides a convenient go–no go point for further study. The desirability, as well as the feasibility, of conducting a detailed system design study can be evaluated in terms of expected cost and benefit. While conducting the remaining steps in the managerial design procedure does not commit a firm to implementation or even guarantee a viable new system design, the potential benefits of change should be fairly clear at the completion of the situational appraisal.

Second, the typical end product of the appraisal will be a confirmation that a great many aspects of the existing logistical system are more right than wrong. This should not be a surprising conclusion. However, it is one that should be reached based on comprehensive factual analysis and not opinion. The delineation of areas where improvement potential exists, as well as those where operations are satisfactory, provides the foundation for determining the need for strategic adjustment. For example, it may be apparent that a serious problem exists in inventory, which holds the potential for cost and service improvement. Correspondingly, if there is no justification for questioning the existing structure of facilities with respect to location or size, then all subsequent analysis can focus on improvement of the inventory component without serious risk of suboptimization.

[2] See Chapter 1, pages 10–11.

The third end product of the situational appraisal should be a clear statement of the logistical alternatives available as options to the existing system. At this point in the study process, it is well worth the effort to construct flow diagrams illustrating the basic networks associated with different alternatives. These diagrams will illustrate the opportunities for engaging flexible operating patterns, clearly outline the transportation and communication requirements, and serve to provide a comprehensive overview of the study situation. Some variables available in identifying logistical options will be difficult to illustrate in a flow-diagram. For example, regional variations, product-mix variations, and differential shipment policies are difficult to illustrate, although they do form the basis of design alternatives. Nevertheless, an attempt should be made to delineate the options. The techniques involved in this form of presentation are discussed in Chapter 11.

A recommended procedure is for the manager responsible for evaluating the desirability of a revamped logistical strategy to develop a logical statement and justification of potential benefits. Based upon the logic of logistical cost (Chapter 8) and customer service alternatives (Chapter 9), the estimated results of a modified logistical strategy should be committed on paper.

COST-BENEFIT ESTIMATE. The final result of the feasibility assessment is a preplanning estimate of what benefits are expected to materialize if a logistical study is completed and implemented. The benefits can be summarized in categories of service improvement, cost reduction, and cost prevention. Naturally the three categories are not mutually exclusive, in that an ideal logistical strategy might realize some degree of all benefits simultaneously.

The category of service improvement simply means that the potential exists to generate more effective performance without spending additional monies or committing additional resources. For example, a reduction in the number of stocking points may increase inventory availability without a sacrifice in other attributes of customer service.

Potential cost reductions are of two types. First, a one-time reduction in capital or managerial resources required to operate the existing system may result from logistical redesign. The impact of reductions in capital deployment is significant in that the continuous cost associated with usage is eliminated and the capital is freed for alternative deployment. The second type of cost reduction deals with the expenditure of out-of-pocket or variable costs to perform logistical tasks. The redesign of the system to employ new technologies often results in a particular function being accomplished more efficiently.

Cost prevention consists of instituting system changes in order to avoid continued involvement in programs and operations experiencing excessive cost increases. For example, many recent entries into private transportation have been at least partially justified on a financial analysis that takes into account the estimated future level of common-carrier rates. Naturally, any cost-prevention justification is based on an estimate of future conditions and is therefore vulnerable to error. While a logistical study would seldom be approved solely for cost prevention, consideration of such ramifications is recommended.

No rules exist to determine when a strategic planning situation offers adequate cost–benefit potential to justify an in-depth effort. Ideally, strategic review should be a continuous process undertaken at specific intervals to assure continued viability of the existing operational system. In the final analysis, the decision to undertake in-depth strategic planning must rest on how convincing the supporting logic is, to what degree the estimated benefits are believable, and an assessment of whether or not the estimated benefits offer sufficient incentive to justify organizational and operational change. These potential benefits must be balanced against the out-of-pocket cost required to complete the strategic plan.

Project Planning

The second step in formulating a logistical strategy is the establishment of the project plan. Four specific tasks must be accomplished at this stage of the managerial procedure: (1) statement of objectives, (2) identification of project scope and time frame, (3) statement of constraints, and (4) development of measurement standards. Each is discussed briefly.

STATEMENT OF OBJECTIVES.   The strategic objectives deal with cost and service expectations for the revised system. It is essential that such objectives be stated specifically in terms of measurable factors. A typical procedure at this point in the study is to state specific service objectives, setting cost considerations aside until later in the study. The following is a typical format of service objectives: (1) the system will be designed to provide 95 per cent inventory availability for category A products, 92 per cent for category B products, and 87 per cent for category C products; (2) desired delivery of all customer orders will be within 48 hours of order placement for 98 per cent of all orders; (3) customer service from secondary service points will be held to a minimum; (4) mixed commodity orders will be filled without back order on a minimum of 85 per cent of all orders; (5) back orders will be restricted to five days' aging; and (6) the 50 most profitable customers will receive these minimum performance capabilities on 98 per cent of all orders.

Given these statements of customer service, a system can be planned that will provide the desired performance. Total cost of the system can then be derived. To the extent that such cost does not meet managerial expectations, various levels of alternative performance can be tested later in the study.

An alternative approach to the statement of output objectives is to fix a maximum allowable total cost expenditure and then design a system which achieves the highest possible degree of service. Such cost-oriented objectives are practical, because results will be within acceptable budget ranges, but they lack the selectivity of the service-oriented approach to system design.

PROJECT SCOPE AND TIME FRAME. Based upon the supporting logic and statement of objectives, the scope of the project must be specified and the time
required for completion delineated. The alternatives and opportunities
specified during the feasibility assessment provide the basis for determination
of study scope. In turn, the scope of the planned inquiry provides the basis
for estimating the time required for completion.

Specifically, it must be decided if the design study is to be concerned with
all or only select parts of the logistical system. In situations where a comprehensive redesign is being conducted for the first time, it is not unusual for the
study to be limited to either physical distribution, materials management, or
inventory transfer. At a later point, potential benefits of total logistical system
integration can be examined.

In addition to identification of the extent of coverage, it is necessary to
specify which logistical components will be included in the analysis. In this
respect, the study scope should be as broad as possible in order to approach
the design problem on a total system basis.

Whatever the managerially determined limits, they will have a significant
impact upon the research results. Alternative strategies to guide the selection
of study scope were presented at the conclusion of Chapter 9.

A major overall management responsibility is to assure that expected results
are realized within time and budget constraints. One of the most common
errors in strategic planning is to underestimate the time required to complete
the specified assignment. Extended time overruns will result in greater than
planned expenditures for the planning effort. Fortunately, several scheduling
techniques are available which can be easily adapted to the logistical planning
project.

Scheduling is concerned with planning and accomplishment of nonrepeti-
tive projects. In addition, scheduling techniques are concerned with the most
efficient utilization of resources during the study. Two scheduling techniques,
the *program evaluation review technique* (PERT) and the *critical path method*
(CPM), are reviewed in Chapter 12. Utilization of scheduling techniques is
not limited to strategic planning situations, thus coverage is deferred to the
chapter dealing with operational planning. The illustration developed in
Chapter 12 is specific to the time phasing and managerial guidance of strategic
logistical planning.

STATEMENT OF CONSTRAINTS. An additional aspect of project planning deals
with design constraints. From the situational analysis, it is expected that
management will place restrictions on the scope of permissible modifications.
The nature of such restrictions will depend upon the specific circumstances
of individual firms. However, two typical examples are provided here.

One restriction common to distribution system design concerns the network
of manufacturing facilities and the product assortment produced at each. To
simplify the study, management may elect to hold existing manufacturing
facilities constant in the system design. Although such constraints reduce the

optimization of a study, they are justified on the basis of financial considerations and capacity for immediate change.

A second category of constraints deals with marketing channels and physical distribution activities of separate divisions. In firms with a traditional pattern of decentralized profit responsibility, management may elect to omit certain divisions from study consideration. Thus some divisions may be managerially determined to be candidates for consolidated physical distribution operations, whereas others are omitted from consideration.

All design constraints serve to limit the scope of the study. However, as one executive stated the problem: "Why study things we don't plan to do anything about?" Unless a reasonable chance exists that management is favorably inclined to introduce change, the subject in question should be structured as a study constraint.

The purpose of developing a statement of constraints is to have a well-defined starting point and overall perspective for the planning effort. If computer models are used to assist in the planning effort, all such constraints can be evaluated later with a minimum of effort. If the planning is conducted on a manual basis, the degree of flexibility to vary constraints is significantly reduced. In contrast to study scope, discussed above, the statement of constraints relates to specific buildings, systems, procedures, and/or practices to be retained from the existing logistical system.

DEVELOPMENT OF MEASUREMENT STANDARDS. In most situations the feasibility assessment will illustrate the need for managerial determination of measurement standards. Such standards will concern the structure of synthetic costs and the cost of performance penalties. Management must provide guidelines for each category as a prerequisite to the formulation of the plan. Once formulated, such standards must be held constant throughout the design analysis. Although considerable managerial prerogative exists in the formulation of standards, care must be exercised not to dilute the validity of the analysis and subsequent results.

An important aspect of measurement is to quantify a list of assumptions which underly or provide the logic supporting the standards. These assumptions should receive top managerial approval because they can significantly shape the results of the strategic plan. For example, a relatively small variation in the standard cost and procedure for evaluating inventory can result in major variations in the strategic plan.[3]

Modeling

The third step in the overall strategic planning procedure is to determine if a computer model should be used to assist in planning. Determination of the type of model and the associated technique of analysis requires creative talent

---

[3] See Chapter 8, pages 256–262.

as well as analytical ability. This is normally the domain of the specialist. However, management still must play an active role in order to maintain control and to develop appropriate data into a usable format. A technical treatment of design technique is the subject matter of Chapter 11. At this point, emphasis is placed on the nontechnical manager's role in the logistical modeling process.

The fundamental purpose of modeling is to attempt to make a valid prediction of how potential logistical configurations will perform in advance of actual implementation. A model constitutes a body of information and restrictions about a unique situation accumulated for the purpose of systems analysis.[4] The model is a substitute for testing actual logistical designs. By developing and testing a model, it is possible to evaluate the impact of alternative policies prior to resource commitment. Thus modeling permits experimentation with different potential system designs without resorting to trial and error or arbitrary modifications to existing operations.

Models are of two general types: (1) physical and (2) abstract.[5] Physical models are replicas of the object under study. Common examples are the scaled replications of aircraft within a wind-tunnel environment used to deduce performance of full-size aircraft. The process of physical modeling is frequently used in construction. Many logistical managers use physical models when planning a new warehouse layout. The disadvantage of using physical models in total system design studies is the complexity, time, and cost requirements of constructing the replications.

The abstract model uses symbols rather than physical devices to represent a system. A variety of abstract models exist, but the two most commonly used in logistical system design are block-flow diagrams and mathematical symbols. In a block-flow symbolic treatment, the system is illustrated by communication and product-flow diagrams. In a mathematical model, the components and interrelations of a system are expressed in terms of equations.

Model development involves equations to handle operating relationships and, to the degree desired, feedback mechanisms. Programming consists of writing computer instructions to handle the required computations. Managerial responsibility in model formulation and programming is limited to a control of expense and constant review of progress. It is not unusual to have weekly briefings on development progress. Although excessive managerial pressures can be a deterrent to creativity, a lack of progress control can result in a substantial waste of resources.

DESIRABLE MODEL ATTRIBUTES.   Regardless of the specific model structure, a well-designed model will reflect a number of desirable characteristics. Four such characteristics are reviewed in this section.

---

[4] A comprehensive classification of model types is found in Jay W. Forrester, *Industrial Dynamics* (Cambridge, Mass.: The MIT Press, 1961), Chap. 4.
[5] Ibid., p. 49.

Modular Construction.   Although modular construction is not critical to all types of system models, the approach is recommended for the development of logistical models. The modular or building-block approach begins with a single module of the system being modeled and then adds modules until the total system is modeled.

The main advantage of modular construction is that it permits a complex system to be divided into a number of smaller subsystems. With identification of basic modules, a variety of system designs can be combined from the modules, thereby introducing considerable design flexibility.

Each module represents a part of the total system that is influenced by limited input variables and produces limited outputs. Ideally, it can be initially represented by a block diagram and the system, in total, can be illustrated graphically by connecting the blocks.[6]

Accuracy.   Naturally, unless a model is accurate with respect to the situation under study, its output will be of little value to management. Accuracy involves both data collection and the verification of model design.

One of the most costly aspects of modeling is the collection of data necessary to formulate all elements of the system model. One benefit of a modular approach is that it permits data to be collected and refined on a buildup basis. To an extent, the collection of unnecessary data and duplication are safeguarded against.

Managerial considerations related to model validation and calibration are further discussed under the project procedure section of this chapter.

Simplicity.   As a general rule, the models constructed should be as simple as the situation under design will permit, thereby reducing the complexity of data collection and model verification. One method of reducing complexity is to aggregate as many modules as possible, thereby eliminating the sheer number of functional relationships modeled.

Another interesting approach to simplifying a model is to concentrate design efforts upon the most important linkages of a planning situation.[7] This has the net effect of neglecting weak linkages. Procedures have been developed to identify the relative importance of linkages in a model's structure.[8]

The notion of strong link concentration is to forget about the occasional shipment that may take place unless it represents a regular relationship. Thus, the emergency shipment of a product from the manufacturing plant to a customer to supplement a critical warehouse out-of-stock situation could very well be a one-time activity that should be eliminated from system redesign efforts. One-time and weak linkages can render a model very complex, while adding little to or even reducing the relevancy of the design solution.

Adaptability.   Adaptability or universality of a model refers to the ease

---

[6] See Chapter 11, pages 338–339.

[7] Important or strong links are defined as those between which important activity takes place.

[8] William K. Kolstein and William L. Berry, "Work Flow Structure: An Analysis for Planning and Control," *Management Science*, February 1970, pp. 324–37.

with which it can be adapted to different analysis situations. From a managerial viewpoint, a high degree of adaptability is desirable in order to reduce the cost of additional model development as planning situations are confronted.

A model constructed along the basis of nodal locations, levels, and linkages has a high degree of adaptability to any planning situation involving temporal and spatial integration. In this respect a logistical system model has a great deal in common with any other network model.[9]

The more specialized the model becomes, the greater its relevancy to a specific planning situation and the less its overall adaptability. However, special-purpose models can incorporate greater redundancy, which may be a desirable feature in model design.

Redundancy in a modeling context increases reliability by providing backup structures. Although important to select types of system performance, such as aerospace guidance systems, system backup assumes greater importance in logistical operating systems such as order processing and inventory control. The important point is that universal models have greater difficulty in incorporating redundancy features.

The four characteristics reviewed are considered important aspects of logistical system design models. The characteristics covered are neither exhaustive nor necessarily the most important characteristics in terms of models in general. The important point is that a considerable degree of judgment must be integrated into model design. No exact rules exist to guide the model builder in these critical design areas.

REQUIREMENTS EVALUATION. For logistical planning the range of available models can be classified on the basis of the mathematical techniques they utilize in arriving at a design solution, their structural capabilities, and the number of echelons considered. Each will be discussed briefly.

Analytic–Simulation. Mathematical models may be classified as analytic or simulation, depending upon the specific analysis technique used to generate design solutions. Analytic techniques seek a precise answer to the design situation confronted. To utilize analytic techniques, it is necessary that all relationships in a system design be capable of full description. When such system definition is attainable, analytically optimum design solutions can be determined.

In complex logistical system design situations, it may be next to impossible to identify all the relationships that exist within the potential combinations of warehouse locations, inventory allocations, transportation alternatives, order processing, and material handling. It is necessary to make a great number of assumptions to avoid overcomplication of the model. In such situations a useful alternative to an analytical technique is to employ simulation. A simulation

---

[9] For an example, see Omar Keith Helferich and Robert M. Monczka, "Development of a Dynamic Simulation Model for Planning Material Input Systems," *Journal of Purchasing*, August 1972, pp. 17–33.

model utilizes computation methods to replicate system design and performance. However, it contains no specific mathematical procedure that assures identification of the best possible solution. A simulation model does not attempt specifically to identify relationships within the model. Emphasis is placed upon the way that various components interact in terms of system performance.

The primary objective in logistical system design is to identify an arrangement of components that will meet specific cost–service performance specifications. Consistent with the systems concept, emphasis is placed on performance of the total system and not on relationships among variables. Therefore, although it is theoretically desirable to isolate optimal design solutions, it is not necessary for improving logistical system design.

The tempo of business change coupled with the inability to consider all facilities and resource commitments variable at a given point in time permits considerable imperfection in the system design process. Even if an optimum system could be conceived and modeled, it is doubtful that construction and overall implementation could be completed in sufficient time to enjoy the perfect arrangement. Thus the selection between analytic and simulation techniques depends upon the type of planning situation confronted.

Both types of techniques have substantial application in overall logistical planning. Analytic techniques can be employed in design situations where the nature of the problem is sufficiently limited to allow a full description of relationships. In Chapters 11 and 12, models using analytic techniques are illustrated. Analytic techniques in logistical management are most frequently used in operational decision making.[10]

In planning situations requiring simultaneous treatment of all components of the logistical system over a time horizon, simulation procedures are used extensively. The two types of simulation most utilized are static and dynamic. Simulation is discussed and illustrated in Chapter 11. It is interesting to note that large-scale models in the logistics field have begun to combine both types of techniques within a single structure.[11] For example, a dynamic simulation model may include one or more analytical techniques to handle specialized design solutions at a given point during the planning horizon, that is, the determination of economic order quantities or the location of a specific warehouse.

Static–Dynamic Structure. The fundamental difference between static and dynamic models rests on time interrelationships. A model is static if it deals with time periods on an exclusive basis with the system in equilibrium during analysis. For example, a static model may replicate system performance over 13 four-week periods during an operating year. As such, the model would cover an extended time horizon. The modeling process is static if each of the time periods is treated independently.

---

[10] Several illustrations are presented in Chapter 12.

[11] Alfred A. Kuehn, "Complex Interactive Models," in *Quantitative Techniques in Marketing Analysis* (Homewood, Ill.: Richard D. Irwin, Inc., 1962), pp. 106–23.

If the time periods are linked in a manner wherein one time period's performance can influence the next time period's design, then the model is dynamic.[12] The 13-period replication is dynamic if each of the time intervals is linked on a recursive basis with linkage accomplished by feedback mechanisms.

The significant point in favor of a dynamic model is the capability it provides to study the interrelation of components of a logistical system. In a dynamic model performance cycles can be replicated on the basis of total elapsed days required to complete the logistical activity. If desired, the time required to perform specific functions such as order communication, warehouse processing, or transportation can be included in the model as either constant values or on a varied basis using probability distributions.[13] The dynamic model incorporates the time and possible delays necessary to perform specific functions. Thus, customer service is capable of measurement in terms of availability, speed, and consistency of performance on a customer-by-customer basis as well as for individual orders using a dynamic model.

The determination of whether a static or dynamic approach should be used in logistical modeling depends, for the most part, on the type of planning situation confronted. As a general rule, if inventory strategy is a significant part of the design task confronted, the most desirable approach is dynamic. A static model may be fully adequate for the purpose of locating a single warehouse. In contrast, total system planning can be more realistically modeled on a dynamic basis.

Single–Multiple Echelon.   In Chapter 3 the performance cycle was identified as the fundamental concept around which integration of logistical functions is achieved. In Figures 3-1 and 3-2 the nature of multiechelon performance cycles was introduced to illustrate the complex nature of the typical logistical channel. More often than not, multiple echelons must be considered if the modeling objective is to plan the total logistical system.

Models can be classified according to their capability to replicate echeloned channel structures. If a particular model can only represent one performance cycle level at a time, it is classified as *single echelon.* For example, a model which has the capability to evaluate the number of distribution warehouses but must assume the remainder of the enterprise facilities as given would be single echelon. In contrast, if all levels of facilities can be included in the modeling process and a simultaneous evaluation can be rendered, the model is classified as *multiecheloned.*

The determination of the need for either single or multiecheloned modeling capacity basically results from the planning objectives and constraints. If a multiecheloned structure is desired, more data are required to operationalize

---

[12] For a clear explanation of dynamics, see Thomas H. Naylor, Joseph L. Balentfy, Donald S. Burdick, and Kong Chu, *Computer Simulation Techniques* (New York: John Wiley & Sons, Inc., 1966), pp. 16–20.

[13] Models are typically classified as either deterministic (constant) or stochastic (probabilistic), based upon this aspect of structure.

the model. If one objective is to evaluate the potential for flexible performance cycles, then data must be collected to permit linkup of all possible movement arrangements. Thus the decision concerning the number of levels or echelons to be included in a planning model should be carefully reviewed. Generally, analytic models are restricted to single-echelon situations, whereas simulation models may be designed to replicate multiecheloned structures.

CONCLUSION—MODELING. The major responsibility of management in model selection is to evaluate the recommendations of the specialist in terms of time and cost. It is to be expected that the specialist will be more concerned with development of broad-gauged models requiring complex integrative techniques. Management must balance this desire for exacting answers, perfect information, and sophistication with related cost and time requirements. In addition, management must understand the capability and limitations of proposed techniques. Although technical evaluation of problem requirements is an area of specialized talent, deciding if a firm can commit the necessary resources is a managerial responsibility. Neglect of this responsibility at an early stage of study development is perhaps the greatest cause for subsequent failure.

Project Procedure

Given the selected method of analysis, the project procedure consists of four steps: (1) definition of data requirements, (2) data collection, (3) georeference classification, (4) model validation and calibration, and (5) analysis. Each will be discussed in this section.

DEFINING DATA REQUIREMENTS. The data required to operationalize a computerized technique can be classified according to their utilization in the modeling process. A well-defined body of knowledge exists concerning the relationship of data to model design. Four aspects of modeling that have data requirements are (1) components, (2) variables, (3) parameters, and (4) functional relationships.

Components. The components of a model consist of the entities that are being described by a set of equations. They are the objects of primary interest in the system design. In terms of logistical system models, the entities or components are facility type and size, transportation, inventory, communication, and material handling. These factors constitute the resources of the firm that must be integrated to formulate a logistical system. Data must be collected on each system component.

Variables. The variables in a model serve the purpose of relating components. A number of variables exist within a complex model structure. The most common are exogenous, status, and endogenous variables.

Exogenous variables are independent of the system being modeled. They constitute inputs to the model. As such, an exogenous variable's impact upon the system causes it to react or perform in a specified manner. Exogenous variables can be classified as instrumental or environmental on the basis of control exercised by the model builder or user.

Instrumental variables can be controlled or manipulated by the model user for experimental design. They are taken as given by the model but are controlled by the user. Thus they can be changed at will for purposes of testing their impact upon system design. In terms of logistical models, order-size policies, inventory dispositions, and customer service standards all represent instrumental variables.

Environmental variables cannot be controlled by the model user since he has no direct influence upon their nature or value. Thus the impact of environmental variables must be taken as given. A prime example of an environmental variable influencing logistical system design is the geographical distribution of product demand. The logistical system must service the product orders that evolve from basic demand determinants; however, no control exists over the geographical distribution of demand for the purpose of improved logistical design.

Environmental variables may have constant impact upon logistical system performance or may impact only at specific points in time. For example, while we hope that demand impact will be continuous, we hope that the impact of a fire, flood, or other acts of nature will occur rarely, if ever. Both types of environmental factors impact the model's performance and must be accommodated in design.

While variables generated by the environment cannot be controlled with respect to actual impact, they can be manipulated by model users to evaluate system design. In this form of evaluation, it is possible to determine how the logistical system would perform if environmental variables changed. As a result, a logistical system design having a high degree of capability to handle the most probable environmental changes with the least system disruption can be determined.

A critical aspect of model design is to define the system's boundary or dividing line between instrumental and environmental variables. The boundary influences the system's design range and will have a major impact upon the accuracy and relevancy of the resultant model.

Exogenous variables can also be viewed in terms of their purpose to the model. In this sense they are classified as set and flow variables. With respect to input, set and flow variables constitute the data necessary to establish and use the model.

Set data establish the prevailing system prior to the design process. To initiate the modeling procedure, it is necessary to define customers by location, size, and product demands. In addition, georeference coding is also required for raw-material sources, suppliers, existing manufacturing plants, inventory accumulations, distribution warehouses, transport capacity, and all other factors involved in the existing logistical system. Set data also include values for various managerially determined constraints on system design. The degree of desired customer service and a statement of available resources are of critical importance. If any given data are considered beyond the boundary of the model but influential to the system design, they are classified as environmental.

Flow data represent the stream of operational demands to be placed upon the system during the study or planning period. At an operational level, flow data will be constructed as a series of shipment requirements by customers or other terminal locations. Such activity may be listed sequentially or randomly generated in order of occurrence for each time period under study. In seeking the best system design, flow data are held constant during analysis. The end result is a system status that will most effectively meet managerially determined service policies at the lowest total cost.

Status variables describe the system's state at any given time. In a logistical model, system state reflects the condition of all components with a particular design relationship or state. Each system state is based upon a set of relationships among components that will have a system service capacity and associated cost.

The starting system state is defined by the set data formulated under initial conditions. In logistical system modeling, initial state formulations must be sufficiently broad to allow inclusion of all potential system configurations. The fundamental purpose of the model is to modify state variables as a result of flow data processing, thereby providing an improved system design.

Here, perhaps better than from any other vantage point, the difference between simulation and analytic models can be illustrated. Analytic models deal with a limited number and range of status variables and seek the best or optimal relationship between those considered. Simulation models are more comprehensive with respect to the range of variables treated. The more comprehensive range is obtained at a sacrifice in determining the optimal relationship or system state arrangement.

Endogenous variables are dependent upon system performance and constitute output of the system. As a result of the interaction of exogenous and status variables, endogenous variables are generated according to the operating characteristics of the model.

The main managerial involvement with logistical design models is with the output printouts. Given an initial system state and both set and flow endogenous variables, the output expresses for management the degree of improvement obtainable from variations in system design. As will be elaborated later, depending upon the model under consideration, such output may take the form of operational status reports, profit-and-loss statements, or special analysis of problem situations.[14]

Parameters. In the design and operation of a model, *parameters* represent variables that do not change as a function of model operation. In other words, they constitute restrictions upon the model.

For purposes of this treatment, a parameter is defined as a design limitation

[14] See pages 434–440.

on a model's structure and boundary. Parameters define the components that will be formulated by system state variables and the set limits of the endogenous variables that define the system boundary. The parameter is different than the managerial constraint identified during the project planning stage.

Constraints are limits placed upon the values of system state variables as well as both endogenous flow and set variables. These limits, both upper and lower, are enforced by the model user in order to exclude specific aspects of the study situation from system design modification. For example, manufacturing plant locations may be held constant in the design of a logistical system.

Both parameters and constraints may be varied by modification of the set data. The general procedure is to hold both constant in initial design of a logistical system. Once a system design is isolated that meets a specific operating requirement, parameters and constraints may be varied for sensitivity impact upon the design solution.

Functional Relationships. *Functional relationships* describe the interaction of all types of variables as the model functions. In modeling terminology, functional relationship, transformation, and algorithm are used interchangeably.

It is necessary to formulate the relationships among all variables included within the system structure. In essence, functional relationships are behavioral because they reflect the impact of change in system state. For example, the addition of a warehouse will result in substantial changes in transport, inventory, and communication demands placed upon the system. The functional relationship formulas provide a means for determining resultant changes in system state occasioned by the modeling process. As such, functional relationships are flow formulations, whereas system states are level equations.[15]

An important part of the transformations of a model is the feedback mechanism. As indicated earlier in the chapter, feedback is essential to rendering the model dynamic. Given an initial system state flow, exogenous variables are processed to determine if an improved system state is possible. The degree of improvement is measured by change in the endogenous variables or output of the model. Such an improved system state results from analysis of operational relationships over a period of time. Feedback transformations are the manner by which time-related performance penalties and delays are formulated in a model.

The impact of feedback transformations influences the derived system state. Thus stability is introduced into the modeling structure. A stable model will strive to maintain its original or initial state and make appropriate modification as disturbing events occur. An unstable model tends to amplify disturbances. Instability results because lags and unplanned interruptions are not dampened out by the ability of the system's functional relationships to take corrective

---

[15] For an expanded discussion, see Omar Keith Helferich, *Development of a Dynamic Simulation Model for Planning Physical Distribution Systems: Formulation of the Mathematical Model* (unpublished Ph.D. dissertation, Michigan State University, 1970), Chaps. 2 and 3.

system state action. The end result may be destruction of the system as it loses complete control.

Given a stable system, a disturbance, such as a two-week out-of-stock on a fast-moving product, would be expected to result in temporary adjustments in stock levels to protect the desired level of inventory availability. However, unless demand stabilized at a higher level, the model would seek to reinstate the original condition. In any event, a stable model would retain the desired performance level with a minimum of oscillation. In contrast, an unstable system would be more likely to experience prolonged oscillation between excessive and deficient inventories.

The typical manager may not view out-of-stock performance in terms of stability. However, the odds are high that instability has been experienced in actual operations. An unstable situation seldom improves until some external force intervenes. In consecutive periods, such external force may well be the controller when inventories peak and the sales manager at times of inventory drought. The development of stability in the logistical system can greatly reduce this conflict.

DATA COLLECTION. In actual system design practice, the process of data collection began with the feasibility assessment. In addition, a fairly detailed specification of data is required in the formulation or adaptation of the system model. However, at this point in the procedure, the detailed data must be accumulated and organized for use in analysis. One aspect of data collection is that the model can often be initially calibrated and validated using assumed or artificial data. Once operational, the model can be subjected to sensitivity analysis to determine the categories of data of particular importance to the design solution. Once identified, the data preparation area can concentrate on the critical information categories.

For purposes of discussion, the types of data required in a logistical design study are grouped as internal and external. Each is briefly discussed.

Internal Data. The majority of data required in a logistical study can be obtained inside from internal records. Although considerable digging may be required to come up with all the necessary pieces, most of the information is available.

The first category of required data is that related to sales and customer orders. The annual sales forecast and percentage sales by month, as well as seasonality patterns, are necessary to structure the total volume to be modeled. An historical sample of customer order invoices is necessary to classify order characteristics. This sample, stratified by size and type of customer, can be used to generate orders to be processed by the system model.

Specific customer data are required, and ideally the data should be classified on a georeference basis. Location, type, size, order frequency, growth rate and special logistical services required are perhaps the most significant grouping of data needed.

For materials management it is necessary to identify the sources of manufacturing and purchasing. In addition, a classification of raw materials and parts by demand and type is required.

While manufacturing plant locations may not be a variable in a logistical design, it is necessary to specify the number and location of plants, the product mix produced, production schedules, and seasonality of production.

With respect to inventory transfer, reorder priorities, shipment policy, warehouse processing times, and cost must be identified. In particular, inventory control rules and product allocation procedures are required.

For each current and potential warehouse, it is necessary to establish operational costs, maximum-product-mix storage, and service capabilities. For the model structure it is necessary to identify the location and size of all existing warehouses as well as locations that may be added during analysis.

In the area of transportation, the number and type of modes utilized, as well as the criteria for selecting each mode, must be established. Rates and transit times by modes, as well as shipping rules and policies, must be quantified. If private transportation is to be included in the analysis, then all relevant data are required.

In the areas of inventory and communication, it is necessary to identify reorder policies, costs of inventory maintenance, order-processing time, and cost. Definition of the existing and potential reliability and capability of the order-communication system is required to provide the basis for alternative systems analysis.

Obviously, the collection of data for a detailed logistical system is a time-consuming and expensive task. The problem is complicated by the fact that synthetic costs and operating data are necessary to accommodate system modifications that require modeling of nonexistent logistical component arrangements.

While the various types of data here noted may be more or less than those required to evaluate a specific type of logistical system modification, the description provides an overall perspective. The prime justification of placing formal data collection following modeling is to limit the chance of collecting unnecessary information.

A final note concerns the quality of the data used in analysis. Simply stated, the design solution will be no better than the data it is based upon.

External Data.   In most logistical planning situations, a selected amount of basic environmental data is required to model the system into future time. Management can normally provide an estimate of expected or desired sales for a planning horizon up to 10 years. The difficulty comes in obtaining a market-by-market distribution of the total forecast.

One solution to the problem is to use demographic factor projections that correlate highly with sales. For example, assume that a multiple correlation exists among sales, school enrollment, family size, and total population. Based on this correlation, future sales in any geographic area can be forecast by projection of these demographic factors.

The task of collecting demographic base data has become relatively simple.

The U.S. Department of Commerce now makes available the Census of Population and Housing Fifth-Count Tallies Classified by ZIP Code Area.[16] These data are available on computer tapes, and provide all necessary information to develop a positive correlation. A variety of projections concerning demographic factors are regularly published by various government agencies and universities. Thus a reasonable data bank of environmental information is readily available.

Additional external data required will be information concerning competitive logistical system designs and the marketing channel. An important interest will be competitive facility locations. In most cases this is readily available from published reports, annual reports, and the general knowledge possessed by company executives. The main purpose in collecting these data is that during the analysis phase of the study, it is desirable to compare the customer service capabilities of one or more major competitors to the system under consideration.

GEOREFERENCE CLASSIFICATION. For modeling purposes, data concerning sales, customers, product raw materials, and demographics need to be classified on a geographical basis. Distribution of such data by individual markets provides the geographical structure of demand or material source that must be serviced. The purpose of the model is to arrange the logistical system components in such a manner as to provide a level of service to individual markets at the lowest total cost. Thus selection of the georeference classification method is an extremely important aspect of the system design procedure.

A number of georeference classification structures have been developed. The six most useful to logistical modeling are (1) customer point locations, (2) county, (3) standard metropolitan statistical area (SMSA), (4) economic trading area, (5) ZIP code, and (6) grid structure.

For purposes of selection in any given modeling situation, the alternative georeference structures can be evaluated on the basis of two criteria: (1) data attributes, and (2) specific modeling requirements. Table 10-2 provides a summary of the major considerations in evaluating each criterion.

Customer Point Locations. The individual customer or material location is the most detailed georeference classification. One disadvantage of developing a model structured on individual customers is that the sheer number can greatly slow processing. However, in some cases where a relatively few customers or supply sources are critical to logistical system design, specific customer detail may be justified.

When it is desirable to classify on the basis of specific customers, their geographic location can be identified by latitude and longitude or by use of a point reference system. A widely used point reference system is PICADAD,[17]

---

[16] For a complete discussion of the usefulness of ZIP data, see *Rand McNally Zip Code Atlas* (Chicago: Rand McNally & Company, 1975).

[17] Donald E. Church, "Picadad: A System for Machine Processing of Geographic and Distance Factors in Transportation and Marketing Data," Bureau of the Census, U.S. Department of Commerce, 1965.

TABLE 10-2
Criteria in Georeference System Evaluation

Comparative georeference system attributes
    Size of unit
    Stability
    Homogeneity
    Flexibility
    Mutual exclusiveness
    Geographical continuity
    Availability of periodically updated data
Model-oriented georeference system attributes
    Availability of relevant data at the basic data unit
    Appropriateness of data unit coverage to the markets serviced by the firm
    Ability to determine distance from logistical facilities to data unit
    Compatibility of data unit to the firm's management information system

---

which stands for PI, place identification; CA, characteristics of area; and DAD, procedure for computing distance and direction. Developed by the U.S. Department of Commerce, PICADAD provides a method to pinpoint almost every city in the United States. A special feature is that the reference system includes the computation procedure for calculation of distance. Determination of whether or not to use a point reference system rests with the level of detail desired. All other systems group geographical areas for purposes of data collection.

County. The county provides a reference system that for the most part is structured on historical political patterns. A great deal of data is available on a county basis. It is the basis for grouping of census data and can be readily identified to larger data sources such as SMSAs and states. Thus the county structure is easily controlled from the viewpoint of data availability and processing.

In terms of model usage, it is sufficiently homogeneous for many products, is mutually exclusive, stable, and provides geographical continuity. Distance can be determined by use of key or central city in the county without introducing significant error.

The primary disadvantage of the county is that it does not represent a trading area. The number of counties, approximately 3,000, is also a disadvantage in system model processing.

Standard Metropolitan Statistical Area. The SMSA is defined as a county or group of 300 continuous counties that contain at least one city or twin cities with a population of 50,000 or more.

The primary advantage of using the SMSA as a georeference base is that 300 data units can be used to represent over 70 per cent of the consumer sales or other demographic information needed to project future demand. Data are easy to collect and a great many are readily available in computer-processing format. As with the county, distance can be determined on a key-city basis.

The major limit is that the total set of SMSA units does not result in a geographically continuous control structure. In addition, the SMSA structure is designed to change as a function of growth patterns.

Economic Trading Area. The concept of an economic trading area (ETA) is to design a georeference system to suit the requirements of a specific firm's demand and management information.

For example, an ETA classification system could be developed on the following basis: (1) all SMSAs; (2) each county where sales exceed a specific minimum that is not included in an SMSA. However, a set of rules for grouping other georeference systems would be acceptable. The main advantage is custom design. Distance can be calculated on a key-city basis.

The primary disadvantage of ETAs is that they will be geographically large. The number would fall between the 300 SMSAs and the 3,000 counties.

ZIP Code. A zip-based georeference system is formulated on the U.S. Postal Service ZIP Code Sectional Center System, which divides the country into 552 areas, including about 314 multicoded cities. The Postal Service describes an area as follows:[18]

1. It includes a hub city that is a national center for local transportation.
2. It includes between 40 and 75 post offices.
3. The most remote post office is no more than 3 hours' normal driving time from the hub city.

It is possible to further subdivide the ZIP areas into up to 20,000 specific areas if the full classification is employed. In fact, the census data, available on a ZIP basis for the first time in 1970, are extended to the most detailed level.

The primary advantage of the ZIP georeference system is flexibility. The classification is geographically continuous and relatively stable. It is common for firms to maintain ZIP codes in their data files, which greatly assist in obtaining internal data. Finally, distance can be determined on a hub-city basis.

The only significant limitation of the ZIP Code reference system is that it is not as homogeneous as some other data classification units. The geographic size of an area can vary greatly.

Grid Structure. Under a grid structure classification base, the United States is divided into geographically standardized blocks. The primary example of this form of classification is the REA grid.[19] REA originally developed the grid for purposes of pricing their transportation service. The concept divides the United States into 1-degree-square blocks based on latitude and longitude.

[18] For a detailed study of geocoding systems, see Pamela A. Werner, *A Survey of National Geo-Coding Systems* (Washington, D.C.: U.S. Department of Transportation, 1972).
[19] Ibid.

Each block is further divided into 256 smaller squares, each containing approximately 41 square miles.

The grid system is relatively the smallest, most homogeneous, completely stable, highly flexible, mutually exclusive, and geographically continuous among the georeference systems available. In addition, it has been modified to accommodate distance by the elimination of curvature distortion.[20]

The primary limitation of a grid reference system is significant. In most cases it cannot be used without significant modification and adjustment of both internal and external data. The relevant data required in logistical design are not grouped in a manner compatible to grids. Depending upon the situation, one or more georeference systems may be combined to formulate the data-classification structure for a system model. For example, it is not uncommon for the ZIP sectional areas to be used as the primary reference base supplemented by identification of a large number of customers on a point basis.

Among the six georeference systems reviewed, the ZIP code appears to be most widely used for logistical system models.[21] The ZIP configuration meets all the desirable attributes specified in Table 10-2. The only serious limitation is that the areas are not uniform in size, which somewhat prohibits analysis based on density. However, the increasing availability of precoded and updated data is the main attribute of a ZIP-based reference system.

Data Formatting and Aggregation. Given the study period, data must be developed for use as flow input and as set constants to the study model. The flow input represents historical records placed into a georeference code for analysis. Set constants represent a restatement of managerial parameters in terms of the system model. The technical aspects of each of these input formats are not a managerial responsibility.

In most situations it is necessary to aggregate data to reduce the amount of detail in a modeling situation. An example of aggregation would be the use of a limited number of products to reflect the activities of several different individual stockkeeping units. While aggregation is necessary, extreme care is required not to dilute data relevancy by excessive aggregation.

To a significant degree, the exactness of data rests upon the purpose of model construction. In analytical formulations, where precise answers are anticipated, extreme care must be taken to maintain accuracy. Some latitude exists in simulations. However, the assumptions of aggregation procedures must be checked prior to use.

MODEL VALIDATION AND CALIBRATION. A critical managerial responsibility is validation of the system model. Because mathematical model building and computer simulation is a complex task, the risk is always present that the technical expert will not understand or have sufficient knowledge of the specific

[20] Richard Lewis, *A Logistical Information System for Marketing Analysis* (Cincinnati, Ohio: South-Western Publishing Company, 1970), pp. 33–34.
[21] Helferich, op. cit., p. 121.

business under study. Thus, before a model is used for system design, its validity must be tested. If the model is not a reasonable approximation to the situation under study, little in terms of improvements can be anticipated.

In development of a validity test two conditions are desirable. First, the original model state should be structured to simulate a known situation. As a start, the first system state is often structured as a replica of the existing system. Second, extreme care must be exercised to use all input flow data associated with the study period. Given these two conditions it is possible to test validity by appraising the model's capability to simulate results of a known situation.

When using simulations, a popular procedure is to operationalize the model on the basis of assumed data. Provided that the components and the functional relationships of the model can be defined, the model can be validated in part on a diagnostic basis to determine sensitivity range. A well-defined body of model-verification theory exists which provides guidance in this critical area of modeling.[22] At least two aspects are important in logistical modeling: (1) surface relevancy (2) internal consistency.

Surface relevancy relates to the believable nature of model outputs. In essence, does the model output reflect what the manager expects to see about the situation under study? Managerial confidence is critical to the ultimate implementation of a design solution. Therefore, a common procedure in system simulation is to start the analysis by replicating the existing logistical system. This provides outputs for managerial review that correlate with operating results.

Within the model, a number of relationships must be validated to assure that the model will not lose its validity once it is utilized in experimental design situations. The manner in which flow data are handled must be free of bias, the functional relationships must be consistent, and the feedback mechanisms must be stable. Mathematical and statistical tests are available to assist in the validation of a model's internal consistency.[23]

Regardless of the care taken in testing model validity, an element of error remains a constant possibility. First, it is impossible to calibrate for all possible situations. This danger increases as the model becomes more dynamic. Second, it is never possible to eliminate or identify all compensating errors in a specific validity test. Although such errors may wash out in a validity test, their interrelation may become significant under alternative test situations. Every effort should be made to develop the best possible model, keeping in mind inherent limitations of the modeling process when evaluation results.

ANALYSIS.   The fifth step in the project procedure is to apply the selected model and associated data to develop a logistical plan. The analysis phase consists of experimental design and sensitivity analysis.

---

[22] Peter Gilmour, *Development of a Dynamic Simulation Model for Planning Physical Distribution Systems: Validation* (unpublished Ph.D. dissertation, Michigan State University, 1971), Chap. 2.
[23] Ibid.

Experimental Design.   The experimental design phase of study completion consists of establishing a set of runs for the model and analyzing the data that result. Assuming that the model is validated, it is necessary to plan a series of model runs or replications to arrive at a design solution.

In a technical sense, the formulation of an experimental design is concerned with measuring dependency. For example, given an independent event such as an increase in orders, what will be the impact on the dependent event, logistical cost? To date, there has been relatively limited development of techniques to assist the manager in analysis of experimental data generated by computer models.[24] If only one cause–effect relationship were of concern, a number of basic statistical measurements could assist in evaluation.[25] The problem is that a logistical design analysis is multivariate. Therefore, basic techniques of solution variance measurement do not offer a great deal of practical help.[26]

In the use of a model, the researcher must arrive at several basic decisions aimed at zeroing in on a solution. The structure and sequence of carrying out these decisions serves as the experimental design for analysis. In logistical system design problems, four basic determinations are necessary to form an experimental design[27]:

1. State the initial conditions and objectives in the form of parameters and constraints to limit the range of analysis.
2. Decide to what degree or over what range of values particular parameters and/or constraints will be permitted to vary in order to establish the necessary measures of system response to arrive at a solution.
3. Define the number and sequence of model applications or runs necessary to arrive at a solution.
4. To the extent practical, measure significant differences in output values (total cost and customer service) as a function of parameter or constraint variance.

The utilization of a logistical design model involves a great deal of trial-and-error analysis preceded by postulation concerning probable outcomes. Thus, in practical application the number of model runs (determination 3) to include in the experimental design will, to a significant degree, be a function of the range and variance of output values. This trial-and-error procedure is referred to as sensitivity analysis.

[24] Geoffrey Gordon, *System Simulation* (Englewood Cliffs, N.J.: Prentice-Hall, Inc., 1969), pp. 18–22.

[25] Naylor et al., op. cit., Chap. 4, and K. D. Tocher, *The Art of Simulation* (London: English University Press Ltd., 1963), Chap. 2.

[26] Gilmour, op. cit., Chap. 2.

[27] Developed from P. J. Kiviat, *Digital Computer Simulation Modeling Concepts* (Santa Monica, Cal.: Rand Corporation, 1967), p. 18; and M. Asimow, *Introduction to Design* (Englewood Cliffs, N.J.: Prentice-Hall, Inc., 1962).

Sensitivity Analysis. In *sensitivity analysis,* the objective is to see how design solutions vary as a result of systematically changing parameter and constraint values. The process of sensitivity analysis provides a way in which management can pretest alternative distribution policies. In many ways, the real payoff from an integrated logistical system study depends upon the range of sensitivity testing. Given a valid model, the design solution will represent the best possible logistical arrangement in terms of management parameters and constraints. However, this does not mean that the study is over. One of the greatest benefits of a system model is the ability to ask "what if" questions without taking a chance with the existing business.

In project planning, management constraints are introduced concerning output objectives, design parameters, and measurement standards. Each introduces an unknown degree of restraint on the problem solution. By holding all other factors constant, the influence of managerial assumptions can be evaluated in terms of total cost and customer service impact.

To illustrate the importance of such a diagnostic procedure, consider a typical problem confronted by management in logistical system design. Namely, what level of performance should we decide to provide our customers ? The reader will recall that one measure of customer service level is concerned with inventory availability, which, in turn, is a function of safety stock size.

Figure 10-3 charts the results of using sensitivity analysis to isolate the cost effect of increasing service availability from the existing level of 92 per cent to as close to 100 per cent as possible. To complete the analysis, the constraint dealing with service was relaxed on a systematic basis and total cost for achieving the specified availability was determined. For example, the constraint was first relaxed from 92 to 94 per cent and the associated design was identified. This procedure was continued until the total cost curve associated with the service function could be constructed. In the example illustrated in Figure 10-3, five computer runs were required to construct the curve. The chart illustrates both total cost and inventory cost.

An objective in sensitivity analysis is to select critical variables by early diagnosis in a design problem. By making value differentials in potentially critical variables and measuring how violently the design solution reacts, it is often possible to limit analysis quickly to those variables that really matter.

In reference to Figure 10-2, a feedback loop is incorporated in the recommended study steps between product procedure and project planning. This linkage reflects the recursive nature of sensitivity analysis. Once the model is fully operational, any or all of the restrictions developed during project planning may be subjected to sensitivity analysis. For example, constraints may be relaxed, measurement standards may be varied, objectives may be altered, and even project scope may be expanded or contracted. The prime requirement to permit comprehensive sensitivity analysis is the availability of data and sufficient model adaptability.

Heuristic Procedures. Modeling, by its very nature, is an interactive process wherein the user attempts to formulate a logistical strategy utilizing

FIGURE 10-3
Illustration of Using Sensitivity Analysis in Logistical Design

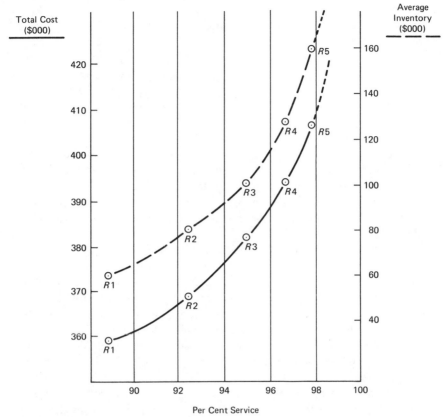

computer capabilities to assist in the plan development. As noted earlier, when discussing experimental design and sensitivity analysis the utilization of a model involves a great deal of trial-and-error analysis preceded by postulation concerning probable outcomes. To reduce analysis cost, a great deal of attention has focused on the development of a logical procedure to limit the range of strategic options to a manageable number. It is becoming increasingly common to refer to the solution approach as a *heuristic procedure*.[28]

A heuristic approach to problem solving closely parallels the thought process of the human mind. In essence, it is a steplike procedure that narrows in on the solution by systematic elimination of the alternatives. Such an approach

---

[28] Kiviat, *op. cit.*, p. 18.

does not necessarily result in selection of an optimal solution. The step procedure requires review at each decision point with related explanation at each step of the procedure. Thus the solution once derived requires little interpretation on the part of the planner.

In logistical planning, modeling constitutes only one aspect of the overall study. Regardless of the technical nature of the model employed, chances are it will be used a number of times under different design constraints to arrive at a solution. The very nature of system design is experimental since management is seeking a more satisfactory level of cost and/or service performance. Thus, whereas the technique employed may be precise in its analytical capabilities, the managerial process of analysis is not.

For example, assume that the desired end result of the analysis is to select the number, size, and location of distribution warehouses. Inventory policy is assumed constant and a number of warehouses is assumed to start the analysis. The total heuristic process attempts to reduce location alternatives to a minimum consistent with cost–service objectives. Managerial intervention is planned at critical points in the search process in order to guarantee acceptable results.

Under heuristic procedures, a given network of facilities is modeled and measured on the basis of cost and service capability. This information is given to management for evaluation. The assumption is made that management has sufficient appreciation of realistic requirements not to eliminate a vital aspect of the solution. As a result of this evaluation, additional distribution facilities are added to or deleted from the network by managerial discretion.

The modified system state is then evaluated. As new facilities are added or deleted, existing warehouses are reviewed in terms of continued desirability. Once again results are compiled for managerial review. This process continues until the most acceptable network of warehouses is determined.[29]

To assist management in the solution process, a number of models offer preprogrammed heuristic procedures. These procedures, often referred to as *machine heuristics*, consist of analysis rules which automatically test the sensitivity of selected parameters which are typically major focal points in strategic planning. The primary purpose of the preprogrammed analysis routines is to increase the efficiency of the modeling process. It is important to remember that machine heuristic procedures are based upon assumptions which will direct the solution process and influence outcome. Naturally, the planner must fully understand the assumptive logic behind the machine heuristics to avoid solution bias.

Formal heuristic procedures serve to highlight the fact that the most comprehensive computer models are at best an aid to management when developing a strategic plan. To a significant degree, modeling is more an art than a science.

---

[29] The initial model using this procedure in a logistical system design was reported by Harvey N. Shycon and Richard B. Maffei, "Simulation—Tool for Better Distribution," *Harvard Business Review* (November–December 1960), pp. 65–75.

Soundly developed heuristic analysis procedures serve to increase the trial-and-error efficiency.

Formulation of Recommendations

The most common question asked by business executives is "What can I expect to see as the end result of logistical planning?" Unfortunately, unless considerable evaluation is completed and a report prepared, the executive will see a voluminous stack of computer printouts. The mental barrier to approaching such a mass of data can greatly reduce the benefit gained from the study as a result of the need to "dig it out." Therefore, the best procedure is to develop a study summary report of significant findings. Such a report will contain the following information:

1. A statement of system customer service capabilities, including an estimate of performance probability.
2. An estimate of total fixed and variable cost expressed as a percentage cost of sales for a specified operating period.
3. A comparison of service and cost projections for the redesigned system in comparison to the current system for identical time periods.
4. Estimated results of several alternative service policies and related costs of performance.
5. A format of required transport, facility, communication, and inventory capabilities under the integrated system.

The results of the overall planning effort will contain infinitely more detail than the information listed above. In the final analysis, recommendations to support implementation must quantify two basic decision elements: (1) cost–benefit evaluations, and (2) risk appraisal.

COST–BENEFIT EVALUATIONS. At the feasibility stage of strategic planning, potential benefits were identified as service improvement, cost reduction, and cost prevention. It was noted that these benefits were not mutually exclusive and that a sound strategy might realize all simultaneously. To evaluate the potential of implementing a particular logistical strategy, a comparative analysis must be completed of present cost and service capabilities to conditions projected under a revamped system. The ideal benefit analysis compares the two systems fully implemented for a base period and then projects comparative operations across the planning horizon. Thus, benefits can be projected on the basis of one-time savings which result from system reconfiguration as well as reoccurring operating economies. The importance of viewing cost–benefit results across the planning horizon is illustrated by the following examples.[30]

---

[30] For a complete discussion of the following examples, see Donald J. Bowersox et al., *Dynamic Simulation of Physical Distribution Systems* (East Lansing, Mich.: Division of Research, Michigan State University, 1973).

Illustration I. The planning situation called for a 10-year evaluation of required warehousing capacity. The existing system consisted of six regional distribution warehouses. A sales growth of 50 per cent was forecast over the 10-year planning horizon. Management specified that customer service be maintained at or above the current level of 80 per cent of all orders being serviced at lowest possible total cost and within a five-day total order cycle.

Heuristic analysis established three design alternatives that management desired to evaluate in detail: (1) expand existing facilities, (2) expand existing facilities plus add two facilities, and (3) expand existing facilities plus add three facilities. The cost–service results of the detailed simulation runs are graphically illustrated in Figures 10-4 and 10-5.

FIGURE 10-4
Total Cost—Illustration I

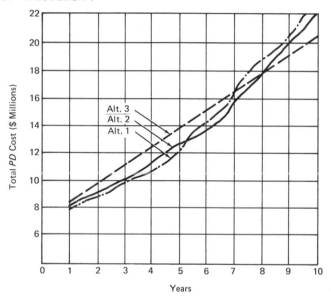

A surprising result was that total logistical system cost over the planning horizon was similar for each alternative. Each alternative experienced increasing costs over time. However, trade-offs between the various physical distribution components in each situation were substantially different. Alternative 1 experienced highest transport costs coupled with lowest inventory costs. The situation was reversed in the case of alternative 3.

Despite similar total system costs, a significant differential existed between the customer service capabilities of the three alternatives. Although not expected, all three systems did realize the stated managerial service goals. Over the planning horizons, however, alternative 3 realized greater than 90 per cent of all orders being serviced within a five-day performance cycle. Thus alterna-

FIGURE 10-5
Performance Cycle Time—Illustration I

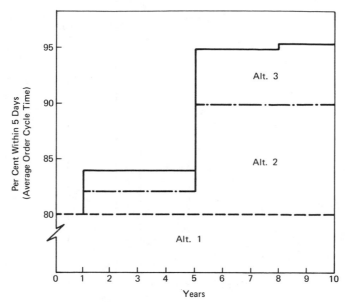

tive 3 was about 10 per cent more effective than alternative 1 at approximately the same total cost.

The preplanning management expectation was that additional warehouses would be required to maintain desired service standards, and that the total system cost associated with adding facilities would increase substantially. The simulated results provided a flexible plan for expanding service capabilities if and when desired as part of the total marketing offering. In the interim, cost–service objectives could be realized by retaining and expanding the existing warehouses.

Illustration II. The planning situation involved inventory planning for a market area consisting of eight states. In this situation the marketing organization desired the addition of a second warehouse to improve service capability and average order cycle by reducing transit time. Expectations were that the total cost of servicing the overall market would increase as a result of adding the second facility. A second alternative for improving customer service was to increase the safety stock at the existing warehouse. Increased safety stock was expected to improve average order cycle time via a reduction in back orders. The existing average order cycle time was 4.6 days; 75 per cent of all orders were filled within 5 days. Marketing desired a 10 per cent improvement at minimum total cost.

Addition of the warehouse (alternative 1) reduced the average order cycle time to 4.1 days, which was the equivalent of increasing the orders filled within

FIGURE 10-6
Order Cycle Time—Illustration II

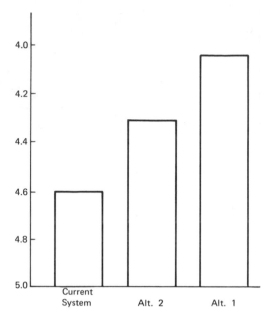

5 days from 75 to 92 per cent. Increasing safety stock at the existing warehouse (alternative 2) reduced the average order cycle by 0.3 day, to 4.3 days. This was equivalent to improving the percentage of orders filled within 5 days from 75 to 87 per cent. Over the 10-year planning horizon, the addition of a second warehouse provided the lowest-total-cost alternative.

The service–cost relationships of the two alternatives are illustrated in Figures 10-6 and 10-7. In this situation the warehouse addition resulted in the lowest cost and provided the highest average customer service. It is interesting to note that the addition of a warehouse was the more costly alternative for approximately the first three years of simulated operations but the least costly for the aggregated 10 years. Thus marketing could realize a 12 per cent increase in service capability for the initial three years at the lowest total cost by increasing safety stocks at the existing warehouse. Establishment of a second warehouse to be operational by the fourth year would realize an additional 5 per cent improvement in service and a continuation of the least-cost arrangement. This relationship of cost and service over the planning horizon is one of the many situations simulated to date which illustrates the importance of a dynamic planning structure.

Illustration III. A final planning illustration shows total system service relationships on (1) the number and sequencing of warehouse locations, (2) inventory cost related to performance delays for an eight-location structure, and (3) market area adjustment to postpone timing of warehouse additions.

FIGURE 10-7
Total Cost—Illustration II

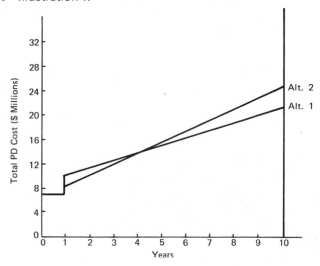

The general relationship of service as a function of the number and sequencing of warehouse additions is illustrated in Figure 10-8. A specific marketing situation was evaluated over a 10-year period in an effort to identify the shortest possible average order-cycle. A locational model was used to select the sequence and number of warehouse locations constrained only by permissible annual capital investment. Inventory performance was held constant at 85 per cent of all orders being filled within the average order-cycle time. Given the initial six warehouse locations, an expansion plan was selected from a list of 35 potential warehouse additions. The facility planning model isolated the expansion sequence by selecting additional warehouses on the basis of the incremental relationship between minimum added cost and maximum service.

In total, performance cycle time was reduced from 6.0 to 4.4 days by expanding the locational structure from 1 to 19 warehouses. As anticipated, improvement in simulated average order time increased at a decreasing rate as additional warehouses were added. No improvement was realized beyond 19 warehouses.

Based upon the expansion sequence illustrated in Figure 10-8, management elected to evaluate the addition of two warehouses beyond the existing six. An analysis was conducted to determine the relationship of inventory investment cost to average performance delays for the eight-warehouse configuration. In effect, the original constraint of 85 per cent of all orders being satisfied within 5.0 average order-cycle days (dashed lines, Figure 8-10) was simulated to obtain the service improvement possible from increased safety stock levels. For the particular number and location of warehouses it was determined that an increase from $7 to $14 million of annual inventory cost

FIGURE 10-8
Relationship Distribution Centers to Total Order Time—Illustration III

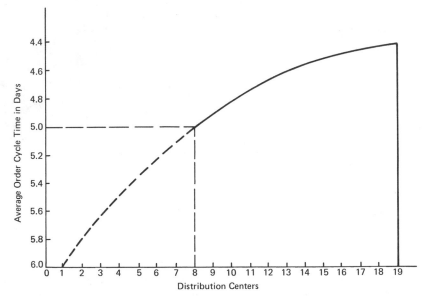

would be required to increase service from 85 to 100 per cent of all orders filled within 5.0 average order-cycle days (Figure 10-9).

Next, the alternative of adding two warehouses was subjected to sensitivity analysis, wherein market area assignments to specific warehouses were allowed to shift a maximum of twice during the 10-year planning horizon. The objective was to determine if a trade-off could be realized between investment and operating cost at little or no sacrifice in customer service. The sensitivity testing resulted in a plan to postpone the first facility by one year and the second facility by two years.

The situations illustrated demonstrate the results and recommendations expected from strategic planning. Each example was selected from an overall strategic planning situation to illustrate the importance of time horizon analysis. The illustrations indicate the depth of cost–benefit justification that should support a recommendation to adopt a specific logistical strategy.

RISK APPRAISAL. A second type of justification necessary to support planning recommendations is an appraisal of the risk involved in the proposed strategic plan. Risk relates to the probability of whether or not assumptions underlying the study will in fact materialize as well as an appraisal of potential hazards related to system switchover.

Risk related to assumptive logic of the plan can be quantified by selected sensitivity runs. For example, assumptions can be varied and the resultant

FIGURE 10-9

Percentage of Orders Filled in 5.0 Average Order-Cycle Days—Eight
Warehouse Configuration—One Year—Illustration III

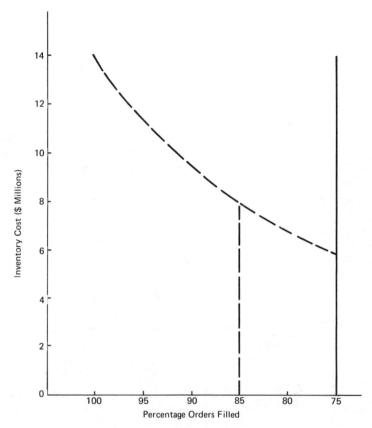

impact upon the performance under the proposed strategy can be calculated.
The end result of this form of appraisal should be a financial evaluation of
downside risk involvement if the predictions upon which the plan is predicated
do not fully materialize.

Risk related to system switchover can also be quantified. The implementation
of a strategic logistical plan, as noted earlier, may take several operating years.
The typical procedure is to develop an implemental schedule to guide system
switchover. To evaluate the risk associated with unanticipated delay a series
of contingency plans can be tested and reduced to an estimated loss of anticipated benefits.

CONCLUSION—FORMULATION OF RECOMMENDATIONS.   A great deal of planning
effort can be wasted if the recommended logistical strategy is not clearly
articulated. No blueprint exists regarding the ideal method supporting a plan

or presenting recommendations. Setting aside the detail, a good test of the strength of the recommendation's supportive logic is to see if the benefits and risks can be summarized clearly into one short statement for executive review. Details can be generated to the extent necessary to support planning conclusions when and if needed.

Implementation

One positive result of using a computer model when developing a logistical strategy is that a time-phased implementation program can be specified. Once management has selected a final strategy study, detail is used to develop an implementational program. It would be a rare situation when an across-the-board revision of a logistical system could be implemented. Thus the planning model is a valuable tool for selection of the steps that will provide the greatest payoff if implemented at once. Thus a five-year (or any other time period) implementation program can be developed with a measure of expected results. Priorities and checkpoints are necessary to guide revision of the existing system. The changing nature of business requires that constant checks be performed to test the continued validity of the system model.

From a managerial viewpoint, a final system design never really exists. The redesign implementation plan should constantly be adjusted to take advantage of change. The organization that develops a logistical planning model, formulates a redesign implementation plan, and then disregards the model forfeits a powerful planning tool. The continuous process of planning is illustrated in Figure 10-2 by a feedback linkage between implementation and feasibility assessment.

From the viewpoint of scheduling and control, the techniques of PERT and CPM offer management a methodology to assist in plan implementation.[31] Since full implementation of a strategic plan can be expected to span several years, operational planning for specific time periods will specify changes in system structure or operating procedure scheduled for implementation.

Summary

In this chapter a typology of logistical planning was presented that classified three requirements: (1) strategic, (2) operational, and (3) tactical. The main distinctions highlighted between the plans were the nature of asset commitment, the time duration of coverage, and the likelihood of the plan materializing.

The second and major section presented a six-step procedure (Figure 10-2) recommended as a managerial guide for conducting logistical planning. To illustrate the logic of the managerial guide, the strategic planning situation was utilized. With some modification the managerial guide is equally applicable

---

[31] See Chapter 12, pages 411–417.

to operational and tactical planning. In fact, when computer modeling is utilized, the model may provide capability to assist in all three planning requirements.

Emphasis throughout the chapter has been placed upon managerial responsibility rather than technical detail. Particular attention was directed to the critical nature of the manager in feasibility assessment, project planning, modeling, project procedure, presentation of recommendations, and implementation. The entire chapter stressed managerial involvement in overall planning administration. Attention in Chapter 11 is directed to a review of modelling techniques available for use in logistical planning.

Questions

1. What is the basic objective in a system redesign study? Is it normally a one-time activity?
2. In performing a feasibility assessment, why is the situational analysis extremely important? What is the role of developing a supporting logic?
3. Why must extreme care be given to measurement of competitors' service when undertaking redesign of a system?
4. Are design constraints specified at the early stage of a study capable of being modified at a later point in the system redesign? Why would this be done and to what extent is it practical?
5. Does the nontechnical manager have responsibility in model development?
6. What is meant by validity checking and calibration?
7. Why is geoclassification of data important to logistical studies?
8. Discuss the major differences among the six georeference classification systems presented in the chapter. Which method of classification does the author appear to favor, and why?
9. What is sensitivity analysis and what part does it play in experimental design?
10. Discuss the formulation of an implementation program as a result of a logistical redesign study. What would you consider to be the major ingredients of such a plan?

Design Techniques

This chapter presents an overview of logistical system design techniques. Throughout earlier chapters the systems approach has been presented as a method whereby complex logistical arrangements can be analyzed. The techniques reviewed in this chapter represent tools capable of applying systems technology to logistical strategic planning.

The initial section of the chapter presents some introductory comments regarding the use of models. Next, an overall classification of techniques reviewed in the chapter is presented in terms of computation characteristics as initially discussed in Chapter 10.[1] The third section describes symbolic replications, which are the most basic and simple to use logistical strategic planning models. Next, two classes of analytic techniques are reviewed. The final section presents two classes of simulation techniques. Each of the sections concludes with a brief commentary on the techniques discussed.

Nature of Strategic Planning and Modeling

A logistical strategy consists of a long-range plan for commitment of capital and managerial resources to the movement and storage operations of the enterprise. The specific objective of the strategic plan is to provide an operating structure capable of attaining the performance goals of the enterprise at the lowest total cost. Thus, it is the strategic plan that delineates where warehouse facilities will be located, where and which assortments and quantities of materials and finished inventories will be stocked, how transportation requirements will be performed, which techniques of materials handling will be

---

[1] See page 300.

employed, the methods and procedures of order processing and procurement as well as all other aspects of logistical operations. Perhaps the *most* important aspect of the strategic plan is that it provides the mechanism by which logistical operations are coordinated into an integrated effort.

The strategic planning process is appropriately viewed as a continuous process. The typical planning situation consists of a series of modifications to an existing logistical system. These planned modifications will be implemented over an extended time period. In this sense the planning situation is more appropriately identified as *system redesign,* as contrasted to a system design. In every organization a limit exists regarding the extent of structural change that can be effectively implemented during a given time period. For example, the opening or closing of two distribution warehouses may represent about all the facility change an organization can handle while maintaining day-to-day operational and tactical control of logistical performance. Thus, the implementation of a strategic plan may span a substantial time period.

The extended time required to activate a total logistical system strategy means that there is a good chance that the original plan will be modified prior to final implementation. Thus, the planning process as well as the techniques of analysis require the capability for periodic reevaluation of system design alternatives during the implementation period. Assuming a vigorous and ever-changing competitive situation, the period of implementation may never end.

To assist management in the formulation and review of strategic plans, a wide range of logistical *models* have been developed. As noted earlier, a model consists of a body of information and restrictions about a unique situation accumulated for purposes of systems analysis.[2] Thus, the model represents a substitute for actual field testing of potential strategies. When analytic or numerical computation procedures are incorporated in the model, it is typically referred to as a planning technique. In such cases, the identification as a technique means that the model provides a computation procedure whereby system design alternatives can be quantified. In this chapter the primary attention is directed to a managerial description of available logistical planning techniques. Planning techniques may or may not require computer processing, depending upon the size and complexity of the planning process. Planning techniques are appropriately reviewed as one and only one aspect of formulating a logistical strategic plan. To clarify this point in the reader's mind, it is suggested that the *Managerial Guide to Logistical Planning* illustrated in Figure 10-2 be reviewed.[3] The techniques of logistical system design are aids to assist in the overall process of formulating a strategic plan.

Owing to the relative newness of both the logistical field and quantitative techniques, an appropriate question is: How extensively are such techniques actually employed in logistical planning? A recent analysis of 75 industrial

[2] See page 301.
[3] See page 293.

TABLE 11–1
Classification of Strategic Planning Techniques in Terms of Six Selected Attributes of Importance to Requirement Evaluation

Category of Planning Technique	Technique Attribute					
	Analytic	Dynamic	Echeloned	Total System	Requires Computer[a]	Adaptable to Sensitivity Analysis
Symbolic replications						
Comparative analysis	Yes	No	No	No	No	No
Break-even analysis	Yes	No	No	No	No	Yes
Flowcharting	No	No	Yes	No	No	No
Analytic techniques						
Gravity location	Yes	No	No	No	No	No
Transportation LP[b]	Yes	No	No	Partial[c]	No	Yes
Simplex LP	Yes	No	No	Partial[c]	Yes	Yes
Mixed-integer LP	Yes	No	No	Partial[c]	Yes	Yes
Separable LP	Yes	No	No	Partial[c]	Yes	Yes
Trans-shipment LP	Yes	No	No	Partial[c]	Yes	Yes
Decomposition LP	Yes	No	No[d]	Partial[c]	Yes	Yes
Variable-range LP	Yes	No	No	Partial[c]	Yes	Yes
Simulation techniques						
Static	No	No	Yes	Partial[c]	Yes	Yes
Dynamic	No	Yes	Yes	Yes	Yes	Yes

[a] In a technical sense, all the techniques can be utilized on a manual basis. The classification is in terms of logistical strategic planning and practicality of application.

[b] LP, linear programming.

[c] These techniques are total-system in terms of the number of echelons modeled, with the exception that inventory level must be determined based on a calculation.

[d] Advanced applications of decomposition linear programming do provide the capability of dealing with three echelons in the design solution.

enterprises revealed that 43 were currently involved in logistical modeling. Among the firms using computerized techniques, 73 different models were reported.[4] The firms that reported being "into" modeling normally were multiple model users. Such models ranged from small-scale special-purpose applications to large-scale total-system-design techniques.[5] Thus, at least for a substantial number of enterprises, the use of computerized techniques to assist in logistical planning is a "here today" activity. This chapter is concerned with techniques having particular applicability to strategic planning. Chapter 12 focuses on applications related to operational and tactical planning situations.

Technique Attribute Classification

One important managerial concern in logistical strategic planning is to select the appropriate technique to assist in overall strategic planning. As would be expected, available techniques offer a wide variety of attributes as well as inherent limitations. The specific purpose of the *requirements evaluation* aspect of the planning procedure is to match technique capability to study requirements.[6] In total, this chapter reviews seven approaches. In the case of linear programming, seven different variations are discussed. Coverage places emphasis upon the computation technique as contrasted to description of a specific model. Table 11-1 lists the techniques discussed in this chapter and classifies each according to six features important to requirements evaluation.

The analytic feature means that the technique is capable of generating a mathematically precise answer to the design situation confronted. The dynamic feature indicates that the technique is time-based and incorporates feedback to achieve across-time performance evaluation. The echeloned feature reflects the technique's capability to handle more than one performance cycle or two nodal levels in the overall logistical structure. Total system capability means that all essential cost and service features necessary to formulate a strategy can be simultaneously evaluated. The need for computerized processing reflects the type of skills and financial commitment necessary to fully deploy the technique. The feature of adaptability to sensitivity analysis reflects the ease of varying objectives, constraints, and standards in the formulation of a finalized strategy.

The discussions that follow focus on specific techniques. Occasional reference to Table 11-1 will assist the reader in organization of the following materials.

---

[4] Robert G. House and George C. Jackson, *Trends in Computer Applications in Transportation and Distribution Management* (Columbus, Ohio: Ohio State University, 1976).
[5] Ibid.
[6] See Chapter 10, pages 303–306, for a discussion of modeling requirements evaluation.

Symbolic Replications

None of the first category of tools available to assist in strategic planning
are techniques in the precise meaning of the term. Thus, they are identified
as symbolic replications. Three such replications are discussed in this section:
(1) comparative analysis, (2) break-even analysis, and (3) flowcharting.

Comparative Analysis

One of the most widely used procedures for evaluating the desirability
between two courses of action is to calculate the comparative total cost.[7] The
procedure is easy to utilize. The primary requirement is identification of cost
accounts appropriate to each alternative method of operations.

For purposes of illustration, assume that a decision is required between
(1) continued direct shipment to a market area, or (2) use of a public warehouse
facility. The typical circumstance that might lead to such a review is a managerial belief that total cost could be reduced by use of consolidated transportation to a warehouse located in the market with local distribution beyond.
Another motivation may be a belief that customer service can be improved,
thereby increasing sales penetration as a result of having an inventory locally
available. Table 11-2 presents a total cost evaluation of the alternatives,
including the managerial assumptions necessary to complete the analysis.
If the warehouse facility is established, transportation cost for customer
delivery can be reduced by $62,500 on the volume currently sold in the market.
However, when all other costs are included in the analysis, establishment of a
warehouse facility will raise total cost by $121,040. Thus, if the primary ob-
jective is to reduce total cost, the most appropriate alternative is to continue
the practice of direct customer physical distribution.

From a marketing viewpoint, the availability of local inventory would
increase the service capability in terms of speed and consistency of delivery,
owing to the reduced distance of warehouse to customer shipments. Given
the assumption that before-tax profit is 15 per cent of sales, additional sales
in the amount of $806,933 would be required to offset the added distribution
costs. However, to assure the validity of the total cost estimates, the comparative evaluation would be again required on the basis of the incremental
additional tonnage added as a result of sales increase.

In terms of capability and comprehensive treatment, comparative analysis
has many limitations. First, the array of shipment sizes must be averaged.
Second, the approach has limited capability to evaluate alternative volume
levels. Third, the analysis is static. Fourth, the range of designs tested is

---

[7] This form of analysis was the initial application of total costing. See Howard T. Lewis,
James W. Culliton, and Jack D. Steel, *The Role of Air Freight in Physical Distribution*
(Boston: Division of Research, Graduate School of Business Administration, Harvard
University, 1956).

TABLE 11-2
Comparative Analysis: Direct Versus Public Warehouse Distribution

	Total Cost	
Account	Direct	Warehouse
Transportation		
Warehouse CL		$100,000
Customer LTL	$225,000	115,000
Customer TL	105,000	52,500
Total transportation	$330,000	$267,500
Other		
Plant processing	$130,000	$100,000
Inventory	87,500	175,000
Warehouse		110,000
Inventory control		7,500
Order processing		1,040
Managerial	17,000	24,500
Total other	$234,500	$418,040
Total cost	$564,500	$685,540
Savings direct	$121,040	

Assumptions:
1. Annual sales to market $7 million, standard cost of manufacturing 50%, total volume 100,000 cwt.
2. Customer order mix 50% TL and 50% LTL and warehouse CL.
3. Freight rates in ($/cwt):
   Plant to warehouse: CL $1.00.
   Plant to customer: LTL $4.50; TL $2.10.
   Warehouse to customer: LTL $2.30; TL $1.05.
4. Total day average inventory:
   Plant direct: 30 days at plant
   Warehouse: 15 days at plant, 10 days rail transit, 35 days at warehouse—total, 60 days.
5. Inventory carrying cost 30% of standard cost.
6. Warehouse cost—public facility, no fixed cost.
   Order processing: $20 per order, one order per week.
   Inventory control: 7.5 cents/cwt.
   Warehouse: $1.10/cwt.
7. Managerial and allocated amount of overall supervision required to manage market area physical distribution activities.
8. 15% profit before tax.

limited to those which management feels are acceptable alternatives. Fifth, facility locations must be assumed and held constant under any given design configuration. Thus the interrelationship of facility location is not treated in design configuration. Finally, the approach is not able to handle trade-offs between customer service and cost requirements with the same precision as other integrative techniques.

These limitations render comparative analysis deficient for large-scale integrative studies. The approach is useful for evaluation of proposed modification to limited parts of an existing system. For example, as illustrated, it can be employed to check if a given market area has reached a sufficient volume to support replacement of direct shipments with a warehouse. The comparative analysis is quick and inexpensive, and it requires a minimum amount of technical expertise or computation capacity. If used with care and on specific types of problems, it can represent a useful short-range planning tool.

Break-Even Analysis

A more sophisticated approach to evaluating system design alternatives is break-even analysis. The objective in *break-even analysis* is to evaluate the changing nature of total cost as a function of volume. Two or more alternative system designs are identified as potential systems. For example, assume that an enterprise is evaluating the alternatives of direct versus private warehouse physical distribution to a specific market. In addition, an alternative exists between establishment of a mechanized versus an automated facility in the event that utilization of warehousing represents the lowest total cost method of physical distribution. The initial step is to isolate the appropriate costs, similar to the procedure followed in comparative analysis. Once costs have been identified, the major difference is that they are then divided for purposes of analysis into fixed and variable groupings for each alternative.[8]

Each alternative will have different cost functions in each category. Some will have higher fixed costs than others. The variable costs of handling more-or-less average shipments will also be substantially different among alternative systems. For any given volume one system will have the lowest combination of fixed and variable costs and therefore will be the lowest-cost logistical alternative under consideration.

Table 11-3 provides an assumed grouping of fixed and variable costs related to transportation, inventory, and materials handling for the alternatives of direct distribution, a mechanized warehouse, and an automated warehouse.

When using break-even analysis, an attempt is made to express variable-cost relationships for each system in a formula. These formulas are linear in relationship and represent the variable cost of an additional average shipment to the market under study. Fixed costs are held constant. By testing alternative volumes of average shipments, it is possible to locate the level at which one system achieves lower cost than the next. The series of formulas represent the models of alternative systems under study.

Using the data presented in Table 11-3, the alternatives are ranked on the basis of relative fixed cost. The analysis starts with the lowest-fixed-cost system. The formulation of this illustration requires that two break-even points be determined: (1) direct versus mechanized warehouse, and (2)

---

[8] To review costing procedures and problems related to isolating logistical costs, see Chapter 8, pages 254–256.

TABLE 11-3
Example Costs for Break-Even Analysis

| | Physical Distribution Alternatives | | |
| | (1) | (2) Warehouse | (3) Warehouse |
Account	Direct	Mechanized	Automated
Fixed[a]	$10,000	$50,000	$100,000
Variable ($/cwt)			
Inbound transportation	—	$0.25	$0.25
Outbound transportation	$3.00	1.00	1.00
Material handling	—	0.75	0.25
Total variable	$3.00	$2.00	$1.50

[a] Fixed cost includes cost of average inventory commitment to each system alternative.

mechanized versus automated warehouse. With x representing the two break points, F = fixed cost, and V = variable costs, the analysis is as follows:

$$x_1 = \frac{F_2 - F_1}{V_1 - V_2}$$

$$= \frac{50,000 - 10,000}{3.00 - 2.00}$$

$$= \frac{40,000}{1.00}$$

$$= 40,000 \text{ cwt} \quad \text{or} \quad 4,000,000 \text{ pounds}$$

$$x_2 = \frac{F_3 - F_2}{V_2 - V_3}$$

$$= \frac{100,000 - 50,000}{2.00 - 1.50}$$

$$= \frac{50,000}{.50}$$

$$= 100,000 \text{ cwt} \quad \text{or} \quad 10,000,000 \text{ pounds}$$

The results are illustrated in graphic form in Figure 11-1.

Given the three alternatives in the illustration, direct distribution from the manufacturing plant would be the lowest cost alternative if the volume was less than 4 million pounds. Beyond 4 million pounds a mechanized warehouse would be justified, however, automation would not be economically feasible until the volume reached or exceeded 10 million pounds.

Break-even simulation has many of the same limitations as comparative analysis. Location is assumed, range of system alternatives is limited, and

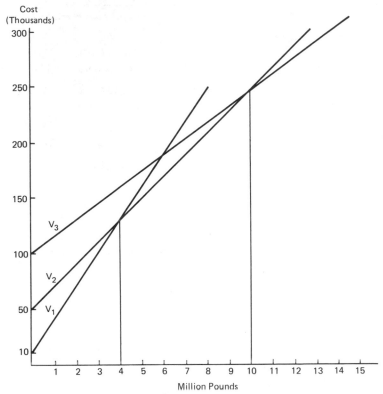

FIGURE 11-1
Least-Cost Chart: Break-even Analysis

service-cost relationships are lacking. Because testing can consider performance at alternative volume levels, break-even analysis eliminates one of the
main deficiencies of comparative analysis.

Break-even analysis has limited usefulness as a planning tool. It is frequently
utilized to aid operational decision making. For example, if alternative methods
of direct distribution exist to service a given market, break-even simulation
can be formulated on the basis of fixed and variable costs of each as a function
of shipment size. Given a particular shipment, it is possible to select the direct
distribution alternative that should be utilized. Even if a warehouse exists in
the service area, the model can provide valuable cost information to help
decide if the shipment should be sent directly from the factory. Under certain
conditions it may be less expensive to bypass the warehouse and ship direct.

Flowcharting

A final tool in the category of symbolic replications is to use *flowcharts* or
flow diagrams to replicate alternative logistical systems. The procedure con-

sists of diagramming the physical product and communication flows as connecting linkages between facility nodes. Once the diagram is completed, cost accounts associated with each node and category of linkage are identified. These costs are then grouped together to formulate a total cost projection for the system configuration illustrated by the flow diagram at a specified volume level. Given the flowchart, the costing procedure is identical to comparative analysis as illustrated in Table 11-2.

Flow diagrams represent the first step in the development of most computer models. However, the emphasis in modeling is on identification of components, variables, functional relationships, parameters, and constraints for purposes of model formulation and programming. In the case of direct use of flowcharting to aid in strategic planning, a different diagram must be developed for each alternative system.

Figure 11-2 illustrates a two production plant/three-distribution warehouse logistical system. This system has the following characteristics: (1) each of the production plants ships to all three distribution centers; (2) distribution warehouses have a communication capacity with each other and with central control; (3) distribution centers can interbranch-transfer when the situation is warranted; (4) when conditions justify, shipments can be made direct from production plants to customers; (5) customer orders are routed direct to distribution warehouses for shipment, if possible; and (6) inventory and production control is maintained at the central inventory control location, which is linked to distribution warehouses by data transmission.

The system detailed in Figure 11-2 represents a major simplification, because no detail is developed for major activity centers. In flowcharting the complete structure of a physical distribution system, the normal procedure would be development of diagrams for each subsystem. The procedure would be even more complex if the flowchart attempted to replicate the total logistical system. A recommended set of symbols for use in logistical system flowcharting is presented in Appendix V.

In terms of capability to replicate or conduct a comprehensive system design, flowcharts have the same limitations as both comparative analysis and break-even analysis. Although flowcharting can be used to identify alternatives, it must be supplemented by some form of costing to serve as an aid to system planning. Thus, although comparative analysis, break-even analysis, and system flowcharting provide tools to assist in limited research, more powerful and comprehensive techniques are needed for tackling complex distribution system studies. The next two sections review such techniques.

Analytic Techniques

Two main categories of analytical techniques useful in logistical system design are presented in this section. The *first* category consists of center-of-gravity techniques, which are useful when the major concern is the location of a single facility such as a warehouse or a terminal. The *second* category

FIGURE 11-2
Two Production Plant/Three Distribution Warehouse System Flowchart

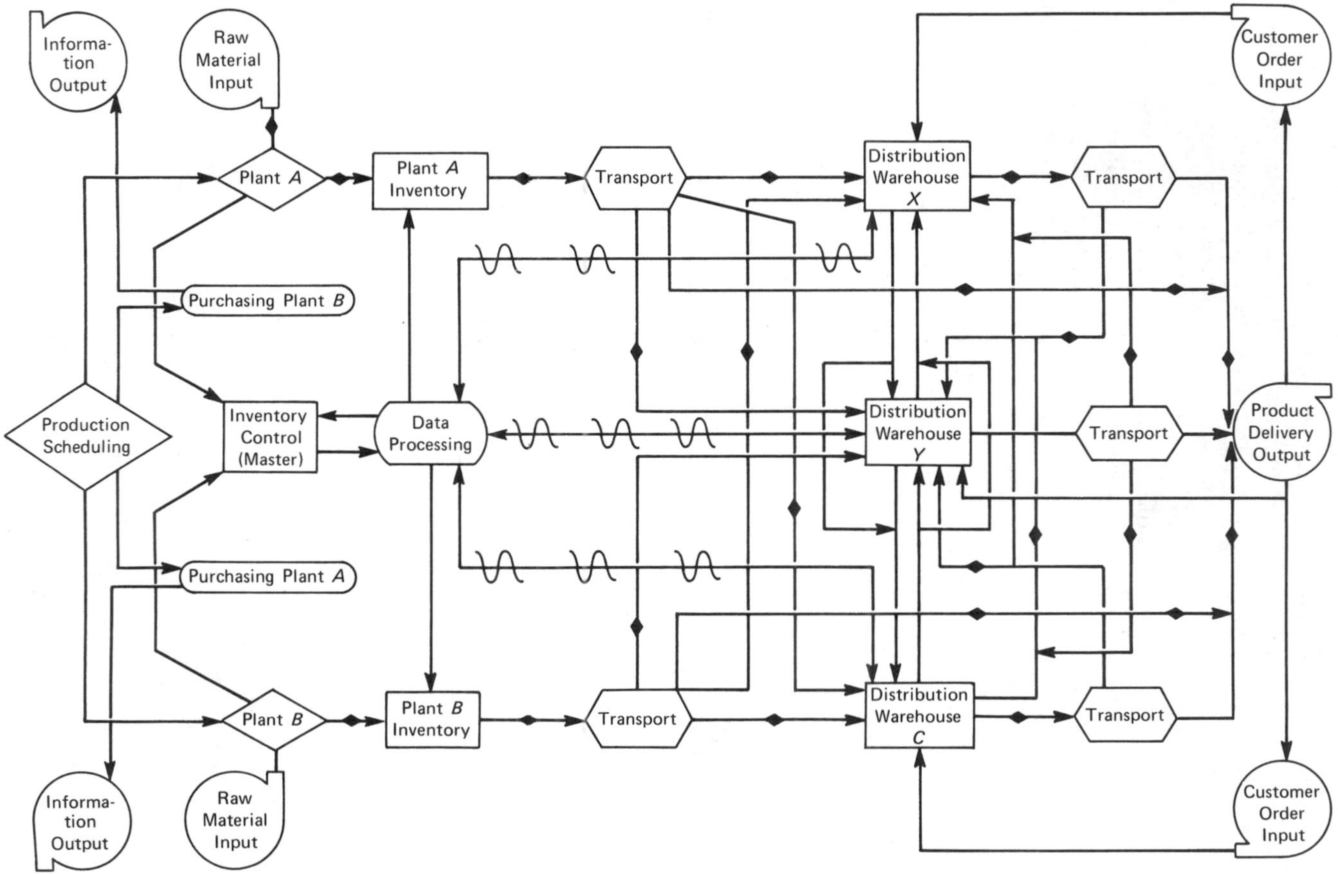

consists of a variety of linear programming techniques that have been adapted to logistical system design problems.

The unique feature of an analytical technique is the capability to isolate a precise mathematical solution to the problem under analysis. Thus, within the framework of assumptions and constraints of the analysis, the solution will represent a mathematical optimum. The main disadvantage of approaching complex design situations with analytical techniques is the requirement that all relationships be fully identified and quantified. To the extent that the technical requirements for formulating a problem on an analytical basis can be satisfied, they represent an ideal application of models to logistical system strategic planning.

Center of Gravity

This part illustrates the use of an analytical technique to assist in the location of a single distribution warehouse or manufacturing plant.[9] A number of methods, both mathematical and nonmathematical, can be applied to the problem of a single location. The cost and complexity of the technique should be matched to the difficulty of the problem. Here an analytical technique for solving the location problem is presented. By use of this technique, it is possible to locate a facility at the ton center, mile center, ton–mile center, or time–ton–mile center within a service territory—whichever results in lowest total cost. Where it is necessary to locate multiple distribution warehouses in a total system network, techniques similar to those discussed in following parts should be used.

The technique employed evolves from analytic geometry. The model is based upon Cartesian coordinates. In a system of Cartesian coordinates, the horizontal, or east–west, axis is labeled the x axis. The vertical, or north–south, axis is labeled the y axis. Together these two axes differentiate four quadrants, which are customarily numbered as illustrated in Figure 11-3.

Any given point in a quadrant can be identified with reference to the x and y coordinates. The y coordinate of a point is called its *ordinate*. The ordinate is found by measuring its distance from the x axis, parallel to the y axis. The x coordinate of a point is referred to as its *abscissa*. This is the distance from the vertical y axis, measured parallel to the x axis. Taken together, the abscissa and ordinate form the coordinates of a given point, the abscissa being given first. Figure 11-4 illustrates the abscissa and ordinate point A in the positive or northeast quadrant. In Figure 11-4 the distance Ox_1 equals the abscissa of point A, and the distance Oy_1 equals the ordinate. Assuming the values of 40 miles for x_1 and 30 miles for y_1, the coordinates of point A would be read as $A(40, 30)$. The use of uniform mileage scales along the axes permits all points in the quadrant to be relatively located.

[9] This technique illustration is adapted from Donald J. Bowersox, *Food Distribution Center Location: Technique and Procedure*, Marketing and Transportation Paper 12 (East Lansing, Mich.: Michigan State University, 1962).

FIGURE 11-3
Cartesian Coordinates

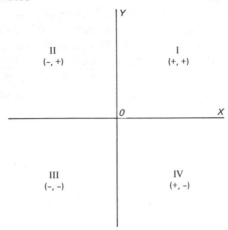

By use of this basic system of orientation, it is possible to replicate the geographic market area in which the warehouse facility is to be located. All delivery points are plotted in the Cartesian plane. Each store is identified by a subscript and placed in the replicated market with reference to its coordinates. In other words, destinations are plotted with reference to their abscissa and ordinate, measured on a uniform mileage scale.

The algebraic method for solving the location problem identifies the coordinate position of the proposed distribution warehouse. The computation is essentially a weighted average of a given number of independent variables, with the dependent variable being the warehouse location. The algebraic process is solved for the abscissa and ordinate of the warehouse. For simplicity, it is convenient to solve independently for the *x*- and *y*-coordinate location of

FIGURE 11-4
Location of a Point in the Positive Plane of Cartesian Coordinates

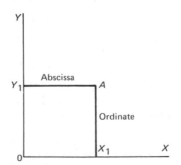

the warehouse. The formula for this calculation depends upon the independent variables, which are expressed in the location measure employed.

In the algebraic formulation the data utilized as basic measurement input represent independent variables. The resultant warehouse location is the dependent variable. The location problem is structured with identical service standards required from all potential distribution warehouse locations. Given this service standard, the objective is to minimize transportation costs.

Generally, it is accepted that transportation costs are a function of time, weight, and distance. Historically, however, when mathematical techniques were employed, not all of these cost factors were included as independent variables in the measurement device. Four solutions to the location problem are presented: (1) the ton–center solution, (2) the mile–center solution, (3) the ton–mile–center solution, and (4) the time–ton–mile-center solution. As the titles suggest, the first three are limited to variables related to weight and distance. The fourth includes both of these plus time as cost-influencing factors.

TON-CENTER SOLUTION.   In the ton-center solution, the point located represents the center of gravity or center of movement in the market area. When obtaining a ton-center solution, the assumption is that the center of movements represents the least-cost location. However, accepting cost as a function of time, weight, and distance reveals the basic limitation of the measurement device—only weight is given consideration.

All outlets are plotted in the Cartesian plane and identified by subscripts. To express tonnage requirements to each destination, annual tonnage is reduced to standard trailer units. The standard trailer utilized is a 40-foot semivan with a capacity of 38,000 pounds. Once each destination location is determined and the total trailer loads to each are known, the warehouse location may be determined.

The location solution is found by adding the products of location and delivery frequency to each destination from the x coordinate and dividing by the total number of trailers. The process is repeated from the y coordinate. The result is a location in terms of x and y for the distribution warehouse. The final location solution indicates the point that provides the balance of weight between destinations over a specific period. This basic algebraic procedure is followed for all mathematically derived location solutions with appropriate modifications necessary to handle the inclusion of different variables. The algebraic formula for the ton-center computation is

$$x = \frac{\sum_{i=1}^{n} x_i F_i}{\sum_{i=1}^{n} F_i} \qquad y = \frac{\sum_{i=1}^{n} y_i F_i}{\sum_{i=1}^{n} F_i}$$

where

x, y = unknown coordinate values of the warehouse

x_n, y_n = delivery locations, designated by appropriate subscript

F_n = annual tonnage to each destination, expressed as standard trailers, identified by appropriate subscript

MILE-CENTER SOLUTION. The mile-center solution isolates that geographical point which results in the least combined distance to all delivery points. The assumption underlying the solution is that delivery costs are a function of mileage. Therefore, if mileage is minimized, a least-cost location is determined. The basic deficiency in the mile-center solution is the omission of tonnage and time considerations.

Unlike the ton-center solution, the mile-center solution cannot be determined simply by solving for the weighted average along each coordinate. To find the mile center it is necessary to establish the distance of each destination from an original warehouse location, thereby obtaining a mileage value. This value is determined by utilizing the general formula for finding the length of a straight line connecting two points. The exact procedure is developed below.

Because the solution requires an initial x and y value for the distribution center, the final solution is found by a trial-and-error procedure. Starting with initial values for x and y, each time a computation is completed, new values are generated for the warehouse in terms of x and y. The location problem is solved when the new values are equated to zero or within an acceptable tolerance of the previous values. For example, if the initial values of x and y are 30 and 40, respectively, the location solution is obtained by utilizing these values to determine the new warehouse coordinates. Assuming that the new values obtained are $x = 36$ and $y = 43$, the procedure has failed to set the new values equal to the original values. Thus additional computation is required. For the second computation, the most recent values, $x = 36$ and $y = 43$, are employed. If the second computation results in the values $x = 36$ and $y = 43$, the location solution equates to zero, and the problem is optimized.

In trial-and-error solutions, an acceptable tolerance of ± 1 mile is usually established for the x and y warehouse coordinates. This means that solutions are correct within a 4-mile-square area. If through trial and error, values for x and y within this tolerance are reached, the location is accepted as the center of the 4-square-mile area. This results in a maximum location error of 1 mile.

The algebraic formula for determining the mile-center solution is

$$x = \frac{\sum_{i=1}^{n} \dfrac{x_i}{d_i}}{\sum_{i=1}^{n} \dfrac{1}{d_i}} \qquad y = \frac{\sum_{i=1}^{n} \dfrac{y_i}{d_i}}{\sum_{i=1}^{n} \dfrac{1}{d_i}}$$

where

x, y = unknown coordinate values of the warehouse

x_n, y_n = delivery locations, designated by appropriate subscript

d_n = location until the trial-and-error procedure is completed

The value for d expressing the distance from a warehouse can be determined from direct measurement on the coordinate plane or by utilization of the following straight-line formula:

$$d_n = \sqrt{(x_n - x)^2 + (y_n - y)^2}$$

where

d_n = distance between destination and warehouse, designated by appropriate subscript

x, y = given coordinates of warehouse

x_n, y_n = delivery location, designated by appropriate subscript

Because the value of d for all destinations changes each time a new set of warehouse coordinates is determined, the distance formula is utilized in each step of the trial-and-error procedure.

TON–MILE-CENTER SOLUTION. The ton–mile-center solution combines the variables of weight and distance in selecting the warehouse locations. The assumption is that costs are a function of ton–miles. The ton–mile solution is superior to the mile-center solution, because it takes frequency of delivery to each destination into consideration in selecting the warehouse location. It is superior to the simple ton-center solution, since the impact of distance is taken into consideration. The solution once more calls for trial and error, since d is included in the formulation.

The ton–mile formulation is

$$x = \frac{\sum\limits_{i=1}^{n} \dfrac{x_i F_i}{d_i}}{\sum\limits_{i=1}^{n} \dfrac{F_i}{d_i}} \qquad y = \frac{\sum\limits_{i=1}^{n} \dfrac{y_i F_i}{d_i}}{\sum\limits_{i=1}^{n} \dfrac{F_i}{d_i}}$$

where

x, y = unknown coordinate values of the warehouse

x_n, y_n = delivery locations designated by appropriate subscript

F_n = annual tonnage to each location, expressed as standard trailers identified by appropriate subscript

d_n = delivery location differentiated in miles from the initial warehouse location and sequentially from each new location until the trial-and-error procedure is completed

TIME–TON–MILE-CENTER SOLUTION.   The fourth location measurement device includes all cost-influencing variables. Because costs are a function of time, weight, and distance, the warehouse location derived as a product of this device should represent a superior least-cost location. The procedure for selecting the time–ton–mile solution is trial and error, because both the time and distance factors are differentiated from a given warehouse location.

The formulation is as follows:

$$x = \frac{\sum_{i=1}^{n} \frac{x_i F_i}{M_i}}{\sum_{i=1}^{n} \frac{F_i}{M_i}} \qquad y = \frac{\sum_{i=1}^{n} \frac{y_i F_i}{M_i}}{\sum_{i=1}^{n} \frac{F_i}{M_i}}$$

where

x, y = unknown coordinate values of the warehouse

x_n, y_n = delivery locations, designated by appropriate subscript

F_n = annual tonnage to each location expressed as standard trailers, identified by appropriate subscript

M_n = delivery location differentiated in terms of miles per minute from the initial warehouse location and sequentially from each new location until the trial-and-error procedure is completed

To arrive at a value for M_n it is necessary to ascertain both the distance and time to all destinations from the given warehouse location. The distance value is determined by use of the basic distance formula. The time in minutes to each destination is found by calculating a time value from the coordinate plane. An estimate of delivery time must include number of miles, type of highway, and traffic. A general rule is that time per mile decreases as the number of miles per stop increases. To account for the basic factors that influence driving time, zones representing attainable movement rates should be established for the market area. These zones consist of two basic types: rural and urban. Such estimates must be developed from engineering time studies for each alternative warehouse location. Given the values of distance and time through rural and urban zones, M_n is calculated in the following manner:

$$M_n = \frac{d_n}{t_n}$$

where

M_n = attainable miles per minute to the appropriate delivery location

$d_n = \sqrt{(x_n - x)^2 + (y_n - y)^2}$

t_n = total time to the location

The location of a single facility is commonly confronted in logistical planning. The very fact that a total system revision is rarely conducted for immediate implementation makes a simple approach to the evaluation of a single-facility location a useful aid to management. In cases where inbound transportation is an important cost, the model can easily be modified to include both inbound and outbound transportation cost. The next section discusses more comprehensive analytical techniques.

Linear Programming

As a category of analytical techniques, linear programming is among the most widely used strategic and operational planning tools in logistical management. In a technical sense, *linear programming* is an optimization technique. The procedure subjects the desired end result to identified constraints and then provides a process for selecting the optimal course of action from among a number of available options.

In order to solve a problem using linear programming, several qualification conditions must be satisfied. First, choice must exist in that two or more activities or locations must be competing for limited resources. For example, shipments must be capable of being made to a customer from at least two locations. Second, all pertinent relationships in the problem structure must be deterministic and capable of linear approximation.[10] Unless these enabling conditions are satisfied, a solution derived from linear programming, while mathematically optimal, will not be valid for logistical planning.

[10] For expanded treatments of linear programming, see George B. Dantzig, *Linear Programming and Extensions* (Princeton, N.J.: Princeton University Press, 1963), Harold Greenberg, *Integer Programming* (New York: Academic Press, Inc., 1971), G. Hadley, *Linear Programming* (Reading, Mass.: Addison-Wesley Publishing Company, Inc., 1962), Samuel B. Richmond, *Operations Research for Management Decisions* (New York: The Ronald Press Company, 1968), Ronald H. Ballou, "Dynamic Warehouse Location Analysis," *Journal of Marketing Research*, Vol. 5 (August 1968), pp. 271–76, and R. A. Howard, "Dynamic Programming," *Management Science*, January 1966, p. 317.

While linear programming is frequently used in logistical strategic planning, it is more widely applied to problems of an operating nature such as assignment and allocation. In this part, the attributes of seven basic variations of linear programming are described in terms of their application to logistical system design. In Chapter 12 three applications of linear programming to operational planning are illustrated.[11]

TRANSPORTATION METHOD. The most widely used form of linear programming for logistics problems is the *transportation method*, which derived its name from early applications directed at minimization of transportation cost. In part, the popularity of the transportation method is that no formulas need be developed or manipulated to arrive at an optimal solution. The general formulation of the transportation method is in terms of a matrix relating demand-and-supply locations.

Table 11-4 illustrates an example matrix formulation of a transportation problem. In the matrix a_1 represents demand, b_j represents the location of supply, and c_{ij} represents the cost of transportation from any supply location b_j to demand location a_i. The matrix represents a network of geographical points connected by links over which the transportation flow can be routed. The matrix illustrated in Table 11-4 represents the classical linear programming problem structure. Given the limited supply at source locations and variable requirements at demand locations, the objective is to satisfy all requirements at the lowest possible transportation cost.

TABLE 11-4
Basic Transportation Method Matrix

Supply Locations	*Demand locations*			
	a_1	a_2	a_3	a_i
b_1	c_{11}	c_{21}	c_{31}	c_{i1}
b_2	c_{12}	c_{22}	c_{32}	c_{i2}
b_3	c_{13}	c_{23}	c_{33}	c_{i3}
b_j	c_{1j}	c_{2j}	c_{3j}	c_{ij}

The computation for locating the optimal solution consists of a routinized addition and subtraction procedure. As noted earlier, typical assignment and allocation problems are illustrated in Chapter 12 from inception to attainment of solution optimality. For the solution to satisfy optimality conditions: (1) the cost of an individual shipment is the product of the quantity and the trans-

[11] See page 386.

portation cost, and (2) the total cost of the objective function must be the sum of the individual costs.

The general application of the transportation method in system design studies dealing with location is to individually isolate the optimum for a variety of different locational structures. For example, if the objective is to select from a list of possible warehouse locations the one additional facility that will result in lowest total system cost, the computation procedure would consist of a series of optimal quantifications. The existing system would be tested with each potential facility "in solution." The final solution would be the combination of existing warehouses plus the additional facility which results in lowest total cost in comparison to all alternatives tested. Because the solution is limited by the preselected locations, optimality is limited to the specific problem formatted.

Beyond specific limitations of all analytical techniques, the basic transportation method fails to incorporate many attributes that are desirable when dealing with comprehensive system planning. First, the method, while simple to use manually on small-scale problems, becomes cumbersome and unruly when applied to situations containing a large number of nodes and links. In comparison to alternative linear programming procedures, the transportation method when computerized does not offer high computational efficiency. Second, the optimal recommendation reached by the transportation method may not be a practical solution in terms of operating constraints. Third, the basic technique does not provide the capability to trans-ship. Given an unmodified version of the basic transportation method, it is not possible to route a shipment through an intermediate location (such as a warehouse) to realize minimum total cost routing. Fourth, the solution does not permit incorporation of economies of scale. Fifth, the basic procedure does not permit the joint handling of a product mix. Finally, the transportation method is not capable of dealing with a multicheloned structure. To varying degrees, alternative versions of linear programming discussed below overcome some of the basic defects of the transportation method.

SIMPLEX METHOD.   The *simplex algorithm* utilizes a generalized mathematical procedure to arrive at the optimal problem solution. While more difficult to use than the transportation method, the simplex procedure is adaptable to large-scale problems and can be programmed for computer processing with relative ease and efficiency.

The simplex algorithm is highly adaptable to varied problems because it can handle a larger number of variables. The basic algorithm consists of an iterative method whereby the problem is solved by identifying successive feasible solutions and testing each for optimality. When a solution is identified that cannot be improved upon, the optimal recommendation is isolated within the constraints of the specific problem formatted. Because of the adaptability of the simplex procedure, the objective function can be minimized or maximized with relative ease.

FIGURE 11-5
Basic Simplex Solution Flow

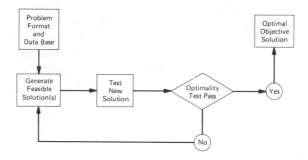

Figure 11-5 illustrates the basic simplex procedure solution flow. In terms of a problem similar to that illustrated in the transportation method, the basic mathematical structure to format the simplex approach is:

$$Z = \sum_i \sum_j C_{ij} x_{ij}$$

with the constraint that all demand be satisfied,

$$\sum_{j=1}^{n} x_{ij} = a_i \qquad (i = 1, \cdots, m)$$

with the constraint that supply not be exceeded at any location,

$$\sum_{i=1}^{m} x_{ij} \leq b_j \qquad (j = 1, \cdots, n)$$

where

Z = minimum solution value (optimal set of x_{ij})
a_i = demand
b_j = supply
C_{ij} = cost from b_j to a_i
x_{ij} = quantity to be shipped from b_j to a_i

The flexible nature of the simplex structure permits a wide variety of constraints and variables to be incorporated into the problem format. As illustrated above, the simplex illustration has all the limitations of the transportation method except ease of computerization. Its main advantage is formatting flexibility. Thus the simplex algorithm can be adapted to overcome some or all of the deficiencies discussed under the transportation method. These adaptations, as they relate to logistical system design, constitute the linear programming variations discussed throughout the remainder of this part.

MIXED INTEGER.   Both the basic transportation method and the basic simplex algorithm represent noninteger forms of programming. An alternative method of problem formatting is to restrict all solution variables to integer values.[12] From the viewpoint of logistical system design, the ideal is to structure the problem format in a combination of noninteger and integer values. This type of problem format is identified as *mixed-integer programming*. The primary advantage of the mixed-integer format is that fixed as well as different levels of variable cost can be included in the determination of the objective solution. Thus demand can be treated on a noninteger basis, while warehouse capacity and transportation equipment can be evaluated on an integer basis. The mixed-integer approach permits a high degree of practicality to accommodate restrictions found in day-to-day logistical operations. However, the range of design operations is restricted in problem formatting in that existing programs can handle only a limited number of integer variables.

SEPARABLE.   A specific application of mixed-integer programming is known as *separable programming*. The essential feature of this variation is that separable programming allows incorporation of the impact of economies of scale into the problem solution. Thus the relationship of the activity level and the cost of function within the problem format is permitted to vary within specific constraints. The separable feature is of particular importance to logistical system design because it permits the solution to incorporate such features as warehouse sizing and scale economies of alternative handling methods based upon assigned volume throughput.

TRANS-SHIPMENT.   The *trans-shipment* feature of a linear programming procedure permits linkage between an origin and destination point to incorporate movement through an intermediate point when additional economies can be realized. From a computation viewpoint, the trans-shipment feature is efficient because it avoids the requirement to determine the least-cost linkage from all origins to all destinations. Thus, in final solution the number of variables can be reduced, since total links can be less than the total number of origin–destination pairs.

From the viewpoint of logistical planning, the trans-shipment feature is significant. It permits evaluation of flexible distribution patterns, which is required in advanced system designs. In addition, the trans-shipment feature permits shipment consolidation, provided that the program has been adopted to handle multiple products. This multiple commodity adaptation is discussed as the next form of linear programming modification. The trans-shipment modification to the transportation method is illustrated in Chapter 12.[13]

DECOMPOSITION.   A major development in linear programming from the viewpoint of logistical planning was the application of *decomposition* to the design

---

[12] Greenberg, op. cit.
[13] See pages 396–398.

FIGURE 11-6
Mixed-Integer Solution Flow with Decomposition Feature

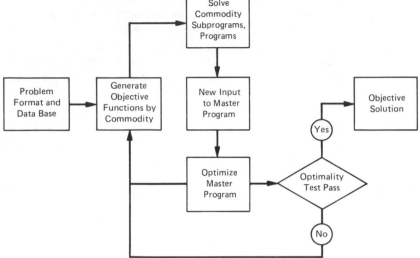

solution.[14] The benefit of decomposition is that it permits multiple commodities to be incorporated into system design. Most firms have a variety of products which are purchased in varied assortments and quantities by customers. While such products may be shipped and stored together, they are not interchangeable from the viewpoint of servicing customer requirements.

To handle this realistic requirement the decomposition technique provides a procedure for dividing the multicommodity situation into a series of single-commodity problems. The procedure for arriving at commodity assignment follows an iterative process wherein costs associated with each commodity are tested for convergence until a minimum cost or optimal solution is isolated.

This decomposition procedure has been incorporated in a *multicommodity distribution system design program* that includes a mixed-integer algorithm for evaluating the configuration of warehouse locations.[15] The procedure for arriving at a system design follows a two-stage iterative process. First, given the location structure, individual commodities are optimally assigned to minimize cost. This aspect of the design procedure is similar to the basic transportation solutions; however, it is formatted on a multiproduct basis

---

[14] For a discussion of the application of decomposition to logistical system design, see A. M. Geoffrion and G. W. Graves, "Multicommodity Distribution System Design by Benders Decomposition," *Management Science*, Vol. 20 (January 1974), pp. 822–44, and Arthur M. Geoffrion, "Better Distribution Planning with Computer Models," *Harvard Business Review*, July–August 1976, pp. 92–99.

[15] Ibid.

using the decomposition technique. Second, a mixed-integer algorithm is utilized to enumerate the facility structure in terms of individual commodity customer assignments. The combined solution is tested for optimality and the two-step procedure is repeated until convergence is within accepted tolerance.[16] Figure 11-6 illustrates the combined linear programming procedure. For a clear understanding of the basic solution flow, a comparison of Figures 11-5 and 11-6 is suggested.

VARIABLE RANGING.   A final feature of linear programming which is significant to logistical system design is *variable ranging*. Variable ranging permits postoptimality analysis of the objective solution to determine its validity range. Thus a specific variable or a combination of variables can be tested to determine if the optimal solution is violated within a feasible range of values the variable might encounter in practical application. In essence, variable ranging incorporates a form of preprogrammed analysis into the linear programming solution procedure. This form of sensitivity-analysis capability was referred to in Chapter 10 as machine heuristics.[17]

Conclusion—Analytical Technique

The basic attribute of an analytical approach to partial or total system planning is the capability for an optimal design solution. This feature alone represents ample justification for continued development of this type of planning tool. The two basic categories of analytical techniques discussed in this section were gravity location and linear programming. Of the two, linear programming offers the greatest potential for comprehensive or total system design. The many modifications to the basic linear programming technique discussed in this section reflect the research and development which has been under way during the past decade.

From the viewpoint of total system design, the major benefit of linear programming is the capability to provide complete enumeration of the range of feasible facility locations. If management wishes to evaluate a list of 50 potential locations, all feasible options can be evaluated in terms of structural configuration to arrive at a system design that satisfies the objective function.

Notwithstanding the value of complete enumeration, linear programming confronts some major problems when dealing with complex logistical system designs. First, to format a comprehensive system design it is necessary to develop explicit functional relationships for the full range of design options. Second, the optimality feature of the technique is relative, being only as valid as the design problem formatting. Too many simplifying assumptions can render the solution optimal but invalid. Third, the capability of existing linear program procedures is typically limited to a system configuration with only

[16] Ibid.
[17] See pages 318–321.

two echelons. Thus warehouse to customers can be included in the problem format; however, total channels cannot be subjected to analysis. Fourth, although not impossible, it is difficult to utilize a wide variety of freight rates in a single design solution. The typical procedure is to utilize a weighted average freight rate which offers some aggregation limitations to the computation results. Finally, existing programs are not able to handle the nonlinear functional relationship between size of safety stock and the number of locations. To accommodate this aspect of analysis, the typical procedure is to calculate the estimated safety stock for purposes of cost presentation but not as a functional variable to the design solution. This final limitation represents a major deficiency, because the application of linear programming to comprehensive system design does not achieve full total cost integration, as discussed in Chapters 8 and 9. While the technique has a great deal of application to operations planning, applicability to strategic formulation is only valid within the limits of computation procedure.

Simulation Techniques

This section covers two basic forms of computer simulation which are widely used in logistical strategic planning. The first category is static simulation and the second is dynamic simulation. The label *simulation* can be applied to almost any attempt to replicate a situation. Simulation is a process by which a model of a particular situation is developed and tested using known facts. As one would expect, the range of simulations in terms of complexity and subject studies is unlimited.

Unlike analytic techniques, simulation does not attempt to provide a mathematically optimal solution. In fact, the best way to view simulation is as a computer program that replicates or quantifies the potential performance of a proposed logistical system design. This capability to quantify system performance permits managerial evaluation of potential policy change or system redesign before resources are committed. While the solution results may not be optimal, such simplicity typically results in lower analysis costs and faster results. Because of the rapid rate of change in modern business, such managerially accepted or "satisfactory solutions" are adequate for a wide variety of system design situations.

Static Simulation

In a *static simulation* an attempt is made to describe an existing or potential logistical system design in the form of a computer model. All components of the total logistical system are replicated, and total cost is generated by utilization of a numeric computation procedure.

The essential feature of static simulation is that the analysis is quantified as of a specific point in time. In this sense the primary difference between static and dynamic simulation is the manner in which *time* is treated. Whereas dynamic simulation evaluates system performance across time, in static simulation no attempt is made to structure time–period interplay. The static simulation treats each operating period within the overall planning horizon as a finite interval. Final results represent a summation of operating performance for each period in the planning horizon. For example, in the formulation of a five-year simulated plan, each year might be simulated as an independent event. Likewise, the simulated activity for the year would be processed on an aggregated basis, as if total performance took place at one point in time.

The static simulation procedure seeks to estimate the outcome of a specified plan or course of future action. If the potential system design is identified, the primary purpose of the simulation would be to quantify total cost and threshold customer service.[18] Used in this sense the static simulator provides a tool for rapidly measuring the capabilities and costs related to system designs and related sensitivity analysis.[19]

An alternative use of static simulation is the numerical computation procedure to assist in the selection of system design. In this capacity, the static simulator can be programmed to evaluate and quantify various networks of warehouses from a potential list of facility locations provided during problem formatting.

When utilized to help identify the facility structure of the logistical system, the typical procedure is to include all plausible locations in the initial simulation. Customer ship-to locations are assigned to each potential warehouse on the basis of the lowest total cost source. One of the main benefits of simulation is that the design problem can be structured on a multiecheloned basis and delivery points can be assigned to warehouses or directly to manufacturing plants, whichever offers lowest total cost delivery. The warehouse evaluation routine can be established to replicate a system design that (1) represents lowest total cost, (2) provides maximum customer service, and/or (3) provides a specified service level at the lowest associated total cost.

Given the design objective, the simulation deletes warehouse locations one at a time from the maximum to a managerially specified minimum or until only one facility remains in the system. The typical delete procedure eliminates the most costly warehouse from the remaining "in-system" facilities on a marginal cost basis. The demand previously serviced by the casualty warehouse is then reassigned to the next-lowest-cost supply point and the quantification procedure repeated. If a full system delete process is desired,

---

[18] The threshold service concept is critical to system design studies. See Chapter 8, pages 269–272, for a complete discussion.

[19] For examples of static simulators used for logistical planning, see Harvey N. Shycon and Richard B. Maffei, "Simulation—Tool for Better Distribution," *Harvard Business Review*, November–December 1960, pp. 65–75, Alfred Kuehn and M. J. Hamburger, "A Heuristic Program for Locating Warehouses," *Management Science*, July 1963, pp. 543–666, *WHAMOL* (Benton Harbor, Mich.: Whirlpool Corporation Physical Distribution Department, 1973), and *Distribution Planning Model-DPM* (East Lansing, Mich.: Cleveland Consulting Associates, 1976).

FIGURE 11-7
Distribution Planning Model—Static Simulation Solution Flow

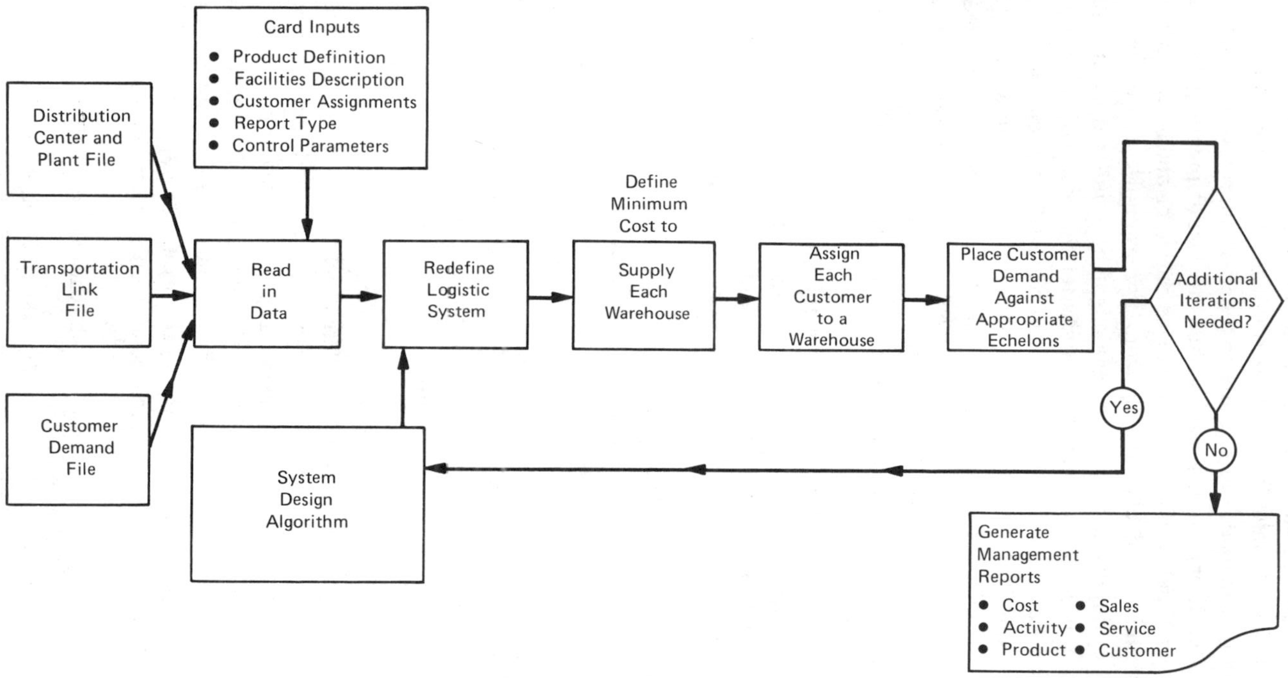

the static simulation will require as many iterations as there are potential warehouse locations under consideration.

The system design solution is obtained by comparison of the total cost and threshold service capabilities among the configurations resulting from the deletion procedure. This analysis is performed by direct comparison of managerial output reports. There is no assurance that the combination of facilities selected as a result of the delete procedure will represent the optimum or even the near-optimum facility configuration. The fact that a warehouse location is no longer available for consideration in subsequent replications once it is deleted is one of the major shortcomings of static simulation procedures.

One of the more advanced static simulators is the *distribution planning model.*[20] Figure 11-7 illustrates the solution flow. The system design algorithm represents the facility delete procedure discussed above. Table 11-5 contains a summary of the capacity of the distribution planning model in terms of operating range and replication capability.

The main advantage of static simulation is that it is simpler, less expensive to operate, and more flexible than other comprehensive design techniques. The replication capabilities of a multiecheloned static simulator create almost unlimited design possibilities. As a result of the process of numerical computation, static simulation does not require explicit functional relationships. If the system or proposed design modification can be described, it can be simulated. The capabilities and operating range of a comprehensive static simulator make the inclusion of multiple products and freight rates relatively easy.

There are three significant disadvantages to static simulation. First, the technique does not have diagnostic capabilities such as those found in analytical techniques. Thus static simulation is a trial-and-error procedure guided by the insight and curiosity of the logistical planner. Second, static simulation omits analysis of time-related aspects of logistical planning because of its single-point-in-time focus. Finally, similar to linear programming, static simulation is unable to generate safety stock directly as a function of the number of warehouse locations. Thus to estimate safety stock the typical procedure is to calculate an expected safety stock for purposes of cost presentation.

Dynamic Simulation

Dynamic modeling was introduced in Chapter 10.[21] The essential feature of a dynamic technique is that operating periods are linked on a recursive basis by feedback mechanisms. Thus the performance of the modeled system during any given time period can and is expected to have repercussions on the nature of future operations.

[20] *Distribution Planning Model*, op. cit.
[21] See pages 304–305.

TABLE 11-5
Distribution Planning Model—Capability and Operating Range

Capability
    Impact of distribution policies on customer service and distribution cost
    Number, location, and annual volume of plants and warehouses
    Assignment of plants to distribution points, and distribution points to customers
    Annual transportation flows
    Impact of stocking policies and stocking locations by product group and customer type
DPM Operating Range
    50 product groups
    3–99 echelons
    300 vendors, production points, and/or distribution points
    Specific point-to-point transportation rates and/or equations by mode, class, or weight interval
    Working stock or safety stock factors input by product group and distribution point
    Inventory costs by product group and distribution point
    All distribution variable costs input as cost per hundred weight, unit, or cube
    All fixed-cost input by distribution point
    Customer service measured as percent and amount shipped within eight mileage service intervals
    Four methods for assigning customers or markets to vendors, production points, or distribution points:
                Least cost
                Best service
                Least cost at a desired service level
                Fixed assignment

Source: Omar Keith Helferich, *Distribution System Design Techniques* (East Lansing, Mich.: Cleveland Consulting Associates, 1976), p. 20.

In the dynamic modeling process the initial state or structure of the model is derived from flow and set data. Flow data provide a stream of operational confrontations for the simulator. Set data establish the system's initial component state, functional relationships, parameters, and constraints. Each time the flow data are processed or generated, a study cycle is completed. The processing of flow data results in operational output. Such output is generated by the interaction of the flow data with components according to functional relationships and within the limitations imposed by parameters and constraints.

If the simulator's design does not incorporate feedback, it is considered static. In such simulators no attempt is made to allow output to influence future set-data values. Thus set data are held constant and the initial condition of state variables of the model will not change as an internal feature of the model based upon output. If the model is dynamic, it incorporates the internal capability of altering system state on the basis of output.

In Figure 11-8 the functional interrelationships of a dynamic simulator are displayed to illustrate the recursive relationship. The initial simulation cycle results in a system state identified as $t + 1$. Operational relationships and feedback influence the system state in two ways. First, for the initial cycle, the study-period deficiencies in system capability are generated in terms of extra demand loads with related operational penalties. Second, given initial system status, deficiencies lead to modifications in system status, shown as $t + 1 \cdots n$. Such modifications are reflected as new values for system-state set variables. This process is repeated until no improvement in system state is possible and the system t_f (final system) has been structured.

FIGURE 11-8
Dynamic Simulation Solution Flow

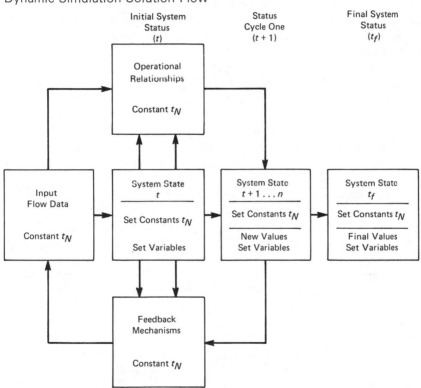

In terms of operating range and capability, dynamic simulation can perform all tasks outlined in the discussion on static simulation, and it incorporates the added feature of time interplay. As noted above, feedback mechanisms treat system output as inputs for the next activity period. Given any single time period, the prevailing system design must have excessive capacity, adequate capacity, or be deficient to the task at hand. The optimum situation would be a system design that remained adequate to the desired performance over the entire design horizon. However, adequate capacity is seldom the case in logistical system design under conditions of uncertainty. Thus the prevailing system capability will be either abundant or deficient. Both situations result in operational penalties. A condition of excess capacity results in higher than necessary total cost. Excess penalties can be handled properly in both static and dynamic models. A deficient condition is more critical.

Deficiencies influence both cost and service performance. For example, inventory shortage at a given warehouse may (1) result in shipment from a secondary location at greater cost and possible reductions in customer service; (2) result in a back order, with related cost and service penalties; or (3) result in an order cancellation, with possible customer loss. In any event, the actual system under analysis must cope with the deficiency in terms of specific action or a significant element important in design is omitted. Likewise, the model used in analysis should be capable of handling deficiencies. Dynamic models include feedback elements to provide a more realistic approximation of actual logistical operating situations.

Of particular concern to logistical system planning is the implementation sequence of design modifications. From a purely operational viewpoint, no enterprise of any substantial size has the capability, nor could it justify the risk, of simultaneously changing all aspects of a logistical system. Thus the sequence of implementing a system modification across time is of critical importance. The nature of dynamic modeling is such that sequential planning can be more comprehensively treated than is possible under either static simulation or linear programming.

Among the most advanced dynamic simulators is the *LREPS model*.[22] The LREPS model has multiecheloned capability. Because of its dynamic nature, the model may be operated on either a probabilistic or deterministic basis with respect to total order-cycle time relationships between echelons of the system being replicated.

Three groupings of variables are defined in LREPS: (1) target variables, (2) environmental variables, and (3) controllable variables.[23] The major target variables are customer service and total cost. Environmental variables are grouped into major categories of demographics, technologies, and acts of

---

[22] For other reported simulation models incorporating dynamic features, see Robert E. Markland, "Analyzing Geographically Discrete Warehousing Networks by Computer Simulation," *The Journal for the American Institute for Decision Sciences*, Vol. 4 (April 1973), pp. 216–36; and Michael M. Conners et al., "The Distributor System Simulator," *Management Science*, Vol. 18 (April 1972), pp. B425–53.

[23] For a complete report on the LREPS model, see Donald J. Bowersox et al., *Dynamic Simulation of Physical Distribution Systems* (East Lansing, Mich.: Division of Research, Michigan State University, 1973); Donald J. Bowersox, op. cit.; Donald J. Bowersox, "Dynamic Simulation of Physical Distribution," *Distribution Worldwide*, December 1972, pp. 24–31; and Donald J. Bowersox, Omar Keith Helferich, and Edward J. Marien, "Physical Distribution Planning with Simulation," *International Journal of Physical Distribution*, October 1971, pp. 38–42. Portions of the following sections and figures are based upon these references by the author.

nature. Each of these categories is broken down into variables that are interactive with the model itself, that is, demographic variables defined in terms of cost-of-living indices, real estate value indices, and demand determinants.

The major controllable variables illustrated in Table 11-6 structure the major logistical and marketing overlap. Included to the right of each variable is a summary of design options for simulated experimentation. Figure 11-9 illustrates the solution flow of the LREPS model. Given the supporting data necessary to simulate a planning situation, the solution flow embodies four steps.

TABLE 11-6
LREPS Controllable System Variables—Operating Range

Variable Groupings	Design Options
Marketing-oriented variables	
Order characteristics	Actual or hypothetical
Product mix	Actual or hypothetical
New products	As desired
Customer mix	Actual or hypothetical
Distribution-oriented variables	
Facility structure	Actual or hypothetical by echelon
Facility connection	Actual or hypothetical between echelons
Inventory policy	Reorder point, replenishment, or hybrid by echelon
Transportation	Truck, rail, air, private and contract truck in any combination between echelons
Communication	Computer, teletype, mail, telephone between echelons
Material handling	Automated or mechanized by echelons

First, daily orders by demand units are generated. This is achieved by randomly selecting blocks of actual orders in such a manner as to satisfy the daily sales requirements of each demand unit. An overall sales forecast is allocated to demand units on the basis of independent market variables. This initial activity is performed by the model's demand and environmental subsystem (D&E).

Second, the actual processing is simulated. All order cycles between demand units and other echelons are simulated, and appropriate elapsed times are computed. The operations subsystem (OPS) of LREPS performs this processing function and thereby constitutes the model's system structure.

As orders are processed at each distribution center, inventories are appropriately reduced. If unavailable, products are back-ordered. As reorder points or periods are reached at one echelon, replenishment orders are dispatched to the next echelon. There time delays are computed and inventory replenishment decisions are made.

FIGURE 11-9
Generalized LREPS System Concept—Solution Flow

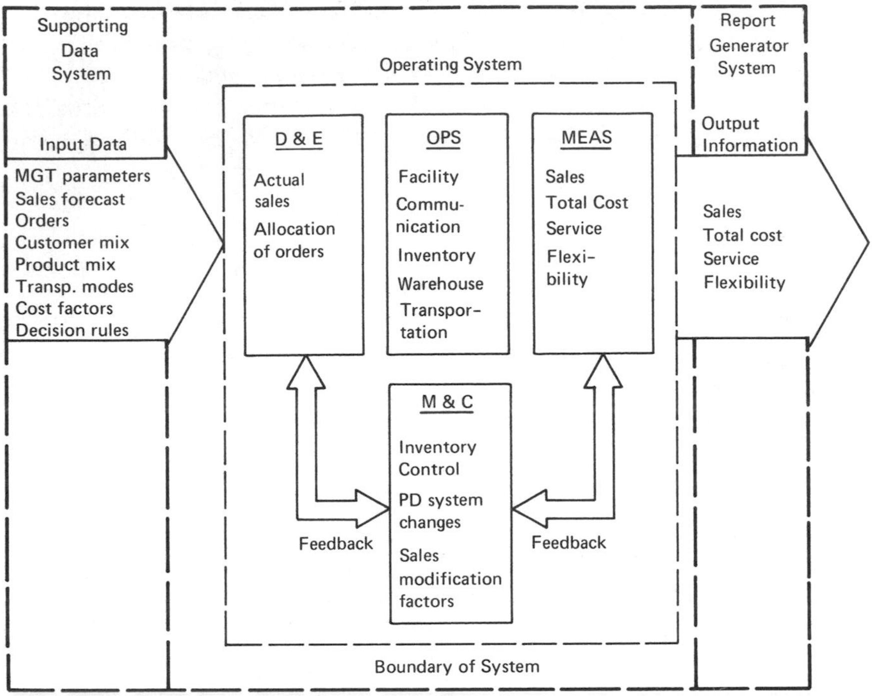

Supporting Data System	Operating System			Report Generator System
Input Data	**D & E**	**OPS**	**MEAS**	**Output Information**
MGT parameters	Actual sales	Facility	Sales	Sales
Sales forecast		Communication	Total Cost	Total cost
Orders	Allocation of orders	Inventory	Service	Service
Customer mix		Warehouse	Flexibility	Flexibility
Product mix		Transportation		
Transp. modes				
Cost factors				
Decision rules				

M & C

Inventory Control

PD system changes

Feedback   Sales modification factors   Feedback

Boundary of System

Third, all information is used to compute target-variable values. Total cost is measured on the basis of cost parameters and mathematical transformations related to each component of the system. Fixed facility investment cost by size and type of facility is based upon annual depreciated amount. Order-processing costs for each distribution center are calculated using regression equations with different cost factors based upon size and location of the facility. Communication costs are calculated using regression equations where the independent variables are the number of orders and lines processed. Inventory carrying and reorder costs are calculated for all nodal and pipeline inventories. Inbound transportation costs to distribution centers are calculated on specific point-to-point rates. Outbound transport costs to demand units are calculated from sets of regression equations based on distance. The measurement subsystem (MEAS) provides necessary measurement for evaluation of system performance.

The interplay here described must be monitored and controlled (M&C subsystem). The introduction of new variable values at the proper time, the addition or deletion of distribution facilities according to management rules, and the impact of changes in the environment are handled internal to the model by this subsystem.

The main advantage of dynamic simulation is that it incorporates the realism of day-to-day operations. Thus a system design can be evaluated in terms of actual customer service capabilities on an order-by-order basis. Unlike linear programming and static simulation, dynamic simulation can measure directly the cost benefits of alternative safety stocking policies. As such, dynamic simulation is the only planning tool that can estimate the full integration of temporal and spatial variables upon system design.

The dynamic simulation procedure is complex. Because of the extreme detail required to replicate feedback, simulating a large-scale system is time consuming and expensive. The detailed interrelationships of simulating a multi-echeloned dynamic structure do not result in a model highly flexible with respect to locational reconfiguration. Finally, regardless of the precise nature of the interrelationships replicated, dynamic simulation, like all forms of numeric processing, suffers from the lack of a precise mathematical solution algorithm. In the final analysis, the process of logistical planning is based upon trial and error as guided by managerial direction.

Conclusion—Simulation Techniques

Capability to format the problem in a comprehensive manner is the main attribute of simulation techniques in approaching partial or total system planning. Simulation techniques do not require exact functional relationships. And, in turn, they cannot provide precise solutions.

Static simulation is a useful tool for evaluating alternative locational arrangements of warehouse facilities and assignment of customer service territories. While relatively easy and inexpensive to use, the delete location algorithm used to select location configuration does not offer complete enumeration of all available facility locations. The static simulation approach fails to incorporate time relationships critical to selected logistical planning situations.

Dynamic simulation is the most comprehensive of the available planning techniques. Because of its feedback mechanisms, dynamic simulation is also complex and requires considerable computer time to replicate performance under alternative design configurations. The main advantage of the dynamic approach is that it incorporates the impact of time into performance evaluation. Analysis of system performance across time provides the foundation for planning inventory strategy in relation to order-by-order customer service performance. Thus, the full impact of the location configuration upon safety stock can be evaluated directly using dynamic simulation.

The comprehensive nature of dynamic simulation restricts its flexibility to adapt to a wide variety of facility location schemes. Therefore, a practical approach to total system planning is to utilize either linear programming or static simulation initially to reduce the range of possible locations. Next, dynamic simulation can be employed to render the final system design and to plan implementation. With the dual-technique application, the major attributes of both techniques can be enjoyed in system strategic planning.

Summary

The focal point of this chapter has been the application of various quantitative techniques to the strategic planning of logistical system design. The orientation has been primarily managerial. Thus a variety of available techniques have been discussed from the viewpoint of their ability to assist in overall logistical planning.

At the outset, a general overview of strategic logistical planning was presented. Next, all the techniques reviewed in the chapter were classified on the basis of their attributes. This classification permits comparison of available techniques in terms of major capabilities. The remainder of the chapter was devoted to a discussion of symbolic replications, analytic techniques, and simulation techniques. In total, seven techniques or procedures for analysis were presented. In the case of linear programming, seven features were discussed, including the significance of each modification to logistical strategic planning. The overall chapter provides a comprehensive review of the range of techniques currently available to assist in comprehensive system design.

The next chapter shifts emphasis to the areas of operational and tactical planning. When dealing with shorter time intervals and less complex situations, the range of models available to assist management increases substantially. The field of small-scale or minimodeling is one of the fastest-growing areas of quantitative application in the logistical field.

Questions

1. What is the main advantage of using symbolic replications to aid in logistical system planning?
2. What is meant by a dynamic model?
3. Why is the generalized model described in Figure 11-8 considered dynamic?
4. What is the major advantage of analytic techniques over simulation techniques?
5. What major advantage critical to logistical system design does dynamic simulation have over static simulation and linear programming?
6. Describe the process by which a simulation technique is utilized in combination with managerial inputs during a logistical system design study.
7. Can a heuristic procedure be utilized with the employment of an analytical model?
8. In the model illustrated for single-location determination, what is the major reason for attempting to include time as a variable in the problem solution?
9. In discussion of large-scale simulations, what is meant by the feature of multi-echelon and multitrack?
10. Why is dynamic representation essential to spatial and temporal unification?

Operations Techniques

Attention in this chapter is directed to the quantitative techniques used in day-to-day logistical management. This orientation contrasts the treatment of design techniques in Chapter 11 in two ways. First, the focal point of technique application within this chapter is to operations decision making given the logistical system design. Second, most techniques presented seek solutions to specific problems without regard to impact upon total system performance. In terms of fit into the various types of logistical planning, the techniques illustrated in this chapter would most appropriately be classified as operational and tactical planning tools.

This chapter follows a unique structure in comparison to other chapters in that no attempt is made to integrate the discussion of individual groupings of techniques. Each group is viewed as a set of tools that can be utilized by a logistical manager if and when justified by the operational or tactical planning situation. The initial section deals with the basic logic of decision making under conditions of uncertainty. Next, techniques related to facility operations are presented. The third section is devoted to solving allocation and assignment problems. The fourth section deals with a set of techniques which can assist in the determination of routing requirements. The final section presents scheduling techniques.

Two groups of techniques that have previously been discussed appropriately fall into the operational and tactical classification. In Chapter 4 forecasting techniques were discussed as an integral part of logistical coordination. In Chapter 6 statistical and simulation techniques applicable to formulating safety stock strategy were treated, as well as analytic techniques dealing with economic order quantity.[1] In both situations the judgment was made to include technique discussion in the chapter developing the functional subject because of uniqueness of application. The techniques discussed in this chapter are not as specialized in application.

Design for Decision

The major variable in logistical operations is the ever-present uncertainty. A logistical manager must always be gauging the probability of disruptions such as unexpected shipment delays, work stoppages, material shortages, and price changes. The essence of contingency tactical planning is to estimate the probability that a disruption will occur and to plan the corrective action consistent with operational goals. To a significant degree, the best approach to coping with the probability of such disruptive events occurring is to maintain familiarity with the prevailing market conditions. Given this knowledge, statistical decision techniques can be utilized to help formulate a logical course of action.

Decision Criteria

A number of criteria have been developed to help managers select between available courses of action. To make a good decision, the manager should evaluate the relative risks and expected payoffs associated with each course of action.

As a general rule, the greater the potential payoff, the greater the corresponding risk. For example, a decision not to stockpile steel because the probability of a strike is minimal will have a high payoff because normal materials management operations can be maintained, excessive storage costs prevented, and cash flow regulated. However, the corresponding penalty associated with complete disruption of manufacturing operations in the event a strike does occur could make the decision very risky.

MAXIMUM–MINIMUM RELATED CRITERIA. A number of logic rules have been worked out to help a decision maker select a course of action that will either maximize payout or minimize risk. These basic criteria are useful in establishing the extremes of a pessimistic or optimistic outlook.

A maximum criterion is based on the assumption that all possible future events will go contrary to the best interest of the enterprise. Therefore, the pessimistic decision maker attempts to minimize future risk at the sacrifice of potential gains in payoff. Using the maximum criterion, the decision maker isolates the minimum risk–payoff relationship for each course of action and then selects the alternative that offers the maximum of the minimum risks.

[1] See pages 159–164.

The minimax criterion is also pessimistic in that the minimum alternative is selected from among a series of maximum-seeking alternatives. In this situation the maximum risk–payoff relationship for each course of action is identified. The alternative offering the minimum risk is then selected as the decision solution.

The most optimistic criterion under this grouping is to select the maximax course of events. Under the maximax outlook, alternatives are ranked similar to the minimax criteria. However, the alternative offering the highest payoff is selected with complete disregard to the associated risk.

The maximum–minimum associated criteria reflect the extremes of the decision-making perspective. In most materials management appraisals, the appropriate decision criterion is found between the extremes of pessimistic or optimistic outlook.

HURWICZ CRITERION.   The Hurwicz criterion makes use of an optimism–pessimism coefficient to incorporate the decision maker's feeling or appraisal of the likelihood of future events. To use this criterion, the decision maker must arrive at a measure of optimism and the potential payoff associated with alternative courses of action.

To guide the decision solution, a weighted average is calculated using the coefficient of optimism and the maximum and minimum payoffs associated with each alternative. The decision solution is based on the highest of the weighted averages.

To illustrate, assume on a scale of 0.01 to 1.0 that the decision maker's knowledge of the situation leads to a slightly optimistic view with a coefficient of optimism of 0.6. Table 12-1 illustrates the maximum and minimum payoff associated with three different courses of action.

Using the Hurwicz criterion, the decision maker uses the following mathematical procedure to evaluate each alternative:

1. Multiply the maximum payoff by the coefficient of optimism.
2. Multiply the minimum payoff by 1 minus the coefficient of optimism.
3. Add the two products together to rank the alternatives.

The result of ranking is illustrated in Table 12-1. Using this criterion, the decision solution selected would be the second course of action.

TABLE 12-1
Example Hurwicz Criteria

| | Product | | Ranking |
Alternative	Maximum	Minimum	Product
1	$10,000	$6,000	$8,400
2	20,000	4,000	13,600
3	8,000	7,000	7,600

EXPECTED-VALUE CRITERION. Using this criterion, a probability or measure of the likelihood of events is directly assigned to each possible outcome. This probability is then multiplied by the expected payoff to rank alternatives on the basis of the weighted value of each option. The fundamental difference of expected value and the Hurwicz criterion is that the best estimate of attainment is applied directly to the best estimate of accomplishment. The expected value criterion is discussed further in the section of this chapter dealing with make versus buy decisions.

Decision Trees

Another approach to the selection process is the use of decision trees. In most complex situations, a number of options are confronted as a result of any initial decision. Formulation of an overall plan requires evaluation of a total course of action. Initial probabilities and payoffs must be appraised followed by the conditional additional probabilities associated with each subsequent course of action. The decision tree enables the manager to assess a relatively complex situation systematically.

Decision trees consist of three parts: (1) the initial decision point, (2) the paths, and (3) the branches. The whole tree represents the decision problem. The paths, which may consist of several branches, represent the various probabilities and events of a particular outcome. The branches represent various outcomes. Each set of decisions has one outcome and an associated probability.

To illustrate, assume that a logistical manager is concerned with the likelihood of a strike and the associated possibility of a material price increase. To assist in formulation of a strategy, it is necessary to estimate the initial probability of a strike occurring. Next, an estimated cost must be determined for fulfillment of the material plan with and without a strike as well as with or without a subsequent price increase.

The probability of a strike is estimated to be 0.6. The conditional probability of a price increase is judged to be 0.7 if a strike occurs and 0.8 if it does not. However, a price increase following the strike would be greater than if it is granted without a strike. Under each set of conditional probabilities, the cost of material management operations has to be calculated in terms of net profit impact. In other words, any loss of product sale caused by failure to maintain supply continuity has been taken into consideration in arriving at the estimated net profit of each event. The decision structure is presented in Figure 12-1.

Table 12-2 provides the end product of the various events and the expected profit impact. Under the best estimate of probable future events and the impact of each upon expected profit, the most desirable course of action is to take a chance that the strike will not occur but that a price increase will. Taking into consideration all associated costs and potential loss of revenue, the odds favor taking the risk that a strike will be postponed.

FIGURE 12-1
Decision Tree Structure

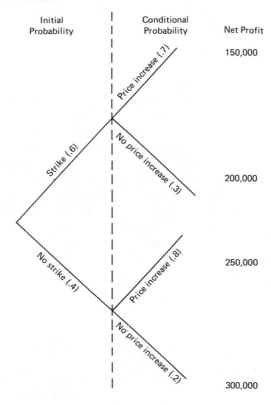

Initial Probability	Conditional Probability	Net Profit

TABLE 12-2
Decision Tree Results

Event	Joint Probability	Expected Profit Value
Strike–increase	0.42	$63,000
Strike–no increase	0.18	36,000
No strike–increase	0.32	80,000
No strike–no increase	0.08	24,000

The decision tree structure and problem illustrated are relatively simple in comparison to those which might be confronted in an actual planning situation. Similar to all decision aids, the value of the decision tree is directly related to the correct assignment of probabilities, which is sometimes very difficult. For example, if the probability of a strike had been judged to be 0.7, the recommended course of action would have been to take the appropriate action necessary to continue to produce during the strike followed by a price increase. Under this set of circumstances, the cost of protection in comparison to the revenue gained from continued operation would have justified stockpiling the material.

Make Versus Buy

A number of situations occur in logistical operations where a decision must be made regarding the external purchase or internal performance of a service or manufacture of a component part. Typical service situations requiring do-or-buy analysis are private versus common carrier, public versus private warehousing, and internal study versus use of consultants. However, the most frequent type of make-or-buy situation concerns the manufacturing alternative of internal fabrication or external procurement. The typical manufacturing situation is illustrated. As a general rule, a manufacturing enterprise desires to make as many parts of its finished product line as economically practical. For the most part, raw materials must be purchased from outside sources, since few firms are vertically integrated to the point where they operate extraction of commodity processing facilities.[2]

Ammer has presented a general set of conditions that are helpful in the

TABLE 12-3
Factors Favoring Make-or-Buy Decisions

Factors Favoring Fabrication	*Factors Favoring Procurement*
1. If the part can be more cheaply fabricated than purchased.	1. If the necessary facilities are not available and there are more profitable opportunities for investing company capital.
2. If the cost is nearly equal (because fabrication reduces the number of vendors the firm must rely upon).	2. If existing facilities can be more economically employed to make other parts.
3. If the part is vital and requires extremely close quality control.	
4. If the part can be produced on existing equipment and is of the type in which the firm has considerable manufacturing experience.	3. If the existing personnel skills cannot be readily adapted to making the parts.
5. If the fabrication process requires no extensive investment in facilities already available at supplier plants.	4. If patents or other legal barriers prevent the company from making the parts.
6. If the requirements for the part are projected to be both relatively large and stable.	5. If the expected requirements for the part are either temporary or seasonal.

[2] Wilbur B. England, *Modern Procurement Management*, 5th ed. (Homewood, Ill.: Richard D. Irwin, Inc., 1970), pp. 72–81, provides an excellent summary of conditions encouraging or discouraging making versus purchasing.

initial appraisal of the decision to make or buy.[3] These are summarized in Table 12-3. Beyond the general conditions favoring making or buying, the final decision results from the most efficient allocation of available capital. To aid in evaluation, the materials manager can apply expected value analysis to project the probable gain of investing in the necessary fabrication equipment as opposed to alternative uses of capital. In general, any investment is expected to provide a return on investment that meets corporate financial planning criteria.

Although the expected-value criterion is one of the most widely advocated methods of evaluating alternative courses of action, it requires considerable knowledge concerning the decision. In the case of the make-or-buy decision, the technique is extremely useful since the costs of each basic option are normally well defined. Assuming that the costs and other pertinent factors are nearly equal, the final decision is one of evaluating alternative application of financial resources. The basic concept is illustrated by an applicational example. Assume that the materials manager has a choice of spending $50,000 in any area that will improve overall costs of procurement. Three major options are available. The first is to invest in fabrication equipment that would result in making rather than buying a specific part. The second option is to improve warehouse receiving facilities to reduce the amount of overtime currently required by dock personnel. The third is to improve the existing methods used to control overall procurement inventories. The problem is to select one of these alternative areas for investing the $50,000.

The first step is to project the potential cost savings of each option over a future time period. Assume that a basic corporate return on investment policy is that all capital investment must be recovered by cost–benefit savings within a three-year period. The best judgment of management is that the payoffs involved in each option are adequate to satisfy the cost–benefit criterion. The estimates of payoff are presented in Table 12-4.

TABLE 12-4
Expected Cost Benefit

Option	Three-Year Cost Reduction
Fabrication equipment	$100,000
Warehouse receiving	95,000
Inventory control method	125,000

However, each projected cost saving involves a certain degree of risk that the expected results will not materialize. The second step is to assign a relative probability to the expected realization of each potential cost benefit.

[3] Dean S. Ammer, *Materials Management*, rev. ed. (Homewood, Ill.: Richard D. Irwin, 1970), p. 271.

Establishment of the probability is a judgment based upon evaluation of relative risk. For example, perhaps a potential vendor of the part in question will develop a new technology that will result in a price reduction if the part is purchased rather than fabricated. Alternatively, the demand for the part may not materialize at the level anticipated, which will result in noneconomical deployment of the new fabrication equipment. Each of the options has similar contingencies that could result in the anticipated savings not materializing. Based on a careful evaluation of all facts, management on a scale of 0.01 to 1.0 estimates the following probabilities of realizing the expected cost reduction: (1) fabrication equipment 0.6, (2) warehouse receiving 0.8, and (3) inventory control method 0.5. The expected comparative value among the three options is calculated by multiplying the probability of attainment and the anticipated cost benefit. The results are presented in Table 12-5.

TABLE 12-5
Expected Value of Capital Expenditure

Option	Cost Benefit	Probability	Expected Value
Fabrication equipment	$100,000	0.6	$60,000
Warehouse receiving	95,000	0.8	76,000
Inventory control method	125,000	0.5	62,500

Using the expected-value criterion to guide the investment decision, the choice would be to complete the improvement of warehouse receiving facilities. Even though this option has the lowest estimated cost benefit, it has the highest expected value, owing to the high probability that the expected cost benefits will indeed be realized.

In conclusion, no statistical or financial aid to decision making can serve as a substitute for management judgment. The perception of the manager in estimating the probability of various events is the key to identifying the appropriate course of adjustment action. The main benefit of decision techniques is that they force a logical and consistent interpretation of the facts as perceived by management. Thus, when decision techniques are used, a systematic method for reviewing alternatives is applied. The benefit gained is consistency.

Facility Operations

Statistical techniques can assist in a number of special situations confronted in the operation of warehouse and manufacturing facilities. Three such technique applications are illustrated in this section: (1) receiving, (2) inspection, and (3) facility sizing.

Receiving

Material and finished-goods receiving are typical areas in an enterprise where waiting lines or queues can develop. Queueing analysis is applicable to any situation where (1) some material, person, vehicle, or other element arrives at a facility for servicing; (2) at times, it is necessary to wait in line; (3) the desired service is received; (4) the object in question leaves the system.[4] Thus, queueing analysis could just as readily be applied to a doctor's office, barber shop, a retail store, the overall manufacturing process, or any other similar situations.

As in most areas of applied mathematics, queueing theory has a specialized terminology that should be understood by the reader. The *arrival rate* refers to the average rate at which trucks arrive at the unloading dock. Normally, it is expressed as the number of arrivals per unit of time. The *service rate* refers to the average rate at which trucks can be unloaded. It is expressed as the number of trucks serviced per unit of time. The *distribution rate* for arrival and unloading has a significant impact upon waiting-line analysis. Basically, two rates exist. If no logical or consistent pattern of arrival and unloading exists, then a *random distribution* rate is experienced. If a pattern is present, then the distribution rate is *predictable.*

The probabilities of arrival and servicing can be expressed in the form of statistical distributions. Arrivals are typically expressed in the form of a *Poisson distribution*, whereas servicing is an *exponential distribution.*[5]

The Poisson distribution or the distribution of arrival times is expressed as

$$P(x) = \frac{(\lambda t)^x e^{-\lambda t}}{x!}$$

where

$P(x)$ = probability of arrival
t = unit of time
λ = average number of arrivals per unit of time
x = arrivals

The equation yields the probability that there will be x arrivals in time t with the average arrival rate of λ units. Figure 12-2 illustrates the Poisson distribution.

---

[4] For an expanded discussion, see Harvey M. Wagner, *Principles of Management Science* (Englewood Cliffs, N.J.: Prentice-Hall, Inc., 1970), Chap. 15.

[5] The reader not familiar with basic statistical concepts should skip this section and resume reading at "Inspection," page 379.

FIGURE 12-2
Poisson Distribution

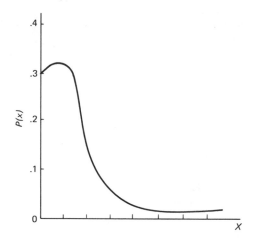

The probability of service time is exponential and is expressed as follows:

$$S(t) = Me^{-Mt}$$

where

$$S(t) = \text{density function for service times}$$
$$t = \text{unit of time}$$
$$M = \text{average servicing time}$$

The average service time overall is $\check{t}s = 1/M$. Figure 12-3 illustrates the exponential density function.

FIGURE 12-3
Exponential Distribution

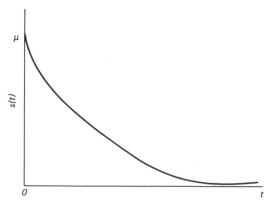

A final term used in queueing analysis is *channel*. Channel refers to the number of processing devices in the situation under analysis. For example, if one unloading dock is available, then the system is *single-channel*. If more than one channel exists in the problem, then it is *multiple-channel*.

The queueing-analysis problem represents a quantification of the receiving situation to allow management to test different ideas or queue-reduction solutions. To illustrate, assume that an unbiased data bank has been collected about arrival and unloading of trucks at a warehouse dock. The average time between arrivals of trucks at the dock is 30 minutes. Table 12-6 presents the measured unloading times for the trucks and the related frequency distribution.

TABLE 12-6
Queueing Analysis Data

Number of Trucks	Unloading Time (minutes)	Percentage Distribution Unloading Time	Weighted Average of Unloading Times
10	35	10	3.50
30	40	30	12.00
40	45	40	18.00
20	50	20	10.00

Based on the data available, the unloading dock can be simulated. The first task is to simulate the arrival of a loaded truck. Based upon the average arrival-time analysis, there is a high probability that at least one truck will arrive every 30 minutes. Using a random-number table, the number of arrivals each 30-minute period can be approximated. In a similar manner, random-number tables can be used to approximate the expected unloading time for each arrival. A sample of the simulated operational data that can be generated using random numbers and the probabilities of arrival and unloading time is presented in Table 12-7.

Once the arrival and service pattern is determined, the queueing solution is to seek the lowest-cost way to complete the unloading. The cost of unloading consists of warehouse labor plus idle time of truck drivers and equipment while in the queue. Assuming that the necessary number of unloading docks or channels are available, the problem is to decide the size of the labor crew that will most economically service the arriving vehicles. The standard work rule is that trucks are unloaded on a first come–first service basis. For purposes of queue analysis, it is assumed if there is one arrival, it will occur at the start of the 30-minute period, and if two trucks arrive, the second will be ready for servicing at the start of the sixteenth minute of the 30-minute period.

TABLE 12-7
Simulated Arrival and Service Data

30-Minute Time Periods	Simulated Arrivals	Simulated Service Time (minutes)
1	0	
2	2	45–50
3	1	40
4	1	40
5	0	
6	0	
7	0	
8	1	50
9	0	
10	2	40–50
11	0	
12	1	45
13	0	
14	1	40
15	1	45
16	2	45–40
17	2	50–35
18	1	45
19	0	
20	0	
21	0	

Figure 12-4 represents the simulated arrival and servicing patterns for the data displayed in Table 12-7. The numbers on the left side of Figure 12-4 represent 30-minute time periods. The dashed line represents waiting time once the truck has arrived. The solid line represents servicing time once the unloading starts. The total time in the queue is the combination of the waiting and servicing time.

Based on Figure 12-4 the total idle time of drivers and equipment is 1,285 minutes, an average time per driver in the queue of 85.69 minutes. Table 12-8 presents the cost of warehouse labor and idle drivers and equipment. The assumption is that idle transport equipment could be utilized if not in the queue.

TABLE 12-8
Queue Cost Factors

Warehouse regular rate/hour	$3.50
Warehouse overtime rate/hour	5.25
Driver and equipment rate/hour	20.00

Based on the data in Figure 12-4, it will be necessary for the warehouse dock crew to work 12.25 hours to complete the servicing of trucks scheduled to arrive on the simulated day. All hours over eight are paid at overtime rates.

The total cost of using a single seven-man unloading crew is presented in Table 12-9.

FIGURE 12-4
Simulated Queue Time Pattern

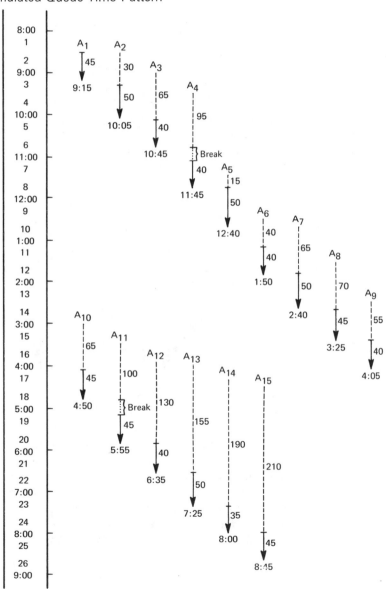

TABLE 12-9
One Warehouse Shift

Warehouse regular rate	$196.00
Warehouse overtime rate	156.19
Driver and equipment rate	409.32
Total cost	$761.51

An alternative unloading procedure would be the addition of more warehouse personnel to unload or service the arriving trucks faster. To illustrate, a second crew of seven men is added under a work schedule that starts at 10 A.M. and ends when the last truck is unloaded. The regular crew is limited to an 8-hour shift.

While the simulated queue pattern is not presented, the result would be a reduction in average waiting time from 85.69 minutes to 25 minutes per truck. Table 12-10 provides the related cost data for the two-crew unloading alternative. A queue pattern for the two-crew unloading alternative similar to Figure 12-4 can be developed from the data presented.

TABLE 12-10
Two Warehouse Shifts

Warehouse regular rate shift A	$196.00
Warehouse regular rate shift B	196.00
Warehouse overtime rate shift B	15.44
Driver and equipment rate	123.75
Total cost	$531.19

In the illustration the queue has been substantially reduced by adding the second crew with a daily saving of $230.32. Based on a 250-day work year, the annualized cost benefit would be $57,580.

This simple illustration points out the type of analysis required by the materials management organization in order to realize smooth operations at the lowest possible total cost. One frequent belief is that when common carriers are used, the in-queue time is not important. Therefore, the proper solution to the queue situation is to use the lowest amount of warehouse labor that will get the trucks unloaded in time for the materials or parts to be ready for manufacturing use. This logic is faulty for two reasons. First, over an extended time, driver and equipment idle time of common carriers will be reflected in the rate per hundredweight charged for their service. Second, most tariffs provide for a specific delay charge unless trucks are serviced within a specified time period.[6]

[6] For an expanded discussion, see page 138.

A number of variations can be applied to a waiting-line simulation to seek better servicing rate or lower costs. For example, when private trucks are used, an attempt can be made to eliminate random arrival by scheduling. Scheduled arrival will reduce the waiting queue. A second potential modification is to relax the first come–first service rule to move trucks with critical materials or higher than average delay charges rapidly through the queue.

In essence, the main point of emphasis in receiving is establishment of an unloading procedure that will meet manufacturing requirements at the lowest total cost. As in most areas of logistics, care must be exercised to assure that all relevant costs are considered in the decision process.

Inspection

One of the basic objectives of materials management is quality maintenance. Inferior quality is the single greatest cause for failure of supplies to be delivered on time. The materials management inspection responsibility is aimed at checking a representative sample of materials and parts to assure they meet specification. Such inspection may be done at the vendor's manufacturing plant or after the material is received. The location of inspection will depend upon the critical nature of the item in question and its overall vulnerability to damage while in transit. The more susceptible a given material or part to inspection rejection, the greater the need to stockpile acceptable items in order to maintain continuity of supply.

The cost of 100 per cent inspection will, in most cases, be prohibitive.[7] Therefore, some form of inspection or quality control by statistical sampling is required. In most fabrication situations, a degree of random fluctuations in specific parts is expected to occur. The purpose of the inspection sample is to measure the degree of fluctuation or damage to determine if the fabrication or transportation process was out of control.

Sampling consists of selecting a predetermined number of items from a large lot or shipment for careful inspection. The sample size and method of selection is structured in such a way to assure that it will be representative of the total group.[8] Based upon a careful inspection of the sample, the inspector follows a predetermined statistical inference procedure with respect to acceptance or rejection of the entire shipment. For each material or part, a predetermined required reliability sets the basic standard for acceptance or rejection.

For example, assume that a shipment of a specific part consists of 400 units. It has been determined that a 10 per cent, or 40-unit, sample is adequate to project the overall condition of the shipment with a 95 per cent confidence of correct appraisal.[9] The sampling procedure under this situation could be

---

[7] Robert E. McGarrah, *Production and Logistics Management* (New York: John Wiley & Sons, Inc., 1963), pp. 7–20.

[8] Ibid.

[9] Ninety-five per cent confidence means that the sample size will be adequate to make a valid inspection 95 out of 100 times. It does not mean that deficiencies will exist 5 per cent of the time.

a complete inspection of every tenth part. If all 40 parts meet specifications, the entire shipment would be accepted. If one defect was discovered in the sample of 40, then several options might be followed.

First, the total lot could be rejected. However, this could result in unnecessary expense of return shipment and possible shortage of a critical part. Second, the total lot could be inspected, with separation of those parts which do and do not meet specifications. A final choice, if only one or a limited number of defects was discovered in the initial sample, is to take a second random sample to cross-verify results. The degree of tolerance in acceptance or rejection, as well as the amount of additional inspection caused by a defect, will depend upon the tolerance range established for the part.

Facility Sizing

Determination of facility size is a subset of strategic planning which must be implemented as part of the operational planning effort. Once the decision has been made to establish a particular facility at a given location, it is necessary to determine size. Facility sizing involves an analysis of activities to be performed at the facility, coupled with an estimate of inventory space requirements. The focal point of concern in the example is inventory since other requirements for space, such as order processing or light fabrication, are unique to each enterprise's plans. Sizing a warehouse facility was noted initially in Chapter 7.[10] The technique described here can be utilized for all types of facility planning requirements. The example is based on a warehouse situation. The overall sizing analysis requires that four tasks be completed: (1) data identification, (2) determination of gross space requirements, (3) throughput analysis, (4) cost analysis. Each is discussed and illustrated.

DATA IDENTIFICATION.   Several elements of basic data are required to estimate facility size requirements. First, demand forecasts are critical to sizing since they quantify the throughput requirements of the facility. The inherent errors of forecast techniques require that the final estimate of demand be calculated on the basis of management prediction. Care should be taken to include only warehouse service area demand that will pass through the facility in the prediction. The second type of data required for sizing concerns the characteristics of products and orders to be stored and shipped from the warehouse. The critical product feature is cubic displacement, since it determines the size required to store a specific amount of product. The critical aspects of customer order patterns are the size, frequency, and variation in time between orders. Data collected on existing product and customer configurations must be modified to reflect potential changes. The third type of data required to complete the analysis are estimates of the fixed and variable costs associated with alternative courses of action. Assumptions regarding each type of data are introduced as appropriate.

[10] See page 226.

DETERMINATION OF GROSS SPACE REQUIREMENTS. The determination of gross space requires five steps. The basic data required to render facility sizing are presented in Table 12-11. The forecasted annual demand of $152 million in facility throughput is presented on a monthly basis in column 1 as the first step in the analysis. The sales forecast provides an estimate of demand level and expected seasonal variation. In the second step of the analysis, sales dollars are converted to cubic throughput requirements, as indicated in column 2 of Table 12-11. In the example situation an average price to cubic displacement ratio of $20 per cubic foot is assumed.

Given sales in cubic feet the third step is to estimate average inventory level. An estimate of average inventory can be calculated on an analysis of past orders or by the use of past inventory turnover experience. For this illustration an annual turn factor of six times has been assumed. Using this turn factor the average inventory for each period in cubic feet is computed to be twice the monthly sales volume. This calculation is presented in column 3, Table 12-11. If the facility is to service a situation where a high degree of seasonality is experienced in either manufacturing or sales accompanied by inventory buildup, the calculation of average inventory based on turns would not provide useful results. In such situations a detailed analysis of the timing of inventory buildup and depletion rate would be required.

The fourth step is to estimate square-foot warehouse requirements. The assumed usable vertical storage height for the product line is 16 feet. The actual figure will depend upon product stacking capability and the planned materials-handling system. To determine area requirements, the monthly average inventory is divided by 16. The results are presented in column 4, Table 12-11.

In the fifth step of the analysis an adjustment must be made to convert required storage space to gross warehouse size. The amount of loss space will vary by the overall functions to be performed at the facility, the product, and the actual layout. For the illustration it is assumed that the usable product storage will represent 75 per cent of gross space. To compute the gross facility size on a monthly basis, the storage area requirement is divided by 0.75. The results are provided in column 5, Table 12-11.

The result of steps 1 through 5 is a monthly gross facility requirement. Next, a throughput analysis is required.

THROUGHPUT ANALYSIS. Given the gross space requirement it is necessary to evaluate month-to-month requirements, in terms of private warehouse or alternative forms of storage, such as public warehouses or transportation equipment. Since the size of a private facility cannot be adjusted on a monthly basis, a form of make-or-buy analysis must be performed to determine the ideal size throughout the year. For illustration it is assumed that the choice is between private construction and public warehouse overflow storage. In terms of overall problem solution, the facility combination that results in the lowest total annual cost would represent the ideal solution.

TABLE 12-11
Facility Requirements Determination

	(1) Monthly Sales ($000)	(2) Monthly Sales[a] (000s of cubic feet)	(3) Average Inventory[b] (000s of cubic feet)	(4) Area Requirement[c] (square feet)	(5) Adjusted Gross Area Requirements[d] (square feet)
January	11,200	560	1,120	70,000	93,333
February	11,800	590	1,180	73,750	98,333
March	13,200	660	1,320	82,500	110,000
April	12,900	645	1,290	80,625	107,500
May	12,100	605	1,210	75,625	100,833
June	13,500	675	1,350	84,375	112,500
July	14,800	740	1,480	92,500	123,333
August	14,800	740	1,480	92,500	123,333
September	13,600	680	1,360	85,000	113,333
October	11,900	595	1,190	74,375	99,167
November	10,400	520	1,040	65,000	86,667
December	11,800	590	1,180	73,750	98,333
Total	152,000				

[a] An average value of $20/cubic foot is assumed on the average for the overall product line.
[b] On the basis of an average of six turns per year, the average inventory level is twice the monthly sales volume.
[c] Assuming an average usable stacking height of 16 feet, the area requirement for the facility is the cube divided by 16.
[d] The actual area required for storage is estimated to be 75 per cent of gross requirements.

The throughput analysis is presented in Table 12-12. A range of possible warehouse sizes is taken directly from column 5, Table 12-11, and is ranked in descending order of monthly gross requirements—column 1, Table 12-12. Assuming that each estimate of monthly gross requirements represents a feasible warehouse size, the relative throughput of private and public utilization is calculated in dollar sales. The sales throughput for private utilization is presented in column 2, and for public utilization in column 3, Table 12-12.

TABLE 12-12
Throughput Analysis

(1) Possible Warehouse Sizes (square feet)	(2) Sales Throughput Through Private Facility ($000)	(3) Sales Throughput Through Public Facility ($000)
123,333	152,000	0
123,333	152,000	0
113,333	149,600	2,400
112,500	149,300	2,700
110,000	148,100	3,900
107,500	146,600	5,400
100,833	141,800	10,200
99,167	140,400	11,600
98,333	139,600	12,400
98,333	139,600	12,400
93,333	133,600	18,400
86,667	124,800	27,200
0	0	152,000

Since the first two levels of capacity in Table 12-12 represent the maximum size needed for any month, the entire annual volume can be stored and shipped from the private facility. Thus the throughput in column 2 represents the total annual sales volume of $152 million. For smaller facility sizes, since these sizes were based on a lower monthly throughput, not all of the volume may be shipped from the private facility. For example, for the third possible warehouse size of 113,333 square feet, the size requirement was based on a monthly volume of $13,600,000. At this capacity level, any monthly volume over that level must be shipped through a public facility. In this case, since the next highest month has a volume of $14.8 million, the volume that must be shifted to the public facility is $2.4 million [(14.8 million − 13.6 million) × 2]. The throughput volume through the private facility in column 2 and the volume through the public facility are then adjusted to reflect this shift. The volume split for the other possible facility sizes are each illustrated.

If the smallest possible private warehouse is constructed, $27.2 million in sales will be serviced using a public warehouse facility. Other options are to use all public warehousing or to build some size of private facility to accommodate from minimum to maximum gross requirements.

COST ANALYSIS.   To arrive at a final solution, a total cost analysis of the available options is necessary. This requires that the fixed and variable costs through the private facility as well as the cost of utilizing a public warehouse be estimated. The results of this analysis are presented in Table 12-13. To complete the analysis several cost factors are needed. First, throughput must be converted to weight, since variable cost is typically a function of pounds. Based on an assumed sales value of $2 per pound, the throughput ratios are restated in hundred-pound equivalents for each type of warehouse in columns 2 and 5, Table 12-13.

To calculate private warehouse costs, a variable cost of $0.25 per hundred pounds was assumed to reflect such factors as labor, handling equipment, and supplies. For private fixed costs, a figure of $0.75 per square foot was assumed to reflect such items as depreciation, insurance, heat, taxes, light, and administrative overhead. No economy of scale as a function of warehouse size was factored into either cost figure, owing to the narrow range of alternative sizes. The appropriate costs are presented in columns 3 and 4 of Table 12-13.

For the public warehouse facility an assumed rate quotation of $0.50 per hundredweight was used to calculate cost. In the case of public facilities, the cost includes both fixed and variable costs of the warehouser, but from the user's viewpoint, charges are assessed on the basis of hundredweight throughput. Once again, the analysis does not include the possibility of rate reductions that might be obtained by offering larger volumes to the public warehouse. These costs are illustrated in column 6, Table 12-13.

The total cost of each alternative is illustrated in column 7, Table 12-13. The ideal size of warehouse would be between 107,500 and 110,000 square feet of gross space.

As noted at the outset of the sizing analysis, the analysis is only as good as the supporting assumptions regarding demand and cost. For example, what would be the effect if variable cost associated with the public warehouse declined to $0.40 per hundredweight or if demand increased 10 per cent?

The sizing application illustrated has for simplicity been limited to a single-year time frame. In actual situations the analysis would be complicated by the need to consider expected life duration of the warehouse as well as changes in demand, cost, and product data across the planning horizon. The ideal solution would be the selection of a facility size that would result in the least total cost based upon discounted cash flow across the planning horizon. The technique illustrated can be expanded to deal with across-time requirements planning.[11]

---

[11] For an illustration, see Ronald Ballou, *Business Logistics Management* (Englewood Cliffs, N.J.: Prentice-Hall, Inc., 1973), pp. 380–96.

TABLE 12-13
Facility Cost Analysis

(1) Warehouse Size (square feet)	(2) Private Facility Throughput[a] (00's of pounds)	(3) Private Facility Variable Costs[b] ($000)	(4) Private Facility Fixed Costs[c] ($000)	(5) Public Facility Throughput[a] (00's of pounds)	(6) Public Facility Variable Costs[d] ($000)	(7) Total Annual Operating Costs ($000)
123,333	760,000	190.00	92.50	0	0	282.50
123,333	760,000	190.00	92.50	0	0	282.50
113,333	748,000	187.00	85.00	12,000	6.00	278.00
112,500	746,500	186.63	84.38	13,500	6.75	277.76
110,000	740,500	185.13	82.50	19,500	9.75	277.38
107,500	733,000	183.25	80.63	27,000	13.50	277.38
100,833	709,000	177.25	75.62	51,000	25.50	278.37
99,167	702,000	175.50	74.38	58,000	29.00	278.88
98,333	698,000	174.50	73.75	62,000	31.00	279.25
98,333	698,000	174.50	73.75	62,000	31.00	279.25
93,333	668,000	167.00	70.00	92,000	46.00	283.00
86,667	624,000	156.00	65.00	136,000	68.00	289.00
0	0	0	0	760,000	380.00	380.00

[a] The product mix is assumed to have an average value of $2/pound.
[b] Based on an arbitrary handling and throughput cost of $0.25/hundredweight of volume moved through the facility.
[c] A $0.75/square foot fixed charge is assessed against the private facility.
[d] Based on an arbitrary handling and throughput cost of $0.50/hundredweight of volume moved through the public facility.

Allocation and Assignment

With allocation and assignment problems the decision maker is certain about the operational planning conditions. Although a number of limitations and restrictions may exist, the objective of allocation is to determine the optimal course of action taking all important factors into consideration. The *allocation* problem exists under conditions of adequate supply as contrasted to the *assignment* problem, wherein a choice situation is confronted as a result of shortage.

The most common technique for solving this type of operational problem is *linear programming*. The capabilities of linear programming were reviewed in Chapter 11.[12] In this chapter one linear programming procedure, the *transportation method*, is illustrated as an appropriate method to solve allocation and assignment problems. The procedure is designed to optimize or maximize a single function referred to as the objective function. Even though it derives its name from its early use in transportation scheduling, the basic method is applicable to other situations.

Allocation: Adequate Supply

The general structure of the allocation problem is that a given number of product source points and product demand points exist in a network and the cost of shipping a volume from each source to each destination is known. The sources and destinations may represent manufacturing plants, warehouses, or customers. The problem is to select those assignments that will minimize shipping cost while satisfying the capacity and demand requirements of each source and destination.

To solve the problem using the transportation procedure, the following data are required:

1. The capacities of each source (e.g., manufacturing plant).
2. The requirements of a destination (e.g., warehouse).
3. The transportation cost per unit from each source to each destination.

The only general restriction beyond deterministic and linear relationships is that a one-for-one substitution must be possible when using the transportation method. For example, if it is decided not to ship 100 units of a product from a specific plant to a specific warehouse, it must be possible to substitute a similar number of units from a different plant.

In the example two plants located in New York and Los Angeles each produce the product in question. Shipments are made from the two plants to four warehouses located across the country.

---

[12] See pages 347–353.

Three types of data are required to operationalize the transportation method. Tables 12-14, 12-15, and 12-16 present the data.

TABLE 12-14
Weekly Availability of Manufacturing at
Each Plant

Plant Location	Manufacturing Schedule
New York	4,000
Los Angeles	3,500
Total manufacturing (units per week)	7,500

TABLE 12-15
Weekly Requirements at
Individual Warehouses

Warehouse	Unit Requirement
Atlanta	1,500
Chicago	2,000
San Francisco	2,000
Pittsburgh	1,000

TABLE 12-16
Transportation Cost from each Plant to Each
Warehouse (Dollars per Unit)

Warehouses / Plants	Atlanta	Chicago	San Francisco	Pittsburgh
New York	+5	+4	+11	+3
Los Angeles	+10	+7	+2	+9

PROBLEM INITIALIZATION. The first step is to develop a matrix that arranges supply, demand, and transportation cost data. However, this matrix must maintain a balance between supply and demand; if supply does not equal demand, a dummy source or destination must be added to account for the difference. In the initial matrix, an "other" or dummy destination is added, since the manufacturing capacity exceeds demand. The transportation cost to the dummy destination is zero, since no product is actually shipped.

An initial solution is necessary to start the procedure. The initial solution can be determined in a number of ways, among which are (1) existing assignments, (2) present lowest-cost solution found by inspection, (3) managerially preferred method, and (4) the northwest corner rule (NCR).[13] The NCR is used in this example because it offers a systematic and logical method to arrive at an initial solution. The following procedures are used when implementing the NCR.

1. Begin in the upper left corner of the matrix and compare the demand of the column with the supply in the row. Place the smaller of these two values in that matrix location. If this fills the demand, move to the next location to the right and fill this demand, if possible. Continue this until the supply is exhausted for the row.
2. Moving to the next-lower row, again compare the demand with the supply. Select the smaller of the two quantities and place it in that location. Move to the next column or row and follow the same procedure.
3. After completing the second row, move to the third and fourth row, and so on, following steps 1 and 2.

Matrix I, Table 12-17, is the cost matrix with the dummy column inserted. Since the transportation method is a maximizing procedure, transportation costs are expressed as negatives. If a negative value is used to express cost, a direct readout of the profit impact is possible. Matrix II shows the initial feasible solution of the problem obtained through the NCR method.

TABLE 12-17
Matrix I: Cost Matrix with Dummy Column

Warehouses / Plants	Atlanta	Chicago	San Francisco	Pittsburgh	Other	Total Supply
New York	−5	−4	−11	−3	0	4,000
Los Angeles	−10	−7	−2	−9	0	3,500
Total Supply	1,500	2,000	2,000	1,000	1,000	

Matrix II, Table 12-18, represents a possible allocation, but not necessarily the least-cost alternative. The matrix must now be evaluated for more economical alternatives. Through analysis of each vacant square in the matrix,

---

[13] An alternative approach to arriving at an initial solution is the Vogel approximation. See Nyles V. Reinfield and William R. Vogel, *Mathematical Programming* (Englewood Cliffs, N.J.: Prentice-Hall, Inc., 1958).

it can be determined if the least-cost solution has been found. If not, a better solution is possible by varying the shipping assignments within the established constraints.

TABLE 12-18
Matrix II: Initial Solution—NCR Procedure

Plants \ Warehouses	Atlanta	Chicago	San Francisco	Pittsburgh	Other	Total Supply
New York	1,500 / −5	2,000 / −4	500 / −11	−3	0	4,000
Los Angeles	−10	−7	1,500 / −2	1,000 / −9	1,000 / 0	3,500
Total Supply	1,500	2,000	2,000	1,000	1,000	

SOLUTION PROCEDURE. To evaluate the matrix, the following steps are performed.

1. Place a zero in the margin of the first row. This is a row value. Now, for each nonempty location in that row, determine the column value by using the following equation:

$$\text{transportation cost} = \text{row value} + \text{column value}$$

or

$$\text{column value} = \text{transportation cost} - \text{row value}$$

Place the column value in the margin of the column. The appropriate column should then be used to find the row value for another row, and the process should be repeated until each row and column have a value. Only nonempty locations are used to find these values.

2. Now every vacant location is evaluated by means of the following equation:

$$\text{vacant value} = \text{row value} + \text{column value} - \text{transportation cost}$$

This is done for all vacant locations and the value is placed, in parentheses, in that location.

3. If all the values in parentheses are nonnegative, the solution is optimal. However, if there are negative values, a better solution exists. A better solution can be obtained by transferring units to the warehouse with the negative value, or the warehouse with the most negative value if there is more than one.

4. If units must be transferred, trace a path starting at the location with the most negative value and put a plus (+) in that location. Continue tracing a path until returning to the original row, alternately placing plus and minus in the nonempty locations. This process, in effect, balances the rows and columns so that units can be shifted to the desired location. Remember, all locations except the first one on this path must be nonempty, and all angles on the path must be right angles.
5. Review the path and find the warehouse with the smallest number of units and a minus in it. This is the number of units to transfer to a new warehouse. Transfer this number of units and balance the remainder of the matrix by adding or subtracting this value from the locations along the path as denoted by the sign. The number of nonvacant locations should equal the number of rows plus the number of columns minus 1 at all times during the solution procedure. If this is not the case, a degenerative situation is said to exist and special steps must be taken to resolve the situation. The necessary procedure will be discussed later.
6. Return to step 1 and evaluate the new matrix.

SOLUTION EVALUATION. Using the rules already given, the solution presented in matrix II, Table 12-18, can be evaluated for optimality. First, obtain row and column values using the nonempty locations. If a value of zero is arbitrarily assigned to R_1, then C_1 can be computed as follows:

$$C_1 = -5 - 0 = -5$$

where R_1 is the row value for row 1 and C_1 is the column value for column 1.
Additional column values can be identified through this procedure until column 3 is reached:

$$C_3 = -11 - R_1$$
$$= -11 - 0$$
$$= -11$$

C_3 is now used to find R_2:

$$R_2 = \text{transportation cost} - C_3$$
$$= -2 - (-11)$$
$$= 9$$

The value of R_2 is now placed in the margin and the process continues as before until all row and column values have been determined. When each row and column have been assigned an appropriate value, each vacant location is evaluated using the following formula:

$$VV_{ij} = R_i + C_j - TC_{ij}$$

where

VV_{ij} = value to be put in the vacant location at the intersection of the
ith row and jth column
R_i = row value for row i
C_j = column value for column j
TC_{ij} = cost (negative) of sending 1 unit from source i to demand point j

To illustrate this procedure, for the matrix location designating Los Angeles (R_2) to Chicago (C_2), the calculation is as follows:

$$VV_{2,2} = R_2 + C_2 - TC_{2,2}$$
$$= 9 + (-4) - (-7)$$
$$= 12$$

The 12 is placed in that matrix location in parentheses. Matrix III, Table 12-19, is the matrix after all row and column values have been found and all vacant locations have been evaluated.

TABLE 12-19
Matrix III : Solution 1

Row Value	Plants / Warehouses	Column Value −5 Atlanta	−4 Chicago	−11 San Francisco	−18 Pittsburgh	−9 Other	Total Supply
0	New York	1,500 / −5	2,000 / −4	500 / −11	(−15) / −3	(−9) / 0	4,000
9	Los Angeles	(14) / −10	(12) / −7	1,500 / −2	1,000 / −9	1,000 / 0	3,500
	Total Supply	1,500	2,000	2,000	1,000	1,000	

Total Cost = $33,000

Upon analysis of matrix III it can be determined that units should be transferred into the New York to Pittsburgh route since it is the most negative. Since the matrix on this path location with the least number of units and a minus sign contains an allocation of 500 units (New York–San Francisco), this is the number of units to be transferred. This is the existing allocation from the New York plant to the Pittsburgh warehouse. When the number of units to be shifted has been determined, the quantities of each of the matrix locations on the path must be adjusted and balanced to maintain the correct relationship between the supply and demand at each location. To do this,

500 units are placed in the New York–Pittsburgh location by subtracting 500 units each from the New York–San Francisco and Los Angeles–Pittsburgh locations and adding 500 units to the Los Angeles–San Francisco location. This is accomplished in matrix IV, Table 12-20, and matrix V, Table 12-21.

TABLE 12-20
Matrix IV: Path to Balance Supply and Demand After Transfer

Warehouses / Plants	Atlanta	Chicago	San Francisco	Pittsburgh	Other	Total Supply
New York	1,500	2,000	500 (−) ⟶ (+)			4,000
Los Angeles			(+) 1,500 ⟵ 1,000 (−)	1,000	1,000	3,500
Total Supply	1,500	2,000	2,000	1,000	1,000	

TABLE 12-21
Matrix V: Reallocation

Warehouses / Plants	Atlanta	Chicago	San Francisco	Pittsburgh	Other	Total Supply
New York	1,500	2,000		500		4,000
Los Angeles			2,000	500	1,000	3,500
Total Supply	1,500	2,000	2,000	1,000	1,000	

Notice that the totals in supply and demand must remain the same after each transfer iteration. Matrix VI, Table 12-22, now brings together the new routes from matrix V, Table 12-21, and the cost data from matrix III, Table 12-19.

The solution procedure is repeated until a solution is isolated, which yields all nonnegative values for vacant locations. In total, it is necessary to generate three matrices before all negative values are eliminated.

As can be seen in matrix VII, Table 12-23, each of the empty matrix locations has a nonnegative value, so this set of assignments provides the optimum method of allocation.

TABLE 12-22
Matrix VI : Solution 2

	Column Value	−5	−4	4	−3	6	
Row Value	Warehouses / Plants	Atlanta	Chicago	San Francisco	Pittsburgh	Other	Total Supply
0	New York	1,500 / −5	2,000 (−) / −4	(15) / −11	500 (+) / −3	(6) / 0	4,000
−6	Los Angeles	(−1) / −10	(−3) (+) / −7	2,000 / −2	500 (−) / −9	1,000 / 0	3,500
	Total Supply	1,500	2,000	2,000	1,000	1,000	

Total Cost = $25,500

TABLE 12-23
Matrix VII : Optimal Solution

	Column Value	−5	−4	1	−3	3	
Row Value	Warehouses / Plants	Atlanta	Chicago	San Francisco	Pittsburgh	Other	Total Supply
0	New York	1,500 / −5	1,500 / −4	(12) / −11	1,000 / −3	(3) / 0	4,000
−3	Los Angeles	(2) / −10	500 / −7	2,000 / −2	(3) / −9	1,000 / 0	3,500
	Total Supply	1,500	2,000	2,000	1,000	1,000	

Total Cost = $24,000

Matrix VIII, Table 12-24, provides a simplified form of matrix VII showing only the loads to be shipped from each manufacturing plant to each warehouse. The savings between the initial matrix and the final one are $8,000. Although this problem could have been solved just as well using trial-and-error techniques, larger problems require a systematic approach. The transportation algorithm provides a technique for manual implementation of linear programming methods. However, for larger problems, the required calculations quickly become tedious. The simplex procedure has two advantages over the transportation method. First, the simplex method is general and can solve other types of linear programming problems. Second, there are many computer software packages available which use the simple procedure to solve linear programming problems.

TABLE 12-24
Matrix VIII: Optimal Shipping Assignments

Plants \ Warehouses	Atlanta	Chicago	San Francisco	Pittsburgh	Other	Total Supply
New York	1,500	1,500		1,000		4,000
Los Angeles		500	2,000		1,000	3,500
Total Supply	1,500	2,000	2,000	1,000	1,000	

DEGENERACY. As noted previously, the degenerate situation arises when the number of nonempty matrix locations is more or less than the number of rows plus the number of columns. An example of a degenerate situation is presented in matrix IX, Table 12-25. After the development of each matrix, the analyst must check for the degenerate condition. Steps must be taken to either increase or decrease the number of nonempty matrix locations before the transportation procedure can be continued.

TABLE 12-25
Matrix IX: Example of Degenerate Solution

Plants \ Warehouses	Atlanta	Chicago	San Francisco	Pittsburgh	Other	Total Supply
New York	1,500	2,000				3,500
Los Angeles			2,000	1,000	1,000	4,000
Total Supply	1,500	2,000	2,000	1,000	1,000	

When the initial allocation method produces too many nonempty matrix locations, the possibility of alternative row and column values is introduced. This would make it difficult to compute the resultant vacant square values (VV_{ij}) so the matrix could not be evaluated further. When this form of degeneracy occurs, the allocations to some of the nonempty matrix locations must be combined until the correct number of nonempty locations is obtained. After this task is completed, the normal solution procedure can continue.

If there are not enough nonempty matrix locations, as demonstrated in matrix IX, Table 12-25, then an additional square or squares must be filled in. This can be accomplished by allocating 0 units to any of the matrix locations which are presently empty. This provides enough nonempty matrix locations to compute the row and column values. Once this new matrix location has been selected and filled in, the problem can be solved in the normal manner treating the location with 0 units just as any other nonempty location.

Assignment: Short Supply

The short-supply problem occurs when the inventory available to ship falls short of that required at the destinations. The problem is to select a product allocation plan that will minimize the loss associated with the shortage.

The transportation method can be used to solve the short-supply problem by structuring a dummy plant (origin) rather than a dummy warehouse to handle the differential between supply and demand. For example, if the New York plant in the allocation example had a decreased amount of inventory available because of a strike or parts shortage, a shortage would exist. In this instance the total supply is 6,000 units while the demand remains at 6,500 units. Since the demand of at least one of the warehouses cannot be fully satisfied, it is necessary to determine the location(s) which the shortage will affect least.

The procedure attempts to minimize the total costs of the system, which, in this example, include the normal transportation cost per unit and a per unit penalty cost associated with the loss of sales if the warehouse is not supplied. Table 12-26 provides estimates of the per unit shortage cost to each warehouse.

TABLE 12-26
Cost of Stockout at Warehouses

LOCATION	COST
Atlanta	2
Chicago	5
San Francisco	4
Pittsburgh	3

These shortage costs are added to the original transportation costs from Table 12-16 to provide a "pseudo" total cost, which includes transportation and penalty cost. For example, since Atlanta has a penalty cost of $2 per unit and the transportation cost from New York to Atlanta is $5 per unit, the approximation for total cost is $7 per unit. The dummy plant supplies an amount equivalent to the shortage (500 units). All costs are shown as negative values. Using the NCR initialization procedure, the first solution is illustrated in Table 12-27. The total cost of the initial solution is $51,000.

TABLE 12-27
Short-Supply Matrix

Plants \ Warehouse	Atlanta	Chicago	San Francisco	Pittsburgh	Total Supply
New York	1,500 / −7	1,000 / −9	−15	−6	2,500
Los Angeles	−12	1,000 / −12	2,000 / −6	500 / −12	3,500
Dummy	−2	−5	−4	500 / −3	500
Total Supply	1,500	2,000	2,000	1,000	6,500

Total Cost = $51,000

The optimal solution for the situation is achieved via the transportation procedure previously described. After four iterations, the final solution, with a total cost of $48,500, is shown in Table 12-28.

TABLE 12-28
Final Short-Supply Matrix

Plants \ Warehouse	Atlanta	Chicago	San Francisco	Pittsburgh	Total Supply
New York	1,000	500		1,000	2,500
Los Angeles		1,500	2,000		3,500
Dummy	500				500
Total Supply	1,500	2,000	2,000	1,000	6,500

Total Cost = $48,500

Trans-shipment

Reductions in transportation cost are often possible by shipping a product to final destination through an intermediate destination point. For purposes of this illustration of allocation, this procedure of shipping through an intermediate point is called trans-shipment.

Normal linear programming methods do not take trans-shipment potential into consideration when reaching a solution. However, with a small change in the solution procedure, trans-shipment potential can be evaluated using the transportation method. The primary modification to permit trans-shipment is that all locations, plants, and warehouses are treated as potential supply and destination points.

For contrast, Table 12-29 gives an initial solution and Table 12-30 a final solution. Neither solution includes trans-shipment. The total cost of this solution is $97.

TABLE 12-29
Initial Solution—
No Trans-Shipment

| | *Warehouse* | | |
Plant	X	Y	*Total*
A	5	1	6
	-2	-4	
B		9	9
	-5	-8	
Total	5	10	15

TABLE 12-30
Final Solution—
No Trans-Shipment

| | *Warehouse* | | |
Plant	X	Y	*Total*
A		6	6
	-2	-4	
B	5	4	9
	-5	-8	
Total	5	10	15

The trans-shipment modification requires that a positive quantity be available at all plants and that all warehouses have demand. This is accomplished by adding an artificial supply available from each plant. The quantity added should exceed the total that is otherwise required or available. Since the total required in the problem is 15, a suitable addition is 20. Thus warehouses X and Y require 20 more than the actual that is exactly available from the plants. Using the NCR method, Table 12-31 illustrates the initial trans-shipment solution. This problem is now solved exactly like a normal transportation problem. The final solution is shown in Table 12-32.

TABLE 12-31
Initial Solution—Trans-Shipment

Plant	X	Y	x	y	Total
		Warehouse			
A	20	6			26
	0	−2	−2	−4	
B		14	15		29
	−1	0	−5	−8	
a			10	10	20
	−2	−3	0	−2	
b				20	20
	−4	−3	−2	0	
Total	20	20	25	30	115

TABLE 12-32
Final Solution—Trans-Shipment

Plant	X	Y	x	y	Total
		Warehouse			
A	11		15		26
	0	−2	−2	−4	
B	9	20			29
	−1	0	−5	−8	
a			10	10	20
	−2	−3	0	−2	
b				20	20
	−4	−3	−2	0	
Total	20	20	25	30	115

This solution shows that 9 units should be shipped from B to X, 15 units should be shipped from X to a, and 10 units should be shipped from a to x. If there had been no trans-shipment, all the locations on the diagonal would have a value of 20. This solution has a total cost of $59, which is a reduction of $38 from the solution without cross supply.

Routing

One of the most common situations confronted in logistical operations is the need to route transportation vehicles. The problem is to select the delivery sequence of the vehicle so it makes all required stops while minimizing traveling time or distance. Three types of routing situations are illustrated in this section: (1) separate origin–destination points, (2) coincident origin and destination points, and (3) routing with vehicle capacity constraints. While the basic problems are similar, for each situation the technique that handles the specific requirement most efficiently is illustrated.

Separate Origin–Destination Points

The objective in this type of routing is to select the sequence of stops that will minimize the distance while visiting all intermediate locations. The data required are origin, list of all delivery locations, and a measure of either distance or elapsed time between all locations. Figure 12-5 illustrates the network assumed for the application example. The locations are identified as points *A* through *F*, and the numerical values represent the distance between any two sets of locations.

FIGURE 12-5
Example of Routing Network Separate Origin–Destination

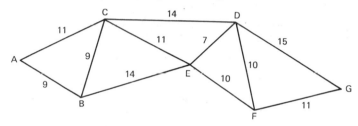

The solution procedure illustrated is known as the *listing method*. The initial step is to list all origins along with the destinations that can be serviced from each location and the related distance. This step is illustrated in Table 12-33.

TABLE 12-33
Origin–Destination Pairings and Distance—Separate Origin and Destination

A	*B*	*C*	*D*	*E*	*F*	*G*
$AB = 9$	$BC = 9$	$CD = 14$	$DG = 15$	$ED = 7$	$FE = 10$	$GD = 15$
$AC = 11$	$BE = 14$	$CE = 11$	$DF = 10$	$EF = 10$	$FD = 10$	$GF = 11$
	$BA = 9$	$CA = 11$	$DC = 14$	$EB = 14$	$FG = 11$	
		$CB = 9$	$DE = 7$	$EC = 11$		

To initiate the solution procedure a value of zero is assigned to the route origin. For the example, *A* is assumed as the routing origin location. A new listing is then completed wherein all routes that lead to location *A* are deleted. This listing and all subsequent iterations necessary to arrive at the final solution are presented in Table 12-34.

TABLE 12-34
Steps to Select Optimum Route—Separate Origin and Destination

Iteration 1: Deletion of A Destinations

$A = 0$	B	C	D	E	F	G
$AC = 11$	$BC = 9$	$CD = 14$	$DG = 15$	$ED = 7$	$FE = 10$	$GD = 15$
$AB = 9$	$BE = 14$	$CE = 11$	$DF = 10$	$EF = 10$	$FD = 10$	$GF = 11$
		$CB = 9$	$DC = 14$	$EB = 14$	$FG = 11$	
			$DE = 7$	$EC = 11$		

Iteration 2: Deletion of B Destinations

$A = 0$	$B = 9$	C	D	E	F	G
	$BC = 9$	$CD = 14$	$DG = 15$	$ED = 7$	$FE = 10$	$GD = 15$
	$BE = 14$	$CE = 11$	$DF = 10$	$EF = 10$	$FD = 10$	$GF = 11$
			$DC = 14$	$EC = 11$	$FG = 11$	
			$DE = 7$			

Optimum route $= A$–$B = 9$

Iteration 3: Deletion of C Destinations

$A = 0$	$B = 9$	$C = 18$	D	E	F	G
	$BE = 14$	$CD = 14$	$DG = 15$	$ED = 7$	$FE = 10$	$GD = 15$
		$CE = 11$	$DF = 10$	$EF = 10$	$FD = 10$	$GF = 11$
			$DE = 7$		$FG = 11$	

Optimum route $= A$–B–$C = 18$

Iteration 4: Deletion of E Destinations

$A = 0$	$B = 9$	$C = 18$	D	$E = 29$	F	G
		$CD = 11$	$DG = 15$	$ED = 7$	$FD = 10$	$GD = 15$
			$DF = 10$	$EF = 10$	$FG = 11$	$GF = 11$

Optimum route $= A$–B–C–$E = 29$

Iteration 5: Deletion of D Destinations

$A = 0$	$B = 9$	$C = 18$	$D = 36$	$E = 29$	F	G
			$DG = 15$	$EF = 10$	$FG = 11$	$GF = 11$
			$DF = 10$			

Optimum route $= A$–B–C–E–$D = 36$

Iteration 6: Deletion of F Destinations

$A = 0$	$B = 9$	$C = 18$	$D = 36$	$E = 29$	$F = 46$	G
			$DG = 15$		$FG = 11$	

Optimum route $= A$–B–C–E–D–$F = 46$

Iteration 7: Final Route

$A = 0$	$B = 9$	$C = 18$	$D = 36$	$E = 29$	$F = 46$	$G = 57$

Optimum route $= A$–B–C–E–D–F–$G = 57$

The second iteration is to select the lowest distance from origin, which is $AB = 9$ in the example. B is then assigned the value 9, and all locations that list B as a destination are deleted. The value of B is obtained by adding the value of A to the distance of the AB route.

The third iteration is to select the least distance route with B as the origin which is BC. A new iteration is then developed in which C is assigned the accumulated distance value of $B + BC$, which is 18. Then all remaining locations with C as a destination are deleted.

This iteration procedure is repeated until all the points requiring delivery are sequenced. The final route of $A–B–C–E–D–F–G$ is reached in nine iterations and has an optimum distance of 57.

In a problem of this size it was not difficult to isolate the optimum route. The primary advantage of the listing method is that it provides a systematic means to reduce routes to a manageable size. In this situation 720 possible routes were quickly delineated. If the number of destinations increases, the problem can become unmanageable by manual methods. For example, with only 10 locations there are 3.6×10^5 possible routes. If the number of locations increases to 20, the possible routes expand to 1.2×10^{17}. For larger problems, computer techniques can be used. However, even computerized solution procedures can soon be overpowered by the sheer quantity of routing options.[14]

Coincident Origin–Destination Points

A typical routing situation is dispatch of a vehicle for multiple delivery and/or pickups, with eventual return to the originating location. The complicating factor is the need to return to the origin as the final destination. This situation is generally referred to as the "traveling-salesman" problem. A wide variety of analytic and numeric techniques have been applied to this problem.[15] The most feasible solution procedures for large-scale problems are nonoptimizing. One such procedure is illustrated.

The example problem reflects a typical warehouse delivery problem. The vehicle departs warehouse location A and makes deliveries to customers at

---

[14] O'Neil and Whybark state that the largest problem they could solve in 2,000 seconds on a CDC 6500 involved 10 customers and 3 vehicles. See Brian F. O'Neil and D. Clay Whybark, "The Multiple-Vehicle Routing Problem," *The Logistics and Transportation Review*, Vol. 11 (December 1975), p. 161.

[15] See Frederick S. Hillier and Gerald J. Liebermann, *Introduction to Operations Research* (San Francisco: Holden-Day, Inc., 1967), pp. 218–22; John D. C. Little, Katta G. Murtz, Dura W. Sweeney, and Caroline Karel, "An Algorithm for the Traveling Salesman Problem," *Operations Research*, Vol. 11 (November–December 1963), pp. 972–89; Arthur V. Hill and D. Clay Whybark, *Comparing Exact Solution Procedures for the Multiple-Vehicle Routing Problem* (West Lafayette, Ind.: Krannert Graduate School of Industrial Administration, Purdue University, Paper No. 551, May 1976); Samuel B. Richmond, *Operations Research for Management Decisions* (New York: The Ronald Press Company, 1968), pp. 461–65; Robert L. Karg and Gerald L. Thompson, "A Heuristic Approach to Solving Traveling Salesman Problems," *Management Science*, Vol. 10 (January 1964), pp. 225–48.

locations $B, C, D, E, F,$ and G. The possible routes and the respective distances are illustrated in Figure 12-6. The first step is to create a table that contains the distances between any two points in the system. In the example a simplifying assumption is made that to reach a customer not directly connected to the warehouse location it is necessary to pass through intermediate points. While this assumption simplifies the illustration, it is not necessary to the solution procedure. Table 12-35 presents the distance relationships of the network.

FIGURE 12-6
Example of Routing Network Coincident Origin and Destination

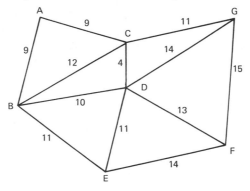

The solution procedure is initiated by random selection of a customer destination from the list. In the example, location B is added with a round-trip distance of 18. Since only one possible round-trip route exists, the distance is optimum. This and all additional iterations necessary to select a final route are illustrated in Table 12-36.

In the second iteration a third customer location is inserted into the list. In the example destination C was selected. The result of the second iteration was

TABLE 12-35
Origin–Destination Distances—Coincident
Origin and Destination

	A	B	C	D	E	F	G
A	0						
B	9	0					
C	9	12	0				
D	13	10	4	0			
E	20	11	15	11	0		
F	26	23	17	13	14	0	
G	20	23	11	14	25	15	0

TABLE 12-36
Iterations to Select Route—Coincident Origin and Destination

Iteration 1:
   $A-B-A = 9 + 9 = 18$

Iteration 2:
   $A-C-B-A = 9 + 12 + 9 = 30$
   $A-B-C-A = 9 + 12 + 9 = 30$

Iteration 3:
   $A-D-B-C-A = 13 + 10 + 12 + 9 = 44$
   $A-B-D-C-A = 9 + 10 + 4 + 9 = 32$
   $A-B-C-D-A = 9 + 12 + 4 + 13 = 38$

Iteration 4:
   $A-E-B-D-C-A = 20 + 11 + 10 + 4 + 9 = 54$
   $A-B-E-D-C-A = 9 + 11 + 11 + 4 + 9 = 44$
   $A-B-D-E-C-A = 9 + 10 + 11 + 15 + 9 = 54$
   $A-B-D-C-E-A = 9 + 10 + 4 + 15 + 20 = 58$

Iteration 5:
   $A-F-B-E-D-C-A = 26 + 23 + 11 + 11 + 4 + 9 = 84$
   $A-B-F-E-D-C-A = 9 + 23 + 14 + 11 + 4 + 9 = 70$
   $A-B-E-F-D-C-A = 9 + 11 + 14 + 13 + 4 + 9 = 60$
   $A-B-E-D-F-C-A = 9 + 11 + 11 + 13 + 17 + 9 = 70$
   $A-B-E-D-C-F-A = 9 + 11 + 11 + 4 + 17 + 26 = 78$

Iteration 6:
   $A-G-B-E-F-D-C-A = 20 + 23 + 11 + 14 + 13 + 4 + 9 = 94$
   $A-B-G-E-F-D-C-A = 9 + 23 + 25 + 14 + 13 + 4 + 9 = 97$
   $A-B-E-G-F-D-C-A = 9 + 11 + 25 + 15 + 13 + 4 + 9 = 86$
   $A-B-E-F-G-D-C-A = 9 + 11 + 14 + 15 + 14 + 4 + 9 = 76$
   $A-B-E-F-D-G-C-A = 9 + 11 + 14 + 13 + 14 + 11 + 9 = 81$
   $A-B-E-F-D-C-G-A = 9 + 11 + 14 + 13 + 4 + 11 + 20 = 82$

Final Route: $A-B-E-F-G-D-C-A = 76$

a distance of 30, regardless of the round-trip route selected. The iteration procedure is continued with the repeated insertion of additional customer locations. The shortest round-trip route is selected each time as the interim solution until all customer destinations are included. The final route of $A-B-E-F-G-D-C-A$ with a distance value of 76 is isolated with six iterations.

The round-trip route identified in the example is the optimum. However, the procedure does not guarantee an optimal solution. Several enhancements have been suggested to improve the procedure for application to large-scale problems.[16]

[16] Karg and Thompson, op. cit.

Routing With Vehicle Capacity Constraints

A third type of routing procedure involves the addition of vehicle capacity constraints to the solution procedure. The problem is to schedule a limited number of vehicles from a central facility subject but not limited to the following constraints [17]:

1. The delivery requirements to all destinations must be satisfied.
2. Vehicle capacity may not be violated.
3. The total time or distance traveled by a given vehicle may not exceed a predetermined amount.

An additional condition or constraint typical of this type of problem is that the number of vehicles in the fleet is limited and they may have different maximum capacities. The objective of the solution procedure is to select the vehicle assignments and the best possible routing. The technique illustrated is known as the "savings" method, which is a nonoptimizing solution procedure. [18]

TABLE 12-37
Demand Requirements and Route Lengths

Load q^i ⟶ z	P_0	P_1	P_2	P_3	P_4	P_5	P_6	P_7	P_8	P_9	P_{10}
200	9	P_1									
75	12	5	P_2								
100	16	8	7	P_3							
150	19	11	11	5	P_4						
200	21	13	14	12	8	P_5					
Y 300	24	19	12	18	12	7	P_6				
50	28	19	18	21	16	11	6	P_7			
200	31	25	25	25	21	14	12	7	P_8		
300	35	26	28	24	25	19	16	11	6	P_9	
200	40	33	31	26	26	23	19	18	15	12	P_{10}

The example problem consists of a fleet of vehicles that are dispatched from origin, P_0, and must make deliveries to 10 destinations identified as P_1 through P_{10}. The destinations are located at a distance of $d_{y,o}$ from the origin and $d_{y,z}$ from each other. Table 12-37 presents the distances for all routes included

---

[17] For a more detailed example, see N. Christofides and S. Eilon, "An Algorithm for the Vehicle Dispatching Problem," *Operations Research Quarterly*, Vol. 20, No. 3, pp. 309–18.

[18] Ibid. For other approaches, see M. Held and R. M. Karp, "A Dynamic Programming Approach to Sequencing Problems," *Journal of the Society of Industrial Applied Mathematics*, Vol. 10 (1962), p. 196; R. L. Hays, "The Delivery Problem," *Report MSR 106* (Pittsburgh, Pa.: Carnegie Institute of Technology, Graduate School of Industrial Administration); G. Clarke and J. W. Wright, "Scheduling of Vehicles from a Central Depot to a Number of Delivery Points," *Operations Research*, Vol. 12 (1964), pp. 568–81.

in the assumed network. For example, $d_{1,0} = 9$, $d_{2,0} = 12$, while $d_{2,1} = 5$. In addition, the requirements of each destination customer are listed in cubic feet in the columns of Table 12-37 labeled "Load q^i." This demand must be satisfied by deployment of the fleet capacity as illustrated in Table 12-38.

The computational procedure is as follows:

1. Initially, assume that there are enough vehicles to allocate one to every customer. Since there are 10 customers, that is the number of vehicles shown in the 300-cubic-foot (ft^3) size in Table 12-38. If a single customer demand exceeds the capacity of the vehicle, split the load and consider only the remainder of the load. For example, if P_1 demanded a 1,000-ft^3 delivery volume, one of the 800-ft^3 trucks would be assigned to it and the remaining 200 ft^3 would be the only volume to be considered in the analysis. Following this procedure, an initial vehicle allocation is determined as illustrated in Table 12-39. One vehicle of the smallest capacity is initially allocated to each customer and provides an initial solution to the problem.

TABLE 12-38
Available Vehicle
Sizes

Size (cubic feet)	Number
300	10
400	3
800	2

TABLE 12-39
Available Vehicle Capacity and Initial
Vehicle Allocation to Customers

Trucks	300 ft³	400 ft³	800 ft³
Available	10	3	2
Allocated	10	0	0

2. The development of a savings matrix is the next step in the algorithm. This savings, denoted $S_{y,z}$, is the time or distance that will be saved if the routes $P_0 \to P_y \to P_0$ and $P_0 \to P_z \to P_0$ are combined to form a single route $P_0 \to P_y \to P_z \to P_0$. The entire savings matrix is shown in Table 12-40. The savings in each of the cells is determined with the following formula:

$$S_{y,z} = d_{0,y} + d_{0,z} - d_{y,z}$$

TABLE 12-40
"Savings" Matrix

Load q_i

	P_0										
200	②	P_1									
75	②	16	P_2								
100	②	17	21	P_3							
150	②	17	20	30	P_4						
200	②	17	19	25	32	P_5					
300	②	14	24	22	31	38	P_6				
50	②	18	22	23	31	38	46	P_7			
200	②	15	18	22	29	38	43	52	P_8		
300	②	18	19	27	29	37	43	52	60	P_9	
200	②	16	21	30	33	38	45	50	56	63	P_{10}

where $d_{y,z}$ is the route length from Table 12-37. To illustrate this computation:

$$S_{1,2} = d_{0,1} + d_{0,2} - d_{1,2}$$
$$= 9 + 12 - 5$$
$$= 16$$

This is the value of 16 at the intersection of column P_1 with row P_2. The remaining values are computed similarly.

The circled values in some of the cells, $t_{y,z}$, indicate whether the customer combinations P_y and P_z are in a tour. This designator has the following values:

$t_{y,z} = 1$ if two customers are linked on a vehicle route
$t_{y,z} = 0$ if the customers are not linked on a vehicle route
$t_{y,z} = 2$ if the customer is served exclusively by a single vehicle

Zero entries are not shown in Table 12-40. For the initial problem, set all $t_{y,0} = 2$, meaning that one vehicle is used to serve each customer. For ease of computation, the matrix of Table 12-40 is ordered from left to right on the basis of increased savings $S_{y,z}$.

3. At this stage the iterative process is initiated until each savings-assignment matrix is evaluated for further route improvements. The procedure is to search the matrix for the largest savings subject to the following conditions for any cell (y, z):

a $t_{y,0}$ and $t_{z,0}$ are > 0.

   b. P_y and P_z are not already allocated on the same vehicle run.

   c. Amending Table 12-40 by removing the trucks allocated to loads q_y and q_z and adding a vehicle to cover the load q_y and q_z does not cause the vehicles allocated to exceed the vehicles available in any column of Table 12-39.

4. Next, a cell is selected where there are two routes that can be combined into a single tour. A value of $t_{y,z} = 1$ is placed in the cell, and all $t_{y,z}$ values are adjusted so that the sum of $t_{y,z}$ across a row, plus $t_{y,z}$ down the column where $y = z$, is always equal to 2. Where $t_{j,0} = 0$, set $q_j = 0$ and make q_j equal the total load on the tour for all other j. This procedure terminates when no further consolidation is possible.

To illustrate this procedure, the delivery problem is traced through its initial iterations. From Table 12-40 the greatest amount of savings can be obtained by combining routes $P_0 \rightarrow P_9 \rightarrow P_0$ and $P_0 \rightarrow P_{10} \rightarrow P_0$, since $S_{9,10} = 63$. The other three conditions expressed in step 3 can also be met; namely, $t_{9,0}$ and $t_{10,0}$ are greater than 0, P_9 and P_{10} are not already on the same route, and $q_9 + q_{10} = 500$, which is below the capacity of an available vehicle. Now that the two routes to be combined have been selected, the mechanics outlined in step 4 of the procedure above must be repeated. The necessary changes in the values of $t_{y,z}$ and q_i are made in the new savings-assignment matrix illustrated in Table 12-41. To follow these through, a $t_{y,z}$ value of 1 is placed at the intersection of column P_9 and row P_{10}. In addition, the values of $t_{y,z}$ must be adjusted to fulfill the conditions specified in step 4. Since the sum of $t_{y,z}$ across row P_9 and down column P_9 must sum to 2,

TABLE 12-41
Savings-Assignment Matrix After One Iteration

Load q_i	P_0	P_1	P_2	P_3	P_4	P_5	P_6	P_7	P_8	P_9	P_{10}
200	②	P_1									
75	②	16	P_2								
100	②	17	21	P_3							
150	②	17	20	30	P_4						
200	②	17	19	25	32	P_5					
300	②	14	24	22	31	38	P_6				
50	②	18	22	23	31	38	46	P_7			
200	②	15	18	22	29	38	43	52	P_8		
500	①	18	19	27	29	37	43	52	60	P_9	
										①	
500	①	16	21	30	33	38	45	50	56	63	P_{10}

$t_{0,9}$ must be set to 1. The same is true for the sum of the $t_{y,z}$ across row P_{10}, so $t_{0,10}$ is set to 1 also. The q_i's are also adjusted to reflect the total volume of the shipment, Table 12-41. In this case $q_9^* = q_{10}^* = q_9 + q_{10} = 300 + 200 = 500$, where q_i is the volume before and q_i^* is the volume after the routing change. Through this change in routing, one 800-ft³ vehicle has been substituted for two 300-ft³ vehicles and a savings of 63 time or distance units has been obtained. The revised vehicle-allocation table is shown in Table 12-42. The

TABLE 12-42
Vehicle-Allocation Table After
One Iteration

Trucks	300 ft³	400 ft³	800 ft³
Available	10	3	2
Allocated	8	0	1

adjustments for the iteration have been completed, so the new matrix can be evaluated for further improvements. After an analysis with regard to the criteria expressed in step 3 of the procedure, it appears that a 60-unit savings can be obtained through a combination of routes $P_0 \rightarrow P_8 \rightarrow P_0$ and $P_0 \rightarrow P_9 \rightarrow P_{10} \rightarrow P_0$. The required adjustments are made in the values of $t_{y,z}$ and q_i and the revised matrix is presented in Table 12-43. The new route is

TABLE 12-43
Savings-Assignment Matrix After Two Iterations

Load q_i

	P_0										
200	②	P_1									
75	②	16	P_2								
100	②	17	21	P_3							
150	②	17	20	30	P_4						
200	②	17	19	25	32	P_5					
300	②	14	24	22	31	38	P_6				
50	②	18	22	23	31	38	46	P_7			
700	①	15	18	22	29	38	43	52	P_8		
									①		
—		18	19	27	29	37	43	52	60	P_9	
										①	
700	①	16	21	30	33	38	45	50	56	63	P_{10}

$P_0 \rightarrow P_8 \rightarrow P_9 \rightarrow P_{10} \rightarrow P_0$ and the volume involved is 700 ft³. Table 12-44 shows the new vehicle allocation.

TABLE 12-44
Vehicle-Allocation Table of Two Iterations

Trucks	300 ft³	400 ft³	800 ft³
Available	10	3	2
Allocated	7	0	1

This iterative procedure is followed until there are no more identifiable route consolidations. In this illustration this requires four more iterations, but the final matrix and allocation table are shown in Tables 12-45 and 12-46, respectively. A graphic presentation of the final route is shown in Table 12-47. A statement of the finalized routes along with the volume assigned to each is illustrated in Table 12-48.

TABLE 12-45
Savings-Assignment Matrix—Final Iteration

Load q_i	P_0										
	P_0										
275	①	P_1									
275	①	①	P_2								
750	①			P_3							
—				①	P_4						
—					①	P_5					
750	①						P_6				
750	①							P_7			
—								①	P_8		
—									①	P_9	
750	①									①	P_{10}

TABLE 12-46
Final Vehicle-Allocation Table

Trucks	300 ft³	400 ft³	800 ft³
Available	10	3	2
Allocated	1	0	2

TABLE 12-47
Graphic Presentation of "Best" Routes

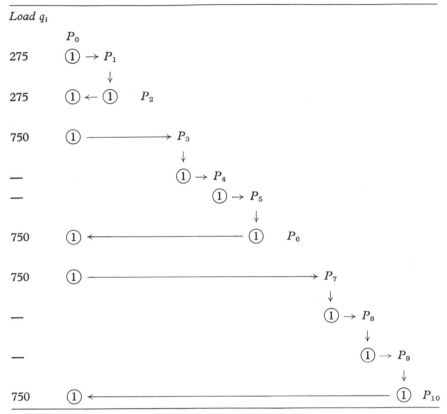

Load q_i

275

275

750

—

—

750

750

—

—

750

TABLE 12-48
Final Routes and Volume

Volume	Route
275	$P_0 \rightarrow P_1 \rightarrow P_2 \rightarrow P_0$
750	$P_0 \rightarrow P_3 \rightarrow P_4 \rightarrow P_5 \rightarrow P_6 \rightarrow P_0$
750	$P_0 \rightarrow P_7 \rightarrow P_8 \rightarrow P_9 \rightarrow P_{10} \rightarrow P_0$

Although this procedure is relatively complex, it does offer a practical procedure for evaluating routing problems with capacity limitations. This solution technique is appropriate for either manual or machine computation.

Scheduling

The major management responsibility in logistical design studies is to assure that valid results are realized within time and budget expectations.

Fortunately, several scheduling techniques are available which can be easily adopted to the logistical research project.

Scheduling is concerned with planning and the accomplishment of non-repetitive projects. In addition, scheduling is concerned with the most efficient utilization of resources during the study. During the 1950s sophisticated project planning and progress evaluation techniques were developed. The techniques help managers maintain control over manpower, money, material, and machinery allocated to a project. Two scheduling techniques, the *program evaluation review technique* (PERT) and the *critical path method* (CPM), are reviewed in this section.[19] Both PERT and CPM are variations of more general critical path planning approaches. First, characteristics common to both techniques are reviewed and then the peculiarities of each discussed. For purposes of illustration, the techniques are discussed in terms of a logistical system strategic design study.

Basic Critical Path Concepts

The heart of critical path planning is a graphic portrayal of the project work plan. This graph, or network as it is commonly called, displays the interdependencies between activities leading to project completion.

The critical path concept is designed to satisfy the following five project management requirements:

1. Evaluate progress towards attainment of project completion.
2. Focus attention on potential and actual problems during the project.
3. Provide frequent and accurate status reports at critical check points.
4. Provide a regular and updated prediction of when the project will be completed.
5. Provide at any time during the project determination of the shortest completion time if priorities and resources are shifted.

The Network

The network is a flow chart of project events joined by lines that represent activities. The activities illustrate project interrelationships and interdependencies. Events are usually represented by circles and activities are illustrated by arrows that connect events. A project event is a significant occurrence. Events signify the start or completion of at least one activity and represent the achievement of a project goal.

Activities in a project network may be real or dummy. Real activities represent tasks that must be completed to advance from one node to another. Real activities expend project resources. Dummy activities illustrate the dependency of one event to another for project-planning purposes. Dummy activities do not expend project resources. All events are numbered in the

---

[19] For a more detailed discussion, see Wagner, op. cit., pp. 150–55.

network chart. Although the activity arrow lengths have no relationship to the time required to accomplish an event, arrows always connect lower- and higher-numbered events.

Pert Project Illustrations

To illustrate project planning and control, the PERT technique is discussed as applied to design of a logistical system. When this planning project is completed, the best set of warehouse locations will be determined along with the customer assignments and inventory policies. The initial use of PERT or CPM to guide project development was noted in Chapter 10.[20]

The illustration that follows could be developed using either PERT or CPM. The primary difference is that PERT deals only with timing, whereas CPM considers the trade-offs between the time and cost requirements of a project.

PROJECT DESIGN. The initial step is to divide the overall project into specific tasks. These tasks become activities in the project network. These activities are initiated and terminated by an event. The events and the activities which link them must be sequenced on the network under a logical set of ground rules which allow the determination of important critical and subcritical paths. These ground rules include the fact that no successor event can be considered complete until all predecessor events have been completed and no "looping" is allowed.

Since activities represent the time necessary to advance from one event to the next, the second step in the scheduling process is to estimate the time necessary to complete each activity. One fundamental difference between PERT and CPM is the nature of the time estimates. CPM uses exact or deterministic times while PERT uses probabilistic estimates. A PERT schedule requires three time estimates for each activity. These are:

1. *Optimistic time*—the elapsed time if the activity proceeds perfectly, represented by a.
2. *Pessimistic time*—the elapsed time if extreme difficulty is experienced, represented by b.
3. *Most likely completion time*—the expected time, represented by m.

The basic activities and time estimates for the example project are contained in Table 12-49.

The third step is to structure the project in a PERT network, identify the necessary dummy activities as well as the interrelationships between events, and calculate the mean elapsed time (T_e) for each activity. The PERT network is illustrated by Figure 12-7. The following formula is used to develop mean

---

[20] See page 299.

TABLE 12-49
Project Activities and Variable Time Estimates

Activity	a	m	b
A. Situation audit	1	2	4
B. Problem definition	1	1	2
C. Selection of analytical tool	1	2	3
D. Specification of alternatives	1	2	4
E. Definition of data requirements	1	1	2
F. Collection and preparation of demand data	2	3	5
G. Collection and preparation of cost data	3	5	8
H. Collection and preparation of freight data	4	5	8
I. Validate data and model	2	3	5
J. Initial model runs	1	2	4
K. Preliminary report preparation	2	4	5
L. Model runs for alternative analysis	3	5	7
M. Analysis of model results	1	2	3
N. Final report preparation	2	3	4

elapsed times giving a weight of 4 to the most likely time and 1 each to the optimistic and pessimistic times:

$$T_e = \frac{a + 4m + b}{6}$$

This formulation approximates a normal distribution with a relatively low coefficient of variation. The resultant data are presented in Table 12-50.

TABLE 12-50
Activity-Weighted Elapsed Time

Activity	a	m	b	T_e
A	1	2	4	2.17
B	1	1	2	1.17
C	1	2	3	2.00
D	1	2	4	2.17
E	1	1	2	1.17
F	2	3	5	3.17
G	3	5	8	5.17
H	4	5	8	5.33
I	2	3	5	3.17
J	1	2	4	2.17
K	2	4	5	3.83
L	3	5	7	5.00
M	1	2	3	2.00
N	2	3	4	3.00

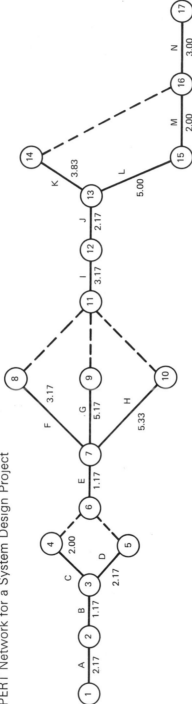

FIGURE 12-7
PERT Network for a System Design Project

———— Activities

— — — Dummy Activities (No time elapses)

The fourth and final step is to identify the critical path for the project. The path with the longest mean elapsed time (T_e) represents the critical path. All other paths are called *slack paths* because the final project completion date does not depend upon completing events along the slack path. Table 12-51

TABLE 12-51
Path Identification and Average Elapsed Time

Path	Activity Average Elapsed Time	Total Elapsed Time
1–2–3–4–6–7–8– 11–12–13–14–16–17	2.17 + 1.17 + 2.00 + 1.17 + 3.17 + 3.17 2.17 + 3.83 + 3.00	= 21.85
1–2–3–5–6–7–9–11– 12–13–14–16–17	2.17 + 1.17 + 2.17 + 1.17 + 5.17 + 3.17 + 2.17 + 3.83 + 3.00	= 24.02
1–2–3–5–6–7–10–11– 12–13–14–16–17	2.17 + 1.17 + 2.17 + 1.17 + 5.33 + 3.17 + 2.17 + 3.83 + 3.00	= 24.18
[a]1–2–3–5–6–7–10–11– 12–13–15–16–17	2.17 + 1.17 + 2.17 + 1.17 + 5.33 + 3.17 + 2.17 + 5.00 + 2.00 + 3.00	= 27.35
1–2–3–5–6–7–9–11– 12–13–15–16–17	2.17 + 1.17 + 2.17 + 1.17 + 5.17 + 3.17 + 2.17 + 5.00 + 2.00 + 3.00	= 27.19

[a] Critical path.

presents the determination of the critical path in the example project. Although not all possible paths have been explored in Table 12-51, the total elapsed time for many of the alternatives has been computed and the critical path has been determined.

Once the schedule analysis is completed, management attention is directed to the activities on the critical path. It is important that these activities be completed on schedule, since any delay will delay the overall project completion date.

The final project schedule is based upon the network having the longest total elapsed time. The highest T_e of this network is the project critical path.

CPM Illustration

The procedure for CPM is very similar to that for PERT. The fundamental difference is that CPM uses exact time estimates and incorporates cost or budget figures. Therefore, CPM is particularly applicable to projects of a deterministic nature, where time and cost data can be projected from past experience or estimated with a high degree of certainty. For this reason, the method is used extensively in the construction industry.

The previous example of the system design project will be used to demonstrate CPM, however, a complete analysis will not be performed. The subset of activities shown in Figure 12-8 will be discussed in detail.

FIGURE 12-8
Partial PERT Network for a System Design Project

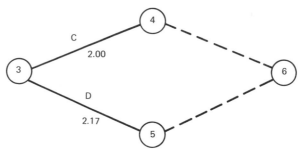

For each of the activities specified in the network, the project manager must develop the best cost and time estimates possible. These estimates include an approximation of the expected time with the normal amount of resources applied as well as speed-up approximations when additional resources are applied. Time and cost estimates for activities C and D are presented in Tables 12-52 and 12-53, respectively. The resource allocation may represent manpower or computer commitments.

TABLE 12-52
Time and Cost Estimates for Activity C

Resource Allocation	Cost	Time
Normal	$2,000	2.00
110% normal	2,250	1.90
120% normal	2,700	1.80
130% normal	4,000	1.70

TABLE 12-53
Time and Cost Estimates for Activity D

Resource Allocation	Cost	Time
Normal	$2,500	2.17
110% normal	3,000	2.10
120% normal	3,700	2.00
130% normal	4,700	1.90

The critical path method analyzes the cost and time trade-offs characteristic of each activity to determine where resources can be applied most beneficially. Since activity D lies on the critical path, CPM would call for the project manager to allocate additional resources to this activity to speed up project completion. By allocating $500 more to this activity, the project length can be decreased by 0.07 period while a $700 allocation to activity C would not shorten the project. An allocation of $1,200 to activity D would enable the entire project to be shortened by 0.17 period. However, any increased allocation of resources to D alone would not result in a shorter project time, since activity C along with D lies on the critical path at this point.

In addition to trade-offs between activities that lie on different paths, there may be trade-offs between activities that lie on the same path. Given that D and H both lie on the critical path, it may be less expensive to cut 0.17 period from the schedule by allocating resources to activity H than by allocating resources to D. However, the time required for the project would be the same in either case.

In addition to providing the information to expedite the project, CPM also provides information concerning resources that may be deallocated without affecting the schedule of the project. In Figure 12-8, for example, the project manager may observe that it is possible to complete activity C with only 90 per cent of the resource allocation if the time is increased to 2.17 periods. Since this is not on the critical path, this would not delay the project completion date. The critical path method also provides the necessary data for estimating time and cost at any point during the project in the event that it becomes desirable to expedite the project.

Since the number of alternative paths and costs considered quickly becomes unmanageable even in small projects, it is usually necessary that the network analysis be performed by computer. Fortunately, many medium and large computer facilities have existing programs that can be used for this purpose.

Summary

The intent of this chapter was to introduce and illustrate a variety of quantitative techniques available for use in day-to-day logistical decision making. In total, the chapter covered five groupings of techniques, related to (1) basic decision making, (2) facility operations, (3) allocation and assignment, (4) routing, and (5) scheduling. No attempt was made to integrate the groupings because of the specialized nature of the technique application. Thus the chapter sections are problem-oriented and stand independently. What the groupings have in common is that they all present techniques applicable to operational and tactical planning situations.

Questions

1. What is the major shortcoming of using various decision criteria in day-to-day operations? What is the major benefit?
2. Why would an enterprise under certain circumstances elect to purchase a component part even though it could manufacture it more economically?
3. In the utilization of queueing analysis, why are arrivals typically expressed in the form of Poisson distribution, whereas servicing is an exponential distribution?
4. Discuss the impact of single versus multiple receiving channels upon the queueing solution.
5. Why is it beneficial and safe to use sampling in this inspection procedure related to quality control?
6. In general terms, why is linear programming a useful tool for consideration when allocating product from plants to warehouses?
7. Describe the basic purpose of the northwest corner rule.
8. Why is it important to include capacity constraints in selected types of routing problems? Provide an illustration.
9. What can one hope to gain by the use of a project scheduling technique?
10. Discuss the differences between PERT and CPM. What is the role of a dummy activity in the PERT analysis?

PART Four

Logistical System Administration and Organization

Administration

Given a logistical system design, administration becomes an important area of managerial responsibility. Logistical administration is concerned with allocation of resources and control of logistical operations. Organization is the structure by which human resources are aligned in a particular logistical operation. The areas of integrated system administration and organization in logistical management are the least understood. A lack of clarity stems from the relative newness of integrated logistical systems and related performance measurement techniques.

This chapter is concerned with administration. Chapter 14 deals with organization. The format of both chapters is based upon management by objectives. Administration becomes effective through the establishment of clearly defined goals and continuous review of progress. The first section of this chapter develops the management by objectives concept. The operational planning and control process is then developed.

Management by Objectives

The essential mission of management by objectives (MBO) is the establishment of goals and controls. In MBO the job description is not important. The important aspect is the individual job accomplishment objectives established for each administrative period. The job objective is identified as the goal. Given a goal or a series of goals, logistical administration then concerns itself with control in order to measure progress toward accomplishment.

421

The recommended concept of professional management is illustrated in Figure 13-1. It is based on an MBO approach, which is summarized as follows:

1. At the beginning of the planning period, top management establishes overall goals or objectives for the entire organization. These overall objectives are then translated into action plans for every manager in the organization so that each has clear, unambiguous objectives for his particular area of responsibility—objectives in keeping with the overall organizational objectives.
2. Next, an organizational structure consistent with and capable of achieving these objectives must be established. Whereas objectives represent the "end," organization represents the "means" or the vehicle by which objectives will be achieved.
3. Position descriptions which clearly define the responsibilities of each individual in the organizational structure must then be developed.
4. The next phase involves establishing performance standards to guide and direct each individual's activities. These performance standards must be supportive and consistent with functional area and overall corporate objectives.
5. This step involves developing a reward structure that fairly and adequately compensates each individual when he achieves the performance standards established for his position.
6. Finally, and perhaps most importantly, each individual's success or failure in achieving his standards of performance *must* be appraised and corrective action taken where necessary. This represents the key to professional management.[1]

Management by objectives depends on the development of a sound operational plan. The approved plan becomes the basis for performance measurement during the operating period. The process of developing an operational plan is time-consuming and tedious. It is complicated by the need to view the total system on an integrated basis. Such integration often requires information beyond that normally available from a firm's standard costing or accounting systems. The next section discusses operational planning.

Development of the Operational Plan

Operational planning is crucial because managerial talent is always in short supply and this shortage is expected to become even more acute in the future. Therefore, top and middle management cannot afford the luxury of becoming fire-fighters bogged down in operational problem solving. One important technique for coordinating the efforts of an organization is the operational plan.

The operational plan for logistical administration is short-range. Operations

[1] Bernard J. La Londe and James F. Robeson, "Corporate Strategy and Organization for Distribution," *Journal of Business Policy*, Spring 1972, p. 55.

FIGURE 13-1
Process of Management by Objectives (MBO)

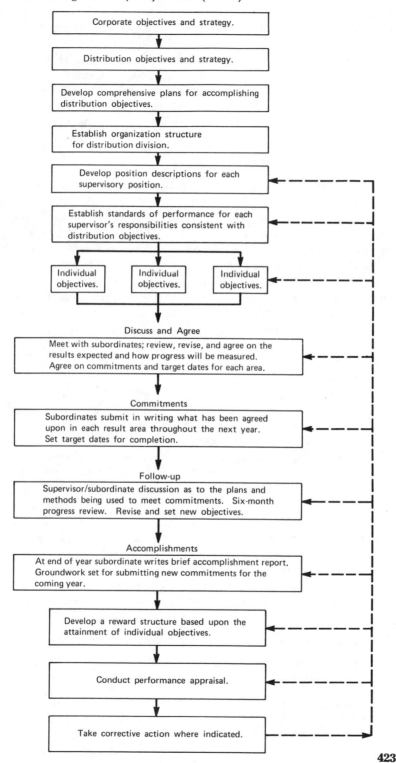

normally will not be projected for more than a single fiscal year. The operational plan covers one segment of the overall system strategic plan.[2] Given a strategic plan (long-range), operational plans (short-range) must be developed to direct day-to-day work efforts. Long-range strategies represent a set of guideposts within which short-range operational plans detail expected accomplishments during a specified time period. Such accomplishments concern system modifications, performance, and budgeting. Each represents a set of logistical management objectives.

System Modification Objectives

During any period, several adjustments in operating structure may be planned for implementation. For example, an enterprise may have a long-range system implementational strategy calling for consolidation of 25 warehouses into 10 regional distribution centers. The full implementational program may cover a number of years and will therefore embrace several different operational plans. The initial operating plan may call for a commitment to build or lease two of the regional facilities and to close a selected number of existing warehouses. Future operational plans may provide for occupancy and use of these first two regional distribution warehouses, the commitment to establishing additional facilities, and closing other outdated warehouses. The implementation of a logistical system redesign normally involves a number of years. Thus, consecutive operational plans will contain specific elements of an overall long-range strategic plan.

Two factors must be clearly understood when considering facility adjustments included in operational plans. First, budget allocations must isolate the expense of the initial setup as well as once-and-for-all savings separate from day-to-day operational expenditures. Second, special efforts required to maintain customer service commitments during the period of system readjustment must be programmed adequately. Each of these expenditures is a function of the long-range plan for system redesign rather than the operation of the existing system. As such, adjustment expenditures are not expected to prevail between consecutive operational planning periods. Unless such one-time expenditures are isolated, the capability for comparative analysis of operational results from one period to the next is substantially diluted.

The operational plan provides for scheduled adjustments in logistical system facilities. It allocates resources and designs its managerial responsibility to achieve desired adjustments specified by the logistical strategic plan.

Performance Objectives

A significant portion of the operational plan consists of objectives to guide day-to-day operations. Operational performance objectives typically consist

---

[2] See Chapter 10, pages 287–292 for a detailed discussion of the time interval and content of various types of planning.

of specific goals as well as the schedule of planned activities to reach the stated goals. For example, during a specific operating period, assume the month of May, a grocery manufacturer may have a marketing objective to introduce two new products and to conduct three promotional activities in a specific marketing area. The physical distribution performance objectives for the operating period prior to May will require an inventory buildup and a degree of advanced product movement to support inventory requirements during the promotional period. The goals may call for 100 per cent availability of the new and promoted inventory items with two-day reorder capability during the first two weeks of the promotion, followed by somewhat less stringent performance during the final two weeks of the marketing effort. The detailed activities planned and the performance schedule to support the new product and promotional activity represent the performance objective aspect of the operational plan.

The development of performance objectives is based upon a combination of forecasts and managerial judgment regarding future marketing requirements. To develop appropriate goals and performance schedules a great deal of coordination is required among all managerial units of the enterprise. For logistical goals to be relevant, they must integrate marketing plans and manufacturing capabilities. Without effective coordination the basic benefits of integrated logistical performance will not materialize.

The statement of performance goals and related activity schedules typically covers a short time interval within the operating plan. While goals may remain constant from one performance period to the next, activity schedules may be significantly different. Many enterprises plan performance on the basis of calendar months. Others select to operate on the basis of 13 four-week periods. The typical performance schedule will cover approximately 90 days, with the detail updated in 30-day intervals.

Thus the performance schedule aspect of the operating plan provides the structure for achieving logistical objectives. It is the short-range "battle plan" which guides the allocation of authorized resources and ranks day-to-day activities by priority. As such, the total logistical effort is synchronized through the statement of performance goals and the scheduled activities necessary to realize goal attainment.

Budget Objectives

Given system modification and performance objectives, the next step in the operations planning process is to budget expenditures needed to accomplish stated objectives. A typical procedure requests budgets from individual management units. Thus, line management, given a statement of objectives, is asked to formulate a request for operational funds. The budgets requested constitute each manager's estimate of resources required to achieve specific objectives. The budget is the key to formulating a logistical cost-control program. Four basic types of budgets are used in logistical controllership:

(1) fixed, (2) flexible, (3) zero level, and (4) capital. The first three are used to control direct expenditures for logistical performance. The last is used when adjustment involving any component of the logistical system is scheduled during the operating period.

FIXED DOLLAR BUDGETING.   As the name implies, the fixed budget is an estimate of functional costs by account associated with an anticipated volume of logistical activity. Given a volume projection, the budgeting process attempts to arrive at the most realistic estimate of costs to be expended for the completion of logistical processing. The budget serves as a base for comparing desired performance in advance of the operational period with actual performance during and after the period. To a significant degree, budgeting is a management game in which top-level and operating executives attempt to arrive at joint estimates of funds required to realize desired performance. Naturally, top management desires lower budgets, whereas operating executives want to build in as much slack as possible. To overcome such bias in the budgeting process, many management groups structure budgets on a line-item basis. On the line-item basis, only a minimum transfer of expenditures between functional accounts is permitted unless plan modification is authorized.

FLEXIBLE BUDGETING.   The flexible budget is designed to accommodate up or down variations in volume during the operating period. Normally, the flexible budget is based on standard costs for performing specific logistical functions. Expenditures are permitted to float automatically to the level of actual operations. Although this method is desirable, a high degree of cost sophistication is necessary for effective flexible budgeting.

ZERO-LEVEL BUDGETING.   Zero-level budgeting is used two ways in operational planning. At an operational-line management level a typical budgeting procedure starts with no authorized funds at the inception of the operational plan. Funding is then authorized from *zero up*, depending upon justification of funds required to achieve stated objectives. A second type of zero-level budgeting is used in planning staff activities. This budgeting requires that all or a specified range of staff services be budgeted back to specific line operations so that the final staff budget includes *zero* unjustified expenditures. Both types of zero-level budgeting are attempts to tie operational expenditures to specific tasks, thus improving the base for subsequent managerial review and control.

CAPITAL BUDGETING.   Capital budgeting controls the extent and timing of logistical investments. As noted earlier, during operational planning a number of logistical system changes may be initiated or completed. The capital budget, for example, may commit cash or credit to construct a new warehouse, install a new order-processing system, purchase or lease transportation equipment, or institute any other planned expenditure.

When major system changes are planned, the capital budget formulation is straightforward. The difficulties arise when capital budgeting involves expenditures for research and development, since at inception such expenditures are nearly impossible to justify on a cost–benefit basis.

A creeping capital commitment ensues when the normal process of operation results in a fixed asset investment that is higher than it was previously. All functional areas of the corporation are subject to such elusive capital deployments, but logistical operations are among the most vulnerable in terms of inventory levels. If inventory is not rigorously controlled, a substantial unplanned capital investment may result.

A final note concerns determination of those costs applicable to a particular capital investment decision. The accepted capital budgeting practice is to consider only investments that require new net capital commitment. If system changes can be implemented that result in operational savings without new commitment, they are not subjected to the rigid control of capital budgeting.

Review of individual budget requests is the critical juncture of logistical administration. Top management must be concerned with the total performance of the system and not the individual parts. Development of an integrated system provides top management with an estimate of the total dollars required to meet specified system objectives. The planning process becomes one of reconciling individual budget requests with total system resources.

Budget requests of middle managers will often exceed funds required for good performance. This is understandable because no single unit manager is in a position to view the total system. A tendency also exists to view performance in any area on a unit cost basis. This bias in unit cost budgeting often forces uneconomic performance in one area without full evaluation of interrelationships to other areas. A traffic manager concerned with unit cost will tend toward low-cost transport selection, which he or she may be able to achieve only by delayed shipments.

Why are individual managers asked to formulate budget requests if such deficiencies are anticipated? The answer is twofold. First, it is essential that the individual manager participate in budget formation to gain a complete understanding of the integrated nature of total system programming. Budget formation is one of the most potent control and training tools available to top management. Second, individual unit managers are often aware of factors that must be considered in a specific operational plan which have not come to the attention of top management. The greatest danger in total system planning is top-management complacency concerning the continued validity of the long-range implementation strategy. Interaction between middle and top management is essential to the development of a realistic but demanding operational plan.

The Final Plan

The final operational plan is a blueprint for short-range performance. This written plan should contain a statement of objectives and detailed cost budgets for each operational unit. The budget package focuses on total system performance and objectives. It is designed to combine all relevant cost centers into a single unified plan. With this method each operating manager will be more likely to aim for his budget performance goal on an overall cost basis, since cost increases or decreases in one function are no longer relevant. It is the total cost performance that counts. This concept of total accountability is one of the essential aspects of management by objectives. For the total system to achieve the highest possible performance, all managers must assume correlative responsibility for everyone else's job.

Plan Modification

Once the final plan is developed, printed, and distributed, some aspects may require modification. Tactical adjustments to the operational plan will be required throughout the total planning period. Such modification results both from planning errors and from adjustments to unanticipated events.

Because individual managers have participated in development of the operational plan, each will be aware of the impact of decisions upon other functional areas. In day-to-day operations, managers may become aware of unanticipated changes that may adversely or favorably affect corporate distribution activities. A change in freight rates, packaging, material handling, and so on comes to the attention of the individual manager, who is in a position to recommend adjustments in the current operational plan.

Significant modifications to operational plans are encouraged, because results are achieved by exploiting timely opportunities. Two rules must be followed, however, in all such modifications. First, tactical modifications must be formally requested prior to any deviation from planned operations. Second, it follows that all such modifications must be evaluated in terms of total system performance. Once proposed modifications are adopted, formal written amendments to the operational plan should be distributed to all involved managers.

Logistical Controllership

The operational plan provides the measurement base for overall control of logistical operations. The control system assures that resources are assigned and monitored to achieve managerial objectives.

Control of a logistical system should always be relative to the operational plan. Without an operational plan, measuring performance is difficult, if not impossible. In the retail field, Christmas toys might be purchased in early spring to realize special discounts and allowances. From a control perspective, such practices, although justified on a total cost basis, may result in significant temporary increases in logistical costs far in advance of the normal season. These cost expenditures, when viewed in terms of the operational plan, cause little more than advanced planning for cash flow. Without the benefit of an operational plan, early expenditure for advanced distribution of Christmas merchandise could appear as an uncontrolled inventory buildup.

Logistical control is management by exception. The comprehensive and detailed nature of logistics requires that management review limit itself to deviations from anticipated results. However, few managers are willing to sit back and wait for an exception to appear. The exception is proof that a problem exists. Although solving such problems is a vital aspect of management, something more is needed: a mechanism for system monitoring. The monitoring network exists to reassure management that the total system is tracking along the desired course. A deficiency noted from system monitoring calls for a diagnostic evaluation of causal factors. The appearance of a significant exception means that a trend leading to a major deviation was overlooked during its formation stages.

The following example from inventory management illustrates the relationship between system monitoring and exceptions. Dollars allocated to an open-to-buy program at a given point in a planning period may be nearly depleted. At the same time a critical item may be approaching a reorder point. Placing the requirement order size as indicated by economic-order-quantity formulations could result in a commitment over and above authorized expenditures. One might assume that the individual merchandise controller would bring this situation to management's attention so that appropriate adjustments can be made.

However, if the original open-to-buy program was sufficient to cover needs, the current deficiency is a result of improperly allocated dollars for a past purchase decision by the same controller. Resort to management means that the controller needs help to rectify his error. Unfortunately, too few individuals feel free to expose themselves to open management scrutiny. This reticence may cause the controller to gamble that existing stock of the critical item will last until new funds are authorized. A rush order is then planned. In reality, the gamble involves customer service policy since it risks a stockout on a critical item. Given the opportunity for review, management might well choose to add dollars to the open-to-buy program to eliminate the risk of an out-of-stock situation. Unless the firm has a comprehensive monitoring system, management may never get the chance to express its choice until the out-of-stock situation turns up as an exception to stated policy.

In inventory control, the monitoring system can signal that a critical item had passed the inventory level of normal reorder without the issue of a purchase order. The inventory control manager would be expected to take appropriate action and request aid from higher management if necessary. The combined procedure of management prevents the monitored trend from becoming a full-scale exception.

This discussion makes it clear that management would rather prevent than correct exceptions. The monitoring system exists for this purpose. The exception reporting system exists to signal a breakdown within a segment of the organization that requires corrective action to prevent recurrence.

Control of a logistical system combines expected levels of performance with related expenditures. The operational plan calls for specified goal accomplishments for two types of compliance activity: (1) system modification, and (2) performance.

System Modification Control

As noted earlier, an operational plan may call for adjustments in the facilities constituting the logistical system.[3] The adjustments are planned, funds are authorized, and implementation is placed on a timetable. One function of the control system is to provide status reports concerning conformity to the agreed-upon plan. Such reports anticipate problems that might occur if the implementational schedule is not met. An unavoidable lag in development is often handled more efficiently by rescheduling than by commitment of additional resources.

Reports concerning planned facility adjustments are most often developed by middle management on a customized basis rather than from automated data processing. Care should be taken to see that such reports are provided on a regular basis and that they are sufficiently comprehensive to include all critical information. In one case of branch-plant relocation, progress reports indicated that all was well. In fact, the new building was ahead of schedule. Appropriate plans were made to hire new workers, personnel were transferred, and the product was stockpiled as scheduled in field warehouses to accommodate customers during the switchover. The undetected problem was that a new series of automated finishing machines were not meeting specifications at the plant of a long-time, reliable equipment supplier. By the time this was detected, the old facility had been closed down and the equipment sold for salvage. The result was that a national-brand appliance was for all practical purposes out of stock in the marketplace for over three months. A deficiency in reporting placed this firm in a situation beyond the control of management. The full implications of the prolonged out-of-stock upon long-range market position are difficult to measure.

Another important aspect of controlling facility adjustments are reports concerning unplanned changes. It is difficult to visualize a situation in which a plant or warehouse is added or deleted without preplanning, but inventories are subject to substantial changes over a single planning period. In general, the more variable the cost associated with a specific activity, the more probable an unscheduled accumulation or depletion. The operational plan should specify maximum and minimum inventory levels by individual stocking location. One important function of total system monitoring is a current report on trends that could lead to unplanned modifications. Such deviations materialize over time and can assume ample proportions once the trend is fully developed. The causal forces may be significant changes in sales patterns or

[3] See Chapter 10, pages 287–292.

internally generated factors. In either case the trends must be detected early to prevent serious readjustment problems and lags.

Performance Control

Assuming that all is well with planned system adjustments, a critical need still exists for measurement of operating performance. The control system of a firm must be capable of measuring efficiency and effectiveness of performance in comparison to the operational plan. This aspect of controllership relates performance goal attainment with budget authorization.

Efficiency is a dollar measure of expenditure to complete a specific assignment. A specified level of expenditure is authorized in the operational plan and management is concerned with the relationship between authorized and actual expenditures. It should be noted that efficiency as developed here is concerned only with the stated plan and subsequent performance. No judgment is made as to whether that plan is the most efficient one for accomplishing the required logistical performance. That decision and related compromises were made earlier during system design. Given a design, a level of resource allocation is structured into an operational plan. Management, from an operations control perspective, is concerned with the efficiency of the authorized resource expenditure.

Effectiveness is a measure of accomplishment of objectives. If the objective is never to be out of stock of a specific item at any location, the system would not be fully effective if a single stockout occurred. Effectiveness, then, is a measure of how well the integrated logistical system performs in terms of goals. A system that obtains 100 per cent operating effectiveness over the total planning period is unique.

The most direct form of logistical controllership is budget control. A typical procedure is to report actual expenditures over a specified time period relative to budgeted or expected expenditures. Analysis of the variance of actual to expected expenditures provides the basis for flexible budgeting adjustments.

Measures of effectiveness and efficiency combine to provide performance controls. Effectiveness indicates whether the desired job is getting done, but efficiency measures actual to planned budget for whatever level of performance the system is generating. For example, considering transportation expenditures, 95 per cent of all orders may be arriving on time. However, the cost for the first three time periods of the plan may be 102 per cent of the budget. The effectiveness thus falls within acceptable ranges, but management may feel that more efficient transportation must be selected. The next part reviews levels of control and data requirements.

Levels of Control and Information Flow

The nature of control requires that several levels of information be developed within the enterprise. As a general rule, the higher the level of management review in the organization, the more selective the control information and the reporting. The following four levels of information are appropriate to logistical control systems: (1) direction, (2) variation, (3) decision, and (4) policy revision. At each level the information may be related to trend monitoring or exception correction.

DIRECTION.   At the level of direction, information flow and control are concerned with execution of the operational plan. A stream of transaction documents signals a need, and the action document identifies appropriate steps necessary to meet objectives. For example, an order is received, credit is checked, the order is assigned to a warehouse, and it is picked, packed, and shipped. Upon shipment, the customer is billed in accord with the agreed-upon terms of sale. The order receipt is a transaction document; the remainder of the activities are generated by action documents.

At specified time intervals, all transaction and action documents are combined in a series of status reports. The status reports summarize individual activities in terms of existing capabilities to meet forecasted transaction requirements. For example, total inventory usage may be summarized by each item in the product line, and a comparison made to current inventories. Prompted by status reports, additional action documents may be issued to replenish stock on specific items.

Two important features should be kept in mind concerning information flow and control at the direction level. First, information at the direction level is concerned with day-to-day activities of the business on an individual transaction basis. Information at the direction level is selectively limited to review of status in accord with predetermined decision rules. In total, information flow at the direction level is concerned with execution of predetermined programs.

The second feature of information flow at the direction level is accumulation of records to formulate a data bank for all other levels of control. It is from this data bank that all reports concerning effectiveness and efficiency are generated, all trends are monitored, and all exceptions are detected. Although managerial discretion at the direction level is limited, all that follows is based upon the accuracy of information processed and generated from transaction and action documents.

VARIATION.   The variation level of control is concerned with accumulation of information which indicates that all is not going according to plan. As indicated earlier, the variation level of control ideally results in interpretation of a trend that could lead to future trouble. However, the variation may first appear as an exception to the desired level of performance at the direction level.

Managerial discretion concerning resource allocation initially occurs at the variation level. First, the manager must ascertain if the situation discovered is an isolated event or if it is symptomatic of a more serious problem. Second, the manager must determine if a solution to the problem is within the scope of his delegated authority or if it will require additional resources. Depending on the manager's interpretation of these two questions, either corrective instructions will be issued to the direction level of operations, or assistance will be requested from the decision level.

It is important to realize that the scope of information reviewed at the variation level is considerably reduced in comparison to the direction level. Management at the variation level is concerned with the broader issues of effectiveness and efficiency related to a series of transactions.

DECISION.   Control at the decision level of management concerns modifications in the operational plan. Situations which have materialized at the direction and variation levels require a reappraisal of the original operational plan. As one would expect, the assortment of information presented at the decision level will be very selective. It is significant to note that the decision level is the initial control level at which a formal change in the operational plan is considered.

Modifications normally will require allocation of additional resources. In accord with the format of control outlined here, the range of decisions will never involve a modification of system objectives. In other words, at this level customer service standards will not be changed if performance has been deficient. Rather a greater expenditure will be authorized as required to meet system objectives. Managerial activities at the decision level must be evaluated in terms of total system consequences. As noted earlier, decisions that modify the plan must be relayed to all managers involved in total system performance.

POLICY.   Control at the policy level involves a basic change in objectives. Once again, the areas of system design and administration merge when questions of policy are confronted. The arena of concern becomes enterprise-wide in scope and includes all members of management. The formulation of new policies requires an evaluation of planned system design as well as total cost of achievement. Requests for policy revisions may originate from any point within the enterprise. Thus far, this discussion of control has centered around information generated from the logistical data base and around deficiencies in either logistical performance or expenditure plans. However, policy situations may initiate from other management areas. For instance, the marketing department may desire an overall upgrading of customer service standards.

Figure 13-2 will help clarify the four levels of control involved in logistical administration. Adjacent to each level, reference is made to the approximate corresponding organizational rank within an enterprise. On the left side of the chart a data pyramid is developed to reflect the selectivity of information considered at each level of control. As noted earlier, each level is concerned with system monitoring as well as exception reporting. However, as information flows from the direction level to the policy level, the subject matter decreases in quantity and increases in importance to the welfare of the enterprise.

FIGURE 13-2
Information Flow and Levels of Control

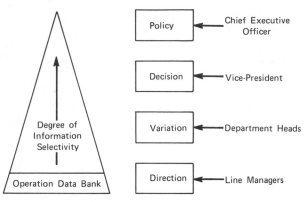

Performance Reporting

The essential feature of all control systems is the quality of reports generated from the management information system. Unless available information can be presented rapidly, accurately, and on relevant subjects, little in the way of positive control will transpire. In general, there are three types of reports used in a logistical control system: (1) status, (2) trend, and (3) special reports. Each type of report is illustrated as it relates to inventory control. Similar types of reports are required for all functional areas of a logistical system to assure compliance to operational plan objectives.

STATUS REPORTS. As the name implies, a status report provides detailed information about some aspect of the logistical operation. One of the most common is the stock status report used in inventory management. The stock status report is used to keep track of multiple-item inventories at more than one stocking location. The amount of information contained in an individual report will depend upon the firm, its degree of inventory management sophistication, and the extent to which automated data processing is used. Table 13-1 provides an example of an inventory stock status report.

In the example, inventory items are controlled from one central management location for distribution warehouses located in Detroit, Chicago, Atlanta, Newark, Tacoma, and Fresno. The unit inventory is maintained on a computer using techniques of scientific inventory management. Individual items have been assigned to stock controllers, who are responsible for inventory status at all six distribution warehouses. This particular report is for a controller referred to as A.

The individual item or unit number is printed in column 1. These item numbers do not appear in numerical sequence, since only items requiring attention are printed. However, if an item requires action at a specific distribution

TABLE 13-1
Example of a Stock Status Report

ABC Company
Distribution Warehouse
Stock Status Report

Date 3-10-80
Controller A

(1) Item	(2) Location	(3) Status	(4) on Hand	(5) on Order	(6) Forecasted Average Weekly Use	(7) Back Order	(8) Suggested Order Quantity	(9) Dollars on Hand	(10) Inventory on Order	(11) Date Placed	(12) Date Due	(13) Quantity
			Unit Inventory							Open Purchase Order Detail		
10-326-01	Detroit	Normal	183		25			457.50				
	Chicago	Out of stock		365	40	45		0	912.50	2-15-80	2-26-80	365
	Atlanta	Expedite	29	145	15			72.50	462.50	3-1-80	3-12-80	145
	Newark	Overstock	293		30			732.50				
	Tacoma	Order	55		10		75	137.50				
	Fresno	Normal	103		23			257.50				
Total			663	510	143	45	75	1,657.50	1,375.00			530
10-327-05	Detroit	Normal										
	Chicago	Normal										
	Atlanta	Overstock										
	Newark	Order										
	Tacoma	Order										
	Fresno	Order										
Total												
10-365-00	Detroit	Normal										
	Chicago	Expedite										
	Atlanta	Out of stock										
	Newark	Out of stock										
	Tacoma	Expedite										
	Fresno	Expedite										
Total												

435

warehouse, status of that item in all other warehouses is printed on the report. Thus, when an inventory controller plans specific action concerning an item the status at all stocking locations can be reviewed. The location is displayed in column 2 and status is reflected in column 3. Of particular interest is the required action printed in the status column 3. Based upon the rules of the inventory control system, the controller is informed of the reason the particular item appears on the stock status report. The remainder of the columns are self-explanatory. They provide the necessary information for the controller to direct the inventory procurement program.

Status reports can be developed for all logistical activity centers. Some relate to individual unit or transaction control; others are financial in nature. The purpose of the status report is to provide line managers with relevant information to fulfill their responsibility in the overall logistical system.

TREND REPORTS. Trend reports are used by administrators at levels of control higher than the line manager. In keeping with the flow of data outlined in Figure 13-2, trend reports are more selective in content than status reports. To illustrate, Tables 13-2 and 13-3 provide examples of trend reports that might be based upon the inventory stock status report.

Table 13-2 provides an inventory recap for all items, controllers, and stock locations. A report of this type is used by department heads to review the overall inventory situation. The data contained in the daily inventory summary are developed as a by-product of the stock status report printed for inventory controllers. Thus management possesses a quick recap of the total system and can evaluate overall performance.

Table 13-2 provides a variety of information. General performance is available on all locations as well as individual controllers. For example, the Newark warehouse is 75 per cent in stock (column 1), 21 per cent of the items have been out of stock longer than five days (column 10), and 92 per cent of the orders scheduled for shipment were shipped as planned (column 12). The report also indicates that controller *C* is having problems. This person is in stock on only 82 per cent of the items (column 7), 15 per cent of the assigned items in stock currently require expedite efforts to prevent future stockouts (column 8), and the items out of stock fall heavily into the critical area of classified merchandise (column 9).

Armed with this information, the department head is in a position to review activities and take corrective action. If desired, special reports can be requested which will provide further detail to help analyze a possible trend. For example, the department head in this case would probably desire detailed information concerning the Newark facility and the activities of controller *C*. There is no end to the selective information that can be generated from a data bank of the type maintained to develop Tables 13-1 and 13-2.

Table 13-3 provides an executive summary of selected critical facts regarding inventory performance. Condensed information of this type would most often be used by executives at the vice-presidential or decision level of an operation

TABLE 13-2
Daily Inventory Summary

Location	(1) Total Items Stocked	(2) Per Cent in Stock	(3) In Stock	(4) On Order	(5) Forecasted
			Dollar Values Inventory		
Detroit	1,075	92	17,385	3,231	7,115
Chicago	1,093	91	20,265	3,695	5,940
Atlanta	1,041	88	15,197	3,780	8,201
Newark	1,073	75	18,243	9,361	11,116
Tacoma	1,075	89	23,116	5,143	4,307
Fresno	1,026	90	19,450	2,184	1,993
Total system	6,383	87.5	$113,656	$27,394	$38,672

Controller	(6) Total Items	(7) Per Cent in Stock	(8) Per Cent Expedite	(9) A	B	C
				Out of Stock by Class		
A	1,250	91	10	30	40	50
B	1,300	89	9	36	71	38
C	1,100	82	15	65	47	91
D	1,275	85	9	15	81	95
E	1,458	95	8	20	70	40
Total	6,383	87.5	10	166	309	314

Location	(10) Items Out of Stock + 5 days	(11) Items Overstocked	(12) Per Cent Orders Shipped on Schedule
Detroit	12	31	96
Chicago	16	11	97
Atlanta	11	38	99
Newark	21	5	92
Tacoma	14	17	87
Fresno	19	0	94
Total	93	120	96

(see Figure 13-2). As noted earlier, an executive who is content to wait for exceptions to appear is rare. Most executives would prefer to see the trend of performance in their areas of responsibility.

Table 13-3 covers a four-week period. The first three weeks are presented in aggregate, and the fourth week is developed on a daily basis. Reports of this nature provide the basis for trend evaluation and are useful in selecting areas for diagnostic analysis. For example, the data in Table 13-3 point out that

TABLE 13-3
Logistical Performance Recap

Performance Area	Week C-3	Week C-2	Week C-1	Current Week by Days				
				1	2	3	4	5
1. System in-stock (%)	88.0	86.0	81.0	82.0	85.0	86.2	87.3	87.5
2. Weighted performance (%)	83.8	84.2	90.0	79.8	83.2	84.0	86.3	87.0
3. Dollars inventory	121,614	119,381	111,843	95,417	98,106	96,412	110,807	113,706
4. Shipments on schedule (%)	99	97	98	99	96	97	98	96
5. Back orders	365	691	780	193	217	238	165	101
6. Selected data								
7. Other system								
8. Activity centers								

although inventory performance over the past three weeks had deteriorated, performance on the most recent days indicates that corrective action has been taken. Of particular interest in Table 13-3 is line 2, weighted performance. The weighted performance is a measure of stock availability in the quantities desired by customers. A system may enjoy a very high level of in-stock items but be out of stock on the items most wanted by customers. Measures of weighted performance generally run lower than measures of system in-stock.

The data presented in Table 13-3 contain inventory trend information generated from the inventory stock status report (Table 13-1) and the daily inventory summary (Table 13-2). In all probability the executive receiving the performance recap would be responsible for additional logistical system activity centers. The report could be expanded to include data on transportation, warehouse performance, order processing, material movement, or any other desired areas. In addition, similar reports can be generated in materials management and inventory transfer operations. Because the information is selective and highly condensed, these reports can often be confined to a single page.

SPECIAL REPORTS.   Special reports may be created at any level of logistical administration and for a variety of reasons. Most often, special reports are developed to provide detail on specific areas of performance. Three types of special reports are common in administration.

The first type is a diagnostic report, which provides detail on a specific phase of operations. For example, a report might be requested to provide greater detail on current back orders and subsequent corrective action. If the firm operates a real-time order-processing system, special diagnostic reports may be obtained from either hard or soft copy by direct interrogation.

The second type of special report is a position paper. Given a current or anticipated problem, a report outlining alternative courses of action and probable consequences is often desirable. In terms of control levels (see Figure 13-2), position papers are usually developed by line managers and department heads for use by executives at the decision level of the organization. These position papers will often request additional resources. If the request is approved, the operational plan will have to be modified. In accord with the levels of administrative control, position papers and related actions may involve a greater allocation of resources, but they will not involve changes in performance objectives.

The final special report is concerned with policy modification. Earlier in this chapter an example of a policy report was discussed when the marketing department requested that customer service objectives be substantially upgraded. Policy reports always are directed to or initiate from the chief executive officer of a firm. Their content almost always involves areas of activity beyond logistics.

In conclusion, the content of control reports is highly customized to the individual enterprise, its organization, and management information system sophistication. The content of reports should be geared to levels of administrative control: the higher the level of control, the more selective the nature of information contained in the report.

For the most part, status reports are used by line managers to direct logistical activities in accord with predetermined operational plans. Trend reports to monitor progress are highly condensed and are used by executives at the variation and decision levels. The higher the control level, the more condensed and selective the trend report. Trend reports prepared at the decision level should contain information related to all aspects of an integrated logistical system. Special reports contain selected information on certain units of the system. From the control center, interrogation of status and performance of individual units located at any geographic point may be initiated. Performance with respect to the operating plan can be evaluated to permit rapid and efficient management response to any externally or internally generated change.

Summary

Logistical administration consists of operational planning and control. Administration in the logistical organization should be guided by management by objectives designed to result in a clear statement of objectives. The control process provides a measure of accomplishment.

Operational planning is concerned with the day-to-day activities of an enterprise within the framework of the strategic plan. The formulation of an operating plan requires the coordination of objectives related to system modification, performance, and budgets into one integrated effort. As noted earlier, consecutive operating plans represent short-range elements of longer-term system implementational strategy. Therefore, logistical system design and administration are unified through the relationship between operational plans and implemental strategies.

The control process is one of the most complex aspects of logistical management. The problem is not one of information availability. In today's business enterprise data are abundant, and continued refinements in management information systems make data increasingly more available. The challenge in logistical controllership is to format required data in a manner which results in consistent performance measurement.

Two types of data are required for logistical controllership. Cost-control data, although readily available, require a great deal of restructuring to be useful to logistical administration. Service performance data normally are not available within the corporate record base. However, the fact that all elements of the total performance cycle are under logistical management control in a unified organization structure renders the data for service measurement attainable. Logistical controllership must isolate cost and performance data to provide management with facts concerning the overall logistical operations. All levels of management control require timely and accurate data. In the final analysis, a logistical operation can only be as efficient and as effective as the control system that guides its destiny. Chapter 14 deals with practices and problems in organization.

Questions

1. Describe the concept of management by objectives. Is this limited to logistics in its application?
2. What types of factors or activities would be included in a typical operational plan?
3. Describe the role of a system modification in an operational plan.
4. Is it a good practice to modify operational plans once established?
5. Discuss the relationship between the operational plan and the logistical control process.
6. Describe the different types of control commonly found in a logistical system. Discuss the difference between control at the direction variation decision and policy levels of an organization.
7. Does variation in control necessarily mean that a problem has developed?
8. In the scheme of decision making presented in the chapter and illustrated in Figure 13-2, is it reasonable to conclude that system redesign decisions would reach the policy level while system administration decisions would be concerned with the direction variation and decision levels? Why, or why not?
9. Describe the differences among fixed, flexible, and capital budgeting. Which method do you prefer, and why?
10. What are the basic purposes of status, trend, and special reports?

Organization

Management is the process of getting things done through others employed by the enterprise. An integral part of all management is personnel motivation. The fundamental responsibility of top management is to create an environment within which each operating executive has maximum opportunity to achieve corporate objectives. To this end, organization structure is a vital part of management.

Traditionally, responsibility for logistical management has been fragmented throughout the organization. One basic premise underlying the integrated logistical concept is that organizational fragmentation of responsibility increases vulnerability to duplication, waste, and at times, complete hindrance of mission accomplishment. With fragmented responsibility, communication flows become distorted and lines of authority and responsibility are blurred.

Organizational structuring of logistics as a separate managerial unit is a relatively new concept. The fact that logistical activities have always been performed within industry has created a great deal of controversy on whether a unified organizational group is necessary or even desirable. This chapter provides an overview of logistical organization practices. An evolutionary approach to logistical unification is described which reflects commonly observed patterns of organizational revamping. Next, several persistent issues in organizational structure are discussed.

Two comments are in order concerning the manner in which organization structure is presented. First, recognizing that organization is a highly customized activity, no attempt is made to present charts of individual enterprises as representative models.[1] No chart fits all structures. Rather, emphasis is placed on the logic of grouping functions given the maturity level of integrated logistics within an enterprise. Accordingly, three types of organizations are discussed as points along a unification continuum. Applicability of these

---

[1] Some representative enterprises who have restructured their logistical organizations recently are Hooker Chemical, Abbott Laboratories, H. J. Heinz, Black and Decker, Bristol-Myers Products, and Johns-Manville Sales Corporation.

general organizational comments will vary, depending upon the individual enterprise's requirements.

A second point worth noting is that acknowledged principles of management are not reviewed. The established principles apply to all forms of management and provide valuable guidelines for designing an organizational structure. Since the principles of management are discussed in detail in basic management textbooks, they are not elaborated on here.

Organizational Evolution

If one accepts the premise that top management in general is not disposed to revolutionary change, it follows that unified logistical organization must evolve over time. As noted repeatedly, all functions of logistics have always been performed by successful enterprises. It is only natural that an attempt to relocate management authority and responsibility in existing organizational units will be resisted. Many logistical managers can testify that attempts at rapid reorganization are often met with rivalry and mistrust—not to mention accusations of empire building. The nature of management organization is that budgets flow with operational responsibility. Likewise, power and visibility result from large budgets. Logistical reorganization, therefore, will be evolutionary in all but a few exceptional situations and will need to be preceded by substantial overall management education.

Type I Organization

Unified organization is not a prerequisite to improved logistical efficiency. Likewise, it is not a guarantee that overall performance will automatically become more efficient and/or effective. The first condition that must exist within an enterprise is awareness that logistical performance can improve through integrated effort. To unequivocally state that integrated organization is essential to total system cooperation erroneously places emphasis on structure rather than end results.

An organization with any degree of formal unification will emerge only after the basic concept and potential of logistics is accepted by management. The typical pattern is for two or more logistics functions to be grouped organizationally without significant change in positioning within the hierarchy. This grouping may occur initially at the staff or line level of organization. Seldom will organizational units engaged in materials management and physical distribution management be joined together at this initial stage. Finally, the initial grouping will seldom make organizational provisions for separate and distinct management of the product allocation system.

Figure 14-1 illustrates a traditional organizational structure with dispersed logistical functions. *Only those functions typically involved in logistical operations are highlighted by the hypothetical organization chart.* In proceeding with the discussion of organization, it will be interesting to note that several specific logistical functions which will be introduced at a later stage do not exist in the traditional organization structure displayed in Figure 14-1.

FIGURE 14-1
Traditional Organizational Structure of Logistical Related Functions

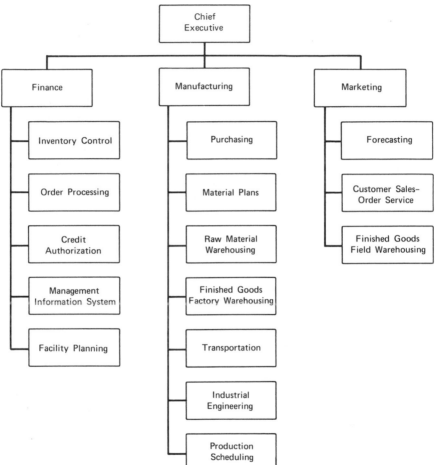

Figure 14-2 illustrates the form of unified organization likely to emerge initially. Although completely separated, physical distribution and materials management are identified as areas of functional control and selected activities are grouped under these new control centers. No definitive studies are available concerning which specific functions are unified initially and whether both physical distribution and materials management emerge as separate control areas at stage I development.[2]

[2] The concept of physical distribution is most commonly found in firms marketing consumer products. Materials management typically is found in manufacturing operations.

FIGURE 14-2
Type I Logistical Organization

FIGURE 14-2
Type I Logistical Organization

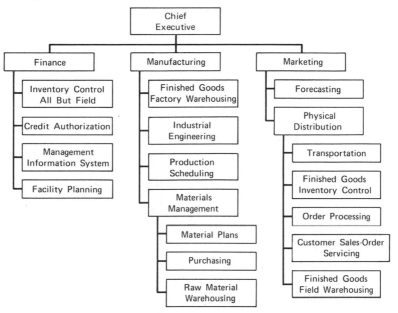

The point is that as recognition of integrated logistics develops within an enterprise, two clusters of unified operations are likely to emerge. In the marketing area, the cluster will be around customer servicing. In the manufacturing area, concentration will be in materials and parts procurement. However, with few exceptions, no traditional functional departments will be repositioned, nor will the level of the newly created organizations be altered significantly. For the most part, type I organizational change involves regrouping within the traditional areas of marketing and manufacturing.

Type II Organization

As the overall enterprise gains operational experience with unified logistics and the cost benefit of the approach is proved, a second stage of reorganization may occur. Figure 14-3 illustrates a type II organization posture.

The main point in the second stage of development is that some portion of the logistical area is isolated and elevated to a position of higher organizational authority and responsibility. A likely candidate for initial independent status is physical distribution if improved customer service is conspicuous in overall enterprise performance. Typical of this enterprise type is the grocery manufacturing business. In industrial manufacturing and processing industries, materials management often increases in operational authority and responsibility as the integrated concept matures. Thus, the focal group elevated to a

FIGURE 14-3
Type II Logistical Organization

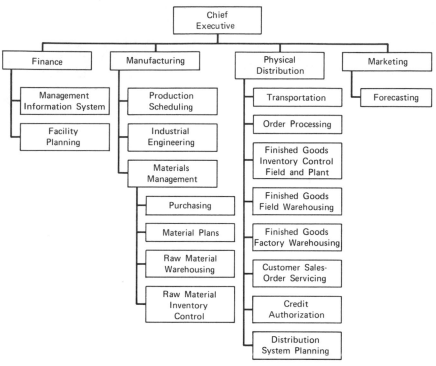

position of higher organizational prominence will depend, to a significant degree, upon the nature of the enterprise's primary activity. The example in Figure 14-3 illustrates a situation wherein physical distribution has been restructured.

In order to structure a type II organization, it is necessary to reallocate functions and to position the newly created organization at a higher level within the overall enterprise structure. In the type II organization, note that the concept of fully integrated logistics is still secondary to the separate fields of physical distribution and materials management. This failure to synthesize all movement management into an integrated system is due in part to a preoccupation with specific tasks, such as order processing and purchasing, which are essential to continued operations. A second limiting factor to total unification is the lack of a fully operational logistical information system at this stage of development. A review of industry literature indicates that most firms with a high degree of sensitivity to logistics have organizations roughly equivalent to a type II organization.[3]

[3] See Bernard J. La Londe and James F. Robeson, *Profile of the Physical Distribution Executive* (Columbus, Ohio: The Ohio State University), p. 1.

Type III Organization

The third type of organization involves unification of all logistical functions and operations under a single management structure. Under type III organization, the concept of logistical management as developed throughout this book emerges as a fully integrated system. Type III organizations with the comprehensive nature illustrated in Figure 14-4 are rare. However, the trend in organization grouping is clearly toward the unification of as many logistical planning and operational functions as practical under single authority and responsibility. The goal is strategic management of all materials and finished product movement and storage to the maximum benefit of the enterprise.

The rapid development of logistical information systems provides an impetus for type III organizations. The information technology is currently available to plan and operate systems that fully integrate logistical operations. Several features of the type III organization are noteworthy. The structure illustrated in Figure 14-4 is discussed by specific organizational units.

First, each aspect of overall logistical operation is structured as a separate line operation. The lines of authority and responsibility are thus clear for each major task to be performed within the logistical effort. Because of the well-defined areas of operational concern, it is possible to establish inventory transfer as an operational unit similar to materials management and physical distribution. Each of the three units is operationally self-sufficient. Therefore, each is able to maintain the flexibility necessary to accommodate the peculiar nature of movement and storage within their respective operational areas. In addition, since all logistical activities are planned and coordinated on an integrated basis, opportunities between operational areas can be exploited.

Second, four functional areas of logistics are represented at the system support services level. This operational unit facilitates total integration of the logistical system. Care has been taken not to describe support services as a staff group. Rather, the group is involved in day-to-day functional management with direct liaison between materials management, physical distribution, and inventory transfer operations.

Third, at the coordination level, the full potential of the logistical information system can be deployed throughout planning and line operations. Order processing triggers the logistical system into operation and generates the data bank for controlling all phases of the operation. The logistical coordination group integrates product-market forecasting, operational planning, production scheduling, and purchasing to guide logistical operations.

Finally, system planning and controllership exist at the highest level of the type III organization. These two groups represent staff services for the integrated organization. The systems planning group is concerned with long-range strategic planning and is thus responsible for logistical system design studies and redesign recommendations.

The logistical controller appears frequently in type II organizations.[4] The

---

[4] See Chapter 13, pages 428–430, for a discussion of logistical controllership.

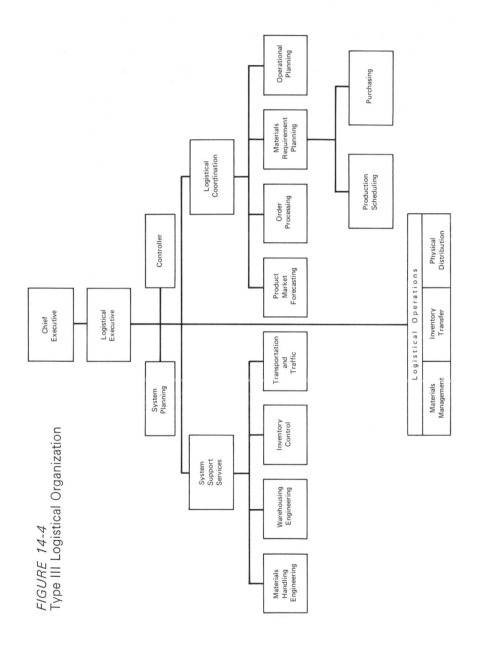

FIGURE 14-4
Type III Logistical Organization

448

controller measures performance of the logistical operation and provides data for managerial decision making. The development of a program for logistical controllership is one of the most critical areas of integrated logistical administration. The task is extremely important because of the large operating and capital dollar expenditures involved in logistics. It is complicated by several barriers to effective costing which are inherent in accepted accounting principles and financial reporting.[5] To develop effective logistical cost control, it is necessary to isolate functional accounts and to reconcile the impact of time upon operational expenditures. The key tool of logistical cost control is the combination of operating and capital budgets that regulate cash flow within the logistical sector. Of equal importance is the measurement of operational effectiveness in terms of the stated logistical mission.

Conclusion—Organizational Evolution

There is every reason to believe that logistical organization will continue to move toward greater unification. The next logical step is unified management control over all movement in the organization except within the production plant. Unification is an evolutionary process. It will continue as long as the payoffs are substantial. While the type III organization posture is a look into the future, some progressive firms are actively studying similar fully integrated organizational concepts.[6] Although organization is not a substitute for mature management, proper organization can increase the effectiveness of a sound managerial approach.

Persistent Issues in Organization

The subject of organizational structure always raises a number of issues. These issues are classified as persistent, because they are easy to identify but difficult to solve. In this section five such organization issues are discussed: (1) centralization–decentralization, (2) line and staff, (3) conglomerate structures, (4) organizational positioning, and (5) interorganizational control.

Centralized Versus Decentralized Structure

The distinction between centralization and decentralization in organization structure is based upon the degree of authority and profit responsibility

---

[5] See Chapter 8, pages 254–256.

[6] For selected discussion of organization issues, see Roger Meissner and Paul Nelson, "What is the Right Name for Us?" *Handling & Shipping*, May 1976, pp. 46–49; Lester K. Kloss, "You, Your Future, and the Future of Physical Distribution Management," *Handling & Shipping*, May 1976, pp. 50–54; or "How These Presidents View Physical Distribution," *Presidential Issue, Handling & Shipping* (1975). For case studies, see Jack W. Farrell, *Physical Distribution Case Studies* (Boston: Cahners Books, 1973).

delegated to specific operating units. Within an enterprise, units or divisions are considered highly decentralized if each is able to function on an almost autonomous basis. In a fully decentralized organizational structure, each division would be responsible for providing its own logistical requirements.

Current trends in logistical organization support centralized positioning. The development of logistical information systems no longer requires decentralization to provide high performance levels. Second, the high cost of logistical facilities and equipment prohibits duplication between divisions. Therefore, while logistical centralization may be contrary to developments in other functional areas of business enterprises, it is in the best interest of logistical organization to realize the inherent benefits of centralized operations.

Line and Staff

Managers have attempted to reconcile the difference between line and staff responsibilities since the advent of organization. The traditional distinction has been that line performs the operational tasks while staff concerns itself with planning.[7] As suggested earlier during the discussion of type III organizations, this distinction may no longer be valid. Today, all managers are involved to a significant extent in both operations and planning. What could be defined as a line function one day may very well be a staff function the next, depending upon the nature and urgency of the task. The impact of total information management upon logistics is beginning to remove the traditional staff–line classification.[8] The two groups are merging into a managerial resource base dedicated to maximum integration of the logistical operating system.

Conglomerate Structures

During the 1960s and 1970s, many enterprises developed a conglomerate structure through ownership and control of other business enterprises. Unlike earlier mergers, the conglomerate approach preserved the organizational integrity of acquisitions. Once ownership transfer was completed, the typical conglomerate practice was to permit the acquired enterprise to continue to operate on a decentralized basis. Earlier discussion dealt with centralization versus decentralization within a single enterprise structure; the conglomerate issue involves management of several jointly owned businesses.

A pressing question in strategic planning for the 1980s is whether selected operating units should be consolidated. The idea of forming a separate service company to provide integrated logistics for all enterprises within the conglomerate as a profit-making distributive organization is one such consideration. The rationale is that the potential cost saving from consolidation would reduce

---

[7] For a discussion of line versus staff, see John F. Stolle, "How to Manage Physical Distribution," *Harvard Business Review*, July–August 1967, pp. 93–100.

[8] See Chapter 2, pages 32–35.

each individual enterprise's existing logistical expense enough to show a substantial return on investment for the service company.[9]

When one considers that, on a combined basis, several major corporations have annual logistical operating costs in excess of $100 million, the service subsidiary concept appears to have potential. A few initial steps have been taken to date toward service company development. If a trend materializes, even the organizational approach outlined as type III (Figure 14-4) would not be sufficiently comprehensive for conglomerate logistical service operations.

Organizational Positioning

Organizational unification has the net impact of improving the relative position of logistical management in the overall enterprise structure. Twenty years ago executives with any form of logistically related title were nearly impossible to locate. Today, functional vice presidents are customary.[10]

The logistical function, however, has not yet achieved the organizational status that would place it on an equal footing with marketing, manufacturing, and finance. In most firms the stage of organizational evolution ranges between type I and type II structures. Although the trend is undeniable, development of the integrated logistical management concept to the point where it is independent and functionally positioned in top management will be realized only over an extended period of time.

Interorganizational Control

In Chapter 2 the need for cooperation between enterprises that form a channel of distribution was discussed in terms of interorganizational dependency. Only through coordination of all functions required for effective logistics can all transaction requirements be satisfied fully. Despite the need for cooperation, individual profit objectives and legal restrictions create conflict between channel members. One issue of organizational concern is the extent to which one member of a channel of distribution can and should influence operational decisions and practices of other channel members. This extension of an enterprise's operational influence to the direction of other channel members results from an unbalanced power ratio.[11]

The acknowledgment that tactics of persuasion and coercion may be used effectively to further channel group objectives could result in a type IV organizational arrangement. Such arrangements could acknowledge the

[9] For an illustration, see *General Foods Logistics System* (Boston: Intercollegiate Case Clearing House, Harvard University, 1974).

[10] La Londe and Robeson, op. cit.

[11] For examples, see Donald J. Bowersox, "Showdown in the Magic Pipeline: Call for New Priorities," Presidential Issue, *Handling & Shipping*, Fall 1973, pp. 12–14; James L. Heskett, "Sweeping Changes in Distribution," *Harvard Business Review*, March–April 1973, pp. 123–32, and Walter F. Friedman, "Physical Distribution: The Concept of Shared Services," *Harvard Business Review*, March–April 1975, pp. 24–36.

dependency relationship between channel members and lead to institutionalization of the process of functional transfer. Although such formalized interorganizational arrangements are not common today, some experts predict their inevitability in the future.[12]

Summary

Logistical organization is an evolutionary process. Traditionally, responsibility and authority for logistical performance has been fragmented. Definite trends are developing toward unification of logistical functions under a single management. This trend has not evolved to the point where logistics has gained equal stature with manufacturing, marketing, and finance, but the gap is narrowing. There is every reason to project that future logistical organizational structures will continue to gain independence from traditional functional areas of management and achieve top executive positioning.

All organizational charts represent a customized approach to structuring the affairs of a specific enterprise. However, all enterprises face some persistent issues when reviewing organizational requirements. Issues related to: (1) centralization–decentralization, (2) line and staff, (3) conglomerate structures, (4) organizational positioning, and (5) interorganizational control were reviewed in the chapter. The final chapter reviews future directions of integrated logistics.

Questions

1. Is the organization of all logistical activities into a single management unit essential to the achievement of efficient operations?
2. What is a type I organization?
3. Why is it common for physical distribution and material management to develop as separate entities in a firm? Is this bad?
4. Describe a type II organization and distinguish it from type I.
5. Why is it logical that forecasting will remain initially with marketing if and when physical distribution becomes a unified organization?
6. What is the major distinguishing difference of a type III compared with a type II organization? Describe the role performed by the logistical controller.
7. Among the persistent issues in an organization, why does centralization versus decentralization remain an issue? Why does logistical operation favor centralized operation?
8. What factors encourage the combination of logistical operations within conglomerate structures?
9. Do you believe that logistics should be positioned at the vice-presidential level? Why, or why not?
10. Is the notion of structured interorganizational behavior consistent with sound management? Is it legal?

[12] Friedman, op. cit.

Dimensions of Change

This brief concluding chapter offers one perspective on the future direction of logistical management.

The Setting—1980 and Beyond

Given the extreme changes that have occurred in logistical management concepts and practices during the past three decades, an appropriate question is: What can we expect to happen during the remainder of the twentieth century? The primary determinant of the shape and form of future logistical systems will be the nature of the demand which must be serviced.

Current projections are that the gross national product of the United States will exceed \$2 trillion by 1980 and surpass \$3 trillion prior to the end of the century. The areas of significant growth will be expenditures for goods and services. In comparison to today, a significantly larger share of the total population of the United States will participate in the "good life" projected for the 1980s and 1990s. In terms of logistical demands, operating systems will need to handle ever-increasing package and tonnage volumes to maintain the expected standard of living. From an operating viewpoint, logistical systems of the future will face complex performance requirements. Even more so than today, logistical systems will be required to support multiple-product distribution to heterogeneous markets and through a variety of marketing channels. The return movement of inventory for recycling and/or recall will become a more integral part of future logistics. This rapidly increasing area of "reverse logistics" will require the logistical system flexibility of efficient two-way movement.

Some planners rest easy with the belief that logistical strain will be eased or counterbalanced by a decline in population expansion. Some go to the extent of projecting a zero population growth rate. Providing the mid-1970 low fertility rate of just over two children per family continues, population will, in fact, grow at a diminishing rate. However, growth will continue at a positive yearly increase, as long as normal immigration continues, until long after the end of the twentieth century. Even if fertility rates drop to an unprecedented low of one child per family, zero growth would not be experienced until near the year 2000.

The significant point is, regardless of the population growth projection one feels most secure with and barring a catastrophic event, it is difficult not to expect an increase in total population exceeding 50 million people during the remainder of the twentieth century. To put this population growth in perspective, at a bare minimum we will need to provide logistical support for one additional person for every four in the United States today.

The prospect for the remainder of the century is the presence of the two main ingredients for growth—money and people. However, significant differences can be expected in life-style and related social priorities. Despite some earlier predictions to the contrary, evidence now supports the position that the consuming public will demand increasingly greater services within products purchased for in-home consumption. For instance, such products as frozen produce might well be cooked and ready for consumption when purchased. To the extent that this develops, more value will be added to the typical product before it begins the logistical process. As a result, the complexity of the total manufacturing/marketing system will increase rather than decrease in the years ahead.

Ever present in future society will be the continued problems and pressures of energy and ecology. The dependence of the logistical system upon a ready supply of energy is and will continue to be a critical concern. The cost of energy is projected to remain a serious problem for the logistical sector during the foreseeable future. From an ecological viewpoint, continued pressures will exist to reduce the negative impact of logistics on the environment. These pressures reflect socially worthwhile goals. However, ecological compliance will be costly. To some degree, ecological considerations will eliminate selected logistical alternatives currently available such as specific forms of packaging and selected materials handling equipment.

Finally, the remainder of the twentieth century is projected to be a period during which selected raw materials will remain in short supply. Thus the problems of maintaining operational continuity, characteristic of the mid-1970s, will be present in the decades ahead.

How Adequate Is Our Present Logistical Potential?

Assuming full maturity of integrated logistics, how adequate is our present capability to meet the demands outlined above? Providing maintenance of a 5 per cent level of unemployment, the logistical infrastructure and managerial practices of today will be hard-pressed if not unable to satisfy future demand. In our society, logistics is second only to personal services as a consumer of labor. Logistics is a labor-intensive process. The situation becomes even more critical when marginal workers must be employed as a result of full employment. Logistical systems are forced to employ more than their rightful share of such marginal workers because of the extensive manual tasks involved. Physical handling of goods does not rank high in employment choice when alternative jobs are available. Thus, marginal entries to the work force are the prime source of manual labor needed to keep the goods moving. The result has been and will continue to be a problem of maintaining adequate labor productivity.

One substitute for labor deficiency is the development and application of new logistical technology. For the past three decades, our logistical system has kept pace with growth by applying new technology to the performance of traditional logistical tasks. For example, load capacity of transportation vehicles has been expanded in water, rail, truck, and air operations. Today, each mode can carry larger payloads faster and cheaper than was considered possible a few years ago. In a similar vein, high-speed data processing and data transmission have provided a method of receiving and processing customer orders faster and more accurately while simultaneously capturing critical operational measurement data. During the past decade significant advancements have been made in automation of both unit-load and package warehouses.

Across the board, technological developments have been applied to keep pace with and overpower increasing tonnage demands placed upon the national logistical system. Considering the track record, even the most severe critic would have to acknowledge outstanding performance. However, after all is said and done, by 1980 the logistical system will continue to utilize massive amounts of physical labor to perform its designated tasks. Despite our logistical system's historical track record of having adequate capability to deliver our industrial output, the existing system is now strained and the situation will become increasingly critical in the decades ahead.

From the viewpoint of technology assessment, the prospects for continued development to satisfy future logistical demands are not encouraging. For example, load capabilities and transportation speeds have reached near maximum for our highway, rail, harbor, and airport infrastructures. Future technology can be expected to pay off at a significantly slower rate. It appears safe to conclude that new technology will not provide the total answer for satisfying tomorrow's logistical demand.

In summary, with demand versus adequacy, the remaining years of the twentieth century are projected to be a period of continued affluence. The sheer numbers of people and their physical requirements will place unprecedented demands upon logistical performance. Complexity of the logistical process will increase as a result of changing life-styles, continued high cost of energy, ecological compliance requirements, and the constant potential of recurring material shortages. Unlike the past three decades, the United States cannot look forward to a steady stream of new technology as the solution to satisfying logistical requirements. Providing no significant change in managerial practice, our existing logistical capacity will be hard-pressed to satisfy projected requirements.

The Solution—Innovative Applications of Available Technology

The problems created by the emerging situation are capable of solution. However, doing more of the same things in logistics that have been done during the past three decades is not the answer. The past practice of over-powering the logistical mission by deployment of new technology will no longer be viable. The challenge for the coming decade is to develop *new* ways to satisfy logistical requirements, as contrasted to attempting to perform *old* ways more efficiently. The solution rests with innovative applications of technology available today within a new and permissive framework. Many traditions and practices which characterize today's national logistics structure are both archaic and symbolic of a bygone era.

Throughout the preceding 14 chapters a selected number of basic concepts were discussed which are vital to the emerging form of logistical operations. The overall field of logistics has evolved over a relatively short period of time from a fragmented operational effort into an integrated philosophy of strategic movement and storage management. During this developmental period, several basic concepts have emerged which are vital to the future development of the logistical process. The following represent eight of the most significant concepts which provide a foundation for solving future problems.

The Systems Approach

The systems approach was and remains the cornerstone of the integrated logistical concept. Few question the logic that significant benefits can be obtained by integrated deployment of human and financial resources toward accomplishment of the logistical mission. The problem is one of application. In far too many industrial and marketing organizations the systems approach is given lip service but not serious implementation. The identification and measurement of trade-off potential within a logistical system is difficult without a serious reexamination of traditional procedures and practices. In most cases, organizational arrangements must be altered to focus accountability. In many situations, new and innovative performance measurement devices must be implemented to open the door for the synergistic potential promised by the systems approach. Countless managers know *what* to do to improve logistical productivity but they do not know *how* to effectively implement systemic planning and management of logistical effort. In this sense the systems approach offers new potential to many organizations, because it has actually never been applied.

Data Transmission

One technological development of the last decade has been the significant increase in data-transmission capability. The result is the capability to introduce time-controlled information flow into planning and administration of a logistical system. By direct transmittal of customer orders to computer processing facilities, valuable time can be saved and deployed for the performance of other necessary logistical activities.

Perhaps the greatest untapped potential of data processing is the opportunity to improve control of the total performance cycle. Such control can eliminate a great deal of uncertainty, which is so difficult to cope with when formulating safety stock policies. Implementation of control devices to increase speed of performance while simultaneously decreasing uncertainty of performance could reduce dramatically the overall need for safety stocks in our national logistical system. In fact, given performance consistency, a great deal of the logic used currently to formulate safety stock policy could be modified substantially. In data transmission we have a "here today" technological capability. The opportunity exists to improve overall performance because few firms are exploiting fully the many benefits attainable from time controlled information flow.

Consolidation

Two different forms of consolidation are fundamental to the design and operation of a logistical system: (1) transportation, and (2) inventory. It is safe to generalize that few firms today realize fully the many benefits available from the two forms of consolidation.

Transportation consolidation results from the realization that movement costs can be controlled by fully coordinating shipping or procurement. Consolidation is essential to benefit from the quantity discounts structured into common-carrier transportation rates. Such consolidation can be realized by grouping orders destined for a specific market, pooling through public warehouse distribution programs, and developing scheduled delivery programs. Despite the basic logic of the potential offered by transportation consolidation, each passing year sees an increasing number of small shipments dragging down the productivity of our national transportation capacity.

Inventory consolidation relates to the number of locations at which inventory is held in anticipation of servicing customer orders. Few dispute that the total inventory necessary to support a logistical mission is directly related to the number of warehouses. By consolidation of facilities, total cost can be lowered because inventory reductions or inventory availability for purposes of customer service can be increased, given the same level of inventory. In spite of the undisputed benefits of inventory consolidation, countless firms continue to operate extensive field warehouses without justifying the network on the basis of total cost or customer service benefits.

Cost-Revenue Measurement

To a significant degree, failure to utilize a systems approach, lack of widespread use of data-transmission capabilities, and failure to fully consolidate shipping or inventory locations are symptoms of inadequate measurement capabilities. Development of integrated logistics has long been hindered by the lack of standard functional costs. In particular, controversy exists concerning the appropriate measurement of cost trade-offs. Most practitioners agree that logistical plans ideally should be formulated on the basis of total cost expended in relation to revenue generated by customer service performance. Marginal cost–revenue measurement offers the necessary refinement over traditional forms of accounting. The total field of logistical controllership, while still in its infancy, provides a new perspective for measurement and control of the logistical process. The capability to set priorities and measure performance accurately offers a readily available way to improve logistical productivity.

Channel Separation

Substantial opportunities for improving logistical productivity can result from viewing the structure of overall distribution channels in terms of specialization of effort. Logistical-channel relationships and performance plans should be formulated using specialists engaged in management of physical movement and storage. The concept of channel separation challenges the long-standing practice of using the same intermediaries for performing marketing and logistical functions. For example, wholesalers traditionally have served as both marketing and physical distribution intermediaries. The tradition of a single-channel structure is not based on inherent economic advantages or legal requirements. It evolved over time as a result of ease of development and for control purposes. The concept of channel separation offers a logical and practical alternative for the future given the control capabilities *now* available for use by logistical managers. The channel-separation concept is not new and has been tested. The technology to make it work is here today. The difficulty with establishing specialized channels is that long-standing and traditional business arrangements must be renegotiated and restructured.

Flexible Operating Structures

Closely related to the notion of channel separation is the development of flexible operating structures. A flexible operating structure consists of a systems capability to service selected customer orders utilizing a variety of shipping locations and/or transportation methods, depending upon the characteristics of the order. Thus orders may be processed to customers in a combination of ways that achieve logistical performance objectives most effectively.

Flexible operations may be incorporated into a logistical system design on either a contingency or standard performance basis. The main benefit of flexible operations is that they offer a format for coping with constantly changing logistical demand. By incorporating flexibility into system design, the operating posture of the system can be adapted to meet day-to-day and even order-to-order requirements effectively. Operating flexibility eliminates the neat and rigid patterns of well-defined warehouse service areas which have become characteristic of countless enterprises. The procedure for meeting a customer's requirement at the lowest total cost using flexible assignment is now gaining an operational foothold.

Essential to flexible operations is development of selectivity in formulating inventory stocking policies and related safety stocks. It is not necessary and most often will not be desirable that all facilities have the same stocking policies. Using fine-line item classification, policies should be formulated to meet specific performance standards. The criteria for establishing such standards may be product profitability, customer profitability, importance of product delivery to customer, or any other combination of standards critical to meeting operating objectives.

The important point is that stocking selectivity combined with flexible operating structure provides a way to realize high levels of output while reducing the level of assets deployed in support of the logistical mission. Similar to each of the concepts discussed, the technology is currently available to establish flexible operating capabilities.

Postponement

The traditional nature of logistical performance is that emphasis has been placed on movement of product in *anticipation* of future transactions. Anticipatory action is also characteristic of our manufacturing, wholesaling, and retail sectors of business. Generally, products are produced, transported, stored, handled, bought, and sold several times until they arrive at a location where they are offered for final sale. Provided that all of the anticipatory work has been performed properly, final transactions are realized in an efficient and effective manner. The concept of postponement is a risk-reducing approach to performing manufacturing and logistical operations. To the extent that final manufacturing or logistics of a product can be postponed until a final customer commitment is obtained, anticipatory action is reduced, resulting in little or no risk of error.

The attributes of postponement may be incorporated into a logistical system on the basis of *form* and/or *time*. Form postponement consists of holding the final manufacturing, assembly, or packaging until customer preference is identified. The classic example is mixing paint to customer specifications at retail stores. The potential for incorporating form postponement into logistical system design is almost unlimited. From an operating perspective, systems that incorporate form postponement must be designed to move nondifferentiated products towards customer locations, with final customizing taking place at warehouse facilities. To the extent that form postponement develops as a common feature of future operations, light manufacturing will become an integral part of the logistical system.

Time or space postponement simply means that the risks of anticipation are eliminated by not moving a product until a customer order is received. In essence, time postponement is required to enjoy inventory consolidation. Likewise, to develop the capability for temporal postponement, it is necessary to exploit the potential of data transmission to offset the loss of valuable time in getting the customer's order into the logistical process.

The significant point about both form and time postponement is that they offer ways to reduce the anticipatory nature of today's business arrangements. Thus, to the extent that postponement can be structured into a logistical system, reliance on forecasting and its related risk is reduced. The concept and the technology necessary to operationally benefit from postponement are available today.

Interorganizational Management

Logistical operations extend beyond the traditional domain of a single enterprise to include many other organizations. The fact that no firm can be self-sufficient was the basic motivation behind the notion of channel separation. Since dependency exists, channel arrangements should be fostered to take maximum advantage of the specialization possible.

Coordination of interorganizational logistical performance provides an opportunity to eliminate duplication and minimize risk for the total channel. The concept of interorganizational management creates opportunities for utilizing third-party specialists and shared distribution facilities. While the track record of shared distribution facilities is not yet noteworthy, the expanded use of third-party specialists is extremely encouraging. A number of barriers exist to future exploration of interorganizational management concepts. While some barriers are legal and/or regulatory, the most serious problem confronted in the development of interorganizational arrangements is traditional practice. The concepts to guide the formulation of interorganizational arrangements are currently available to management.

Concluding Statement

The projected demand for logistical services during the remainder of the twentieth century is frightening. Even a conservative estimate of growth will push the existing logistical infrastructure far beyond its demonstrated capability. Over the past three decades advancements have been made in the philosophy of integrated logistics. However, almost all actual improvements in operating capability have resulted from technological developments. In a sense, we have overpowered our problems of logistical growth by technology. Now, for the first time since World War II, the continued development of logistically related technology is not encouraging.

A variety of approaches to help meet future logistical requirements do exist within the philosophy of integrated logistics. Each represents a new or different way of formulating and conducting logistical operations using currently available technology. To be fully implemented, each concept requires a major change in current logistical operating practices. *The significant point is that innovative applications of today's technology to cope with tomorrow's logistical needs must rest with management.* While many legal and/or regulatory barriers exist to hinder innovative change, the most serious problem is management attitude and inflexibility. The time is now for the implementation of the philosophy of integrated logistics.

Appendixes

Simchip—A Logistical Game

Simchip is a logistical management decision simulation based on four firms supplying five market areas with potato chips. Each firm produces potato chips in 1-pound bags and distributes to the five areas in the week following production. The overall objective of the simulation is to make maximum gross distribution profits for a time period specified by the umpire. Product sales result in revenue generation. Warehouse and inventory costs, production costs, transportation costs, and distribution costs result in expense generation.

The purpose of Simchip is to demonstrate the basic interrelationship between several important elements of logistics. The game has not been designed to present all possible alternatives in a dynamic setting, but to focus on the key elements of the task to provide important background perspective for the student.

In order to focus on the logistics task, some simplifying assumptions have been made. These assumptions include a simplified market structure, a limited product line, and the elimination of promotional and advertising decisions.

The explanation of Simchip is divided into three general parts. The first part, entitled "Information on Key Variables," presents detailed data on all the variables used in the simulation. The second part, entitled "Explanation

465

of Forms and Procedures Used by the Player," explains the forms and procedures used in actually playing the game. The third section illustrates the forms utilized by the players in recording decisions.

The game may be played for as many periods as specified by the umpire. The reader should carefully review all materials in the appendix and thoroughly understand the simulation procedure before completing any decision forms.

Information on Key Variables

Market Data

Consumer demand for the product is the key determinant in the firm's sales. Each firm starts the simulation with an equal share of the total market. Consumer demand based on past sales history fluctuates ± 15 per cent. As the simulation develops, each firm's market share will vary depending on the efficiency of production and physical distribution.

Raw Materials

	Cost	Package	Pounds/ Cubic Foot
Potatoes	$ 4.21/cwt	100-lb bags	6.66
Salt	1.735/cwt	100-lb bags	12.50
Oil	16.21/drum	50-gal drum, 400 lb	44.44
1-lb bags	22.00/M	1,000 bags, 260 lb	9.64

Warehouse and Inventory

Each firm has two types of warehouse facilities available for raw materials storage.

Private.   12,500 square feet, 20 feet clear.

80% usable cube = 200,000 cubic feet.

Warehouse overhead charge = $1,443/week.

Warehouse operation = throughput = total receipts + total production (from status report) $\div$ 2 $\times$ $0.16/cwt.

Public.   A public warehouse will be used after 200,000 cubic feet have been placed in a private warehouse.

Cubic Feet	Cost/Cubic Foot
0–100,000	$0.015
100,000–500,000	0.010
500,000 and above	0.005

(*Note:* Cost includes delivery from warehouse to factory.)

Raw-Material and Finished-Inventory Carrying Cost

Ending raw-material inventory (at cost) × 10% ÷ 52.
Finished-goods inventory carrying cost = waste × unit wholesale price ×
20% ÷ 52.

Production Capacity

CAPACITY. Each firm operates a cooking plant at its home market location
(see Figure EI-1). This plant has a cooking capacity of 20,000 pounds/day
normal, 5,000 pounds/day overtime, and an additional 20,000 pounds by
scheduling Saturday production. Production must be completed in the week
prior to the following week's anticipated sales.

FIGURE E1-1
Simchip I—Market Structure

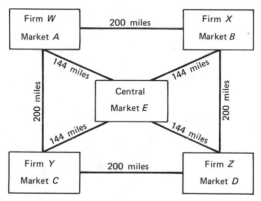

PRODUCTION OVERHEAD. Fixed overhead charge regardless of production—
$3,750/week. A portion of this overhead is for the reusable cartons utilized in
delivery.

COOKING COSTS. The production of finished potato chips requires raw
potatoes, oil, salt, and bags. Costs are incurred as raw materials are converted
to chips.

Cooking Conversion—1,000 Pounds of
Finished Chips

Potatoes (lb)	4,370	$183,970
Salt (lb)	50	0.868
Oil (lb)	400	16.210
Bags (lb)	1,000	22.000
		$223.048
	Total cost	Cost/lb
	223.05	$0.223

Cooking Costs—Regular

Basic (lb)	lb/day	Saturday/lb
10,000	$0.220	$0.319
11,000	0.215	0.319
12,000	0.210	0.319
13,000	0.205	0.319
14,000	0.200	0.319
15,000	0.195	0.283
16,000	0.190	0.283
17,000	0.185	0.283
18,000	0.180	0.283
19,000	0.175	0.283
20,000	0.170	0.283

Cooking Costs—Overtime

Basic (lb)	Per lb
0–2,500	$0.284
2,501–5,000	0.246

Transportation Costs (Inbound Raw Materials)

Transportation of raw materials is accomplished by rail, common-carrier motor truck, and private truck. All raw materials are received from Central City.

Company Truck (No Lead Time)

	Capacity (lb)	
	Truck A	Truck B
Potatoes	60,000	24,000
Salt	50,000	20,000
Oil	96,000	38,000
Bags	10,000	4,000
	Cost	
	Truck A	Truck B
Basic	$100/week	$65/week
Per mile	$0.15	$0.10
Average mile/hour	40	45
Loading–unloading time	4 hours	4 hours
Driver's wages	$6/hour	$6/hour

Central City—Rail (2 Weeks Lead Time) (No Maximum)

0–480,000 lb	$0.15/cwt
480,000–960,000 lb	0.13/cwt
960,000–1,440,000 lb	0.125/cwt
1,440,000–any Q lb	0.120/cwt

Central City—Truck (1 Week Lead Time)

	LTL	TL
Potatoes	0–30,000 lb $0.50/cwt	30,000–50,000 lb[a] $0.35/cwt
Salt	0–25,000 lb $0.55/cwt	25,000–60,000 lb[a] $0.35/cwt
Oil	0–48,000 lb $0.30/cwt	48,000–96,000 lb[a] $0.20/cwt
Bags	0–5,000 lb $0.85/cwt	5,000–10,000 lb[a] $0.65/cwt

[a] Maximum weight/shipment.

Distribution Costs (*Finished Product*)

Company Truck

	Truck A	Truck B
Per mile	$0.15	$0.10
Average mile/hour	40	45
Unloading time	1 hour	1 hour
Driver's wages	$6/hour	$6/hour
Capacity		
Cartons	1,620	600
Pounds	9,720	3,600

Common Carrier

	LTL: 0–9,000 lb	TL: Over 9,000 lb
Central (144 miles)	$3.50/cwt	$3.00/cwt
Adjacent (145–200 miles)	$3.90/cwt	$3.40/cwt
Distant (over 200 miles)	$4.20/cwt	$3.80/cwt

Distribution in Market Area—Basic Cost/Market $250.00[a]

	Cost/cwt
Under 2,000	$0.27
2,001–5,000	0.26
5,001–10,000	0.25
10,001–15,000	0.24
15,001–20,000	0.23
20,001–25,000	0.22
25,001–30,000	0.21
Over 30,000	0.20

[a] The cost is added once each decision period for each market in which distribution is made. This cost represents storage in transit and distribution in the various market areas.

Explanation of Forms and Procedures Used by the Player

Status Report

The status report provides the basis for planning each period's actions and aids in preparing the operating statement. It is filled out by the umpire. The form contains your company's share of each market and the amount of waste you had last period. You are to assume that you will sell the amount proposed if you produce and distribute that amount to each market. The percentage share may be compared to past percentages to get an idea of your distribution in each market as compared to that of the other companies. Waste is the amount produced and distributed to each market that was not sold.

Remember, this is a simulation and your score will be determined by how well you control your logistic system. Coordination among team members is of prime importance!

Decision-Recording Form

PRODUCTION SCHEDULE. This schedule will be completed, showing production for each day and the total for the week.

RAW-MATERIAL INVENTORY STATUS. Beginning inventory and purchase orders due will be provided by the umpire at the start of the simulation. After this, you will be responsible for completing this form in duplicate and returning one copy to the umpire each period. The starting inventory will be the same figure as last period's ending inventory. Usage (obtained from the production worksheet) and receipts (obtained from the warehouse worksheet) are applied to beginning inventory to obtain ending inventory.

All new orders placed and those placed in previous periods and not received during the period are deleted.

DISTRIBUTION SCHEDULE.   This schedule is provided in three parts:

Total Distribution.   This form is to be filled out completely showing the market and the day of distribution. Total q will show the daily distribution; total p will show the total distribution to each market. These two totals must be equal.

Company Truck Distribution.   This schedule will show your truck schedule for each day of the week and the total pounds distributed. If the truck is used to pick up raw material, the route will be entered in the market column and miles recorded. [*Example:* Your firm is located in market B. You make a raw material pickup in Central (*E*). Market column would show *B–E–B–*; miles, 288; pounds and distribution stops, blank. If you loaded your truck with 9,000 pounds of chips and delivered 4,500 to market D and 4,500 pounds to *E*, and then picked up the raw material, the form would be Market, *B–D–E–B*, miles, 488; pounds, 9,000; distribution stops, 2.]

Common-Carrier Distribution.   This schedule will show the daily distribution by market and pounds when using a common carrier.

Note: The combined totals of parts 2 and 3 must equal the total distribution in part 1.

Operating Statement

The worksheets provided are cross-referenced to assist you in preparing your operating statement.

General

The decision recording form and the operating statement will be completed and turned in to the umpire on the day announced by your instructor. Fill out these forms completely and accurately, for they are subject to audit at any time during the simulation. File each period's worksheets so that you will be able to support your figures.

STATUS REPORT

Company _____   End of Period _____

Market	Proposed demand in pounds	Per cent share last period	Waste last period in #
A			
B			
C			
D			
E			

Total   _____ _____ _____

Sales Computations:

    Total distribution in $ = distribution last period x .845¢
    Total waste in $ = waste last period x .845¢

Total Distribution Less Total Waste = Total Net Sales

    $ _____ - $ _____ = $ _____

DECISION-RECORDING FORM

Company _____   End of Period _____

Production schedule:

M	T	W	TH	F	S	S
#	#	#	#	#	#	#

Raw materials inventory status:

	Potatoes #	Oil #	Salt #	Bags #
Starting inventory				
Usage (–)				
Receipts (+)				
Ending inventory				
Order due				
# period				
_____ _____				
_____ _____				
_____ _____				
_____ _____				
_____ _____				
_____ _____				
Total Committed				

DISTRIBUTION SCHEDULE

1. Total distribution:

	M	T	W	TH	F	S	Total(p)
Local							
Mkt							
Mkt							
Mkt							
Mkt							
Total(q)							

2. Company truck distribution:

	Truck A				Truck B				Total #
	Routing	Miles	Pounds	Stops	Routing	Miles	Pounds	Stops	
M									
T									
W									
TH									
F									
S									

Total   ____ ____ ____   ____ ____ ____ ____

3. Common carrier distribution:

	Market	Pounds	Market	Pounds	Market	Pounds	Total #
M							
T							
W							
TH							
F							
S							

OPERATING STATEMENT

A. Sales (in Dollars) $ _____

B. Warehouse and Inventory Costs

    B-1. Warehouse overhead $ ___1443___

    B-2. Warehouse operations $ _____

    B-3. Extra warehousing (public) $ _____

    B-4. Raw material inventory carrying cost $ _____

    B-5. Finished good inventory carrying cost $ _____

       Subtotal $ _____

C. Production Costs

    C-1. Overhead $ _____

    C-2. Cooking conversion $ _____

    C-3. Cooking costs—regular $ _____

    C-4. Cooking costs—overtime

       Subtotal $ _____

D. Transportation Costs—Inbound Raw Materials

    D-1. Company truck

        Fixed charge $ ___165.00___

        Variable charge $ _____

    D-2. Common carrier—rail $ _____

    D-3. Common carrier—truck $ _____

       Subtotal $ _____

E. Distribution Cost—Outbound (Finished Product)

    E-1. Company truck variable $ _____

    E-2. Common carrier truck $ _____

    E-3. Distribution in market $ _____

       Subtotal $ _____

        Total Cost $ _____

         Profit for Period $ _____

WORKSHEET — WAREHOUSE AND INVENTORY COST

B-1. Warehouse Overhead (Private) $ _____

B-2. Warehouse Operations (Raw Material Handling)

      Raw Material Receipts During Period

	#	Order No.
Potatoes	_____	_____
Salt	_____	_____
Oil	_____	_____
1 # Bags	_____	_____
Total Receipts (a)	_____	

      Raw materials used
        during period (#)
        (Production worksheet) (b) _____

        Total (a) & (b)_____ ÷ 2 x .16/cwt =_____

B-3. Extra Warehousing (Public)

      Cubic ft. used during period   _____
      x Appropriate rate   _____
      Extra warehousing cost for period $_____

B-4. Raw Material Inventory Carrying Cost

      Beginning Raw Materials Inventory

        Potatoes_____ x 4.21/cwt = _____
        Oil   _____ x 4.05/cwt = _____
        Salt   _____ x 1.735/cwt = _____
        Bags   _____ x 22.00/Bale =_____
                        Total (a) $_____

      Ending Raw Materials Inventory

        Potatoes_____ x 4.21/cwt = _____
        Oil   _____ x 4.05/cwt = _____
        Salt   _____ x 1.735/cwt = _____
        Bags   _____ x 22.00/Bale =_____
                        Total (b) $_____

        Total (a) and (b) $_____ ÷ 2 = (c) $_____
        (c)_____ x 10% ÷ 52 =
        Period raw material inventory carrying cost $ _____

B-5. Finished Goods Inventory Carrying Cost

      Period waste (status report)_____
      x Unit wholesale price_____ $ .845
      $_____ x 20% ÷ 52 =
      Period finished goods inventory carrying cost $ _____

C. Production Costs:

C-1. Overhead .... $ _3750_____

C-2. Cooking Conversion

    Quantity cooked this period _____ (finished)

    Potatoes   _____ x $.0421/lb = _____

    Salt   _____ x $.0017/lb = _____

    Oil   _____ x $.04/lb   = _____

    Bags   _____ x $.022/bag = _____

                         Total Conversion Cost_____

C-3. Cooking Costs — Regular

    Quantity cooked x   rate/lb   =   total cooking cost

    M _____ x _____ = _____

    T _____ x _____ = _____

    W _____ x _____ = _____

    TH_____ x _____ = _____

    F _____ x _____ = _____

    S _____ x _____ = _____

                           Total _____

C-4. Cooking Cost — Overtime

    Daily output in excess of 20,000 lb x rate

    _____ x _____ =

    _____ x _____ =

    _____ x _____ =

                        Total _____

D. Transportation Costs:

Inbound Raw Materials:

D-1. Company Truck ..... Fixed Charge $ _____

    *Total mileage per period x rate

    Truck A _____ x _____ $.15 _____ = _____

    Truck B _____ x _____ $.10 _____ = _____

    (Driving time + loading time) x driver's wages

    (_____ + _____) x $6 = _____

                   Total _____

*Separate truck mileage between raw materials hauling and finished goods delivery.

D-2. Common Carrier — Rail

    Total lbs   x   Rate

    _____ x _____ x

    _____ x _____ x

    _____ x _____ x _____

              Total _____

D-3. Common Carrier — Truck

	Total Lbs/ Shipment	x Rate (LTL OR TL)	
Potatoes	_____	x _____	= _____
Salt	_____	x _____	= _____
Oil	_____	x _____	= _____
Bags	_____	x _____	= _____

                       Total _____

E. Distribution Cost:

Outbound Finished Product

E-1. Company Truck

*Total mileage per period x rate

Truck A _____ x _____ $.15 _____ = _____

Truck B _____ x _____ $.10 _____ = _____

Driving time + unloading time   x   drivers' wages   =

(_____ + _____) x $6.00   = _____

                                        Total _____

*Separate truck mileage between raw materials hauling and finished goods delivery.

E-2. Common Carrier — Truck

Market	Pounds	x	Rate (LTL or TL)		
_____	_____	x	_____	=	_____
_____	_____	x	_____	=	_____
_____	_____	x	_____	=	_____
_____	_____	x	_____	=	_____
_____	_____	x	_____	=	_____
_____	_____	x	_____	=	_____

                                        Total _____

E-3. Distribution In Market

No. of markets in which distribution is made x fixed distribution charge =

_____ x $250. _____   = _____

Pounds delivered in Market:

A _____ x _____ = _____

B _____ x _____ = _____

C _____ x _____ = _____

D _____ x _____ = _____

E _____ x _____ = _____

                                        Total _____

Plant Location Factors

Current economic literature contains many contributions aimed at developing a general theory of industrial location. Several such contributions were reviewed throughout the text. These theoretical studies address the problem of explaining geographic distribution of plant capacity. The main criterion permeating the majority of published works is the rational allocation of scarce resources. Thus, most location literature has been devoted to explaining socially acceptable goals generated from classical competitive economics.

However, the principle of free economic action and profit maximization may lead to personal goals inconsistent with social goals. Given imperfections in social and economic organization, individual entrepreneurs may find profit opportunities derived from astute location decisions. It may appear that economic theory and applied business practice are, therefore, incompatible. This view is quite incorrect. The function of location theory is to abstract from practice so that all elemental forces affecting location may be identified. Once these forces are appropriately defined, they implicitly form the foundation of public policy, which is aimed at achieving maximum economic welfare. One result of location theory is, therefore, the formation of adequate public policy to guide the nation's economic welfare. Given this orientation, the

479

complete acceptance of general location forces for the purpose of solving an individual location problem may be inappropriate. However, theory aids in identification of fundamental forces affecting location and thus assists in the organization of an applied method for locating a specific plant. Applied methodology can be developed within the guideposts so conveniently developed by economic theorists.[1]

Least-Cost Location Factors

Location theorists point out that all location factors can be grouped and summarized under three broad categories: (1) least-cost factors, (2) profit-maximizing factors, and (3) intangible factors. To select a proper plant location, a complete evaluation of the influence of each category of factors on a particular location problem is necessary. Thus it is important that all location factors be clearly understood. This and the following two sections are devoted to a detailed discussion of each category.

Location cost factors may be divided between transfer costs and production costs.[2] Transfer costs are defined as the costs that result from the movement of raw materials to the proposed plant site and those that are incurred by shipping finished products to market.[3] Production costs include all other costs related to plant operation. To achieve the least-cost location, the sum of all transfer costs and production costs must be minimized.[4] Intangibles may be defined as those elements affecting costs which may not be classified in transfer or production accounts.

Transfer Costs

Transfer costs as a factor in plant location traditionally have been considered by assuming that all other location influences are negligible.[5] Such an assumption tends to minimize important location forces and, therefore, should be employed with considerable caution. On the other hand, this approach allows

---

[1] For a comprehensive review of location theories, see M. J. Webber, *Impact of Uncertainty on Location* (Cambridge, Mass.: The MIT Press, 1972), Chaps. 2 and 3; and Melvin L. Greenhut and H. Ohta, *Theory of Spatial Pricing and Market Areas* (Durham, N.C.: Duke University Press, 1975).

[2] Hoover presented as the core of his thesis two influential cost categories—transfer and process. Although not utilized in a similar manner these cost categories have been adopted for the present treatment. See Edgar M. Hoover, *The Location of Economic Activity* (New York: McGraw-Hill Book Company, 1948).

[3] Transfer costs are defined to include all cost components as developed in the total cost discussion. For a complete discussion of all costs included in transfer costs, see Chapter 4.

[4] Only costs that vary between alternative locations are influential in plant location. For example, the cost of raw materials, per se, is not important unless this basic cost is geographically variable.

[5] For example, see D. Philip Locklin, *Economics of Transportation*, rev. ed. (Homewood, Ill.: Richard D. Irwin, Inc., 1972), p. 67.

a detailed and unrestricted treatment of this very important factor. Transfer costs frequently are a dominant element in plant location. Because they are readily quantifiable, transfer cost analysis provides a convenient starting point for solving locational problems. In Chapter 11 an analytical technique is developed which may be employed to arrive at the geographical point of least transfer costs. However, it is essential to keep in mind that transfer costs are only one of many location influences. The point of least transfer cost normally will have to be amended to accommodate other location elements in selecting the profit-maximizing plant site. Five principal methods of movement are available to transport raw materials and finished products: rail, truck, air, water, and pipeline. The particular method capable of solving a given movement problem depends upon the commodity to be moved, distance, weight, size of shipment, speed required, cost, and so on.[6] Given the alternative methods capable of moving a particular commodity, the specific method or combination of methods employed is selected on the basis of cost and type of service required. Cost in all cases should be held to a minimum under the standards of service necessary to satisfy market requirements. Thus, when service requirements are satisfied, the combination of methods that results in the lowest total transfer cost may be determined by utilizing the total cost techniques introduced in Chapter 11. The combination of transfer methods and resultant costs can be materially altered by the geographic point at which the production plant is located. Consequently, in selecting a plant location, it is necessary to isolate the one best geographical point from which service requirements may be satisfied at the lowest total transfer cost.

Intercity transfer costs may be divided into two components: the costs associated with accumulation of raw materials and those related to product distribution. Accumulation costs result from the movement of raw materials or semifinished products to the point of manufacture. Distribution costs are derived from shipment of finished products to the final market through all intermediary steps. A particular plant location may be pulled toward the market or toward the source of raw materials, depending on which location minimizes the sum of accumulation and distribution costs. In some cases, as will be shown, a location between the market and the source of raw materials may yield the lowest total transfer costs.

Materials-Oriented Industries

The plants in a particular industry may be located near the source of raw materials because of the unique location of the raw material or because of a great weight loss in the process of production. Extractive industries as characterized by agriculture, mining, and lumbering must be located at the point where raw materials are available in economic quantities. In agriculture,

---

[6] The capabilities and limitations of various modes of transport are discussed in greater detail in Chapter 5.

the supply and quantity of land suited to particular crops plays the dominant role. In mining, it is the location of deposits; in lumber, it is the location of forests.

Industries in which, because of the nature of the product, great weight loss is experienced in production tend to locate plants near the source of raw materials.[7] Sugar beet refining and cotton ginning are excellent examples.[8] The net result of such locations is to reduce total transfer costs, because the weight shipped to market is significantly less than the weight of raw materials. A third element causing plants to be located near raw materials is the perishability of the materials. Many agricultural canning and freezing processes are examples. The great canning and freezing complex in central New Jersey, with its vast fresh fruit and vegetable acreages and large processing centers, illustrates this condition. To some unmeasurable extent, this location factor is offset by technological improvement in transportation equipment, for example, refrigerated cars and trucks.

In summary, several major forces influence transfer costs for particular industries, thereby making the point of least transfer cost one in close proximity to the source of raw materials. These forces are (1) great loss of weight in raw materials during processing or production, (2) availability of raw materials for extractive industries, and (3) perishability of the raw material.

Market-Oriented Industries

Industries that add weight during the production of finished products, experience large differentials in rates between raw materials and finished products, or produce a highly perishable finished product tend to locate plants near the market.[9]

A typical weight-gaining process is found in the beverage industry. Water, a major ingredient in the final product, causes substantial weight gains during production. Because adequate water supplies are found in most potential locations, it is economically desirable to ship concentrates rather than finished products. The weight added to the final product by the addition of water causes transfer costs to be lowest when it is added near the market.[10]

[7] Webber, op. cit., pp. 11–13.

[8] For example, about one sixth of the weight of sugar beets is retained in the extracted sugar. This is also important in cane sugar production; the mature cane is about 10 per cent fiber, 18 per cent sugar, and 72 per cent water. Stanley Vance, *American Industries* (Englewood Cliffs, N.J.: Prentice-Hall, Inc., 1955), p. 557.

[9] There is considerable confusion in current literature regarding whether perishability, service, and so on are location forces requiring a market orientation as a result of transfer expense, or location forces requiring a market orientation owing to consumer preferences. Unquestionably, both forces are important. A clear separation could be obtained only by studying specific industrial location problems.

[10] In some cases where other than "any quantity" rates prevail, for example, if rates in carload lots are lower than rates on less-than-carload lots, it may be possible to increase weight without increasing total costs. Furthermore, within a limited range, increased weights may decrease cost. See Locklin, op. cit., pp. 73 and 78.

It is interesting to note that in the total marketing effort of the firm, advertising may somewhat modify the impact of transfer cost factors. If advertising can develop a product image that commands a higher price, this increased revenue may absorb the added transfer expense associated with a location at a point distant from the market. This is of particular importance to firms selling to a national market in which the production process does not allow the use of concentrated syrups. In the beer industry, for example, the accepted meaning of a "premium beer" is that it sells at a price above that of locally brewed products. Although there may indeed be quality difference, it is not the only foundation for classifying a beer as premium for marketing purposes. However, the basic market orientation rule is not greatly influenced by this special case. If concentrates can be employed, the location impact of advertising may be channeled toward more productive sources while lower transfer rates are enjoyed. Primary examples of such physical distribution decisions are the policies followed by the major soft drink producers.

Even when weight differentials between raw materials and finished products are negligible, the plant may be attracted to a market location. A general characteristic of rates is that lower rates are placed upon cruder materials, with the rate increasing as the product reaches final stages of fabrication.[11] Therefore, transfer rates tend to increase with the stage of manufacture. Historically, this condition reflects the value of the service principle in rate making. That is, in some loose way it was assumed that the higher the value a commodity could command, the more easily it could absorb a higher freight rate. The monopoly position enjoyed by the railroads up to the 1930s allowed such discrimination. Newer modes of transportation in competition with the railroads have impaired the railroad's ability to continue such practices.Value of service in modern rate-making theory refers to the rate that may be charged by a competing form of transport equivalent service. Under this new concept, the spread between raw-materials rates and finished-product rates is likely to diminish in the future. To the extent that this differential diminishes, such discrimination will become of lesser consequence in plant location.

If the final product is characterized by extreme perishability, there may be additional reasons why a market-oriented location should be selected. Special handling and the requirement for extreme speed may tend to increase the cost of transferring commodities such as baked goods, ice cream, and delicatessen foods. Under such conditions, production close to markets minimizes such transfer expense.

In summary, transfer forces pulling plant locations to a market proximity are (1) weight gains during production, (2) differential freight rates between raw materials and finished products, and (3) perishability of the finished product.

---

[11] Ibid.

Location at Other Points

A third group of industries traditionally has been labeled "foot-loose." This is because the transfer costs related to their particular manufacturing process allow selection of a plant location either at markets, at raw materials, or at an intermediate point. If a particular industry is truly foot-loose, transfer costs may play a small role in determining plant location. For example, research and development firms are quite independent of the transfer forces under consideration.

But this is not the situation for all the firms that select plant sites at points separated from raw materials or markets. In some special cases, a plant located at an intermediate point represents the least-cost transfer location. The earlier discussion illustrating why plants are attracted to materials or markets was based upon the assumption that freight expense for a through movement was less than the expense incurred from movements to and from an intermediate point. Although this is normally true, there are some notable exceptions.

Probably the best-known exception to the general rule is the granting of in-transit privileges by the transport companies. The most widely utilized in-transit privileges are milling and fabrication. In both cases, the raw material may be shipped to a production point, then to final destination, at a combined cost slightly higher than the through rate. Utilization of this artificial removal of the "diseconomy" of short hauls is particularly influential when the pull of the materials and the pull of the market are otherwise almost equal. Examples of in-transit privileges can be found in the grain and steel industries. In-transit privileges allow management considerably more freedom in the selection of plant sites. The net effect of in-transit privileges is to promote the dispersion of industry.[12]

Intermediate location may also stem from the use of trans-shipment points. Location at trans-shipment points can be highly beneficial to industries processing raw materials which have low transport costs into final products normally associated with high transport costs. In such cases location at junction points may greatly reduce aggregate transport costs. Water facilities are among the cheapest methods of movement for the transport of bulky raw materials. Processing may then take place during the rehandling operation. This has the net effect of reducing unnecessary rehandling cost. Location at such junction points means that raw materials may move via water transportation, and finished products may be shipped via the cheapest satisfactory means of reaching the market. The importance of Pittsburgh and Youngstown as steel centers may be attributed in part to the availability of water transportation facilities.

---

[12] For more detailed discussions, see Martin Beckman, *Location Theory* (New York: Random House, 1968), James T. Kreafsey, *Transportation Economic Analysis* (Lexington, Mass.: Lexington Books, 1975), P. Dicken and P. E. Lloyd, *Location in Space: A Theoretical Approach to Economic Geography* (New York: Harper & Row, Publishers, 1972), and Edward J. Taaffe and Howard L. Gauthier, Jr., *Geography of Transportation* (Englewood Cliffs, N.J.: Prentice-Hall, Inc., 1973).

Additional factors that pull plants to intermediate locations result from the need to utilize several raw materials or serve several different markets. A firm that utilizes a number of raw materials in processing can usually realize lowest transfer costs by locating at collection points. A collection point is a location that has minimum aggregate accumulation costs for various raw materials. On the other hand, a distribution point is a location that has minimum distribution costs to various markets. When one material or one market cannot be identified as the primary determinant of lowest transport costs, an acceptable compromise location at intermediate least-cost points may be the alternative.

In summary, if an industry can be categorized as truly foot-loose, plants may be located at any point, and transfer costs may not be a dominant location element. Particular industries tend to locate plants at intermediate points, depending upon certain economic forces. In these special cases, transfer costs will be minimized at an intermediate location.

Distorting Influences

The transfer factors thus far indicated combine to point out the one best location that results in lowest total transfer costs for each plant. Several factors may act to displace the least-cost location, based only on minimum transfer costs. Processing costs, competition, and intangible elements that displace this location will be considered shortly.

At this point, some additional transfer factors of an institutional nature must be considered. One such element is simply the availability of transportation facilities. Extensive industrial development of the northeastern United States may be attributed in part to this condition. At one time, no geographical point within this region was farther than 10 miles from a railroad.[13] The influence of topography and its effect upon transportation facilities cannot be overemphasized. Waterways are restricted to rivers, valleys, lakes, bays, and relatively level areas where canals can be constructed. Other natural barriers influence the character of various modes of transportation. The transportation network is a powerful element that limits the availability of locations to points along the current configuration of transfer routes.

Rate discrimination among commodities and geographic areas will also modify location decisions. Utilization of base-point pricing or uniform blanket rates may completely distort the influences of transportation costs. In addition, rate policies of the various carriers can influence the location of industries. Although rates are subject to regulation, the point must be kept in mind that effective rates are set by the carrier. Close proximity to facilities does not necessarily mean lowest rates. Another important point is that published rates do not necessarily reflect the rate at which freight actually moves. It is necessary to make a detailed study of rates under which relevant commodities actually move rather than to accept published rates.

[13] Locklin, op. cit., p. 49.

In conclusion, transfer costs as location factors can attract plants to the point of raw materials, or of markets, or to some intermediate point. Which prevails will depend upon the service necessary to meet individual market requirements and the cost of achieving this service at alternative locations. Because of the general importance of transfer costs in plant location, techniques that minimize this factor offer convenient starting points for the solution of location problems.

Production Costs

Production costs consist of all expenses necessary to convert raw materials into finished products. The production costs related to any given manufacturing process are geographically variable. Such geographical differences may be directly traced to forces of immobility. To the extent that any factor necessary for production of a product is mobile, it will tend to move to the geographical area of greatest reward.[14] From the viewpoint of production costs, the most economical location is one that combines the cheapest critical immobile factors with the necessary array of inexpensive mobile factors. Major production costs may be grouped into three categories, each of which is, in varying degrees, an important location factor. These are (1) rent, (2) labor, and (3) power.

RENT. In broad perspective, rent includes the following production costs: land, taxes, and capital.

Land Cost. Land prices may reflect wide regional differences. These cost differences result from the immobile characteristics of land and the wide variation in the natural endowment of individual sites. Variations in costs among specific sites stem primarily from scarcity. The general rule is that the more intensive the demand for land in a given area, the greater will be the cost. Normally, land cost diminishes as distance increases from the city center. Although the cost of land within the central city may be high, it usually offers certain economies that offset this high purchase price. Among these advantages are more adequate transport supply and a more flexible labor market. The price of a parcel of land must, therefore, be considered in light of other location advantages it may provide.

For any manufacturer, there are two classes of plant sites. First, sites with existing structures may be purchased or rented. Although vacant plants are found in abundance, the adaptability to specific location requirements may be limited. Because the average life of a real estate improvement is often in excess of 20 years, this durability results in a standing stock of plant facilities that have limited adaptability to individual tenants. The second alternative is to purchase vacant land. Construction normally requires a substantial

[14] Hoover adequately summarizes the influence of mobility on location in the following quote: "The price of a freely mobile factor would be the same everywhere and would not affect the location of production or other factors at all." See Hoover, op. cit., p. 69.

capital outlay that tends to bind the firm to a permanent location, thus decreasing mobility. Whether to rent or buy is primarily a financial question to be considered in light of company policy.

Tax Cost. The influence of tax cost on location decisions is elusive, to say the least. Common knowledge dictates that a firm will attempt to locate at the point of least aggregate tax cost. It also follows that the 50 bodies of state tax laws, not to mention uncounted community ordinances, will render distinctly different tax assessments in various geographical areas. Yet empirical studies point out that tax costs are, at best, relatively unimportant, secondary influences in location. Greenhut reviews four studies, which all agree that the incentives offered by lower taxes were not the determining factors in locating industries.[15] The location influence attributed to taxes was concluded to be of primary concern only in selecting between various sites within a particular area. Taxes may play a minor role in the decision to relocate, but the combined role of these and other costs casts the influence. Tax costs are especially influential when political boundaries, such as state lines, separate the communities under consideration. In addition, taxes are primary cost factors for firms with a high proportion of assets which are taxable under state and local ordinances. For example, if a firm requires a large acreage of land to undertake production, property taxes may become important location elements. In such cases, the firm tends to move toward areas offering comparatively lower property tax levies.

Capital Costs. The cost of capital is an important factor in plant location, but this does not mean that the manufacturer must be geographically near the source of funds. Capital is the most mobile of the elements influencing location. The major significance of capital rests upon availability and cost. For a business to grow, it must have ready access to capital at reasonable cost. Neither of these requirements is directly related to location. Availability is more nearly connected to the financial status of the firm requesting loans and the character of executives employed by the firm than it is to location. The cost of capital is a direct result of the money market, although this, too, may depend upon the intrinsic character of the firm. Historically, capital has been considered an influential factor in location. Today, financial requirements are rarely, if ever, critical determinants. The decline of the influence of capital upon location is generally attributed to the rise in mobility of capital funds.

LABOR. The location influence of labor affects manufacturing firms in different ways. These variations tend to pull the location of particular industries toward the geographical point that will best satisfy labor requirements. Although the cumulative influence of labor upon location is difficult to measure, for some companies it is the greatest single influence motivating plant relocation.

---

[15] Melvin L. Greenhut, *Plant Location in Theory and Practice* (Chapel Hill, N.C.: University of North Carolina Press, 1956), p. 126. For a technical analysis, see also Melvin L. Greenhut, *A Theory of the Firm in Economic Space* (Austin, Tex.: Lone Star Publishers, Inc., 1971).

Since there are great variations in labor requirements among industries, a number of firms are attracted by low labor rates. Traditionally, wage levels in the United States have been lowest in the southern states. Accordingly, many firms that are labor intensive and operate on low margins locate in the South to take advantage of large numbers of low-wage, unskilled workers. Wages paid are important determinants of location but only one aspect of the labor-cost factor. From the viewpoint of the employer, productivity, skill requirements, stability, and labor legislation also must be considered.

Location advantages of an area that offers low wage rates may be offset by low productivity rates. Hoover points out that high wage rates do not necessarily attract job seekers or repel employers.[16] Low production costs may be found in areas with relatively high wage rates. The essential concern for the manufacturer is the productivity of labor and labor's response to maintaining low overhead costs. Hot climates are normally considered areas of low productivity. Although this statement has not been substantiated, to the extent that it is true, the low-wage advantage of the South may be offset by decreased productivity.

Firms that require highly skilled labor normally locate in close proximity to the areas that offer such skill. When other critical factors force manufacturers to move from areas of skilled labor, this loss may be offset by bringing skilled operators to train the local unskilled labor force. It is possible to offset the lack of skilled workers, but this is a costly and time-consuming process.

Regardless of the planning and analysis taken prior to locating in a particular area, low labor costs will not be realized if the local labor force proves unstable. High labor turnover is expensive. Retraining and loss of productivity are cost factors that cannot be recovered easily.

Labor laws can also cause cost differences between geographical areas. Virtually all industries are subject to state labor laws. Workmen's Compensation insurance rates normally are applied against payrolls at rates varying substantially among the states. Although not a limiting factor to some firms, compensation charges may represent a substantial cost to the manufacturer when a large work force is employed.

The size of the necessary labor force can also limit location possibilities. Those manufacturers who require large work forces normally are restricted to densely populated areas. In any community, the available supply of labor is basically represented by the workers unemployed. Response of labor to geographical wage differences is often restricted because of movement expense. Although the mobility of labor may be somewhat "sticky," migration can materially affect the local labor supply in times of increased demand.

POWER. Historically, the location of power resources has been an outstanding factor in the selection of plant sites. But power, like capital and labor, has gained mobility throughout the years. For some early industries, the most

---

[16] Hoover, op. cit., p. 103.

attractive sites were located at the fall lines of navigable streams. At this point, water could be harnessed to turn power wheels at minimum cost.

Technological developments have altered the location influence of both power and fuel. Although some plants are still attracted by the availability of cheap and abundant power, in most industries the cost of power as a percentage of total cost is small. Aluminum reduction plants are examples of firms attracted to water-power sites. Natural gas, in the production of glass, and accessibility to coal and coke in steel production are other examples of power-oriented industries. Because of more or less uniform availability, the location of the average plant will not be chosen solely because of power or fuel cost differentials.

In summary, the location factors of rent, labor, and power can influence the cost structure of a plant located at different geographical points. To the degree that production factors are immobile, costs will vary geographically. Thus, to find the point of least production cost for a given plant, it becomes necessary to evaluate alternative cost structures resulting from different potential locations. To a large extent, these geographical cost differences result from forces of external economies of location. Therefore, prior to concluding the discussion of location cost factors, attention is directed to external economies of location.

External Economies of Location

External economies of location refer to cost reductions which result from the geographical clustering of plants.[17] The forces of concentration explain why the least-cost locations for many plants tend to congregate within a few industrial areas. For particular plants such cost reductions may be direct or indirect. Direct cost reductions evolve from the increased demand for interchangeable factors of production and transportation resulting when a large number of plants locate within a single industrial complex. Indirect cost reductions stem from other benefits realized from location in close proximity to an industrial population.

Examples of direct cost reductions are (1) lower total transfer costs resulting from better transport facilities, (2) reduced production costs due to a ready supply of technically trained labor, and (3) specialization of supplies allowing lower unit costs for materials, supplies, and services. These direct cost reductions explain to a large extent the forces underlying least-cost analysis.

Indirect cost reductions are not as easily qualified. Greenhut refers to this category of influences as a group of generally neglected location forces.[18]

---

[17] External economies of location, as the phrase is used here, are similar to the forces referred to by Weber as agglomerative. He defined an agglomerative force as "An aggregate cost-reducing influence resulting from spatial interdependence." In external economies of location, economies of spatial interdependence are considered from the viewpoint of direct and indirect reductions. The original discussion of agglomerative forces did not develop this distinction in great detail. See Carl J. Friedrich (trans.), *Alfred Weber's Theory of Location of Industries* (Chicago: University of Chicago Press, 1928), p. 134.

[18] Greenhut, *Plant Location in Theory and Practice,* op. cit., p. 168.

He points out that indirect cost-reducing factors may be separated from basic cost factors, because they emphasize the relationship between physical distance and costs in terms other than those of transfer and labor costs. Insurance is an example of a cost factor reduced by locating in an industrial community. A particular type of insurance may be available because of better protective facilities or familiarity of an insurance company with local hazards. Although the cost of insurance is a direct expense, the reduction in cost resulting from excellent protection represents the influence of indirect economies of concentration. Advertising costs can also be reduced by location in highly populated areas. Lower expense may be incurred to achieve equal population coverage.

The combined influence of external economies of location is to attract plants to industrial complexes. Individual firms attempt to locate plants in close proximity to other plants in order to enjoy mutual benefits of spatial concentration. To a large extent these same forces may influence a particular firm to centralize individual plants in order to realize maximum benefits from external economies.[19]

Intangible Location Factors

A final group of location forces influencing site selection is often classified as intangible factors. Intangible factors may be divided into two categories for discussion purposes. The first category contains cost–revenue influencing factors that result from personal contacts of company executives. The second group is personal preferences that influence site selection.

Cost–Revenue Influencing Factors

Plant locations may be altered to capitalize on the personal contacts and influences of management. Such factors may directly influence the availability of materials, capital, and sales. The availability of capital may be related to personal friendships and confidences that exist between management and creditors. Special requests for rush materials or spare parts in order to eliminate production bottlenecks may be given urgent consideration if friendly relations exist. Last of all, additional sales may be realized by community contacts developed by executives.

All of these intangible factors influence the cost–revenue structure of a particular firm. Without this aspect of personal consideration, location forces are impersonal results of cost and competitive factors. With consideration of personal influence, locations may be altered to increase profitability. Obviously,

---

[19] Hoover expands this consideration to include individual benefits realized by centralizing all plants owned by an individual firm. See Hoover, op. cit., p. 80.

this influence is paramount to small manufacturing firms, which in some cases may find their only economic justification based upon such personal relationships.

Personal Preferences

Personal preferences influence plant location as a result of adjustments made to accommodate human needs and desires. A particular community may be selected because it offers desirable types of recreation, housing, or educational facilities. A particular region may be selected because it offers an enjoyable climate. Although such factors cannot be conveniently analyzed within the framework of economic analysis, the fact remains that purely personal considerations can be important determinants of plant location. Intangible considerations alter the ideal economic location. The freedom available in selecting sites to fit intangible specifications is somewhat narrow if profit-maximization principles are strictly employed. For any particular firm, these factors may be influential only in selecting between communities located within close proximity to each other.

Plant Location—General Procedure and Checklist

General Procedure

Plant location procedure consists of an organized development of location factors within a working framework. Selection of a plant site is a compromise among various location forces. Because location is conceivably possible at an infinite number of geographical points, the final decision requires an orderly elimination of undesirable locations until the one best plant site is selected. Fortunately, the natural and logical process of plant location provides a satisfactory location procedure, which consists of plant analysis and field analysis.

Plant Analysis

The first step in applying location theory to practice is an appropriate evaluation of the three categories of location factors as they apply to the individual plant location problem. This stage of evaluation is referred to as plant analysis. For plants currently operating, one purpose of plant analysis is to determine if relocation is desirable. With the assumption that a new location is desirable, careful analysis of all location elements will determine what specifications the new location must meet. Similarly for new plants, analysis must be completed to isolate relevant location specifications.

It is during plant analysis that location theory can be applied to the specifics of an individual problem. The critical cost factors for the new plant should be identified, and a detailed cost study of current operations should be completed. This will allow comparative cost analysis between the current location and potential new sites. In most cases identification of cost factors requires extensive data collection. The net result is ideally a number of specifications that can be transposed into dollar costs. For example, the amount of labor required, the point of raw-material procurement, the power requirements, and the many other factors noted earlier should be quantified in order to guide field research. A detailed study of market areas and competitive forces should be completed in order to determine what general geographic areas appear to contain a profit-maximizing location. Finally, the impact of intangible elements should be given complete analysis.

The final result of extensive plant analysis is a set of location specifications designed to guide the process of site selection. If one or two location factors evolve as critical, they should be identified during plant analysis. Only after the location problem has been analyzed in the magnitude here indicated is field analysis ready to be undertaken.

Field Analysis

Field analysis consists of three steps necessary to reduce the geographic area of concern to a few potential locations. Evaluation of location alternatives should be completed at the regional, community, and site levels of consideration. Field analysis procedure is not viewed as a limiting process. Selection of the one best community need not be made prior to conducting a search for satisfactory factory sites. Several search areas can be considered simultaneously, including their alternative communities and respective factory locations.

Individual states are not considered focal points of attention. Without doubt, some states offer advantages for location while others have distinct disadvantages. But the potential geographic territory included in a search area is indifferent to political boundaries. Consequently, several different states may be considered simultaneously as location prospects.

Regional Evaluation

The first step in selecting a specific site from a potential geographic area is regional evaluation. The task at this stage of selection is to determine which areas qualify for detailed field examination. The total area under consideration will vary according to the specifications of individual firms. In cases where inexpensive labor is the primary location influence, examination may be limited to only a few regions. If proximity to markets is a primary requirement, regional possibilities will be in the general locale of major market areas. Competitive or intangible influences may limit the regional areas to just a few. Whatever the specifications, the first step is to identify the geographic areas that meet the broad location requirements.

The second step is to determine which of the alternative regions will be most economical for achieving location objectives. Consideration begins with the assumption that all costs are regionally variable. Each potential region is evaluated by examining the expense of satisfying location requirements. The differential in cost between alternative regions will vary with particular industries. For any particular firm, regional evaluation will identify geographic areas that will satisfy location requirements at least cost. The regions that present possibilities for most economic operation become the search areas for particular communities.

Community Evaluation

Up to this point, the firm considering plant location has, by the process of elimination, selected a few general areas within which communities capable of satisfying location requirements must be identified. Community evaluation should include the availability of necessary facilities. Such factors as availability of utilities, adequate labor force, and transportation must be examined. If a particular community appears to have the necessary characteristics in this respect, a more detailed investigation is undertaken.

Detailed investigation consists of measuring all facilities in terms of potential costs of manufacturing. If all facilities are available at a reasonable cost, investigation is extended to include intangible characteristics of the community. The character of local politics and the community's attitude toward industrial development must be considered. Of primary concern is the question of compatibility between the firm and the community: Will the proposed building and manufacturing operations meet with the approval of the community? Not understanding all implications of such intangible factors can result in a serious and expensive mistake on the part of the firm. The firm must also consider if the community fulfills the environmental desires of the personnel to be transferred. Living conditions must be examined in terms of such factors as recreational facilities, cost of living, and adequate housing. If the community offers incentives, complete details should be examined. Analysis of these and all other factors of importance will point out which communities are the best potential locations for conducting manufacturing operations. Evaluation of potential sites still remains.

Site Evaluation

Evaluation of available sites represents the last step in plant location. Only if the community meets all other requirements will the search be necessary.

Selection of a site to construct a new plant can normally be completed in all industrially minded communities. In location problems where an already constructed plant is sought, evaluation of sites may be necessary prior to community delineation.

In selecting a site, attention must once again be directed to cost analysis and consideration of intangibles. In addition, physical requirements and topographic features must be considered. Naturally, the direct cost of procurement is one governing factor. Other costs, such as obtaining rail sidings, utility hook-ups, and highway access, also require evaluation. From the intangible aspect, the firm must determine if the neighborhood is consistent with the desired image of the firm. For some firms, close proximity with "linked" industries may be desirable.

Only after satisfactory plant sites have been determined is the location process near completion. At this point, the firm's executives are armed with the necessary facts to make an intelligent location decision. Sufficient information should now be available to determine the area, community, and site that offers the best plant location.

Because all location factors have been under consideration throughout plant and field analysis, the forces of cost, market competition, and intangible location factors have guided the selection procedure. To aid in selecting between alternative sites, comparative cost analysis is helpful. The total costs of operation at each potential site should be compared to total costs experienced at the old location. Such cost analysis will clearly point out the benefits gained from relocation.

Plant Location Checklist

I. Plant Analysis
   A. Logistical Analysis
      1. Logistical system analysis
         a. Current Production Points
         b. Current Warehouse Locations
      2. Long-Term Expansion Plans and Policies
      3. Primary Transfer Requirements
      4. Modes of Transportation Capable of Satisfying Transfer Demands
         a. Raw-Material Movement
         b. Finished-Products Movement
   B. Production Analysis
      1. Raw-Material Requirements
         a. Present Point of Purchase
         b. Quantity Purchased
         c. Alternative Purchase Points
      2. General Characteristics of Production Process
         a. Special Factors Dependent upon Location

3. Labor Requirements
   a. Number of Skilled and Unskilled Workers
   b. Degree of Labor Organization Acceptable
   c. Number of People To Be Transferred
4. Power and Utility Requirements

C. Market Analysis
   1. Geographical Location of Major Market Segments
   2. Competition Analysis
      a. Production Locations
      b. Major Markets Serviced and Relative Strength in Each

D. Managerial Location Preferences

E. Location Specifications for New Plant
   1. Logistical Requirements
   2. Production Requirements
   3. Market Requirements
   4. Managerial Preferences

F. Cost Analysis at Present Manufacturing Location
   1. Transportation
   2. Production

II. Field Analysis
   A. Regional Analysis
      1. Least-Cost Transfer Location
         a. Arrival at Alternative Points Using Different Raw Material Purchase Points
      2. Selection of Region(s) To Be Given Detailed Analysis
      3. Analysis of Location Factors Variable Between States
         a. Legal Structure
         b. Political Environment
         c. Corporate Laws and Tax Structures
         d. Labor Laws and Labor Conditions
         e. State Financial Status
         f. Industries Currently Located in State
         g. Cost-of-Living Index
      4. Selection of State(s) To Be Evaluated in Detail Based upon Regional Analysis and Location Specifications

   B. Community Analysis
      1. General Description of Community(ties)
      2. Population and Growth Patterns
      3. Industrial Climate
         a. Existing Industry
         b. Local Laws
         c. Labor Situation
         d. Community Attitude Toward Industry
         e. Amount of Cooperation Available

      4. Supporting Facilities and Services
        a. Transportation Facilities
        b. Utilities
        c. Municipal Services
      5. Living Conditions
        a. Cost of Living
        b. Housing Conditions
        c. Educational Facilities
        d. Recreational Facilities
        e. Character and Quality of Local Government
      6. Selection of Community(ties) on the Basis of Location Specifications To Be Evaluated for a Plant Site
  C. Site Analysis
      1. Geographical Considerations
        a. Size
        b. Soil Content
        c. Drainage
      2. Utility Availability
      3. Availability of Required Transportation Facilities
      4. Costs
        a. Procurement
        b. Landscaping, etc.
      5. Selection of a Site(s) Based upon Location Specifications
III. Final Location Selection
  A. Proposed Costs at Alternative Sites
      1. Continuing Production and Distribution Costs
      2. Initial Establishment Costs
  B. Comparative Analysis of Proposed Costs with Costs Experienced at Current Location
  C. Final Selection of New Location Based upon Least-Cost Comparison

Marketing Approach to Distribution Channel Structure

Unlike those concerned with logistics, marketing managers have traditionally acknowledged that distribution channels consist of a fantastically complex network of organizations grouped in a variety of combinations.[1] Each organization linked in a distribution channel exists for a reason and performs services in anticipation of a return on investment and effort. The marketing task is never considered complete until the final owner has been satisfied with respect to pretransaction anticipations. In fact, a considerable degree of marketing effort centers around measurement of pretransaction anticipation and post-transaction satisfaction. Thus marketing horizons are not limited by the operating boundaries of the enterprise. The basic acknowledgment of a wider spectrum of planning and the realistic approach to interorganizational relationships renders a channel approach superior to that of a single firm. The marketing approach eliminates the limitations of dealing only with vertically controlled systems.[2]

---

[1] The purpose of this appendix is to provide a brief overview of the conventional marketing approach to channel description. A great deal of the terminology is based upon *Note on Marketing Channels* (Boston: Harvard Business School, 1965), ICH 10M65, EA-M-480.

[2] See Chapter 2, pages 32–33.

498

Four general approaches are used by marketing writers to study and describe channels: (1) descriptive institutional, (2) graphic, (3) commodity groupings, and (4) functional.

Descriptive Institutional Approach

The institutional approach to channel analysis focuses on the identification, description, and classification of middlemen institutions. Such institutions are grouped with respect to the marketing services they perform. Figure EIV-1 typifies the analytical framework. At the first level, the distinction is made between merchant and functional middlemen. Merchant middlemen take title to the goods with all the ownership risks. Functional middlemen escape the risks of ownership but provide some necessary service to both client and customer.

At the second level, the distinction between range and type of wholesale services is made. Full-function middlemen typically buy in large quantities, break-bulk, assemble, assort, sell, and deliver. In performing these activities, the full-function middleman maintains a warehouse, employs a sales force that calls on the trade regularly, provides for physical distribution, extends trade credit, manages the collection of accounts, and serves in an advisory capacity or as an informational link to both suppliers and customers. The limited-function wholesaler is so designated because his range of services falls short of that provided by a full-function middleman. On the other hand, the split-function middleman usually operates as both a retailer and wholesaler.

The third level of Figure EIV-1 represents descriptive criteria commonly applied to the various categories of wholesalers specified by the first two levels. Every student of business administration should have a working understanding of marketing institutions, because they serve as the basis for all other methods of studying channel structures.

FIGURE EIV-1
An Analytical Framework of Middlemen in the Structure of Distribution

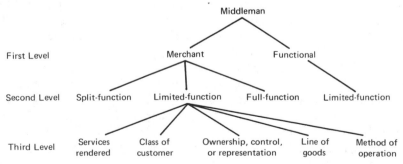

Merchant Middlemen

Included in this section are those wholesalers who buy and sell of their own initiative, thereby dealing with the risks of ownership.

REGULAR WHOLESALERS.   The service, or regular, wholesaler operates a full-function enterprise. Usually the firm is independently owned and handles consumer goods. The regular wholesale firm purchases in large volume from producers and manufacturers, accepts delivery at one or more of its warehouses, breaks down and stores its purchases, sends out its sales force to canvass the trade, assembles orders in relatively small quantities, delivers orders to its customers, extends credit, assumes the risks of inventory and receivables, offers advisory service to its customers, and supplies marketing information to both customers and suppliers. The regular wholesale firm predominates as a retail source of supply in many mass-distributed consumer-goods lines.

INDUSTRIAL DISTRIBUTOR.   The industrial distributor is also classified as a regular or full-function wholesaler. As such, these distributors provide essentially the same services enumerated previously. The industrial distributor is differentiated from other full-function wholesalers by customers serviced and by the nature of inventory sold. Customers purchase goods for consumption, use within their enterprise, or as an unfinished item subject to further processing. Although retailers are not technically excluded as a class of customer, in practice they are a minimal source for the distributor. Most of the distributor's trade comes from manufacturing firms, public utilities, railroads, mines, and service establishments (e.g., doctors, barbers, beauticians, hotels, and restaurants). The industrial distributor often specializes in servicing one industry segment, such as automotive or mining.

DROP SHIPPERS.   Drop shippers are limited-function wholesalers in that they seldom take physical possession of the goods. Commodities such as coal, lumber, construction materials, agricultural products, and heavy machinery are bulky and require the economies of shipment by carload lots. The drop shipper purchases the carload from the supplier in anticipation of a future order. Once a buyer is found, the drop shipper assumes the responsibility and ownership of shipment until it is accepted by the customer. Because no warehouse facilities are maintained, the drop shipper's risk of title bearing varies with the time lag between purchase and sale of the carload. Apart from this risk, the drop shipper also incurs the risks and costs of credit extension and receivables collection. A distinction between the practice of drop shipping and the drop shipper is important. Drop shipping is the practice of shipping an order direct from the supplier to the customer, although a middleman might be involved in the transactions. For example, central purchasing might purchase a large quantity of bulk merchandise. Instead of direct shipment to the firm's distribution warehouse; the company might allocate portions of the shipment directly to its retail store. This practice is termed *drop shipping*. The drop shipper, on the other hand, is a distinct middleman who arranges for shipment, takes title, assumes responsibility for shipment, and functions as a merchant middleman in the overall distribution channel.

CASH-AND-CARRY WHOLESALERS. Cash-and-carry wholesalers are limited-function middlemen who operate on a cash basis with no merchandise delivery. Chiefly found in the grocery trade, they were established to serve the small retailer whose order size was not large enough to justify delivery. By stocking staple merchandise, employing no salespersons, and eliminating delivery services and credit, such middlemen can economically serve the small retailer. To take advantage of such services, the retailer must travel to the warehouse, find and assemble an order, carry it to a central checkout location, pay cash, load it on a truck, and transport the order to the retail location.

WAGON DISTRIBUTORS (JOBBERS). Utilized mainly by the grocery trade, the wagon distributor is a limited-function wholesaler who specializes in high-margin specialty items or quick-turnover perishables. This intermediary purchases from producers, may or may not maintain a warehouse, and employs one or more drivers to call on the trade regularly. Sales and delivery are performed simultaneously. The customer selects merchandise from the truck's limited assortment and closes the transaction with a cash payment.

RACK JOBBERS. Rack jobbers or service merchandisers are classified as full-function intermediaries in that they perform all the regular wholesaling functions plus some retailing functions. Dealing in extensive lines of nonfood merchandise, driver–salesmen regularly service grocer accounts. Typically, a sales representative on call performs a stock control function to ensure that display racks are adequately stocked, properly price-marked, and arranged in an attractive manner. Generally, a rack jobber will be responsible for stock rotation. The retailer is usually billed on a consignment basis, paying only for merchandise sold since the jobber's last visit.

ASSEMBLING WHOLESALERS. Primarily dealing in agricultural products, the assembling wholesaler reverses the common procedure in terms of order size. This category of wholesaler buys the output of many small farmers, assembles and grades the product, ships in economical quantities to central markets, and sells in larger quantities than those purchased.

SEMIJOBBERS. Semijobbers are designated split-function middlemen, because they operate at both the wholesale and retail level of the channel of distribution. Usually semijobbers are limited- or full-function wholesalers who indulge in some retail sales; conversely, they are retailers who find it advantageous to be classified as wholesalers for at least a small portion of their operation. An illustration of the former is automotive suppliers. The second case is not typical of any particular retailing segment but is illustrative of a strategy aimed at gaining lower prices or developing business in two separate market segments.

Functional Middlemen

Wholesalers in the functional category do not take title; nevertheless, they perform many wholesale functions. All middlemen included in this classification are, by definition, limited-function wholesalers, because they do not assume the risks of ownership.

SELLING AGENTS.   Selling agents serve their clients in lieu of a sales organization. They are contracted to sell output of one or more manufacturers as long as the lines handled are supplementary and do not compete directly. Because their principals are generally small firms, as illustrated by the textile industry, they are often called upon for financial assistance in terms of loans, carrying credit for the client, or collecting receivables. Furthermore, agents serve as collectors, analysts, and dispensers of marketing data. For these services, selling agents are remunerated on a commission basis.

MANUFACTURERS' AGENTS.   Manufacturers' agents are similar to selling agents in that they act as substitutes for a direct sales organization, are hired on a continuing contractual basis, represent relatively small enterprises, provide market intelligence, and are reimbursed by commissions. They differ from selling agents inasmuch as they do not sell the entire output of their clients, are limited to a specific geographic territory, and have little control over prices, discounts, and credit terms. A manufacturer's agent or representative usually represents a number of manufacturers who produce noncompetitive but related lines.

COMMISSION MERCHANTS.   Unlike agents, commission merchants rarely are used on a regular contractual basis. Instead, they are engaged for a single transaction, or, more commonly, to facilitate the disposal of a particular lot of goods. Once contracted, the commission merchant takes possession but not title of the goods, provides warehousing facilities, and displays either a sample or the entire lot to prospective purchasers. Once negotiations begin, the commission merchant is usually empowered to accept the best offer, as long as it exceeds a previously stipulated minimum price. To facilitate good offerings and speed the closing of transactions, the commission merchant may choose to extend credit at his own risk. In practice, commission merchants commonly extend credit, bill the customer, collect the account, provide a final accounting, and remit the proceeds less commission to the principal. Such a wholesaling operation is of vital importance to the marketing of livestock, grain, and other agricultural products.

BROKERS.   Brokers serve as catalytic agents to classes of buyers and sellers that would normally have considerable difficulty in meeting for purposes of negotiation. A broker's entire function is to stimulate and arrange contacts between the two groups. It is understood that brokers do not permanently represent either buyer or seller. Furthermore, they do not handle the goods, rarely take physical possession, nor do they provide financial assistance to clients. The brokerage fee is paid by the principal, whether it is the buyer or the seller. In no case can a broker legally receive a fee from both parties to a transaction. Brokers are widely used in foreign trade by small manufacturers of convenience goods and by wholesale grocers.

AUCTION COMPANIES. Auction companies are widely used in marketing fruit, tobacco, and livestock. They provide a physical setting conducive to marketing specific lots of commodities. Facilities are usually available to all those offering commodities and to all those bidding for them. The auction company is paid by the seller at a flat fee per transaction or a percentage of the sale.

PETROLEUM BULK STATIONS. Stations provide the storage and wholesale distribution for the petroleum industry. Such establishments may be owned by refining companies and operated on a basis similar to that of manufacturers' sales branches. Alternatively, they may be owned and operated independently.

Graphic Approach

Flow graphs are a useful technique to identify the flow of ownership title of raw materials and finished products. These graphs illustrate the range of alternatives in institutional selection at all levels of the marketing process.

The graphic approach to describing a structure of distribution is shown in Figures EIV-2 and EIV-3. In Figure EIV-2 the most common variations in consumer-goods channels are illustrated. Of the four channels shown, the most

FIGURE EIV-2
Typical Channel Structure Alternatives in Consumer Goods Distribution

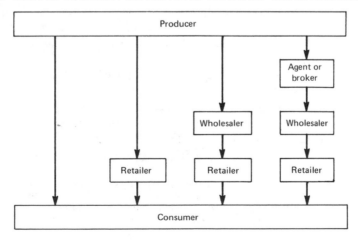

typical for the consumer is the wholesale–retail–consumer channel. Most mass-produced consumer goods reach the market through a wholesaler and retailer. The channel selected by the manufacturer depends upon the characteristics of the product, the buying habits of the consumer, and the overall marketing strategy of the firm. For example, a large personal sales force is required for successful marketing of a product nationwide directly to the consumer. Such companies as Avon Products and Fuller have selected this method of distribution. On the other hand, a manufacturer with limited capital resources and a limited product line might elect to hire a broker or an agent to sell products in consumer channels.

FIGURE EIV-3
Typical Channel Structure Alternatives in Industrial Goods Distribution

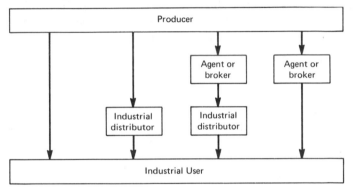

In Figure EIV-3 a description of alternative channels for industrial-goods distribution is presented. Most high-volume items in industrial markets move directly from producer to consumer. Industrial distributors often handle supplies, replacement parts, and small orders of bulk items. In this sense the industrial middleman performs much the same function as the wholesaler in consumer channels. One major difference between consumer and industrial channels is that incidence of functional middlemen such as selling agents, brokers, and manufacturers' agents is much greater in industrial than in commercial channels.

The structures described in Figures EIV-2 and EIV-3 should be regarded as general patterns. There are a great number of possible variations in channel structure in addition to those shown in these charts depending on the product, the customer, and the entrepreneurial vision of the channel members. The neat graphs of distribution channels have been confused by the expanded tendency toward *scrambled merchandising*.[3] An organization once considered

---

[3] *Scrambled merchandising* refers to the identical product being offered for sale in several different types of retail outlets, for example, garden rakes sold at gasoline service stations as well as in hardware, garden, discount, and department stores. Also referred to as *channel jumping* and *conglomerate marketing*. See Chapter 4, page 64.

only a wholesaler may now function within the channel as a retailer as well as a wholesaler. Retailers and manufacturers in turn have assumed many traditional duties of wholesalers. This extension of activities has been referred to as *integrated wholesaling*.[4] Under integrated wholesaling, the retail operation performs the functions traditionally assumed by the wholesale intermediary.

The main advantage of a graphic approach is that it illustrates the many links in modern marketing. By the use of graphs the multiplicity of institutions is focused in a logical sequence. However, the simplicity of flow diagrams tends to understate some complexities of designing the proper channel structure for an individual firm.

Commodity Groupings

In an effort to limit the range of considerations in channel planning, several studies have been completed with the objective of defining channel structure in detail for specific commodities.[5] Generally empirical in nature, commodities studies combine a description of institutions with a graphic illustration of primary ownership flows. Although they are very useful in specific situations, such commodity-channel treatments are too specific for general planning.

Functional Treatments

The functional approach to channel structure developed as a result of attempts to provide a logical explanation of the overall marketing process. Figure EIV-4 illustrates the most commonly agreed-upon listing of functions. A function, in a marketing sense, represents a major economic activity that must be performed to some degree in the marketing of all products. In the marketing of many products, a given function may be performed by a number of institutions and intermediaries between the points of original sale and final sale. For example, storage may be performed by a producer, wholesaler, retailer, and even by a user. On the other hand, market financing might be performed by only one institution in the total process of marketing a product. Beckman and Davidson[6] have summarized these functional relationships as follows:

Marketing has been defined as a process—one in which no person or institution is self-sufficient. It involves many participants and consists of various functional components. One must consider each of these functions and their interrelationships to understand the totality of the process.

[4] Theodore N. Beckman and William R. Davidson, *Marketing*, 7th ed. (New York: The Ronald Press Company, 1962), pp. 348–64.

[5] For a historical review of the development of marketing channel logic and selected industry examples, see Richard M. Clewett, *Marketing Channels* (Homewood, Ill.: Richard D. Irwin, Inc., 1954).

[6] Beckman and Davidson, op. cit.

FIGURE EIV-4
Marketing Functions [7]

The functional approach to marketing provides a framework for evaluation of alternative channel structures with respect to total channel capability.

Initial listing of marketing functions has been greatly expanded by subsequent developments of functional analysis. Functional analysis concentrates upon the interrelation of various functions in the total marketing process. Particularly noteworthy are the developments of Alderson with respect to the role of middlemen in the marketing process.[8] In the Alderson treatment, the essential role of marketing intermediary is one of reconciling a narrow conglomeration of products from single sources into a wide inventory assortment at the point of final sales. This involves several steps, which can be best accomplished by a specialized middleman.

The entire process of changing conglomerations to assortments was labeled *sorting* in the Alderson treatment.[9] The marketing channel serves to perform the sorting activity, which consists of four steps. The initial step involves the *sorting out* of large conglomerations and results in one large supply being reclassified into small lots of various types of goods according to the requirements of the sorter. Next, a larger supply, perhaps from different locations, is *accumulated* over a period of time to provide a larger grouping of specialized but homogeneous goods. The third step in the sorting process consists of *allocation*. In allocation the total supply is apportioned either within corporate facilities or among market outlets. Finally, *assortment* takes place, which constitutes the building of individual supplies into a combination of different products or an assortment in accordance with an anticipated pattern of demand. Alderson's process of sorting is illustrated in Figure EIV-5. In Figure EIV-5 the four aspects of sorting are illustrated in the sequence most commonly found in the marketing process.

Staudt, Taylor, and Bowersox[10] have built upon Alderson's concept of

---

[7] Ibid., p. 390.

[8] Wroe Alderson, *Marketing Behavior and Executive Action* (Homewood, Ill.: Richard D. Irwin, Inc., 1957).

[9] Ibid.

[10] Thomas A. Staudt, Donald A. Taylor, and Donald J. Bowersox, *A Managerial Introduction to Marketing*, 3rd ed. (Englewood Cliffs, N.J.: Prentice-Hall, Inc., 1976), pp. 278–82.

sorting and have generalized four principles that justify the existence of marketing intermediaries: (1) the principle of minimum total transactions, (2) the principle of massed reserves, (3) the principle of proximity, and (4) the principle of postponement.

FIGURE EIV-5
Alderson's Process of Sorting

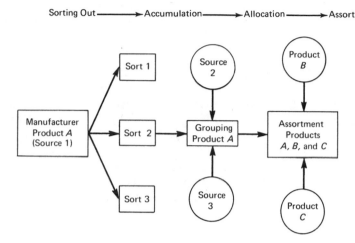

The *principle of minimum total transactions* acknowledges that the total process of sorting is reduced by having a limited number of middlemen. This principle has wide application in finished-goods and agricultural-commodity distribution. In essence, the principle advocates specialization in the marketing process. Figure EIV-6 illustrates the principle of minimum total transactions.

FIGURE EIV-6
Principle of Minimum Total Transactions

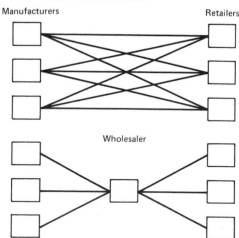

The *principle of massed reserves* is concerned with the storage of goods in the distribution channel. Goods in the form of inventories exist at each stop in the process of concentration and dispersal. Such stops are defined at the producer level, accumulation level, assortment level, and the household. The amount of goods in inventory when intermediaries are used is less than would otherwise be required.[11] This principle assumes exacting inventory control and consistent product delivery.

The *principle of proximity* states that the specialized intermediary should be located close to the marketplace. Close proximity provides better positioning to render final assortments in a manner most satisfactory and timely to market demand.

The principle of postponement was introduced in Chapter 9 as a strategic consideration in logistical system design.[12] With postponement, physical changes in product form and identity should be delayed as long as practical in the manufacturing and distribution process.[13] Inventories should be retained in homogeneous lots to reduce the risk associated with the sorting process detailed by Alderson.

In total, the four principles lend credence to the logic of including specialized middlemen in a channel of distribution. To a significant degree, the objective of each principle is more effectively realized by cooperation within a middleman structure.

[11] See pages 281–283.
[12] See page 281.
[13] Staudt, Taylor, and Bowersox, op. cit.

System Terminology and Flowcharting Symbols

Flowcharting of any system represents the alignment of the steps followed by the system in performance of a specified activity. Flowcharts are used in automated data processing (ADP) for outlining sequential steps in both general systems and computer programs. In distribution system design, flowcharts provide a means by which physical and information flows can be visualized. To date no standardized set of symbols has been developed for use in specialized logistical flowcharts. The purpose of this appendix is to outline some standard symbols for use in such flowcharting.

In the field of automated data processing, standard symbols have been developed. In general, three basic symbols are used:

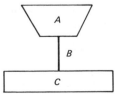

Symbol A is the notation for an input or output of a given system flow. Symbol B is used to describe the direction of flow within a system. The

509

direction is normally read from top to bottom and from left to right. It is not standard practice to use arrowheads, if the flow is in either direction. In the event flow is to the opposite or reverse direction, an open arrowhead is used to indicate this condition. Bidirectional flow is charted by dashed lines or double lines. Symbol *C* represents a processing function. The processing symbol is used for illustrating a major activity on the data flow. For example, the preparation of a payroll is indicated by a processing symbol.

These basic symbols are supplemented by a variety of special symbols that define in greater detail the type of input, output, or processing to be performed in a data-processing system. A great deal of effort has been centered on the development of these standard symbols. Both basic and special symbols are fairly interchangeable between major data-processing systems. When physical distribution systems are flowcharted for computer processing, these basic notations should be used. However, when flowcharts are developed for visualizing a logistical system, standard symbols used in ADP are too restrictive. More descriptive symbols are desirable.

Nine basic symbols are required to develop a logistical flowchart. Each is listed below with a brief description.

Fixed Location
Activity Center

Symbol *A* is used to denote those logistical activities that are performed at a fixed location such as a distribution warehouse.

Transit Activity
Center

The transit activity center is noted by symbol *B*. It is useful to distinguish between fixed-location and transit activity centers because of the wide range of alternatives in transit performance.

Input/Output

Symbol C is used to illustrate inputs and outputs of the logistical system.

Activity Centers
External to Physical
Distribution System

A great many activity centers or other areas of the corporation come into direct involvement with the logistical system. These external activity centers are indicated by symbol D.

Data Processing

Symbol E is used to indicate points of data-processing control. It is at these points that computer facilities are employed in the logistical system.

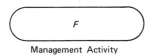

Management Activity

From time to time, special managerial action is generated as part of the overall system. Although such action is a part of almost every system segment, when special attention is desired symbol F is recommended.

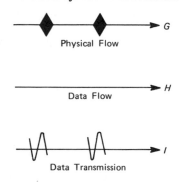

Physical Flow

Data Flow

Data Transmission

Three different symbols are used to illustrate flow in the logistical system. Symbol G is used to illustrate physical product flow. Symbol H is employed for information flow, and the special symbol I is used to denote the existence of data-transmission equipment.

In addition to these nine basic symbols, any number of special symbols may be used to illustrate additional or more detailed logistical activities. An example utilizing these symbols was presented in Figure 11-1, page 338.

Selected Bibliography

ACKERMAN, KENNETH B. *Warehousing.* Washington, D.C.: Traffic Service Corporation, 1977.

AMMER, DEAN S. *Materials Management,* rev. ed. Homewood, Ill.: Richard D. Irwin, Inc., 1970.

BALLOU, RONALD H. *Business Logistics Management.* Englewood Cliffs, N.J.: Prentice-Hall, Inc., 1973.

BLANCHARD, BENJAMIN S. *Logistics Engineering and Management.* Englewood Cliffs, N.J.: Prentice-Hall, Inc., 1974.

BOWERSOX, DONALD J., BERNARD J. LA LONDE, and EDWARD W. SMYKAY. *Readings in Physical Distribution Management.* New York: Macmillan Publishing Co., Inc., 1969.

BROWN, ROBERT G. *Statistical Forecasting for Inventory Control.* New York: McGraw-Hill Book Company, 1959.

BRUCE, HARRY J. *How To Apply Statistics to Physical Distribution.* Philadelphia: Chilton Book Company, 1967.

BUFFA, E. S. *Production Inventory Systems: Planning and Control.* Homewood, Ill.: Richard D. Irwin, Inc., 1968.

CONSTANTIN, JAMES A. *Principles of Logistics Management.* New York: Appleton-Century-Crofts, 1966.

COYLE, JOHN L., and EDWARD J. BARDI. *The Management of Business Logistics*. St. Paul, Minn.: West Publishing Co., 1976.

DANIEL, NORMAN E., and J. RICHARD JONES. *Business Logistics*. Boston: Allyn and Bacon, Inc., 1969.

DAVIS, GRANT M. *Transportation Regulation: A Pragmatic Assessment*. Danville, Ill.: The Interstate Printers and Publishers, Inc., 1976.

ENGLAND, WILBUR B. *Modern Procurement Management: Principles and Cases*, 5th ed. Homewood, Ill.: Richard D. Irwin, Inc., 1970.

FETTER, ROBERT B., and WINSTON C. DALLECK. *Decision Models for Inventory Management*. Homewood, Ill.: Richard D. Irwin, Inc., 1961.

FORRESTER, JAY W. *Industrial Dynamics*. Cambridge, Mass.: The MIT Press, 1961.

FRANCIS, RICHARD L., and JOHN A. WHITE. *Facility Layout and Location*. Englewood Cliffs, N.J.: Prentice-Hall, Inc., 1974.

HADLEY, G., and T. M. WHITIN. *Analysis of Inventory Systems*. Englewood Cliffs, N.J.: Prentice-Hall, Inc., 1963.

HAZARD, JOHN. *Transportation Management, Economics, and Policy*. Cambridge, Mass.: Cornell Maritime Press, 1977.

HEINRITZ, STUART F., and PAUL V. FARRELL. *Purchasing*, 5th ed. Englewood Cliffs, N.J.: Prentice-Hall, Inc., 1971.

HESKETT, JAMES L., ROBERT M. IVIE, and NICHOLAS A. GLASKOWSKY. *Business Logistics*, 2nd ed. New York: The Ronald Press Company, 1973.

LA LONDE, BERNARD J., and PAUL H. ZINSZER. *Customer Service: Meaning and Measurement*. Chicago: National Council of Physical Distribution Management, 1976.

LAMBERT, DOUGLAS M. *The Development of an Inventory Costing Methodology*. Chicago: National Council of Physical Distribution Management, 1976.

LEE, LAMAR, JR., and DONALD W. DOBLER. *Purchasing and Materials Management*, rev. ed. New York: McGraw-Hill Book Company, 1971.

LEWIS, HOWARD T., and JAMES W. CULLITON. *The Role of Air Freight in Physical Distribution*. Boston: Harvard University, 1956.

LOCKLIN, D. PHILIP. *Economics of Transportation*, rev. ed. Homewood, Ill.: Richard D. Irwin, Inc., 1972.

MAGEE, JOHN F. *Physical Distribution Systems*. New York: McGraw-Hill Book Company, 1967.

MAGEE, JOHN F. *Production Planning and Inventory Control*. New York: McGraw-Hill Book Company, 1958.

McCONAUGHY, DAVID. *Readings in Business Logistics*. Homewood, Ill.: Richard D. Irwin, Inc., 1969.

McGARRAH, ROBERT E. *Production and Logistics Management*. New York: John Wiley & Sons, Inc., 1963.

MOSSMAN, FRANK H., PAUL BANKIT, and OMAR KEITH HELFERICH. *Logistics System Analysis*. Washington, D.C.: University Press of America, 1977.

MOSSMAN, FRANK H., and NEWTON MORTON. *Logistics of Distribution Systems*. Boston: Allyn and Bacon, Inc., 1965.

ORLICKY, JOSEPH. *Material Requirement Planning*. New York: McGraw-Hill Book Company, 1975.

PLOWMAN, E. GROSVENOR. *Elements of Business Logistics*. Stanford, Calif.: Stanford University Press, 1964.

SCHIFF, MICHAEL. *Accounting and Control in Physical Distribution Management*. Chicago: National Council of Physical Distribution Management, 1972.

SCHORR, JERRY, MILTON ALEXANDER, and ROBERT J. FRANCO, eds. *Logistics in Marketing*. New York: Pitman Publishing Corp., 1969.

SMYKAY, EDWARD W. *Physical Distribution Management*, 3rd ed. New York: Macmillan Publishing Co., Inc., 1973.

STARR, M. K., and D. W. MILLER. *Inventory Control: Theory and Practice*. Englewood Cliffs, N.J.: Prentice-Hall, Inc., 1962.

STERN, LOUIS W., and ADEL EL-ANSARY. *Marketing Channels*. Englewood Cliffs, N.J.: Prentice-Hall, Inc., 1977.

TAFF, CHARLES A. *Management of Traffic and Physical Distribution*, 5th ed. Homewood, Ill.: Richard D. Irwin, Inc., 1972.

WEBBER, M. J. *Impact of Uncertainty on Location*. Cambridge, Mass.: The MIT Press, 1972.

WHEELWRIGHT, STEVEN C., and SPYROS MAKRIDAKIS. *Forecasting Methods for Management*. New York: John Wiley & Sons, Inc., 1973.

Name Index

Subject Index